Understanding and Teaching Reading:
An Interactive Model

Understanding and Teaching Reading: An Interactive Model

Emerald Dechant
Fort Hays State University, Hays, Kansas

NEW YORK AND LONDON

First Published by
Lawrence Erlbaum Associates, Inc., Publishers
365 Broadway
Hillsdale, New Jersey 07642

Transferred to Digital Printing 2009 by Routledge
270 Madison Ave, New York NY 10016
2 Park Square, Milton Park, Abingdon, Oxon, OX14 4RN

Copyright © 1991, by Lawrence Erlbaum Associates, Inc.
All rights reserved. No part of the book may be reproduced in any form, by photostat, microform, retrieval system, or any other means, without the prior written permission of the publisher.

Library of Congress Cataloging-in-Publication Data
Dechant, Emerald V.
    Understanding and teaching reading : an interactive model / Emerald Dechant.
      p.   cm.
    Includes bibliographical references and index.
    ISBN 0-8058-0824-8. — ISBN 0-8058-0839-6 (pbk.)
    1. Reading. 2. Word recognition. 3. Reading comprehension.
    4. Reading, Psychology of.   I. Title.
LB1050.2.D43   1991
372.4'1—dc20 90-43492
                                        90-43492
                                          CIP

Publisher's Note
The publisher has gone to great lengths to ensure the quality of this reprint but points out that some imperfections in the original may be apparent.

Contents

PART I. THE READING PROCESS   1

Chapter 1   Introduction to the Reading Process: A Definition of Reading   3

PART II. CORRELATES OF READING ACHIEVEMENT AND OF READING FAILURE   39

Chapter 2   The Sensory Nature of the Reading Process   43

Chapter 3   Reading: A Memory Process, A Perceptual-Cognitive Process, A Linguistic and Communicative Process   79

PART III. BASIC STRATEGIES IN READING   105

Chapter 4   The Schema Model of Reading   107

Chapter 5   Developing the Predictive Strategy in Reading: Integration of the Meaning and Within-Word Cues   127

PART IV. ORGANIZING AND STRUCTURING THE READING LESSON — 163

Chapter 6 Introducing Children to Reading: The Language Experience Story, Basal Readers, Trade Books, Expository Texts, Individualized Reading, Whole Language, and Literature-Based Reading — 165

Chapter 7 Programming the Reading Lesson: Using a Modified Directed-Reading Activity — 193

PART V. THE WORD IDENTIFICATION AND WORD RECOGNITION PROCESS — 235

Chapter 8 Developing Instant Recognition of Letters and Words: Using the Integrated Reading Method — 245

Chapter 9 Development of Grapheme/Phoneme Correspondence Knowledge and of the Structural or Morphemic Analysis Skills — 293

PART VI. THE COMPREHENSION PROCESS — 339

Chapter 10 Lexical Access and Semantic Encoding: Strategies for the Development of Meaning for Individual Words — 347

Chapter 11 Assembly and Integration of Propositions and Text Modeling: Strategies for the Development of Meaning for Units of Increasing Size: Phrases, Sentences, Paragraphs, and Total Text — 387

Chapter 12 Strategies for the Development of Higher Levels of Comprehending — 425

References — 467

Author Index — 505

Subject Index — 515

Preface

Few people today question the values of reading. In fact, most extol its virtues. Reading is a key to success in school, to the development of out-of-school interests, to the enjoyment of leisure time, and to personal and social adjustment. It helps children to adjust to their peers, to become independent of parents and teachers, to select and prepare for an occupation, and to achieve social responsibilities. As our culture becomes more complex, reading plays an increasing role in satisfying personal needs and in promoting social awareness and growth. Through reading, we may broaden our tastes and our understanding of others; we make our life full, significant and interesting. But, above all, in the modern school, effective reading is the most important avenue to effective learning.

Reading is so interrelated with the total educational process that educational success requires successful reading. Experience has taught us that those who fail in school usually have failed first in reading. But why do we need another book on reading and on the teaching of reading? The simplest answer to this question is that, despite the effort of thousands of dedicated teachers, there are unfortunately millions of children leaving our schools without adequate ability in reading. It is estimated that 23 million adults are functionally illiterate; they do not possess the reading and writing skills needed to understand and to use the printed material usually encountered in the work place and in everyday living (Stedman & Kaestle, 1987). They are unable to read job or credit applications, directions on medicine bottles, or the manuals that accompany cars or appliances. Illiterate adults account for 75 percent of the unemployed. Forty percent of fourth-grade poor readers would rather clean their room than read (Adams, 1990). An even larger number of children are not reading up to their grade or ability level. And, many cannot read the textbooks used on their grade level. It is obvious that the ultimate goal and value of schooling, which is literacy (Poplin, 1988a, 1988b), is not being attained. The illiteracy problem in this country is real. It is a personal tragedy, and it is a collective tragedy. If anything, it has grown over the last 20 years.

There is something seriously wrong. The reasons for this collective failure are multiple, but surely our teaching of reading has to be suspect.

It may not be so much "what are we doing wrong" but rather "what are we not doing right." Since the 1970s, the teaching of reading has probably focused too narrowly. It just may be that we have forgotten that reading is a twofold process. It is not simply comprehension and it certainly is not mere word recognition. Rather, it is both. In 1969 Chall (1969) found that a coding emphasis (i.e., being able to sound the word) made it easier for children to read with understanding. In 1979 and again in 1987 she (Chall, 1979; 1987) reaffirmed her conclusions. There are still no data to contradict her findings.

The first obvious component of reading is that the words be recognized. The second, and most important component is comprehension. Reading is a synthesis and an integration of two processes: identifying and recognizing words *and* comprehension. Thus, this text is about these basic processes of reading. It is about the issues that center on word recognition and comprehension: direct visual access or the phonological route to meaning; the psycholinguistic nature of reading; bottom-up, top-down, and interactive models of reading; the schema model; structuring the classroom lesson for instruction; whole language; skill teaching; monitoring comprehension; asking questions and responding to the questions; predicting ourselves through print; identification of words; and interpretation of phrases, sentences, and total text.

Reading usually cannot occur unless the pupil can identify and recognize the printed symbol. The acquisition of a sight or recognition vocabulary needs to be a goal of reading instruction. Efficient reading depends on having a vast store of words that are recognized spontaneously. Readers eventually must commit the word so well to memory that they can respond to it automatically without having to figure it out. Each word then becomes a sight word that is instantly recognized and with which the reader can associate meaning. This is precisely what poor readers cannot do.

This text takes a strong position on the importance of word recognition, and on developing automaticity in recognizing words. It affirms that "without word recognition, meaning cannot take place" (Harris & Sipay, 1985, p. 13). In the view of the writer, comprehension is limited by the degree to which the reader is unable to process printed symbols, that is, by the degree to which the reader has not attained automaticity and accuracy in identifying words and in giving the visual configuration or word a name. Beginning readers, poor readers, and in some circumstances even good readers are aided when they can identify and sound out the word. And so are their comprehension, their use of context cues, and their use of the predictive strategies in reading. The simple fact is that the difference between good and poor readers often occurs at the word identification level.

As important as word recognition is, it is only one aspect of the reading process. Reading is about meaning and the comprehension of meaning. Comprehension is *the* goal and purpose of reading. Without it there is no reading.

Reading always involves encounters with words, but reading single words is not reading. It is more like practice for real reading—something like hitting balls over the fence in batting practice. "The 'game' in reading is comprehending a text" (Perfetti, 1985, p. 13). Reading is not merely pronouncing the words but understanding the text and developing a cognitive representation of the text.

If the basic processes of reading are word identification and comprehension, it follows that a major goal of reading instruction should be development of proficiency in these processes. Even though in this book we have separated word recognition and comprehension for purposes of analysis, the two processes are fully interdependent and one cannot be understood without the other. A good reading program must target the integration of the meaning with word identification and recognition skills. Good teaching must guide the pupil's development in both, especially in their integration.

As you read this text you will be exposed to much psychological research and theory. However, you will quickly learn that there are few questions in education that have clear-cut answers and that there is no automatic, one-to-one relationship between theory and application. The theorist, even the learning theorist, cannot replace the educator, and psychology of reading cannot substitute for the art of teaching reading. The theorist offers advice, gives direction, and prevents errors; ultimately, however, the educational programs must emerge from the distillation of theoretical principles with practical know-how (Kendler, 1961).

Psychology does not consist of a catalogue of educational formulae that tell the teacher how to teach, the administrator how to administer, and the parent how to parent. It would be nice if psychology had attained this degree of refinement, but there are no ready-made pills available for educational ills.

William James pointed out:

> You make a great, a very great mistake, if you think that psychology, being the science of the mind's laws, is something from which you can deduce

definite programmes and schemes and methods of instruction for immediate schoolroom use. Psychology is a science, and teaching is an art; and sciences never generate arts directly out of themselves. An intermediary inventive mind must make the application, by using its originality.

The science of logic never made a man reason rightly and the science of ethics . . . never made a man behave rightly. The most such sciences can do is to help us catch ourselves up and check ourselves if we start to reason or behave wrongly; and to criticize ourselves more articulately after we have made mistakes. . . . Everywhere teaching must *agree* with psychology, but need not necessarily be the only kind of teaching that would so agree; for many diverse methods of teaching may equally well agree with psychological laws. . . . (James, 1920, pp. 7–11)

James also noted that research, theory, and psychological principles make us "more clear as to what we are about." If research and theory are to have a significant effect on teaching procedures and techniques, theory and practice must be tied up in a very definite way. We simply cannot be an "ammunition wagon" loaded with knowledge that we do not know how to use; we must be a rifle (Rogers, 1961, p. 281).

There are many outstanding books about reading and about the teaching of reading. Too often, unfortunately, these books have focused either on the research and the psychology of reading, or on the teaching of reading to the exclusion of one or the other. A common plea from teachers today is that research and psychology be translated into teaching behavior. Teachers want to know the psychological bases of reading, or the facts and principles that should guide methodology. But, they also want to know the educational implications of theory and research. Our aim in this text is thus:

1. To increase the teacher's knowledge base: to *identify, report, organize,* and *discuss* those bits of data, research, and theory that are most relevant to the teacher's understanding of the reading process.
2. To help teachers to become better at translating theory and research into in-class decisions: to help teachers to *interpret* and *apply* theory and research data to everyday classroom teaching and to the problems encountered daily in developmental and remedial teaching.

This book thus focuses on the teaching strategies that good teachers need to use and on the learning strategies that pupils must learn to apply if they want to be efficient identifiers of words and efficient comprehenders of what they are reading. It identifies what to teach in reading, especially in the areas of word identification and comprehension, and provides the strategies and techniques to teach what needs to be taught.

Although the text has primarily a developmental emphasis, it has been written with an eye toward correction and remediation. In this writer's view, good teaching is good teaching, whether it be developmental or remedial. There seems little quarrel with the view that the principles guiding remedial instruction should be basically the same as those that govern good developmental reading instruction (O'Bruba, 1974). Strategies that are educationally sound developmentally are probably sound when applied remedially.

The primary audience of this book is fourfold: (a) undergraduate junior and senior students majoring in elementary education; (b) graduate students majoring in reading who will take advanced courses in reading methods, in the psychology of reading, and in corrective and remedial reading; (c) elementary teachers who seek continuing development in and understanding of the reading process; and (d) students preparing for a career in special education, especially those focusing on learning disabilities. We believe the text will be of significant value also to remedial teachers, reading specialists, reading coordinators, reading supervisors, and elementary principals.

The text is divided into six parts: "The Reading Process," "Correlates of Reading Achievement and of Reading Failure," "Basic Strategies in Reading," "Organizing and Structuring the Reading Lesson," "The Word Identification and the Word Recognition Process," and "The Comprehension Process." These six parts consist of 12 chapters.

We have not aimed at developing another model of reading. Rather, we have attempted to present the facts about reading, have drawn some conclusions from these facts, and have expressed some opinions as to which of the existing models best explains the reading process. It is questionable whether anyone fully understands all the complexities of reading. To some extent all models "are little more than general frameworks which provide some (theoretical) biases about which aspects of reading are really important" (Rayner & Pollatsek, 1989, p. 25). Models reflect how we interpret the majority of the evidence on the reading process. If a model means a way of summarizing the evidence in which we place the most credence, this text is indeed engaging in model making.

This book will not answer all the questions about how children learn, or fail to learn to read. As Huey (1908) long ago remarked, if one could understand what the mind does during reading it would be the acme of a psychologist's achievements. We may inadvertently offer some wrong answers, or even ask some wrong questions. We agree with Smith (1988) that "some current views about reading and reading instruction must be wrong" (p. 221). Our success in teaching reading should be better if we understand the process more completely. We thus seek the truth about reading.

We recognize that the teacher may be the single most important determinant of the child's achievement in reading. The teacher probably matters more than the specific type of instruction used. Good theory cannot substitute for good teaching. While we do not fully agree with Smith (1988) that children learn to read by being read to and by reading (this is not the complete answer), we fully agree that "the function of teachers is not so much to teach reading as to help children read" (p. 4). Crowder (1982) pointedly observed that it is the highest vanity for teachers to believe that learning is caused by what they do. Learning to read depends more on what the pupil does than on what the teacher does (Smith, 1988) and the teacher's role is to make it a bit easier (Rayner & Pollatsek, 1989). We hope this book will help the teacher in that task.

PART 1
The Reading Process

Part 1 consists of a single chapter, namely, chapter 1, "Introduction to the Reading Process: A Definition of Reading." This chapter describes reading as developing a representation or mental model of text by relating what is on the page to one's own fund of knowledge or experience. The closer the representation of the reader is to the mental representation of the writer when he put his ideas into print, the better the reader will comprehend what the writer intended, and the better the communication between writer and reader will be. Chapter 1 further describes reading as a synthesis of word recognition and comprehension. Reading involves the recognition of printed stimuli, but the development of meaning or comprehension is the essence of reading. Reading is about meaning. Chapter 1 also introduces the discussion of reading as a sensory process, as a high-level thinking process, and as a language, a psycholinguistic, and a communication process. It examines both the phonological and direct visual access routes to meaning, and the role of the semantic and syntactic contexts in the construction of meaning. It discusses the surface and deep structure of reading and affirms that the interactive model explains reading better than do either the top-down or bottom-up models singly.

Chapter 1
Introduction to the Reading Process: A Definition of Reading

   I. Introduction
  II. Reading as Interpretation of Experience
 III. Reading as Interpretation of Graphic Symbols
  IV. The Word Identification Process
   V. The Comprehension or Decoding Process
       A. Smith's View of Comprehension
       B. Levels of Comprehension
  VI. The Surface and Deep Structure of Language
 VII. Additional Characteristics of Reading
       A. Reading as a High-Level Thinking Process
       B. Reading as a Language and Psycholinguistic Process
VIII. The Semantic and Syntactic Context in Reading
       A. Semantic Processing
       B. Syntactic Processing
  IX. Models of Reading: Bottom-up, Top-Down, Interactive
       A. Bottom-up Models
       B. Top-Down Models
       C. The Interactive Model
   X. The Phonological and the Direct Visual Access Routes to Meaning
       A. Subvocalization
       B. Prelexical Phonological Recoding
       C. Direct Visual Access
       D. Postlexical Phonological Recoding
  XI. Summary

CHAPTER 1

Introduction to the Reading Process: A Definition of Reading

Chapter 1 examines important issues in reading: What is reading? What is the role of word recognition and comprehension? What are the surface and deep structure in reading? To what extent is reading a thinking process? What are the implications of defining reading as a language, a psycholinguistic, and a communication process? Is reading only a psycholinguistic guessing game or is it something more? What are the roles of the semantic and syntactic contexts? What model, the bottom-up, the top-down, or the interactive, best explains what happens in reading? And, is access to meaning achieved through a process of direct visual access (i.e., going directly from the printed word to meaning), a process of phonological recoding (i.e., going from the printed word to sounding of the word and then to meaning), or both? We first examine definitions of reading.

Definitions of reading are generally divided into two major types: (a) those that equate reading with interpretation of experience generally, and (b) those that restrict the definition to the interpretation of graphic symbols. The first is a broader category and encompasses the second; most reading definitions are related to one or both. Let us consider more closely some of the definitions which make up these categories.

READING AS INTERPRETATION OF EXPERIENCE

With the first type of reading definition, in which reading is equated with the interpretation of experience generally, we might speak of reading pictures, reading faces, or reading the weather. We read a squeaking door, a clap of thunder, a barking dog, or another's facial expressions. The golfer reads the putting greens, the detective reads clues, the geologist reads rocks, the astronomer reads stars, the doctor reads the symptoms of illness, and the reading teacher reads the symptoms of reading disability.

The definition of reading that came out of the Claremont College Reading Conference fits this first category. In the Conference's Eleventh Yearbook, Spencer (1946) wrote, "In the broadest sense, reading is the process of interpreting sense stimuli. . . . Reading is performed whenever one experiences sensory stimulation" (p. 19). Benjamin Franklin in 1733 in *Poor Richard's Almanac* had such a definition in mind when he wrote: "Read much, but not too many books" An important implication of the definition of reading as interpretation of experience is that pupils must be readers of experience before they can become readers of graphic symbols. They must first be readers of the world. Pupils cannot read symbols without having had those experiences that give the symbol meaning. This last implication will interest us more at a later point in this text.

READING AS INTERPRETATION OF GRAPHIC SYMBOLS

Turn now to the second type of definition of reading, that which equates reading with the interpretation of graphic symbols. Most definitions of reading given in professional textbooks are of this second type. Writers have furnished us with multiple descriptions of reading, often with varying nuances and emphases. They have described reading as involving the comprehension and interpretation of the symbols on the page (Harris—Sipay, 1975, 1985); as a complex interaction of cognitive and linguistic processes with which readers construct a meaningful representation of the writer's message (Barnitz, 1986); or as giving significance intended by the writer to the graphic symbols by relating them to what the reader already knows (Anderson, Hiebert, Scott, & Wilkerson, 1985; Dechant, 1964, 1970, 1982; Duffy & Roehler, 1986).

Reading is also described as the reconstruction of the message encoded graphically by the writer; as constructing meaning from print (Gillett & Temple, 1986); as making sense of written language (Gillett & Temple, 1986); and as a process of information search or information processing. It is described as an interactive process involving both the reader's previous fund of knowledge and the words in the text; it is a process of putting the reader in contact and in communication with the ideas of the writer which are cued by the written or printed symbols; it is a process of building a representation or a mental model of text (Perfetti, 1985). In this text reading means building a representation of text by relating what is on the page to one's own fund of experience. When the reader's representation of text essentially approximates that of the writer, genuine reading occurs.

THE WORD IDENTIFICATION PROCESS

Reading is additionally described as a synthesis or integration of word identification and comprehension, in which the absence of either makes true reading impossible.

In reading, the obvious need is that the words on the page be identified and recognized by the reader. Reading begins as a sensory process and as a word identification process. Word identification or encoding of the printed word involves three basic processes (see Figure 1-1): visual discrimination and identification of the symbols; visual memory for the symbols; and, generally recoding, pronunciation of the symbols, or association of sound with the symbols.

The purpose of all communication is the sharing of meanings; the purpose of all reading is comprehension of meanings. But it is the symbols or words that must carry the burden of meaning between the communicators. The written symbols are the writer's tools for awakening meaning in the reader. Communication through writing and its reciprocal, reading, requires such a sign system. Without the graphic input there can be no reading. Good readers often are such because they are capable of rapid and accurate word recognition. They have automatized the word identification skills. They have committed thousands of words to their sight or recognition vocabulary and can recognize them instantly with minimum language cues.

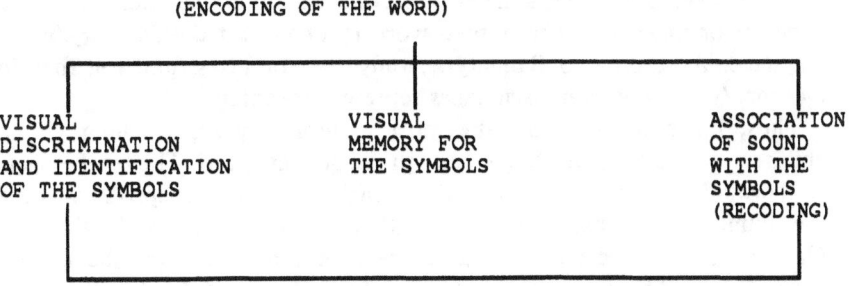

FIGURE 1-1. The word identification (recognition) process (encoding of the word)

It is obviously important that readers make a visual discrimination of the symbol, whether it be *car, sνωθι sαυτον,* or *phlogiston,* and that they visually discriminate one symbol from the next. Readers must identify the graphic symbols or develop a percept of the graphic stimulus. They need to be able to process the visual array of letters and words. Beginning readers in particular need to learn to perceive the significant contrastive features, those elements of the visual configuration that distinguish one letter from another letter or one word from another.

Matching of letters and words is not enough. The task readers face is not one of looking for words that match. They must be able to see the difference in words. They need to discover the critical differences between two letters or two words, between a given word and any other word. They need to learn what the distinctive features of written language are.

Unfortunately, visual discrimination of the symbols alone is generally not enough for beginning readers to go to meaning. Such readers commonly need to be able to see that *cat* represents /kăt/, and that *sνωθι sαυτον* represents /gnōthē soutŭn/. They benefit when they can move from the graphic code (which they see) to the sound code (which they have already learned), when they can associate sound with the printed symbol, and when they can recode from the graphic to the spoken code. Reading, thus, for some readers is not simply visual discrimination of the symbols. It often includes the ability to recode. Both aspects are generally significant elements of the reading process, especially in the learning-to-read process. Indeed, a major goal of word-identification teaching is to help children develop a code that permits them to move quickly and easily from the written to the spoken code; in other words, to see why *cat* represents /kăt/, and why *cent* represents /sĕnt/.

A common model for reading is based on reconstructing a spoken message from a printed text and making the same meaning responses to the printed text that one would to the spoken message. Bannatyne (1973) noted that visual symbols (the graphemes) represents sounds (the phonemes), not concepts or meanings. The printed word is a code for the auditory/vocal language. According to Bannatyne, only the sounds strung together in auditory/vocal words and sentences represent meaning.

Thus, for many teachers, the most natural way for teaching young children to read has been to go through the spoken word. The teacher says to the child: "Look at this word. This word is /kăt/." The spoken word is the familiar stimulus, while the written word is the novel stimulus. Gradually, with repeated associations between the written and the spoken word, the child brings to the written word the same meaning he previously attached to the spoken word.

Undoubtedly, beginning, and even mature, reading often includes recoding. Reading comprehension is clearly related to the ability to pronounce (recode) the printed words. Poor readers tend to have poor recoding skills. They make more than twice the number of oral reading errors per 100 words that good readers do. The beginning reader recodes more frequently than the fluent reader. The question of whether or not all readers characteristically recode to gain access to meaning will concern us later in the chapter. Our answer will be different for beginning and for fluent readers.

THE COMPREHENSION OR DECODING PROCESS

We have already noted that the central purpose or *sine qua non* of all reading is the comprehension of meaning. Reading is thus more than word identification. If reading were simply a word-identification or word-naming process, children would be good readers when they could identify the word immediately at sight or when they could recode or name the printed symbols or words. Reading is more than the ability to identify or to pronounce the words on the printed page, or to go from the graphic to the spoken code. It is more than giving the visual configuration a name. This is recoding, but is not decoding. Decoding requires the reader to reconstruct the message encoded graphically by the writer. Decoding occurs only when meaning is associated with the written symbols and only when the meaning that the writer wanted to share with the reader has been received.

It is not enough to put one's own stamp of meaning on the words. The reader must follow the thought of the writer (Goodman et al., 1987; Langman, 1960). Comprehension occurs only when the reader's construction or representation of text agrees substantially with the writer's representation or his intended message. Only then does true communication via reading take place.

Hittelman and Hittelman (1983) note that "reading is the process of reconstructing from printed patterns the ideas and information intended by the author" (p. 4). In a later text (1988), Hittelman says: "Reading entails both reconstructing an author's message and constructing one's own meaning using the print on the page. A reader's reconstruction of the ideas and information intended by an author is somewhat like a listener's reconstruction of ideas from a speaker's combinations of sounds" (p. 2). In the same text Hittelman notes that "Reading comprehension is partly the reconstruction of an author's intended meaning" (p. 416).

Reading is not simply a matter of communicating signs or symbols, letters or words. It is concerned with the communication of meaning. Thus Gephart (1970) remarks, that reading refers to an interaction by which meaning encoded in visual stimuli by an author becomes meaning in the mind of the reader.

Obviously, reading of graphic symbols consists of two processes: the visual process involved in bringing the stimuli to the brain and the mental process involved in interpreting the stimuli after they get to the brain. Before this can be called reading, however, the signals must be interpreted and the reader must bring meaning to the graphic symbol. Reading requires more than the interpretation of the graphic symbols. It requires a reconstruction of the events behind the symbols.

Frank Smith's Views of Comprehension

Throughout this text we have singled out Frank Smith's views because of the high regard that we have for his discussion of reading and because of his influence on the understanding of reading in the last 15 to 20 years. Smith has set the agenda in reading. He has framed the debate. He is the sounding board used by each of us to evaluate our positions. And, all of this in a lucid, inimitable style that invites quotation. We are particularly interested in Smith's top-down model of reading and his views on comprehension, on the importance and role of nonvisual information, on the predictive process in reading, and on the whole language versus skills/subskills controversy.

Smith (1988) observes that comprehension is "the basis of reading and learning to read" (p. 6) and indeed of all learning. He reiterates again and again that cognitive structure, which he terms *nonvisual information*, determines whether the reader comprehends or not. From his perspective, comprehension is directly related to the amount of nonvisual information, in other words, to what the reader knows. Comprehension for Smith (1988) is a state, the opposite of confusion. It is "the possibility of relating whatever we are attending to in the world around us to the knowledge, intentions, and expectations we already have in our heads" (p. 53). Smith (1988) further defines comprehension as identification and apprehension of meaning, and as "making sense of print," (p. 54).

Smith (1988) notes that the good reader's eyes are always ahead of the brain's decisions (i.e., comprehension), "checking for possible obstacles to a particular understanding. Readers concerned with the word directly in front of their nose will have trouble predicting—and they will have trouble comprehending" (p. 17). It is of course true that such a reader's difficulty is that he cannot make sense of what he is reading, but from another perspective it appears also clear that the reader's problem would be alleviated if he were more efficient in identifying the words. Smith himself intimates as much when he writes: "Comprehension requires sharing knowledge with the author about the manner in which a . . . text is conventionally constructed" (p. 226).

Smith also defines comprehension as "the reduction of a reader's uncertainty" (p. 154). "Without comprehension, there can be no reduction of uncertainty" (p. 53). He adds: "Conversely when uncertainty reduction is taking place, there must be some comprehension" (p. 53). Smith continues to define a message that does not convey information as noise. He notes that any part of a text that a reader lacks the skill, familiarity, or knowledge to comprehend becomes noise, and thus reading is intrinsically more difficult for the novice than for the experienced reader.

Smith's definition of comprehension may appear to disagree with our earlier observation that comprehension is a process of apprehending the message intended by the writer. Not so. Smith notes that the good reader is one whose comprehension approximates the information level that the writer encodes in print. In another place he observes that "just because meaning has to be brought by the reader [to the text] does not mean that *any* meaning will do" (p. 218). However, he also states that not all uncertainty needs to be eliminated.

In his earlier writings relying on information theory, Smith perceived the writer as a transmitter of a message, the reader as a receiver of that message, and the visual system as a communication channel through which the message flowed. In a more recent work, Smith (1988) differentiates between information and meaning and asserts that information is not what the brain is primarily concerned with. He no longer believes that reading is the acquisition of information from text, or that it is a matter of receiving particular facts put into a text by the writer, or that writers encode messages in text which readers in turn must decode. He suggests that the brain deals with meaning and understanding. He notes: "Either information becomes understanding when it gets into the brain . . . or it remains an isolated fact" (p. 247). Smith identifies information in its most restrictive sense as "how the brain resolves uncertainty related to visual input from the eyes" (p. 62). Information moves the reader closer to a decision (e.g., the identity of a single letter); it allows the reader to choose among alternatives (e.g., the 26 letters of the alphabet); and it permits reduction of uncertainty by elimination of alternatives.

Smith argues that a situation with multiple alternatives is one with a great deal of uncertainty and in which multiple decisions are possible. He thus relates the degree of uncertainty to the number of alternatives. If the reader or decision maker can reduce the alternatives to one, the decision is complete, and "the amount of information is equal to the amount of uncertainty that existed" (p. 52). "Information" for Smith, is knowing that a word begins with a particular letter (e.g., The boy fell d_ _ _ _ the stairs) or that it is of a certain length. Smith (1988) notes that "either of these pieces of information will reduce the number of alternative possibilities of what the word might be" (p. 52). He adds: "Just as the measure of uncertainty is concerned with the number of alternatives among which the decision maker has to choose, so information is concerned with the number of alternatives that are eliminated" (p. 52). Even knowing that a letter is a vowel reduces the alternatives from 26 to 5.

Levels of Comprehension

Turn your attention now to the levels of comprehension. The encoding of the meaning of a single word is the most elemental form of comprehension. Just and Carpenter (1987) note that the first problem readers face is to encode the word and then to access its meaning in their internal or mental lexicon. The meaning of the single word or the word concept is the knowledge about a word that is stored in the brain and the representation or concept associated with the word (Just & Carpenter, 1987). The encoding of the meaning that is appropriate to the context is a second level of comprehending. It is at this point that semantic and syntactic contexts start to play a critical role in comprehension. A third level is comprehending units of increasing size: phrases, sentences, paragraphs, and total text. Readers must be able to extract meaning from units larger than a single word, phrase, or sentence. They must be able to develop a representation of extended text, of paragraphs and multiple paragraphs.

And, comprehension depends upon the reader's ability to understand on variant, qualitatively different levels: the literal, organizational, inferential, evaluative, and appreciative levels. Furthermore, the reader needs to learn to comprehend when reading orally, when reading for study processes, (i.e., integrative comprehension), and when reading in the content areas. Finally, the reader needs to learn to comprehend at an appropriate rate. Figure 1-2 identifies these subsets of comprehension. Chapters 10, 11, and 12 of the text will discuss each of these more fully.

THE SURFACE AND DEEP STRUCTURE OF LANGUAGE

Earlier we referred to the graphic, semantic, and syntactic cue systems in reading. Psycholinguists have termed the graphic cue system "the surface structure" and have identified meaning with the "deep structure". They affirm that meaning resides in the deep structure of language, and they maintain that the two levels of language (the surface and deep structure) are related in a complex way through a grammar implicit in each reader, which is termed transformational grammar and which, as Smith (1988) observes, cannot be taught explicitly.

The deep structure refers to the meaning, and comprehension may be described as the translation of the surface structure into the deep structure (Marzano, Hagerty, Valencia, & Di Stefano, 1987). The surface structure includes the number, size, and contrast of the printed marks on the page.

INTRODUCTION TO THE READING PROCESS   13

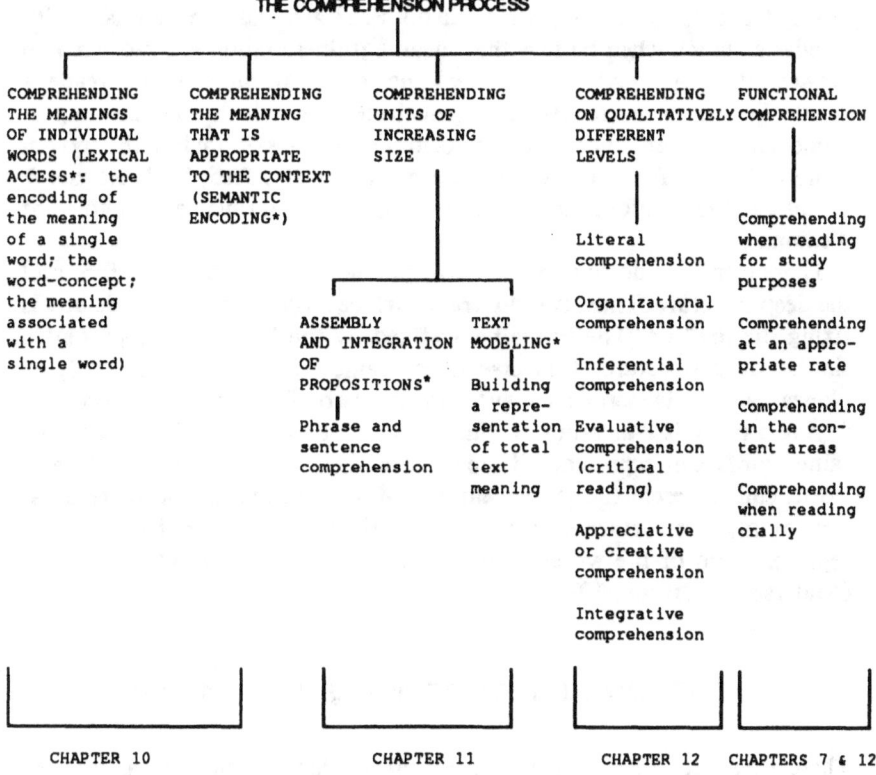

*The terminology is from Perfetti (1985).

FIGURE 1-2 The Comprehension Process

According to Smith (1988), surface structure is the visual information of written language; it is the source of information that is lost to the reader when the lights go out. The surface structure refers to the observable features of language. It includes the syntactic form that the sentence takes.

Smith (1988) notes that meaning does not lie at the surface of language, but rather in the mind of the reader, or in what we term the within-brain context. We agree with Smith that meaning is not implicitly contained in the printed or written marks on the page. The evidence overwhelmingly supports the view that the meanings brought to the surface structure differ from individual to individual and in the same individual from time to time.

We would argue, however, that the symbols on the printed page elicit meaning within the mind of the reader and that meaning is therefore at least indirectly affected by the writer's peculiar choice of words, by his ordering and structuring of words, and by the interrelationships among words. In fact, without the surface structure, there can be no deep structure. We thus argue that cues to meaning reside at both surface and deep levels. Smith implies as much when he says that meaningfulness requires a close match between the way a text is constructed and the organization of the reader's mind. Furthermore, readers read much text in which the meaning is immediately evident once they transform the written symbol into the spoken symbol. Indeed, fluent readers often comprehend (Perfetti, 1985; Rayner & Pollatsek, 1989) before the within-text context can influence the choice of meaning.

There clearly is no one-to-one correspondence between the surface and the deep structure. Thus, two different surface structures (e.g., "The boy is fixing the tire" or "The tire is being fixed by the boy") may represent a similar deep structure. Conversely, the same surface structure ("Flying planes can be dangerous") may represent two different deep structures (flying a plane is dangerous or planes may be dangerous). Obviously, the same words can represent different meanings, and conversely different words can represent the same meaning. Moreover, the mental representation of a given surface structure will at times be much richer than the representation of the writer or than the words in the text literally entail (Anderson & Ortony, 1975).

ADDITIONAL CHARACTERISTICS OF READING

There are aspects of reading that need further elaboration. We will address ourselves briefly to these, beginning with "Reading as a High-Level Thinking Process."

Reading as a High-Level Thinking Process

Definitions of reading often emphasize that reading is a perceptual, an interpretative, and a conceptual, cognitive process. Smith (1988) notes that reading cannot be separated from thinking. Reading is described as thinking through print. Conceptual thought is required to react with meaning. Reading requires higher-order thinking, in which readers interpret what they read, associate it with their past experience, and project beyond it in terms of ideas, relations, and categorizations.

Such descriptions point out that reading requires the communication of a message or of meanings and the apprehension of meanings. Researchers note that reading is so difficult to analyze because it involves the most intricate workings of the human mind (Huey, 1908). Einstein remarked that reading is the most difficult task that man has ever devised for himself. Just and Carpenter (1987) note that reading is an intellectual feat, a complex cognitive skill.

Thorndike (1917) suggested years ago that the reading of a paragraph involves the same sort of organization and analysis as does thinking. It includes learning, reflection, judgment, analysis, synthesis, problem solving, selection, organization, comparison of data, determination of relationships, and critical evaluation of what is being read. Hildreth (1958) pointed out that reading requires inference, weighing the relative importance of ideas and meanings, and seeing the relationships among them. What this all means is that the cognitive processes play a large role in the understanding of text. Clearly, comprehension in reading depends upon the possession of word meanings, but especially upon reasoning with word meanings. Two readers, aged 8 and 12 years, possessing equal word recognition skills and reading the same text, will surely comprehend differently. This is so because the processing resources of readers are often limited by the deficiencies of their personal schemata or their world of experience. Furthermore, children are programmed differently and have different concepts. Some children can think thoughts that other children cannot. The cognitive capabilities of readers clearly set some limits on reading achievement (Perfetti, 1985).

It is thus unrealistic to expect reading comprehension to exceed the conceptual level of the learner. It is unrealistic to expect children to be able to deal with abstract concepts and the symbols that represent them if they have not attained an adequate level of conceptualization. Reading comprehension thus must await conceptual development. The greater the number of concepts that readers have formed and fixed through words, the better tends to be their understanding of what is read.

Reading as a Language and Psycholinguistic Process

Definitions of reading frequently emphasize the fact that reading is a language process. Reading has a strong basis in language. Perfetti (1985) notes that linguistic processes are central to reading and to the understanding of reading. He observes that the central processes of reading are essentially mental operations on linguistic structures (i.e., the semantic, syntactic, and phonological structures) that begin with visual input. He adds that reading is a linguistic phenomenon because it includes both recognition of words and comprehension. Marshall (1985) considers the core of the reading process to be the assignment of linguistic structure to the written form. An orthographic form or the spelling of the word must be associated with a phonological, morphological, and a semantic representation.

Because reading is perceived as reflecting thought processes and psychological, learning, and linguistic processes, reading is often described as a psycholinguistic process. The psycholinguistic view is simply that reading is better understood when it is viewed in terms of linguistic processes and that language processes are important in the processing of print (Perfetti, 1985).

Smith (1988) observes that psycholinguistics has unfortunately become something of a battlecry for some, a term of opprobrium for others, and a rationale for a meaning or top-down emphasis. Clearly, other models of reading are compatible with the psycholinguistic position. The psycholinguistic position suffers from another ambiguity. It is aften associated with the "psycholinguistic guessing game" hypothesis, first espoused by Goodman. In the last twenty years psycholinguistics in reading circles has to a great degree been associated with the names of Goodman (1966, 1967, 1973, 1976a, 1985) and Smith (1971, 1973, 1988).

Goodman (1973) defined reading as "a psycholinguistic process by which the reader reconstructs . . . a message which has been encoded by a writer as a graphic display" (pp. 22–23). For Goodman, reading begins with a graphic display as input and ends with meaning as output. Goodman suggests that the eyes of readers move across a line of print picking up minimal visual cues. These cues, together with knowledge of language, their world knowledge, and the meaning of previous text, allow readers to make guesses as to what will follow and what the words are. When the reader guesses incorrectly, his eyes will regress to previous material for additional cues.

Smith (1971, 1973, 1988) points out that fluent readers maximize the use of cues contained in the semantic and syntactic language and minimize their dependence on graphic analysis, analysis of the surface structure, and print-to-speech processing. They operate at a deep structure level and predict as they read, sampling the surface structure or focusing upon the most relevant cues as they test out their predictions. When the predictions are not confirmed, they then engage in more visual analysis.

Goodman suggests that to comprehend a passage, readers must be in a continuously alert, anticipatory frame of mind, forming tentative judgments and interpretations, suspending judgment, and correcting or verifying guesses as they go along. Reading is described as a constructive process: the good reader constructs progressively refined hypotheses about text in order to understand and remember it. He or she uses the semantic and syntactic context and the knowledge that he or she has stored in the form of schemata to construct a representation of the author's message.

Psycholinguistics observe that poor readers, in contrast to good readers, maximize the graphic input and minimize the semantic and the syntactic input. Poor readers are often so involved in working out the pronunciation of the word that they have little time left to attend to meaning. They fail to extract semantic and syntactic contextual cues essential for word and meaning identification, and they fail to utilize such cues even when they are presented with them. They seem to be identifying words as if the words were unrelated items unaffected by syntactic or contextual relationships. Good readers, on the other hand, concentrate most of their processing ability on the extraction of meanings, using both semantic and syntactic context in reading. They sample the text to validate linguistic expectancies of the information content of the text rather than analyzing the passage in a word-by-word manner.

This text accepts the psycholinguistic position, particularly that of Smith, but with some modification of emphasis. Our primary concern is, and has been, the effect that the "psycholinguistic guessing game" hypothesis has had on the teaching of reading. Today's reading methods texts too often project an almost total reliance on context cues with only minimal emphasis on the within-word cues (i.e., phonic and morphemic cues) in predicting oneself through print. However, we agree with Perfetti (1985) that reading is not characteristically or essentially a "psycholinguistic guessing game." Readers can acquire and skilled readers in fact have at their disposal a lot of information (e.g., the graphemic and morpho-phonemic rules) beyond semantic and syntactic cues that makes reading something more than a guessing game. Perfetti (1985) notes:

> The orthographic system provides a constrained set of possibilities for any given string of letters. And the coding principles provide very narrow choices for any orthographic string. Of course, *lead* may map onto *led* or *lead* out of context. But it can't map onto *window* or *deer*. The skilled reader has adequate knowledge to identify almost all words with very minimal context. For the skilled reader, reading is psycholinguistic but it is no guessing game. (p. 9)

Just and Carpenter (1987) and Nicholson (1986) observe that recent research has disproved the "guessing game" hypothesis and its implications. Rayner and Pollatsek (1989) observe that guessing behaviors "play a minimal role in the process of reading" in skilled or fluent readers (p. 26). Nicholson and Hill (1985) found that both good and poor readers' reading accuracy was not improved when reading in context compared to reading words in isolation. Yelland and Bradley (1985) concluded that context is not an important tool in normal word recognition. Gough (1976) observed that guessing indicates that the child did not decode (recode) the word rapidly enough. Rayner and Pollatsek (1989) observe that children learning to read do indeed often guess, but that by the time children reach fourth or fifth grade reading "does not involve guessing behavior (or an over-reliance on contextual information)" (p. 462).

Unquestionably, context, especially for pupils who have not developed recoding proficiency and are left only with a context-cues strategy, may help readers to predict the meaning of the unknown word and even to identify the word. If the predicted word is the same as the target word, this is to the good. If, however, the predicted and target word are not the same but are only semantically and syntactically related (e.g., reading *lamb* for *sheep*), the reader is said to be making a "good" miscue by Goodman. Unfortunately, such a "good" miscue is not what is desired or even required. The reader has not recoded correctly, and as we will note later, this may lead to unwanted consequences, including difficulties in comprehending.

The reason beginning readers and poor readers rely more on context and guessing than do good readers is that they are too slow in recoding (Stanovich, 1980). Even good readers may rely more on context when the word is difficult to recode or when the context is especially rich. Clearly, the difficulties of some readers in interpreting the writer's message is often directly traceable to weaknesses in word identification, lack of orthographic knowledge, inability to recode (i.e., to transform a letter string into sounds), and inability to activate word-name codes from memory (Perfetti, 1985).

Rayner and Pollatsek (1989), two bottom-up theorists, are predictably critical of the interpretation of Goodman and Smith. They note that the limitation of this approach to teaching reading is it's failure to recognize that one of the cueing systems is more central in the process of learning to read than are others. In their words, "Children who have mastered the alphabetic principle and learned the code have knowledge that enables them to read no matter how much the semantic, syntactic, and pragmatic cues conspire against them" (p. 351). Rayner and Pollatsek add that the theme of "psycholinguistic guessing game" advocates "seems to be that learning to read, like learning to speak, is a natural act and the child teaches him- or herself how to do it" (p. 351)."

My reading of Smith and Goodman is that their model of reading is not incompatible with developing the alphabetic principle or a code emphasis. That many of Goodman and Smith's followers have sought to develop a so-called "psycholinguistic method" is unfortunate. It certainly has led to aberrations in defining psycholinguistics, an unfortunate disparaging of the function of the graphic-logographic-orthographic-phonological-graphophonemic cues, rejection of code instruction in reading, and indeed a misinterpretation of the term, psycholinguistic guessing game.

The psycholinguistic emphasis in reading has clearly changed our perceptions in reading (Stoodt, 1989). Reading specialists today do accept the principles that:

1. Reading is not a precise, exact, sequential process, involving merely word-by-word recoding (Goodman, 1966, 1967, 1976a, 1976b; Smith, 1971, 1978, 1988).
2. Reading is a meaning-centered process and instruction should focus on meaningful content.
3. Context is an important factor in reading.

INTRODUCTION TO THE READING PROCESS   19

4. Reading is language based.
5. Children read best when they hypothesize and predict, confirm or disconfirm their predictions, and revise their inaccurate predictions.

We well discuss the predictive process in reading more fully in chapter 5. We will qualify statement 5 above when discussing global and focal prediction. In addition, we will examine the research, both pro and con, that relates to the psycholinguistic guessing game hypothesis. We will try to show that reading is intended to be more than a psycholinguistic guessing game and that in fluent readers it in fact is.

THE SEMANTIC AND SYNTACTIC CONTEXT IN READING

We have already alluded to the benefits of context in reading. Reading with understanding, interpreting the printed symbols, giving significance to the graphic symbols, and decoding are mediated through semantic and syntactic cues. Thus to comprehend, readers must access and process the semantic and syntactic information contained in words and sentences: they must associate semantic meaning (a meaning acquired through experience and conceptualization) and syntactic meaning (a meaning inherent in language structures) with the symbols. In other words, there are two basic contexts in reading, the semantic and the syntactic, and readers must use both of them if they expect to be good readers. We will first examine the semantic context or semantic processing.

Semantic Processing

When readers associate meaning with symbols, a meaning that they have acquired through experiences, they are utilizing a semantic cue, are doing semantic processing, and are making use of the semantic context. Semantic cues are meaning-bearing cues based on experiences: they are bundles of experiences which have been given vocabulary tags by a writer. Words thus contain the "distilled essence of a thousand experiences (H. Smith, 1962, p. 63)."

When pupils "read" the word *cat* or $\gamma\nu\omega\theta\iota$ $\sigma\alpha\upsilon\tau\omicron\nu$ and can pronounce the words as /kăt/ and /gnōthē soutŭn/, they are still not yet reading. Readers must take meaning to the symbols. They must call upon their previous experiences with *cats* and associate these experiences with the printed symbol. The real live cat thus is the referent for the word *cat*. Readers can really read $\gamma\nu\omega\theta\iota$ $\sigma\alpha\upsilon\tau\omicron\nu$ only when they realize that these words mean "know thyself" and when they have had the experiences necessary to give meaning to the concept of knowing oneself. Reading thus is correctly described as the process of giving the significance intended by the writer to the graphic symbols by relating them to one's own fund of experiences (Dechant, 1964, p. 12; 1970, p. 19). Meaning is supplied by readers as they process the symbolic system by relating it to experience and conceptual structures.

Clearly, comprehension comes from the reader's fund of experience and is actually supplied by readers as they process symbols by relating them to experience. We read in order to gain experience, and yet it is also true that we get more out of reading if we have more experience. The good reader constantly processes information, tests it, reformulates it, and acts upon it in the light of prior experience. It should now be clear why it was noted earlier in the chapter that children must be proficient readers of experience before they can become proficient readers of graphic symbols. They cannot be good readers if their past experiences have not furnished them with a cognitive base relevant to the information contained in a particular written communication (Hollander, 1975). Children cannot read symbols without having read experience—without having those experiences that give the symbol meaning.

The importance of the semantic context in the development of meaning for words on the printed page may be summarized as follows:

1. The semantic context contains the experiential content of meaning. It is the experience that gives meaning to a word. The experience is what the word stands for. It is a word's referent. There simply is not a one-to-one correspondence between the written word and meaning. What the reader must add is the sum total of the retained and organized effects of past experience. Meaning is not a property of language. The words themselves have no intrinsic meaning.
2. Reading involves the reading of past experience; reading is more a matter of bringing experience, and hence of meaning, to the printed page than of getting meaning from the printed page (Dechant & Smith, 1977; Dechant, 1964, 1970, 1982); Smith & Dechant, 1961).
3. Semantic meaning leads to tentative meaning choices that must be tested against the graphic information but also against the syntactic information.
4. There are really two semantic contexts: that within the text and that within the mind of the reader. The words on the printed page, the within-text context, stimulate the reader's mental representation of experience or the within-mind context. Both are significant in building a representation of text.

5. Generally, the contextually appropriate meaning is selected by the reader when he needs to reduce uncertainty. It wins out from the myriad of possible meanings. Context biases one meaning more heavily than another. Thus in the phrase, "the running brook" the reader will select the meaning "flowing" from the 109 meanings that the word *run* may have.

Syntactic Processing

Readers must process the graphic-semantic cues, but this step needs to be supplemented by syntactic processing. To be a good reader, it is not enough to process the semantic context, or to focus on the semantic or referential meaning (what the symbol "steeple" represents or, in other words, its referent). Readers must also process the syntactic context; they must use language structure to decode meaning.

Good comprehenders are such because they can process total language structures that are termed phrases, sentences, and paragraphs, and not simply words, to decode meaning. They see the grammatical relations among the words in phrases, clauses, and sentences (Just & Carpenter, 1987). They have more experience with and knowledge of language structure, of syntactics and idiomatic usage. They have less need for visual information. They are better in processing sentences.

Lefevre (1962, 1964), a linguist, started the emphasis on the significance of language structures for reading comprehension. He pointed out that syntactic cues, both the morphological or intra-word cues (such as inflectional endings, contractions, prefixes, suffixes, and accent) and the inter-word cues (such as word order, function words, and punctuation) affect meaning. Thus, the addition of *s* to a word (cat*s*, hit*s*, Mary*'s*) changes the meaning of the words; the prefix *trans* changes the meaning of the root *port* in *transport*; and the addition of the suffix *fy* changes *false* to *falsify* and creates a new meaning. Lefevre emphasized that the grasp of meaning is integrally linked to the processing of these language structures in a sentence.

Syntax permits the grouping of words to suggest specific nuances of meaning. Thus the same words might be grouped in different ways to suggest various meanings: "The weak girl is playing a game of tennis" or "The girl is playing a weak game of tennis"; "The boy sat in the chair with the broken arm" or "The boy with the broken arm sat in the chair." In such sentences, readers must first recognize the distinction in the arrangement before they can perceive the distinction in meaning.

Syntax thus serves a most useful function in comprehension. The syntactic context is the language-based content of reading. It is almost impossible to read a sentence correctly or to comprehend it without mastery of the grammar of a language. Decoding is clearly effected through syntax and sentence structures (Smith, 1971). Syntax determines how words are arranged into sentences, but more importantly it is a set of rules by which sense is made out of what one reads. The syntactic context determines how the visual-semantic or graphic-semantic associations are to be interpreted, and it determines which of the many semantic meanings that might be associated with a symbol is the appropriate one in the syntactic and structural context in which the word is placed. In the sentences "He is playing records" and "Will he record a new song?" it is the syntax that provides the cue as to which word is *record'* and which is *re'cord*.

In his earlier writings (1971, 1978), Smith believed that grammar or syntax is the bridge between surface and deep structure. Today, Smith (1988) disagrees, arguing that one must comprehend the sentence before one can identify a word's grammatical function. He still accepts that transformational grammar provides a link between surface and deep structure.

Clearly, readers will do a better job of comprehending or decoding if they can process the patterned regularities among the elements of the sentence (i.e., the word order, the inflectional endings, intonation patterns, the function words, and the punctuation). All of these signal information and redundantly define and confirm the meanings assigned to words, in addition to mediating and communicating meanings. The question is: What is the best way to decode? The answer seems to be: by utilizing simultaneously and interactively the graphic cues, the semantic cues, and the syntactic cues. The evidence is that increasing knowledge of syntax, in addition to increasing knowledge of semantics, will result in improved ability to process sentences (Frasure & Entwisle, 1973).

As suggested earlier, reading is message reconstruction (like reading a map), and for the most part comprehension of meaning depends on using all the cues available. Readers will be better decoders of meaning if they understand sentence structures and if they concentrate most of their processing ability on the extraction of meanings, using both semantic and syntactic context in reading. Readers must check the validity of their predictions in reading by seeing whether they produced language structures as they know them and whether they make sense. If the word is both semantically and syntactically acceptable, readers are likely to comprehend what they are reading and assimilate a new meaning.

In summary, an adequate response in reading thus demands much more than the mere identification and recognition of the configuration of the written word. The perception of a graphic symbol must, of necessity, involve simple perception of forms (the printed word), but also must include the more complex aspects which will ultimately allow for the perception of meaning. Reading occurs only when the reader understands what the symbols stand for or represent.

MODELS OF READING: BOTTOM-UP, TOP-DOWN, INTERACTIVE

Since reading deals with word recognition and comprehension, there is some question whether pupils use or should use a bottom-up approach (Gough, 1972, 1976; LaBerge & Samuels, 1974) to comprehension and reading, a top-down approach (Goodman, 1966, 1967, 1973, 1976a, 1976b; Smith 1971, 1978, 1988), or an interactive model (McCleland, 1986; Rumelhart, 1976, 1980; Rumelhart & McCleland, 1981, 1982. The bottom-up approach involves sensing print on the retina, analyzing letter features and letter clusters, detecting and combining the letters into words, organizing words into phrases and sentences, associating meaning with these sentences, and storing and reasoning with these meanings. The top-down approach includes searching for meaning, selectively reacting to print, and confirming or rejecting predictions made. The interactive model essentially emphasizes parallel processing of print. Three current exemplars of the different models of reading are those of Smith 1988 (top-down), Rayner and Pollatsek, 1989 (bottom-up), and Perfetti, 1985 (interactive model).

Bottom-up Models

Bottom-up models operate on the principle that the written text is hierarchically organized (i.e., on the grapho-phonic, phonemic, syllabic, morphemic, word, and sentence levels) and that the reader first processes the smallest linguistic unit, gradually compiling the smaller units to decipher and comprehend higher units (e.g., sentence syntax). The emphasis in this approach is on text processing. In the bottom-up models, if the text processing falls down anywhere on the hierarchical ladder, remediation is applied at this point. Bottom-up models, at least in the beginning stages, give little emphasis to the influences of the reader's world knowledge, contextual information, and other higher-order processing strategies.

Gove (1983) suggests that advocates of the bottom-up strategy believe that: (a) readers must recognize each word in a selection to comprehend the selection; (b) readers should give primary emphasis to word and sound/letter cues in identifying unrecognized words; (c) reading acquisition requires a mastery of a series of word-recognition skills; (d) letters, letter/sound relationships, and words should receive primary emphasis in instruction; (e) accuracy in recognizing words is significant; and (f) knowledge of discrete subskills is important. The reader thus first learns to identify letter features, links these features to recognize letters, combines letters to recognize spelling patterns, links spelling patterns to recognize words, and then proceeds to sentence, paragraph, and text-level processing (Vacca, Vacca, & Gove, 1987).

In Rayner and Pollatsek's (1989) bottom-up model, processing begins with eye fixation and the initial encoding of the printed word. This initial encoding process involves two separate processes occurring in parallel: foveal word processing and parafoveal processing. Foveal processing examines the letters in parallel (not serially) in the word that is being fixated. Parafoveal processing is concerned with extracting visual information to the right of the fixation. This involves letter and word information (including the length of the word). The size of the perceptual span or the region of effective processing extends from the beginning of the word being fixated to about 15 character spaces to the right of the fixation.

Lexical access of the fixated word occurs next. It may be very rapid, especially if it is aided by a parafoveal preview of the letter information from the prior fixation. Lexical access can proceed via two routes: a direct route from the printed word to the lexicon or an indirect route to the lexicon involving phonological recoding. The phonological route is probably the primary means for recognizing words that are relatively infrequent or unfamiliar in print but which are in the spoken lexicon. It appears that lexical access develops over time (with full development occurring at about fourth or fifth grade) and involves careful visual analysis of the stimulus as well as phonological awareness.

The lexicon is, together with real-world knowledge and the text representation (which is actually a part of the real-world knowledge and a product of what has been read), a component of long-term memory. The meaning of the word, along with such syntactic information as its part of speech, is obtained rapidly from the lexicon. Furthermore, an acoustic representation as well as activity in the speech tract or inner speech are activated. Inner speech holds information in short-term memory. When lexical access is completed, attention shifts to the next word and a saccade or eye movement is made toward that word.

A simplified version of Rayner and Pollatsek's bottom-up model is presented in Figure 1-3.

After or concomitantly with lexical access, the meaning of the currently fixed word is integrated into an ongoing text representation which is being built in working memory. The working memory has three components or modules: (a) a module that holds inner speech, (b) a syntactic parser, and (c) a thematic parsing module. When the word is difficult to integrate or is an infrequent word, the eye fixation will continue; the eye may even make a second fixation on it. The inner speech module in short-term memory holds an ordered and relatively literal record of what has been read. Readers with difficulty in comprehending may refer to it or simply look back in the text.

The syntactic parser parses strings of words into their appropriate

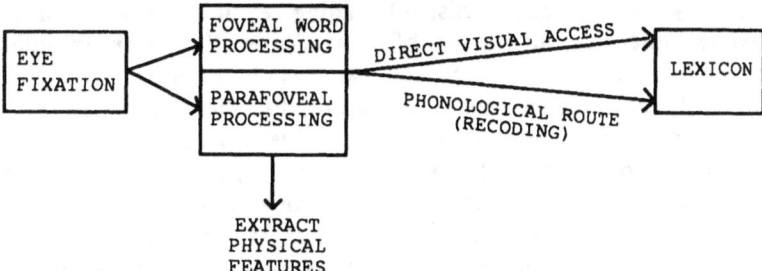

FIGURE 1-3. Rayner and Pollatsek's Bottom-Up Model

syntactic constituents. It receives input from the lexicon about the syntactic class of each word as it is read. When a word can serve as two parts of speech and the parsing of the sentence up to that point allows either interpretation, parsing is delayed until additional information is available.

The thematic module monitors the semantic content of the text, using both previous text and real-world pragmatic information to arrive at the semantically and pragmatically best interpretation. When the thematic processor detects that syntactic parsing is inconsistent with either real-world information or with prior contextual information, the reader either makes a number of fixations in the same region of the text or makes a regression. Research (Rayner & Pollatsek, 1989) suggests that syntactic processing occurs prior to semantic processing and that semantic processing lags behind the eye by at least one fixation.

Top-Down Models

Top-down models suggest that processing of print begins in the mind of the readers with meaning-driven processes or with an hypothesis about the meaning of some unit of print. From this perspective readers identify letters and words only to confirm their hypotheses about the meaning of the text. Thus, the top-down approach has been described as concept-driven. The top-down approach emphasizes that reading is not simply a bottom-up process and that meaning is not entirely residing in the text. The knowledge, experience, and concepts that readers bring to the text, in other words, their schemata, are a part of the process. As noted earlier, reading in this context is more a matter of bringing meaning to than gaining meaning from the printed page (Dechant, 1964, 1970, 1982; Dechant & Smith, 1961, 1977).

Gove (1983) suggests that advocates of the top-down strategy believe that: (a) readers can comprehend a selection even though they do not recognize each word; (b) readers should use meaning and grammatical cues to identify unrecognized words; (c) reading requires the use of meaning activities rather than the mastery of a series of word-recognition skills; (d) the reading of sentences, paragraphs, and whole selections should be the primary focus of instruction; (e) reading for meaning is the primary objective of reading rather than mastery of letters, letter/sound relationships, and words; and (f) the most important aspect about reading is the amount and kind of information gained through reading.

In the top-down approach, the reader is said to be using the deep structure of the language to interpret the surface structure. The top-down view of reading *á la* Smith and Goodman puts a high degree of reliance upon the formation and testing of readers' hypotheses about what they will read next. It is thus often described as an hypotheses-testing model. The central feature of the model is a selective, tentative anticipatory process (i.e., hypothesizing what will come next). However, Rayner and Pollatsek (1989), bottom-up theorists, observe that visual processing of text is very fast and that "the extent to which readers engage in hypothesis testing or guessing behaviors seems to play a minimal role in the process of reading" (p. 26).

In most top-down models, the reader is said to scan the surface structure and to proceed directly to the deep structure. The reader begins at the semantic and syntactic level and samples other sources of information only as needed. Recoding, whether on an aural or oral level, occurs after, not before, the apprehension of meaning. Figure 1-4 graphs these interrelationships.

From a top-down view of reading, the reader's contribution to meaning is an essential ingredient in the comprehension of text. Reading thus becomes an inferential, constructive process, characterized by the formation and testing of hypotheses about the text (Spiro, Bruce & Brewer, 1980). Reading is perceived as a subset of problem solving rather than simply automatic matching of linguistic responses to linguistic stimuli.

The Interactive Model

The interactive model (McClelland, 1986; Perfetti, 1985; Perfetti & Roth, 1981; Rumelhart 1976, 1980; Rumelhart & McClelland, 1981, 1982; Stano

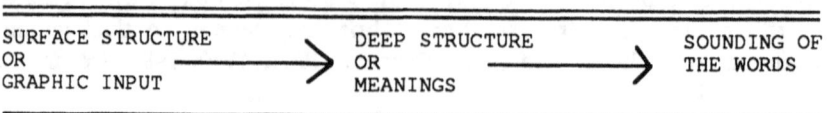

FIGURE 1-4. The Top-Down Model

vich, 1980), the model which is espoused in this book, suggests that meaning comes from many sources, that the reader simultaneously uses all levels of processing, that any one source of meaning can be primary at a given time, that utilizing information from one source often depends on utilizing information from the others, and that the reader constructs meaning by the selective use of information from all the sources of meaning without adherence to any set order.

The sources of meaning, from an interactive perspective, include the following:

1. *Logographic knowledge:* This results in instant recognition of words on the basis of the salient and global features: their length, shape, or configuration as defined by the pattern of ascenders and descenders. It is recognition of words on the basis of gross aspects of words independent of the letters. Preschool children identify words such as *K-Mart* or *Stop* in this way.
2. *Graphemic knowledge:* This focuses on the distinctive features of the graphemes, both individual letters and letter clusters (e.g., *ch, sh, th, wh*). This is information specific to the letters making up the word. The features that characterize the graphemic input are identified.
3. *Phonological knowledge:* The phonological knowledge includes the word's acoustic, articulatory, and phonemic structure; each word has a phonological identity.
4. *Orthographic knowledge:* A word has an orthographic structure or identity; it has a specific internal structure, an idiosyncratic spelling. Each word has a distinct arrangement of grapheme sequences. Orthographic knowledge consists of recognition of the sequence of letters which bear a systematic relationship to the word's acoustic and articulatory structure.
5. *Morphemic knowledge:* Some readers identify words by an analysis of the morphemic or meaning parts of words. They learn to sound the morphemes; recognizing *returnable* as *re-turn-able*.
6. *Grapheme/phoneme correspondence:* This is knowledge of the grapheme/phoneme correspondences. These symbol/sound associations help readers to identify and recode words.
7. *Lexical knowledge:* Lexical knowledge refers to individual word meanings; it includes also the morphemic information.
8. *Semantic knowledge:* This is the experiential content of sentences and paragraphs; it gives the word semantic identity. It includes the meanings that the reader has acquired through experience and that form the reader's personal schema.

9. *Syntactic knowledge:* This is the recognition of the word order and each word's grammatical function. Together they give the word its syntactic identity.
10. *Schematic knowledge:* This is the prior knowledge that the reader brings to the text. It includes the reader's cognitive base, the reader's fund of linguistic experience, the reader's topical knowledge, and the reader's knowledge of the rhetorical structures that signal the organization of texts.

Figure 1–5 identifies the basic differences between bottom-up, top-down, and interactive models.

In interactive models, reading is perceived to involve parallel and simultaneous processing of all the sources of information (May, 1986). The top-down and bottom-up models are serial models, emphasizing sequential processing. Leu and Kinzer (1987) observe that "reading proceeds as each knowledge source in one's mind interacts simultaneously with the print on the page and with other knowledge sources" (p. 44).

Advocates of the interactive model suggest that readers process letters and words at the same time as they formulate hypotheses about the meaning of what is on the printed page. Karlin and Karlin (1987) note: "Word recognition facilitates the production of hypotheses about meanings, and these hypotheses help develop further hypotheses about what the words are. Comprehension depends upon how well readers do both" (p. 23). McCormick (1987) suggests that the reader "simultaneously initiates word identification and predicts meaning: the lower level processes (word identification) and higher level processes (meaning) help each other at the same time" (p. 28).

Perfetti (1985) suggests that the facts of word recognition and those of accessing a word in permanent memory are best handled by a model that

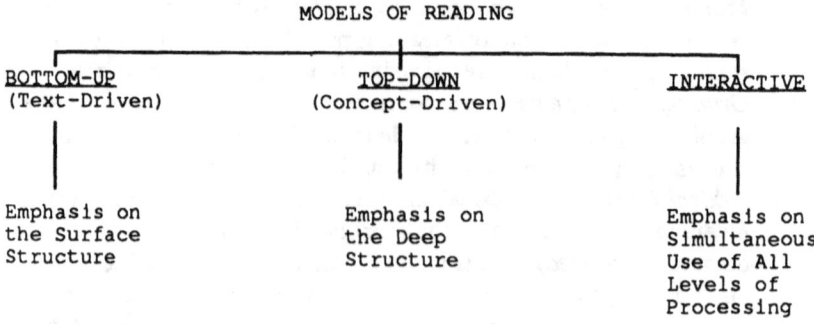

FIGURE 1-5. Models of Reading

assumes that all processes (low-level and higher-level processes or bottom-up and top-down processes) interact and that Rumelhart and McClelland's interactive model best meets this requirement. Rumelhart's theory suggests that each level of information (grapheme, phoneme, word, etc.) is separately represented in memory and that information passes from one level to the next in both directions; in other words, it is strongly interactive. It is not simply processing from the bottom up or from the top down.

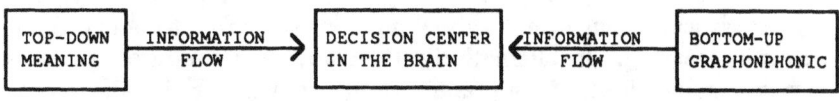

FIGURE 1-6.

The interaction of letter level and word level is only part of the interactive system. The word level can obviously receive activation from the context. Perfetti (1985) suggests that the working-memory or short-term memory, as it processes the text, activates the words in permanent memory and that the activation spreads automatically to semantically related words. As the text increasingly constrains the choice of words, the easier it is to identify the word. In other words, the context lowers the threshold for perceiving the word. Speed of identification rises with increases in the degree of constraint imposed by the context (Perfetti, 1985). The evidence shows that high semantic activation (context) can compensate for inadequate feature or letter activation.

In the preface we intimated that literacy problems might be the result of putting undue emphasis on certain aspects in the teaching of reading. We suggest that using a strictly top-down strategy is not sufficient. Relying exclusively on context and personal schemata leads to numerous comprehension errors. Context cues used alone are inefficient predictors of meaning. The reader must be flexible and genuinely interactive in reading. He needs to learn parallel processing. Our teaching should focus the pupil's attention on the whole (the language experience story, the paragraph, the sentence), but simultaneously also on the parts. Good teaching moves from whole to part to whole.

Rayner and Pollatsek (1989) describe their model as a "bottom-up model in which the reader gets some help from the top-down processes" (p. 26). We think of our approach more as a top-down model in which readers get some help from the bottom-up processes. We believe that the interactive model provides the best explanation of reading: the interactive model proposed in this text begins with a top-down emphasis, moves to bottom-up when needed, and returns to top-down emphasis. It moves from whole to part to whole.

THE PHONOLOGICAL AND THE DIRECT VISUAL ACCESS ROUTES TO MEANING

Clearly, the information about a word stored in the mental lexicon has to be accessed for reading comprehension to occur. The goal of all reading is for the reader to associate the visual configuration, which we know as a word, with a meaning. However, there are two distinct theories for how the process works. First, in encountering printed words, the reader may characteristically transform the visual input into a spoken form in order to access its meaning. Or, alternatively, the reader may use direct access to meaning, going directly from graphic symbol to meaning. In other words, after the registration of the graphic stimulus in the occipital lobe, the visual input may take on semantic and phonological characteristics or simply semantic characteristics?

In reading there are thus basically two routes to meaning (see Figure 1-7): (a) the phonological route from the visual word form to the phonological processing system to the semantic system, and (b) the direct visual access route from the visual word-form system to the semantic system, which allows for direct access to meaning.

Direct visual access depends upon a match between the visual stimulus and its lexical equivalent. The lexical route maps a word's visual characteristics onto a stored lexical representation (Swanson, 1989). In this instance the reader sees the word, the word is registered in the occipital lobes, and then sent directly to the semantic system. Phonological access requires the conversion of the printed word into its phonological code, which is then matched to the lexical equivalent.

Traditionally, in teaching children to read, the child is shown, for

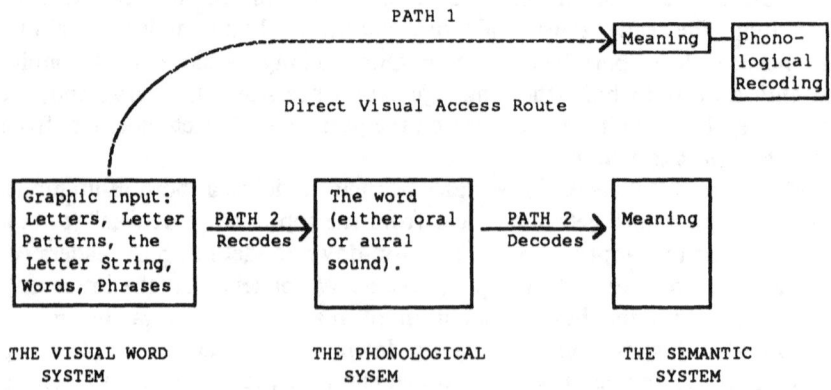

FIGURE 1-7. Alternate Paths to Meaning

example, the word *cat*, the teacher pronounces the word as /kăt/; and the child says the word /kăt/. The process may be illustrated as follows, using the classical conditioning paradigm:

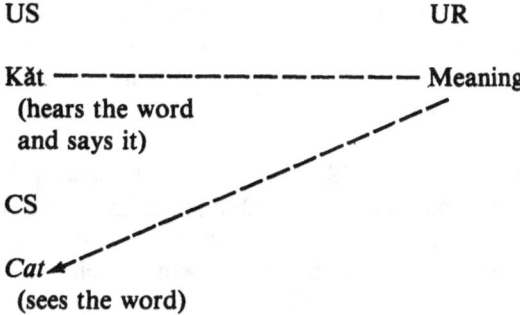

Gradually, with repeated associations between the written and the spoken word, the child brings to the written word the same meaning she previously attached to the spoken word. Of course, this works only if the spoken word has already been comprehended and if its meaning is readily available in her cognitive structure.

There may even be a third possibility, the morphemic decomposition route (Taft, 1985). Van Orden (1987) and Leong (1989) found that morphemic knowledge is important for word deciphering and syntactical understanding. Morphemic decomposition involves decomposing of the word (e.g., *resurvey*) by accessing the meaning of the individual components (e.g., *re* and *survey*) (Just & Carpenter, 1987) or by analyzing a compound word into its two separate words.

The research suggests that the phonological path (i.e., the print-to-sound-to-meaning path) and the direct access path (i.e., the direct print-to-meaning path) typically operate in parallel in the skilled reader (Juel, 1983).

We call to your attention a common experience of teachers. The word *steeple* appears on the page and the context is such that the pupil reasons that *steeple* refers to "that something up on the roof of a church." The pupil has used direct visual access to meaning. However, he "reads" the word wrongly as *tower* /touər/. Sounding of the word is obviously faulty. In this instance, attainment of meaning is not adequate to the task of identifying the word. Although the pupil attains lexical access and even proffers a name for the visual configuration, it is not the correct name. Good readers will achieve lexical access and will identify the word simultaneously. For them, encoding of the word and lexical access operate in parallel.

Whether readers use the phonological route, the direct visual access route, or both depends on: (a) whether the reader is a fluent reader, a beginning reader, or a poor reader; (b) on the difficulty level of what is being read; and (c) upon the age and maturity of the reader.

Huey (1908) observed that "it is perfectly certain that the inner hearing or pronouncing (the inner voice or speech) or both, of what is read, is a constituent part of reading" (pp. 117–118). Huey believed that "inner speech" plays a crucial role in comprehending text. Each of us experiences the feelings of hearing our voice say the words when we read silently. Also, many of us move our lips, and there is significant muscle activity in the speech tract.

Rayner and Pollatsek (1989) note that inner speech (including both subvocalization and phonological recoding) is an important part of reading. We would add that this is true whether one uses the phonological or the direct visual access route. Sounding of the word, even though it may be at a subvocal level, seems to occur either before or after lexical access.

Subvocalization

Moving the lips and subvocalizing while reading silently are not as undesirable as some educators believe. It seems likely that speech traces are a part of all, or nearly all, thinking and probably even "silent" reading. Jacobson (1932) found that the muscles controlling the eyes contract during imagination as though the individual were looking at the object. Furthermore, when persons think, the muscles of the tongue and upper lip vibrate as if they were saying the words. Edfeldt (1960), studying electromyographic (EMG) records of college students, found that all engaged in inner speech while reading. The muscles in the speech tract (lips, tongue, chin, larynx, throat) did in fact move during reading. Inner speech, however, is not the same as real or overt speech because we can read "silently" much faster than we can read aloud. Summarizing the research from the EMG records obtained by inserting needle electrodes inside the muscles or by placing surface electrodes on the speech organs, Rayner and Pollatsek (1989) report an increase in speech tract activity during reading and greater EMG activity for difficult text than for easy text and for beginning readers than for skilled readers. Recent analysis of brain wave research indicates that when the brain decides to speak, the Broca-Wernicke area of the brain sends out word waves a fraction of a second before the word is vocalized, telling the vocal cords, the mouth, and throat to form the words. The interesting point is that the brain sends out the word waves even if the person does not speak the word but only thinks it.

That speech aids thinking was recognized by early philosophers and psychologists. The Greeks used the same word, *logos*, for both thinking and speech. Kant suggested that to think is to speak to oneself. And Watson (1920) referred to thought as the subvocal use of language. Certainly, little children frequently use speech to make sense out of their world. They constantly talk to themselves, dripping speech as it were, because for them, inner thinking and mental imagery are closely associated with vocal expression. Speech aids their thinking. It appears that subvocalizing and vocalizing similarly aid young children in comprehending what they are reading.

Perfetti (1985) notes that speech muscle activation occurs in silent reading even among skilled readers when the reading is difficult (vocalization usually indicates that the pupil is having difficulty in reading and often is a crutch used to improve comprehension), when the reader is trying to remember, or when the text contains many low-frequency words (Seidenberg et al., 1984) or words whose visual form is unfamiliar (Just & Carpenter, 1987; Kleiman & Pumphrey, 1982; Rayner & Pollatsek, 1989). Smith (1988) suggests that subvocalization may serve a useful function in providing rehearsal to help hold in short-term memory words that cannot be immediately understood. Adams (1990) observes that subvocalizing is a normal part of silent reading, that even skilled readers usually vocalize the printed words, and that skilled readers cannot comprehend a complex sentence if they are prevented from subvocalizing the words.

Rayner and Pollatsek (1989) note, "One important feature of inner speech is that it probably is an indicant of the more 'constructive' aspects of reading, whereby the reader is adding something to the printed record in order to help decipher its larger meaning" (p. 219). They add that inner speech aids comprehension by bolstering short-term memory. Inner speech processes thus appear to support both memory and comprehension. Rayner and Pollatsek (1989) observe that when inner speech is experimentally eliminated or interfered with, comprehension suffers unless the comprehension task is very simple.

Prelexical Phonological Recoding

Prelexical phonological recoding or phonemic recoding has been variously named the prelexical speech code, acoustic coding, phonetic recoding, and speech recoding (Downing & Leong, 1982; Just & Carpenter, 1987; Rayner & Pollatsek, 1989). Rayner and Pollatsek note that phonetic recoding "suggests a process of converting written words into articulatory features" (p. 189). The term prelexical speech more accurately portrays what occurs when the reader is using the phonological route to meaning. Unquestionably, many readers recode the graphic input into speech (either as spoken words or as internal speech) and then, using their own speech as aural input, access or decode the words' meaning.

Although converting words to sounds is not absolutely necessary for the identification of words or for accessing word meaning (Barron, 1986;

Rayner & Pollatsek, 1989), the prelexical speech code (which is generated directly from print independently of and prior to lexical access) plays a significant part in lexical access or accessing the meaning of words, especially in beginning readers and unskilled readers (Just & Carpenter, 1987; Van Orden, 1987). They master reading only with a great deal of help from acoustic intermediaries (Doehring, 1976). They rely on the phonological information in recognizing words (Bruck, 1988) and in checking on the accuracy of their word recognition (Jorm & Share, 1983). Even skilled readers use phonological coding when attempting to identify low-frequency words (Bruck, 1988; Stanovich, 1986). They may even use the slower phonological route to meaning or activate the prelexical speech code concurrently with visual-based lexical access (Jorm & Share, 1983).

Perfetti and McCutchen (1982) and Perfetti (1985) suggest that speech processes occur automatically as a part of lexical access and that even skilled reading is benefited when it includes implicit speech or recoding. The reader needs to secure a referent for the word and this is facilitated by having a phonetically indexed name code (the code is the name of the concept). This code is automatically activated as a part of lexical access in the skilled reader. It allows access to the information stored with a word in memory even after the word has been accessed. The name of the word serves as a referent code because semantic information for a word is connected in memory by its linkage to the word's name (Perfetti, 1985). It follows then, Perfetti observes, that reading may be more efficient if phonetic information is a part of lexical access. Phonetic activation is not necessarily the first step to lexical access, but when it reaches a high level of activation prior to completion of lexical access, it is correctly termed recoding.

Barron (1980, 1981), Ehri (1980), and Just and Carpenter (1987, p. 93) also observe that the lexical entry for a word or the print lexicon is jointly constituted from its visual form, its phonological form, its syntactic characteristics, its orthographic characteristics, its semantic characteristics, and its relation to other concepts. The sound of the word is said to be linked in the mental lexicon with all the other characteristics of the word. Fowler (1981) and Just and Carpenter (1987) thus observe that the word must be sounded in some way because the phonological form is a necessary part of the word. When any of the word's other characteristics are activated, the sound of the word is also activated.

Perfetti (1985) adds that comprehension occurs at all points during the process. The word's meaning can be accessed directly, but since there is a memory for the word itself in the form of a phonetic name and since this name is also a part of propositional encoding (i.e., the comprehension of isolated sentences), automatic phonemic activation makes a word available in memory and thus serves comprehension. Just and Carpenter (1987) remark that the prelexical speech code is generated more readily when the code is not restricted to individual letters and their sounds, but includes groups of letters (i.e., consonant clusters, phonograms, and morphemes). Thus, a multiunit activation process makes the prelexical speech code a more plausible route. Rayner and Pollatsek (1989) note that "phonological codes appear to be activated for most words we read" and add that "this phonological information is held in working memory and is used to comprehend text" (p. 216). Gough (1972) believes that the phonological code is needed because linguistic information can be retained longer in short-term memory than can the orthographic information. Rose (1969) found that the fadeout of a visually acquired stimulus is rapid if it is not recoded in acoustic form. An acoustic factor seems to be involved in immediate memory and recall.

Direct Visual Access

Buswell (1947) believed that silent reading should be a process of association between perceptual stimulation and meaning "without a mediating subvocalization." Psycholinguists generally maintain that the fluent reader decodes directly from the graphic symbol to meaning. Smith (1988) observes that written language does not require reading to sound to be comprehended. Such processing is termed direct visual access.

The direct visual access route to the lexicon involves the categorization of the word in the visual input system, then in the cognitive or semantic system, and ultimately in the phonological system for phonemic analysis. The word is recognized directly as a visual ideogram, the meaning is accessed, and the word is sounded only after lexical access. Many mature and proficient readers follow this route. They have automatized the process of analysis and synthesis and recognize the word immediately as a whole, either from its general contour or its context (Gaddes, 1980). In this alternate route, the visual word images are processed directly without phonemic transcoding. We shall indicate later (chapter 8) that this is also the approach used by beginning readers who have not yet learned how to get at the sound of a novel word. They rely more on grapheme information (Rayner & Pollatsek, 1989). That is why we recommend the teaching of some "sight words" before teaching phonics.

Perfetti (1985) notes that the word can be identified before phonemic activation reaches a high level (i.e., before recoding occurs), but not without at least some phonemic activation. If the identification process is slow, the phonemes are highly activated before a word decision is made, and word identification is affected by phoneme activation. If the word is identified quickly, the complete phonemic activation may not occur. Just and Carpenter (1987) likewise think that the letters of the word initiate the activation of the corresponding visual word percept, which in turn activates the word's meaning, producing lexical access. However, when the letters of the word activate lexical access they simultaneously activate the prelexical speech code. The prelexical speech code, like the visual word percept, then initiates the activation of the word's meaning. But, because visual access is more quick and more accurate, it reaches threshold before the prelexical speech code can and before it activates lexical access.

Postlexical Phonological Recoding

Postlexical phonological coding occurs when lexical access precedes phonological coding or when the speech code (i.e., inner speech) is generated after lexical access or as a by-product of lexical access. Clearly, meanings of words can be accessed without sounding the words (deaf children do learn to read), but even then, sounding of words either before or after lexical access is beneficial in that it holds words in working memory while other processes, such as working out the syntactic structure of the sentence, finding the referent for a pronoun, or extracting meaning from the sentence, are completed.

Both prelexical and postlexical codes (i.e., sounding of words) (Just & Carpenter, 1987; Rayner & Pollatsek, 1989): (a) help readers to retain the serial order of words in a text, thus aiding syntactic processing; (b) supplement memory and recall because the sounded words represent the features of stress, intonation, and pauses; (c) convert the printed symbols into a speech code (which is longer lasting in working memory than is the visually based code and holds them in memory until meaning can be passed on to long-term memory; (d) help to check on the visual word identification process; and (e) aid comprehension. The sounds of the word contain prosodic information (i.e., rhythm, intonation, stress) which are present in speech but are less so in written language. The phonological code helps the reader to reorganize the written sentence into a prosodic structure or into rhythmically organized information in working memory.

A stronger case can be made for the role of inner speech in postlexical comprehension processes than in aiding lexical access. Subvocalization, even though it aids comprehension of difficult text (Hardyck & Petrinovich, 1970), is of generally less importance to comprehension than is phonological recoding, particularly postlexical phonological recoding (Rayner & Pollatsek, 1989). Rayner and Pollatsek (1989) conclude that both phonological recoding and subvocalization are involved in short-term memory processes used in comprehending discourse; subvocalization is probably not involved in lexical access whereas phonological coding probably is. In the phonological coding process the grapheme/phoneme conversion rules are applied to sound out letter patterns, which are then blended to form the word. The process may be completely independent of lexical influences or may involve lexical influences (Olson, 1985). Furthermore, word recoding may occur without the application of grapheme/phoneme conversion rules. The sound of an unfamiliar word may be obtained by analogy to words that have a similar orthographic pattern.

Phonetic coding falls off sharply by about the third grade, with direct access increasing above that grade level (Olson, 1985). Rayner and Pollatsek (1989) suggest that by fifth grade pupils generally have mastered phonics.

Rayner and Pollatsek (1989) note that phonological codes lag roughly two words behind the eyes in reading, whereas the "inner voice" in silent reading is more closely tied to eye position.

If reading depends on either prelexical phonological coding, postlexical phonological coding, or both, it follows that readers need to be able to hear phonemes, to translate them into word sounds, and to associate them with comparable written or printed words.

SUMMARY

Chapter 1 has reviewed various definitions of reading, classified definitions into those that define reading as interpretation of experience and those that define reading as interpretation of graphic symbols, and discussed the importance of word recognition, comprehension, and semantic and syntactic structures. Reading was described as building a representation of text, and as a word recognition and comprehension process in which integration of these two subprocesses is an essential ingredient. Reading always involves a sign system (the words or symbols on the printed page) and decoding (the association of meaning with the symbols). The chapter also presented the view that readers can be good readers only if their past life experience has furnished them with a cognitive base relevant to the information contained in a particular written communication, and if their level of experience with language itself, with syntactic and idiomatic usage, has been adequate.

Finally, the basic theme of the chapter is that reading is clearly a process which is complete only when comprehension is attained. The critical element is that the reader reconstruct the message encoded in the written language. Full comprehension occurs when the reconstruction agrees with the writer's intended message. The chapter also suggests that the path to meaning may be direct (i.e., direct visual access), indirect (i.e., through the recoding or phonological route) or both; that reading proceeds best when the reader uses both bottom-up and top-down processing, particularly when the reader integrates the two in interactive or parallel processing; and that comprehension depends as much or even more on the information stored in the reader's brain than on the information stored in the text.

PART II

Correlates of Reading Achievement and of Reading Failure

Part II consists of two chapters: chapter 2, "The Sensory Nature of the Reading Process," and chapter 3, "Reading: A Memory Process, A Perceptual-Cognitive Process, A Linguistic and Communicative Process." These chapters expand on reading as a sensory process (involving vision and visual perception, eye movement, and often auditory perception); as a memory or information-processing process; as a perceptual-cognitive process involving the associating of meaning with symbols, the construction of meanings, going beyond the printed page, and taking meaning to the printed page; as a linguistic process (i.e., reading functions best when it is taught in a speaking-listening, writing-reading, whole-language context); and as a communicative process (i.e., the reader must share the meanings communicated by the writer).

We have headed Part II "Correlates of Reading Achievement and of Reading Failure" because the processes discussed in chapters 2 and 3 are not reading. They are rather the enabling or prerequisite skills for the attainment of readiness and the development of literacy. Reading readiness may be described as the teachable moment for reading: the point in time when the pupil is ready to learn how to read.

Children generally come to school wanting to learn to read. When they discover that what can be said can also be written, they show an even greater interest. The most frequently repeated phrase during the readiness period is "What does it say?" Children early develop print awareness by "reading" names on cereal boxes, candy wrappers, store buildings, traffic signs, and so on. And, they develop story sense by being read to. Smith (1988) observes that children are ready to learn to read whenever they have "a purpose and intelligible opportunity for reading, not in terms of settling down to a concentrated period of systematic instruction but in an explorer's interest in signs and labels, in telephone directories and catalogs, and in stories" (p. 211). Children are more ready to read when they possess a large speaking and listening vocabulary and when they have a sense of story (Stoodt, 1989). They are ready to read when they know that written language is meaningful and that it is different from spoken language.

It is not easy to describe or even to list all the variables that affect readiness and achievement in reading. However, research and experience indicate that for success in reading, the child should either possess or develop in school certain minimum levels of proficiency in a number of areas. Conversely, in children having difficulty learning to read, there is rarely one factor that explains the difficulty. Multiple causality is generally indicated, and the difficulty is generally related to cultural, economic, environmental, psychological, social, emotional, and educational factors.

Of primary importance for children learning to read are attention, motivation and interest, and the self-concept of the learner. "Learning does not occur without a prior focussing of attention and without appropriate motivation" (Cotman and Lynch, 1988, p. 48). Children need to attend to what needs to be learned, they must want to learn, and they need to feel that they can learn. Smith (1988) observes that:

> Children do not learn to read who do not want to, or who see no point in doing so, or who are hostile to the teacher, or to the school, or to the social or cultural group to which they perceive the teacher and the school as belonging. Children do not learn to read who expect to fail, or who believe that learning to read will be too costly, or whose preferred image of themselves, for whatever reason, is that of a nonreader. (pp. 211-212)

Major concerns in reading, and especially in the readiness-kindergarten period, are the development of a knowledge of the alphabet, letter recognition, ability to name the letters, directional orientation (moving in a left-to-right progression while reading), word consciousness, acquisition of a basic sight vocabulary, awareness of the relationship between a printed word and the sound representation of that word, development of basic word-identification skills, and development of word meaning and simple comprehension skills. These areas of knowledge are treated in later chapters. Each is a bit of necessary knowledge for the pupil to acquire.

But, for the moment, our emphasis is on the variables that make the acquisition of this information either relatively easy or inordinately difficult. As noted earlier, teachers of reading must be concerned with the pupil's vision and visual perceptual processes, with the pupil's eye movement patterns, and with hearing and auditory perception processes. The teacher must also understand the influence of such negative factors as lack of world knowledge; memory deficits; inadequate experiences with life itself; low socioeconomic status and impoverished home environment; cultural differences; low level of conceptualization; deficient environmental stimulation; and divergent cultural, societal, and parental expectations.

Other negative influences include inadequacy of instruction, lack of experience with being read to, difficulties in symbolization and language (articulatory defects, speech defects, lack of sentence sense, etc.), too early introduction to reading, poor management of skill development, inadequacy of instructional materials, poor social and emotional adjustment, faulty learning style, low intelligence, motivational inadequacy, health problems, gender (the ratio of boys to girls with learning difficulties is 3 or 4 to 1), neural deficits, left or mixed hand preference, defective direction sense, and glandular dysfunction, malnutrition, prematurity, low birth weight, developmental delay, and hyperactivity or hypoactivity.

It is impossible to identify and discuss in two chapters all the variables that relate to readiness and achievement in reading. We focus in chapter 2 on the sensory aspects of reading and in chapter 3 on the memory, perceptual/cognitive, linguistic, and communicative aspects of reading.

Possession of the enabling skills, singly and collectively, does not assure success in reading, but their absence may retard and even totally inhibit the learning of reading. Thus, readers who cannot develop a visual discrimination and a visual memory for the writer's words, who cannot recode these words, and especially those who cannot associate meanings with these words, cannot perceive the message of the writer. For them communication via reading does not occur.

Figure Part 2-1 relates the sensory, perceptual/cognitive, language/communicative, and memory processes to reading tasks, and identifies the enabling skills needed for efficient performance of the task. Because reading is a sensory process, involving vision, eye movement, and hearing, we address this aspect first.

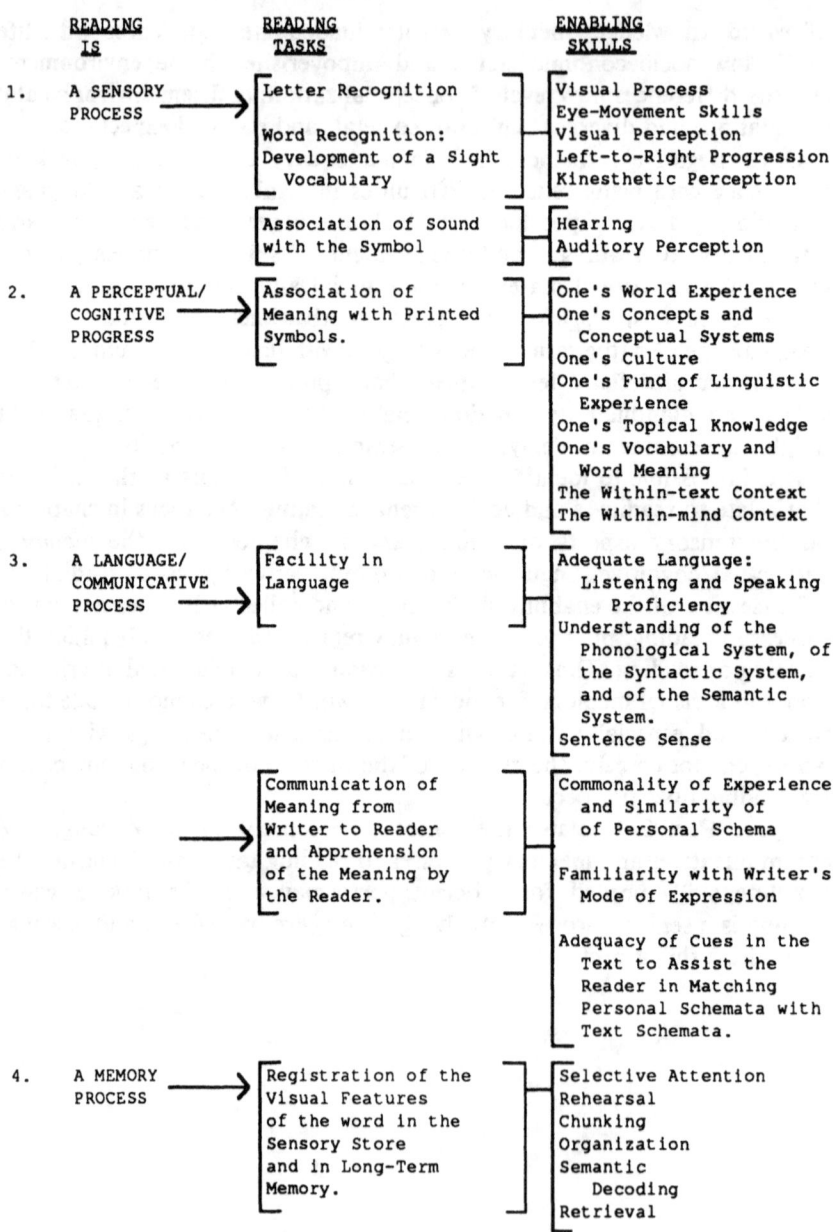

FIGURE Part 2-1. The Enabling Skills in Reading

Chapter 2
The Sensory Nature of the Reading Process

    I. Introduction
   II. The Visual Processes and Reading
       A. The Structure and Functions of the Eyes
       B. The optic Nerve and the Optic Chiasma
       C. The Lateral Geniculate Nuclei
       D. Area 17 in the Occipital Lobe
  III. Visual Defects and Reading
       A. Lack of Visual Activity
       B. Refractive Errors
       C. Binocular Errors
  IV. Eye Movement Skills and Reading
       A. Fixation
       B. Fixation Time
       C. Saccade Length and Duration
       D. Perception Span
       E. Fixation Frequency
       F. Eye-Memory Span and Eye-Voice Span
       G. Thought Unit Reading
       H. Regressions
       I. Return Sweep
       J. Rate Improvement
   V. Eye Movement Deficits and Poor Reading
  VI. The Rayner-Pollatsek Model
 VII. Visual Perception and Reading
VIII. Hearing and Reading
  IX. Auditory Perception and Reading
       A. Auditory Discrimination
       B. Auditory Memory
       C. Auditory Figure-Ground Discrimination
   X. Summary

CHAPTER 2
The Sensory Nature of the Reading Process

Reading as a sensory process focuses on the graphic input, the letters and words on the page. Without the graphic input, there can be no reading. If indeed reading is a process of comprehension and word recognition, and if word recognition requires the pupil to visually discriminate each printed symbol from every other symbol, to identify the symbol, and to develop a memory for the symbol, then it follows that the visual processes should have a bearing on word identification and that the teacher of reading should be interested in understanding the effects that vision, eye movement, and visual perception have on reading achievement.

THE VISUAL PROCESSES AND READING

Reading begins as a visual skill. Vision is the first step in reading. Visual information is a must in reading. "It is what goes away when the lights go out" (Smith, 1988, p. 65). The reader must visually process the graphic symbols, the letters and words. The eyes bring the stimuli to the reader, and it is only through vision that the reader is able to deal with the significant contrastive shapes and features of the graphic symbols which form the sign system or the surface structure in reading. It is vision that allows the reader to identify or encode the word and then to recognize the word on subsequent occasions.

The Structure and Functions of the Eyes

As we have already noted, reading begins with visual sensation. Sensations are the result of physical stimulations of the sensory receptors. Perceptions are defined as meaningful interpretations of these sensations. Perception gives an awareness of whole objects or events in the external world.

Stimuli are referred to as proximal and distal. Proximal stimuli (e.g., light rays) lead to sensation; distal stimuli (e.g., chair) are what is perceived in perception. When the light rays from the words strike the retina of the eye or, more correctly, when patterns of light fall on the sensory neurons in the retina, the receptor organs or cells within the eye translate electromagnetic energy or light reflected from the word into electrochemical neural impulses or messages to the central nervous system. It is this process which initiates the identification, recognition, and interpretation of printed symbols.

The electromagnetic waves or rays of light vary in frequency, amplitude, and spatial and temporal patterning, but what perceivers see is color, form, texture, and movement. They see an object; they see a word. They do not perceive the light rays.

Unfortunately, readers, looking at a page of print, do not see all the words on the printed page equally well, with equal acuity, or with equal keenness of vision. Rayner and Pollatsek, (1989) observe that in terms of acuity, a line of print falling on the retina divides into three regions: the foveal, the parafoveal, and the peripheral. The foveal area extends some 2° about the fixation point, the parafoveal, about 10°, and the peripheral encompasses everything beyond the parafoveal region. Acuity is sharpest in the foveal area. Rayner and Bertera (1979) found that when the central seven characters around the fixation point were masked, reading was still possible from the parafoveal vision, but only at a rate of 12 words per minute. When both the foveal and parafoveal were masked (i.e., the central 11 to 17 character spaces around the fixation point), reading became almost impossible.

When the reader reads, the light reflected from the word enters the eye (see Figure 2-1) through the cornea, a transparent convex-shaped protective membrane that bends the light rays together. The light next passes through the pupil. Inside the pupil, the light passes through the lens which focuses the light on the retina. The lens changes shape to focus on objects either closer or farther away. The lens also inverts the image of the objects on the retina. The retina, an inner lining of the back of the eyeball, contains the rods and cones, the receptor cells, that respond to light.

The fovea is a small depression at the center of the retina that consists

THE SENSORY NATURE OF THE READING PROCESS

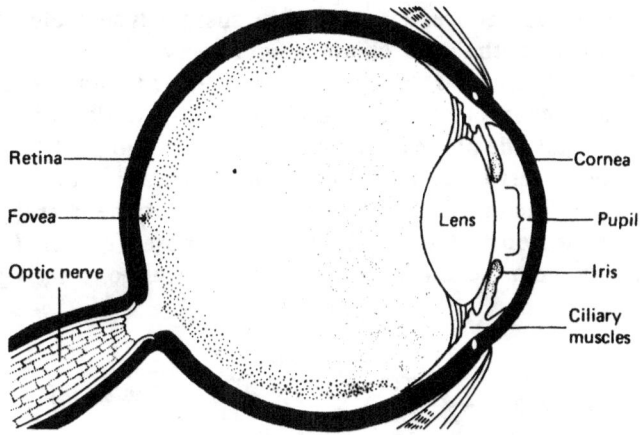

FIGURE 2-1. Cross Section of the Human Eye (Gazzaniga, 1973, p. 21)

almost entirely of cones. The peripheral region is composed only of rods. The cones open mainly in daylight and are specialized for processing detail and for the discrimination of wavelengths or hue. The rods detect movement, permit discrimination of brightness or shades of gray, and control night vision.

Reading begins when the eye fixates upon the words on the page. The eye fixation lasts for some 250 milliseconds and takes in 15 to 20 letters. Each forward fixation moves the eye 7 to 9 letter spaces to the right. The result is an image of the portion of the page upon which the eyes focused. This image lasts for a very brief period of time (from ½ to 1 second) after the external stimulus is removed. Stabilization of this image is brought about by the formation of a visual afterimage, which lasts for about 20 to 30 seconds and then gradually disappears.

The Optic Nerve and the Optic Chiasma

Cells in the retina convert the light energy (reflected from the letter or word) into electrochemical or neural impulses (or electrical codes) that are carried via the optic nerve, a pencil-thick bundle of nerve fibers, to the visual projection area (area 17 or the striate cortex) in the visual cortex in the occipital lobe in the brain. The impulses that travel from the retina to the brain undergo a series of transformations on the way. After the electrical code leaves the retina, it travels along the optic nerve to the optic chiasma. Each eye views both left and right sides of the visual world.

However, the brain receives left and right visual fields separately because a crossover occurs at the optic chiasma: optic nerve fibers from the nasal halves of the retinas cross, while those from the temporal halves do not. The optic chiasma is thus a visual switching yard. It sends half of the optic fibers to the right side of the brain and the other half to the left (see Figure 2-2). The optic nerve fibers(and hence the electrical impulses or signals) from the right visual field of both eyes next travel to the lateral geniculate nuclei (LGN)and on to the left visual cortex; those from the left side of each retina or from the left visual field of both eyes go to the right visual cortex.

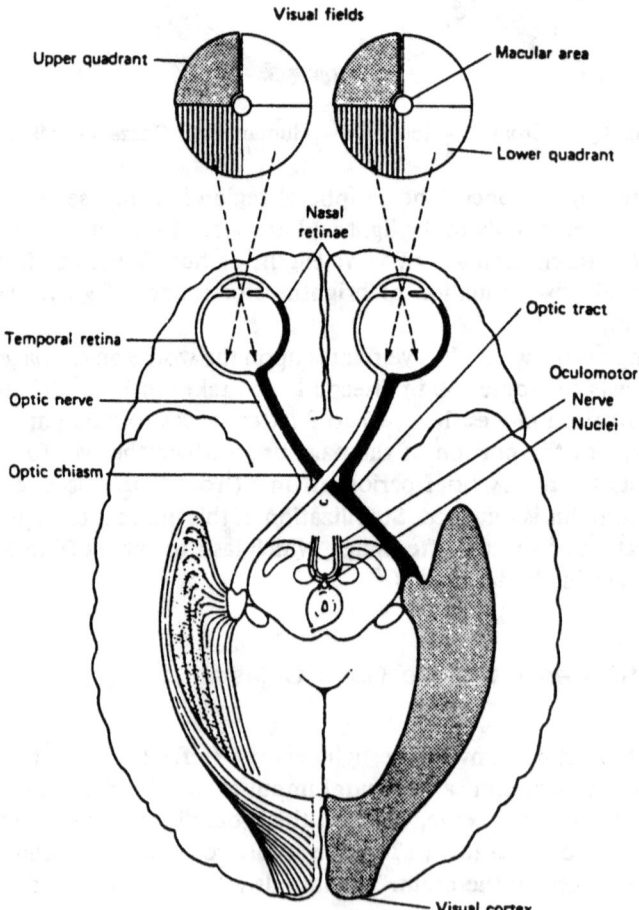

FIGURE 2-2. The Visual Pathway to the Occipital Lobe
(Robeck & Wallace, 1990, p.   )

The Lateral Geniculate Nuclei

The lateral geniculate nuclei of the thalamus (see Figure 2-2) are important way stations in the total visual process. They function as the interconnecting centers for visual impulses passing to the occipital lobe and provide the initial processing of visual signals. They are the loci where the optic nerves synapse with the brain neurons. All the geniculate fibers project directly onto area 17 in the occipital lobe and are the primary visual input to area 17 (see Figure 2-3).

Not all nerve fibers of the optic nerve follow the path described in Figure 2-2. Some nerve fibers go directly to the superior colliculi in the midbrain and direct the eyes to the appropriate target. Other fibers in the superior colliculi control the reflex movements required in adjusting the size of the pupil of the eye, and still others direct the eye muscles to change the shape of the lens. The cells in the superior colliculi detect the presence of novel objects in the periphery of the visual field, determine whether what is seen is important (and adjust the eye movements accordingly), and regulate visual grasp or orientation responses.

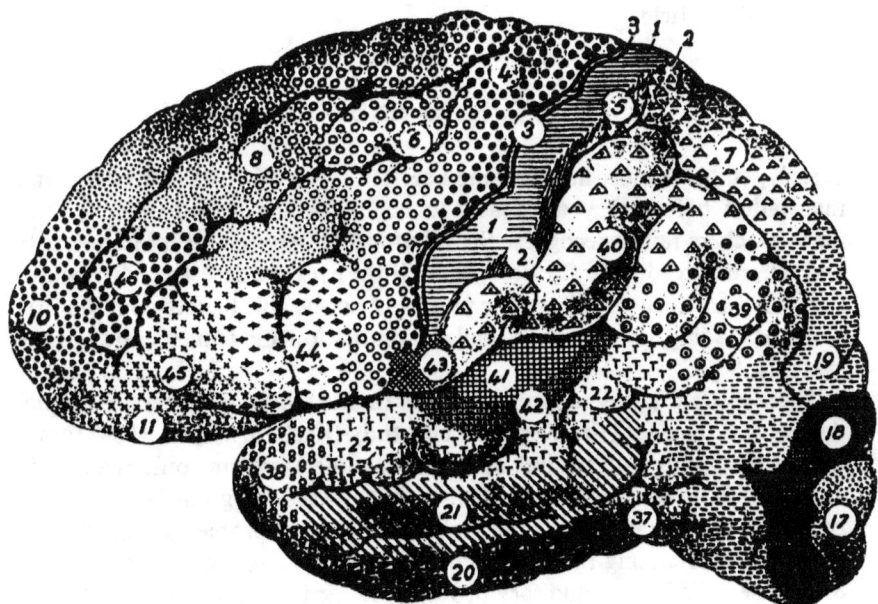

FIGURE 2-3. The Projection and Association Areas of the Brain (Duke-Elder and Scott, 1971, p. 471)

Area 17 in the Occipital Lobe

From the lateral geniculate nuclei the nerve impulses travel to area 17, the visual cortex in the back of the occipital lobe of the brain. It is in the visual cortex that seeing really begins. After the visual stimulus reaches area 17 (see Figure 2–3), it is processed for visual identification, visual memory, sounding, and meaning. Area 17 is the primary visual register or analyzer; it receives visual input or the neural impulses from the retina and is responsible for the apperception of the sensation of light, the fusion of two separate images in binocular vision, the perception of color, form, and contour, and localization in space. It also is responsible for synthesis and stabilization of the visual impulse.

At the cortical level, words to the right of the fixation point in the environment are represented in the left cerebral hemisphere, while those in the left field of vision are represented in the right hemisphere. Each half of the brain is thus concerned with half of the visual field. For this reason, destruction of the optic nerve results in blindness in one half of each eye. Rayner and Pollatsek (1989) note that words are processed more efficiently when presented in the right visual field (i.e., left hemisphere processing), whereas faces and pictures are processed more efficiently when presented in the left visual field.

VISUAL DEFECTS AND READING

Clearly, children must have attained certain levels of visual efficiency and maturation before they are ready to begin reading. Unfortunately, too many teachers fail to recognize the relationship between visual immaturity and failure in reading in the first grade. If the eyes are defective, difficulties in reading are likely to follow: the pupil will not be able to carry out the first phase of reading, namely, the visual discrimination and identification of the symbols.

There are few, if any, definitive studies on the relationship between visual defects and reading. However, a recent study (Keefe & Meyer, 1988) found that of 106 adults with reading difficulties, some of whom could read "only a few words," some "just a little," others at "low second-grade level," or still others "at third-grade level," the incidence of visual problems ranged from a high of 89% among those who could read only a few words to a low of 65%. The incidence of auditory problems ranged from a high of 78% to a low of 40%.

Children must be able to focus the eyes at 20 inches or less as well as at 20 feet or more. They must have skill in depth perception, binocular coordination, ability to center, and ability to change fixation at will. And,

THE SENSORY NATURE OF THE READING PROCESS 51

they must see clearly, singly, and for sustained periods. Unfortunately, many children are not visually mature enough to cope with the printed page before the age of eight. Children are born farsighted. This prevents adequate focus of images of near objects on the retina. As the eyeball lengthens, farsightedness gradually decreases and the child becomes capable of adapting to the demands of near vision. However, at age six, 10% to 15% of children are still too farsighted to see clearly such small stimuli as the printed word without developing headaches, fatigue, and nervousness. Farsightedness is only one of the visual defects that may hamper efficiency in reading. Figure 2-4 identifies others.

Lack of Visual Acuity

Visual acuity or keenness of vision, usually measured at near point, 14 to 18 inches, and at far point, 20 feet or more, does not seem to have the significance for reading achievement that some other visual factors have. And, lack of visual acuity is not necessarily damaging in reading. To read the average book, one needs only 20/60 visual acuity at near point (especially in the left eye). The emmetropic or normal eye sees with 100% of acuity only a very small portion of the visual field, perhaps no more than four or five letters, with increasingly less accuracy as the distance from the area of foveal vision increases. When the book is held 16 inches from the eyes, the reader sees about 2¼ inches of printed material. The pupil should have 20/30 visual acuity at far point. An acuity score of 20/30 means that at 20 feet the smallest letter the observer can read is one that should have been seen normally at 30 feet (Goldberg et al., 1983).

A recent study (1987) by Geiger and Lettvin at MIT, reported in the *New England Journal of Medicine*, of a small group of dyslexics suggests that dyslexics have poor foveal vision, but much better peripheral vision. The result is that they take a wide-angle view rather than a direct view of words,

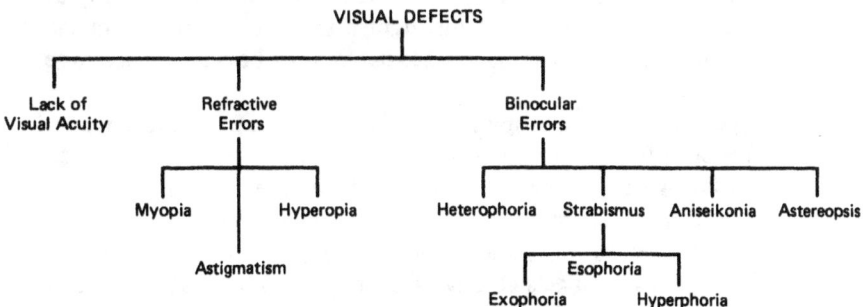

FIGURE 2-4. Visual Defects

seeing the peripheral word better than the word in foveal vision. Remediation consists of looking through a piece of paper with a small hole in it when reading.

Refractive Errors

Refractive errors, which include myopia, hyperopia, and astigmatism, are due to damage, disease, or weakness in the lens or other portion of one or both eyes, causing a defect in conformation of the eyes. These errors result in a faulty focus of the light rays on the retina. In myopia the eyeball is too long, with the result that the light rays (and hence the image) come into focus in front of the retina, instead of on the retina. In hyperopia, the eyeball is too short with the result that the image falls behind the retina, and near vision is blurred. In astigmatism, the curvature of the cornea is uneven. It is spoon shaped rather than spherical. Generally, refractive errors can be corrected by glasses. Glasses, however, do not increase the sensitivity of the eyes. They help the eye to focus and lessen eye strain, but they frequently fail to provide normal vision.

1. Myopia, or nearsightedness, forces the pupil to hold the book closer than the normal 16 inches or so. Distant vision generally is blurred. Myopia makes it difficult to see far point objects, such as what is on the chalkboard. Near vision remains unimpaired since the light rays from near objects fall on the retina. Usually concave lenses are prescribed for myopic conditions. Children may become myopic through premature attempts to adapt their eyes to the demands of close vision; myopia may be symptomatic of a general weakness of connective tissue; the sweep in reading from the end of one line to the beginning of the next may lead to congestion and pressure on the posterior pole of the eye, causing it to become myopic; and hurried and excessive use of peripheral vision or "teaching Johnny to read" at an early age may cause myopia. Myopia generally does not distinguish the good reader from the poor reader. It may even be associated with better than average progress.
2. Hyperopia, hypermetropia, or farsightedness, appears to have an adverse effect on reading when it is severe; if it is linked to phorias; when it is present in one eye while the other is normal or myopic; if it is present beyond fifth-grade level; or when it is accompanied by a squint (Spache, 1976). Hyperopia makes it difficult to see objects clearly at near point. The reader thus has difficulty in seeing images at the typical reading distance of 14 to 16 inches. Severe hyperopia affects the ability of the eyes to

converge. Hyperopia results from a shorter-than-normal distance between the cornea and the retina. As a result, the visual image is still not in focus by the time the light waves reach the retina. In an attempt to compensate for the loss of focus, the ciliary muscles must contract strongly, especially when the child is trying to get a clear image of close objects. The adjustment required puts a strain on the eye muscles and may cause blurring of vision, a short visual attention span, or headaches. Convex lenses are usually prescribed.
3. Astigmatism, the inability to bring the light rays to single focal point, causes vision to be blurred and distorted. Unless the distorted image is corrected by the use of cylindrical lens, the child fatigues easily and usually dislikes close work or prolonged distant vision. Astigmatism is a major cause of ocular asthenopia or eyestrain. Headaches are common, similar letters and words are confused, and the pupil experiences difficulty in sustained reading. Astigmatism may be a handicap to successful reading when the learner has a severe case or when it is present in only one eye.

Binocular Difficulties

Binocular difficulties or lack of fusion have the communality of giving the child a double image (diplopia), but to be a successful reader the pupil should be able to focus at 20 inches or less. The visual images of the same object are focused simultaneously on the retina of each eye, and to see clearly these images need to be fused so the perceiver sees a single object. To read with efficiency and ease, the reader can either become monocular or develop an efficient binocular system. Anything between these two extremes is likely to cause fusion problems and to lead to difficulties in reading.

As a rule, it is the left eye which does most of the leading, suggesting that the eyes are not synchronized during saccadic movement. Presumably, when the deviations become too large, binocular difficulties occur.

When the ocular maladjustments are minor, children may suppress the stimulus. When they can suppress it only partially or temporarily or when the maladjustments are major, they may see two of everything or a blurred image. They are likely to lose their place, to omit words, to mix letters and words, to regress, or to be excessively slow in reading. Continued suppression of the vision of one eye can lead to functional blindness in that eye. When the pupil uses only one eye (suppressing the use of the other even though both eyes are structurally intact), the condition is described as amblyopia (the "lazy eye" condition).

Binocular difficulties manifest themselves as strabismus, heterophoria, aniseikonia, and astereopsis.

1. Strabismus (from the Greek word meaning "to squint") is a severe muscular imbalance or fusion difficulty stemming from a paralysis of an eye muscle or from an incoordination or lack of proper balance among the six pairs of muscles that move the eyeballs. Sometimes the convergence of the eyes is insufficient or one eye aims too far outward (exophoria or wall eyes), too far inward (esophoria or crossed eyes), or one eye aims in a different vertical plane from the other (hyperphoria). A severe case of strabismus may result in double vision; a less severe case in general blurring of the image. Hyperphoria may lead to jumping of lines or misplacement of a word to a line above or below. Esophoria is frequently associated with nearsightedness and exophoria with farsightedness. Exophoria occurs more frequently among poor readers than does any other phoric condition. It leads to omissions, regressions, and loss of place and causes greater divergent movements at the beginning of lines. Phorias combined with farsightedness are closely related to reading problems. Bax and Whitmore (1973) found that strabismus is a risk factor in learning disorders.
2. Heterophoria is a milder form of eye muscle imbalance. It results in fatigue. As readers tire, their eyes tend to deviate even farther. Attempts to counteract this deviation increase fatigue. A vicious cycle is set up in which children become inattentive and irritable, lose their place, omit words, and regress.
3. Aniseikonia, which results in a difference in size between the two ocular images, makes fusion more difficult, and the reader may become tense, experience fatigue, and have headaches. The condition is more prevalent among poor readers.
4. Astereopsis is the inability to perceive depth. Stereopsis gives a tridimensional effect and occurs because the two eyes receive slightly different images. It often is the best indication of binocular coordination. The eyes of the average adult are separated 65 millimeters. Because of this separation, the images on the two retinas are positioned slightly differently. This disparity is responsible for depth perception or stereopsis.

Other eye movements required for clarity of vision and focus that are associated with varying degrees of reading inefficiency are pupillary adjustment, convergence and divergence, accommodation, compensation for head movements while reading, pursuit (smooth movement used to read signs while driving or moving print on a screen), and physiological nystagmus (involuntary oscillating eye movements, and involuntary, rapid, back-and-forth movement of the eyeballs) (Griffin, Walton, & Ives, 1974).

The pupillary reflex automatically adjusts the size of the pupillary opening to the amount of illumination, permitting more light to enter in dimly lit situations and less light in brightly lit conditions. The convergence reflex, which is also automatic, controls the eyes' tendency to turn in to focus on an object. Stein and Fowler (1984) found that in dyslexics the eyes are pointed in slightly different directions. Dyslexics often demonstrate unstable vergence control; they have difficulty making the small movements that keep both eyes pointing at the center of attention (Rayner & Pollatsek, 1989). Taylor (1962) found in a survey of some 2,000 children with academic difficulties that 95% of these lacked sufficient eye coordination and had difficulties with fusion. They failed to show the convergence required to direct the eyes toward a single fixation point at 13 inches of reading distance while maintaining appropriate divergence or eye balance. Taylor adds that deficiencies in binocular control lead to inadequate word perception and the consumption of an excessive amount of energy in maintaining single vision. The pupil will fatigue easily and will experience distraction, poor comprehension, constant moving of the head, and difficulties in concentration.

The accommodation reflex automatically adjusts the shape of the lens (from narrow to flat to elongated and wide) to the distance of the object so the image on the retina will be kept in sharp focus. In adjusting to distance, the lenses and the posture of the eyes must be carefully coordinated. The eyes separate or diverge for distance and converge for near-point focusing. While this is going on, the lens bulges or flattens to keep the image clear. The eyes are virtually parallel when seeing an object more than 10 feet away, but are turned substantially inward when focusing on an object a foot away. The accommodation-convergence reflex is often not mature before the age of six.

Ocular-motor pursuit refers to the ability to make smooth and continuous movements so the eyes can follow a moving object and quick, saccadic movements with intervening fixations when the object observed is stationary. Ocular pursuit also is needed to shift the eyes along a line in a book, to shift from one line to the next, and to make quick and accurate shifts of vision between the desk and the chalkboard (Pope, 1976).

It is difficult to evaluate the specific effect of the various visual disturbances. Visual problems are more likely to influence an individual's desire to read, due to discomfort and fatigue, rather than the ability to read per se. They act as irritants and lower the efficiency of the individual. However, eye defects, unless they are gross in nature, rarely preclude a child from becoming an adequate reader. The eyes can make amazing accommodations so that words may be seen clearly. With the proper motivation the pupil may learn despite visual handicaps. Children can ignore a distortion from one eye if they see clearly with the other or if they adjust their reading positions to compensate. The pupil may suppress the vision in one eye or alternate from one eye to another. The result is monocular vision. Generally, however, for effective vision the child must be able to use the eyes in unison.

The simple fact is that some children with defective vision become good readers and that others without any visual difficulty do not learn to read. However, this does not indicate that good vision is unimportant to reading. Eye defects are a handicap to both good and poor readers. Smith (1988) notes that "there are no evident visual defects that are specific to reading, but this does not mean that there are no general visual anomalies that will interfere with learning to read" (p. 211). Vellutino (1987) argues that reading disability is a symptom of dysfunction during storage and retrieval of linguistic information rather than the consequence of a defect in the visual system. Benton (1985), however, notes that the question of visual processing is not closed. He points out that reading requires the abstraction of orthographic features, a process which necessitates adequate visual processing. Before the mind can can perceive and comprehend, the eyes must apprehend. The real significance of vision and visual efficiency in reading is that our imaging or perceptual processes, indeed our ability to read with meaning, are clearly dependent upon the stimulus information received through the eyes (Smith, 1971).

EYE-MOVEMENT SKILLS AND READING

Efficiency in reading clearly depends upon adequate visual functioning, but also upon the movements of the eyes during reading, upon gaining cognitive control of the eye movements, and upon the oculomotor habits of the reader.* A major purpose of the eye movements is to bring all words close to the fovea (Rayner & Pollatsek, 1989). Much of what is known about how the eyes react during reading has come from the work of Emile Javal (1878) who was the first to report on the nature of eye movement during reading. He noted that in reading the eyes do not move in a continuous sweep across the page. Rather, they move in quick, short movements with pauses or fixations interspersed. Javal described the eyes as moving "par saccades"— by jerks or little jumps with intervening fixation pauses or stops. The eyes generally move forward about 7 to 9 character spaces with each saccade. All visual information comes in during the fixation. Even though the eye is essentially immobile during fixation, there are very small rapid movements,

---

*We are deeply indebted to Rayner and Pollatsek (1989) in this section and refer the reader to their text for a more extensive, and indeed intensive, discussion of eye movement.

called mystagmus, going on constantly to help the nerve cells in the retina to keep firing (Rayner & Pollatsek, 1989).

The fine discrimination of the retinal cells is possible only because the eye is constantly making these tiny oscillating movements. Without this involuntary tremor, there can be no normal vision and the eye would be seriously damaged (Pritchard, 1971). Stabilizing of the image on the retina results in a disappearance of the image within about 1 minute of inspection, leaving a bland, gray field of light. The tremor occurs at the rate of 50 oscillations per second.

Spache (1976) some years ago observed that eye-movement screening probably provides the best objective evidence of what precisely the individual is doing visually while reading. He noted that eye movements confirm the effects of the visual deviations upon reading as no other diagnostic tool can do. It is only recently (McConkie & Zola, 1984, 1985) that eye-movement data have been used to infer the moment-to-moment cognitive processes during reading. Eye movements provide a window on the difficulty or ease of understanding text (Hall, 1989). Rayner and Pollatsek (1989) note that " where readers look and how long they look there provides valuable information about the mental processes associated with understanding a given word or set of words" (p. 23). They add that "the record of how the eyes move during silent reading of text is by far the best way to study the *process* of reading" (p. 112).

They also point out that the eyes are sensitive to and the eye movements vary with the text being read, the length of the words, the difficulty of the material, the spaces between words, the frequency of the word in the language, the desire and attempt of the reader to read well, and the predictability of the word from sentence context.

Eye movements are characterized by fixations, interfixation movements, regressions or refixations, and return sweeps. The time elements in reading are fixation and movement time. Most eye movements or saccades move forward, but about 10% to 15% even in skilled readers move backward. These backward saccades are termed regressions. Return sweeps are the movements the eye makes when moving from the end of one line to the beginning of the next.

Research (Perfetti, 1985; Rayner & Pollatsek, 1989) suggests that the eyes fixate most of the words in text. Readers fixate a high proportion of the content words (over 80%) such as nouns, adjectives, verbs, and adverbs, and a smaller proportion of the function words (about 40%) such as *the* and *a* (Just & Carpenter, 1980, 1987). Not many words are skipped. Fixations tend to fall on the first half of the word; this is probably so because the eye encodes fewer letters to the left of the point of the fixation than to the right.

When the reader fixates on a word, the reader is likely to process not only that word, but some additional information to the right of it. Information further than about 15 character spaces to the right of the fixation is not processed (Rayner, 1986; Rayner & Pollatsek, 1989). The information seen in extrafoveal vision is processed less well than that in foveal vision, but is nonetheless processed (Rayner & Pollatsek, 1989). The word in the parafovea may be fully identified, identified only partially, or skipped entirely.

Rayner and Pollatsek (1989) offer a word-identification model of eye movement. Their analysis of eye-movement control reveals the following sequence of events:

1. Meaningful information strikes the retina: The fixation begins.
2. The eye-mind lag: This is the time it takes for information to arrive in area 17 of the occipital lobe (see Figures 2-3 and 2-4) where words are identified.
3. The encoding of the visual information: This includes the computation of the boundaries of words from the position of spaces, the determination of whether the word is orthographically acceptable, identification of the word, the accessing of the word's pronunciation and meaning, and the joining of the word meaning to prior context in order to continue the construction of the syntax and the the meaning of the phrase, sentence, and paragraph.
4. Decision time: When the word is identified, the reader must make a decision to move to the next word or line. This requires only a modicum of time.
5. Eye-movement program latency: This is the time between deciding to move to the next word or line and the beginning of the eye movement or of the actual saccade.
6. Saccade time: The fixation is completed and the eye moves to the next fixation.

After an extensive analysis of the research, Rayner and Pollatsek (1989) conclude that it takes an average of about 50 msec. for the word to be registered in the brain, (steps 1 and 2), another 80 to 120 msec. for the word to be encoded (step 3), and 50 to 70 msec, to decide that an eye movement needs to be made and to begin execution of the same (steps 4, 5, and 6). The rapid rate of processing may be the result of partial encoding of the word in the prior fixation and the determination of where to move the eye may actually be done in parallel with word identification. Rayner and Pollatsek (1989) note that the beginning reader's average fixation duration is about 350 milliseconds, her average saccade length is 2 to 5 characters, and roughly one-fourth of her eye movements are regressions. As children mature, their fixations are shorter, their saccades are longer and fewer, and their regressions are fewer. Eye movements tend to stabilize by about fifth grade, with the exception of regressions which continue to decrease until the end of high school. It is likely that beginning readers focus all or most of their attention on the fixated word and make only minimal use of the parafoveal and peripheral vision and thus have a reduced perceptual span. The perceptual span of beginning readers extends about 11 character spaces to the right of the fixation (Rayner, 1986).

Rayner and Pollatsek (1989) conclude that the beginning reader's slow reading and less efficient eye movements are not the result of a smaller perceptual span or of the eye movements as such, but rather reflect central cognitive processing deficiencies and nonautomatized encoding and word-recognition processes. They note that regressions on a fixated word probably reflect higher-order difficulty with the text and not additional time to identify the word.

Rayner and Pollatsek (1989) note that skilled readers take from 150 to 200 msec. to identify a word. Individuals who read 300 words a minute do in fact take about 200 msec. to process a word, provided they are reading every word. Low-frequency words take about 30 msec. longer than do high-frequency words (Inhoff & Rayner, 1986). It takes the reader approximately 60 to 70 msec. of processing time to identify a word, leaving some 130 to 140 msec. for such higher-order processes as constructing the correct syntactic structure, relating word meanings, and fitting text into what one knows.

Rayner and Pollatsek believe that the issue of when information is extracted in a fixation is not conclusively settled. Blanchard et al. (1984) argue that visual information can be extracted at any point in the fixation and that higher-order cognitive processes are driving the reading process. When the higher-order processes are ready for the next word, the reader looks at the visual information to determine what the word is.

A brief summary of eye movement data may provide an understanding of the relation of eye movements to reading.

Fixation

Because the input of visual information resulting in perception is not continuous (the eyes move by saccades with intervening pauses or fixations), the material is divided into chunks that are reassembled by the brain into a spatiotemporal, continuous visual world (Gaardner, 1970). The fixation is the stop that the eye makes so it can react to the graphic stimuli. It seems possible to gain information only once during a fixation (Smith, 1971; Smith, 1978), or during the pause during which reading occurs.

During the fixation pause, the intake process is essentially suspended and the inner process of reading occurs. Rayner (1983b, 1983c) and Smith (1988) report that skilled readers acquire most of the information needed for reading during the first 50 msec. of the fixation. It takes about 50 msec. for the word to be registered in the brain.

There is a close relationship between the number of letters in a word and where the reader fixates (Rayner & Pollatsek, 1989). As word length increases, the probability of fixating the word increases. There is also a preferred viewing location in words between the beginning and middle letters of words. Furthermore, the eyes are less likely to land on the period or the spaces at the end of the sentence. However, the last word in a sentence tends to receive a longer fixation than do other words. Carpenter and Just (1981) refer to the latter as "sentence-wrap-up" time: apparently the reader is assembling sentence parts or adding interpretations to parts of the sentence that were incompletely or incorrectly interpreted. Readers can sometimes identify one or two words to the right of the fixated words. They generally do not fixate the last word of a line, but the word may be fully processed in the parafovea (Rayner & Pollatsek, 1989).

Blanchard, Pollatsek, and Rayner (1988) found that the word may be fully identified in the parafovea (and thus may be skipped), or it may be partially activated. The latter may speed later identification of the word.

Fixation Time

Fixation time generally varies from 66 to 416 msec., with the average being 218 msec. (Rayner and Pollatsek, 1989). Fixation times are sensitive to word frequency and to the predictability of the word in a text (Morris, 1987); fixation times are longer on longer words, on words of lower frequency, and on words that are less predictable. Inhoff and Rayner (1986) found that the difference in fixation time between high-frequency words and low-frequency words is about 30 msec.

Single long fixations on a word or consecutive fixations on the same word are aggregated into units called gazes (Just & Carpenter, 1987). Gaze duration is the total time on the word before the eyes move on (Rayner & Pollatsek, 1989).

Readers spend characteristically more time on some words than on others, with gazes ranging from a 10th of a second to 1 second. The length or duration of the gaze on a given word reflects the processing time expended on receiving, understanding, and integrating the word (Just & Carpenter, 1987). Perfetti (1985) notes that the number and length of fixations on a word reflects linguistic and cognitive demands of lexical access: that is, some of the fixation time is going to cognitive processing.

Word length and word frequency do affect the gaze. Rayner and Pollatsek suggest that gaze duration is a better measure of encoding or word identification time than is the duration of the first fixation on a word, as

Inhoff (1984) suggests, since it represents the total amount of time spent on a word before the eye moves on.

Smith (1978) notes that excessive fixation time or excessive prolongation of a fixation in reading is similar to an unblinking stare at a picture. It is an indication that the viewer can make little sense of what is being looked at. In a later text, Smith (1988) notes that "A person who stares is not seeing more, but rather is having difficulty deciding what was looked at in the first place" (p. 75).

Saccade Length and Duration

The average saccade length is about 8.5 (7 to 9) characters, but the range is from 1 to 18 characters or letter spaces (Rayner & Pollatsek, 1989). McConkie (1982) suggests that the average saccade covers about 8 to 10 letter spaces. Saccade length is sensitive to word frequency and predictability (e.g., when a word is skipped), but it is also sensitive to word length(Rayner & Pollatsek, 1989). The eye tends to jump further when a long word is to the right of the fixation then when a shorter word is there.

Saccade duration in reading varies with the distance moved, with a typical saccade taking about 20 to 35 msec. Rayner and Pollatsek (1989) observe that the eyes move about four or five times per second.

Recognition Span

The recognition span, or the amount and the size of the unit seen, recognized, organized, and comprehended during a single fixation (its length in terms of words), depends upon readers' facility in word recognition, the difficulty of the material, their familiarity with the material being read or the knowledge of the readers, the physical characteristics of the material, and their ability to assimilate ideas. The less readers know about what they are reading, the less they will be able to apprehend in a single fixation.

Smith (1988) points out that what distinguishes the fluent from the less-skilled reader is the number of letters or words that can be identified in a single fixation. Smith adds that the more sense the letters make, or the more the brain is capable of using prior knowledge, the more can be seen. Readers generally are able to see four or five random letters, two or three unrelated words, or in a meaningful sentence context perhaps four or five words (Smith, 1988). Random letters, are not predictable and thus demand a great deal of visual information for each identification.

The recognition span is obtained by dividing the number of words read by the number of fixations made while reading:

$$\frac{\text{Number of words read}}{\text{Number of fixations}}$$

The average recognition span (see Table 2-1) for first graders is 0.45 of a word and for college students it is 1.11 words.

Perception Span

The perception (or visual span) is the quantity of numbers, letters, or words that is seen in a single fixation. This can be measured by a tachistoscopic exposure. Poor readers frequently have a wider visual span than good readers because they do not organize what they see. The size of the perceptual span is limited, extending from the beginning of the fixated word to about 15 character spaces to the right. (Rayner & Pollatsek, 1989). The reason the perception span is as narrow as it is is because we do not see very far into the periphery when reading (Hall, 1989).

Fixation Frequency

Fixation frequency or fixation rate is determined by the purposes of the reader, the difficulty of the material, familiarity with the content, and the

Table 2-1
Averages for Measurable Components of the Fundamental Reading Skill

Grade +	1	2	3	4	5	6	7	8	9	10	11	12	Col.
Fixations (incl. regressions) per 100 words	224	174	155	139	129	120	114	109	105	101	96	94	90
Regressions per 100 words	52	40	35	31	28	25	23	21	20	19	18	17	15
Average span of recognition (in words)	.45	.57	.65	.72	.78	.83	.88	.92	.95	.99	1.04	1.06	1.11
Average duration of fixation (in seconds)	.33	.30	.28	.27	.27	.27	.27	.27	.27	.26	.26	.25	.24
Rate with comprehension (in words per minute)	80	115	138	158	173	185	195	204	214	224	237	250	280

Stanford E. Taylor, Helen Frackenpohl, and James L. Pettee, *Grade Level Norms for the Components of the Fundamental Reading Skill* (Columbia, SC, Educational Developmental Laboratories, Inc., 1960), Bulletin No. 3, p. 12.

First grade averages are those of pupils capable of reading silently material of 1.8 difficulty with 70% comprehension. Above grade one, averages are those of students at midyear reading silently material of midyear difficulty with at least 70% comprehension.

format in which the materials are presented. The average first grade student makes between 15.5 and 18.6 fixations per 3 ½ inch(21-pica) line. The average college student makes 5.9 fixations on a line of the same length (Buswell, 1922). The average first grader makes about 224 fixations per 100 words, the average college student about 90 (see Table 2-1).

Eye-Memory Span and Eye-voice Span

Generally, in silent reading the good reader has an eye-memory span (the distance the eyes have traveled ahead of the point at which interpretation occurs) of from 15 to 20 letters. In oral reading the eye-voice span, (the number of words or letter spaces that visual processing is ahead of oral reading) is slightly less. The eye-voice span of good comprehenders tends to be about 8.7 letter spaces. The average eye-voice span is approximately three words, for second graders and four and a half words for fourth graders (Levin & Turner, 1966). It tends to increase with age and is influenced by the meaningfulness of the material.

A wide recognition span contributes to a wide eye-voice span in oral reading and to a wide eye-memory span in silent reading. A narrow recognition span contributes to a narrow eye-voice span and forces the pupil to pronounce each word as it is recognized in order to obtain meaning from the text.

In beginning readers struggling to identify words, the eye is generally not ahead of the voice. This tends to change by the end of first grade and the beginning of second grade.

Thought-Unit Reading

Thought-unit reading is sometimes wrongly identified with the suggestion that it is possible or even common to read three or four words per fixation. Thought units are not visual units. The reader groups words, using a knowledge of syntax to do so. Meaning depends upon the syntactic (not visual) structure that the reader projects on a series of words. Even though pupils read in thought units, they rarely comprehend more than one word per fixation. Thought units generally consist of a series of fixations.

Mature readers with a wide eye-memory span and a wide eye-voice span do not commit themselves to an interpretation until they have read a sufficient amount of material. Such readers delay their interpretation of the visual intake until they have perceived enough material to grasp a thought unit, and they keep in mind sufficient context so as to make the best interpretation.

Regressions

Regressions are a reverse eye movement, a return to a previously fixated word for a repeat fixation, or a fixation or saccade in a right-to-left direction on the eye-movement photograph (see Figure 2-6). They are likely to occur when the flow of thought is interrupted, out of habit or lack of confidence (pupil feels the need for constant rereading), when eye deficiencies prevent accurate perception, when directional attack in seeing is inadequate, or simply because certain material was missed. Regressions are especially influenced by difficulties in comprehending higher-order aspects of text (Rayner & Pollatsek, 1989). The flow of thought may be broken in a number of ways: through failure to recognize the basic meaning of a word, failure to recognize the meaning suggested by the context, or failure to relate the meaning of one word to that of other words.

The number of regressions made per 100 words varies from reader to reader. The average first grader makes about 52; the average ninth grader about 20; and the average college student about 15 (see Table 2-1). Rayner and Pollatsek (1989) suggest that regressions occur 10% to 15% of reading time. The good reader makes a regression about once every 2 seconds. The really good reader makes about 9 or 10 regressions per 100 words. Low-frequency words are more likely to be refixated than are high-frequency words (Inhoff & Rayner, 1986).

When children make many regressions it is more likely that they are having difficulty making sense of the material than that regressions are the cause of this difficulty (Smith, 1971, 1978). "The number of regressions that readers make is an indication of the complexity to them of the passage they are trying to read" (p. 78).

Although regressions may result in immature reading, regressions for verification, for phrase analysis, and for reexamination of a previous sentence are beneficial. Regressions thus may at times be just as productive an eye movement as a saccade in a forward direction (Smith, 1971, 1978, 1988). The regressions of the poor reader are usually not for verification or phrase analysis. They tend to occur within the same word and are caused primarily by inaccuracies in seeing.

Return Sweep

After a line has been read the eyes make a return sweep to the beginning of the next line. The return sweep takes from 40 to 54 milliseconds. Return sweeps are quite complicated because they often start five to seven character spaces from the end of the line and generally go to about the third to seventh character space of the next line (Rayner and Pollatsek, 1989, p. 114). The proper line may be missed entirely or the eyes may fix on a point before or after the first word of the new line. Inaccuracies here may require refixation. Figure 2-5 illustrates how the various eye movements are represented on the eye-movement photograph.

Rate Improvement

Rate improvement depends, to a great extent, on the shortening of the fixation pauses and on the lengthening of the eye-memory and the eye-voice spans. Smith (1988) notes that reading is accelerated by reducing dependency on visual information. The latter is done by making use of meaning. Rayner and Pollatsek (1989) observe that as the text grows in difficulty, the rate slows down, the average fixation duration increases, the average saccade size decreases, and the number of regressions increases. They comment that reading rate can be increased by making either fewer fixations or shorter fixations (or both), but most of the increase is generally due to making fewer fixations.

EYE-MOVEMENT DEFICITS AND POOR READING

Eye-movement surveys indicate that a great number of children have not developed the habit of perceiving materials in a left-to-right progression while making a minimum number of fixations and regressions (Taylor, 1959). Undoubtedly, both good and poor readers show irregularities in eye movement. In fact, Rayner's (1983a, 1983b) data led him to conclude that with reading materials of appropriate difficulty, both good and poor readers exhibit the same eye-movement patterns. Olson (1985) likewise found that when texts are adjusted in difficulty to the word recognition level of the pupil, eye-movement differences between good and poor readers are negligible. Vellutino (1987) notes that if deficiencies in motor and visual-motor development or defects in eye movements caused perceptual impairment and reading problems, one would be at a loss to explain how so many children with various visual-tracking defects become literate. Moreover, eye training, visual tracking, eye muscle exercises, and perceptual training have simply not been shown to be fruitful in remediating eye movement (Casbergue & Green, 1988).

However, the evidence is substantial that poor readers exhibit substantially more eye movement or oculomotor difficulties (Griffin, Walton, & Ives, 1974; Lefton et al., 1979; McConkie, 1982; Pavlidis, 1983, 1985) than do good readers even when allowance is made for differences in recoding words and in comprehension and even when the reader is reading easy material (Griffin, Walton, & Ives, 1974; Pavlidis, 1983). Poor readers exhibit the following eye movement charcteristics:

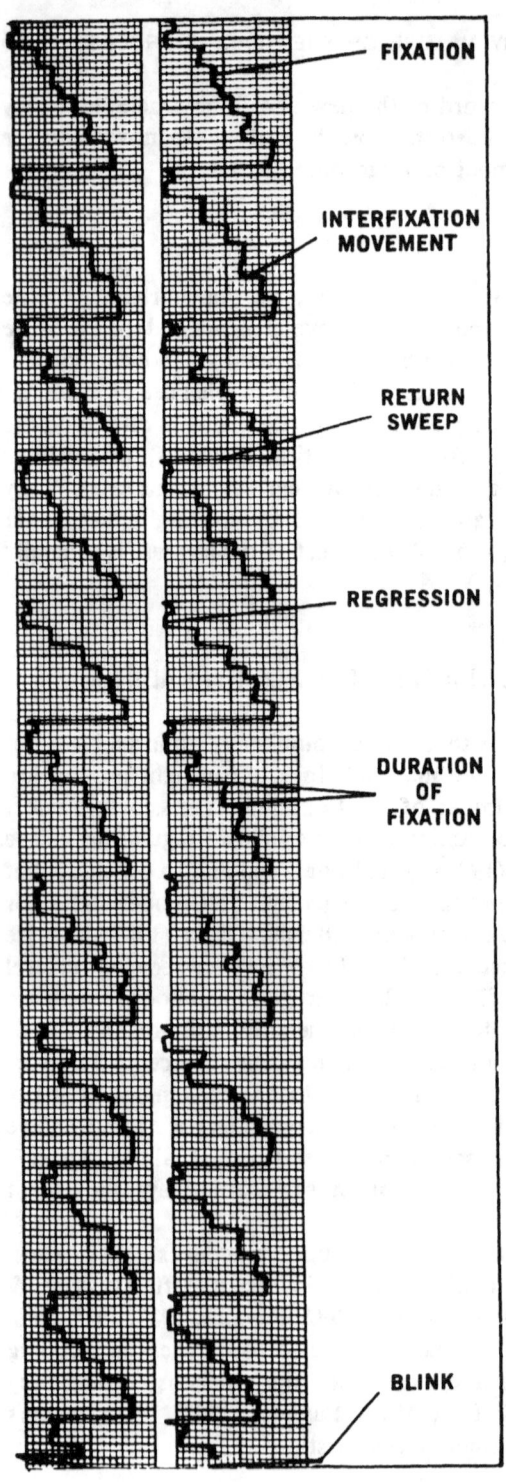

FIGURE 2-5. An Illustration of the Components of Eye Movement (Educational Developmental Laboratories, Columbia, S.C.) of McGraw-Hill)

1. They make too many fixations, fixations that are too long or too short in duration, saccades that are shorter than normal, and too many regressions for their age and grade level (Griffin, Walton, & Ives, 1974). The fixations of poor readers are highly variable and their regressions occur in clusters, often within the same word. When the fixation is too short, the result may be a recognition span that is too narrow—it does not include as many letters or words as it might.
2. They sequence eye movements too rapidly, thus skipping material or they perseverate, sequencing too slowly, with resultant overfixation (Griffin, Walton, & Ives, 1974). In the latter situation, the pupil reads slowly and hesitantly.
3. They show more right-to-left saccades than do normal readers (Pavlidis, 1985). Rayner and Pollatsek (1989) cite four earlier studies in which dyslexics did not exhibit this same behavior.
4. They show inflexibility in eye movements: Immature and disabled readers often do not change their eye movements to fit the difficulty of the material or change of purpose for reading.
5. They lack rhythm in reading. Their eye-movement patterns are erratic (Pavlidis, 1985; Rayner, 1985). They exhibit chaotic oculomotor control.
6. They have difficulty in moving from the end of one line to the beginning of another (the return sweep is faulty). The pupil makes multiple, small, leftward saccades rather than a single large return movement. This is often accompanied by jumping or skipping of lines.
7. They have relatively low reading efficiency, generally below their age or grade level. The relative efficiency (R.E.) is computed thus:

$$\frac{\text{rate(wpm)}}{\text{fixations and regressions per 100 words}}$$

An R. E. of .29 is equivalent to a 1.0 grade level; one of 1.71, to 9.0 grade level; and one of 2.95 to a 14.0 grade level.
8. They have short eye-memory and eye-voice spans.

Numerous causes can be offered to explain the eye-movement difficulties of some readers. One is the inability to make use of peripheral vision. Fisher (1980) points out that fixations last on an average about 250 milliseconds, 50 milliseconds of which are devoted to encoding the stimulus. The period of 50 milliseconds, during which an image or icon of the stimulus is formed and stored, sustains the visual image acquired during a fixation (e.g., the *c* in *cat*) through the eye movement or saccade that follows (a period of time in which the eye does not see) and permits the joining of what is seen in the subsequent fixation (e.g., the *at* in *cat*) with the content of the previous fixation to form the complete word *cat*. The good reader uses the remaining time to peripherally preview the text that follows. Fisher observes that the disabled reader cannot make use of this peripheral vision in processing of the word. However, Just and Carpenter (1987) and Rayner and Pollatsek (1989) note that parafoveal and peripheral vision alone do not appear to permit the needed acuity to do adequate reading.

Other causes commonly adduced to explain eye-movement difficulties are: (a) inadequate maturation: children's eye movements improve with age; (b) difficulty of the material; (c) the format is not appropriate for the pupil, with the print being too small, the type face being inappropriate, or the lines of print being too long; (d) the pupil takes too much pain to read well; (e) the pupil lacks facility in word recognition; (f) the pupil is not familiar with the material being read; (g) the pupil has difficulty assimilating ideas; (h) the pupil has difficulties in binocular coordination; or (i) the pupil points at words, prohibiting smooth movement of the eyes across the line of print.

Physical health conditions also have a direct bearing on eye movements. For example, making too many fixations may be caused by tumefaction of the pituitary gland; diabetes mellitus, as well as a low basal metabolic rate, can cause an excessive number of regressions. Neural lesions may also cause eye-movement difficulties. Lesions may occur in the occipital lobes (areas 18 and 19), in area 4, the motor area of the brain, in the posterior part of the corpus callosum, in or near the two superior or upper colliculi (rounded protuberances on the posterior surface of the midbrain that serve as conduction centers in the visual tracts), in the left angular gyrus, or in the cerebellum. Areas 18 and 19, together with area 8, control the voluntary and involuntary movements of the eyes. Figure 2-4 shows the loci of these brain areas.

Neural conditions that cause eye-movement difficulties may also be chemical in nature. Too much cholinesterase at the point of the synapse may prohibit sustaining the fixation long enough for a proper image to be obtained. The result is inaccurate perception, rapid shift of attention, and inaccurate reading characterized by frequent substitutions. Too much acetycholine at the point of the synapse may make the fixation unnecessarily long and may lead to slow reading and difficulties in reading.

Impulsivity and perseverative behavior are also common causal factors. In the impulsive reader the fixation is often too short; he looks only at the first letter of the word and guesses wildly at the rest. In the perseverative reader, the fixation span is often too long; his reading is extremely slow.

There are indeed multiple factors than can cause or at least explain eye movement difficulties. However, eye movement difficulties more commonly are the result of poor reading (and this explains why poor readers exhibit more eye movement difficulties) than the cause of poor reading.

Most of the research (Olson, 1985; Rayner, 1983c, 1985a, 1985b; Rayner & Pollatsek, 1989) indicate that oculomotor behavior is primarily symptomatic of the underlying perceptual and assimilative processes or of central cerebral processes, and provides cues to the pupil's more basic word recognition and comprehension difficulties. Efficient reading results in efficient eye movements rather than vice versa. Poor readers make extra fixations and regressions because they do not understand, and such pupils need training to improve word recognition and comprehension rather than training in eye movement.

THE RAYNER-POLLATSEK MODEL

Eye movements play a significant role in Rayner and Pollatsek's (1989) model. Reading in their model begins with an eye fixation, involving both foveal and parafoveal processing. Foveal processing is concerned with processing the letters in a fixated word in parallel; parafoveal processing involves the extraction of information to the right of the fixated word. Information from the latter is used in determining where to look next. The region of effective processing, i.e., the perceptual span, extends from the beginning of the fixated word to about 15 character spaces to the right of the fixation.

After lexical access has been achieved, attention shifts to the next word to the right of the fixation and is followed by saccade to the next word. Usually, the word to the right is not identified until the saccade brings the fovea to the preferred location in the second word. The letters at the beginning of the second word, which are viewed by the parafovea, often are processed in parallel with the target word. This prior processing speeds the processing of the second word. Sometimes the second word in the parafovea is identified before a saccade to the right is made. The reader may then shift attention to the third word and makes a saccade to it. If the second attention shift occurs while the reader is still fixating on the first word, the program for the saccade to the second word may be aborted and the eye will move directly to the third word. Usually, such a cancellation of the first saccade results in a 30 msec. increase in the duration of the first fixation. If the first saccade cannot be canceled, the reader may fixate on the second word only briefly and move to the third word. This circumstance explains the very short fixations that occasionally occur in the eye-movement photograph and why readers sometimes initially fixate on the end of the word. Generally, the sequence of events is foveal word processing (with parafoveal processing occurring in parallel), lexical access, attention shift to the next word, saccade to the next word, and a repetition of the cycle (Rayner & Pollatsek, 1989).

When lexical access is complete, the meaning of the fixated word is integrated into the ongoing text representation which is built in working memory. If the identified word cannot be integrated, because it does not fit the semantic and syntactic context, a signal is sent to the ongoing eye-movement control, telling the eyes to remain fixated on the word, to make a number of fixations in the same region of the text, or to make a regression for reanalysis.

VISUAL PERCEPTION AND READING

Even though adequate vision and efficient eye movements may be related to reading success in certain instances, adequacy of visual perception is more significant. Ever since there has been concern in reading with the visual discrimination and identification of words and with the development of a visual memory for words, visual discrimination and visual memory have been accorded a primary position.

Visual perception is concerned with the ability of the reader to extract visual information from the printed page, to analyze the patterns, and to retain these patterns. It is what goes on in areas 18 and 19 of the occipital lobe (see Figure 2-4). Visual discrimination will concern us again in chapter 8.

The visual perception skills include visual discrimination of shape; visual-motor integration, figure-ground discrimination, visual closure, perception of parts-to-whole relationships, visual constancy, visual memory, and perception of orientation.

In reading, visual discrimination of the shapes of words includes: (a) the ability to match letters and words, (b) the ability to identify and recognize letter symbols visually, (c) the ability to discriminate visually each letter from every other letter, (d) the ability to analyze and to synthesize printed words and to develop a gestalt for a word or to experience the "flash" global identification of a word as a whole, and (e) the ability to discriminate between and recall look-alike words.

Perceptual deficits, per se, do not appear to account for severe reading disability, even though many severely disabled readers do have visual perception difficulties (DiLollo, Hansen, & McIntyre, 1983; Slaghuis & Lovegrove, 1985).

HEARING AND READING

Reading is not exclusively a visual process. An essential process in word recognition, at least in the beginning reader, is the association of sounds with the printed symbol, the ability to give the visual configuration a name, or recoding. The pupil needs to be able to convert *cat* into /kăt/. Children cannot do so if they are not able to hear the various phonetic elements of words, if they do not speak the sounds correctly, and if they confuse spoken words.

Hearing is the process by which sound waves are received, modified, and relayed along the nervous system by the ear. Auditory acuity is the recognition of discrete units of sound; it is keenness or sharpness of hearing. Smith (1977) notes that auditory acuity is not essential for reading, even though it may be prerequisite for reading instruction.

The auditory pathways move from both ears to the transverse temporal gyri of Heschl. The sounds that are heard by the ears are registered in Heschl's gyrus. It is located in the upper and middle portion of the temporal lobe, areas 41 and part of 42, adjacent to the fissure of Sylvius (see Figure 2-4), which is the projection area for auditory input.

From the inner ear sound waves set up vibratory patterns that are converted into electrochemical or neural impulses in the auditory nerve in the cochlear nuclei. The auditory nerve enters the brain stem at the level of the medulla oblongata, divides, and ascends on both sides to the inferior colliculi. The two auditory pathways then travel by way of the medial geniculate bodies to Heschl's gyrus in each temporal lobe (Figure 2-6).

As in vision, half of the auditory nerve fibers cross the midline to the opposite side of the brain, while others ascend on the same side. Thus each ear is represented in both the right and left cortex. For this reason both ears can continue to function normally, even though the auditory cortex of one side is destroyed. Decoding of the sounds of oral speech occurs in the auditory speech analyzer or Wernicke's area (area 22 and part of 41 and 42).

When readers use the prelexical or phonological route to meaning, the visual input and the auditory input are shared in the angular gyrus (area 39 in the brain). This visual-auditory association, as we saw earlier, also occurs in direct visual access, but after lexical access. When the child has normal perception of the pure tones of the audiometer, it indicates that the Heschl's gyri are functioning normally. Difficulty discriminating between "deer" and "dare" indicates a possible lesion in Wernicke's area (Luria, 1973). A lesion in Heschl's gyri produces a language disorder known as word deafness. The individual so afflicted cannot comprehend spoken language.

Difficulties in the development of the brain mechanisms responsible for auditory processes may result in difficulties in auditory discrimination, auditory analysis/synthesis, auditory sequential memory, and articulation; specifically, in hearing the difference between phonemes (e.g., *f* and *v*), in perceiving a word as a series of sounds that must be ordered in correct sequence (spaghetti versus pasghetti), in blending, in remembering temporal sequences, in the ability to learn the auditory counterparts of letters, and in the ability to recall what letters sound like.

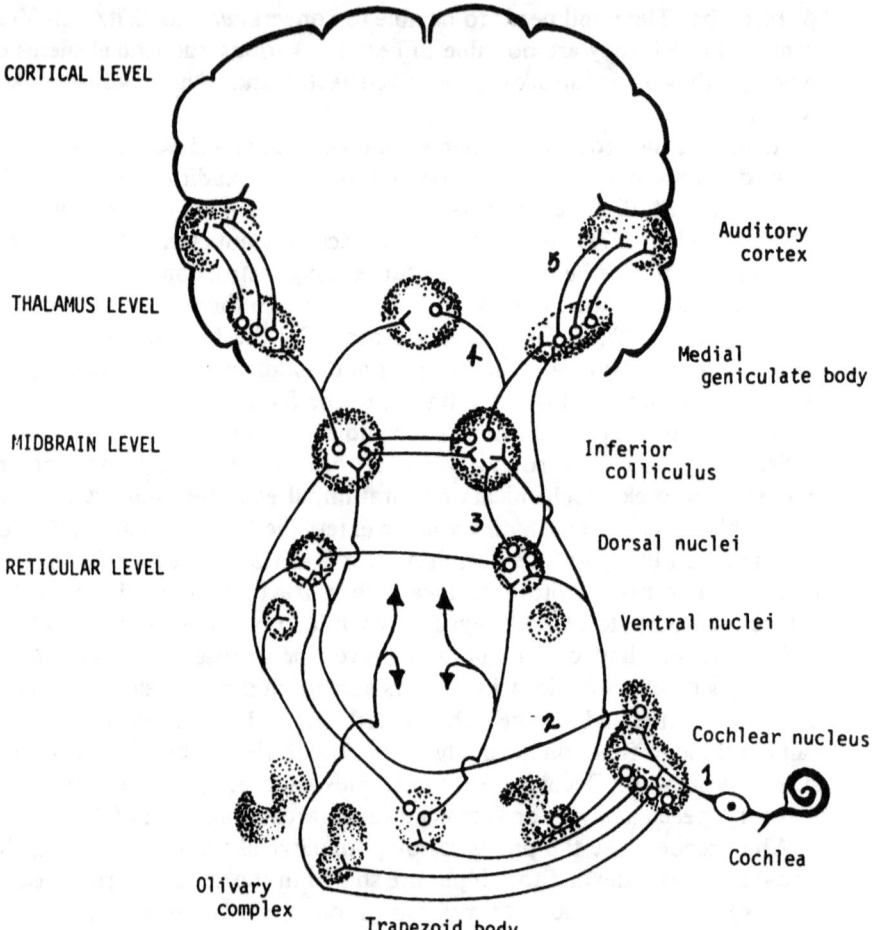

FIGURE 2-6 Auditory Pathways (Robeck and Wallace, 1990).

Loss of hearing is associated with retardation in school and can precipitate or aggravate a reading deficiency. Reading disability may be precipitated by a conductive hearing loss or sensori-neural loss. A conductive loss is a reduction in loudness that stems from an impairment in the conductive process in the middle ear. It reduces the intensity of the sound reaching the inner ear. Either there is wax in the ear, blocking the external auditory canal, the eardrum is punctured, or there is a malfunction of the three small ossicles (bones) (Malleus, Incus, Stapes) in the middle ear (see Figure 2-7).

A sensori-neural or perceptive loss stems from lesion of the end organ, the cochlear hair cells, or the auditory nerve of the ear and affects clarity and intelligibility of speech. Persons with such a loss hear the speech of

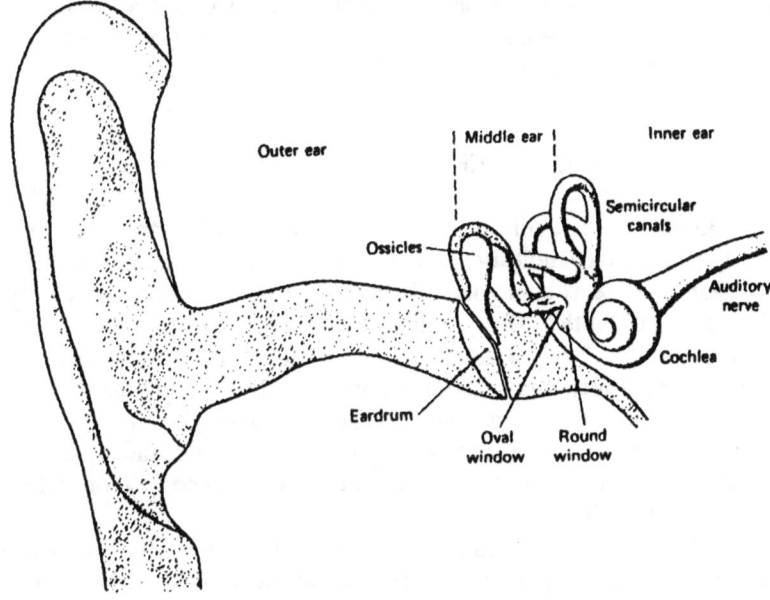

FIGURE 2-7 The Human Ear (Robeck and Wallace, 1990, p. 80).

others but may not understand what they hear. Sensorineural deafness prevents the learner from hearing and distinguishing the high-frequency sounds, especially such sounds as /f/, /v/, /s/, /z/, /sh/, /zh/, /th/, /t/, /d/, and /k/. Articulation generally is affected. The pupil often shows signs of misunderstanding the teacher. The pupil who suffers high-frequency loss and has a teacher with a high-pitched voice is particularly at risk. The inability to hear high-frequency sounds is often related to reading problems.

Severity of hearing loss is directly related to severity of effect. When the pupil's hearing ranges between 11 to 15 db, the pupil should be seated close to the teacher. When the hearing level falls between 15 and 25 db, the pupil may have difficulty sustaining attention. At hearing levels between 25 and 40 db, the pupil has difficulty hearing faint speech for distant sounds, may benefit from lip-reading instruction, may need speech training, and , at the upper level (35 db level), should have a hearing aid. The child with the 40 db loss across the speech range will have particular difficulty with the sounds /ch/, /f/, /k/, /s/, /sh/, /th/, and /z/. Between hearing levels of 40 and 55 db, the pupil can understand speech only at distances of approximately 3 to 5 feet. The pupil needs a hearing aid, speech correction, auditory training, lip reading, and preferential seating. When the hearing level is between 56 to 70 db, the pupil has difficulty hearing even with a hearing aid. Persons whose hearing level is 71 db or more cannot learn speech through hearing and are considered to be deaf; anyone whose level is 35 db to 69 db is considered to be hard of hearing.

AUDITORY PERCEPTION AND READING

Just as in vision, the auditory problems of poor readers are often not the inability to hear but auditory perception deficiencies. Inadequate auditory perception is twice as common as is hearing loss in children with learning and reading disabilities. Dysfunctional auditory processing is thus more a matter of disability in auditory perception than of hearing or auditory acuity as such. Furthermore, studies show that the percentage of children with auditory perceptual problems is higher than average among children in low socioeconomic groups and is even higher than that among disadvantaged children who belong to racial minorities or who come from bilingual homes (Arnold & Wist, 1970).

Undoubtedly, some persons are poor readers because they are deficient in auditory processing. These deficiencies reveal themselves as slow language development; inadequate articulation and difficulties in speech; poor performance in auditory discrimination, especially of beginning and ending sounds of words; poor sound blending; poor auditory memory; inability to learn phonics or grapheme-phoneme correspondences; inability to match a visual with an auditory sequence; inability to name a visual configuration; inability to break the alphabetic code; problems in following oral direction; better recall when shown what to do rather than when told; frequent phonetic spelling errors; and reading better silently than orally (Bader, 1980; Lerner, 1976, 1985).

Auditory perception skills include auditory discrimination, auditory memory or sequencing, auditory figure-ground discrimination, and auditory comprehension or decoding. They also include phonological awareness, phonemic segmentation, auditory or phonetic blending, detection of rhyming, and alliteration. We defer the discussion of these to chapter 8.

Auditory Discrimination

Among the auditory perception skills, auditory discrimination, the ability to distinguish between phonemes, has been given primary attention by teachers of reading, and rightfully so. One fact is clear: pupils who learn to read easily are usually pupils who can discriminate between the sounds of language.

Inadequacies in auditory discrimination manifest themselves in the following ways:

1. Some pupils cannot tell whether two words spoken to them are alike or different, and cannot tell whether the difference is at the beginning, middle, or end of the word; they confuse words with similar sounds (*pin* and *pen*). In other words, they cannot synthesize sequences of phonemes within words and cannot analyze words into their auditory units.
2. They are unable to discriminate among the phonemes of the language. They may have special difficulty in identifying and differentiating the late-developing sounds: /z/, /s/, /r/, /wh/, /ch/, /j/. And, they often have difficulty with the high-frequency sounds: /f/, /v/, /s/, /z/, /sh/, /zh/, /t/, /d/, /p/, /b/, /k/, /g/, /h/, /ch/. Discrimination of the consonants is much more dependent upon the intensity or the decibel level of the signal than is that of the vowels. Consonants thus are affected by loss of intensity far more rapidly than are vowels.
3. They often make sound substitutions in reading.
4. They may have problems in articulation.
5. They have difficulty making a correct association between printed symbols and sounds as well as a special difficulty with phonics.

Beginning readers often have no concept of the phonemes and do not perceive that speech can be analyzed into phonemes in a definite sequence. Children must learn that words consist of sounds, that sounds follow sequentially, that the same sound may occur in more than one word, and that one word generally has different sounds than another word. And they need to realize that words that sound alike frequently look alike and that the letters work as a code for speech.

The facts concerning auditory discrimination as they relate to reading disability have been summarized in previous writings by Dechant (1977, 1982), and are:

1. Approximately 20% of the normal speaking population has poor auditory discrimination ability.
2. There is a positive relationship between auditory discrimination and reading. Although there are negative studies, Kavale (1981), after an analysis of 723 coefficients of correlation, concluded that auditory perception is an important correlate of reading ability, even when allowance was made for IQ.
3. Auditory discrimination is more closely related on the primary grade level to reading efficiency than is mental age or visual discrimination, but less so than is articulation ability.
4. Poor auditory discrimination is related positively to inaccuracies in articulation and pronunciation as well as to reading disability and to poor spelling.

5. Ability to match a picture with a spoken word that has the same sound at the beginning as the name of the picture is a significant predictor of reading achievement.
6. Children have varying degrees of ability in auditory discrimination. Auditory discrimination ability rarely shows any significant development after age 8 or 9, but seldom is fully developed before age 8. The average six-year-old cannot consistently distinguish between /g/ and /k/, /m/ and /n/, /p/ and /b/, and so on. Since only 24% of children have accurate auditory discrimination at the end of second grade, deficits in this area expose children to the risk of academic failure.
7. Auditory discrimination ability is most needed in programs with a strong phonic emphasis.

Auditory Memory

Another auditory perceptual deficiency is inadequate auditory memory. Auditory memory span was studied before the turn of the century by Jacobs (1887). A short, sequential memory or attention span and a poor memory for auditory sequences may result in inaccuracies of articulation, in difficulty in repeating sentences, or in reversals of phonemes or syllables in spoken words. It may show itself as reversals of words in sentences or as slowness in developing syntactic phrasing ability; it may lead to substitutions, distortions, omitted words, and the like when reading aloud. Poor auditory memory may result in inability to remember words spoken or to tell how many sounds there are in spoken words; oral spelling errors and reversals when writing are also frequent.

Auditory memory seems to have a special significance for reading at the first-grade level and in phonics-oriented programs. Deficiency in auditory memory and auditory sequential memory has been related to reading disability by many researchers, including Bannatyne (1966) and Newton et al., (1979). Doehring's (1968) findings indicated that visual sequencing is more important than auditory sequencing.

The ability to recall sequences is developmental in nature, with children gradually becoming able to recall longer series of digits. There is generally little change in scores on tests of auditory sequential memory between ages 7 and 8; the most significant changes occur between ages 6 and 7.

Auditory Figure-Ground Discrimination

Other readers frequently cannot focus attention on a relevant sound (such as the teacher's voice) while ignoring irrelevant or background sounds (e.g., hall noises, pencil sharpeners). Pupils are aided in making auditory figure-ground discriminations by amplification of the sound (Johnson,

1969). Amplifying the sound may serve the same function that color does in print.

Auditory processing difficulties as a group, may have these major effects:

1. Auditory deficits may cause reading difficulties when there is a severe hearing loss, particularly high-tone deafness, or when instruction puts a premium on auditory factors. The exclusive use of the phonic method, especially of synthetic phonics, with a child who has suffered a hearing loss may prevent achievement in reading.
2. They make it impossible to understand what is read orally.
3. They deprive pupils of the auditory feedback that helps them to understand what they are reading silently.
4. They make it impossible for the pupil to use auditory cues together with context cues to identify words.
5. They inhibit classroom learning because the pupil cannot understand material presented orally or because the pupil cannot understand oral directions.

Perceptual deficits in and of themselves probably do not cause reading disabilities; they are more likely to play a contributory role. Children's reading problems result more frequently from difficulties in making verbal associations with or naming the visual image, from cognitive linguistic deficiencies, from memory and sequencing deficiencies, and from intersensory integration difficulties. Perceptual factors are more likely to play a more significant role in the earlier stages of learning to read and linguistic factors play a greater role at later ages.

SUMMARY

Chapter 2 emphasized the sensory nature of the reading process, focusing principally on reading as a visual process, as involving eye movement, and as a hearing process. It also discussed the relationship of visual and auditory perception to reading and described how "what is seen" and "what is heard" are registered in the brain. Chapter 3 continues the examination of additional enabling skills in reading.

Chapter 3
Reading: A Memory Process, A Perceptual-Cognitive Process, A Linguistic and Communicative Process

    I. Introduction
   II. Processing of Information: The Role of Memory
      A. The Sensory or Iconic Store, the Sensory Register, or the Visual Information Store
      B. Short-Term Memory, Primary Memory, or Working Memory
      C. Long-Term Memory Store or Long-Term Memory
  III. The Perceptual and Cognitive Nature of Reading
      A. Terminology
      B. Theories of Perception and Cognition
  IV. Language and Reading
      A. Listening and Reading Proficiency
      B. Oral Language Proficiency and Reading
      C. Knowledge of Grammar and Reading
      D. The Reading/Writing Connection
   V. The Communicative Nature of Reading
  VI. Summary

CHAPTER 3
Reading: A Memory Process, A Perceptual-Cognitive Process, A Linguistic and Communicative Process

In chapter 2 we noted that reading begins with seeing of the word or, more correctly, with the light rays reflected from the word striking the retina of the eyes. The process of word recognition begins in this fashion and ends when the encoded word or the representation of the visual form is registered in the occipital lobe as a word percept. The word percept, which represents the pattern formed by the constellation of letters in a word, is a representation of the visual form of the word without any meaning (Just & Carpenter, 1987). Our first concern in chapter 3 is the processing of information, particularly of visual information, in reading. We are interested in how the word seen on the printed page is integrated into the reader's long-term memory. We need to account for "that something" which is stored in the brain, the engram or permanent change that occurs in the nervous system when one learns.

PROCESSING OF INFORMATION: THE ROLE OF MEMORY

The model we are presenting here is more in the nature of a metaphor than a literal description. It is termed the information-processing model. It does not address the actual loci of memory activities; rather, it explains how we remember, perhaps better, how we study memory.

The human information-processing system significantly limits the reader's capacity for processing textual information (Hall, 1989). As was noted in chapter 2, we are limited in the amount that we can perceive in a single fixation and in how quickly the eyes can move. In this chapter we will note our limitations in the number of chunks of information that can be held in short-term memory and in the speed with which we can retrieve information from long-term memory.

Information processing involves the gathering and the representation of information in the mind (i.e., encoding of information), holding the information in memory, and retrieving it when it is needed (Woolfolk, 1990).

The information-processing model portrays the human information processor in terms of three types of information storage: the sensory or iconic store, the short-term memory store, and the long-term memory store. Each is distinguished from the other two by the type of processing it does and its capacity for processing.

The information-processing model has two advantages: (a) it provides a model for human memory, and (b) it provides insight into how we learn and remember. Processing of information is generally presumed to proceed through the following stages:

1. The imprinting of sensory cues (i.e., the visual features of the word) on the receptor organs, which in reading are the eyes. Only minimal cues are imprinted and for only a very short time.
2. Registration of the patterns of neural impulses in the sensory store. This is analogous to iconic memory if visual information is stored or echoic memory if auditory information is stored. It is the immediate sensory recognition of a stimulus and lasts only from about a quarter of a second to a full second.
3. Selective attention to and perception of relevant features. If the perceiver attends to the stimulus, it is transferred to the short-term memory. There is always selectivity about what and how much is remembered. A great deal of sensory information never reaches short-term memory because the sensory input is not attended to.
4. Transfer into working memory where rehearsal and chunking preserve an encoded or transformed version of the stimulus for no longer than about 20 to 30 seconds.
5. Transfer of the information into a more abstract symbolic representation for storage in long-term memory. Lexical access and semantic encoding are involved in the transformation of the information into meaningful form.
6. Transfer into long-term memory. Long-term memory has an unlimited capacity and includes one's total nonvisual information. Vellutino (1987) points out that during the final stage of memory processing the encoded form of the stimulus is either categorized

and stored in long-term memory, discarded, or inadvertently lost from working memory.

The above description of the stages in processing information point to three operating aspects of memory (Smith, 1988): input (how the information gets to the brain), capacity (how much can be held in memory), and persistence (how long the information can be held in memory). To these should be added retrieval (getting the information from memory).

Presently, the multiple storage theory of memory is in vogue. It is a result of the emphasis on the organism as an information-processing system. The three stages of processing, as summarized earlier, are: (a) the sensory or iconic store, (b) short-term memory, and (c) long-term memory.

The Sensory or Iconic Store, the Sensory Register, or the Visual Information Store

This is the visual image, the icon, the immediate memory, or the preliminary processing that converts the input into a sensation and holds it for about 250 milliseconds. The information received decays rapidly as new information is taken in. The sensory store consists of the impressions that stimuli from the external world make on the senses. In reading, it is the registration in visual-sensory memory of the images of the words scanned; it is what remains after stimulation of the retina and termination of the stimulus. Stanley and Hall (1973) found that dyslexics need a 30 to 50 millisecond longer separation of parts (to perceive two parts of a figure) than do normal readers, and they need a 30–50 percent longer image duration in the sensory store. For efficient reading, the image of the word in iconic memory must be retained long enough for its features to be transferred to short-term memory. If it fades too quickly, learning will be slow and jerky. Increasing exposure of the word for the short iconic reader and decreasing it for the long iconic readers may be desirable. Greater contrast between print and background for short icon images and less contrast for long icon images may have similar effects.

Short-Term Store, Primary Memory, or Working Memory

This is the conversion of information into meaningful units. In reading it is the analysis of the meaning of the words and sentences. The amount of information that can be processed is much less than in the sensory store, perhaps no more than five to seven items. Generally, the information is retained for only a few seconds (approximately 30 seconds) while processing

84　CHAPTER 3

is going on. Short-term memory is more resistant to decay than information in the sensory store. How much is retained depends on how the information is formed, either as single letters, single words, or a related set of words. By "chunking" information, learners can store many more than seven items or letters; they can easily store seven words or seven "chunks" of information. Short-term memory is what is in one's immediate consciousness or awareness at any given time. It is called the "working memory" because it holds information for further processing. Perfetti (1985) notes that the working memory is a limited capacity processing system that is constrained by the number of memory elements that can be simultaneously activated. These elements include permanent memory nodes such as words as well as the linkages between nodes or words. Working memory is used in the comprehension of sentences. It stores the results of partly processed sentences and groups words into tentative structures. Short-term memory serves as a "buffer memory" where one retains in the forefront of one's mind whatever one is attending to at a particular moment (Smith, 1988). It is of "central importance in reading. It is where you lodge the traces of what you have just read while you go on to make sense of the next few words" (p. 90). Smith identifies short-term memory as that part of long-term memory that we use to attend to, and make sense of, a current situation.

Figure 3-1 diagrams the interactions between the various phases of memory. The arrow between short-term memory and sensory store is double-ended to indicate that the brain is selective about the visual information that it attends to, and the arrows between short-term and long-term memory are double-ended to represent their continual interaction.

Smith (1988) observes that the child who has seen only ELEP in the word *elephant* cannot read four or five more letters, and still hold ELEP in memory. As the elements of one fixation go into short-term memory, other elements of a previous fixation are pushed out. Holding ELEP, in the

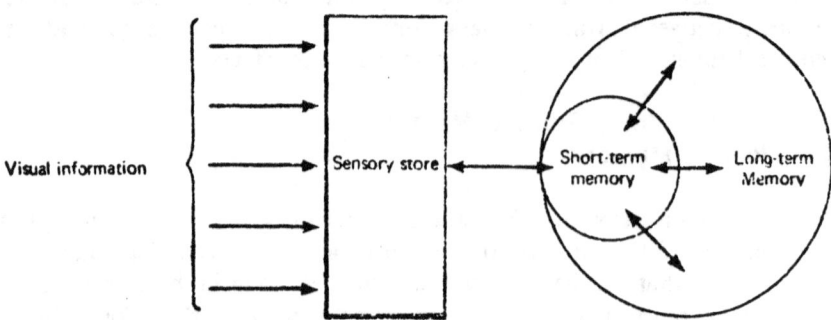

FIGURE 3-1: An Alternative Representation of Memory (Smith, 1988, p. 95)

forefront of ones attention, obviously makes reading much more difficult. Smith adds:

> Not much reading can be done if half your attention is preoccupied with earlier bits of letters and words that you are still trying to make sense of. (p. 91).

Smith notes that nothing stays around very long in short-term memory. To retain information, one must keep giving it ones attention and one must constantly rehearse. Rehearsal is critical in moving information into long-term memory. Rehearsal is a matter of repeating information to oneself. A person wanting to make a telephone call often finds that he looks up the number, but in the midst of dialing forgets it and has to look it up again. Looking it up again is a form of rehearsal. Disabled readers are generally defective in rehearsal. Children before the age of six years simply point to or name; six-year-olds rehearse; 10-year-olds categorize and rehearse, while older children use a conceptual organization or chunking to remember (Kirk, 1983a, 1983b).

Forgetting of items put into short-term memory seems chiefly to be caused by interference from similar messages, or by the inhibitory influence of preceding and succeeding irrelevant or interfering actions (proactive and retroactive inhibition) on the neural traces rather than by gradual decay. When attention is directed to something else, the original content is lost (Smith, 1988). Short-term memory thus is limited in capacity, is modality-specific (material entering through different modalities is stored differently), and loses items primarily by displacement (presentation of new items removes traces of earlier items).

Learners differ in their short-term memory capacities. Disabled readers on an average have a shorter memory span, hold images for a shorter time in memory than do normal readers, have shorter memories for letter strings, and generally are deficient in remembering linguistic material. Their short-term memory deficits appear to be specific to tasks requiring phonetic coding. They have difficulty in the phonological domain, generally lack metalinguistic awareness, and are less accurate at comprehension of spoken sentences. Vellutino (1979, 1987) explains short-term and long-term memory deficits of disabled readers as the inability to employ linguistic devices to aid recall.

Long-Term Memory Store (LTM) or Long-Term Memory

Long-term memory is analogous to learning; it is the repository for all one's information, one's cognitive structure or nonvisual information. It is the process by which information is stored permanently for recall on demand. In reading, it is the storage of the sense of the sentences. Materials enter long-term memory through organization, chunking, or semantic decoding. Long-term memory is distinct in that its capacity appears to be unlimited: "Nothing has to be lost or moved aside in long-term memory to accommodate something new. We never have to forget an old friend's name to make room for the name of a new acquaintance" (Smith, 1988, p. 92). Long-term memory is also distinct in its persistence. It does not need rehearsal. But retrieval from long-term memory is another matter. Our information is not always immediately accessible. Retrieval depends upon how the information is organized in one's brain. Smith notes: "Basically, everything depends on the sense that we made of the material when we originally put it into memory. . . . It is not just that nonsense that goes in will be nonsense when it comes out, but that it is extremely difficult to get nonsense out at all" (p. 93).

Finally, commitment of information to long-term memory is slow. To hold a telephone number in long-term memory, so that it can be dialed the next day, will require a good half minute of concentration, 5 seconds for each digit (Smith, 1988). Smith observes that meanings are readily put into long-term memory and notes that meanings are far easier to retain and retrieve because "meaningfulness implies that the input is related to what we already know and makes sense to us" (p. 96). Information is generally stored in long-term memory in schematic networks. We will address this issue again in chapter 5.

THE PERCEPTUAL AND COGNITIVE NATURE OF READING

As was noted in chapter 1, identification of and memory for the graphic symbols are not enough in reading. The graphic symbols must be interpreted. The critical element is not what is seen on the page, but, rather, what is signified by the written symbol. Reading occurs only when meaning is brought to graphic stimuli. Printed pages do not of themselves transmit meaning. Meaning is not something inherent in the word. The essence of meaning comes from the reader's fund of experience and from the mind of the reader. Meaning comes essentially from within the reader; it is a function of perception and cognition. The pages that follow thus focus on reading as a perceptual process and as a cognitive process.

Terminology

After the visual features of the words on the printed page are registered on the retina, they are transmitted to the visual cortex in the brain where they are interpreted. Some theorists term the entire receptive process perception. Others draw a distinction between sensation (the passive reaction of the receptor cells, not involving memory) and perception (the remainder of the receptive process). Others subsume perception under cognition. Still others distinguish between sensation, perception, and cognition. Thinking, meaningful language, problem solving, and so on are assigned to cognition, while the nonsymbolic processes or nonabstract properties such as size, color, and shape are relegated to perception. We accept this threefold distinction, even though the words, perception and cognition, are often used synonymously in common parlance. Thus, we earlier (Chapter 1) accepted Just and Carpenter's (1987) view that the end product of the encoding of the printed word is a word percept and that the meaning of a word or the mental representation that is associated with a word and that is stored in the brain is the word concept.

Theories of Perception and Cognition

The ancient Greeks interpreted the perceptual process as one in which "copies" of objects passed down sensory tubes. In more recent times, Gestalt psychologists pointed to the phenomenon of apparent movement, generally called the phi phenomenon, as proof that responses were not totally controlled by external stimuli. Motion pictures are an excellent example of apparent movement. The projected images from the individual frames of the film have no movement, and yet the observer perceives movement. Certainly what is apprehended by the viewer involves data not presently available to the senses. Gestalt psychologists thus emphasized that a central process is a codeterminer of behavior, that this central cerebral process is a representational process, and that these cerebral processes represent properties which are not present in the immediate stimulus situation at all. They pointed out that, in some way, the incoming sensory data are retained, processed, and reorganized by the viewer. Some intermediary step takes place between the sensory input and the response.

Perception, as presented here, refers to the meaning that is attached to the information received through the senses. It is the interpretation of the sensation. Smith (1975) observes that the eyes merely look, but the brain sees. When perception goes beyond the apprehension of the size, color, and shape of what is seen—when there is a consciousness of the experiences evoked by a symbol or when it is a sensation clothed with the perceiver's wealth of past experiences it is rightfully called cognition. When what is seen involves "the interaction of the sensory systems with those parts of the brain that are concerned with storage and retrieval of past experiences" (Atkinson, 1971, p. 106), it is more cognition than perception.

The perception of a graphic symbol must of necessity involve the simple perception of form, shape, color, and size, but the more complex perception and cognition of words must include the organization and modification of various sensory data in order for a particular series of printed letters to evoke meaning. Reading occurs only when the reader understands what the symbol represents. Reading is the reconstruction of the events behind the symbols.

Readers do not see the object, person, or experience of which the author writes. Their eyes are in contact with a word (the distal stimulus), in fact with the light rays (the proximal stimuli) that are reflected by the word. It is impossible for readers to see meaning, and yet they take meaning to the word. Readers are perceiving something beyond what they see. They are using information that is not present to the senses. Their reactions to the printed word are determined by the experiences that they have had with those objects or events for which the symbol stands.

Gestalt psychologists used the term perceptual field, which is equivalent to the terms cognitive structure, schema, and nonvisual information, to refer to the complex of meanings each of us has at a given moment. They noted that an individual's perceptual field is based on his world experience and that since no two individuals have had the same experiences, they cannot have the same perceptual field or personal schema in today's terminology. The significant fact for Gestalt psychologists was that the perceptual field (more correctly, the cognitive field) is a major determinant of the reader's reactions to a word. Two readers see the word *democracy* and take completely different meanings to the term. Each one's behavior is determined by his or her own cognitive field.

A number of interesting corrolaries flow from this view:

1. Recognition of a word is not reading. Meaning must be associated with the graphic symbol.
2. A word has no intrinsic meaning as such. There is no direct or invariable connection between the symbol and the referend, the datum, object, or event. Meaning is supplied by readers as they process their symbolic system by relating it to their prior experiences and conceptual structures. Words take on meaning by relation to the extralinguistic world of objects, ideas, and experiences (Crystal, 1976).
3. Readers use previous experience to interpret the words of the writer. If experience is inadequate, it is likely that the meanings for words will be similarly inadequate, and communication and comprehension of meanings will not occur.
4. The cognitive field (or the meanings possessed by an individual) is much smaller than it might be. The cognitive field of any individual includes only a small fraction of meanings that might be

present. Cognition of a word usually does not represent the complete meaning intended. Some persons thus bring a greater number and a much higher quality of meanings to words than do others, but few exhaust the total aggregate of meanings.

5. The meanings that comprise the cognitive field come primarily from the learner rather than from the word and are determined primarily by the sum total of the reader's experiences—in other words, the total field of psychological, cultural, and social forces as they impinge upon the reader's perceptions at the moment of action. Simply put, all readers read something of themselves into the written or printed word. In a very real sense, reactions to words are always intentional, individualistic, specific, and concrete and never quite communicable.

6. As the number of meanings and experiences connoted by a word increases, the more difficult it is to understand the full meanings of such a word. Reliability of initial perception of a word decreases as the number of meanings that may be associated with the word increases.

7. The teacher must constantly test the validity of the learner's perceptions and his meanings for words. The pupil's experience may have been too meager. Sometimes behavior is directed by only a part of the field. In reading it happens when pupils latch on to only a very limited or literal meaning, or react concretely to a communication that calls for a generic response. It also happens when the pupil identifies a word by some such part characteristic as an ascending or descending letter and confuses the word with another that has a similar characteristic.

Meanings are obviously very personal. If a group of persons were to look at the same object of art, there likely would be as many different interpretations (perceptions) of that art object as there were viewers. Lange, noting that the poet's image of a landscape differs greatly from that of the botanist, and the painter's from that of the geologist, remarked:

> Were we in perception chiefly passive, could the things of the outer world impress themselves immediately upon our minds and thus stamp their nature upon it, they would necessarily always leave behind the same ideas, so that a variety of apprehension would be impossible and inexplicable (1902, p. 3-4).

Porter (1958) points out that each human being represents literally billions of varied experiences which have been assimilated and ordered in specific ways, and each attempt at communication, at understanding or being understood, bears the mark of this prodigious personal context. He suggests that words rarely ever mean precisely the same thing to any two individuals.

It is thus not likely that two persons will have exactly the same perception/cognition of the same experience. Cognition is rarely totally veridical but is at best an inadequate and approximate representation of concrete reality. However, individuals do strive to achieve the closest possible agreement between the realities of their environment and their own cognition of them. Whenever reality and one's cognition of it are totally congruent (i.e., environment/concept concordance), the cognition is said to be totally veridical or to have ecological validity (Brunswick, 1957).

In reading, veridicality is especially difficult to attain. Words are abstractions that have acquired their meaning from specific experiences. And if experience has been inadequate or the symbolic processes of perceiving have caused inaccuracies or have left a deeply entrenched inaccurate interpretation, a high degree of veridicality may be almost impossible. Generally, the greater the number of experiences, the more relevant and consistent they are, and the richer their quality, the greater are the chances for veridicality in cognition and the greater are the chances that the reader will understand or comprehend what the writer is trying to convey. But even the most veridical cognition may be an inadequate representation, as indeed the "best" interpretation in reading may be equally inadequate. Complete comprehension is extremely difficult to attain. Nonetheless, even though expecting readers to fully extract the writer's thoughts is probably futile (Flood, 1986), approximation of total veridicality is a desirable goal.

LANGUAGE AND READING

Reading is also a linguistic process; it is a language art. Just and Carpenter (1987) note that reading begins with the printed words on the page, with the reader's prior knowledge of the topic, and with the reader's knowledge of language. They add: "The perceptual processes visually register written language, transforming from printed symbols to language. The comprehension processes interpret language, transforming from linguistic symbols to a more abstract symbolic representation—that is, from language to thought. Obviously, both perception and comprehension are crucial to reading" (pp. 4-5). Furthermore, they remark, "Reading is fundamentally the comprehension of language. The various levels of language, including words, phrases, sentences, and entire text, are operated on by some of the component process of reading" (p. 7).

Research generally teaches that reading is clearly dependent upon linguistic, conceptual, cognitive, and general knowledge abilities that are similar to those required for aural language comprehension. People interact with one another through speech and writing, through listening and reading. Listening is the other half of talking, and reading is the other half of writing.

It is because reading is a language process that development in reading closely parallels development in speech. Thus, the oral language base which children bring to the reading experience is a critical factor in reading success (Koskinen et al., 1988; Wilson & Cleland, 1985). Conversely, inadequate language development is a common cause of poor reading.

Liberman, Rubin, Dequés, and Carlisle (1985) note that the problem of most beginning readers who have difficulties in reading is basically linguistic in nature, resulting from the ineffective use of phonologic strategies, deficiencies in lexical access, and difficulties of representation in short-term memory. They point out that the alphabetic orthography represents the phonological structure of the spoken word, that languages are used to convey meanings, and that words are the basic units by which languages do that. They further note that a word has a uniquely linguistic, complex, phonological structure that must be somehow apprehended before one can deal with a message conveyed by language, whether it be written or spoken.

Clearly, beginning readers must "get at the word", they must be able to discriminate the graphic symbols, but they must also acquire a certain degree of linguistic sophistication (Liberman et al., 1985), or the ability to deal with the structure of language in an analytic manner. They must be able to segment the units of speech (i.e., the phonemes, syllables, and words) that are represented by the orthography. They must be able to decipher the phonological codes which are representations of the auditory properties of given words in the form of phonemes. Without the ability to activate and access the phonological properties of printed words, beginning readers may not be able to achieve lexical access or to remember verbally coded material.

Vellutino and Scanlon (1985) point out that in processing written words readers must be familiar with the graphic and orthographic features of words, but they note that readers must also be familiar with the linguistic features of words (i.e., their semantic, phonological, and syntactic features).

As noted in chapter 1, the semantic codes are "the linguistic representations of meaningful concepts, as encoded in both individual words and groups of words" (Vellutino & Scanlon, 1985, p. 181). The research (Liberman & Shankweiler, 1979) suggests that children with more highly differentiated and more highly elaborated semantic networks (i.e., children with a greater vocabulary and a richer fund of world knowledge) are better able to achieve lexical access or to process verbally encoded information. The research also shows that many readers are handicapped by linguistic deficiencies. Yule and Rutter (1976) noted that disabled readers often exhibit abnormalities of speech and language development and add that language impairment renders the child at risk. Whether the child will actually show reading retardation depends on his temperament and motivation, the nature of the home environment, and the quality of his schooling. Newton et al. (1979) suggest that the English written language (being alphabetic) requires skill of which certain young children, who end up becoming severely disabled in reading, are particularly deficient. There is thus a mismatch between the skills of the child and the task demands of the written language system. Vellutino (1979, 1980) found that the major problem of disabled readers is linguistic deficiency or a deficiency in verbal coding: the inability to retrieve words representing given concepts or to name words, a deficiency in syntax, and the inability to code information phonetically.

Vellutino and Scanlon (1985) found that phonological coding deficits are a major cause of both word identification and verbal memory problems in disabled readers. Conversely, phonological coding ability was indicated as a major determinant of reading ability at an early point in skills development and may well set upper limits on the acquisition of various reading subskills. Olson (1985) suggests that disabled readers generally exhibit linguistic deficits, especially in the ability to analyze the component phonemes in spoken words and in phonetic coding; that phonetic coding deficits may be a continuing or permanent characteristic of disabled readers; and that disabled readers may never catch up to normal readers in this characteristic, reaching an asymptote in phonic coding by about 12 years of age.

Unfortunately, reading theory and teaching have concerned themselves largely with psychological, sociological, physical, and neurological matters, but have not concerned themselves rigorously enough with language. Pearson (1978) notes that the failure of diagnosticians to look at reading failure in the context of language has been one of the most serious educational shortcomings. He adds that it has led to situations where it is common to treat children whose basic problem is a language difference as if they had a reading deficiency. Clearly, if the pupil cannot formulate sentences or turn ideas into words, the deficiency is in general language ability. Thus, for some children, reading failures are often secondary to primary language disturbances (i.e., verbal expression and comprehension), and with these children it is necessary to emphasize the primary linguistic skills prior to reading.

There is little debate today that the teaching of reading functions best and progress in reading occurs most readily when it is taught as an integral part of the language arts program. Reading is a language-related process; it is best studied in relation to language and as one phase of the total communicative process.

Listening and Reading Proficiency

Listening or auditory comprehension is the first language art that the child develops, and together with speaking, it has an important effect on the development of competency in reading. Poor readers tend to be poor listeners, while good readers tend to be good listeners (Just & Carpenter, 1987). The correlations between listening and reading between grade 4 and college generally range from .60 to .70 (Sticht & James, 1984). Reading requires vision and comprehension; listening calls for hearing and comprehension. Listening requires cultivation of auditory abilities. It involves the same basic perceptual and mental processes as reading, and listening and reading both involve the reception and interpretation of linguistic messages and ideas from others. The language is the same in all the language arts; only the media for communication are different.

As we have previously described them (Dechant, 1982), the relationships between listening and reading are as follows:

1. Listening provides the vocabulary and the sentence structure that serve as a foundation for reading. Reading success depends upon the child's aural-oral experience with words. In a very real sense, children read with the ears, mentally pronouncing the words to themselves. Words most easily read are those that have been heard and spoken.
2. Without the ability to hear and discriminate sounds, the child cannot learn phonics. Listening develops the auditory discrimination skills that are the basis for phonetic analysis in reading.
3. Ability to listen to and provide an ending for a story is a good indicator of readiness for reading.
4. The teacher's effectiveness in teaching reading often depends upon his or her ability to capitalize on the pupil's listening ability.
5. Listening ability (if scores on a listening comprehension test are higher than the scores on a reading comprehension test) is an indicator of the pupil's potential ceiling in reading ability. In general, when listening ability is low, reading ability also tends to be low.
6. Children from lower socioeconomic homes are often at a distinct disadvantage in learning to read because they have spoken and heard language patterns that interfere with the comprehension of oral and written materials.

7. For children in the lower grades, slow learners, poor readers, those with visual deficiencies at near point, and perhaps boys generally, listening often is a more suitable medium of learning than is reading. Generally, the lower the reading ability and the lower the scholastic aptitude, the greater is the advantage of listening over reading (Swalm, 1972). Reading comprehension generally catches up with listening comprehension during the fifth grade. However, since reading allows the pupil to go back and reread, reading becomes more effective as the difficulty of the material increases.
8. The development of listening comprehension is more relevant to reading achievement than is becoming a competent speaker of standard English (Harris & Sipay, 1975). Smith (1988) notes that children who have difficulty understanding speech may have difficulty learning to read.

The child learns language by ear. The vocabulary and skills in language structure that the pupil brings to school were learned first through listening. Indeed, the foundations of good comprehension are set in early childhood, in listening comprehension (Teale et al., 1987). If it were not for the child's earlier listening development, the child would not, or at least only rarely, learn to read. The teacher of reading should take advantage of these previous learnings, and should help the child to associate the visual symbols with the sounds previously learned.

Oral Language Proficiency and Reading

Oral or expressive language proficiency, like listening proficiency, is associated with reading proficiency. Conversely, slowness in developing speech, slowed automatized naming or verbal processing of words, mispronunciation, missequencing of syllables, poor learning of verbal associations, inadequate use of phonic structure and word segmentation, slow word and sound processing, and impaired word finding all are associated with difficulties in reading (Rudel, 1985). Poor readers often lack sentence sense, speak with excessive hesitation, do not talk in simple sentences, cannot tell a simple story, cannot associate words with experiences, and do not understand the relationships between spoken and written language.

That speaking proficiency or command of the spoken language is important for reading is substantiated also by the following generalizations:

1. Speaking provides the vocabulary and sentence patterns for reading.

2. The child's proficiency in the communication and language skills, both speaking and listening, is one of the best indicators of the child's readiness for beginning reading.
3. Words and sentences most easily read are those that have been spoken and heard.
4. The more alike the patterns of language structure in the reading material are to the patterns of language structure used in speaking, the better the pupil's reading comprehension tends to be.

Liberman and Shankweiler (1979) observe that reading is somehow parasitic on speech. However, written narrative usually employs a different vocabulary and syntax. It cannot rely on gestures and facial expressions. In writing, the meaning must be carried solely through linguistic means (Purcell-Gates, 1989). Written language is not oral language written down. "Written texts tap a wider range of general knowledge, show different forms of discourse organization, use different anaphoric devices, and provide less contextual support than spoken discourse does" (Robeck and Wallace, 1990, p. 63). Perfetti (1985) observes that speech and print are different for the reader in two significant ways: (a) readers must master a new coding system by learning to break the alphabetic code; and (b) they must learn to deal with a written language that is much less contextualized than is the spoken language.

Language deals with the naming or labeling of one's thoughts or ideas; it is the use of symbols to express one's concepts. Symbolization is of course fundamental to language. Cognitive development (conceptualization) precedes expression in language (symbolization). Nevertheless, the interaction between thought and language is pervasive. It is nearly impossible to use one's conceptual skills if one cannot express thoughts and concepts symbolically. Langer (1948) noted that "Without language symbols there seems to be nothing like explicit thought whatever" (p. 103). Language facilitates intra-individual communication and cognition. The verbalization of ideas permits the pupil to think about things and events.

The teacher of reading is especially concerned with clarity of pronunciation. It is essential that children learn to articulate all the vowels and the consonants without distortion, omission, substitution, addition, or transposition; to enunciate all syllables clearly; to pronounce accurately; to give the total visual form its proper sound; and to accent the appropriate syllables. Children must have an adequate vocabulary and they must have mastered, at least to some degree, sentence structure. Without these skills children probably will not be good oral readers, will have problems with phonics and with learning the proper grapheme-phoneme correspondences, and may also have difficulty in transmitting meaning.

Speech deficiencies (particularly, those characterized by the imperfect production of the phonetic elements, leading to distortion of /j/, /l/, /r/, /s/, /sh/, /z/, /ch/, /hw/, /zh/, and /th/, or substitution of /k/ for /g/, /b/ for /d/, /p/ for /d/, /t/ for unvoiced /th/, or unvoiced for voiced sounds), lisping, stuttering, cluttering, cleft palate speech, delayed speech, and speech characterized by dialect are all classified as articulatory defects and each in its own way is related to reading disability and reading difficulty. Oral reading and the learning of phonics are almost always more difficult for the person with a speech defect, especially when the speech defect is characterized by indistinctness, blurring of the consonants, thick quality, or cluttering. Delayed or retarded early speech development or a substantial incidence of articulatory defects (dyslalia) between the ages of two and one-half and four (Catts, 1986) almost always affects reading adversely. Furthermore, if children cannot phrase properly or cannot repeat phrases correctly (Catts, 1986), if their emphasis on words is wrong, and if the pitch and intonation are improper, they probably will not read with full meaning, and comprehension is likely to suffer.

The inference is that language training should accompany reading instruction every step of the way. Every reading lesson should be an extension of language teaching and a means of developing the child's linguistic skill. There is little point in teaching children to read until they can use sentence language in conversation. And it is unwise for the reading text to run any considerable distance ahead of the child's own oral language expression; otherwise, the pupil is virtually trying to learn a foreign language, and valuable instructional time is lost.

Knowledge of Grammar and Reading

Language has a defined structure and this structure, revealed in sentences, plays a significant role in conveying meaning. The structure of spoken language includes three major components: the phonological, syntactic, and semantic or meaning systems (Ringler & Weber, 1984). Written language has a slightly different system: the grapho-phonic, the semantic, and the syntactic. The grapho-phonic and the semantic systems are interrelated through the syntactic system. It is the rules of syntax that allow the grapho-phonic system to communicate meaning. The focus here is on the syntactic system or on the grammar of language. The reader is referred to the discussion of syntactic processing in chapter 1.

Grammar consists of morphology and syntax. Morphology is a study of word meaning and word structure; and syntax, of how words are grouped into utterances. Morphology allows for the introduction of minute changes to bring out a special meaning; the various uses of *s* (cats, cat's, hits) are examples of this. Syntax is the grouping of words to suggest variant (and specific) nuances of meaning. The syntactic codes are grammatic rules that (a) define the functional properties of words, either identifying the form class (e.g., noun, verb, adjective) or in the case of inflectional endings the grammatical properties (e.g., number, person, tense) that qualify the meaning of words, and that (b) order words in the language. Children with greater knowledge of the syntactic codes comprehend and encode meanings better than do those with less knowledge; they encode the surface characteristics of words with greater success.

Genuine reading proficiency may be described as the ability to read language structures, especially sentences and paragraphs. If the pupil reads something the way the writer would like it to have been said, with appropriate stresses, rhythm, cadence, phrasing, pitch, and intonation, true communication of meaning is possible. Conversely, it is almost a certainty that if pupils do not develop sentence sense and an appreciation for the metaphor and melody of language, they are well on the way to becoming disabled readers. Lefevre (1964) stressed that misapprehending the relationships between spoken and printed language patterns is the most decisive element in reading failure.

Words do not give meaning to sentences; rather, words receive their meaning from the sentence or the syntactic context. The pupil who has become a word reader has fallen into the error of not reading the phrase or sentence unit that gives meaning to the word. The sentence circumscribes the word, giving it the distinct meaning intended by the writer.

Immature syntax (i.e., less fluent language and grammatically incorrect language) is a major problem of disabled readers. Deficiencies in syntactic abilities especially affect comprehension.

The Reading/Writing Connection

There is no intent here to give a detailed discussion of the interrelatedness of writing and reading. Neither is the purpose to discuss penmanship. The focus is rather on encoding, the process of translating ideas and thoughts into print, and on composing, the putting together of a coherent message.

Research has clearly shown the importance of the relationship between reading and writing and the benefits of correlating them (Kucer, 1987; Stotsky, 1983; Tierney & Leys, 1984, 1986; Wittrock, 1983). Learning to read is reinforced by writing, and learning to write is reinforced by reading (Jewell & Zintz, 1986). Goodman and Goodman (1983) observe that writing experiences are likely to have a positive effect on reading comprehension because the schemata for predicting texts in reading are basically the same as those used in constructing texts during writing. Tierney and Pearson (1983) point out that writing and reading are both acts of composing, involving essentially similar processes of construction and reconstruction of meaning. Squire (1983) notes that "composing (composition or writing) and comprehending are process-oriented thinking skills which are basically interrelated" (p. 581). Elkind (1976) observes that "the more children write, the more they will get from reading" (p. 358). Hittelman (1988) believes that "as students have opportunities to experience the trials and satisfactions of structuring their own language (writing), they will be better prepared for interpreting the structuring of others" (p. 29).

The encoding of thoughts, which is writing, and the retrieval of thoughts, which involves reading, are obviously closely related. Nonetheless, the caveat of Russell (1989) is well placed:

> Writing is certainly more difficult than reading, and one must at least pause at the prospect of making writers out of the people one has failed to make readers. People who fall asleep at the words of Mark Twain are unlikely to find writing an exciting avocation. Still, to read and to write is to reside in the same place, to draw from the same well; they are related, if not symbiotic. To write is to capture divergent and loosely related thoughts and assign them form and structure. To read is to take form and structure and parlay them into divergent and rich thought. Both require not only an imagination, but also the inclination to use it. (p. 2)

Children, long before they begin formal education, write in some form. Children's writing development moves from scribbling to drawing their thoughts in picture form, to letter-like forms, to strings of letters, to printing their name, to invented spelling, and finally to conventional orthography (Sulzby & Teale, 1985). The spelling patterns which children invent follow a general developmental sequence that appears closely linked to an emerging concept of the word and is predictive of eventual movement into reading (Henderson & Templeton, 1986; Teale, Hiebert, & Chittenden, 1987).

As early as 1971, Read demonstrated that the invented spellings of preschoolers show a predictable pattern in their choices of the letter symbols used to represent the spoken language. Children are able to devise a primitive phonetic transcription based on the names of the letters. The invented spelling approach to reading teaches children phonemic segmentation skills and letter-sound knowledge (Nicholson, 1986), and develops a strong interest in reading. The invented spellings of children are surprisingly uniform. Thus most children tend to come up with inventions such as the following: BOT (boat), GRL (girl), DA (day), WALK (walked). Initially, children's writing is "talk written down." It is this form of writing that children quickly learn to read. The teacher promotes writing/reading activity by engaging children in activities which have them express their thoughts, by recording the verbalizations on the blackboard, and by having them read what they have thought, spoken, and written.

Undoubtedly, reading and writing interact, but it is also clear they are more independent of each other than is generally assumed (Langer, 1986; Shanahan, 1984, 1988). Shanahan goes on to observe that we need to teach both writing and reading, that the teaching of both should begin in the earliest grades, that the relationship between writing and spelling changes developmentally across reading levels, and that teaching must make the reading/writing connection explicit.

Durkin (Aaron et al., 1990) questions whether all children should do a lot of writing right away, adding that there are many unanswered questions about the connection between reading and writing and about the facts of early writing and of invented spelling. Her caveat cannot be taken lightly.

THE COMMUNICATIVE NATURE OF READING

Chapter 1 noted that in addition to being a sensory, perceptual/cognitive, and language process, reading is also a communication process; it is a process of putting the reader in contact and communication with the message encoded by the writer in the graphic symbols. Writing has no purpose without a reader. Reading always involves an interaction between the writer and reader. It is the culminating act of the communication process, initiated by the thoughts of the writer and expressed through the symbols on the page. Without a reader, communication via the printed page is impossible. Reading takes place only when the child shares the ideas that the communicator intends to convey.

Communication always involves two elements: (a) the ideas, messages, or experiences that are to be communicated; and (b) the signs or symbols that are used to convey these ideas or experiences. It is a sensorimotor process involving the use of signs. It includes the motor reactions of the sign-maker — the speaker or writer — and the reception of the sign by the listener or reader. In human communication, these signs are words, and they receive their meaning from and through experience.

Reading is clearly a communication process. The writer communicates meanings or, more correctly, encodes a message in written symbols, and the reader apprehends meaning by decoding the message encoded graphically by the writer (see Figure 3-2).

The graphic cues, letters and words, are the sign system in which messages are encoded. Communication requires such a sign system. But, reading is not a matter of communicating symbols or signs. It is concerned with the communication of a message. Words mirror reality and the world, bear meaning, and act as media of communication. They contain a content, "determined by an identity of reaction in man . . . to the same things, to the same stimuli" (Anshen, 1957, p. 13).

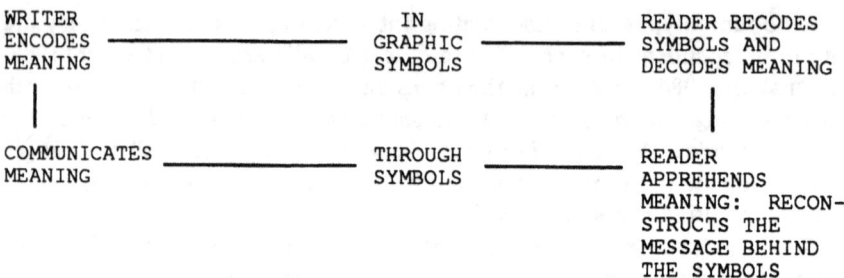

FIGURE 3-2: The Communicative Nature of Reading

Unfortunately, the potentials for a breakdown in communication between writer and reader (and hence a breakdown in comprehension) are ever present. The very personal nature of perception and of experience almost prohibits accurate and complete communication between writer and reader. The writer (transmitter) and the reader (receiver) are two ends of a communication channel along which information flows. As a message passes through the communication channel, it takes on a variety of forms. At each part of the communication process, it is possible that the message will be changed or comprehension of the message will be garbled in some way. The poor comprehender is obviously one who has not received the message sent by the writer. Specifically, lack of communication in reading or failure to achieve an accurate reconstruction of the meaning of the writer may occur for various reasoning reasons (Dechant, 1982; Levine, 1984):

1. There is rarely total communality of world experience, and hence of meanings and cognitive field, between writer and reader. Each reader's store of semantic meaning is not totally adequate. Because experiences, cognitive field, or personal schemata differ from individual to individual, words rarely mean precisely the same thing to any two individuals. There is little likelihood that any two readers will give exactly the same interpretation to any given paragraph. Perfect communication is rare. Generally, the writer and the reader communicate only if they have common concepts and if they assign the same labels to the concept. Messages and meanings are most easily shared when communicators (i.e., writers and readers) have similar backgrounds or when there is some commonality of experience.
2. Writers are not completely familiar with all the ways of expressing meaning. Writers sometimes do not have the skill to say what they want to say; they lack the required rhetorical knowledge. It is the writer who determines which ideas from his long-term memory and from his individually held cognitive structures he wishes to

share. And, it is the writer who superimposes upon print the syntactic arrangements and the rhetorical structures. It is he who organizes text in certain ways, who plans the sequence of presentation, who highlights key ideas, and who chooses transitional elements (Levine, 1984).

3. Readers are often not familiar with the writer's specific modes of expression. They lack the linguistic competence (i.e., knowledge of vocabulary, semantics and syntax, and the rhetorical skill) needed to comprehend the writer's intended message.
4. Each reader is limited by the speed at which the eye can travel over a passage of text making information-gathering fixations and by the amount of information that can be acquired in a single fixation.
5. Because all communication channels, and indeed most readers, have limited capacities, noise (extraneous signals that impede the transmission of informative signals) may overload the system. In reading, noise may be a typeface that is difficult to read, poor illumination, distraction of the reader's attention, or the unwanted emotional noise caused by the reader assigning connotations to words different from the writer. Smith (1971, 1978) notes that because of noise, reading is intrinsically more difficult for the beginning reader than for the experienced reader. Everything is much "noisier" for the beginner. Lack of attention is a major noise factor in poor readers.
6. The writer does not provide adequate semantic and syntactic context or redundancy. Redundancy exists whenever information is duplicated by more than one source. The larger the context, the greater the redundancy tends to be. Presenting a word both visually and orally is a form of redundancy that helps the learner. The more redundancy there is, the less visual information the reader requires to identify words and to associate meaning with them. Conversely, the less redundancy there is, the more visual information is needed. Lack of experience with life itself, with materials and their content, and with words and their identification, is a major inhibitor to redundancy. When readers must get a great amount of visual information—when they must identify every single letter or even every word—they will be slow readers and will usually have difficulty reading for meaning.
7. It is impossible to share concepts directly; all the writer can do is to put on paper words that symbolize the concept. Words can only create a symbolic representation in the mind—never exact reality. Moreover, words do not always convey accurately what is intended. Nevertheless, because experiences and perceptual/cogni-

tive fields tend generally to be more similar than different, the interpretations given to sentences (one's comprehension of them) are similar enough to allow for communication between writer and reader.

8. Comprehension occurs only when the reader's reconstruction of the events behind a symbol substantially agrees with the writers' intended message (Dechant, 1982; Levine, 1984). It is not enough to put one's own stamp of meaning on words. Reading takes place only when the reader shares the ideas that the communicator intends to convey (Langman, 1960). Semelmeyer (1957) points out that reading should bear the same relationship to experiences or events that a map bears to the territory which it is supposed to represent. Reading is a process in which the reader reconstructs a message encoded graphically by a writer and the message must at least approximate what the writer intended. The reader must follow the thought of the writer.

9. The reader may and even must gain meaning from the printed page. In other words, the writer can communicate a new meaning. This occurs when the writer's symbols stimulate readers to combine or reconstruct their own concepts in a novel way or to construct new meanings through manipulation of relevant concepts already in their possession.

10. The reader may be immature conceptually. The reader is often thinking on a concrete level. For communication through writing and reading to occur, readers usually must be able to make a generic response to their experience. Thus, Bruner (1957b) notes: "If perceptual experience is ever had raw, that is, free of categorical identity, it is doomed to be a gem serene, locked in the silence of private experience" (p. 125). A major cause of poor or inadequate comprehension and inadequate communication of meaning is immature conceptualization. The more specific the reader's reaction to printed words, the less effective tends to be the communication between writer and reader; the more generic the reactions, the more effective tends to be the communication. The learner acquires only gradually and with broadened experience new layers of meaning, and the reader's perceptions and interpretation, indeed his comprehension, become increasingly wider, more diversified, and more complex.

11. Communication of meaning often suffers because readers rely too heavily on text-based information and fail to use their world knowledge in the comprehension of text. Conversely, some readers rely too much on their prior knowledge and fail to consider textual information (Harris & Sipay, 1985). Both top-

down and bottom-up strategies are significant in the comprehension of text. Readers must at times monitor information from the bottom up, replacing their hypotheses and expectations with new ones triggered by the text (McNeil, 1984). On the other hand, an overemphasis on bottom-up processing (staying too close to the print) may not fit what is read into the appropriate context; similarly, an overemphasis on top-down processing may result in inferences, expectations, and hypotheses that are not warranted by the text.

Reading is communication through written language. Proficient readers are those who can make appropriate associations between written and spoken symbols, who understand language structures, and who have an adequate language base that allows them to bring meaning to the printed page. Readers cannot rely only on their own concepts and experiences in comprehension. If the reader did so, communication would often not take place. If only the text cues were used, then all of us should agree on the interpretation of text, which is certainly not the case. Reading is clearly an interactive process that relies both on the reader's world of experience and on the cues offered by the text.

SUMMARY

Chapter 1 initiated the discussion of reading as a sensory process, as a perceptual/cognitive or high-level thinking process, and as a language, a psycholinguistic, and a communication process. Chapter 2 greatly expanded on the sensory characteristics of reading. Chapter 3 examined the remaining relationships. It identified how meanings are developed, how they are associated with written symbols, and what it means to go beyond the printed page. It emphasized that meaning is a function of perception and cognition. Chapter 3 further examined reading as a language and linguistic process and as the comprehension of language. It stressed that words have a uniquely linguistic and phonological structure and that the teaching of reading functions best in a total language arts context of listening, speaking, writing, and reading. Finally, the chapter emphasized the communicative nature of reading. Reading ultimately involves a communication and a sharing of meaning between writer and reader.

PART III
Basic Strategies in Reading

In recent years two views have guided the teaching of reading. First, readers must develop the metacognitive awareness that text must be interpreted with respect to what one already knows, to one's personal schemata. Second, reading is a process of predicting oneself through print, and readers' efficiency in reading depends upon their ability to learn the predictive strategy. These two views and the strategies developed from them are discussed in two chapters: chapter 4, "The Schema Model of Reading," and chapter 5 "Developing the Predictive Strategy in Reading: Integration of the Meaning and Within-word Cues."

Chapter 4's basic theme is that the schema-theoretical model of reading should guide all reading instruction. It affirms that (a) reading is best taught within the schema theoretical framework, (b) schema theory is an important unifying and organizing concept and an integral part of the total strategy in reading, and (c) reading and comprehension depend to a great degree on the concepts, topical knowledge, and upon the language and life experiences that readers bring to the text. It also argues that proficiency in reading depends as much on what the pupil brings *to* the printed page as on what is *on* the printed page. From the schema theoretical view, the most critical element is the reader's ability to fit what is in the text to existing knowledge or schemata (Dupuis et al., 1989).

Chapter 5 is designed to develop the predictive strategy in reading. This strategy requires the pupil to integrate the meaning (i.e., picture, semantic, syntactic, and morphemic) with the within-word or word structure cues (i.e., configuration, phonic, morphemic, and identification by analogy cues). It requires the conjoint use of the graphic, orthographic, grapho-phonological, lexical, semantic, and syntactic cues. The efficient integration and application of the meaning and within-word cues aid learners in predicting themselves through text, in searching for meaning, in reducing uncertainty, and in developing a representation or model of text. Reading is not an unguided guessing game. It should at a minimum be an educated guessing game, in which the odds for success are improved by the use of all the word-recognition/comprehension strategies. The chief deficiency of some prominent top-down models of reading is not that they accord primacy to the meaning cues, but that they accord them exclusivity: they essentially ignore the within-word cues. Some primary predictive tools are thus not utilized.

Chapter 4
The Schema Model of Reading

    I. Introduction
   II. Cognitive Structure
  III. The Role of Meaning
  IV. Schemata and Their Role
      A. Schemata Defined
      B. Reader and Text Interaction
      C. Schemata and Semantic and Syntactic Context
   V. Storing and Retrieval of Schemata
  VI. Assimilation and Accommodation
 VII. Schemata and Differences Between Good and Poor Readers
VIII. Nonvisual Information
  IX. Ambiguities in Schema Theory
   X. Summary

CHAPTER 4
The Schema Model of Reading

Some years ago we (Smith and Dechant, 1961; Dechant, 1964) noted that printed pages do not of themselves transmit meaning. The essence of meaning comes at least partly from the mind of the reader. Interpretation and comprehension in reading are clearly dependent upon what is stored in the mind of the reader. We further observed that the reader is stimulated by the author's words, but he vests the author's words with his own meaning. Reading typically is the bringing of meaning *to* rather than the gaining of meaning *from* the printed page. The reader comprehends text more in terms of what he is than in what it is. In reading, the critical element is not what is seen on the page but, rather, what is signified by the written symbol. The critical element in the reading act is the reader's meaningful response to the written symbol. Reading includes the graphic symbol but the primary part of the reading experience is the invoking of meanings and interpretations drawn from the reader's past experiences, and relating them to the symbol.

Moreover, we observed that the reader's perception and cognition, and hence the comprehension of what is read, are determined almost exclusively by the reader's experiences. The prime determinant of whether children will learn to comprehend while reading is experience. We thus defined reading as the process of giving the significance intended by the writer to the graphic symbols by relating them to one's own fund of experience (Dechant, 1961). A reader cannot be a proficient reader of graphic symbols without previously having been a proficient reader of experience. Meaning is supplied by readers as they process the symbols by relating them to experience and to their existing store of information. The good reader is constantly processing information, and incoming information is continually being tested, formulated, and acted upon in the light of prior experience. Clearly, meanings and comprehension cannot far outrun direct concrete experiences. A meaning that is not closely anchored to some clear experience is likely to be wide of the mark; it cannot be more adequate than experience.

These observations of ours were predated by earlier writers and researchers. Lange (1902) wrote: "The mind apprehends outer impressions in accordance with its wealth of knowledge gained through former activity" (p. 8). William James (1890) noted that "whilst part of what we perceive comes through our senses from the object before us, another part (and it may be the greater part) always comes . . . out of our head" (p. 103). Lange (1902) added that "we see and hear not only with the eye and ear, but quite as much with the help of our present knowledge, with the apperceiving content of the mind" (p. 21). Horn (1937) noted that the writer "does not really convey ideas to the reader; he merely stimulates him to construct them out of his own experience" (p. 154).

The position taken in *Psychology in Teaching Reading* (Smith & Dechant, 1961; Dechant & Smith, 1977) and again emphasized in chapter 3 is that reading is a perceptual/cognitive process, that the interpretative response required in reading requires cognition, and that cognition is a sensation clothed with the perceiver's wealth of past experience. Reading requires the reader to go beyond the sensory data, the graphic symbols on the page, to ascertain meaning. Readers are perceiving something beyond what they sense or see. They are using information not present to the senses.

In reading, the incoming sensory data, that is, the graphic symbols, must be retained, processed, and reorganized by the reader. The information from the retinal system must be interpreted by the brain: it must be converted into a cognition or a representation based on past experiences. In short, central processes, perception and cognition, are codeterminers, of reading. Reading is a representational process. What the reader perceives, his mental image of what he "reads," is a construct. The reader constructs a representation of the text, and this representation includes elements that are not explicitly contained in the printed page.

Our focus in chapter 4 is on the schema model of reading. This model is clearly based on a view of the reading process that has been delineated by early writers and researchers. Today it represents a repackaging of what has been known and practiced in the teaching of reading for many years. In a sense, it is a rediscovery and restatement of prior knowledge in a new way. It is a new vocabulary tag that has been given to practices that have been used by thousands of effective teachers and by millions of good comprehenders throughout the history of reading. There is much from earlier theory and observation that is relevant to schema theory today, but it is also true that a formalized schema theory offers additional, if not entirely new, perspectives.

A guiding theme of this text is that reading, and indeed comprehension, depend to a great degree on the concepts, topical knowledge, and language and life experiences that the reader brings to the text. Thus, proficiency in reading depends as much, perhaps even more, on what the pupil brings to the printed page than on what is on the printed page. The reader's knowledge is often more important to the attainment of comprehension than is the text itself, but reading and comprehension result only when the reader and the text interact. Readers, must combine existing knowledge with new information in the text, integrating what they know with what the text presents in order to construct meaning from text. These ideas about reading have come to be associated with the term *schema theory*.

Schema theory is a cognitive theory that emphasizes cognition; conceptual learning; the process of understanding; mental events; conscious experience; acquiring, processing, organizing, storing, and retrieving of information; thinking; reasoning; problem solving; and meanings.

The content of inquiry in schema theory is anything that has been experienced. It is the total phenomenal world of the individual. The German word *Erlebnis* is a useful word to express this concept. It includes the private world of inner personal meanings, the phenomenal world of the individual. It suggests that the meaning that an experience has for an individual, or the meaning the text may have for the reader, may be more significant than the words themselves.

COGNITIVE STRUCTURE

The major focus of schema theory is the concept of cognitive structure, also called the spiral of knowledge (Poplin, 1988), scripted knowledge (Yekovich & Walker, 1988), or simply schema. The schema framework is a model of the structure of knowledge. Schema theory assumes that the mind uses schemata or mental organizing structures to guide perception and cognition and to categorize objects or events. Cognitive structure or schematic structure is the organization of our long-term memories.

Cognitive structure consists of hierarchically organized concepts or subsumers (Ausübel, 1968) arranged much as categories are arranged in Bruner's coding system (Bruner, 1966). It consists of ideas or concepts that have been organized hierarchically from the most inclusive at the apex to the least inclusive at the base. Bruner identifies the hierarchical arrangement of related concepts or categories as a coding system. Subsumers are similar to schemata or categories. Consumers are higher level or superordinate concepts that incorporate or include (subsume) other ideas. An example of a schema is the hierarchical structure of real numbers:

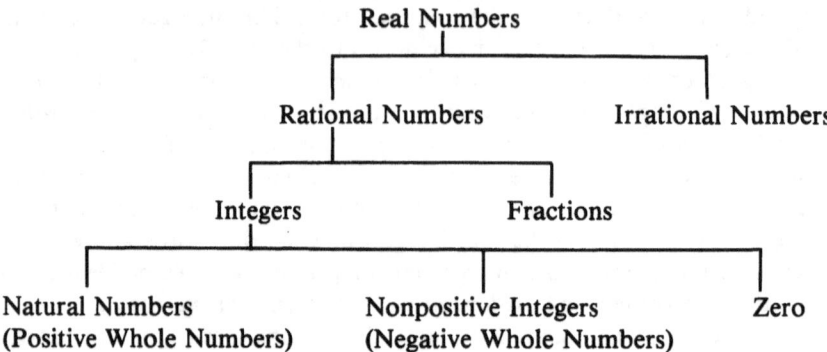

The schema structure, what Yekovich and Walker (1988) call scripted knowledge, consists of declarative memory components, plus separate scripts or procedural memory components. The latter, the procedural components of a script, include the knowledge of how to do something (e.g., painting a room or going to a restaurant) or those aspects of schemata which deal with routines and sequences. Procedural schemata are especially important in problem solving and skill learning. Declarative knowledge is the semantic network representing factual knowledge as conceptual nodes (i.e., an example of a concept) and relational links.

THE ROLE OF MEANING

Meanings are the essence of cognition. In her theory of holistic constructivism, Poplin (1988a, 1988b) defines learning (and hence comprehension) as the construction of meaning or as the process whereby new meanings are created by the learner. In this context, objects, experiences, events, or words take on meaning when they elicit a mental representation in the content of consciousness; that is, when they are related to a concept already in one's cognitive structure. The newly constructed meanings are products of the transformations that occur between the new experience to be learned and all other previous experiences (i.e., one's schemata).

Reading thus is a continuous construction and reconstruction of new, richer, connected, and more complex meanings. When a child reads a book for the second time, she brings different meanings to the text because of the new experiences between the first and second reading. The child continuously brings different schemata to the reading and walks away from reading with yet another new and different meaning.

Children develop meaning through new experiences prompting new meanings, repeated or recalled experiences, or contemplation. Poplin notes that recalled experiences are frequently united and transformed into new meanings as parallels are drawn, communalities are ferreted out, thoughts are rearranged, questions are rephrased, or new solutions are discovered. When these happen, the learner will not perceive the original experience in the old way again. As Heraclitus noted, one never steps into the same river again. The spiral never stops turning and it never stops changing and growing. And the whole, that is, the reconstructed meaning, the new meaning that was constructed by integrating the new with the old, is more than the sum of the individual events. Breaking events into their molecular structure, breaking sentences into words, without relating them to each other, is to lose some sense of their essential nature. A sentence is more than its parts. Water is more than hydrogen and oxygen. A melody is more than an accretion of notes. Poplin observes that "the transformation of new experiences involves a process of creating meaning about the ideas as a whole, the specific parts, and then back to the whole again."

Each new experience (or act of comprehending) leads to a new spiral of knowledge, to a new whole or gestalt. The reader transforms each new reading experience into new insights, into a new cognitive or phenomenal field; thus, comprehension is highly personal, constructed within the context of the reader's own experience. Each reader's spiral of knowledge delimits what will be comprehended and what will not. Indeed, the written words themselves cannot and do not capture the phenomenological richness of meaning or the rich memory representation that one experiences when reading anything to which one can bring meaning.

It is obvious that, from the perspective of schema theory, the reader is not simply a person who passively receives information from the text, poured in as through a funnel.

SCHEMATA AND THEIR ROLE

A major thesis of this text is that schema theory is an integral part of the total strategy in reading, that text must be interpreted with respect to what one knows, one's personal schemata, and that schemata play a critical role in the comprehension of text. The assumption is that there are prestored schemata which determine "how all the information in the text is understood and stored in memory" (Rayner & Pollatsek, 1989, p. 304).

Schemata Defined

Schemata are organized knowledge structures that aid the reader in comprehending text; they are the building blocks of cognition (Rumelhart &

Ortony, 1977; Rumelhart, 1980): They are conceptional abstractions, the scaffolding with which and on which the reader constructs the meaning of the text.

The term schema was first used by Sir Frederick Bartlett in 1932. Schema is a synonym for real-world knowledge (Rayner & Pollatsek, 1989). It is a concept that includes all the associations, experiences, and relationships that have been connected to the concept. Schema is the cognitive base which the reader draws upon to match new incoming information with prior information stored in memory, thereby deriving meaning from what is read.

Specifically, the term schema refers to:

1. The reader's fund of world experience: the total of retained, interrelated, and integrated experiences that define the reader's prior knowledge and information, which is stored in long-term memory (Widomski, 1983). Meaning resides in the experiences of the reader. Semantic information or the semantic context reflects the experience and background information that the reader brings to the text. As noted in chapter 1, when readers associate meaning with a symbol, a meaning that they have acquired through experience, they are utilizing a semantic cue and are making use of the semantic context.
2. The reader's cognitive base: the conceptual systems, understandings, concepts, and vocabulary of the reader.
3. The reader's fund of linguistic experience: the reader's knowledge of language and of the linguistic systems (the grapho-phonemic and syntactic). The reader is a store of semantic information but also of syntactic information. Syntactic information is the knowledge of the grammatical relationships within sentence patterns. It is the reader's basic understanding of graphemes, recognition of the letters of the alphabet, concept of directionality or that print moves from left to right. It is the reader's understanding of the importance of word order, recognition of the function of capitalization and punctuation, understanding of the relationships between spoken and written language, sense of story and its structure, and understanding of the format and style of various literary genre. It includes knowledge of the coherence of text and of the rules of inference.
4. The reader's topical knowledge: Reading is aided when readers have knowledge of the specific topical area in which they are reading.
5. The reader's knowledge of the rhetorical structures that signal the organization of texts: Readers are aided when they understand

story grammar or when they know the patterns used in expository text (McNeil, 1987).
6. The reader's purpose and expectancy: why he or she is reading and what each expects from it (Dupuis et al., 1989). Smith (1988) refers to this as the specification of text or the reader's expectations about what he will find in the text.

Schemata tend to have three characteristics: (a) they are composed of variables whose content is determined by the person's past experience; (b) they are usually embedded within a larger schema and will have smaller schemata embedded in them (Rayner & Pollatsek, 1989); and (c) they vary in their degree of abstraction.

Schema theory suggests that readers must use their understanding of the world in general or their encyclopedic knowledge (Adams & Collins, 1979, 1985), the topic addressed in the text, and their knowledge of how language works to construct and reconstruct meaning from text. Smith (1975) observes that "the only effective and meaningful way in which anyone can learn is attempting to relate new experiences to what he knows (or believes) already" (p. 1) Wilson (1983) notes that comprehension is less a set of isolated skills than a process of connecting text information to the information stored in the reader's head. Meaning is obtained when readers fit the materials read into their own knowledge system or their own schemata. Rumelhart (1984) suggests that all knowledge is packaged into units or schemata and that readers comprehend when they find a configuration of schemata or hypotheses that offer a coherent account of the text. He adds that the reader is constantly evaluating hypotheses about the most plausible interpretation of the text. As readers read sentences, they activate, evaluate, refine, and discard schemata. Readers generate hypotheses about the possible content of the story and evaluate these schemata against the sentences as they read them. "If they find the new information confirmatory they maintain and further elaborate their hypotheses and construct another consistent with the input data (Rumelhart, 1984, p. 17)."

Reader and Text Interaction

Schema theory presupposes that there is a symbiotic relationship between the reader and print. Reading and comprehension occur when the reader and print interact. Reading comprehension depends on what is in the mind of the reader as well as what is in the text. Yekovich and Walker (1987) observe that when a text is read an episodic memory representation is formed. This representation is a composite trace, consisting of the text information and the reader's knowledge.

Anderson, Spiro, and Anderson (1977, 1978) note that the meaning of a communication depends in a fundamental way on a person's knowledge of the world or on the fitting of what is read into one's knowledge system, but it also depends upon the analysis of the context as well as on the characteristics of the message. From this perspective Rumelhart's interactive model of reading seems to be preferable to the top-down models that overemphasize the reader's prior knowledge and the bottom-up models which assign primacy to the print.

The reader's schemata are significant for reading and determine the level of reading and comprehension that the reader will attain because meaning basically comes from the mind of the reader. Printed pages, of themselves, do not transmit meaning. Readers extract meaning from what they read on the basis of the visual information (the surface structure of the language) they receive from the environment through their receptor systems, but also and principally on the basis of the knowledge and experiences contained within the brain (the deep structure of language), which are available to memory (Smith, 1988). Smith (1988) adds that language and what is read cannot be comprehended unless the receiver (the reader or listener) makes this critical, active contribution.

Schemata and Semantic and Syntactic Context

In chapter 1 we observed that comprehension is a matter of interpreting the semantic and syntactic context or the deep structure of language. This is where the reader's schemata have their primary function. They are the building blocks for the semantic and syntactic context. The semantic context takes on meaning because the reader is a virtual storehouse of past experience (i.e., schemata) and can relate this experience to the graphic symbols.

There are literally two semantic contexts: the one is in the mind of the reader, the second resides in the text. The text itself constrains the meaning choices by the choice of words, the way the words are ordered, the rhetorical devices of the writer, and the text form. The schemata in the mind of the reader determine the breadth and depth of meaning that the reader can bring to the printed page.

Research has amply demonstrated that the reader who brings the most background, knowledge, and experience (i.e., the most developed schemata) to the printed page gains the most knowledge from the printed page and comprehends the best. Chall (1947) found that, when she gave an information test about tuberculosis to sixth and eighth graders, those who scored the highest on this test were also those who comprehended the most when they read a selection on tuberculosis. Chall observed that we read in order to gain experience, and yet we get more out of reading if we have more experience.

A later study compared second graders who knew a lot about spiders with those who knew less and found that those with greater prior knowledge, after reading about Webby, the Spider, answered inferential questions better than did those pupils who knew less (Pearson, Hansen, & Gordon, 1979). Marcellesi (1985) found that French second graders with more favorable backgrounds comprehended better than those with less favorable backgrounds. Children whose families were primarily professional and white collar had a better general word knowledge and a better understanding of narrative structures.

The importance of these and similar studies (Chiesi, Spilich, & Voss, 1979; Spilich, Vesonder, Chiesi, & Voss, 1979; Langer & Nicolich, 1981; Marr & Gormley, 1982; Perfetti, 1985) is that when readers have a great deal of relevant and consistent experiences or prior knowledge to relate to symbols, the probability of success of their predictions is high, and their chances for comprehension and recall are increased. When the experience is limited or inconsistent, the reverse is true. The doctor of medicine gets more from reading a book on medicine than does the average layman because of the knowledge that he can bring to the text.

Thus, a basic value of the schemata the reader brings to the printed page is that they help the reader to make inferences and predictions. They allow the reader to understand far beyond what is stated in the text. They allow the reader to fill in information not provided by the writer and to infer what the writer meant.

STORING AND RETRIEVAL OF SCHEMATA

Schema theory provides an explanation of how knowledge is stored in the mind (Mason & Au, 1986). An underlying thesis of schema theory is that all knowledge is organized hierarchically and stored in the brain in the form of mental frameworks, concepts, or cognitive structures (i.e., schema) (Ausübel, 1978; Durkin, 1984).

Schema theory postulates an architecture of knowledge representation or elaborate frameworks of interconnected ideas that contain slots, nodes, or "place holders" that record the particulars of an event (Kardash, Royer, & Greene, 1988). The core of the schema is its invariant part; the slots are the variable characteristics. They contain specific types of information and permit the assimilation of additional information. Data that fill the empty slots are easily acquired, easily remembered, and easily retrieved (Kardash, Royer, & Greene, 1988).

Just and Carpenter (1987) observe that schema slots help to identify the referent of a word or the interrelationships between the different parts of the text. In the sentence, "Mother went into the kitchen to get glasses," the inference is that she got drinking glasses rather than eye glasses. Language uses these short cuts. If a text had to describe every detail explicitly, it would be extremely lengthy and boring. Hittelman (1988) thus observes that schemata are: (a) templates in the memory against which incoming information is matched; (b) organizers that specify how all previously learned information will interact with and shape new information; and (c) processors that specify how the incoming information must be arranged.

The real question is: "How does the reader's knowledge get inserted into the composite memory trace of the text?" Yekovich and Walker (1987) believe that actuation occurs on the nodes (i.e., slots) and that these activated nodes are inserted into the memory trace: reading (i.e., perceptual encoding) the word *brush* directly activates *BRUSH* in memory, thus raising its activation level. Since the word *brush* has more than one meaning (e.g., painting brush, hair brush), usually one meaning is selected for insertion into working memory while the others are deactivated rapidly. This means that one set of nodes is activated and other sets are deactivated. Activation is likely to spread through the declarative network through residual or indirect activation from the source node *BRUSH* to its associated or secondary nodes (e.g., paint, roller, walls, etc.).

The likelihood of the spread to the secondary nodes depends upon the number of previous associations between the source node and the secondary node. Whether a memory node is inserted into the composite memory trace depends upon its level of activation. Concepts with a high level of activation are readily accessible in the composite memory, have greater utility in comprehension, and are more available at retrieval.

ASSIMILATION AND ACCOMMODATION

Schema theory clearly rests on the principle that the most important single factor influencing learning is what the learner already knows. Good readers are such because they activate prior knowledge and associate it with the material to be read. They ask, "How does this add to what I already know?" They fit the new material and information to their existing schemata much like new wine in old bottles. They have learned that information is comprehended, retained, and recalled best when related to analogous ideas or information within the memory of the reader (Marr & Gormley, 1982).

The prior knowledge serves as an "ideational anchorage" or schemata to which successive bits of information may be attached. Unfortunately, many pupils (and perhaps even teachers) lack the metacognitive awareness that one should interpret text with respect both to what one knows and what is in the text (Baker & Brown, 1984b).

McNeil (1984, 1987) describes the fitting of the new into the old as assimilation. Ausübel's (1968) derivative subsumers are analogous to the process of assimilation. They are inferences based on the reader's schemata. In assimilation each new experience is related to and becomes a part of previous experience which, in turn, becomes the basis for new interpretations and meanings. Gillett and Temple (1986) observe (a) that "the information in our own schemata color greatly the experience we have, so that a person with more elaborate schemata will get more out of the experience than a person with less elaborate schemata" and (b) "by interpreting a new experience in the light of our existing schemata, we ever so slightly modify and enrich those schemata" (p. 65).

Reading also often requires a restructuring of one's schemata, called accommodation. Accommodation is the changing of existing cognitive structures to make room for the new inputs. Ausübel's correlate subsumers are analogous to accommodation. They require an extension or revision of the existing cognitive knowledge or schemata.

Thus, when the reader encounters new information, she may (Eggen & Kauchak, 1988):

1. Incorporate new facts into her existing schema. This is a process of assimilation and results in accretion of new learning. The material to be comprehended and remembered is attached to old structures without changing the structures.
2. Modify her schema to accommodate new information. This results in fine tuning of the cognitive structure.
3. Restructure her schemata. In this situation the reader cannot make sense of what she is reading with existing schemata, and must restructure her cognitive structure by creating entirely new schemata.

Good readers are not satisfied with asking: "What do I already know?" They are open to new perspectives and meanings. They restructure their personal schemata when they experience cognitive dissonance, an incongruity or conflict between what they read and what they know. They construct meaning with the help of both the text and their own schemata. They integrate what they know with what the text presents.

Poor readers, unfortunately, frequently interpret the text so as to fit their own schema (MacGinitie et al., 1980; Marie & MacGinitie, 1982). They choose not to assimilate that which causes them too much disequilibrium, and may fit the text into something that more closely resembles their previously held schemata. Some students may turn off reading completely if they have repeated experiences of not comprehending. The strategy of such readers is one of nonaccommodation. They ignore anything that does not conform to their schemata. They fail to learn from text. They read novel meanings into the text, meanings that were not intended and that lead to highly individualized constructions. They fail to comprehend text that conflicts with their prior knowledge or beliefs (Lipson, 1984).

Because schema includes a wide range of knowledge (the concept *cat* includes knowledge of the cat's food, its color, its sleeping habits, etc), each word in the text is likely to call forth the reader's complete schema, including all the information related to it (Anderson & Pearson, 1984). One is reminded of Hebb's (1958) cell assembly and phase sequence theory in which cells or cell systems (A, B, C) are functionally interrelated and the activation or firing of either A, B, or C automatically causes the firing of the other two and indeed the firing of any other cells that are functionally related to them. The total neural circuit starts operating as soon as any portion of it is activated.

Because schemata depend upon the life experiences of the individual and since rarely do two individuals have exactly have exactly the same experiences, it is unlikely that any two persons will have exactly the same schemata and interpret text exactly the same way. Their schemata are idiosyncratic and so is also their comprehension of what they read. This is true of the schemata of the writer as well. And yet the writer's and reader's perceptions and schemata are commonly similar enough so that communication between writer and reader does occur.

The point is that reading comprehension is an interactive process in which both the text and the world knowledge of the reader play key roles (Rumelhart, 1976; Durkin, 1980; Strange, 1980). Vacca and Vacca (1986) thus note, "There must be a point of contact between the reader's knowledge of the world and the ideas communicated by the textbook author. Reader and text must interact for comprehension and learning to take place" (p. 103).

Comprehension of informational material is aided by existing schemata, but reading in and of itself also fills in some of the empty slots, as it were, within the reader's schemata. Readers can and often do learn from what they read. Comprehension is a process that depends upon the schemata that the pupil has, but the process also develops schemata. Readers construct meaning with the help of both the writer's words and their own schemata. Reading comprehension is clearly an interactive process, involving both information supplied by the writer's written discourse and information brought to it by the reader.

SCHEMATA AND DIFFERENCES BETWEEN GOOD AND POOR READERS

If, as has been suggested, schemata play a critical role in the comprehending of text, or if a reader comprehends text only in relation to what he or she knows, then it follows that good readers should be differentiated from poor readers by possession of more elaborate and refined schemata. And, indeed this is so: good readers do have more elaborate schemata. Good readers also can activate their schemata more efficiently than do poor readers. However, Perfetti (1985) observes that efficient schema activation is text-driven in part. A familiar text form and a familiar topic more or less automatically activate appropriate schemata, provided the reader has the necessary knowledge in the first place and the reader's text processing is sufficient to trigger the appropriate schemata: that is, the reader has an adequate vocabulary, can remember the meanings of words, and can make adequate use of context clues.

Readers' comprehension is at risk when:

1. They do not have the appropriate schemata (Rumelhart, 1975, 1980, 1984); they cannot or do not use their prior knowledge (Holmes, 1983b); or there exists a mismatch between the reader's previous experiences and his current experiences (Poplin, 1988). Schema theory implies that the reader constructs meaning by making use of prior knowledge to predict himself through print. The development of background information (or schemata) is particularly important for pupils with poor reading skills. Stevens (1982) found that increasing the student's conceptual background markedly improved the comprehension of lower-level readers.
2. The writer has not provided the appropriate clues to suggest the schemata or to activate the pupil's prior knowledge (Baker & Brown, 1984b; Rumelhart 1975, 1980). The text is too complex, convoluted or stylized. The text lacks story structure and quality. (Elkind, 1974, 1976; Guthrie, 1977). Aspects of text that present difficulty are topic, concepts presented, syntax, organization, format, semantic requirements, genre (e.g., short story, poem, drama, etc.), the idea density, and the absence of cues sufficient to suggest the schemata.
3. The reader may be able to provide an interpretation of the text but cannot come up with the interpretation intended by the author. This misunderstanding may occur because the pupil is unaware of a shift in schema during reading (Vacca & Vacca, 1986). It may also occur when the reader and writer do not have similar language

competence, similar rhetorical skills needed to understand how texts are structured, or similar topical knowledge.

Perfetti, (1985) offers additional considerations for explaining failures in comprehension. The important element may not be that of having adequate schemata or even of selecting the right schema instead of the wrong one, but rather of knowing that there are control processes to apply to texts that help get appropriate schemata activated. This kind of knowledge is usually referred to as metacognition (Perfetti, 1985) and will be discussed further in chapter 7.

Apart from adequate schemata and adequate monitoring, differences in comprehension also occur because of inadequacy in what Perfetti calls local processing. Clearly the working memory capacity of some readers is less than that of others. Good readers remember words from sentences better than do poor readers. Good readers also differ from poor ones by the quality of their semantic encoding, that is, by (a) the availability of a semantic entry in memory or the size of one's vocabulary and (b) the encoding of a word meaning appropriate for the context or the ability to infer meanings of unfamiliar words from context (Perfetti, 1985). As a result, if a text contains many unfamiliar words and if the reader cannot make adequate use of context cues to infer the unknown meaning, the reader's comprehension is at risk. The problem is further aggravated by the fact that poor readers, in addition to having fewer semantic entries, also lack breath and depth in meaning. Their semantic entries have less semantic detail.

NONVISUAL INFORMATION

I am titling this section "Nonvisual Information" because it is the term that Frank Smith uses in *Understanding Reading* (1988) to refer to the prior knowledge that each of us carries around in our brain, stored in our long-term memory, which enables us to make sense of the world and of the written information that comes to the eyes when we read. Smith observes that because reading is an interaction between reader and text, it always involves "a combination of visual and non-visual information" (p. 66). "Nonvisual information" is synonymous with cognitive structure and represents the organization of knowledge in our heads. "Meaning is the most important non-visual information" (p. 81). The nonvisual information permits the reader to predict and to comprehend what is being read. Smith notes that children learn "by relating their understanding of the new to what they know already, while modifying or elaborating their prior knowledge" (p. 180). He adds that the system of knowledge in our brains is "organized into an intricate and internally consistent working model of the world, built up through our interactions with the world and integrated into a coherent whole" (p. 7).

The nonvisual information is a history or summary of one's past experiences. It consists of the various kinds of abstract mental events that permit the person to make sense of the world. It consists of abstract descriptions of events or situations (these are the schemata) with slots for specific detail. Thus, nonvisual information refers to the representational world. Words on the printed page have referends; they refer to something. The referent is the direct experience, the event, or the object, but what the reader sees or experiences must be converted into a representation. This representation of the referent is stored in the mind of the reader in the form of schemata or as declarative or procedural memory components (Yekovich & Walker, 1987). However, the world within the brain is, after all, only a representation of the real world. The "world as perceived" is not necessarily synonymous with the real world or with its referent. It is thus that comprehension of the printed symbols is not necessarily synonymous with its referent or with what the writer intended the words to say.

Smith repeatedly presents the view that one can make sense of the world "only" in terms of what one knows. For him, the cognitive structure is the sole determinant of the quality of the reader's comprehension. Our concern is with his choice of the word *only*. Indeed, what readers bring to the printed page is generally more important than what they get from it, but surely the writer's choice of words plays a role. The words chosen by the writer and their placement within the sentence help the reader to combine his prior knowledge in novel ways, thus creating a different cognitive structure.

Smith's nonvisual information or cognitive structure has three basic components: (a) categories or the category system, (b) rules for specifying membership in the categories or feature lists, and (c) a network of interrelationships among the categories. Categories, from Smith's perspective, are the basis of one's perception of the world. They are formed by treating some objects (e.g., domestic cats, cheetahs, cougars, lions, etc.) or events as being the same, yet different from other objects or events. Smith believes that we are born with the ability to categorize. This assumes that everyone can categorize, but surely this is not so. Some children have a perception of difference, but may not be able to identify the invariable characteristics that permits one to group objects on the basis of "sameness." Smith acknowledges that categories are conventions: "to share a culture means to share the same categorical basis for organizing experience" (p. 10).

For Smith, the category system is a part of our cognitive structure or nonvisual information that is essential for making sense of the world:

"Anything we do that we cannot relate to a category will not make sense" (p. 10). This implies that everything can be categorized and further assumes that only the reader who possesses categories can comprehend. Categories have at least one set of rules which specifies whether an object belongs to a given category. The rules are the significant attributes or distinctive features that differentiate an object from other objects and a category from every other category. Smith observes that "These are not usually rules that we can put into words . . . knowledge of this kind is *implicit*—we can only infer that we have the categories or rules by the fact that we can make use of them" (p. 12). However, the evidence seems overwhelming that experience, including instruction, accounts for the development of most categories and for the development of the rules that specify categories. Finally, the category system is a network of interrelationships among the categories. It is for this reason that objects may share categories.

Smith accords nonvisual information extraordinary explanatory power. He suggests that comprehension is directly related to the amount of information that the reader already has. He thus observes that comprehension is the "possibility of relating whatever we are attending to in the world around us to the knowledge, intentions, and expectations we already have in our heads" (p. 53). Smith notes, "If I have difficulty understanding an article on nuclear physics, it is not because I am unable to draw conclusions, make inferences, follow arguments or solve problems, but because I do not know enough about physics" (p. 21). We would argue that sometimes the reader cannot reason with the information that he possesses or that is presented on the printed page.

We agree fully with Smith that "insufficiency of non-visual information will make reading more difficult" (p. 66) and accept that memorization of letter names, phonic rules, or a large vocabulary do not a reader make. However, we do believe it is overly simplistic to say that "learning to read is not a matter of a child relying upon instruction, because the essential skills of reading—namely the efficient uses of non-visual information—cannot explicitly be taught" (p. 199). It is too facile to suggest that children learn everything that needs to be learned simply by being read to or by reading.

AMBIGUITIES IN SCHEMA THEORY

Schema theory is only one view of how we remember information and how we comprehend when reading. The supportive evidence in favor of schematic intervention is greater than for any other existent model. However, Kardash, Royer and Green (1988) did not find support for the thesis that schemata influence the nature of the information being stored or that activated schemata exert an influence on the encoding of textual information.

There are other uncertainties. Prior knowledge can on occasion interfere with comprehension (Lipson, 1982, 1984), especially if the text asserts something contrary to what the reader predicts (Alvermann, Smith, & Readance, 1985). This is likely to happen when there are differences between the world view of the reader and the cultural perspectives of the text.

Clearly, more elaborate and refined schemata aid comprehension. But it is also true that inadequate, distorted, ill-defined, vague, or incomplete schemata affect comprehension negatively. Malicky and Brake (1983) found that second graders when reading silently sometimes relied too heavily on background knowledge and produced information beyond the constraints of the text. They were comprehending but were not interpreting the material the way the writer wanted it to be interpreted. Young readers, especially, are often reluctant to relinquish their sometimes inaccurate information in favor of the text information and may distort the text information to fit it to their prior information.

Another seeming contradiction exists. Some researchers assert that information that does not fit the reader's schema is not well remembered and may even be lost. On the other hand, schema theorists believe that such information is better remembered than is information that is essentially similar to what one has in one's schema or that is too typical. Rayner and Pollatsek (1989) observe that the latter may be poorly stored in memory because it is redundant.

SUMMARY

Chapter 4 addressed schema theory and identified schema with cognitive structure and with the organization of our long-term memories. One's schemata were defined and related to one's real world knowledge. Chapter 4 noted that the schema concept is not new but a repackaging of older theories and observations. It acknowledges the recent elaborations that have led to further understanding of the reading process.

Schema theory focuses on meanings as the essence of cognition, reading, and comprehension. It reiterates that reading is concerned with the construction and reconstruction of meaning and notes that schema development depends on the acquisition of new experiences, including wide and extensive reading. The latter is another reason why children learn to read by reading. Wide reading expands readers' schemata and their cognitive structure.

Chapter 4 provided the rationale for viewing schema theory as an integral part of the total strategy in reading and explained why text must be interpreted with respect to what one knows. It emphasized that total text modeling or developing a representation of text depends upon schema activation and the search of one's cognitive, informational, and linguistic schemata to effect a match with the text.

Chapter 4, however, also affirmed that reading is not merely bringing meaning to the text. The text itself is a co-determinant of skilled reading. It observed that reading comprehension is an interactive process in which readers vary their focus along a continuum from primarily text-based processing (involving the understanding of the type of discourse, of the text structure and text genre, of the conventions involved in the particular mode of discourse, and of its complexity) to primarily reader-based processing (Pearson, 1984). Readers, indeed, construct meaning by reference to what they already know, but also by relating what they are reading to text just read. The reader's schemata help to chunk or group the incoming information, and, after reading, help the reader to remember what was read. The more the reader knows about what is in the text and the more familiar the reader is with the text structure, the better the reader will understand, integrate, and remember what is in the text. Finally, chapter 4 affirms that comprehension is rarely totally veridical because readers do not bring exactly the same schemata to the text. In fact, sometimes the reader miscomprehends rather than changing her schemata.

Expansion of the reader's schemata has to be a primary concern of the reading teacher. Chapters 7 and 10 will address this issue.

Chapter 5:
Developing the Predictive Strategy in Reading: Integration of the Meaning and Within-Word Cues

    I. Introduction
   II. Prediction in Smith's Description of Reading
  III. Global Versus Focal Prediction
  IV. The Word Identification/Comprehension Strategies
   V. The Meaning Cues
      A. Making Global Predictions
      B. Making Focal Predictions
      C. Picture Cues
      D. Semantic Context Cues
      E. Syntactic Context Cues
      F. Role of Context in Smith's Top-Down Model
      G. The Role of Context in Rayner and Pollatsek's Bottom-up Model
      H. Summary of the Effects of Context on Word Identification and Lexical Access
  VI. Automatic Semantic Activation
 VII. The With-in-Word Cues
      A. Logographic or Configuration Cues
      B. Graphemic Cues
      C. Orthographis Cues
      D. Phonic Cues
      E. Morphemic Cues
VIII. Integration of Cues
  IX. Summary

CHAPTER 5
Developing the Predictive Strategy in Reading: Integration of Meaning and Within-Word Cues

In recent years there has developed a great fascination with Goodman's (1967) description of reading as a psycholinguistic guessing game. The basic thesis of this position is that readers predict or develop hypotheses as they read, constantly confirming, rejecting, and refining tentative decisions, and sampling the surface structure only when predictions are not confirmed. We will argue that this method works well in making global predictions, but it often is not very efficient in making focal predictions. The simple fact is that context is a relatively reliable predictor in making global predictions; it is not reliable in making focal predictions.

The evidence clearly shows that children's linguistic talents often do not permit them to use the context alone to handle all of the problems of word recognition (Perfetti, 1985). Goodman's oversight is that he does not realize that the graphic cue system is an important and coequal cueing system together with the semantic and syntactic context. He accords almost total efficacy to the meaning cues and only gingerly accepts that the within-word cues, the orthographic structure of words, relating letters to phonemes, and recoding or activating the word's name code from memory may be useful, perhaps even necessary, in processing text.

The proposition that reading is a prediction process has a long history. One is reminded of Tolman's learning theory (1945, 1951) and of the writings of Thorndike (1917), Norberg (1953, 1956), Herrick (1956), and Leary (1950). Tolman felt that the learner learns an expectancy. The animal in the maze learns that a given path leads to the food box. Readers learn that in the presence of certain signs (such as the word *run* in the sentence, "Bill can run like a deer"), one can expect to comprehend if one follows the customary behavior route (i.e., if *run* is defined as "to move swiftly"). Conversely, when the word is used as a part of phrases such as "a cattle run," "a run on the bank," or the "ordinary run of people," readers learn that interpreting the word *run* as "to move swiftly" does not lead to correct interpretation.

Text: 1. "Bill can *run* like a deer."
       2. "The bankruptcy caused a *run* on the bank."

Hypothesis: The word *run* means "to move swiftly."

Confirmation of the Hypothesis: In the first sentence the word *run* does in fact mean "to run swiftly."

Rejection of the Hypothesis: In the second sentence the word does not mean "to run swiftly" and the pupil will have to change her hypothesis.

In Tolman's theory, learners are learning meanings. If comprehension is achieved, the meaning for the word is confirmed. If comprehension does not occur, behavior must be varied. Confirmation of correct responses tends to perpetuate them and knowledge of incorrect responses should lead pupils to vary their behavior until correct responses are obtained.

PREDICTION IN SMITH'S DESCRIPTION OF READING

In his top-down model, Smith (1988) clearly identifies prediction as the core of reading and as the basis of comprehension. "Reading depends on prediction" (p. 16). His model suggests that the reader must sample text in order to confirm his or her prediction of what is coming next in the text. According to Smith (1988), prediction "brings potential meaning to texts, reducing ambiguity and eliminating in advance irrelevant alternatives" (p. 18). He notes that it is this ability to predict which is the basis of our comprehension of the world, including our understanding of spoken and written language. He observes that all our predictions are derived from only one source, the nonvisual information in our heads. He describes prediction as "the prior elimination of unlikely alternatives" (p. 18), through the use of redundancy. For Smith, redundancy exists when the same information is available from more than one source (e.g., from the visual information, the orthography, or the semantic/syntactic context). Smith reasons that "we predict to reduce our uncertainty and therefore to reduce the amount of external information that we require" to reduce the uncertainty(p. 18). Every prediction the reader makes limits other possibilities; it reduces alternative hypotheses.

Smith (1988) is quite emphatic that prediction is not "reckless guessing" (p. 18); it does not mean "staking everything on one wild guess (which would indeed run the risk of frequent error)" (p. 31). In a statement that might surprise some "top-down" followers of Smith, he observes that prediction simply means that the uncertainty of the reader is reduced to a few probable alternatives, and adds that information at the surface structure level of the utterance can reduce or dispose of the remaining uncertainty.

Clearly the reader should be taught to look for and to read for meaning rather than for words as such, but the words cannot be ignored in the confirming and disconfirming process. It is because readers look for meaning that skilled readers tend to substitute synonyms for the target word, whereas poor readers tend to substitute words that do not make sense. Smith notes that good readers make fewer mistakes, but they go back and correct the mistakes that make a difference. "Children who are not reading for sense have no chance of becoming aware of even important errors" (p. 152).

For Smith, and indeed Goodman, prediction initiates a process of inquiry similar to hypothesis testing (Garrison & Hoskisson, 1989). Predictive reading is one way to help children develop the capacity for self-correcting thought (Garrison & Hoskisson, 1989). But, it also presents a danger. Readers are often quite ready to accept the evidence that supports or confirms their hypotheses, but, as we observed in Chapter 4, tend to discredit or reject the evidence that does not fit their cognitive structure or their nonvisual information. Clearly, the reader's nonvisual information is a prime determinant or source of the reader's prediction, but such predictions are not always correct.

Smith (1988) notes that readers must have a developing and constantly modifiable set of expectations about what they will find in text and about where the text as a whole might be leading. This, according to Smith, is the reader's specification of text. But obviously writers must have their own specification. This is a constantly changing outline in their mind about the structure or content of a text. Furthermore, there must be a point at which readers and writer interact and this is the text itself. We conjecture that when the writer's and the reader's specifications of text are the same, the reader's comprehension of text is complete and communication between writer and reader is perfect.

Let us briefly summarize what Smith appears to be saying:

1. Readers use nonvisual information or schemata to predict and to understand.
2. The greater the reader's knowledge of the semantic and syntactic constraints, his understanding of the deep structure of the language, his visual and orthographic knowledge, in other words, the greater the redundancy, the more accurate will be the reader's prediction, the more likely it is that the reader will be able to eliminate "unlikely" alternatives, and the more likely it is that the reader will reduce uncertainty.
3. Prediction is designed to reduce uncertainty to a few probable alternatives; the reader may dispose of the remaining uncertainty by using information that can be found at the deep structure level but also "in the surface structure (Smith, p. 31)."
4. Readers predict meaning, and they can or, in fact, use the distinctive features of letters and words to confirm or disconfirm particular meanings (Smith, p. 18, 31).

GLOBAL VERSUS FOCAL PREDICTION

A critical issue centers on which cues the reader uses to predict himself through print. Resolution of this issue depends upon an understanding of the difference between global and focal prediction (Smith, 1988) and upon a realization that strategies which work for global prediction are not necessarily the same as those which work for focal prediction. There is the added consideration of whether readers characteristically rely on conscious prediction of what comes next in text or whether, in fact, semantic activation or activation of meaning is sometimes automatic.

Global predictions are expectations about the story or text as a whole. They guide the reading or decision-making process until the intended goal is reached. They direct the reader's expectations about what he will find in text. They reflect our more general expectations about where the text as a whole might be leading (Smith, 1988). Global predictions persist through the entire length of a book (Smith, 1988). They may take the form, for example, of making predictions about the total story, its overall content, or theme from its title.

Focal predictions, on the other hand, are detailed predictions relating to specific events in the total story. Focal questions relate to predictions about sentences and words, and about specific events.

Smith (1988) makes the observation that just as predictions about text may range from a focal level (words, sentences, paragraphs) to a global level (chapters, stories, books), so also can the intentions of both writer and reader range from a focal to a global level. Smith notes: "From the writer's point of view it might be said that a book is comprehended when the reader's predictions mirror the writer's intentions at all levels from focal to global" (p. 171). In a sense the writer is constantly trying to manipulate the reader's predictions.

The same analogy can be drawn for the representations of text. There thus are conventions for books as a whole: genre schemes, story grammars; for paragraphs: discourse structures; for how sentences are organized into paragraphs: conventions of cohesion; for the organization of words in sentences: conventions of grammar and idiom; for the words: conventions of semantics; and for the physical representation of words: the conventions of spelling.

The specification of a text, similar to the specifications of a house, is thus a cluster of expectations and intentions. From the writer's perspective, it is what the writer wanted or intended to write; from the reader's point of view, it is what he wants or expects to get from the text.

Both writer and reader must know the genre schemes (e.g. conventions of layout, typography, style), the discourse structures, story grammars (and even more importantly the correlative structures in their heads), and the written language conventions (spelling, punctuation, formation of the letters, type, capitalization, paragraphing). These structures and conventions form the basis for prediction (p. 41) and for our comprehension and memory of text. They help the reader to predict what the text will be like and the writer to anticipate what readers are likely to expect. Smith observes that "conventions make prediction possible" (p. 45). He adds:"This understanding of the appropriate conventions, together with prior knowledge related to the subject matter, is the essential nonvisual information that readers must contribute to the act of reading" (p. 46).

In this chapter the concern is more with focal prediction than with global prediction. We are more interested in how the reader predicts an unknown word in a sentence context than in how the reader predicts the ending of a story. Our emphasis is on that aspect of focal prediction involved in encoding of words and in lexical access.

THE WORD IDENTIFICATION/COMPREHENSION STRATEGIES

We have concluded from earlier chapters that readers who can recode or sound words have an indirect access to meaning if the word so sounded is in their aural-oral vocabulary. They can then take the meaning associated with the spoken or heard word to the written word.

Furthermore, we know from research that proficiency and automaticity in word identification have a direct impact upon comprehension by freeing readers to focus their attention, concentration, and effort upon the comprehension process (Samuels, 1976a). Readers who have automatized the word recognition skill comprehend better than those who have not done so. Their minds are free to explore the deep structure. Golinkoff (1975–1976) found that good comprehenders are capable of rapid and accurate word recognition. They have automatized the recoding skill. A basic inference to be drawn from these facts is that developing recoding and automaticity in word identification is a significant strategy in acquiring the predictive strategy in reading and in developing comprehension.

If indeed the reader's nonvisual information is the basis of prediction and therefore of comprehension, as Smith (1988) suggests, we can also infer that our concept of the reader's nonvisual information or cognitive structure should be expanded to include all or most of the word identification/comprehension strategies, including both meaning and within-word cues.

We agree with Smith (1988) and with most top-down theorists that information about semantic and syntactic constraints reduces the reader's uncertainty in advance and permits the reader to predict with greater accuracy. Readers, both skilled and unskilled, do in fact use the semantic and syntactic context and their own nonvisual information to make global predictions about text. And, beginning readers, poor readers, and skilled readers at times use solely the context or meaning cues in making focal predictions.

We argue, however, that information about the graphic, orthographic, and graphophonic constraints generally plays a significant and indispensible role in making focal predictions, especially predictions about a given word, and that unfortunately many top-down theorists have discounted this important information. Moreover, we argue that children who learn and use all the word identification/comprehension strategies in an integrated way to predict themselves through print tend to become or in fact are skilled readers.

Table 5-1 identifies the word-identification/comprehension strategies. These strategies, including meaning cues, variant within-word cues, or a combination thereof, and dictionary cues, are all needed for effective identification of words and focal prediction, as well as global prediction and comprehension. The role of the nonvisual information is primary in the latter.

TABLE 5-1: Word-Identification/Comprehension Strategies

I. Meaning Cues
   A. *Picture Cues*: Picture cues help to discriminate graphically similar words and to increase the ease with which beginners can be initiated into contextual reading. On more advanced levels picture cues may take the form of maps, charts, graphs, diagrams, or tables. Picture cues help the pupil to identify the meaning and hence the word and are therefore both a word identification and a comprehension cue.
   B. *Semantic Context or Semantic Cue Systems*: Pupils are using a semantic cue when they associate with words meanings that have been acquired through experience. There are two types of semantic context: (a) the within-text context or the words on the printed page which are the work of the writer, and (b) the within-mind context, consisting of the reader's cognitive structure or schemata, the nonvisual information that the reader brings to the text.

   The within-mind context or the schematic cue system is the prior knowledge that the reader brings to the text. It includes the reader's world experience, cognitive base, fund of linguistic experience, lexical knowledge, morphemic knowledge, and knowledge of the meaning and within-word cues. It is the pupil's world experience or those parts of the pupil's schemata which are the product of the pupil's world experience.
   C. *Syntactic Context or Syntactic Cue System*: Pupils use the syntactic context when they infer the unknown meaning and word from the grammatical or syntactic elements within a sentence. Syntactic context refers to the cue systems in the flow of language or in the structure of the sentence. The syntactic context may also refer to those meanings or those parts of the pupil's schema which are the product of the pupil's language experience. Six different types of cues constrain the range of possible syntactic interpretations and conjointly impose multiple constraints on text (Just & Carpenter, 1987).
      1. *Patterns of Word Order*: These identify the kernel sentence patterns (e.g., noun-verb, noun-verb-noun, noun-verb-noun-noun, noun-linking verb-noun, and noun-linking verb-adjective) and the basic transformations of kernel sentences (e.g., passive questions, negatives, imperative sentence patterns, and sentences beginning with *it* or *there*).

(continued)

TABLE 5-1 *(continued)*

   2. *The Word Class* (i.e., whether the word is a noun, verb, adjective, conjunction, preposition, etc.). Word class presents a problem when a word is used in two or more ways (e.g., as a conjunction: She sang *before* she left, or as a preposition: She sang *before* the group).
   3. *Intonation Patterns*: These suprasegmental phonemes represent the rhythm or the melody of the language and include pitch, stress or accent, and juncture or pauses in speaking. Juncture in writing is conveyed by punctuation marks and by spacing between words.
   4. *Structure or Function Words*: The function words include prepositions, subordinate and coordinate conjunctions, determiners (*a, the*) and quantifiers (e.g., *few, all, seven*, etc.). They communicate the syntactic or semantic function of a constituent rather than its content (Just & Carpenter, 1987).
   5. *Redundancy Cues*: Redundancy occurs when the same information is available from more than one source. Thus, in the sentence, *The boys eat their lunches*, there are at least four cues that redundantly indicate that the subject is plural.
   6. *Affixes*: Affixes also cue a word's syntactic role and often indicate word class. For example, *ly* (slowly) identifies the word as an adverb. The word's meaning is often determined by the affixes; thus, affixes may be a strong cue to a particular word's syntactic role in a sentence (Just & Carpenter, 1987).
   D. *Morphemic Cues*: Morphemic cues are both structural and meaning cues. Many morphemes, especially free morphemes or words and the lexical, bound morphemes (e.g., prefixes and suffixes) suggest or carry meaning in their own right and thus are rightfully considered to be meaning cues. The relational, bound morphemes (e.g., *s*) do not carry meaning in and of themselves. They take on meaning only when attached to another word.
II. Cue Systems Within Words: The Structural Cues System
   A. *Logographic Cues*: The word's physiognomy, shape, length, and contour or configuration as defined by the pattern of letter ascenders and descenders.
   B. *Graphemic Cues*: The distinctive features of the graphemes, both individual letters and letter clusters.
   C. *Orthographic Cues*: Orthographic cues include the sequence of letters which bears a systematic relationship to the word's acoustic and articulatory structure. The spelling of a word or the letter sequence is a significant cue to the pronunciation of the word.

TABLE 5-1 *(continued)*

D. *Phonological and Phonic Cues*: The word's acoustic articulatory, and phonemic structure and the sound-letter relationships, including recurrent spelling patterns and phonograms.

E. *Analogy Cues*: Identification by analogy is "looking for cues to a word's pronunciation and meaning from words that look the same" (Smith 1988, p. 144). This technique is an extension of the use of phonic cues. Thus, pupils may combine the beginning sound of the word *milk* (which they know) with the end sound of the word *last* (which they also know) to sound out the word *mast* (m - ast).

Stanovich (1980) suggests that skilled readers do not apply letter-to-sound rules when confronted with unknown words but rather look for similarities to words they know. In other words, they identify words by analogy.

Olson (1985) likewise observes that word recoding may occur without the application of the grapheme-phoneme conversion rules. The sound of an unfamiliar word may be obtained by analogy to words that have a similar orthographic pattern. Marsh et al. (1981) suggest that children learn identification by analogy as a consequence of learning the grapheme-phoneme correspondences (thus, by about grade 4), but Goswami (1986) reports that children as early as age 5 can use identification by analogy.

III. Meaning of Context Cues Combined With Phonic and Morphemic Cues: The position taken in this chapter is that the integrated use of both meaning and within-word cues allows for the greatest degree of predictive efficiency. Pupils should be taught to use both meaning and within-word cues to predict their way through text.

IV. Dictionary Cues: Dictionary cues (or such external resources as parents or teachers) may be the only viable resource when pupils can pronounce the word, but cannot take meaning to it, or when they, after using the full complement of meaning and within-word cues, can neither pronounce the word nor take meaning to it.

Ringler and Weber (1984) observe that the most frequently used word-identification/comprehension strategies involve use of the semantic and syntactic context cues, analysis of the meaning parts of words (morphemic analysis), and associating grapheme-phoneme relationships (phonic analysis); in short, a combination of meaning with within-word, structural, or graphic cues. Jewell and Zintz (1986) observe that language may be described as an interrelated network of cues that signal meaning. They identify the most important such signals as phonological cues, grammatical cues (word order, inflections, word endings, function words, etc.), semantic cues, and redundancy cues.

Relying exclusively on the meaning cues to predict oneself through print is giving undue emphasis to the top-down approach. Concentrating totally on the within-word or structural cues makes the reader too dependent on the bottom-up approach. Using both meaning and within-word cues conjointly, giving preference to one or the other as the situation demands, results in an integrated approach to word identification and to comprehension. Perhaps the most significant contribution of the strategies in Table 5-1 is that using them in an integrated and correlated manner helps the reader to predict the meaning and hence the word that fits graphophonic cues, thus developing the predictive strategy in reading. It is important, at this point, to reiterate that reading is not simply barking at print; not simply recoding; not simply pronouncing of words. And, reading materials do not simply furnish graphophonic cues. Reading is message sharing and the message reveals itself through all the cue systems: the visual-graphic, the phonological, the orthographic, the grapho-phonic, the lexical, the semantic, both the within-text and the within-mind context, and the syntactic.

THE MEANING CUES

The meaning cues, as identified in Table 5-1, include picture cues, the semantic context, both the within-text context and the reader's schemata, the syntactic context, and the morphemic cues. Each of these cues can help the pupil to make global (e.g., how the story will end) and focal predictions (e.g., what will be the next word).

From the top-down perspective, the processing of print begins in the mind of the reader with hypotheses about the meaning of some unit of print. Reading for meaning is and should be the reader's primary objective. Children need to be taught to anticipate, predict and look for meaning.

Making Global Predictions

The meaning cues are particularly effective in making global predictions, in determining how the story will develop, what will happen next, what the main idea is, what the writer's intentions are, or where the text as a whole may be leading. Slot-filling inferences that fill in missing information, elaborative inferences that embellish the text, and inferences linking one part of text with another all involve global predictions.

Global predictions depend essentially on the reader's nonvisual information and within-text context cues, and generally involve conscious prediction or conscious semantic activation from context. The top-down theories of Goodman and Smith are founded on conscious prediction from context. We believe that conscious prediction from context indeed works best when readers are engaged in making global predictions.

Making Focal Predictions

Meaning cues or conscious prediction from context also have efficacy in making focal predictions, but at that level the prediction is not nearly as accurate or reliable. And, as we shall see later, the reader is best served in making focal predictions (particularly when these involve the identification of a specific word) when he integrates the meaning cues with the within-word cues. Effective prediction at the focal level depends heavily upon mastery of the within-word cues. The goal in predicting words in print is automatic semantic activation. We will return to this issue later.

However, even when making focal predictions, readers should be taught to use the within-mind and the within-text context to predict what, in terms of meaning, best completes a sentence. They should be taught to search their mental lexicon for the aural-oral word that fits the meaning. Pupils come to the reading situation with a cognitive structure, or schemata that include a complement of word identification and comprehension strategies. They have some knowledge of the meaning and within-word cues (inadequate though it is), and the teacher's task is to help them utilize these strategies in identifying or predicting the meaning and the word. The teacher's task is to assist pupils to call forth from their personal schemata that information which will permit them to predict meaning and to identify the unknown word in a sentence context.

Unfortunately, poor readers often are such because they fail to extract contextual cues essential for identification. They seem to be identifying words as if the words were unrelated items unaffected by syntactical or contextual relationships (Steiner, Morton, & Cromer, 1971). They struggle unsuccessfully to sound out words whose meaning is completely obvious from the surrounding context. They often cannot choose the contextually supported meaning and cannot match meaning with the appropriate symbol. They are frequently so preoccupied with grapho-phonic details, in which they generally are deficient, that they substitute a word into the sentence that makes little or no sense.

Many children, when meeting an unknown word, stop and wait for the teacher to name the word. If the teacher names the word, the teacher is merely teaching the child to depend on the teacher rather than on context and graphic cues for the meaning and pronunciation of the word (Breen, 1988). At a minimum, pupils should learn to read the entire sentence before attempting to pronounce the word. They should learn to read on when the individual sentence context is inadequate. And, they should learn to check the accuracy of their prediction by seeing whether the word makes sense and whether it fits the grapho-phonic cues. In utilizing this process of predicting, sampling the text, and verifying, the teacher is encouraging the pupil to approach reading as a meaning-getting process.

However, Smith (1988) correctly observes that readers also need to "look at words or letters (or more precisely the *distinctive features* of words or letters) that will confirm or disconfirm particular meanings" (p. 31). Unfortunately, beginning and poor readers, lacking competency in the use of the within-word identification strategies, almost totally rely on meaning cues and on the context (and perhaps the beginning letter) to make both global and focal predictions (Marsh et al., 1981; Mason, 1980; Stanovich, 1980).

Reading at the beginner-reading level is generally a matter of conscious anticipation and conscious prediction from context. Beginning readers will misread words (e.g., *cat* for *kitty*), using the sentence context and their own nonvisual information to read the word. They will be able to read *K-Mart* or *stop* on a sign, but cannot read the same words in isolation. They necessarily must predict from context since they have not automatized the word identification process.

Poor readers are like beginning readers in this regard. They clearly rely more on context than do skilled readers (Perfetti & Roth, 1981). Perfetti, Goldman, and Hogaboam (1979) found that 8- to -10-year-old skilled readers used sentence context more infrequently than did less skilled readers. Other studies (Rayner & Pollatsek, 1989) show that as children become more proficient in word recognition, their reliance on context decreases.

In this chapter, as noted earlier, we are concerned primarily with focal predictions. Our concern is with questions such as: What strategies should the reader use when making focal predictions or when trying to figure out a word in a sentence? How does the pupil learn to predict and to anticipate upcoming meaning in a line of print (Jewell & Zintz, 1986) or to figure out a word by the way it is used in a sentence? What strategies should the pupil use on the level of individual word identification and the association of letter and sound patterns?

Picture Cues

It is our contention that all readers should learn the "conscious prediction from context" strategy. They need to know how to use the meaning and context cues, including semantic and syntactic context cues, and picture cues to predict what comes next in print. If the sentence, The boy hit the ball over the fence, is presented with a picture showing a ball sailing over or above a fence, the chances are quite good that the pupil will project the meaning "over" on the space occupied by the word *over* and will make a correct prediction that the word must be *over*. This does not necessarily mean that pupils can identify the word in isolation or when they read it in print without the accompanying picture. Picture cues, a picture or illustration accompanying text, are the pupil's first attempts to make use of the context. They provide very strong meaning and identification cues. They are particularly helpful to readers when the words are similar or when the concept is too difficult for the pupil to develop it through the use of words alone.

The evidence on the use of pictures is conflicting. When too many pictures accompany reading materials, reading often becomes an exercise in picture reading, rather than in identification and understanding of the elements that characterize the word or that give it its idiosyncratic form. The pictures may even be distracting to a few beginners and to poor readers. Studies indicate that pictures may present ambiguous or misleading information and may interfere with reading progress, especially among beginning and poor readers (Harber, 1983; Rose & Furr, 1984; Samuels, 1967, 1970; Singer, Samuels, & Spiroff, 1973). The interference effects of pictures are especially noticeable in the acquisition of a sight vocabulary by distracting children's attention from the stimuli that are critical to word identification. Rose and Furr's (1984) study confirmed these observations. They found that the acquisition of new words is considerably faster when the words are presented without pictures. They note that pictures distract the reader's attention from the distinctive characteristics of the printed stimulus and cause the reader to attend to irrelevant stimuli. Teachers are wont to call the pupil's attention to the pictures (e.g., "What is this a picture of?" . . . "That's right. It's a duck."). An alternative or conjoint instructional strategy is to focus the pupil's attention on the relevant and salient features of the word itself.

Robeck and Wilson (1974) also found that learners remember the most from their reading when deeper involvement is required and when picture cues are kept at a minimum. Rose (1986) found that learning-disabled elementary-aged readers comprehended nonillustrated reading passages better than illustrated passages, perhaps because such pupils generally have greater difficulty filtering out extraneous stimuli. Denberg (1976–77), however, found that increasing the amount of available information through the medium of pictures had a strong facilitative effect on word identification. The additional pictorial information actually encouraged the beginner to use rather than bypass the incomplete information that he or she is able to extract from the printed page. Pictures thus may increase the ease with which beginners can be initiated into contextual reading and may enhance the fluency of their reading.

Semantic Context Cues

If, on the other hand, the sentence, "The boy hit the ball over the fence," appears without picture context, and if the unidentified word is *over*, the pupil may need to identify the word by using the semantic and syntactic context.

The first strategy that readers should learn is to use their predictive or hypothesizing skills and their background of information and meanings to project a meaning that fits the semantic context, and hence a word for the "empty space." Readers are aided when they approach reading as a search for meaning, when they are asked to identify, recode, and decode words that are a part of the flow of language, and when words are part of the semantic and syntactic context. Leary (1950) early pointed out the value of teaching a word in context: "Train a child to anticipate probable meaning, to check the context clue with the form of the word, to search the context for a description or explanation that will identify the word, and he will have acquired the most important single aid to word recognition. For regardless of what word he perceives, if it doesn't 'make sense' in its setting, his perception has been in error". Leary adds that making readers meaning conscious is as much a part of word recognition as it is of comprehension. Farr and Roser (1979) note that "using context analysis to unlock a word is the behavior most in tune with the purpose of reading," which is after all the search for meaning (p. 188).

Vacca (1981) describes context analysis as the use of the information surrounding a troublesome word to get at the word's pronunciation and meaning. It is an inference requiring the reader to see a relationship between the unfamiliar word and the surrounding words or context. Heilman (1972) notes that at practically all points on the reading continuum, the one ability that sets good readers apart from poor readers is the degree to which they can use context to get at unknown words. Similarly, Gray (1969) said that context cues "are perhaps the most important single aid to word perception" (p. 25). According to Arnold and Miller (1976), context cues are especially useful when the arrangement of words in a sentence is such that only one word is likely to fit into a particular slot in that sentence. Unfortunately, such is rarely the case.

Contextual signals work as cues to an unknown word's meaning only if the reader has adequate reasoning and inferencing ability, possesses adequate past experience, has adequate knowledge of the topic, has a sufficient store of meanings, and knows the other words in the selection. If indeed apprehension of word meaning depends at least partially on the ability to use context cues, and if the latter depends upon the reader's conceptual and experiential background or schema, then it becomes imperative for the teacher to expand the pupil's schema, thus enhancing the reader's skill of using context cues.

Context cues reside both in the mind of the reader and in the text. Those in the mind are the schemata, including language schemata, that the reader brings to the text. Text context cues reside in the words and sentences that surround the unknown word. In the first instance, the meaning is supplied by the reader as he processes the graphic symbols by relating them to their referents, to his own experiences, and to his own conceptual structures. In the second instance, meaning is supplied by the writer's personal choice of words, the order of the words, the systematic arrangement of the grammatical constituents, the relationships between the words, and so forth. The words in and of themselves do not possess intrinsic meaning, but the writer helps the reader to predict the pronunciation and meaning of words by the way she uses the word. The words themselves and their order constrain the meaning choices. It is the writer who superimposes upon print the syntactic arrangements and the rhetorical structures, who organizes the text, and who chooses the transitional elements. If reading were only a matter of bringing one's schemata to the text, or of putting one's own stamp of meaning on the printed page, the reader would not be able to learn from text. It is the text context which causes the reader to reorganize his schemata in a novel way and to construct new meanings and new schemata, and which triggers new hypotheses and expectations.

Readers thus must learn to use both the semantic context in the mind and the text context (e.g., the definitions, synonyms or antonyms, descriptions, comparison/contrast cues, example cues, and punctuation, that accompany the word) to identify novel words and to associate meaning with them. Both a top-down and bottom-up strategy (i.e., an interactive strategy) are indicated. The exclusive use of top-down processing will surely lead to inferences, expectations, and hypotheses not warranted by the text. Poor readers are such precisely because they substitute novel words and read novel meanings into the text, that is, words and meanings that were not intended by the writer and that lead to highly individualized constructions. The value of the conjoint use of the within-mind and the within-text context is that they help the reader to make inferences and predictions as to what the unknown word is and what the writer means.

Using the within-mind or semantic context, pupils must learn to project onto the "blank space" occupied by the word which they cannot identify (e.g., *over*) various meanings that fit their personal schemata. Thus, the pupil can conjecture that any one of a vast number of meanings (above, against, around, at, behind, beside, by, in front of, into, near, off, on, on top of, outside of, over, through, toward, under, upon, etc.) is possible in completing the sentence, "The boy hit the ball ____ the fence."

Although there is a finite number of meanings and words that fit the semantic context, it is obvious that in the sentence, "The boy hit the ball ___ the fence," the within-text context is not definite enough to identify the specific word intended. However, it is also true that in the context of "boy-hit-ball-fence," the child's life experiences and his within-mind context will lead him to predict *over* more frequently than other acceptable meaning. The child's mind set is more likely to envision a home run and thus to project the meaning "over the fence." It is equally true that in a story context, where the semantic context might be larger, the semantic context might be adequate to identify the correct word. Thus if the sentence were followed by other sentences, such as "The boy hit the ball ___ the fence. He got his dog to fetch the ball. It was lying on the other side of the fence," the reader will be more likely to project the meaning of *over* and will read the word as *over*. Certainly, words like *against, by, near, at, toward, in front of*, etc. have been eliminated. Words like *through, over, above, under, behind*, and *around* are obviously still possible.

Syntactic Context Cues

Perfetti views syntactic cues as one of the automatic semantic triggering mechanisms. The pupil can and should use the syntactic context in addition to the semantic context to project the correct meaning and word onto the sentence. Word and meaning choices must be semantically and syntactically acceptable. Pupils must ask whether their choices are consistent with their experience-based reservoir of meanings and with language. In the sentence, "The boy hit the ball ___ the fence," only prepositions are syntactically acceptable, and to this extent the syntactic context limits the choice of words to only one of the parts of speech, but obviously each of the prepositions suggested earlier fits the syntactic context. In this instance the syntactic context does not substantially reduce uncertainty. In another instance, "The boy *with the broken arm* sat in the chair" versus "The boy sat in the chair *with the broken arm*," the syntactic context may be the chief determinant of meaning.

Syntax refers to word order or the systematic arrangement of the grammatical constituents. It is a set of rules that govern how morphemes are combined into sentences, as well as the sequence of words that identifies the grammatical role of the word. It is the syntax or the sequence of words that provides us with a code to communicate a configuration of concepts (Just & Carpenter, 1987, p. 129).

Syntactic analysis is the inferring of the unknown word from the arrangement of words in a sentence. English is a highly positional language; thus, the arrangement of words is often such that only certain parts of speech are likely to fit into a particular slot in the sentence. Children, from the beginning, must ask themselves: Does the word I have identified make sense in the sentence and does it result in a syntactically correct sentence? When pupils substitute a part of speech into a slot in which it does not fit, they do not understand that what they read must sound like real language.

Rayner and Pollatsek (1989) suggest that semantic analysis and syntactic analysis can go on independently but parallel to each other; they can proceed sequentially or they can be part of the same analysis. They add that only one syntactic structure is constructed. If that one is not appropriate, the reader will make another attempt. Their analysis leads them to conclude that syntactic analysis often precedes semantic analysis.

Even at the earliest stages of reading, students make use of context cues, and become increasingly responsive to context between the ages of seven and nine. The use of context cues is developmental, especially of syntactic context, with pupils becoming more proficient as they grow older and as they increase in reading abilities (Harris & Sipay 1985). Children move more and more toward coping with reading as an aspect of language. They want their responses to make sense, both on the level of single words and on the level of language structure (Schlieper, 1977).

The Role of Context in Frank Smith's Top-Down Model

Frank Smith's top-down theory clearly accords context a primary role in reading. He (1988) observes that children learn to read when they have the opportunity to generate and test hypotheses in a meaningful, collaborative context. He adds, "If a child is not sure about the likely meaning of what is being attended to, the context (before and after) can provide clues. And the subsequent context will provide the feedback about whether the child's hypotheses were right or wrong" (p. 200). Meaning is difficult to come by, according to Smith, "if the reader attempts to identify and understand every word as if it had nothing to do with its neighbors" and he adds that the reader can learn "the meaning from the text itself" (p. 162). In his view, the reader faces two tasks: (a) to bring meaning to entire sequences such as phrases, clauses, and sentences, and (b) to bring meaning to an individual word (i.e., at the focal predictive level) where the passage is generally comprehensible.

The first of these tasks will be our concern in chapter 11. Smith observes that meaning of a phrase or sentence is not obtained by adding up the meanings of individual words. We certainly agree, but we also should note that sometimes it is. The reader does indeed use the meaning of the individual words to construct the meaning of a phrase such as "in the house." The task generally gets more difficult as the unit of meaning increases, but it is not all that infrequent in sentences such as "I ran into the house."

The second task, that of bringing meaning to individual words, is of course our concern here and deals with the issue of prediction at the focal level. Smith observes that the meaning of the whole phrase, sentence, or paragraph is used to predict the meaning of the individual word and asserts that adult readers learn most of their vocabulary in this way.

The process of bringing meaning to individual words is perceived by Smith (1971) as one involving the reduction of uncertainty; as when the reader uses meaning cues to predict the 1 word of perhaps 20 possible words that is correct. He (1988) also observes that context has its effect because it reduces the uncertainty of individual words through sequential redundancy. It places constraints on what each individual word might be. Sequential redundancy exists when the probability of a letter or word is constrained by the presence of surrounding letters or words in the same sequence. Smith differentiates between distributional and sequential redundancy. Distributional redundancy is "associated with the relative probability that each of the alternatives in a particular situation can occur" or have an equal chance of occurring (p. 243). Thus the letter *e* occurs about 40 times more frequently than does the letter *z*.

Redundancy may take the form of simple repetition. As we have already noted, it may also come in the form of visual, orthographic, semantic, and syntactic information that the reader already possesses. Smith speaks of the *language context*, that is, the body of words in a text or what we have referred to as the within-text context. He asserts that meaningful context exerts its constraints on word occurrence in two ways, semantic and syntactic: "These are two types of restriction upon the particular words an author can select—or a reader predict—at any time. . . . Choice of words is always limited by what we want to say (semantics) and how we want to say it (syntactics)" (p. 277). But, words can also be constrained by the *situational context*: there is a very small and predictable set of alternative words likely to occur on a tube of toothpaste or for that matter in "hitting-ball-fence." Smith adds that there is also an important context in the reader's expectations. He defines context as including the text as a whole, the purpose of the author, and the reader's general intentions and expectations.

Word identification plays a secondary role for Smith. He argues that the features of words in sequence may be analyzed without the words themselves being identified and that readers can go straight to meaning. He thus notes: "*Reading does not usually involve or rely on word identification*" (p. 177). In another context, Smith asserts, "Reading usually involves bringing meaning immediately or directly to the text without awareness of individual words" (p. 161). He adds that meaningful context "makes reading for meaning possible and word identification unnecessary." One would certainly agree with Smith that indeed in perhaps 15% to 20% of the time context alone (not within-text context alone or within-mind context alone, but both) constrains word occurrence to such a degree that prediction is perfect and uncertainty has been reduced to zero. But context alone is often an inadequate predictor; it may even lead the reader astray.

The best data suggest that words are represented in the brain in a form accessible in a variety of ways (i.e., through meaning and grammatical function, but also through sound, spelling, identification by analogy, etc.) and the good reader uses all of these methods of identification.

We later will cite research that shows that poor readers use within-text context more than fluent readers. Smith (1988) observes that all readers need context more when reading is difficult, and argues, quoting Thompson (1981), that when poor and good readers read the same text, their tasks are not equivalent. One is reading difficult material and the other is reading easy material.

Context, for Smith, encompasses the totality of the reader's nonvisual information, including the words on either side of the target word and including the understanding of the text as a whole. He observes that adjacent words on the page are in reality visual information—they are additional features to be analyzed if individual word identification is emphasized and difficult.

Smith points out that the less nonvisual information a reader brings to bear, the more visual information, the reader will need to identify words. He notes that beginning, slow, and less fluent readers demand a great deal of visual information because they are weak in the other sources of information or because they have an unduly high criterion for correctness. They do not want to be wrong and so they are unwilling to take a chance. "Conversely, experienced readers need attend to fewer distinctive features from individual words or from surrounding words as they read." Smith adds: "It could also be argued that children who cannot identify particular words on sight in contrived experimental or instructional situations are forced to use context as much as they can since phonics won't work for them" (pp. 284-285). But this is exactly our point. This is why poor readers rely more on context. We agree with Smith that "reading is not a matter of identifying word after word" (p. 285), even though the eyes focus on most words during reading. Smith argues that the visual focal point does not necessarily indicate that the words are being identified one at a time.

Smith (1988) appears to convey mixed messages. Context is definitely to be used to test hypotheses; context may even give meaning to text without awareness of individual words; and the meaning of the whole (i.e., phrase, sentence, paragraph) should be used to predict the meaning of individual words. He notes that the reduction of uncertainty is the outcome of sequential redundancy, which occurs when the same information is available from more than one source. He includes in such information the visual information and the word's orthography. He even decries reckless guessing.

But, Smith clearly relies on conscious prediction from context as the major strategy in identifying words in context. It is difficult not to conclude that Smith accords conscious activation from context, both semantic and syntactic, along with the intentions, expectations and the nonvisual information of the reader, almost total preeminence in the reading process, both at the global and focal predictive levels. He observes, as noted earlier, that reading usually involves bringing meaning to text "without awareness of individual words" (p. 161), even though readers clearly fixate on most words). In his view, meaningful context makes word identification unnecessary.

Smith's position is not strongly supported by recent research. Jenkins, Matlock, and Slocum (1989) report the research of Hermann, Anderson, Pearson, and Nagy (1987), Nagy et al. (1987), and others. In their assessment, these studies indicate that readers can learn word meanings from context, but the probability that they actually will do so is low. Nagy *et al* (1985) note that many, in fact probably most, contexts give little information about word meanings. Even though it appears possible to increase pupils' ability to learn from context through instruction, Graves (1986) concludes that "teaching students to use context is difficult. In fact, there is no report that presents a thorough and convincing case that students can be taught to better use context to unlock the meanings of novel words encountered during normal reading" (p. 73). Nagy *et al* (1985) note that, even though incidental learning from context is the major mode of vocabulary acquisition during school years, it proceeds in small increments.

Schatz and Baldwin (1986) found that contexts were often as likely to be misleading as to be helpful. Their students showed an accuracy rate of only 14% in supplying definitions or synonyms from context. Stein and Jenkins (1989) found a prediction-from-context accuracy rate of only 15%. Jenkins, Matlock, and Slocum studied fifth graders who scored at the 81st and 82nd percentile in reading comprehension and vocabulary on the *California Achievement Test*. Even after training , they found a mean accuracy rate ranging from 3.12 to 3.40 on a contrived context test and from 1.41 to 1.71 (score of 10 was maximum) on a basal reader test.

Readers simply are not highly skilled in using context cues as the sole cue to meaning and to the word. In fairness to Smith, we must reiterate that he defines context in its broadest sense, namely as the totality of the pupil's nonvisual information. It is thus more than the words surrounding the unknown word.

The Role of Context in Rayner and Pollatsek's Bottom-Up Model

We have chosen the model of Rayner and Pollatsek (1989) as representative of bottom-up theories. They (1989) argue that higher-order processes (i.e., context) have a relatively minor effect on word identification in skilled readers. They essentially believe that the reader "first identifies each word in turn (perhaps somewhat modified by prior context) and then puts these lexical entries together to form higher order structures such as phrases, sentences, and paragraphs" (p. 236).

Rayner and Pollatsek (1989) add that context effects are "not necessarily due to speeded lexical access of the predictable words. It is possible that the predictable context speeds processing of the target word by allowing it to be fit into the sentence context more easily" (p. 224). Furthermore, they point out that the variances in the length of the reader's eye fixations depend more on word length and word frequency than on context. They also argue that the savings in identification time of words in context are really not savings in lexical access so much as savings in text integration or the time it takes to integrate the word into discourse structure. Rayner and Pollatsek's position is of course contradictory to Goodman and Smith's prediction-from-context models, which assume that readers, even skilled readers, rely heavily on context to identify words.

Summary of the Effects of Context on Word Identification and Lexical Access

We are relying heavily in the discussion that follows on the research and writing of Rayner and Pollatsek (1989), Smith (1988), Perfetti (1985), and Just and Carpenter (1987), supplemented by our own analysis of the research. This research indicates that:

1. Identification of words and lexical access or word meaning are clearly facilitated by context or, more specifically, by conscious semantic activation from context. Both good and poor readers use context to identify words (Duffelmeyer, 1984; Perfetti, 1985; Smith, 1988). Context or semantic activation assists lexical access (Perfetti, 1985), especially in the case of the beginning and the poor reader (Carnine et al., 1984; Jenkins & Dixon, 1983; Marsh et al., 1981).

2. Conscious semantic activation from context contributes most to comprehension when the reader's encoding skill is inadequate (Anderson et al., 1985; Perfetti, 1985). It is thus most used by beginning and poor readers. The schema of these readers simply includes more knowledge of semantic and syntactic cues than it does of the within-word cues. Perfetti (1985) observes that good readers often find it easier and more reliable to go from word identification to meaning rather than from meaning to word identification. On the other hand, readers weak in featural and orthographic knowledge find it easier to seek out the semantic-syntactic route. This explains why in some instances the poor reader is more sensitive to contextual restraints than is the good reader. Rayner and Pollatsek (1989) note that "as children gain more experience reading and word recognition processes become more automatic, their reliance on context decreases" (p. 386). Our study of the stages in word recognition support this observation.

Perfetti (1985) points out that high-ability readers are better able to predict the next word in a text than are low-ability readers. Although low-ability readers are just as good at prediction in highly constraining contexts, they are less accurate in loosely constrained contexts. This fact may appear incongruent with the low-ability reader's greater dependence on context. Perfetti notes that it is actually quite compatible. The lower predictive abilities of low-ability readers are indeed quite helpful so they use them. Because their basic word-identification processes are slow acting, active predictive efforts are having an effect. Thus, Perfetti argues, it is completely consistent that an individual whose contextual abilities are limited should use them heavily. Bruck (1988) found that dyslexics seem to rely more on context to facilitate word recognition than do children in general. This supports the view of Stanovich (1981) that a "deficiency in a lower level process [e.g., word recognition] will lead to a greater reliance on higher level knowledge sources [such as context]" (p. 247).

Nicholson, Lillas, and Rzoska (1988) found that both poor and good six-year-old readers read words better in context, but the percentage gain was larger for the poor readers than for the good readers. However, among the eight-year-olds, only the poor readers showed better scores when reading in context. The good readers actually performed less well. The researchers, contrary to Goodman's interpretation of similar data, observe that their study shows that learning to read involves learning how to recode or decipher.

3. All readers use their world knowledge to make global predictions in reading. Global predictions generally involve conscious anticipation from context.
4. Beginning, poor, and even fluent readers, if the text is especially difficult or the words themselves are novel, will use their nonvisual information to make even focal predictions in reading. This is so because beginning readers and poor readers frequently lack adequate within-word information to predict the target word directly from the structure of the word.
5. Focal predictions may involve either (a) conscious prediction from context without the full processing of the visual information (as in the case of the beginning and poor reader), or (b) automatic semantic activation. Perfetti (1985) observes that the reader may actively and consciously anticipate possible word candidates during reading (we have found that beginning and poor readers often do so), but labels this "a pernicious version of the psycholinguistic guessing game" (p. 26). He adds that the skilled or fluent reader does not have time to guess when fixating three or four words per second and observes: If the reader is a skilled reader, why should he even bother? Perfetti suggests that the skilled reader uses automatic semantic activation. Just and Carpenter (1987) likewise call attention to the "conscious activation" model and identify it with the reader using the context to predict what occurs next. They suggest that reading, in this view, is a matter of prediction followed by an eye fixation to some upcoming word to either confirm or disconfirm the prediction. They unequivocally reject this thesis and cite Stanovich and West (1983) to support their position that skilled readers do not make explicit guesses about upcoming words.
6. Conscious focal predictions from context are not very effective because:
   a. The prediction is likely to be wrong (Rayner and Pollatsek, 1989). Readers are not particularly good in predicting the next word in print even with unlimited amounts of time (Gough, Alford, & Holley-Wilcox, 1981).
   b. Conscious focal predictions take "processing resources away from the higher-order processes needed to put words together to form syntactic and semantic structures" (Rayner and Pollatsek, 1989, p. 22).
7. The time needed to name words is facilitated in helpful contexts and inhibited by anomalous contexts, but it is also true that the better the reader is, the less the effect of context tends to be

(Gough, 1984). Context clearly affects the speed of lexical access, even though only slightly. Children, in fact, are faster in naming words in context than in isolation (West & Stanovich, 1978). The savings in processing time amounts to 15 to 30 msec. Words that are highly predictable in text are generally fixated for a shorter time (30 to 50 msec.) than are nonpredictable words (Balota, Pollatsek, & Rayner, 1985; Ehrlich & Rayner, 1981). Rayner and Pollatsek (1989) observe that the predictable context may speed processing of the target word by allowing it to be fit into the sentence more easily. Perfetti (1985) also observes that context adds information to the identification process, causing the word-activation process to execute more rapidly. Ehrlich and Rayner's study (1981) found that predictable context does indeed shortcut visual processing of the target word.

8. Context affects word identification in reading by speeding the extraction of visual information from the parafovea or peripheral vision (Balota, Pollatsek, & Rayner, 1985) rather than from the fovea. Context, in fact, helps the reader to skip over the next word entirely, thus saving some 200 msec. of reading time (Balota, Pollatsek, & Rayner, 1985).

9. Stanovich and West (1983) found that even in instances of direct prediction from context, the context effect is not top-down, but rather intralexical, i.e., the result of a "spreading activation" mechanism or automatic associative priming. Associative priming refers to the automatic priming flowing down from the previous words or previous context in the sentence to the lexical entry of the word immediately following. Stanovich and West (1983) explain predictability effects as the sum of the priming effects from the word preceding the target word. Priming occurs when a prior word (*dog*) speeds the processing of a second word (e.g., *cat*). Priming aids lexical access when there is a short interval between the priming word and the unknown word and when the priming word and the unknown word are strongly associated with each other. Rayner and Pollatsek (1989) suggest that when the lexical entries of related words in the definition are activated, they send automatic activation through links between them and the word being accessed, producing lexical access. Carroll and Slowiaczek (1986) indeed found that readers made shorter gaze durations or fixations on the target word when the priming and the target were within the same clause, suggesting an application of the automatic priming mechanism.

Automatic priming depends on short-term memory. The reader keeps the priming word active in short-term memory as a result of

building a meaning for the sentence (Foss, 1982).Conscious prediction, on the other hand, relies on long-term memory or the reader's schema. In this circumstance, the context is well established by the time the reader comes to predicting, for example, how the story will end.
10. Context has a number of auxiliary effects:
    (a) it can compensate for impoverished feature information (Perfetti, 1985);
    (b) it encourages the reader, if he has not identified the word, to try again (Rayner & Pollatsek, 1989);
    (c) it helps pupils to re-identify words they previously identified (Emans, 1968); and
    (d) it helps the pupil to identify words that are not identifiable in any other way.

AUTOMATIC SEMANTIC ACTIVATION

Perfetti (1985), as already noted, rejects conscious prediction as the mode of word identification and of lexical access for the skilled reader. He suggests that skilled readers engage in automatic semantic activation and proposes that such processing may occur as a result of automatic semantic activation from feature-detection and letter activation processes that bring about recognition and lexical access from the bottom up. This occurs when the reader can encode the word or identify the word fast enough to facilitate the comprehension of the next word (Just & Carpenter, 1987). Automatic semantic activation may also occur as a result of automatic syntactic priming mechanisms (i.e., from the initial encoding of a syntactic pattern: thus, *the* will trigger a noun). Prime triggering mechanisms are the grammatical categories represented in the memory network and syntax in general (Just & Carpenter, 1987). These mechanisms involve fitting the word into the syntactic context. Finally, automatic semantic activation may occur because of what is in the mind of the reader. This is the within-mind context. It is the mental model of the text's meaning constructed by the reader. The reader's knowledge of the world and of the text topic, i.e., the reader's schemata or the within-mind context, are obvious triggering mechanisms (Just & Carpenter, 1987).

Clearly word identification and lexical access are different in skilled readers and in beginning and poor readers, and this difference, we conclude,results from the skilled readers' much greater knowledge of the within-word cues. Skilled readers bring to the text information adequate to the word-identification task. They have automatized the word-processing skills, the within-word or word structure information, processing words in a fraction of a second. They go directly from the graphic input or the visual word form to lexical access. They do not have to rely on the surrounding words or the context to predict what word comes next in the text. They are so fluent and identify the word with such ease and accuracy that the word's pronunciation and meaning are activated automatically from the word itself.

Rayner and Pollatsek (1989) observe that skilled readers' foveal vision triggers so much information that applying context is of little benefit. Perfetti and Roth (1981) note that lower-level processes make a contribution that is independent of context. They are sufficient for identification in and of themselves.

It is when semantic activation is not automatic (either as result of inadequate instruction or the inability to acquire this skill incidentally) that the reader is often making futile stabs in the dark. His reading is less than skilled and he is forced to engage in conscious prediction. This, of course, brings us to our next issue: How does one develop automatic semantic activation from feature-detection processes?

THE WITHIN-WORD CUES

From our perspective, if indeed within-word cue knowledge makes it possible to engage in automatic semantic activation, readers are benefited: (a) when they have internalized the within-word cues (i.e., the information has become a part of their nonvisual information) and (b) when teachers of reading have acquired this information themselves and can impart what is relevant to children, thus expanding the within-word cue information of the reader. Chapters 8 and 9 address what needs to be taught. We will focus here on the use of the within-word cues or surface structure in predicting oneself through print, especially in becoming more proficient at accurate focal predictions. Smith includes the visual information and the orthography in the sources of information that can reduce or dispose of uncertainty. He adds that the distinctive features of words can confirm or disconfirm particular meanings.

Return to the problem of predicting the word *over* in the sentence, "The boy hit the ball over the fence." Meaning cues alone or guessing from context are often inadequate and inefficient in predicting the exact word. We have already noted that for many readers, especially for skilled readers, it frequently is more advantageous to use feature-detection and letter-activation processes that bring about word recognition from the bottom up and to resort to their repertoire of within-word identification strategies in order to reduce uncertainty.

In chapter 8 we outline in some detail the stages of word identification.

Marsh et al. (1981), Mason (1980), and Lomax and McGee (1987) essentially agree that readers go through stages in mastering the word-identification process. The first two stages appear to involve a simple rote association between the word and the name of the word. In stage 1 the learner relies chiefly on his nonvisual information or world knowledge. The pupil will pay little attention to the graphemic cues, with the possible exception of the initial letter. In stage 2 the reader pays increasing attention to the graphemic cues or to the shared letters between the target word and another known word and to the word's shape, length, or final letter.

Marsh et al. (1981) identify stage 3 as the sequential recoding stage: it is the beginning of an appreciation of the alphabetic principle. Orthography or spelling of the word at this stage becomes a formidable cue. This sensitivity to the orthographic structure occurs at about the second-grade level. The reader begins paying attention to all the letters in the word, not simply the beginning letter. The young reader learns to process letters in parallel and to sound out letters. He learns to process a series of letters and to relate this series to a series of sounds (i.e., sequential recoding) in a left-to-right sequence.

Stage 4, the hierarchical recoding stage, is the phonic knowledge refinement stage. It is the stage during which readers process words as adults do. It generally happens at the fourth or fifth grade level or between the ages of 8 and 10 years. It is the stage when readers finally develop expertise in the use of the within-word cues, the logographic, graphemic, orthographic, phonic, and morphemic cues.

Logographic or Configuration Cues

Logographic or configuration cues, that is, word shape and length, are within-word cues, but they are not especially helpful in word identification. There are too many words that have the same configuration as a given target word (e.g., *over*). Furthermore, the reader's memory is not adequate to the task of memorizing thousands of independent word configurations.

This does not imply that configuration cues are meaningless. The teacher should call the pupil's attention to the configuration cues, the word's physiognomy, its shape, length, and contour, as it is fashioned by the letters: thus *book* looks like book. Obviously, a word can sometimes be identified by its shape. Children early note that words have specific shapes or configurations, that some are short and others are long, and that some have ascending letters and some have descending letters.

Graphemic Cues

Graphemic cues or letters and letter clusters are more important in identifying words than are configuration cues. Skilled readers encode words more in terms of letters than of shape (Just & Carpenter, 1987). Children acquire graphemic cue knowledge in sequence: focusing first on the beginning letter, on shared letters between words, on the end letter, on the middle letter, and on letter clusters, and gradually moving to the perception of letters in parallel and in a left-to-right sequence.

Orthographic Cues

As noted earlier, the orthographic cues are important cues in word identification. Spelling bears a systematic relation to the word's acoustic and articulatory structure and is a significant cue to the sounding of the word.

Phonic Cues

The phonic cues have a particularly important role to play in the identification process and especially in the recoding process. Research (Ehri & Wilce, 1985) shows that young children's growth in reading is supported by their knowing how to use the phonic cues. These cues are particularly effective in extracting information from the orthographic code. The reader who has mastered the grapheme-phoneme correspondences, who has learned to break the orthographic code, is able to look at the word (e.g., *cat*) and to recode or translate the written symbol into the spoken symbol (/kăt/). Since the pupil may very well have dictated the sentence, "The boy hit the ball over the fence," in his experience story, the pupil already has an aural-oral meaning for the word *over*; thus, if the pupil can convert the word *over* to /ōvər/, he has reduced uncertainty to zero and now can read the sentence and identify the word. The pupil must come to see that the word *over* is the only word that fits both the semantic and syntactic context and the graphic cue system. It is the only reasonable choice. The pupil must reason thus: "One possible meaning is '*over*'. . . . There is only one word that fits both the semantic and syntactic context that starts with *o* and that ends with *er*, and that thus fits the graphic cues. The word is *over*. The word must be /ōvər/." At the very least, if the pupil only knows that the word begins with *o*, he has eliminated all of the other prepositions suggested earlier with the exception of *on* and *off*. And if the pupil sees that *over* has two vowel letters whereas *on* and *off* have only one, the pupil may have eliminated those words from further consideration and will have confirmed his prediction. The pupil should ask: "What word have I spoken that begins with an *o* and that fits the semantic and syntactic context and the graphic cues?" We are, of course, speaking of the pupil's early attempts at using the phonic cues. Observe that these are conscious attempts at the first- and second-grade levels. It is only when the process becomes automatic that automatic semantic activation does occur.

Phonics helps children to identify a word by helping them to work out the pronunciation of the unknown word. It is a cue to the name of configuration. Phonics may be the only method that allows poor readers to tap the thousands of words that are already in their aural-oral vocabulary. The phonogram or letter-cluster cues, spelling patterns, and analogy cues are all significant cues and teaching of these should be an integral part of each child's teaching. Using the within-word cues, especially the grapho-phonic cues, may effectively reduce uncertainty to zero, and consequently increase predictive efficiency to the level of 100%. It improves the probability of prediction, makes the pupil's guess, if indeed it is a guess, an educated one, and certainly makes word identification less of a psycholinguistic guessing game. It improves the pupil's predictive efficiency. It stacks the odds in the pupil's favor.

Studies (Vellutino, 1987) consistently show that severely disabled readers, because of their poor grasp of phoneme values, are much less proficient than normal readers in learning to use letter sounds to decode pseudowords (meaningless word-like letter assemblages), and that kindergarten and first-grade children who have some ability to segment spoken words into syllables and phoneme-size units learn to read better than children who have little or no such ability. Vellutino (1987) notes that children who can identify phonemes have an increased ability to map alphabetically and an enhanced capacity to identify printed words.

Reading disability clearly is associated with phonological coding or sound mapping deficits (inability to represent or access the sound of a word in order to help remember the word), deficient phonemic segmentation (inability to break words into component sounds), poor vocabulary development, and trouble discriminating grammatical and syntactic differences among words and sentences. Vellutino (1987) notes that poor phoneme segmentation is a manifestation of a more general problem in phonological coding, characterized by the storage in memory of impoverished representations of letter sounds and word names. It causes difficulties in learning the names as whole entities. Words are therefore stored without complete phonological codes in the pupil's mental lexicon. Asked to call up the proper word, the child finds that he or she has not retained enough clues to the name of the word.

Morphemic Cues

Additionally important within-word cues (and indeed meaning cues) are the morphemic cues. Morphemes are both meaning and structural units. Thus, the *s* in *cats* or the *trans* in *transport* are meaning cues because they change the meaning of the base word (*cat* versus *cats*), and they are within-word cues because they change the structure of the word. Words frequently have inflectional endings (such as *s, es, ed, inc,* etc.) or have undergone inflectional changes (such as changing *y* to *i* and adding *es*). They may contain prefixes and or suffixes; they may be compounds or contractions; they often consist of more than one syllable and the accent may differentiate one word from another (record' versus re'cord). Each of these morphemic elements can at various times be used to reduce uncertainty. Conversely, a basic reason for the poor reader's deficiencies in sight vocabulary is often a weakness in identifying these morphemic units.

Morphemic analysis and automatic syntactic priming mechanisms play, as Perfetti (1985) notes, an important role in developing automatic semantic activation. They are best used in combination with context and phonic analysis. The unknown word is divided into its parts (note that in such an instance morphemic analysis precedes phonic analysis), the parts are sounded, and are then blended into the whole word. The resultant is then tested to see if it makes sense in the sentence. Obviously, this technique works best if the word is within the pupil's aural-oral vocabulary.

INTEGRATION OF CUES

In general, the good reader combines nonvisual information and meaning and context cues with phonic and morphemic cues to produce the best possible prediction (Vellutino, 1987). Swenson (1975) notes that pupils need to integrate their recognition of the grapheme-phoneme correspondences with the meaning of the text. Smith (1977) adds, "It is the sense of the text that enables readers to use spelling-to-sound correspondences effectively."

Good readers are such because they have so integrated and automatized their use of all the cues that they appear to be unaware of which cue they are using at the moment. Heilman (1961) notes that persons who have mastered the process of reading may lose sight of the many factors which must mesh if success in reading is to be achieved. Luria (1973) emphasizes that a word is "a complex multidimensional matrix of different cues and connections (acoustic, morphological, lexical, and semantic)" and that "in different states one of these connections is predominant" (p. 306).

As soon as readers can make use of beginning grapheme-phoneme correspondences, especially consonant correspondences, they can combine this partial pronunciation with the use of context and sentence meaning to unlock words. Indeed, beginning readers do so. In the sentence, "Jimmy fell ____ the stairs," the context can help to identify any number of possibilities that will meet meaning and syntax requirements; for example, *off, up, against, into,* and *down*. However, the child who knows that the unknown word begins with the letter *d* (and hence with the /d/ sound) can select the one word that meets meaning, syntax, and grapho-phonic criteria. Using both meaning and phonic analysis, the pupil can be more certain that the word is *down*.

I have often asked students in my college classes to tell me the meaning of the word *taciturn* in a sentence such as "Mary was taciturn all evening." A few students can pronounce the word, but this does not help. They simply have not associated the word with an aural-oral or real experience. Other students neither know how to pronounce the word nor are able to take meaning to the word. They cannot make a prediction or make a wrong prediction. However, as soon as the word is put into a with-in-text context (Ed was taciturn, while Mary was very talkative), everyone in class knows immediately what the meaning is. As soon as this fuller context is provided, the students can read with understanding. They can predict themselves through the passage. They will check their prediction against the added semantic and syntactic context and against their nonvisual information and will confirm, reject, or refine their previous prediction.

The illustration is demonstrative of the fact that readers do, in fact, make predictions and seek confirmation of their predictions when reading, that they learn meanings, and that both the semantic and the syntactic context function for readers, interacting with their personal schema to help them make a prediction.

Studies also show that when good readers err they tend to substitute words that harmonize with the semantic and syntactic context. Poor readers, on the other hand, substitute words that do not fit contextually. Perhaps this is because of the greater experience underlying the good reader's perception. As Norberg (1953; 1956) points out, when the retina is stimulated the observer perceives whatever represents, for him, the best prognosis for action based upon his experience. Thus, the good reader's prognosis is superior to that of the poor reader primarily because the good reader's nonvisual information is superior. What is in the mind of the good reader, namely, her knowledge of the world, the text topic, and language, and the word identification/comprehension cues, provides a better model of the text's meaning. Even more importantly, poor readers often fail to realize that their substitutions do not make sense. They do not listen critically to themselves. They simply have not attained the level of conceptual development that permits them to see the error.

Anticipation and prediction of meaning from context is more likely to be effective if:

1. Pupils have learned the core words of the language; that is, the words in the *Dolch Basic Sight Word List* or in similar lists.
2. Pupils have well-developed schemata and can adequately sample the text to determine the meaning of the passage. Young readers, slow learners, conceptually deficient learners, poor readers (Car-

nine et al., 1984; Jenkins & Dixon, 1983), and learning-disabled children (Pflaum & Pascarella, 1979, 1980; Rosner et al., 1981) often are so deficient in conceptualization and experience and in the use of the text context that they cannot play the "psycholinguistic guessing game" with proficiency and skill. Not all children possess adequate conceptual development; not all can comprehend with equal proficiency.
3. Pupils have already developed an aural-oral meaning for the word.
4. The meaning that fits the blank slot in the sentence or paragraph can be represented by only one word. Obviously this often is not the case since many other words at times represent essentially the same meaning; thus, *small, little, tiny, microscopic, puny, diminutive,* and *lilliputian* share some commonness of meaning. The reliability of the initial perception of a word decreases as the number of meanings that may be associated with the word increases.

Obviously, readers make use of the within-mind and within-text context to predict themselves through print. We have found that this works quite well in making global predictions. It is less effective in making focal predictions. Such prediction is at risk when the pupil lacks adequate knowledge of the within-word cues. The pupil's only recourse may be to have the teacher tell him what the word is. Unfortunately, this is what often happens. The child needs to be given the opportunity to predict. The teacher on her part may need to fill more slots in the pupil's schemata with information about the within-word cues.

We argue, of course, that the development of skilled or fluent reading involves a continuing, progressively refined process of developing automatic semantic activation from print. Just and Carpenter (1987) note that all processes, both high and low level, can concur. But, they point out that in the good reader the encoding and lexical processes are so fast that the high-level processes (i.e., context) have little effect on word recognition. Automatic semantic activation from print is not the totality of reading, but clearly readers are benefited when they develop accuracy, fluency, speed, and automaticity in word identification.

Juel (1988) reports that children lacking recoding skill read little, have little opportunity to increase their vocabulary and enhance their schemata, and have a shaky foundation for reading comprehension.

Fortunately, even though children's initial reliance is on conscious semantic activation from context in making focal predictions, they become increasingly less dependent on prediction of words from context and rely more on automatic semantic activation from feature-detection activation processes. In other words, they rely more on the within-word cues.

Moreover, skilled readers do not rely only on top-down or bottom-up processes, but they use both in an integrated way. In other words, the interactive model (see chapter 1) best explains what actually happens in reading.

SUMMARY

Chapter 5 attempted to deal with the issue of predicting oneself through print and secondarily with addressing the psycholinguistic guessing game hypothesis. We affirmed the role of prediction in reading, defined global and focal prediction, and concluded that different strategies are needed for each. Chapter 5 also examined the role of context, differentiated between the within-text and the within-mind context, and concluded that context, especially the within-text context, is inadequate in reducing uncertainty to zero in most situations. In addition, chapter 5 offered automatic semantic activation as a desirable goal in reading and suggested that this is only possible through the internalizing of the within-word information.

PART IV
Organizing and Structuring the Reading Lesson

Part IV relates to the use of appropriate materials in the teaching of reading, to the use of a whole language, and to the format for organizing a reading lesson. The guiding themes in Part IV thus are:

1. That children will progress best in reading when they are introduced to reading via the Language Experience Approach and a combination of basal readers, trade or literature books, and content or expository texts.
2. That reading is best taught in an individualized whole-language context where the emphasis is on the integration of all the language arts (including speaking-listening, writing-reading, and spelling), where literature-based reading is coequal with basal readers and graded trade books, and where the individualized-reading principles of seeking, self-selection of materials, and self-pacing are a part of the total program, especially in the enrichment phase of the reading lesson.
3. That an optimal format for organizing a classroom reading lesson is, with some modification, the Directed Reading Activity (DRA). What happens before, during, and after reading is important.

Even though the reader's schema and the use of the predictive strategy play a significant role in the comprehension of text, they alone do not assure the pupil's growth in reading. Reading development requires appropriate materials. Every child has a right to read; a child's right to read readable and interesting materials is just as basic. Children learn to read by reading, and materials provide the context in which pupils learn to read. It is certainly true that many children do not read books because they cannot read well enough. It is perhaps more tragic when they cannot read well because they do not read books.

Chapter 6, "Introducing Children to Reading: The Language Experience Story, Basal Readers, Expository Texts, Individualized Reading, Whole Language, and Literature-Based Reading," describes how to introduce the pupil to reading through the Language Experience Approach. Such an approach capitalizes upon the pupil's schemata; it is based on the child's experiences and language. However, because children need to acquire new experiences and need to experience growth in language, their association with materials needs to be broadened to include basal readers, graded and ungraded trade books, especially the wonderful world of quality literature texts, and context area texts. The main theme of chapter 6, however, is not the materials. Rather, it is the interrelatedness of all the language arts: speaking-listening, writing-reading, and spelling. Teaching reading should flow from a total-language context. It should begin with whole language. Individualized reading and whole language put special emphasis on one segment of reading materials, namely children's literature. Chapter 6 affirms that children are best served when they are exposed to the wide variety of reading materials.

Chapter 7, "Organizing and Programming the Reading Lesson: Using a Modified Directed Reading Activity," presents a detailed model of how to organize a reading lesson. The Directed Reading Activity (DRA) format, with modifications from the Guided Reading Thinking Lesson (GRTL) and the Directed Reading-Thinking Activity (DR-TA), provides a structure centered around six steps: (a) developing readiness for reading a selection, (b) guided silent reading, (c) checking and evaluating comprehension, (d) oral re-reading of the materials, (e) expanding word recognition and comprehension skills (including oral reading skills, study skills, and content area skills), and (f) enrichment and follow-up. The DRA model programs for the activation and expansion of the reader's schemata, for the use of a predictive strategy when reading, for the development of a pre-, during-, and post-reading question and discussion strategy, for the use of monitoring or metacognitive skills, and for the development of fluency in reading.

There may be better ways of organizing a reading lesson, but what would one leave out in a reading lesson? Is it developing readiness for reading? Is it the oral rereading of certain elements of text? Is it skill teaching? Or is it enrichment and follow-up activities? Call it DRA or something else, the classroom reading lesson must concern itself with all of the above.

Chapter 6
Introducing Children to Reading: The Language Experience Story, Basal Readers, Trade Books, Expository Texts, Individualized Reading, Whole Language, and Literature-Based Reading

    I. Introduction
   II. The Language-Experience Approach
       A. Steps in Developing the Language-Experience Story
       B. Advantages of LEA
  III. The Basal Reader Approach
  IV. The Individualized Reading Program
   V. The Whole-Language Perspective
  VI. Whole Language and Literature-Based Reading
 VII. Whole Language and Skill Teaching
VIII. Summary

CHAPTER 6

Introducing Children to Reading: The Language-Experience Story, Basal Readers, Trade Books, Expository Texts, Individualized Reading, Whole Language, and Literature-Based Reading

Chapter 4 emphasized that schema theory offers the best context for reading and for comprehending. The pupil's personal schema sets the limits for his or her level of comprehending. It is an equally valid corrolary that pupils cannot comprehend unless they have something to comprehend. Smith (1988) focuses our attention on the importance of reading itself in promoting the learning-to-read process. He observes that children find meaning in print only through meaningful reading.

Reading development does not occur in a vacuum. The pupil does not simply read "reading," he reads "something." He reads the language-experience story, the basal reader story, graded and ungraded children's literature or trade books, and content or expository texts. Figure 6-1 identifies the reading materials most used in developing competency in reading. It graphs the sequence for using reading materials and symbolizes the use of all the variant types of materials throughout the child's reading development. The language-experience story, the basal reader story, and the trade book story are termed narratives; the content texts are called expository materials.

THE LANGUAGE-EXPERIENCE APPROACH

After children have learned to identify and name the configuration which represents their name, they should be introduced to formal reading instruction through the use of the Language-Experience Approach (LEA). Fortunately, most children come to school knowing how to read their name,

168   CHAPTER 6

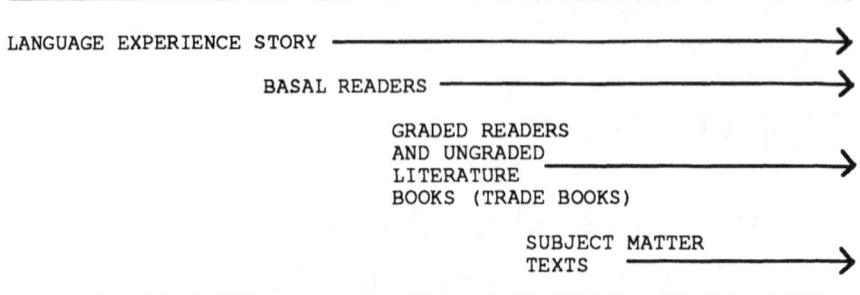

FIGURE 6-1: Materials for Teaching Reading

and many will have learned to "read" names on stores, package labels, road signs, and other words in their environment.

The language-experience approach, involving the use of self-made materials, seems preferable to other approaches, especially at the beginning stages of reading instruction. It capitalizes on children's natural language and on their experiences, content knowledge, interests, and syntactic knowledge. LEA assures that readers bring to bear their own schemata, their information base, to what they are reading (Roney, 1984). It thus minimizes the likelihood of a concept gap. And, since in LEA children develop their own text, it assures that the reading materials contain language patterns and structures that the pupil has mastered in speech.

The language-experience approach began in the 1920s when Flora J. Cooke at the Chicago Institute and later at the Francis Parker School began putting children's oral experiences on the blackboard. It grew and developed as part of the Progressive Education Movement, which de-emphasized the importance of systematic and sequential presentation of material in favor of purpose, interest, and meaning. In 1934 Nila Smith termed this approach the "experience method," and now it is commonly termed the language-experience approach.

The language-experience approach was presented in *Language Experiences in Reading* by Allen and Allen (1966), in *Language Experiences in Reading Program*, by Roach Van Allen, Richard L. Venezky, and Harry T. Hahn (1974), in *Language Experiences in Communication* by Roach Van Allen (1976). *Teaching Reading as a Language Experience*, by Mary Anne Hall (1970) and *The Language Experience Approach to Reading* by Denise D. Nessel (1981) both provide a description of a total language-experience program. *Language Experience Activities* by Roach Van Allen and Claryce Allen (1976, 1981, 1982) and *Feathers in My Cap: Early Reading Through Experiences* by Ellen Cromwell (1980) present numerous activities useful in a language-experience program. Other suitable references to LEA are Allen (1982), Allen et al. (1988), Silvernail (1987), Veatch (1984, 1986–1987,

1987), and Veatch et al. (1979). Teacher Support Software (P. O. Box 7130, Gainesville, Florida 32605) offers a software package emphasizing language experience for use on an Apple computer.

The basic tenets of the language-experience approach may be summed up in a few sentences: What I can think about, I can talk about. What I can say, I can write. What I can write, I can read. I can read what others write for me to read (Allen & Allen, 1966). In LEA, children talk about their experiences, the teacher writes the anecdotal description on the blackboard or records it on an "experience chart", and the children then read what they spoke and the teacher wrote.

Steps in Developing the Language-Experience Story

The steps in developing and using the experience story for instructional purposes, which may be adapted for either group or individual use, include the following:

1. Provide for commonality of experience (for example, a field trip) or identify an experience that the children have shared as a group. The experience story may grow out of a simple picture.
2. Have children discuss and describe their experiences. Children have a natural inclination to want to talk about their experiences, either as individuals or as a group. They love to tell about a mountain trip, fishing at a lake, planting a garden, harvesting wheat, building a bird house, making popcorn, a day at a circus, their Christmas or Thanksgiving, making a kite or a paper airplane, or caring for an aquarium. The teacher helps children to identify significant ideas, to decide on the sequence, and to choose appropriate vocabulary. Heller (1988) recommends that discussion of the common experience involve activation of the children's prior knowledge, setting a purpose for writing the story, and perhaps prereading of a model language-experience story.
3. Record the story or narrative on the chalkboard. The story in the early grades may be short, consisting of perhaps three or four lines. At beginning reading levels, each new sentence should begin on a new line. After the first draft has been written, assist children in revising their sentences. Ringler and Weber (1984) describe three types of experience charts: the personal experience or narrative chart; the work or directions (how to do it) chart; and the reading strategy or skill-teaching chart (e.g., summarizing of text).

4. Read the narrative as a whole, moving one hand from left to right in a smooth flowing motion under each word.
5. Have the children read the whole story aloud with the teacher.
6. Have individual children read the story one sentence at a time. Children's memory spans are usually adequate to "read" back simple sentences.
7. Transcribe the story onto chart paper (this is the experience chart). Make two charts: one of which becomes a part of the children's book of stories and the second of which is used for teaching purposes.
8. Cut the story on one of the charts into sentence strips and help pupils to read the sentences fluently.
9. Isolate parts of the story for specific emphasis, such as the teaching of a specific word, of a specific grapheme-phoneme correspondence, or of a specific meaning or comprehension skill.
10. Have children read the story again as a whole. This may take the form of silent, choral, or individual oral reading.
11. Make a file of experience charts and label them "Our (My) Big Book."
12. Begin a card file of sight words, help children develop a picture dictionary, and start each child's phonogram book. The card file or word bank, consisting of a 3-by-5 inch file box with index cards, may contain word categories for such diverse groupings as words for things, people, or animals; words for days of the week; words for weather; and words for different colors. It may contain groupings of question words, of words that tell when, where, how many, and words that describe actions (Wynn, 1988).
13. Have children re-read the stories occasionally.

Teaching basic reading skills through use of the experience story emphasizes a top-down approach:

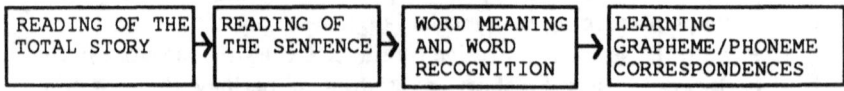

The steps suggested earlier focus first on the reading of the total story, then, gradually, the paragraphs, the sentences, and the words, and finally, on analysis on a grapheme/phoneme level. Isolating words for teaching word-identification skills (including grapheme/phoneme correspondences and morphemic skills) should occur within the sentence context.

Advantages of LEA

LEA allows for a gradual transition from the informal home language to the formalized language in books. Moving from the known (child's spoken language) is good educational procedure and experience charts make this possible. In LEA the language is real, natural, and relevant to the child. The cornerstones of the language experience approach are the child's language and experiences (Hall, 1976, 1978). Children's language determines the language patterns of the reading materials and their experience determines the content. In reading their own experience chart, children read about their own experiences in their own language. LEA is thus consistent with schema theory. The pupil necessarily will have adequate schemata to comprehend what is read.

LEA also teaches children the interrelationships between the language arts (Barnard & Kendrick, 1980). First-grade children have learned that what they can think they can say. Now they learn that what can be said can be written and what can be written can be read. The child learns that sounds can be put into written form and that the beginning, middle, and ending sounds can be graphically symbolized. Figure 6-3 illustrates the steps in LEA and at the same time shows the interrelationship between the LEA and the language arts.

Pupils gain immeasurably by writing and making their own text. Such activities teach them "how to reconstruct the intended meaning of others" (Hittelman, 1983, p. 82) when they are reading. The LEA provides the opportunity to learn about technical aspects of writing (e.g., spaces between words, directionality); it demonstrates the planning, drafting, and revision stages of writing; and it gives children valuable experience in the sustained monologue required in writing (Shanahan, 1988).

LEA is effective because it prevents a mismatch between the pupil's oral language and the written language of the instructional material; it effectively bridges the gap between reader and text. It deals with the problems of the reluctant reader and the disadvantaged reader. It is a simple and meaningful introduction to reading and has built-in motivational elements because children like to read what they have written. The material contains words and meanings that the child wants to know and is interested in. It teaches the pupil to put meaning into print and to reconstruct meaning from print. It develops sight vocabulary; it teaches left-to-right direction in reading; it allows for the teaching of letter-sound correspondences; and it develops spelling, knowledge of language structure, and organization of ideas.

The LEA approach to teaching reading also emphasizes that learning to read should proceed from whole language or total stories to parts and back to wholes. It emphasizes natural reading (Jewell & Zintz, 1986) and focuses on comprehension. It is a natural way to introduce children to reading (Jewell & Zintz, 1986). LEA provides a compelling avenue for demonstrating the meaningfulness, relevance, and utility of reading in the child's world (Jewell & Zintz, 1986). It fosters the development of permanent reading interests and reading for pleasure and information. It teaches children that reading is an extension of listening and speaking. LEA starts reading in the language the child knows best, be it standard or nonstandard English. It presents reading as a language and communication process, and it stresses that reading is an active process of constructing meaning.

The effectiveness of the LEA approach is substantiated by research. Zajano (1977), Asplund and Sunal (1980), Reifman et al. (1981), Silvernail (1987), and Allen, Wright, and Laminack (1988) each report reading gains from LEA experiences.

Hundreds of useful activities can grow out of the experience story. The pupils may be asked to write a title for the narrative, to arrange the sentences in proper sequence, to illustrate the story with drawings or photographs, or to develop skill in reading the sentences with expression and with proper intonation and fluency. The grapheme/phoneme correspondences and the use of morphemic cues can be taught, using the words that children have made a part of their sight vocabulary.

The language-experience approach is not a method. It is rather a philosophy about the type of materials to use in beginning reading. The approach is particularly useful as a way of teaching beginning reading and as a lead-in to basal readers, trade or literature books, and content texts. It can also stand alone, but generally conventional instructional materials in the form of basal or other readers are needed in the latter half of the first grade. The pupil's reading fare needs gradually to be expanded to include picture books, folktales, fables, epics, sports, mystery, animal, adventure, or romance stories, biographies, historical or science fiction stories, realistic fiction books, poetry, plays, humorous books, nonfiction books, and content texts.

Perhaps the major objection to LEA is that the materials derived from

ORAL-AURAL LANGUAGE	WRITING	READING
Children express thoughts, share experiences, and listen to language.	The teacher (or the pupils) records the children's message.	Children read what they have dictated and what has been written.

FIGURE 6-3: The LEA and The Language Arts

stories which children dictate are based on children's present performance rather than on their language potential. Materials based upon what the child knows do not extend performance levels. Part of learning to read is identifying and interpreting words and language patterns not normally used in one's speech. It is for this reason that children need to read materials other than those which they constructed. Some educators believe that the stories should be recorded in the language patterns of the child, whether grammatically correct or not. Others suggest that the vocabulary and the sentences be simplified and be made grammatically correct. The debate continues. However, materials should always be written with standard spelling and capitalization and should be punctuated appropriately.

The microcomputer (with a word processing program, a printer, and a large monitor) may be quite useful in the language experience approach (Grabe & Grabe, 1985). Using it, the teacher first types the story as the children dictate it. Modifications, additions, or deletions suggested by the children are easily made using the word processor. The printer generates copies of the finished story, producing personal copies for each child. Another program presents the pupil with a blank title page and a sequence of pictures that in a general way tell a story (e.g., child launches kite; kite is flown near tall tree; kite lodges in the top of the tree). The children view the sequence of pictures and then discuss what might have happened. After the discussion the teacher enters text under the pictures. First a title is added such as "Stuck in the Tree." Then the children are asked to dictate a description of the action portrayed in each picture. This has children deal with the setting, the problem, and the resolution of the story. Children then read the story and are given a printout that is their personal copy of the story.

THE BASAL READER APPROACH

Although teachers use experience charts or the language-experience approach in introducing reading, few have thought of it as comprising the total reading fare. The need for expanded growth in language and broadening of experience is difficult to satisfy by LEA alone. Children's reading must take them beyond their experiences. Moreover, most children profit greatly from a steady progression through graded materials.

Such graded materials have come to be known as basal reading materials. They are designed to provide continuity in reading development and put special emphasis on skill teaching. They aim at systematic and sequential instruction, leading the pupil by logical, sequential steps to the mastery of the basic reading skill. They are programmed for continuous progress from level to level or from grade to grade, and they provide for systematic repetition and review. They order reading tasks, in scope and sequence charts, as if we actually did know the nature of the learning hierarchy in reading. Unfortunately, the reading task is so complex that it is highly questionable whether such a hierarchy in fact exists (Downing, 1982; Samuels, 1976b).

The basal reading programs provide a rather complete complement of teaching materials, including comprehensive teacher guides, practice workbooks, testing materials, ditto masters, instructional aids such as charts, word cards, "Big Books," game boxes, supplementary paperback library books, and dictionaries. However, the major components of basal programs are the readers themselves, which today are graded in difficulty from preprimers to sixth- or eighth-grade readers, or by levels. The *Ginn Reading 720*, Rainbow Edition, for example, is a 15-level program for grades K–8. The *Houghton Mifflin Reading Series* is another sample of a series that is organized by levels.

Basal readers are usually accompanied by a workbook that leads the child step by step through a carefully developed program of instruction. The workbook introduces the vocabulary and provides the experiential background needed for successful reading. It is especially useful in meeting individual needs, in stimulating interest in reading, in providing opportunities for practice, in varying instructional procedures, and in making optimum use of pupil and teacher time. The workbook offers the repetition, self-competition, and day-to-day records that make it possible for the pupil to grow and for the teacher to diagnose and to remediate the pupil's inadequacies. A teacher's manual is also provided to guide the teacher in day-to-day teaching.

It is important to note that workbooks and manuals may also work against good reading instruction. Teachers may become too reliant upon one or both. It is true as well that basal readers in their attempt to provide systematic instruction, controlled vocabularies, gradual and sequential introduction of skills, and mastery of the basic reading skills through repetition, ready-made seatwork, and review have perhaps failed to some degree in providing purposeful reading. It is unfortunate that too often basal reading teaching is at odds with the whole-language emphasis in reading today. It need not be so. A major drawback of basal readers is that activities and workbook exercises often are not coordinated with the narrative.

Despite the well-documented problems associated with basal reading programs, basal readers have been shown to be helpful in developing reading proficiency in most children, and certainly have helped thousands of teachers, especially inexperienced ones, to offer a fully developed reading program. The inconvertible truth is that probably 95% or more of elementary school teachers use a basal reading approach, even though the percentage of such usage is declining.

A recent book by Goodman et al. (1988) has little good to say about basal readers. Basal bashing is in vogue in some circles, but if recent opinion in *Reading Today* (October-November, 1989) is any criterion, perhaps their doom is not yet near. Basals, not unlike literature, are what teachers and children make of them. They are one piece of the puzzle. Basal readers can be used effectively even in a whole language setting. There is a place for the language experience story and for basal readers, and, as we shall emphasize shortly, for individualized reading and for literature-based reading.

THE INDIVIDUALIZED READING PROGRAM

We discuss individualized reading here more from an historical perspective than as a separate approach to reading. Teachers of reading spoke of individualized reading long before they spoke of "whole language." Today the whole-language approach has incorporated the basic concepts of individualized reading: namely, those of seeking, self-selection of materials, self-pacing, and flexible subgrouping in the classroom. Individualized reading (and, as we shall see later, whole language) represents a preference for literature-based reading. The principal reading materials in individualized reading are quality literature texts, even though the language-experience story has been integrated into the individualized-reading program.

Interest in individualized reading began in the early 1960s. In their thorough discussion of this approach, Veatch and Acinapuro (1978; Veatch, 1987) describe individualized reading as a self-selecting personalized approach. They emphasize use of the child's own language, particularly words that the child finds interesting and meaningful (thus incorporating the language-experience approach), self-selection of reading materials (thus putting high reliance on trade books), self-pacing, individual teacher-pupil conferences, and flexible subgrouping or specific task grouping. The philosophical base of this approach is Olsen's (1952) concepts of seeking, self-selection, and pacing. Individualized reading thus suggests that children seek what they are physiologically and psychologically ready for, and that they show their readiness through the spontaneous selection of the materials that they want to read. Self-selection is considered to be a necessary aspect of individualized reading. Teachers have always encouraged children to explore reading materials apart from those they have used in the classroom. In individualized reading, the pupil is encouraged to take a more active part in this selection of the materials.

The advantages claimed for individualized reading are many. Perhaps the most significant is the attitudinal change in the learner. Pupils tend to be more interested in reading, read more at home, show more interest in improvement and develop more favorable attitudes toward school in general, and often show improvement in work habits, self-motivation, and self-confidence. They seem to engage in more independent thinking and show better self-management.

In individualized reading, the purposes for reading are primarily individual and only secondarily group-related. The group serves as a sounding board for the individual to test the accuracy of the ideas acquired and to permit each child the luxury of sharing the knowledge and insight that has been acquired. The teacher thus works with the individual, detecting and providing for the pupil's needs as the pupil's work reveals them. The teacher keeps an accurate record of the pupil's accomplishments and inadequacies and helps him or her to pace activities in accordance with interests, aptitudes, and previous achievements.

Individualized reading does not seem suitable for pupils who cannot work independently or who cannot select or pace themselves wisely. It is not economical when instruction can be provided more simply and quickly in a group situation than in a one-to-one teacher-pupil conference. Additional disadvantages of individualized reading include the prospect of insufficient skill development; the heavy clerical burden that is put on the teacher; the difficulty of providing an adequate number of individual conferences; the problem of judging the difficulty of books and of guiding children in selection; the teacher's need to be familiar with a great number of books; and classroom control (Zintz, 1980).

If the individualized reading approach is used, the teacher should keep a card on each book which includes questions to test the pupil's comprehension, the numbers of those pages that have material suitable for oral reading, and a list of the vocabulary. Children should generally make their selections from a list or shelf of books preselected by the teacher. Each such shelf of books might contain one basal reader that the child must read prior to going on to other books. The effectiveness of the program depends on the number and quality of the reading materials. The need for many supplementary readers, magazines, and tradebooks on all levels of instruction in such a program is obvious. Equally important is the teacher's familiarity with the content and the reading difficulty of the books.

Today, individualized reading and language experience are merged. As Fields and Lee (1987) observe, the language experience approach lends itself to individualized instruction, and we would add that both of them lend themselves to whole language.

THE WHOLE-LANGUAGE PERSPECTIVE

Today, there is a major focus and emphasis on the "whole-language program" (Goodman, Smith, Meredith & Goodman, 1987). However, Smith (1988) decries the fact that "whole language" unfortunately has become a battlecry for so-called whole-language methods and materials, which Smith calls a "contradiction in terms" (p. 218). He argues that whole language "was originally a term connoting a philosophy of learning, opposed to artificial decontextualized exercises and drills. But as whole language has gained influence and prominence in education, the perspective has become distorted, the theory has become a method, and publishers have begun to produce 'whole language materials' " (p. 218).

A major theoretical premise of whole language is that children acquire language through using it and that they should therefore acquire reading fluency in a similar way. Numerous writers, including Smith (1988), emphasize that children learn to read by reading. Harp (1989) notes that one clear belief emerging through the Whole Language Movement is that literacy is acquired through use, and not through exercises (Altwerger, Edelsky, & Flores, 1987). Harp adds that children learn to comprehend reading material by reading; reading is comprehending; and no comprehension means no reading.

The term *whole language* today may have four encompassing interpretations: (a) that reading is best taught in a total or whole language arts context of reading, writing, speaking, and listening; (b) that reading is an holistic whole-language process rather than a skills-subskills process; (c) that whole-language teachers hold a "humanistic-scientific" view rather than a "behavior-mechanistic" view of learning (Goodman, et al., 1987, p. v); and (d) that reading is best taught through quality literature texts rather than through basal readers, and in a context of seeking, self-selection of reading materials, self-pacing, and flexible subgrouping on an interest or needs basis.

There is not much quarrel with the first of these views. Good teachers have been teaching reading in a total language context for years. The instructional philosophy of such teachers today is termed "whole language." It reflects the view that meaning and "natural language" are the basis of literacy learning (Smith, 1988). The position we present in this text is that reading should occur in the context of whole, real, and functional language and that it should begin with total or whole units (e.g., the language-experience story). And, it should involve the simultaneous and integrated teaching of reading, writing, speaking, and listening. Reading activities should include the daily reading of trade books, magazines, newspapers, bibliographies, poetry, and so on. Furthermore, language arts should be integrated with the content areas.

The second view, that reading is not and cannot be a skills-subskills process, will be addressed in the latter part of this section. Briefly, proponents of this view suggest that attempts to isolate component processes of reading result in tasks very much unlike reading. Harp (1989) thus observes that comprehension is not a subskill that can be practiced independently and separately from the act of reading. Whole-language advocates hold that reading should be taught as a language process. They reject the notion that reading is an accretion or summary of its parts or skills.

The third interpretation of whole language is less clear cut. Casting the issue in a learning-theory context raises many questions. Learning theory data are not so definitive that one can easily choose one theory over another. It seems possible that a teacher might be a whole-language advocate and be guided by a behavioristic theory of learning. Perhaps, Smith's (1988) description of whole language as a philosophy of learning better fits the data.

Traditionally, two sets of learning theories have evolved: behavioristic or stimulus-response theories and field or cognitive theories. Poplin (1988a, 1988b) categorizes learning theories as reductionism and holistic constructivism. From our perspective, the two alternative sets of theories (whether stimulus response versus field, or reductionism versus holistic constructivism) have a complimentary and a corrective effect. It is not an either-or position. The writer believes with Smith (1971) that learning, and indeed learning to read, cannot be understood if only one of the theories is adopted. "No theory can claim to offer a complete account" (Smith, 1988, p. 296).

Reductionism is defined by Poplin (1988a) as the natural process by which we break ideas, concepts, and skills into parts in an attempt to understand and deal better with the whole. The reductionists, as defined by Poplin, believe that:

1. A complex whole such as human learning is identical with its parts (e.g., neural processes, hypothetical/psychological processes, specific skills, or specific strategy behaviors) and that a complex whole can be entirely explained in terms of the description of its parts and of its causes (e.g., mental states are caused by neural processes; therefore, mental states are nothing but neural processes). Reductionists assume that that which has fewer parts or elements is more simple than that which has more. By extension, the speech-writing relationship is only a phoneme-grapheme relationship and reading is only a grapheme-phoneme relationship. Reductionists emphasize molecular rather than molar events.

2. The teaching/learning process is most effective when it is reduced or segmented into its parts.
3. Learning is a result of conditioned associations. Associations are formed primarily as a function of stimulus conditions that are external to a basically passive learner. Learning involves three variables—stimulation, response, and reward. Reductionists believe that all behavior is understood in terms of habits established by the reinforcement of a response or observable behavior in the presence of a particular stimulus. The teacher is the responsible agent who decides what is to be learned by the learner, and who provides and manipulates the external stimuli and the reinforcement that will lead to the desired learning.

Reductionists perceive learning as an additive process; it is the learning of habits. It is the establishing of a bond between a particular stimulus and a response. Reductionism assumes that the mere adding of stimulus-response (S-R) connections will result in a new and qualitatively different type of functioning. Reductionists attribute the child's difficulty in reading to a lack of S-R connections. The emphasis in the classroom is on giving information and on reciting and building more S-R connections. Education is the learning of as many responses as possible.

Poplin (1988a) identifies four models of reductionism and rejects each of them:

1. The medical model with its emphasis on neural processes, neurological functioning or malfunctioning, aberrant processing of information, diagnostic testing, and diagnostic-prescriptive teaching.
2. The psychological-process model with its emphasis on discrete hypothetical processes, on prerequisite skills (visual, auditory, and kinesthetic perception), on teaching to the sensory modalities, and on intra- and intersensory training.
3. The behavioral model with its emphasis on task analysis, on segmentation of learning, on isolated skill training, on time on task, on short-term instructional and behavioral objectives, on mastery learning, preprogrammed and sequentialized materials, and precision teaching, on behavior modification through manipulation of the external environment and through the application of reinforcement, and on the use of programmed learning systems and materials, skill-based workbooks, worksheets, skill practice, and rote learning activities.
   Constructivists reject the behavior-model's emphasis on coding

skills, letter-sound correspondences, word parts, and controlled vocabulary in reading; on vocabulary and pronunciation in language; and on punctuation, spelling and mechanics in writing. They also reject the view that taking natural language apart and cutting it into little pieces can benefit the learner the most or that the whole of reading can be taught by skill teaching. They disagree with the notion that there is a hierarchy of language skills *á la* the basal readers, that language learning can be readily sequenced and ordered, and that learning to read consists of sequential, hierarchical steps and scope and sequence charts.

4. The cognitive-science information-processing models, the cognitive-psychology information-processing model, or the cognitive-strategy models, with their emphasis on eye movements, on the use of computers, on the teaching of strategy behavior, on direct instruction, on the sequential and hierarchical steps in teaching a strategy, on ways to remember, on study skill techniques, on learning and cognitive styles, on cognitive behavior modification, and on metacognition, which may be defined as instructed "self-talk." Smith (1988) suggests that in information-processing models the metacognitive processes are yet another special set of skills which have to be learned. The information-processing model (Rayner & Pollatsek, 1989) views reading as a highly complex process relying on a number of subprocesses.

Heshusius (1989) notes that each of the above models reduces (hence reductionism) the child to understand him. Each claims that the child's learning problem lies within the child (each is deficit driven), each segments learning into parts, and each favors a bottom-up approach to literacy.

Holistic constructivists have a different set of beliefs than reductionists. They maintain, and I believe, rightly so, that their differences with reductionism are not merely attitudinal as Kimball and Heron (1988) suggest, nor merely terminological, as Carnine (1987) would have us believe. Their formulations are not merely "fuzzy," "intuitive" (Lloyd, 1987), "naive," or "mystical" (Kaufman, 1987). There are indeed attitudinal and terminological differences, but these differences, they note, have led to very different instructional processes (Rettinger, Waters, & Poplin, 1989).

Holistic constructivists are more concerned with central or within-brain intermediaries (e.g., understanding and meaning) than with S-R connections. They emphasize the pupil's thought process rather than the observable response. They perceive reading as a creative and constructive activity that is purposeful, selective, and anticipatory (Smith, 1988). They perceive learners as experience-seekers, as creative decision-makers, rather than creatures of habit (Smith, 1988). Learners are perceived as "selective and self-directed in their interactions with the world" (Smith, 1988, p. 295).

Constructivists define learning/reading as the natural, continuous construction and reconstruction of new, richer, and more complex and connected meanings. Learning is the acquisition of knowledge, but it is not simply the taking in of information. Learning is not simply additive or incremental, it is transformative. New knowledge is not simply added to previous knowledge; it rather transforms the old. Learning is understanding relations. Learning is the modification or elaboration of what is already known as a consequence of our interactions with the world around us (Smith, 1988). Children learn by constructing and reconstructing richer and newer meanings.

An emerging emphasis (Heshusius, 1989) in holism-constructivism is that meaning, context, personal purpose, and social interchange alter the learning situation, redefine learning, and change the nature of the task. Knowledge and knowing are perceived "as direct outcomes of processes of social interactions" (Heshusius, 1989, p. 409). Holists believe that the context within which learning occurs is an important determinant of what is learned. This is particularly so when what is learned has personal use and purpose for the learner, and when the learner feels that he has ownership in the very formulation of the problem.

Constructivists emphasize molar rather than molecular units in learning. They believe that the properties of the parts can only be understood from the dynamics of the whole. Parts receive their meaning from the context in which they occur. The whole is both different from and more than the sum of its parts, and is not predictable from its parts .(Heshusius, 1989). Holists note that a melody is qualitatively different from a series of notes, water is no longer water when broken into its elements or molecular units, and a picture is more than spots of paint. The whole is thus more than a simple combination of elements, of psychological processes, skills, or strategies. A word is more than a series of letters; and the meaning of a sentence is more than the sum total of the meanings of the individual words of that sentence. Reading is not a process of combining individual letters into words and strings of words into sentences from which meanings spring automatically.

Reading for holists is more than grapheme-phoneme correspondences. Learning/reading involves more than the mastery of facts, skills, processes, or strategies. Constructivists argue that learning is not best accomplished in a piecemeal incremental fashion (e.g., by task analysis or by formulating behavior objectives taken from scope and sequence charts).

For the holistic constructivists, learning occurs by reorganization rather than by accretion. Their emphasis is on the importance of structuring and the seeking of "insightful" solutions rather than on trial-and-error solutions. The laws of organization are not principles of connection; rather, constructionists describe structures as emerging. The learner learns relationships and differentiations, expectancies and meanings rather than movements or S-R connections. While working with the addition of fractions, children often solve a problem such as $3/8 + 2/8 = ?$, but many of them are stumped when they face problems such as $? = 8/8 + 2/8$. Before they have any continuous success with this type of problem, they have to work with rewriting the formula, addend + addend = sum. Once they discover the relationships of the various parts of the formula, their difficulties are alleviated. The teacher's role is to structure the situation so that the pupil can perceive relationships.

Reality for the holistic constructivists is "meaning." An object may exist but have no meaning for a given individual. A child has no meaning for playing jacks if he has never watched or played the game. The words "bumper crops" have no meaning to a child who associates bumper with automobile bumpers.

Constructivists see the teacher's role as one of guiding and facilitating. The teacher is perceived as "a cheerleader" and a "kid-watcher." Constructivists reject the view that learning occurs most efficiently under controlled situations, when the teacher serves as selector, controller, deliverer of content, interrogator, and manager of behavior. They believe that the learner should not be reduced to a passive responder or sponge (Poplin, 1988a, 1988b). Passively responding to the teacher's agenda is not active involvement in the learning process. The reading and comprehension processes are not static. The reading process must involve the learner in actively inferring, connecting, and summarizing (Irwin & Baker, 1989).

Constructivists stress natural curiosity, affect, intuition, interest, self-concept, connectedness, expectation, and relevancy as primary forces in learning. They see learning as an effortless process, which does not need irrelevant inducements or extrinsic reinforcement. The latter become "necessary only when a child is confronted with something that does not make sense. And forcing a child to attend to nonsense is a pointless enterprise in any case" (Smith, 1988, p. 189). If a child needs reinforcement for learning, "the child does not see any sense in attempting the learning in the first place" (Smith, 1988, p. 189).

Pupils are always learning. "Learning is a continuous process, a natural state of the brain, and children therefore are likely to be learning all the time" (Smith, 1988, p. 189). One cannot stop learning. The learning spiral never stops turning. Even slow learners often become so interested in what they are doing that their learning disability becomes invisible. Making sense of things, making sense of what is read, is a never-ending search for and construction of personal meanings.

From the holistic perspective, learners are inherently active and constructive rather than passive and reactive; they are self-generating, constantly constructing meanings and constantly judging the personal relevance of what is to be learned relative to what they already know (Heshusius, 1989). They are self-regulating and self-organizing and are constantly transforming reality.

Holists observe that learners will generally avoid transformation of anything that creates too much mental disequilibrium or mental discomfort. They will stop trying to learn what is too difficult or irrelevant for them. Heshusius (1989) aptly notes that the observer shapes and creates the observed. A poor reader thus often works actively at not reading when the mental disequilibrium is too great. In his deeply felt desire not to be labeled a poor reader, a situation which he deems intolerable and threatening, the learner may save face by removing himself from the context. Heshusius (1989) cites other examples from McKean (1985) and Erickson (1984). A mentally retarded child may not be able to trace his way out of a simple paper maze, which he finds irrelevant, but finds a way to escape from a 24-hour supervised institution. Someone may be unable to work a simple arithmetic problem on a worksheet, but readily deals with the same problem when giving or receiving change at a grocery store. Learners tend to translate or transform new experiences into a context that is meaningful to themselves. Thus, the transformations of children from different cultures often result in the taking of different meanings to and from the printed page.

Constructivists believe that errors are essential to learning. According to Poplin (1988b):

> The spiral of knowledge is best served when students perceive that what they now see or need is not explainable or solvable by previous knowledge; thus new knowledge must be constructed—and the spiral begins to productively deal with the incongruence (equilibration). This happens, provided that previous experience with the content is developed to the point where errors can be recognized by learners themselves.... The recognition of error (disequilibrium) is a critical part of the complex system of self-regulation and self-preservation in learning. (p. 409)

Constructivists focus on errors in conceptualization or on those that do not maintain the meaning rather than on errors in form and mechanics. The errors of the learner are perceived as opportunities for diagnosis, for developing insight into how the learner reasons (Heshusius, 1989), and for finding out why the pupil answered as she did (Irwin & Baker, 1989). Was she using the wrong prior knowledge? Or did she forget to use prior knowledge? Did she fail to make a critical inference? Constructivists believe that rather than concentrating on pupil deficits, the teacher should seek out pupil strengths and interests. Learners learn (Smith, 1988) by demonstrations (i.e., the opportunity to see what can be done and how) and by engagement (i.e., being involved in the demonstration). Children learn in a social context by seeing what other people do and by being helped by these people to do.

In summary, constructionists believe that reading and comprehension are schema theory–based rather than associationistic; that reading involves global processes more than analytic processes; and that the reader should be more concerned with meaning than with the memorization and accumulation of isolated facts.

Although there are vast differences in approach between reductionists and constructivists, good teachers are able to integrate both. It is unfortunate that some whole-language advocates, at least in their public writing, seem to totally disparage the reductionist position. There is a real danger that the whole-language advocacy may result in all reading teaching becoming exclusively top-down with little or no focus on bottom-up.

WHOLE LANGUAGE AND LITERATURE-BASED READING

The whole-language movement, to its credit, has given renewed attention to surrounding children with "real" books (Tunnell & Jacobs, 1989). Hiebert and Colt (1989) observe that a literature-based program provides children with many varied opportunities to read high-quality literature in authentic reading situations.

Numerous studies (Boehnlein, 1987; Eldredge & Butterfield, 1986; Larrick, 1987; Reutzel and Fawson, 1988; Tunnel, 1986; Weaver, 1988; White, Vaughan, & Rorie, 1986) have lent support to literature-based reading, especially when it is teamed with recoding lessons (Eldredge & Butterfield, 1986: Trachtenburg, 1990). Trade books offer children extraordinary richness in vocabulary, sentence structure, and literary form.

The basic characteristics of a whole-language literature-based program are (Tunnell & Jacobs, 1989; Weaver, 1988):

1. Pupils both tell and read stories daily. Uninterrupted sustained silent reading (USSR) is a part of the daily program.
2. Children's literature provides much of the reading content. Children experience an early, natural exposure to literature, and are given numerous opportunities for reading "real" literature (Stoodt, 1989). However, giving a story a new format does not

necessarily make it "real" literature. A good story in a basal reader may be as "real" as a story in a trade book.
3. Advocates of whole-language literature-based programs often believe that reading skills are acquired in much the same way as learning to speak. We would caution that it is not that simple. Smith (1988) notes there is a distinct difference between the comprehension of written language and speech: In reading, "the reader must use the distinctive features of print to test predictions and reduce uncertainty" (p. 160.). He adds further that the conventions for using vocabulary and grammar are different in speech and reading. There are additional rules governing spelling, punctuation, formation of letters, size of type, capitalization, paragraphing, page layout, etc. Smith also observes that teaching children that reading and speech are the same will cause children to have difficulty in learning to read and in predicting and comprehending the conventions of written language. Undoubtedly children learn to read by reading, but reading alone cannot compensate for effective teaching of reading.
4. The emphasis is on natural text, on using children's literature written in a natural, uncontrolled language. There is no control of vocabulary, and even readability control is minimized.
5. Cooperative learning (Hiebert & Colt, 1989) is fostered. The neurological impress method, repeated reading, paired cooperative reading, peer tutoring, and team activities are frequently used in beginning reading programs. (See chapter 7 for a description of these). Teachers spend a significant portion of time reading aloud to children from enjoyable trade books. Being read to "is the essential element in the backgrounds of natural readers" (Tunnell & Jacobs, 1989). Children who cannot read are especially "dependent on being read to, or at least on being assisted to read" (Smith, 1988, p. 161).
6. There is a natural and reciprocal relationship between listening to literature and the desire and ability to read (Roser, 1987).
7. Teachers serve as models: teachers present new books with whole-hearted enjoyment; they themselves read during sustained silent reading sessions; and they value reading. Even more important is that they convey their interest and enthusiasm to children.
8. The program puts special emphasis on changing pupil attitudes: it seeks to develop learners who love to read. It teaches children not only "how to read, but to want to read" (Trelease, 1985, p. 6). The curriculum thus puts major emphasis on children's interests, abilities, and needs. Smith (1988) aptly notes: "Reading is inter-

esting and relevant when it can be related to what the reader wants to know" (p. 167).

9. An element of self-selection of literature-based materials is usually present.
10. The program has a meaning orientation with skill teaching occurring in meaningful, actual reading contexts (Heymsfeld, 1990). Trachtenburg (1990) emphasizes contextualized phonics teaching and recommends a whole-part-whole sequence in integrating phonics with quality literature. She notes that this framework integrates learning to read with real reading and will produce learners who not only can read, but who will choose to read. Surely, children develop accuracy and automaticity in word identification at least partly as a consequence of frequent and extensive reading. However, (Aaron et al., 1990) note: "I would not want to say all you've got to do is read children's books. Somebodys got to teach children, including phonics and hopefully other word recognition techniques along with it—and systematically" (p. 308).
11. A pre-and/or post-reading activity occurs each day. One of the key facets of whole language is instruction in authorship (Lamme, 1989): children write and develop their own materials. The writing-to-reading emphasis is an integral part of the whole-language emphasis (Rettinger, Walters, & Poplin, 1989).
12. The emphasis, especially in the primary grades, is on discovery learning rather than on reception-learning.

In summary, we believe that reading is taught best and children are benefited most where whole language is a guiding principle in teaching reading and when the pupil is exposed to texts of various types (e.g., the language-experience story, basal readers, literature books, and content texts). Basal readers and quality literature are not mutually exclusive; rather, their conjoint use is strongly indicated. And, we caution that to this date the difficulties, the disadvantages, or the shortcomings of the exclusive use of whole language have not been adequately addressed.

WHOLE LANGUAGE AND SKILL TEACHING

The position that we took in chapter 1 is that reading is an interactive process which begins as a top-down process, but almost simultaneously and in parallel moves back and forth between a top-down and bottom-up process. How does this view fit with what we have described to this point in this chapter? We argue along with Smith (1988) that whole language is not a method; it is a philosophy, a point of view, particularly about the optimum environment for learning. In Smith's (1988) words:

> The analysis I have made *cannot* be translated into a system for teaching, though it can indeed be translated into an *environment* for learning. In fact, the analysis explains environments in which children do learn to read . . . These are environments in which written language makes sense, and in which an autonomous program-independent teacher has a critical role. (p. 206, italics added).

The holistic-constructivist lens reveals a different view of the classroom, a view we want to emphasize. It is a view that should guide us. It is, however, not totally explanatory of children's behavior and learning. Learning must indeed be learner centered, contextualized, and holistic; it must emphasize independence or self-directedness in learning. It needs to pay more than lip service to the learner's inherent activeness, a learner who is in a constant, steady state of neural excitation and who is growth oriented. We also argue that whole language and stimulus-response learning are not contradictory of each other, and neither are whole language and skill-teaching. Whole language can be combined effectively with skill-teaching (Heymsfeld, 1990). Strategy instruction, for example, in its best form is not just another behavioral intervention. It does not have to be training of isolated skills (Reid, 1988). Skill teaching, strategy instruction, reciprocal teaching, and direct instruction can be personalized, contextualized, socialized, and interactive.

We argue that parts are best understood within the dynamic and mutable context of the whole, and phonics and morphemics teaching should indeed occur only "in the context of the students' own sentences and stories" (Poplin, 1988b, p. 408). Teachers need to examine the whole and its parts, regularity and diversity, isolability and interrelatedness (Reid, 1988).

Beginning readers are not language beginners, but they are beginners in reading. It is because of this that, even though teaching is best (e.g., the language-experience story) when it begins with wholes, reading teaching must often go to the parts. The perceptual whole is not an absolute whole. It differs from learner to learner. For some child the perceptual whole may be a sentence; for another it may be a word or even a letter.

We agree with constructionist Poplin (1988b) that the search for meaning "involves a process of creating meaning about the ideas, as a whole, the specific parts, and then back to the whole again" (p. 408). She adds, "Learning involves a process of going from whole to part to whole with accurate forms (parts) being secondary to the whole (Poplin, 1988b, p. 414)." It is exactly this approach that we advocate in this chapter and that later we espouse in the Integrated Reading Method. Reading instruction should begin and end in whole language. The word must be put back into the context of the sentence and the sentence into the paragraph context.

Poplin (1988b) observes that we begin as young children, writing whole meaningful messages by scribbling, and as we become more conscious of the language, we begin to intuitively understand the parts — the spelling and grammar — of our language. However, she adds that if spelling and grammar rules are overemphasized or if the instruction in accuracy of form is premature, the learner may become dysfluent:

> This dysfluency is most noticeable in a decrease in production in writing or the failure to achieve any fluency at all, due to excessive and premature attention to producing the parts.... In reading, dysfluency is noted when children begin to depend too much on sounding out words in the text, thus stalling the process and frequently causing a concomitant loss in understanding. The whole must be fully grasped before the parts can be related to current knowledge; otherwise, there is no scaffolding to attach the specifics, the parts. (p. 414)

Thus, Poplin, even though a staunch holistic constructivist, clearly points out that learning involves a whole-part-whole dynamic. It is a fact that for some learners, whose perceptual whole may be less than a word, sentence, or a story, beginning instruction may have to focus on parts. But even that part is a whole to them. Thus indeed all learning must of necessity begin with the whole. Reductionist teaching strategies are clearly effective in teaching the parts. The major inadequacy of the reductionist strategy is that too often it starts and ends with the parts (Poplin, 1988b).

We agree with Goodman et al. (1987) that the central or primary goal of reading teaching is the construction of a meaning "that substantially agrees with that of the author" (p. 249). But we also call attention to their observations that a subsidiary goal includes strategies for sampling and selecting graphic-phonic cues. A few pages later, Goodman et al. observe that teachers should assure "that children develop the alphabetic principle" (p. 254). They add that "we learn to use print-sound relationships in the context of trying to make sense of print" (p. 398).

The top-down theorist Smith (1988) repeatedly addresses himself to part: He gives a tripart description of memory, divides knowledge into categories and schemata, has chapters on teaching of letters and words, and talks about using mediated word identification and mediated meaning identification from context. He argues against letter-by-letter identification of words and leaves "no room for decoding to sound" (p. 163). He does, however, see a role for phonics when the child knows the meaning of the word but does not know its name.

Smith (1988) observes that "meaning is the most important nonvisual information" (p. 81). But, throughout his text he identifies nonvisual information with a knowledge of "specific aspects of written language such as the way spelling patterns are formed" (pp. 80–81); with knowledge of "anything that can reduce the number of alternatives the brain must consider as we read" (p. 81); "with an understanding of the conventions of texts" (p. 198); with knowing "about the way letters go together in words" (p. 155); with knowing "about the way words go together in grammatical and meaningful phrases" (p. 155); and with the knowledge of discourse structures and story grammar.

There is absolutely no constructive way of reading Smith's text without going from whole to part to whole. Similarly, we argue that whole language can be harmonized with the whole-part-whole or interactive position. It can be reconciled with the teaching of strategies and the development of skills. But skill teaching needs to involve the pupil actively in seeking meaning; it needs to be interesting, relevant, a part of a real event (Goodman, 1986). Skills cannot be taught in isolation from the use of the application of the strategy to meaningful reading tasks and to real-world problems (Gersten, Carnine, & White, 1984). Skill teaching is not a goal onto itself; possessing a set of discrete skills ensures nothing (Eisner, 1983). Strategy instruction should teach the pupil to take conscious control over the process. Skill teaching needs to be in an environment in which teacher and pupil are constantly interacting.

The holistic-whole language and the skills-subskills views each have a long history. Guthrie (1973) suggests that reading is a unitary process in good readers in which subskills are integrated into a holistic or unitary process. The holistic emphasis is on the interrelatedness of all the facets of reading: readers and the knowledge they bring to the reading material (Stevens, 1980), the interactions between the reader and the reading material, and the reading environment. Reading is clearly more than an aggregation of small, sequential, and hierarchial enabling skills (Valencia & Pearson, 1987; Wixson et al., 1987). Davis (1968), on the other hand, factored reading into subskills. Traditionally, comprehension has been developed through the direct teaching of specific reading subskills (such as identifying the main idea, recognizing important facts, following directions, making inferences). The subskills approach has resulted in the development of various taxonomies (Barrett, 1972, 1974; Barrett and Smith, 1974, 1979; Bloom, 1956, 1968; Lanier & Davis, 1972).

This book has been developed within a holistic-subskills context, in which the teaching of subskills is integrated into a whole reading act. The important principle is that reading begins with the total act, with the reading of meaningful materials. In the words of Downing and Leong (1982), "It cannot be emphasized too strongly that reading is a skill where children need to perform different levels of subskills in an integrated manner"

(p. 319). Jenkins and Pany (1981) note that "the purpose of learning a subskill is to transfer its use to natural reading contexts; and the goal of reading instruction is to transfer *all* subskills a reader has learned to reading texts in a fluent manner with adequate comprehension." We also argue that the concept of subskills and task analysis is valid and that the development of skills and subskills must be a continuing concern of the classroom teacher. Task analysis has proved to be an effective procedure for developing a progressive series of linked steps (Kimball & Heron, 1988).

Skill teaching need not focus only on the components. It need not be static. The holistic or separate skills views of reading are both right and, to some degree, both wrong. Seeing a word as simply a whole and seeing it as a "whole with parts" are not the same, and we argue that the latter is preferable. Conversely, skill teaching and task analysis in isolation, without a meaningful context, and without an eye on the goal will fall far short of the target.

Poor readers are such precisely because they have not integrated the subskills; they have not integrated the skills in their minds in such a way as to be in tune with a writer; like the child who cannot swim, they have learned to breathe and to move their arms and legs, but they often cannot integrate and coordinate these in such a way as to be able to swim (Burmeister, 1983).

If both the holistic and subskills emphasis are valid (and we believe they are), then skill teaching necessarily becomes a major focus and a necessary component of good teaching of reading. Combining the best aspects of whole language and direct instruction seems best.

SUMMARY

Chapter 6 emphasizes that children learn to read by reading and that this means reading of something. We recommend that reading begin with language experience. The language experience–individualized reading approach has much to offer. The language-experience approach, in particular, assures that the pupil initially reads materials based on his own experiences, his own schemata, and his own language.

The next chapter discusses the directed reading activity, in which the sixth, or final, step is designed to provide enrichment and follow-up activities in the daily reading lesson. It is here that individualized reading and literature-based reading seem to fit best, and where, from this writer's perspective, all the beneficial aspects of individualized reading are optimally utilized. Every reading lesson should allow for some free and wide reading so that every child can experience the pleasure of reading. Individualized reading, allowing for self-selection of a book that is written on the pupil's own independent level, provides this in an optimal way.

Chapter 6 also points out that it is in the merging of language experience, individualized reading, and a literature-based program that whole language functions best. It is in such a program that children daily are read to, read, tell stories, and write. With this combined approach, children experience cooperative learning and see the teacher as a model. These children both learn to read and to want to read.

Whole language means teaching reading in a whole-language arts context. It establishes an environment where the emphasis is on meaning; where learners are viewed as active experience-seekers and decision-makers; where learning is thought to be transformative rather than simply additive; where molar units are emphasized and where the whole (reading) is not simply the aggregate of skills or strategies; and where the teacher is thought of as a guide, facilitator, and collaborator.

Chapter 6 also stresses that whole language and skill-teaching are compatible and that the interactive model, moving from whole to part to whole, explains what happens in reading better than do either the top-down or bottom-up model singly.

Chapter 7
Programming the Reading Lesson: Using a Modified Directed-Reading Activity

I. Introduction
II. Developing Readiness for Reading a Selection
    A. Developing and Focusing Attention and Motivation for Reading
        1. Attention
        2. Motivation and Interest
    B. Developing a Purpose for Reading
    C. Activating and Building Upon the Pupil's Schema in the Comprehension of Text
    D. Facilitating the Schema-Building Process
        1. Developing Automaticity in Word Recognition
        2. Developing Meaning for Words
    E. Raising Questions Prior to Reading
    F. Developing a Hypothesizing/Predicting Strategy
    G. Developing Readiness for Reading Expository Materials
III. Guided Silent Reading
    A. Segmentation of Text and the Global Purpose
    B. Continuing the Hypothesizing/Predicting Strategy
    C. Continuing the Self-Questioning Strategy
    D. Monitoring Predictions and Comprehension
IV. Evaluating and Developing Comprehension
    A. Levels of Comprehending
    B. Additional Strategies for Use in the Content Areas
    C. Using Questioning With Groups
    D. Evaluating Pupil Comprehension
V. Oral Rereading of the Materials
VI. Extending Word Recognition and Comprehension Skills
VII. Enrichment and Follow-up Activities
VIII. Summary

CHAPTER 7
Programming the Reading Lesson: Using a Modified Directed-Reading Activity

Whether the pupil is introduced to reading through the language-experience approach, the basal reader, individualized reading, trade books, a combination of all of these, or whole language, there is a continuous need to structure and integrate teaching of reading and of word-identification and comprehension skills. The Directed Reading Activity (DRA), originally described by Betts (1946), is helpful in doing this. It is a highly useful format for structuring a reading lesson. This is particularly so when it incorporates the best of the Directed Reading-Thinking Activity (DRTA) (Stauffer, 1975), the guided reading-thinking lesson (Hittelman, 1983, 1988), and the Guided Reading Procedure (Manzo, 1975, 1985). Collectively, these identify what should happen before, during, and after reading.

Some may suggest that there is no need for structuring the reading lesson. To them we simply reply that such a suggestion implies "that thinking in advance of acting is inappropriate" (Mallan & Hersh, 1972, p. 41). Vacca and Vacca (1986, 1989) note that good lesson planning is a "framework for making decisions—nothing more, nothing less" (1986, p. 349). The simple fact is that what the teacher and the pupil do before, during, and after reading does make a difference.

We do not suggest that each directed reading activity must take place in a single class session. Several sessions may well be needed. Nor are we suggesting that each of the six steps of the DRA must be given equal emphasis every day. The need for pupil guidance clearly varies from day to day and from assignment to assignment.

The six steps of the directed-reading activity are:

1. Developing readiness for reading a selection
2. Guided silent reading
3. Evaluating and developing comprehension
4. Oral reading of the material
5. Extending word recognition and comprehension skills
6. Enrichment and follow-up activities

DEVEOLOPING READINESS FOR READING A SELECTION

The importance of readiness was identified by Fredrick Herbart in the 1840s. He made preparation the first step in his five-step teaching model. Thorndike (1913) formulated the Law of Readiness and the Law of Set. The readiness concept simply suggests that what happens prior to learning makes a difference in the quality and quantity of what is learned. Teachers must come to realize that time spent preparing students for the reading experience is at least as important as time spent discussing the reading (Early & Sawyer, 1984). Schema theory suggests that pupils are aided when they activate appropriate schemata before reading. There is a real need for some word recognition and comprehension instruction to occur before reading.

Developing readiness or a mental set for reading includes focusing of attention; creating curiosity, interest, and motivation for reading; setting a purpose for silent reading; relating the concepts in the text to the previous experiences of the reader; expanding the conceptual and experiential background of readers, including their vocabulary; raising questions prior to the reading; and developing a hypothesizing/predicting-confirming/rejecting strategy.

Developing and Focusing Attention and Motivation for Reading

Studies consistently point to the importance of getting the pupil's attention, creating interest, and motivating the reader to want to read. There is a direct relationship between reading success and these factors.

Attention

The pupil must attend to the reading task. The pupil must be "set" to respond. Learning and memory occur only if the pupil will attend to and concentrate on the task at hand. Inability to maintain sustained attention, inability to screen out distractions, short attention spans, hyperactivity, and impulsiveness are all major problems for poor readers. Stott (1973) observes that overriding causes of reading failure often are lack of attention and withdrawal from the learning task.

Motivation and Interest

Readiness for and achievement in reading, indeed learning to read and improvement in reading, are dependent also on certain motivations and upon interest. To achieve in reading the pupil must want to learn. Motivation, interest, and attention are closely related. Interest is a major initiator of motivated behavior. It predisposes an organism to certain lines of activity. It promotes the tendency to give selective attention to something. To increase reading skill, promote the reading habit, and produce a generation of book lovers, there is no other factor so powerful as interest. When pupils are interested, they are more likely to spend more time and more energy on the reading task.

Interest determines not only the area within which children will make their reading choices, but more importantly it determines how much children will read and whether they will read at all. Furthermore, there is a direct relationship of interest to reading comprehension. Asher, Hymel, and Wigfield (1976) found that both boys and girls comprehend better materials in which they are highly interested. Children who are motivated and interested tend to maximize their comprehension. A positive attitude towards reading aids comprehension (Matthewson, 1976, 1985).

The whole concept of readiness is to help pupils to establish a need to know. Step 1 of the DRA should develop a mental disequilibrium which leaves the pupil unhappy at not knowing. In his book *Language in Thought and Action* (1964), Hayakawa terms motivation the *cerebral itch*. The variables that relate to reading are numerous, but motivation is primary. Reduce motivation to zero and all other factors pale into insignificance. Without it, intelligence and many other positive factors are neutralized; with it, the pupil can make amazing compensations for such negative factors as physical deficiency, limited experience, and even low intelligence.

The first aim of reading should be to produce children who *want* to read and who *do* read. The reading habit may be the most important academic aim of the school. Psycholinguists (Krashen, 1987; Smith, 1978, 1988) emphasize that pupils learn to read and indeed grow in reading ability primarily by reading.

The teacher can focus attention and create interest and motivation for wanting to read a selection by:

1. Reading to children and sharing one's love for reading. No activity motivates children to read and develops a love of reading more than a teacher who communicates enthusiasm and an appreciation

of literature through his attitudes and example (Perez, 1986). Children tend to become good readers when they are read to by parents and teachers, when parents and teachers serve as models, and when varied materials are available to the child (Jewell & Zintz, 1986). The value of reading orally to children is well documented (Jewell & Zintz, 1986; Krashen, 1987). The single most important activity for building the knowledge required for eventual success in reading may be reading aloud to children (Anderson et al., 1985; Michener, 1988). Children read more when there are books around, when their homes contain many books, and when they are read to (Krashen, 1987).
2. Providing materials that are interesting and of appropriate difficulty. Introduce children, especially poor readers, to low-difficulty, high-interest materials. Provide a wide selection of easy reading materials—materials which pupils read, not must read. Guide children to books they can read on an independent level. While interest in a book is a powerful motivational factor, interest alone is not enough to make a difficult book easy to read. The book needs to be interesting and readable.
3. Helping each child to find materials of appropriate content. Do not emphasize literary content only. The stories should be about children and heroes and about people with whom the reader can identify. Children should discover in books the way to a world of information and adventure.
4. Giving children an opportunity to share their reading experiences through book reports, panels, or round-table discussion. Permit pupils to discuss the author, plot, theme, setting, and style.
5. Helping pupils look upon themselves as readers. Self-concept is closely related to reading success. A pupil who does not see himself or herself as a reader is not likely to develop the reading habit.
6. Organizing reading around meaningful activities (Eeds, 1981), especially with slow learners. Teaching should stress life-related functional reading. Reading should help pupils to cope with daily living (e.g., reading directions for building something, reading about how to get a checking account, etc.); it should help pupils to communicate (have students read historical books, let them write letters to one another, etc.); and it should help pupils to make sense out of life's experiences. The older pupil needs to learn the working vocabulary required in a future job, how to read and fill out application blanks, to be able to read telephone books, city directories, road maps, street guides, menus, recipes, directions, radio and theater programs, advertisements, catalogues, want-

ads, and newspapers, and to become thoroughly familiar with the dictionary and tables of contents and indices.

Dechant (1982) as do many other writers, presents numerous additional activities to whet children's interest in reading.

Developing a Purpose for Reading

Readers also comprehend better when they have a purpose for reading. If pupils are to understand what they are reading, they must know why they are reading. They must know whether to read for information, to solve a problem, to follow directions, to be entertained, to obtain details, to draw a conclusion, to verify a statement, to summarize, or to criticize (Dechant, 1964). Purpose may involve updating knowledge or integrating new information with old, confirming and disconfirming predictions, identifying the structure of the text, applying a strategy and understanding how, when, and why the strategy works, or reading for pleasure and appreciation (Blanton, Wood, and Moorman, 1990).

The teacher commonly sets the purpose or directions for reading by giving a few introductory remarks about the content of the story and by offering a guiding statement such as "read to find out, . . " The ultimate purpose is good comprehension of the text. The purpose-setting activities should provide a framework for the organization of events and concepts within the text so that the various facets of the text become interrelated and thus more memorable. Usually, a single purpose for reading is more effective than are multiple purposes (Blanton, Wood, and Moorman, 1990).

Developing a purpose for reading or setting overall goals for comprehension usually takes the form of a global question that requires the learner to read the entire selection and synthesize what has been read (Pieronek, 1979). The global question develops a searching attitude on the part of the reader (Singer, 1978). It calls the pupil's attention to the material and motivates the pupil to want to read the material. It may take the form of "As you read this story I want you to think of the following question, . . ." Hittelman (1983) recommends that the pupil rather than the teacher identify the purpose for reading. If the pupil can do so, this is surely desirable, but initially in most situations the purpose may well represent the coordinated product of both teacher and pupil. Nonetheless, instruction in purpose setting should equip pupils to set their own purpose (Blanton, Wood and Moorman, 1990).

The question technique, in the form of a purpose-generating question, is clearly an effective way for developing a purpose for reading (Rowe and Rayford, 1987). Purpose-generating questions help to activate personal schemata and aid in making predictions about passage content. The purpose-setting question should be answerable only after the pupil has read all or most of the story. Purpose should be sustained throughout the reading and a discussion of the purpose should be the first post-reading activity (Blanton, Wood, and Moorman, 1990). The purpose question guides the reader to an overall view or to the basic idea of what is read.

The purpose for reading should always include:

1. The determination to make sense out of what is read. The search for meaning is the ultimate purpose for reading. Poor readers and young readers often focus primarily upon reading as a recoding process rather than as a meaning-getting process.
2. The bridging of the gap between what is known and the new information in the printed material. In short, a purpose of reading should be to make sense out of written material by relating new information to that which is already known.
3. The intention to think with the information, to make predictions and to hypothesize. Many times, the pupil's major concern is simply to answer the teacher's questions. It is more likely that pupils whose purpose is to form predictions and to either confirm or reject those predictions, will think with the material as they read. Thus, a major study strategy of setting purposes for reading may be accomplished (Tierney, Readance, & Dishner, 1980; 1985) by having pupils predict what the story will be about from the title of the story, from illustrations that accompany the narrative, from a few key words, from a few key sentences, or from the introductory or closing paragraph.

Activating and Building Upon the Pupil's Schema in the Comprehension of Text

Activating the pupil's existing schemata is another important way to develop readiness for reading (Reutzel, 1985b). It is not enough that readers have schemata; the schemata must be activated as semantic context (McIntosh, 1985). Reader's schemata determine to what degree they can bring meaning to the printed page. They determine what pupils will comprehend and how well they will comprehend (Tierney & Cunningham, 1984). In short, what the pupil knows affects what is learned from reading.

New words in the text will take on meaning only if they arouse previous conceptual associations; if new concepts are related to the old and familiar concepts. New concepts can be learned only in relation to concepts already known. The old concepts provide anchors for the new information. Pupils should be constantly asking themselves: "How is this concept like a concept that I already know and how is it different?" The teacher needs to ask constantly: "What does the child know that is enough like the new concepts so that I can use it as an anchor point?" (Pearson, 1985).

The reader's schema is what the reader brings to the printed page. Schemata guide comprehension, and helping pupils to organize their prior information and to apply it to what is being read is critical to improving their comprehension (Gillett & Temple, 1986). Good comprehenders use their knowledge of the world (semantic context) and their knowledge of how language works (syntactic context) to construct meaning from text.

Schemata that have special significance in reading and comprehension are those of the different types of discourse: namely, (a) narrative schemata or story grammars consisting of setting, theme, plot, and resolution, and (b) expository discourse consisting of superordinate, coordinate, and subordinate concepts and ideas. Providing pupils with the schemata of narrative and expository discourse and their respective organization improves pupil's comprehension when they read such materials.

The teacher (Dechant, 1982; Early & Sawyer, 1984; Flood, 1986) additionally aids pupils in relating what they are reading to their personal schema by:

1. Setting purposes for reading. This often takes the form of providing objectives.
2. Having students write down what they already know about the topic.
3. Having pupils read about similar content in other books or reading from other books to the pupils prior to reading the assignment.
4. Delivering a short lecture on the subject before the pupil reads.
5. Having pupils read the table of contents and then discuss the logic of the chapter organization. The teacher might ask pupils to suggest alternative ways of organizing the chapter (Roe, Stoodt, & Burns, 1983). The teacher should point out the material's organizational features and diagram the content (e.g., making visuals of a text, especially of the main headings, and projecting them on a screen).
6. Using concrete materials, field trips, role playing, films, filmstrips, illustrations, or other graphics to illustrate the content or having pupils listen to tapes.
7. Having pupils preview or survey what the selection is about. Previewing, especially of expository materials, provides an opportunity to review prior knowledge (Irwin, 1986a). As pupils preview, the teacher might have them discuss what they already know, write key concepts on the board, and speculate what they might expect from the reading.

8. Asking pupils questions prior to the reading that require them to examine what they already know about the topic. McIntosh (1985) observes that poor readers need more encouragement to recall the limited amount of information that they possess. They need more probing and more inferential questioning. Questioning helps pupils to make predictions about the text. This is simply another form of inferencing (Dehn, 1984). Pupils need to learn that they carry meaning as much or more so than does the text, that text is something to interpret rather than something simply to remember (Hansen & Pearson, 1982).
9. Conducting within-class discussions and brainstorming with pupils prior to reading (Roe, Stoodt, & Burns, 1983; Vacca & Vacca, 1989). Within-class discussion and brainstorming should bring students' prior knowledge to the foreground, so that when they read they will be ready to confirm prior knowledge, add new information to old categories, question any false notions that they have held, deal with misconceptions, establish new categories to accommodate new information, and develop new vocabularies.
10. Helping the pupil bridge the gap between the text and the information already possessed by the pupil through use of additional strategies that have been explicitly developed to activate pupils' prior knowledge and to guide them in the reading of text. Among these are: the Pre-Reading Plan (PReP) by Langer (1981, 1982) and the Anticipation Guide (Bean & Peterson, 1980; Readance, Bean & Baldwin, 1981; Tierney, Readance, & Dishner, 1985; Wood & Mateja, 1983). Estes (1984) recommends the Anticipation, Realization, and Contemplation (ARC) format. ARC has pupils identify everything they know about a topic (anticipation), read the article and check the validity of what they had previously stated (realization), and confirm, reject, revise, and add to their information (contemplation).
11. Providing students with an advance organizer either in summary or outline form, a structured overview, semantic web or map, or a preview guide which contains the major ideas that the teacher wishes students to understand. Story maps are very effective as pre-reading organizers (Beck et al. 1982).

    Advance organizers are brief written summaries that precede a longer selection and that offer a summary introduction or a conceptual framework to the remainder of the selection. They bridge the gap between what the reader already knows and what he needs to know to read the text with understanding. Advance organizers are usually developed by the teacher or the writer.

    Advance organizers (Ausübel, 1960, 1963, 1968) provide "ideational scaffolding." They encourage the development of the ideational or organizational framework needed to facilitate comprehension (C. Clark & Bean 1982; Harris & Sipay, 1985). Ausübel (1960, 1963, 1968) describes advance organizers as "preparatory paragraphs which enhance the discriminability of the new learning material from previously-learned related ideas" (p. 214). He adds that to be maximally effective they must be formulated in terms of the language, concepts, and propositions already familiar to the learner, and they must be accompanied by appropriate illustrations and analogies. Advance organizers maximize the cognitive readiness of learners prior to a new task, enhance learning, and aid retention. They enhance the predictability of text by providing a frame of reference for readers to link what they know to what they will learn (Vacca & Vacca, 1986). Their affects on learning are clearly positive (Luiten, et al., 1980). Less able students seem to benefit most from advance organizers.

Advance organizers organize the reader's information base so as to help the reader comprehend incoming information. They are analogous to schema or conceptual preparation (Swaby, 1984). Advance organizers alert the reader to the concepts that are needed to understand what will be read. They are especially effective when: (a) they compare the information in the text with what the reader already knows, (b) the pupil has the relevant information but does recognize it as relevant (these Ausübel labeled comparative organizers), and (c) the pupil is lacking relevant information to which the new material can be related (these are labeled expositive organizers). Ausübel reasoned that when students relate new learning to existing cognitive structures, they will assimilate the new information, subsume new data under more general data, and develop a top-down, hierarchical superordinate-coordinate-subordinate knowledge structure or idea relationship.

Facilitating the Schema-Building Process

Another important phase for developing readiness for reading is building the concepts and the vocabulary necessary to participate successfully in the thinking and problem-solving process of reading. Roth, Smith and Anderson (1984) emphasize the importance of getting pupils "mentally set for instruction" (p. 289), both by calling up relevant prior knowledge and by providing necessary background information. If there is a concept gap between the readers and the content of the story, the teacher must try to fill it. Using the Language Experience Approach to introduce reading to the child minimizes the likelihood of such a concept gap. Nevertheless, Durkin (1984) notes that at a time when the significance of world knowledge for comprehension is receiving widespread attention, there are still far toomany teachers who do not develop background information for reading a narrative.

The most significant aspect of this strategy is that of providing those enriching experiences, direct or indirect, concrete or vicarious, which fill in the pupils' present knowledge and expand their personal schema or cognitive structure. In discussing advance organizers we noted that a basic deficiency of many poor readers is the lack of an adequate information base or the non-use of the information base that they possess. The strategy in this section is concerned with the need for expansion of readers' knowledge base, including their world knowledge, their cognitive base, and their linguistic knowledge.

McIntosh (1985) recommends the use of direct enriching experiences. He suggests that if pupils are to read about the Panama Canal and if they do not know what a canal is and why locks are needed, that such activities as building a canal in a sandbox, looking at drawings, visiting a water purification plant which uses a lock-type system, or viewing films may be used to build upon prior knowledge. The reader's schemata are subject to constant growth and modification (each schema is incomplete), and thus a key role of the teacher is to help the pupil to expand the pupil's information base by providing certain experiences before reading.

Reutzel (1984) observes that since information stored in memory appears to be organized into networks, schema creation and enhancement are aided when new information is organized in a network configuration. Furthermore, schema creation is aided when: (a) instruction emphasizes the relationships between the old and the new; (b) pupils are provided with a method for structuring new information; and (c) teachers present information in an organized manner. Crafton (1983) reports that having pupils read two different passages on the same topic leads to more inferences, greater use of prior knowledge, greater personal involvement, and better recall.

The pupil's schemata need to be expanded particularly in the following areas:

1. The teacher needs to develop word-identification skills to the level of automaticity; this greatly aids comprehension.
2. The teacher needs to expand the quality and quantity of the pupil's word meanings prior to reading and must help pupils to construct new meanings. Comprehension depends on this.

Developing Automaticity in Word Recognition

Just as the comprehension processes all interact with each other, they also interact with word identification processes (Irwin, 1986a). Comprehension is significantly aided when the pupil can identify or recode words quickly and with ease. Automaticity in word recognition frees the mind for comprehension (LaBerge & Samuels, 1974; Samuels & LaBerge, 1983). When the pupil does not know the word at sight, his attention is distracted from comprehension of the sentence.

No one today questions the importance of semantic and syntactic context cues in deciphering the meaning of sentences and paragraphs. The research (Johnson & Baumann, 1984) also shows that effective use of context cues depends upon the development of automaticity in identifying words. An important phase, then, of step 1, "Developing Readiness for Reading," is the pre-teaching of words that the pupil cannot identify. Pupils cannot make use of their personal schema and of their predictive strategies if they cannot identify and recode most of the words. If the pupil is a poor comprehender in reading but possesses adequate listening comprehension ability (poor readers often understand the material when it is read to them but not when they read it), it is likely that word recognition is the principal comprehension problem.

Developing Meaning for Words

Even more important for comprehension than development of automaticity in word identification is lexical access or the development of adequate meanings for words. Many readers have difficulty in comprehending because they have not stored in semantic memory the meanings of words adequate to comprehend what they read. Irwin (1986a) thus notes that expanding the pupil's meaning vocabulary is a critical part of making sure that the pupil has adequate background knowledge. Words and meanings enhance the reader's personal schema and their comprehension. Studies consistently show that in developing comprehension skills the most important and at the same time the most elemental bit of information for the pupil to acquire is a rich vocabulary. A reader's knowledge of the key vocabulary is a better predictor of comprehension than is any other measure.

Another important phase of Step I of the DRA is thus the preteaching of the key meaning vocabulary in which the pupil is deficient. Guidelines (Cooper, 1986; Tierney & Cunningham, 1984) for pre-teaching words are:

1. Teach the significant key concept words for the selection.
2. Develop the words in written context, clearly reflecting the context in which they were used in the selection.
3. Thoroughly teach the words.

4. Relate the words being taught to the concepts needed to understand the selection.
5. Teach the words in semantically and topically related sets.

Chapter 10 will discuss how the teacher can help the pupil to access semantic information and to acquire the word meanings necessary to comprehend what is read. Obviously, children must be taught strategies for identifying, recoding and decoding words that may be new to them. Hittelman (1983) shies away from presenting the "new words" prior to the reading of the story, reasoning that "only by meeting unfamiliar words in the natural context of a story can the students use their word recognition [and comprehension] strategies" (p. 185). Such an approach is particularly recommended as children advance in grade level. Children should then be learning to predict the word and its meaning, using context, phonic, and morphemic cues to do so. It appears reasonable that if there are 10 words that the pupil probably does not know, either because he cannot identify them or cannot associate meaning with them or both, and if the length of the selection is about 100 words, then the teacher should preteach at least 5 words, thus bringing the reading selection up to the pupil's instructional level (the level at which the pupil can attain 95% accuracy in word recognition and at least 75% accuracy in comprehension). This still leaves numerous opportunities for pupils to practice their predictive skills.

Pre-teaching of word identification and word meaning has significant benefits in the beginning grades. Pupils are aided when the teacher selects and pre-teaches from the story to be read: (a) those words that they cannot identify but with which they have associated aural-oral meaning; (b) those words that they cannot identify and with which they have not associated a meaning; (c) those words that they can recognize and with which they have associated a meaning, but not the specific meaning that fits the context; and (d) those words that contain grapheme-phoneme irregularities or that are embedded in a weak context.

Raising Questions Prior to Reading

The teacher can also aid the pupil's readiness for reading by raising questions and by teaching the pupil to raise questions prior to reading the material. The teacher may initially ask the pupil: "What do you think this story is about?" "Do the title, the illustrations, the introductory sentence, or the main headings give you any cues as to what the story is about?" Gradually, pupils should learn to ask such questions of themselves. Pre-reading questions are useful adjuncts in building background for story comprehension, especially when they are oriented toward predicting and relating text to prior experiences and knowledge (Pearson, 1985).

Developing a Hypothesizing/Predicting Strategy

Prediction is the core of reading and the basis of comprehension (Smith, 1988). Reading is clearly a predictive process. Teaching, as we pointed out in chapter 5, should focus on both global and focal prediction and should teach the pupil to use his personal schemata and his within-word cue knowledge to predict himself through print. The teacher may have pupils develop an appropriate title for a series of sentences, predict how a story will end, predict what a specific word is in a sentence, and so forth. This strategy was discussed at length in chapter 5.

The LEA approach, perhaps more so than any other, meets all the requirements of Step 1 of the DRA, and it for this reason is recommended in this text as the optimal way for introducing the pupil to reading. It has built- in attention and motivation; it is founded upon the pupil's personal schema; it makes the purpose for reading an integral part of the total process; and it uses only words which the pupil has either heard or spoken. It is deficient to some degree in that it limits growth and expansion of the reader's schema.

Developing Readiness for Reading Expository Materials

Readers obviously do not read only narratives; they read expository materials. Reading of expository materials clearly requires new skills. It is our experience that the DRA format, with some modifications, is an appropriate organizational and instructional design also for expository materials. The teacher in the content areas should put greater emphasis on:

I. Identification of key concepts and understandings that need to be developed, of the vocabulary that corresponds to the key concepts, and of the important data that support the key concepts. There is little doubt that to master a content area one must learn its key concepts, in other words, its language. Each subject matter field has its own unique language to represent its important concepts. A study of the vocabulary lays the groundwork for the development of concepts. Words are labels for concepts. The pre-reading phase of vocabulary study provides the opportunity to show pupils the inter-relationships of key concepts and to create interest in and awareness of content area words.

II. Identification and discussion of the organizational framework of the unit. Taylor and Beach (1984) found that reading and recall of expository text is aided when the pupil can deal with text as a whole; can reflect on the logical relationships between the superordinate, coordinate and subordinate ideas; and can use a hierarchical summarization strategy. Pupils are greatly benefited when they are taught:
   A. To perceive text organization. A significant aspect of comprehending expository materials is the reader's knowledge of the structural characteristics of such texts (Roe, Stoodt, & Burns, 1983). Readers comprehend better (Niles, 1974) when they use knowledge of how text is organized to follow and predict what is being read. They are aided when they are taught that subject-matter textbooks are usually written in an expository style, that they contain introductory material, explanatory or informational material, and summary material, and that they are organized into superordinate, coordinate, and subordinate concepts. Pupils are aided in reading expository text when the text is coherent, when there is unity of purpose within the material, and when the knowledge base within the material is appropriate for the reader.
   B. To identify patterns of organization: enumeration, time order, comparison-contrast, cause-effect, description, collection (a number of descriptions in sequence including specifics, attributes, and settings), problem-solution, and comparison (Meyer & Freedle, 1984).
   C. To identify and use the signals or cues to paragraph organization.
   D. To use the table of contents, subheadings, typographic aids (e.g., capitals, italics, indentations) index, glossary, introductory paragraphs, summaries, questions, and graphics of all kinds as cues to paragraph and text organization.
III. Development and use of semantic maps. Semantic mapping draws heavily on the activation of prior knowledge (Johnson, Pittelman, & Heimlich, 1986). It works effectively in pre-and post-reading situations. As a pre-reading technique it teaches key vocabulary words, activates children's prior knowledge, and motivates pupils to read the story or informational material. It is equally as effective with with content area materials as with narratives. As a post-reading activity, it helps pupils to recall, organize, and graphically represent the pertinent information. Reutzel (1985a) found that post-reading story mapping does improve reading comprehension with elementary children.
IV. Having pupils anticipate what will be learned from reading the selection. This involves surveying and previewing, locating needed

information, interpreting what is read, reacting with the text, hypothesizing, and raising of questions, especially those of: "What do I need to know?" and "How well do I already know it?" Vacca (1981) observes that a teacher reduces the uncertainty pupils bring to content material by helping them raise questions about what they will read.

V. Having pupils stop their reading periodically to review the main points: this checks for comprehension breakdowns (Schmitt & Baumann, 1986).

VI. Using study guides: Such guides are usually typewritten and are keyed to the textbook. They identify the reading task and present a plan for the pupil to follow in reading or studying. The study guide is the most frequently used strategy for helping students comprehend informational text (Wood, 1988). Guides of various types are available: Concept and pattern guides (Vacca, 1981), guide-o-ramas (Cunningham & Shablak, 1985; Wood & Mateja, 1983), the learning-from-text guide (Singer & Donlan, 1980), the textbook activity guide (Davey, 1986), and the interactive reading guide (Wood, 1988).

VII. Using the gloss procedure: Otto, White, and Camperell (1980) developed the gloss procedure. It involves the use of marginal notations to direct the pupil's attention to places in the text that require the application of certain strategies and skill (e.g., calling the pupil's attention to the topic, to definitions provided by the text) so comprehension can occur. For additional information on the gloss strategy, see Richgels and Hansen (1984) and Richgels and Mateja (1984).

VIII. Using a variety of sources: Many teachers rely on a single text, but it is often desirable to use the textbook to begin the unit and then to branch out into other materials and resources.

Another method for aiding comprehension of expository materials is the structured overview. Developed by Barron (1969), it is a pre-reading activity (it may also follow reading) that relates words to more inclusive vocabulary concepts. It presents the chapter's key ideas and their interrelationships in a visual format (Heilman et al., 1986), either as a diagram, flow chart, semantic web, or outline. It is an advance organizer in graphic form. The structured overview can be accompanied by chapter summaries, sematic webbing or semantic mapping, story guides, use of films or filmstrips, having pupils listen to a tape, lecturing about the content, or reading to pupils.

The structured overview may be used to show the interrelationships in an entire text, in a unit covering several chapters, in one chapter, or even in a part of a chapter. Given to students or developed by them before actually reading the material, it highlights important concepts and new vocabulary, provides background information, defines the reasons for reading and studying the material, identifies the objectives of the lesson, identifies the main ideas, helps pupils see the interrelationship between the ideas presented, provides the stimulus for effective questioning, and effectively outlines or organizes the material (Heilman et al., 1986). The survey/previewing technique is particularly effective in building a structured overview. Initially the structured overview may be developed by the teacher or conjointly by the teacher and the pupil, but more mature pupils should learn to develop one by themselves.

An example of a structured overview is offered by Thelen (1982):

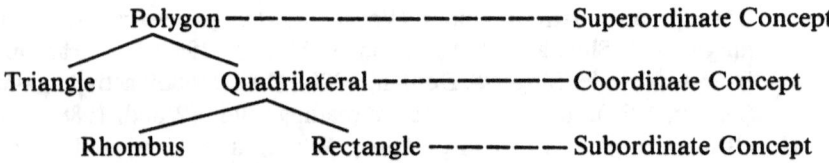

The concept "polygon" is the most inclusive concept, subsuming all others. The concept "quadrilateral" is subordinate to polygon, coordinate to triangle, and superordinate to rhombus and rectangle.

Barron (1969, 1979) identified the steps for developing a structured overview:

1. Analyze the vocabulary and list all the important words (e.g., triangle, quadrilateral, polygon, rhombus, square, rectangle).
2. Arrange the list of words beginning with the superordinate or the most inclusive concept (i.e., polygon). Then choose the words classified immediately under the superordinate concept (i.e., triangle and quadrilateral) and coordinate them with each other. Then choose the terms subordinate to the coordinate concepts (rhombus and rectangle).
3. Arrange the terms into a schematic diagram.
4. Add additional words the pupils are expected to understand (i.e., square as a subordinate to the coordinate quadrilateral).
5. Evaluate the overview: Does the overview clearly show major relationships?
6. Introduce students to the learning task: Relate previous learnings to the overview.
7. Relate new information to the overview.

GUIDED SILENT READING

Step 2 of the DRA involves more than simply reading. It requires appropriate segmenting of the material, developing a purpose for each of the segments, continuing the hypothesizing/predicting strategy, asking additional questions during reading, and monitoring of what one reads. Pupils need guidance in the search for and the retrieval of information during reading. They need to be shown how to think through print (Vacca & Vacca, 1986).

Segmentation of Text and the Global Purpose

Because the vocabulary and the amount of information contained in reading materials is often overwhelming and because the reader's attention span is often quite limited, the teacher may find it necessary to reduce the amount of material to be read in one sequence. The teacher may help the pupil by dividing the story or expository material into appropriate segments (e.g., by dividing the narrative at the best prediction points, or by presenting new information in manageable, logical chunks), by asking a global purpose question for each of the segments, and by interspersing additional questions throughout the text. The purposeful global question may simply be: "Read this segment to identify how Sammy found his dog." On a beginning reading level a segment may not be more than three or four sentences, and should not take more than three or four minutes to read. Breaking the story into segments has the added advantages of stopping the reader and allowing for prediction-generating questions such as: "What do you think the main character will do next?" "What kind of outcome do you expect?" Segmentation of the story should parallel the unfolding of the story elements, perhaps occurring at a break after the setting has been identified or the story problem is revealed.

Continuing the Hypothesizing/Predicting Strategy

As already noted, an important strategy for the pupil to use both prior to and during reading is to develop a hypothesizing/predicting–confirming/rejecting strategy. Reading is a continually repeating process of predicting what lies ahead in a line of print and in the text generally. Research (Ringler & Weber, 1984) clearly shows that readers who develop prediction strategies, who make ongoing predictions and interpretations of text, who learn to hypothesize, to confirm or reject and to change hypotheses, tend to become good comprehenders. Reading requires the use of a problem-solving strategy. Reading is hypothesis-driven. While reading, pupils should relate the materials to their purposes and to the expectancies and hypotheses that they form. They must guide their reading by making individual global predictions about the selection (e.g., predicting story elements including the actions of the characters, the problem, the attempts at solution, and the final outcome) and then read to find out whether the predictions are correct.

The Directed-Reading–Thinking Activity or DR-TA (Stauffer, 1969), with its emphasis on constructing meaning, not simply repeating information, is a useful strategy in getting readers to ask questions and make predictions while reading. After the story has been divided into appropriate segments, the students read each segment using a three-step process of predict, read, and prove. Pupils are directed initially to read the title or to look at the pictures and to predict what the story is about. The teacher might thus ask: "From the title can you guess what this story is about?" or "From the picture, can you guess where the story took place?" The pupils then read the story or check upon their predictions. They are encouraged to verify, change, or adjust their prediction while reading. Finally, pupils are required to prove their predictions by asking and answering questions, such as "Was I correct?" or "How do I know that I was correct?" Pupils should be required to cite exerpts from the text that prove their predictions or that caused them to make new predictions.

Efficient hypothesizing is most difficult at the beginning of a text passage. With only a limited amount of information, with only a small sample of print, with perhaps limited experiences, and with a multitude of plausible hypotheses, the poor reader often jumps to conclusions with insufficient evidence. The good reader with his enriched personal schema can limit the number of relevant hypotheses. If pupils are reading expository text that is beyond their experiential-language-conceptual-comprehension level and cannot use the prediction strategy, the teacher may need to: (a) find books at lower readability levels, (b) make different assignments for different children, (c) rewrite the textbook materials, or (d) prepare similar types of text for children to hear and to read along (Zintz & Maggart, 1984).

When pupils do not understand a passage or when their predictions have proved to be wrong, they can use varying fix-up strategies (Baker & Brown, 1984b, Irwin & Baker, 1989):

1. Ignore the contradiction or incongruity and read on for additional context.
2. Suspend judgment and continue reading.
3. Revise tentative hypotheses.
4. Reread the current sentence
5. Reread the previous context.

6. Try to form a mental image
7. Read orally
8. Read more slowly
9. Go to an expert source for further information: Seek the help of one who knows.

The reader additionally needs to ask: "Why was my prediction incorrect?" "Do I need to make corrections?" This phase is the monitoring phase, which we have identified as a separate comprehension strategy.

Continuing the Self-Questioning Strategy

While reading silently the reader also needs to ask questions. Self-posed prediction questions are especially important. They call for educated guesses based on the knowledge that the reader has and on what has been read up to that point. Such questions define the task for the reader, thereby helping the reader to identify the hypotheses that are most worth developing. Clark et al. (1984) recommend a self-questioning that involves: (a) having pupils read the passage and asking *wh (who, what, where, when, why)* questions as they read, (b) having pupils answer the questions as they read, and (c) having pupils mark the answers with the appropriate symbol, perhaps a happy face to identify a *who* question.

Nolte and Singer (1985) report that the comprehension of fourth and fifth graders was enhanced when they were taught a process of comprehension that involved having the pupils model questions at pertinent points in a story (turning story grammar structures into story-specific structures), then phasing out teacher questions and phasing in student self-questioning.

Monitoring Predictions and Comprehension

Comprehension monitoring (also called cognitive monitoring, metacognition, and metacomprehension) is an important additional comprehension strategy. Readers need to learn to monitor their own understanding of text. They need to ask whether the story makes sense and whether it fits their perception of what a story is. They need to monitor their predictions, to evaluate whether and to what degree comprehension is occurring, to evaluate text for internal consistency and for compatability with prior knowledge, and, if they don't understand to apply fix-up strategies.

Younger and less able readers, in particular, need help in monitoring their reading. They have an inactive approach to text processing, and fail to identify and use effective strategies (Ryan et al., 1986). They rarely ask: "Do I understand? If not, why not." Good readers, on the other hand, are able to detect passage inconsistencies and to search previous and subsequent text for information. They know when they have or have not understood something, and they know what to do when comprehension has broken down.

Monitoring ought to occur simultaneously at the story, passage, or whole text level, the sentence level, and the word level. Does the passage make sense in view of what I already know about the story? Do the sentences make sense? Do they fit what I have just read? How do the sentences tie together? Are the statements incongruous with my own prior experience? How does the whole text fit together?

Gillett and Temple (1986) note that "Comprehension monitoring consists of a range of activities, from the almost reflex phrase-by-phrase checking that alerts us if we read a word improperly ("There was a bear in the refrigerator—no, sorry—there was a *beer* in the refrigerator. . . ") to the more conscious and deliberate setting of expectations of what we will find out in a piece, with subsequent checking to see if we are finding out what we expected to." (p. 66). They add that reflexive comprehension monitoring leads readers to make spontaneous corrections when they read words incorrectly, and also observe that "when children do not spontaneously correct their errors, there is cause for concern, as this suggests that they do not expect their reading to make sense" (p. 67)

Metacognition refers to those self-regulatory mechanisms that good readers use to check upon and evaluate the effectiveness of their comprehending of text. These mechanisms include checking outcomes, planning appropriate strategies, checking the effectiveness of the strategies used, revising strategies, and using compensatory strategies (Hittelman, 1988). Conversely readers who are inefficient monitors or who are deficient in metacognitive strategy often cannot predict the difficulty of a task, cannot determine what is important to remember, cannot choose a strategy to maximize learning, cannot assess their own knowledge or their progress on a task, fail to recognize an increase in difficulty level, do not plan ahead, do not monitor the outcomes of their performance, and do not know when a task has been mastered.

Current cognitive learning models emphasize: (a) the knowledge base which the reader brings to the printed page or the schemata, and (b) the learning-thinking strategies or the tools of intellectual activity. The learning-thinking strategies have generally been divided into three categories: the executive or metacognitive strategies (which are of interest here), the non-executive or cognitive strategies, and the affective and motivational strategies.

Metacognitive or comprehension-monitoring strategies allow the reader to control, monitor, evaluate, and modify ongoing learning, thinking, and reading. They include: problem identification, selecting a process for problem-solving, strategy selection, selecting a mode for representation (table, outline, semantic map), allocation of resources, monitoring progress, and sensitivity to feedback. These are the regulatory mechanisms. They involve checking to see whether one understands, predicting outcomes, evaluating the effectiveness of one's strategies, planning the next move, and apportioning of time and effort. Metacognitive strategies are involved in setting goals and in assessing attainment of the goals. Executive control processes deal with how individuals plan and direct, select, and orchestrate the various cognitive structures for the attainment of some goal (Schumacher, 1987). They coordinate the functioning of the human cognitive system.

The cognitive strategies implement the strategy: they are the information-processing skills applied in task performance (e.g., identification of the main idea). They relate to the process of learning (the skills and strategies that can be used in acquiring and processing content) rather than to the products of learning or to what is learned. They are the skills actually used in analyzing, memorizing, and related processes. These are the how of learning—the how-to-learn strategies. They involve knowing what to do. The non-executive strategies are goal-directed sequences of behavior and include (Weinstein & Mayer, 1986): rehearsal strategies (e.g., repetition, highlighting of the important points in the text), elaboration strategies (e.g., forming mental images, forming analogies, paraphrasing, summarising), and organizational strategies (e.g., grouping, classifying, outlining, identifying the main idea, developing concept-summarizing tables, etc.).

Motivational strategies consist of attention, interest, and motivation. The affective strategies involve emotions, feelings, attitudes, predispositions, and values.

Cross and Paris (1988) note that metacognition is a complex array of knowledge and skills that includes *declarative knowledge* (i.e., knowledge of what factors influence reading; knowing, for example, that skimming is a reading strategy); *procedural knowledge* (i.e., knowledge of how skills operate and are applied; for example, knowing how to skim); and *conditional knowledge* (i.e., knowing when to apply particular strategies and knowing why they are significant; for example, knowing when to skim and why).

Metacognitive processing involves: (a) a conscious awareness of what skills, strategies, and resources are needed to perform a task effectively, (b) control of one's own cognitive and comprehension processes and (c) the ability to use self-regulatory evaluative, and remedial mechanisms to ensure successful completion of the task (e.g., checking the outcome of any attempt to solve the problem and evaluating the effectiveness of one's attempt) (Collins and Smith (1980; Baker & Brown, 1984b). It is knowing when to use a strategy and why it is relevant or important (Schmitt & Baumann, 1986). It is knowing how and when to do what (Woolfolk, 1990).

Yekovich and Walker (1987) note that the metacognitive strategies: (a) coordinate the various reading processes (e.g., word identification versus lexical access), (b) coordinate the allocation of appropriate cognitive resources (e.g., optimizing the use of short-term memory), and (c) control the selection and use of knowledge to fill in gaps in text through inferencing (Perfetti, 1985). The reader is sensitive to metacognitive strategies when he adjusts his reading speed and gaze duration on individual words, when he chooses to read slowly or more rapidly, when he pauses, when he skims or scans, and so forth.

Spring (1985) observes metacognitive instruction should be designed to help readers (a) to become spontaneous assessors of what they know and what they do not know (What do I already know? What do I need to do when I am done?); (b) to be purpose setters, (What are the task demands of this text? What are my objectives?); (c) to be selectors of appropriate reading/learning strategies (Should I outline, summarize, or ask questions?); (d) to be monitors of their own understanding (Do I understand the text-reader interactions? Am I using prior knowledge to make inferences? Do I understand the new learnings? Can I apply fix-up strategies to unclear text?); and (e) to be evaluators of their success in terms of the demands of the task and the purposes set.

Studies (Leal et al., 1985; Paris & Jacobs, 1984; Short & Ryan, 1984; Short et al., 1983; Wong & Jones, 1982) suggest that metacognitive instruction and self-monitoring strategies increase children's awareness of reading strategies, aid comprehension, increase recall and notetaking ability, and make children aware of important units of text. The good reader is likely to be more proficient in comprehension monitoring. The poor reader, on the other hand, needs to be taught to gauge his level of understanding, to use mental imagery, to skim the text in advance, to underline or highlight key points, to read with objectives in mind, to take notes from text, to construct semantic maps, to categorize information via a diagram or table, to summarize, to reread, to paraphrase sections of text while reading, to read ahead, to rate the importance of idea units before reading, to turn the headings into questions, to ask the teacher, to consult the dictionary or glossary, or to engage in self-questioning (Britton & Glynn, 1987; Ryan, et al., 1986). Self-questioning is an effective mode of activating monitoring of comprehension. Visualization or mental imagery, the creation of pictures in the reader's mind prior to, during, and after the reading, is another significant metacognitive strategy in reading (Fredericks, 1986; Palincsar & Ranson, 1988; Sadowski, 1983), leading to better recall and comprehension. Imagery seems to be more effective before than after reading.

Palincsar and Brown (Brown, 1981; Brown & Palincsar, 1982; Palincsar & Brown, 1984a, 1984b) offer a four-fold strategy for monitoring one's comprehension: (a) stopping at a given point and summarizing what has been read; (b) asking oneself whether what has been read is clear and clarifying it if it is not by rereading or discussion; (c) asking oneself questions; and (d) predicting what will come next in the text. Self-monitoring has adjunctive benefits: It combats an inactive learning style, and it forces pupils to continually evaluate their level of attending.

Smith (1988) argues against comprehension monitoring. He believes that thinking about one's own thinking, understanding, or learning is not distinct from thinking. He does not perceive comprehension monitoring as "a special set of skills," (p. 22) but as the constant activity of the brain. He feels it is not an "essential prerequisite for literacy" (p. 209). He adds that learners learn many things without being able to talk about or even being aware of what they are learning. Later he observes: "One can hardly be unaware of whether one is comprehending or confused . . . of course, we can believe we understand something when we are in error. . . . But to make a mistake is not a failure of metcognition metacognition, of being out of touch with our own thought processes. It is simply a matter of being wrong" (p. 228).

The second step of the DRA is obviously not simply reading. Pupils must learn to search for and retrieve information during reading. They need a problem-solving strategy, and they need to learn to think through print. An active response to meaning is requisite. It is during and through reading that the pupil learns to treat sentences and paragraphs differently, to read selectively, to distinguish important from less important ideas, to perceive relationships, and to respond actively to meaning (Vacca, 1981).

EVALUATING AND DEVELOPING COMPREHENSION

If pupils are to make the best use of reading, they must constantly employ a reading-for-meaning strategy. Steps 1 and 2 of the DRA foster such an approach. They develop attention and motivation for reading, fit what is being read into the reader's personal schema, expand the pupil's experience and knowledge base, develop a purpose for reading, teach a hypothesizing/predicting–confirming/rejecting strategy, and present a pre- and during-reading question strategy. Step 3 of the DRA adds the post-reading question strategy, both as an assessment strategy and as a teaching strategy (Durkin, 1978–1979).

Studies generally support a before, during, and post-reading question strategy. Memory (1983a, 1983b) found that low-average sixth-grade readers showed better comprehension when they were given questions about main ideas before reading. A similar effect was not shown with better readers. However, Rothkopf (1970) found that questioning after the reading was more effective for understanding and retention than was the before-reading strategy.

André and Anderson (1978-79) found that self-generated questions are more effective than teacher-formulated questions, and seem particularly helpful with pupils who have low verbal ability. The question technique tends to be more effective than careful reading without questions and rereading of the same material. However, Wagner (1984) found that rereading can enhance expository text comprehension. Apparently, pupils use the first reading as a time to collect and analyze information and the second reading to organize new and old information into a meaningful whole. Undoubtedly, questions are most used to assess pupil comprehension, but they are best used when they help pupils to clarify meaning, to organize and integrate textual information, and to activate the reader's prior world knowledge or topical knowledge.

Questions, whether raised by student or teacher, increase inspection time, cognitive effort, attention, and concentration of the reader (Durkin, 1981; Reynolds & Anderson, 1981); develop and clarify purposes for reading; and stimulate discussion about what has been read. They constitute one of the most useful tools of teaching. They may exert their major effect by causing the reader to pay closer attention to what is being read. Rothkopf (1970) calls this the mathemagenic effect or attending phenomenon.

McGaw and Grotelueschen (1972) note that questions also promote "backward review" and "forward shaping." Questions help the reader to associate the new with what is known (Rickards & Hatcher, 1977-78) and they serve as advance organizers. They help in organizing what has just been read (Beck, 1984a). Raphael and Gavelek (1984) suggest that they may serve as a summary and may create a need for a review of text, thereby strengthening recall.

Smith (1988) puts more emphasis on the relation of comprehension and the asking of questions than do most writers. He notes that comprehension involves "the reduction of a reader's uncertainty, asking questions and getting them answered" (p. 154). He adds:

> Comprehension . . . is relative; it depends on getting answers to the questions being asked. A particular meaning is the answer a reader gets to a particular question. Meaning therefore also depends on the questions that are asked; a reader gets the meaning of a book or poem from the writer's . . . point of view only when the reader asks questions that the writer . . . implicitly expected to be asked. (p. 167)

Smith notes that "comprehension of text is a matter of having relevant questions to ask (that the text can answer) and of being able to find answers to at least some of the questions" (p. 166). He also observes that the reason children do not understand what they are reading is because they cannot ask the "correct" questions.

The ability to ask questions is indicative of the amount of information that reader can bring to the printed page. Individual differences in nonvisual information is thus the reason why some readers can ask only literal comprehension questions, while others can ask inferential questions. Smith contends that the reader who does not comprehend a book is the one who cannot find relevant questions and answers. He observes that comprehension tests asked after reading are in fact measures of long-term memory: "If I say that I comprehended a certain book, it does not make sense to give me a test and argue that I did not understand it" (p. 19). We would argue that the real question is the level of the reader's comprehension (is it on a literal level, inferential level, etc., and is it directed to a knowledge of facts or does it go beyond facts?).

Questions may take the following forms:

I. Free Recall Questions: Free recall questions have pupils recall information or the idea units without the aid of specific questions. A general directive, such as "Tell me what you remember from the selection," is preferred. Free recall provides an insight into the pupil's ability to focus on and to recall the important ideas in text: in narratives, to recall the story structure (setting, theme, plot, and resolution); in expository text, to recall the superordinate, coordinate, and subordinate concepts, and such expository text structures as cause-effect, comparison-contrast, main idea–detail, or problem-solution (Paratore & Indrisano, 1987).

II. Probe Questions: Probe questions may take the form of: "Can you tell me more about _____ ?" "Is there anything more that you remember?" or "Why do you think she said that?").

III. Structured Questions: Children learn and remember best that information which is directly questioned. (Wixson, 1982, 1983a, 1983b). Raphael (1982a, 1982b, 1984, 1986) recommended the QAR (question-answer relation) technique as a strategy for teaching pupils to answer questions. The strategy teaches that sometimes the answers to questions are right in the text (The "Right There" technique); that sometimes they require the pupil to put together some information in in the text with what one already has (The "On My Own" technique). Raphael (1986) has modified this strategy to include just two main strategies: (a) "In the Book," which includes "Right There" and "Think and Search" and (b) "In My Head," which includes "Author and You" and "On Your Own."

A. Textually explicit (TE) or literal comprehension questions: These call for literal comprehension and may also include organizational and integrative-comprehension questions. The answers to such questions are found right in the text. Textually explicit questions may be most appropriate when the pupil is reading directions, following recipes, or reading about a scientific experiment (Wixson, 1982, 1983a, 1983b).
B. Textually implicit (TI) or inferential comprehension questions: These call for inference and may include all higher levels of comprehending except that of literal comprehension. The answer is implied or inferred from reading between lines. Textually implicit questions should be used when the integration of ideas within a text is required (Wixson, 1982, 1983a, 1983b).
C. Scriptally implicit (SI) or schema-implicit questions: These call for the application of one's prior background of experience and knowledge. They require the pupil to put together some information in the text with what one already has. Scriptally implicit or schema-implicit questions are most effective when there is a need for the integration of the information suggested by the text with the reader's existing knowledge (Wixson, 1982, 1983a, 1983b).
IV. Process Questions: Process questions help teachers to understand what processes the pupil used or how he comprehended (Irwin & Baker, 1989). Such questions may take the form of schema questions, inference, and monitoring questions. Inference or predictive questions of a process nature might take the form of: "What inferences did you have to make to understand the passage?" "What cues did you use to make your prediction of how the story would end?" A comprehension-monitoring question of a process nature is: "Where did you have difficulty understanding what the author meant?" "How did you resolve the problem?" (Irwin & Baker, 1989, p. 23).

At a minimum, questioning ought to involve schema-related questions (e.g., "How did this passage relate to what you already know?"); global, purpose-generating questions (e.g., "What is this story all about?"); structured-overview questions (Did the pupil understand the relationships between the ideas presented? Did the pupil have a semantic-map image of the material?); prediction and inference questions (Did the story end as the reader predicted? Did the pupil correctly infer the meaning of words and idiomatic phrases or the main idea?); vocabulary questions (involving questions whose answer is explicitly stated in the material, may be inferred from life experience, or must be inferred from the context); organization-type questions (requiring an understanding of paragraph organization and of narrative and expository structures; metacognitive or comprehension monitoring questions (Did the story make sense? Did the story fit the reader's perception of what a story is?); and evaluative questions (e.g., "Could this story really have happened? Is the ending believable?").

Levels of Comprehending

Each of the question types identified to this point is actually a literal, inferential, organizational, or evaluative question. Thus, for example, the global, purposeful question is an organizational question; it requires readers to summarize, synthesize, or organize what they have read. Chapter 12 will focus on the higher-level comprehension questions.

Observe also that many of the question types recommended earlier measure the use of context cues. Among these are the global, purpose-generating question, the predictive-type question, the vocabulary question, the phrase question, the main idea question, and the inference question.

Additional Strategies for Use in the Content Areas

Questioning strategies that have specific value in reading of expository materials have been formulated in the DR-TA, GRP, and Guided-Reading-Thinking programs.

The Directed Reading-Thinking Activity (DRTA) (Stauffer, 1969) fosters critical reading. It is a guided group discussion activity that focuses on the formation and testing of pre-reading predictions. It has pupils predict possible story events and outcomes and then has them read to confirm or disprove their hypothesis. Pupils are required to test their answers by a predict-read-prove sequence. The teacher activates the thought process by asking: "What do you think?" She agitates thought by asking: "Why do you think so?" And, she requires evidence by asking: "How can you prove it?" Such questions help readers to explore the logic behind an answer: "Why is that a good answer? Why is it a valid answer?" Discussion is an integral part of DRTA and questions generally are open-ended and encourage divergent thinking.

The steps of the DRTA are:

1. Begin with the title, subheadings, and illustrations, and ask: "What do you think this selection will be about?" "Why do you think so?" When reading in content areas the pupil is encouraged to ask: "What do I know about the topic?" "What don't I know?" "What do I need to learn?" Record student speculations or predictions on the chalkboard.
2. Have students read silently to a predetermined logical stopping point.

3. Repeat questions in Step 1. Some predictions will be refined (these may be recorded on the blackboard) and additional ones will be introduced. Add the questions: "How do you know? Can you prove it?" Encourage discussion, offer clarifying ideas, and promote inquiry.
4. Have pupils read to another suitable point. Ask similar questions.
5. Continue this way to the end of the selection. Students should be asked here: "Were your predictions accurate?" "Did you have to revise your predictions?" "Why?" "What were your new predictions?"

DRTA is an effective strategy in helping pupils to develop the hypothesizing, predicting–confirming/rejecting strategy of which we spoke earlier. It helps pupils to predict their way through print. Its major focus is to have pupils read a portion of text, stop and predict what will happen next, read further and check whether their predictions were correct, and repeat the process.

The Guided Reading Procedure (GRP) (Manzo, 1975, 1985) is based on one primary premise: namely, that all the higher levels of comprehending depend upon the ability to comprehend literally. It encourages clarification of key concepts, grouping of the unknown with the known, identification of any inconsistencies between what was remembered and what was actually written, outlining of the content, and immediate review. Whereas DR-TA emphasizes open-ended and divergent thinking, GRP stresses convergent thinking and gradual progression from the literal to the higher levels of comprehension.

The Guided-Reading-Thinking Lesson (Hittelman, 1988) has the pupil:

1. Examine information to determine what is or what is not already known.
2. Hypothesize about probable meanings.
3. Find proof of probable meanings.
4. Suspend judgment when information is not already available to confirm or reject hypotheses
5. Make decisions when information is available to confirm or reject hypotheses or decide to seek information elsewhere.

Further elaborations of the questioning strategies may take the form of feedback and sharing. These specifically may include discussion, retelling, games, role playing, writing, presentation in class, reports, tests, and inquiry (finding out, problem solving, discovering for oneself, etc.). The discussion strategy, especially when it is combined with workable subgroups, is particularly recommended when pupils are reading on substantially different levels and when pupils are reading in the content areas. The teacher will need to identify materials on the same content that essentially match each discussion group's competency level. The discussion should lead to literal, interpretative, and critical experiences with concepts. Having children talk about what they read enhances reading comprehension (Gambrell, Pfeifer, & Wilson, 1985). Rose, Cundick, & Higbee (1984) found that retelling significantly increased the reading comprehension of elementary-age learning-disabled children. Morrow (1984, 1985, 1986) found that retelling or verbal rehearsal improves story comprehension, the sense of story structure, and the organization and retention of text.

Using Questioning With Groups

A continuing concern of the teacher is how to use the questioning strategy with a group of students. When DRA is used in a group situation, pupils at a particular reading level usually meet with the teacher. The teacher motivates them toward the selection by posing questions about the theme, the setting, and other story features. The pupils read the selection silently and orally answer specific teacher-developed questions. Unfortunately, with this strategy it is difficult to provide for individual differences. Even within the same subgroup it is difficult to evaluate each pupil's progress.

Charnock (1977) suggests that above second-grade level each pupil be required, at least sometimes, to write out his or her answers to specific questions about the story. Occasionally pupils can meet as a subgroup, read and discuss the story, and then develop group responses to the questions. Sometimes pupils may pair with a friend to answer the questions. Charnock adds that this approach allows for better class management, better monitoring of pupil abilities and progress, and more original thinking with print. He notes that some children dislike being put on the spot to answer a tough question, resent those who know it all, and are slowed by the less skilled and the less perceptive.

Evaluating Pupil Comprehension

In evaluating the pupil's comprehension, it is important to give consideration to each of the following observations:

1. Pupils cannot be expected to comprehend materials containing a substantial number of words that they cannot identify or name. Whenever the pupil's comprehension score falls below 70–75%, the material is probably on the pupil's frustration level and is too difficult. A pupil's comprehension should be evaluated on materials that are on the pupil's instructional level.

2. When comprehension is assessed by having pupils answer questions about materials read, memory becomes an important determinant of the response. The longer the interval between reading and questioning, the more likely it is that memory processes are being assessed. To evaluate comprehension the teacher may give pupils the question and have them find the answer. The concern always must be: "Did the pupil fail to answer correctly because he did not remember, he did not comprehend, or both?"
3. The teacher needs to make certain that the questions are dependent about the passage—that they cannot be answered without reading the content. Questions are useless if they only measure what was in the reader's schema before he or she read. Reading comprehension is measured only if the pupil, after reading, can answer questions that the pupil could not answer prior to reading.

ORAL REREADING OF THE MATERIAL

Step 4 of the DRA is oral rereading of the material. There is indeed a difference in comprehending when reading orally and when reading silently. Our focus here is on oral reading comprehension. Oral rereading allows the teacher: (a) to evaluate children's oral reading comprehension or their ability to interpret what is read; (b) to develop and evaluate the pupil's ability to read with sentence sense, to phrase properly, to read with appropriate rhythm, to read the punctuation, and to read with appropriate speed and fluency; (c) to diagnose oral reading errors; and (d) to evaluate the pupil's use of voice and the ability to communicate the writer's meaning to others.

Oral reading comprehension is a major goal of reading education. Oral reading requires all the sensory and perceptual skills required in silent reading, such as visual discrimination, rhythmic progression along a line of print, and the ability to take to the word those experiences that the writer, by his or her peculiar choice and arrangement of words, hoped to call to the reader's attention. Oral reading also requires skills beyond those needed in silent reading. Habits of oral reading usually are quite different from those in silent reading. In oral reading there are generally more fixations, more regressions, and longer pauses. Oral reading generally is slower than silent reading. In oral reading, reading rate is limited by pronunciation; in silent reading, it is limited only by the ability to grasp meaning. Oral reading calls for interpreting to others; silent reading, only to oneself. Good oral readers:

1. Interpret the author's meaning accurately.
2. Correctly transmit the author's meaning to the listener.

3. Make a proper interpretation of the author's feelings, moods, and nuances of meaning, interpreting and conveying the emotions and moods of the characters.
4. Read in meaningful thought and phrase units.
5. Demonstrate clarity and accuracy in articulation, enunciation, and pronunciation; the pupil's reading is essentially free from errors of omission, addition, substitution, and reversal.
6. Give an accurate translation of the writer's punctuation marks into pauses and stops. Phrasing is proper. Inflection of the voice is appropriate.
7. Read fluently and smoothly, keeping the eye well ahead of the voice. The pupil has an appropriate eye-voice span.
8. Have suitable quality and volume of voice: the voice is audible.
9. Have suitable pitch: the voice is not too high pitched.
10. Avoid labored precision in reading aloud. The pupils is not a word-by-word reader.
11. Have appropriate tempo and rate: The reading is neither too slow nor too rapid.

Oral reading teaches the pupil that writing is a record of the oral language. The pupil right from the beginning should read aloud the whole sentence, with proper pitch, stress, and juncture. This practice develops an awareness of the intonation patterns, rhythm, and melody of the language. Unfortunately, the intonation pattern cannot be fully represented by writing. The tone of voice (the para-language) and the gestured bodily movements (the kinetics) are only crudely represented by underlined words, exclamation points, or word choice.

Oral reading permits the teacher to see whether the pupil enunciates clearly, pronounces correctly, uses good phrasing, interprets the pronunciation correctly, uses proper voice inflection, has poise and proper voice control, uses proper posture, keeps the eyes well ahead of his or her speech, and uses an appropriate eye-voice span.

Oral reading also has diagnostic values. It is especially helpful in measuring accuracy and fluency in reading and gives clues to a child's eye movements and speech defects. Children need to be carefully evaluated by the teacher to see whether they can recognize words instantly and with accuracy. By listening to a pupil's oral reading, the teacher can detect errors of mispronunciation, substitution, hesitation, repetition, omission, addition, and word-by-word reading. These errors reflect many of the mistakes that the pupil is making in silent reading. Oral reading particularly helps the teacher to detect whether pupils are word callers, jerkily attacking one word at a time, reading as though they were reading a grocery list, paying no attention to the importance of grouping or clustering of words into thought units, and giving little consideration to meaning. Such pupils not only do not comprehend the materials, but cannot properly communicate the meaning to others. If the pupil makes more than 5 errors per 100 words, it suggests that the materials are too difficult for the learner.

A few practical observations might add to this discussion:

1. Do not (except for diagnostic testing as with an informal reading inventory) have the child read orally without previous silent reading. In the primary grades, particularly, where pupils have not yet developed an adequate sight vocabulary and adequate recognition skills, pupils should not be allowed to read aloud to the class without a preliminary silent reading.
2. Have the pupil read the sentence in a manner in which it would be spoken. Help the pupil to grasp the meaning intended and to evoke the mood and feeling the writer intended. Emphasize naturalness of tone. Perhaps the best evidence that readers have comprehended and that they have received the message intended by the writer is if they can read the material the way the writer would have read it.
3. Correct mispronounciations without embarrassing the child. Tell children the words if they hesitate too long. The research of Pany and McCoy (1988) indicates that corrective feedback on all oral reading errors (including such admonitions as "Try another way" or supplying the word) enhanced recognition of isolated words, improved word recognition in context, and enhanced comprehension. The latter is congruent with the theory that reducing the amount of attention for recoding frees the learner's capacity for higher-level comprehension processing.
4. Do not expect children to perform adequately on materials which they cannot read on an instructional level.
5. Help children to expand their eye-voice span. Good readers tend to have a much wider span and more moment-to-moment variations in span than do poor readers. This allows the good reader's voice to proceed smoothly and allows for proper phrasing, appropriate organization and grouping of words, proper inflection, and proper emphasis and stress.
6. Check to see whether the pupil's errors in oral reading are the result of simple carelessness, inattention, habit, immaturity, tenseness, or eye or visual defects; indeed whether they are the result of inadequate sight vocabulary, inadequate word recognition skills, or comprehension deficiencies.
7. See to it that the oral reading is purposeful. Have students read aloud those specific sentences that answer the questions posed earlier; a particular part of the story to prove an answer;

conversational parts; part of a story which describes an illustration; clues from the story that permit readers to predict the story's outcome; dialogue that reveals the feelings of a specific character (Ross, 1986). Such activities allow the teacher to check upon both the pupil's comprehension and on accuracy and fluency in reading.

8. Use phrase-reading activities to develop fluency in reading and reading in thought units (e.g., matching phrases with single words, reading to pupils and emphasizing phrase units, choral reading, reading in unison with the teacher, using punctuation as cues to phrasing, coloring, encircling, or underlining the phrases of a sentence, inserting slash marks to identify the phrases in a sentence, encircling the correct phrase of three alternative phrases to complete a sentence, rearranging scrambled phrases into a correct sentence order, practicing on common prepositional phrases).

9. Read to the pupil and use choral reading, dramatization, and such methods as the neurological impress method or echo reading (Heckelman, 1969) the repeated readings method (Samuels, 1979, 1985), the imitative method, with the teacher modeling and one of more students imitating the model, the simultaneous listening and reading methods (Aulls & Gelbart, 1980), paired reading (two or three children reading together) or assisted reading (Hoskisson, 1979) to provide the pupil with a model for reading in a fluent, conversational manner. In imitative reading the student follows the line of print and then rereads the same sentences, imitating the teacher's inflection (Wood, 1983). Choral reading emphasizes the prosodic cues such as intonation, stress, and duration. (Miccinati, 1985). Studies (Pearson & Fielding, 1983; Tierney, Readance & Dishner, 1980, 1985) show that learning to read with melody and rhythm does help children to comprehend text. Ross (1986) notes that oral reading aids comprehension by helping the pupil to discover units of meaning that should be read as phrases rather than word by word.

Each of the above strategies emphasizes fluency in reading. Unfortunately, fluency is a neglected goal of reading, even though lack of fluency is clearly characteristic of poor readers (Allington, 1983).

EXTENDING WORD RECOGNITION AND COMPREHENSION SKILLS

Step 5 of the DRA focuses on skill teaching, especially on the teaching of those word-identification and comprehension skills in which the pupil was shown to be deficient in Steps 3 and 4. The teacher should ask: Does the pupil have difficulty developing word meaning skills; phrase, sentence, paragraph, and story skills; higher-level comprehension skills (literal, organizational, inferential, evaluative, etc.); reading-study skills; rate skills; content area skills; or oral reading skills? Does the pupil have difficulty developing a purpose for reading; using personal schema in the comprehension of text; developing a questioning strategy; learning to monitor comprehension; or developing fluency in reading? Does the pupil have difficulty with inferential comprehension questions? Can she read critically? Can she organize and synthesize what she has read? Is she using a predictive strategy when reading and can she make predictions and confirm or reject the predictions made? Is the pupil able to use previous knowledge and what he is presently reading to test the validity of his own hypotheses and predictions? What strategies does the pupil use to construct main ideas? How does the pupil relate prior knowledge and experience to the text? How does the pupil generate summaries? How do pupils acquire the deep meanings? How do readers construct relations among the words and sentences of the text and between the text and their schemata and how do they build a model of the text?

Pearson and Dole (1988) note that poor readers improve in comprehension when:

1. Readers are provided explicit comprehension instruction (Baumann, 1988) or inference training by provision of extensive practice in answering inferential questions (Gordon & Pearson, 1983; Brown, Palincsar, & Armbruster, 1984; Hansen, 1981; Hansen & Pearson, 1983; Raphael & Pearson, 1985; Raphael & Wonnacott, 1985). Systematic guided practice and feedback in answering inferential level questions improve readers' answers to both literal and inferential questions (Hansen, 1981; Hansen & Pearson, 1983).
2. Readers activate relevant background knowledge and are given strategy training in integrating new knowledge with prior knowledge (Brown, Palincsar, & Armbruster, 1984; Brown & Palincsar, 1985; Hansen, 1981).

Gordon and Pearson (1983) used a four-fold strategy in developing inferential comprehension: (a) the teacher models the strategy, taking complete responsibility for asking and answering the inference question and for finding and describing how to get clues from the text to support the answer; (b) the teacher and student work together in using the strategy, with the teacher asking and answering the question and the student finding the clues and describing how to get clues from the text to support the answer; (c) the teacher asks the question, the pupil answers it, the teacher identifies the cues, and the student provides the rationale; and (d) the teacher asks the question and the student completes the next three steps of the process. This four-step process involved modeling, guided practice, and independent practice.

Raphael (Raphael & McKinney, 1983; Raphael & Pearson, 1985; Raphael & Wonnacott, 1985) added a fifth step: that of application. In step 1 (modeling and strategy) the teacher asked the question, answered it, assigned the QAR relationship (i.e., whether the answer is "right there" in the printed material, whether it requires a "think and search" effort, or whether it is an "on my own" situation) and justified the classification. Step 2 is guided practice, with the teacher being responsible for asking the question, answering the question, and assigning the QAR relationship and the student being responsible for justification of the classification. Step 3, also guided practice, has the student responsible for both assigning and justifying the classification. Step 4, independent practice, has the teacher asking the question and the pupil answering the question, assigning the QAR relationship, and justifying the relationship. Step 5, independent practice, which indicates true ownership of the strategy, has the pupil assume responsibility for all steps.

The pupil also needs to master the recoding skill. As noted earlier, good comprehenders tend to be good recoders, and inability to comprehend may result from under-instruction in recoding (Eeds-Kniep, 1979). It is not enough that pupils have mastered the grapheme/phoneme correspondences or that they can blend sounds. Their knowledge must go beyond accuracy to automaticity (Samuels, 1976a; 1988). Efficiency in comprehension and fluency in reading are dependent upon speed recoding.

Teaching in the area of word identification and recoding might take the form of reviewing phonic skills, tracing over dotted outlines of words, making a booklet of rhymes or phonograms, building words with alphabet cards, learning to add *s* at the end of the word, dividing two syllable words into their parts, doing exercises requiring the use of context in conjunction with the beginning consonant to identify a new word, and using programmed work sheets. However, such activities are not enough. The pupil needs to learn to use the meaning cues (picture cues, semantic context, syntactic context, and morphemic cues) to become self-directive in the word-identification process. He needs to master the grapheme/phoneme correspondences and develop a code for identifying words.

The major focus of chapters 8 and 9 is to identify what skills need to be taught and how to teach them in the area of word recognition. These chapters focus on the development of the within-word cues. Chapters 10 to 12 serve the same function in the area of comprehension. They emphasize the meaning cues. It is the skills that are discussed in chapters 8 through 12 that should be the major focus of skill teaching in Step 5 of the DRA.

Before turning our attention to the final step of the DRA we might offer some thoughts on skill/strategy teaching. Remember that skill teaching in reading should occur in a whole-language context. We focus first on what should occur before teaching.

Actions prior to skill teaching involve:

1. Getting the learners' attention and cognitive awareness; motivating the learner, promoting interest in the task, and developing a purpose for reading (Brown, Palincsar, & Armbruster, 1984).
2. Presenting skill teaching in a meaningful context, not in isolation, but in natural text reading (Baumann, 1984a, 1984b).
3. Relating skill teaching or what is being taught to pupils' personal schemata (Cooper, 1986). This phase involves an exploration of the pupil's background knowledge of the skill to be taught: "Today we are going to learn about [name of the skill]. Do any of you know anything about this skill?" (Blanton, Moorman, & Wood, 1986). This step helps pupils to organize their prior knowledge and helps the teacher to find out what learners know and what they do not know.
4. Letting students know exactly what they will learn in the lesson. The issue is: What will be taught? To answer this question the teacher must know what the pupil already knows and what is to be learned next (Hunter, 1982, 1989). Instructional objectives ought to specify the "what" or the content and the criterion behavior that validates successful accomplishment or shows that the learner has indeed learned. Objectives ought to specify what the learner should be able to accomplish at the end of the instruction.
5. Getting the learner set to learn: by asking a review question, having pupils write a short summary of what has already been learned, developing an anticipatory set (i.e., any activity that focuses attention, develops readiness for the task, and helps the learner to become mentally and physically ready for the task), letting pupils know why the content is important to them, and identifying the information that the pupil must have so he can attain the objective of the lesson.

You may want to review the multiple strategies that we suggested in Step 1 for developing readiness.

Actions during skill teaching involve:

1. Naming the skill, identifying activities that require the use of the skill, explaining the relevance of the skill, and identifying the

settings in which the skill might be applied (Blanton, Moorman, & Wood, 1986).
2. Having pupils verbalize or explain the skill in their own language (Blanton, Moorman, & Wood, 1986).
3. Modeling of skill or strategy (Blanton, Moorman, & Wood, 1986; Cooper, 1986; Duffy and Roehler, 1982; Duffy, Roehler, & Herrmann, 1988; Herrmann, 1988; Mason & Au, 1986): The teacher should verbalize and demonstrate the skill, show pupils what they are going to learn, discuss why the strategy is important, how to carry out or use the strategy, and when to apply the strategy, provide examples from text, and articulate rules or generalizations. Modeling should include both the modeling of the behaviors required for satisfactory performance on the task and the modeling of the mental processes undergirding strategic reading. The latter makes invisible reading processes visible; it lets the pupil know the cognitive secrets involved in the teacher's success on the task. The teacher must "think aloud" as it were, explaining, for example, the mental processes involved in answering an inferential question or in activating and accessing prior knowledge. Modeling is an exercise in metacognition and pupils will not be able to engage in metacognitive processes if they are not aware of the processes and skills needed to complete a task successfully and if they cannot tell whether they are performing the task correctly. Telling students how to do something is simply not enough. The pupil needs to be shown. Demonstration and coaching are critical elements in effective teaching (Hiebert & Colt, 1989). During the modeling stage the teacher takes complete responsibility for carrying out the strategy.
4. Checking the pupils' understanding of what has been taught. We refer the reader to step 3 of the DRA discussed earlier. The question strategy plays an important role.
5. Guided practice: Pupils need to be given the opportunity to practice the skill or strategy. Children need guided practice in the use of the skill (Cooper, 1986). This is the accuracy phase, in which the skill is mastered through practice and in which the skill is consolidated. The skill needs to be taught thoroughly, even to the point of automaticity. Guided practice means that the teacher and pupil collaborate in the acquisition of the strategy. Each pupil is given the support he needs to execute the strategy, but no more. Guided practice is accompanied by constant feedback and monitoring and by correction of mistakes.
6. Application or independent practice: Pupils need to apply their newly developed skills to alternative instructional materials (to

other basals, to workbooks, etc.), to real-world materials (to magazines, trade books, newspapers, etc.), and to other reading tasks (Raphael, 1982a; 1982b). Responsibility for task completion should gradually shift from teacher to student (Gordon & Pearson, 1983; Hansen & Pearson, 1983; Raphael, 1982a; 1982b; 1984). The emphasis is on automaticity and fluency, with the pupil assuming full responsibility. At the application level the pupil moves from knowledge (i.e., possession of the information) and comprehension (i.e., understanding of the information) to application (i.e., applying the information to new tasks), to analysis (i.e., analytic thinking, creative thinking, problem solving and categorical thinking), to synthesis, and to evaluation.
7. *Closure*: This occurs when the skill is integrated into the total reading process.

Pupils benefit from skill teaching when they learn to summarize what they have learned, when the teacher provides specific and immediate feedback about their performance, when they verbalize how and when to use the skill, when pupils learn how to develop hypotheses, when they can image what they are reading, when they can link new information with prior knowledge, when they can monitor their own process of comprehending and when they are aware of where they get information to answer questions in text (Baker & Brown, 1984a, 1984b; Duffy, et al., 1986; Raphael, 1982, 1984; Roehler, et al., 1987), when they can use fix-up strategies when their comprehension lags, and when they are given the opportunity for independent practice.

ENRICHMENT AND FOLLOW-UP ACTIVITIES

Step 6 is an integral part of the reading lesson. It may not even be placed last. It is in many ways the most important step of the directed reading activity. It is a time for independent, sustained silent reading, in which the virtues of whole language, literature-based reading, and individualized reading are perhaps most visible. We agree fully with Hiebert and Colt (1989) that the ultimate test of an effective literacy program is the ability of children to read independently. Step 6 assures that children are given the opportunity to read on their own. It gives credence to the view that children learn to read, to a great extent, by reading (DuCharme, 1987; Krashen, 1987; Smith, 1988). The purpose of Step 6 is to foster a love for reading.

It is in Step 6 that individualized reading, with its emphasis on seeking, self-selection of materials from a pre-determined shelf of books that are written on the pupil's independent level, and pacing, is particularly effective. Each classroom should have sections of books spanning children's interests and ability levels from which the child can select a book to read on an independent level. Wide and extensive reading is a major factor in developing children's reading skills. Every reading lesson should allow some time for children to read what they like and what presents few reading problems for them. Good readers are not children who can read, but who do read, who want to read, and for whom reading becomes an abiding interest.

Step 6 should not be limited to only reading. It may well involve dramatization, telling of a story, shared oral reading, searching encyclopedias and other books for additional information, or following a recipe to make cookies.

An important activity is to have pupils carry out writing activities that correlate with the story or content read; for example, writing a paragraph about one's favorite character. Other activities may have pupils act out a story. The teacher should occasionally read aloud or play recordings of oral reading. And, students can sometimes read aloud school bulletins, poems, and content area materials that they have read independently.

An important aspect of Step 6 is review. Each reading lesson should culminate with a review of what has been taught: of the words that were learned, of the specific phonic and morphemic strategies that have been covered, and of the outline or semantic web that summarizes the theme or moral of the story. At times the review may simply involve a rereading of the specific story parts.

SUMMARY

The DRA provides the format for organizing the reading lesson and for the development of the basic objectives of reading instruction. The DRA is not a method of teaching reading. It is a model or format for organizing and structuring a reading lesson and for teaching reading. It is particularly appropriate for the development of both comprehension and word recognition skills. It identifies what should be happening before, during, and after reading.

PART V
The Word Identification and Word Recognition Process

The Preface and chapter 1 outlined the basic theme of this text: reading is both a word-identification process and a comprehension process and reading requires an integration of these two processes. The development of these two processes is thus a major goal of reading instruction. The teacher must understand these processes, must know how to develop them, must know how to correct and remediate when and where deficiencies occur, and must be able to help the pupil to integrate them.

Chapter 5 observed that the comprehension processes interact with the word-identification processes and that comprehension is dependent upon the reader's word-processing skills. Comprehension is aided when pupils can identify words quickly and accurately (i.e., automaticity in word recognition is a significant strategy in comprehension), and when pupils can recode most of the words. The reading comprehension of even skilled readers is likely to be disrupted and impaired if most of the words are not recognized or if they are not identified accurately and rapidly. Accuracy and fluency in word recognition are clearly essential to comprehension (Pany & McCoy, 1988; Torgesen, 1986).

Nicholson (1986) notes that fast recoding affects comprehension because it enables children to expand their lexicon of word meanings and it helps the reader to process sentences efficiently, to access the mental lexicon more quickly, to get words more quickly into short-term memory, to read more words of text and thus to benefit more from the context, to develop meanings more rapidly, and to be more accurate in reading, leading to greater access to precise meanings.

Chapter 5 also observed that the pupil who can use the within-word cues to recode the word has an indirect access to meaning, that combining of meaning cues with the within-word cues is what results in an integrated approach to identification and comprehension, and that reading is message sharing. The message reveals itself through the schematic-semantic, syntactic, and lexical cues, but also through the visual-graphic, phonological, orthographic, and graphophonemic cues. Reading, consequently, must be concerned with the development of accuracy in recoding, with automaticity, with automatic semantic activation, and with the learning of the within-word identification strategies (especially the phonic, phonogram, and spelling pattern cues and the morphemic cues).

Part V's main focus is thus on the *what*: what needs to be taught and what needs to be learned by the pupil to develop word identification skills. Part V emphasizes that when the pupil's personal schema and knowledge of the context or meaning cues, and indeed of the within-word cues, are unable to help the pupil predict meaning, to reduce uncertainty, to identify the words correctly, and to comprehend the text, the pupil's information base, especially as it relates to the within-word cues, must be expanded and enlarged. The pupil needs to learn to deal with the regularities and the irregularities in the graphic and visual features of words, with the orthographic and internal structure of words, and with the phonologic information contained in the printed word.

Unfortunately, there has developed in the last 20 years a tendency to downgrade the importance of the within-word cues, of accuracy in reading, and of automaticity in recoding. It is often suggested that it is possible to read with and for meaning without accuracy and, indeed, that accuracy and automaticity have relatively little value. We believe that this position leads to many problems in attaining true meaning and veridical message sharing. Meaning and its apprehension are primary in reading, but surely it is wrong to suggest that accuracy in reading is something that can be discounted, that inaccuracy is something for which the reader can easily compensate, or that the ability to recode fluently and with accuracy does not need the teacher's full attention.

THE NEED FOR WORD RECOGNITION INSTRUCTION

Perfetti (1985) presents strong arguments for the key role of word identification with which we essentially agree:

1. Differences between good and poor readers are directly traceable to and often occur at the word-identification level. Pupils need to develop an increasing ability to recognize and process printed symbols efficiently.

2. Readers differ in orthographic knowledge and in the use of orthographic structure, which is a feature of all alphabetic writing systems. High-ability readers take advantage of the orthographic structure of words more so than do low-ability readers. The English orthographic structure is such that is constrains the arrangement of the graphemes. Thus *q* is always followed by *u*, and *tr* can begin a word, but it cannot end one.
3. High-ability readers and low-ability readers differ in recoding, in activating a word's name code, or in learning the alphabetic code. Recoding, defined as the transformation of a printed letter string into a phonetic code, or printed input into a speech form, or the activation of word-level codes or the name of the word from memory, is a process that sharply differentiates children who differ in reading ability. Skilled readers are both faster and more accurate in recoding, and they have mastered the alphabetic principle.
4. Eye-movement research supports the view that reading of single words plays a dominant role in reading. Research shows that the eyes in reading come to rest on or fixate on most of the words of the text, that only five or six letters to the right of the fixation are perceived, and that words beyond the word being fixated are not processed sufficiently for their meaning to be encoded. Research clearly indicates that successful reading depends on fixating many words, not just a few.
5. Efficient readers are not dependent solely upon context even though they will still use the context to build a text model.
6. Efficiency of word access or efficiency in recalling words beyond accuracy (i.e., when it is automatic) is an important instructional goal. Without it, comprehension will not reach its potential. Comprehension depends upon fluent word recognition (Samuels, 1988).

Top-down theorists often downplay the significance of the rules mapping letters to phonemes or recoding. They imply that the pupil's linguistic talents will allow him or her to use context, especially the sentence and story context, to handle the problems of word recognition. Thus, Smith (1988) writes: "Reading is not normally a matter of extracting and putting together the meaning of individual words, but of bringing relevant meaning to texts" (p. 286).

Juel's findings (1980) are particularly provocative. She found that among second and third graders the skilled readers were text-driven or bottom-up readers, but the nonskilled readers were context-driven or top-down readers. The good readers appeared to rely on the context only when the within-word cues were weak; they became top-down readers only when trying to cope with the words of low frequency or with words that were difficult to recode. Good readers appear to use knowledge about the graphemes that they have stored in the form of schemata to construct an interpretation of the author's message.

Perfetti (1985) suggests that context-free word recognition is a salient characteristic of reading ability and that an important development in reading ought to be a decrease in dependence upon the within-text context. Juel and Roper-Schneider (1982) also note that mastery of context-free word recognition is one of the major factors that differentiates between good and poor readers. Gough (1984,) likewise observes that skilled readers are so good at recoding that they ordinarily do not use the within-text context.

In Perfetti's (1985) view:

> "The main failing of the top-down approach of Goodman . . . is that it does not recognize that one of the cueing systems (that is, the graphic cue system) is more central than the others (especially in the word identification process). A child who learns to code has knowledge that can enable him to read no matter how the semantic, syntactic, and pragmatic cues might conspire against him. No matter how helpful they are to reading, these [latter] cues are not really a substitute for the ability to identify a word." (p. 239)

Perfetti adds: "It has yet to be demonstrated that there are individuals who have comprehension strategy deficits without [recoding] fluency problems" (p. 244).

Obviously, word-recognition instruction, including recoding, should be a primary objective in beginning reading instruction. Perhaps all, or at least most, comprehension instruction is effective only within the limits placed by the reader's word-processing skills. The pupil must learn to discover the coding principles of the writing system. The evidence clearly indicates that it is either impossible or difficult to become a skilled reader without mastering the conventionalized code that maps the writing system to speech. Young children with difficulty in reading almost invariably have imperfect knowledge of the coding system. "Readers of low ability have inefficient— slow and effortful—coding as the major obstacle to reading achievement" (Perfetti, 1985, p. 10). Nevertheless, successful reading depends upon increasingly less expenditure of effort and energy on the coding skills and a greater expenditure of energy on the increased demands of the text and on the application of higher-level comprehension processes. Coding is not less useful as the pupil matures in reading; its use is more refined.

The implications seem clear. Even though reading is a search for meaning, it also involves skill in recognizing words. Word recognition and accuracy in reading play a primary and essential role in reading. The reasons for this are many. Reading always involves encounters with words. There can be no comprehension and communication of meanings from writer to reader without the sign system or the words on the printed page.

Liberman et al. (1985) observe that one must get to the word before one can get to its meaning; that the word must be apprehended before one can deal with the meaning conveyed by the words. The words are the reader's first contact with meaning. They provide the stimulus to the excitation of the reader's cognitive, predictive, and schematic processes and it is to them that the reader brings meanings. But word recognition of itself is not sufficient for comprehension.

Even though some readers can and do go directly to meaning through direct visual access or whole-word reading strategies, many readers, especially beginning readers, use the phonological route to meaning. Unfortunately, readers cannot resort to these rules, or this information, if they have not been taught it. A basic thesis in reading today is that pupils should bring to bear in the comprehension of text their personal schemata, undoubtedly some of which include their aural-oral experiences with words. If the ability to comprehend depends on the ability to associate what is on the printed page with what the reader knows, then it seems logical that pupils will want to match the printed word with its aural/oral equivalent and associate with it the meaning that they have associated with the aural/oral form of the word.

Readers do make mistakes in reading. They miscue. There is a tendency among some educators to downplay these miscues when the miscue maintains the "approximate meaning." If proficiency and accuracy in oral reading is a legitimate goal in reading (and we certainly think it is), then it seems an equally valid goal to have the pupil develop accuracy and indeed automaticity in pronouncing the words on the printed page. Fluency in reading and certainly reading orally to others and presumably sharing a message with others orally requires this.

When a pupil reads "house" for "home," the teacher may be satisfied that the pupil is reading for meaning, but surely this is only partially true. House does not have the same connotations as home and the schemata of "house" and "home" contain quite different associations in almost all of us. If the pupil reads "small" for "minute," there is indeed some sharing of meaning, but the reader may not be comprehending what the writer intended. Presumably, the writer's selection of the word minute had a purpose. The writer selects specific words that are designed to elicit concrete and specific or perhaps abstract reactions from the reader, and if the reader reacts only with a "within-the-ball-park" meaning or one that in general way skirts the meaning intended then sharing of meaning is likely to be quite superficial.

The problems created by misreading content words may often not be serious, but surely it is another matter when the pupil misreads punctuation (period, comma, colon, etc.), omits or adds negatives, alters the tense (present, past, future), fails to process the possessive, alternates the comparative with the superlative, changes the active to passive or the passive to the active, or adds or omits prefixes and suffixes.

Reading in the content fields or in an expository text presents additional problems. A minor substitution (for example, in tense, number, punctuation or even in content words) can result in total misunderstanding of the intended message. There is even a potentially more serious problem when the pupil reads inaccurately safety words, traffic signs, medicine labels, directions of various types, maps, and other important guides.

Bellare (1986) observes that it is a totally negative approach when the teacher treats some miscues as acceptable, thereby condoning and allowing carelessness; and it is unrealistic and misleading when the instructor presupposes that readers can react to the message if they are not able to identify and generally to recode the words. The reader must read what is on the printed page, not what he thinks is there. The research shows that the more automatic the word identification process, the greater is the pupil's potential for comprehension. There is ample evidence that to be a good comprehender the pupil needs to automatize the encoding and recoding process. If encoding and recoding (sounding of the word) takes too long (the research certainly indicates that poor readers use context cues because they are too slow in the use of within-word cues), the pupil may not be able to retain the initial information presented by the sentence long enough to effect comprehension for the sentence. The less time spent on word identification, the greater is the amount available for comprehension. The reason accurate, rapid word identification is significant for reading comprehension is the fact that words cannot be organized into meaningful groups without it. The recognition of words must be rapid enough so that it does not overload short-term memory. Stanovich, Cunningham, and Feeman (1984) suggest that word recognition must be automatic in order to provide sufficient meaning for comprehension, so as to free the cognitive capacity of the reader to effect comprehension. Skilled readers are such precisely because their recognition speed is faster than that of poor readers and they need to allocate only minimum attention to word recognition, freeing their attention for comprehension. Conversely, poor, beginning, and young readers are slower in word recognition and consequently need to allocate most of their attention to word recognition. Beginning readers (LaBerge & Samuels, 1976, 1985; Lesgold, Resnick, & Hammond, 1985; Perfetti, Finger, & Hogaboam, 1978) who develop automaticity in word identification are better able to comprehend text.

Working memory and attention are specific factors that affect sentence processing. Overlearning diminishes the need for conscious attending, thus reducing the processing resources needed and thereby freeing those resources for allocation to comprehension processes. Clearly, the greater the amount of processing time spent on word identification the less there is available for comprehension.

WORD IDENTIFICATION VERSUS WORD RECOGNITION

Since Part V deals with the word-recognition process, it seems useful here to offer definitions of word identification and word recognition.

Word identification refers to the ability to develop a visual memory for a word not previously encountered or learned. It is the initial acquaintance with a word. A broader definition extends the meaning of word identification to include the recall of the spoken symbol that the visual symbol represents. Word identification is thus sometimes defined as the first unlocking of the pronunciation of a word. In this book the word "recoding" rather than "decoding" has been used for this process.

Word recognition, on the other hand, is the perception and recollection of a previously identified word. It is a subsequent acquaintance. Pupils recognize the word form that they previously identified as being the same one they now know. Identification and recognition are not the same process and the means of identifying a word may be completely different from those of recognition.

THE SYMTOMATOLOGY OF READERS HAVING DIFFICULTY IDENTIFYING WORDS

The discussion to this point has intimated that a major difficulty for some readers is that of identifying words. Pupils reveal their difficulties in the following ways:

1. An unusual amount of difficulty with high-utility words, with the core words, without which it is impossible to use the context in reading.
2. Asking again and again for help with the same word.
3. Inability to identify and recode words on their age or grade level.
4. Recoding of even familiar words more slowly and experiencing greater difficulty with visual recognition and recall than is average for the pupil's age and grade level.
5. Unusual difficulty recalling similar-appearing words or words of graphic similarity; such as bed and fed.
6. Inability to develop a gestalt for the word. The pupil does not experience the "flash" global identification of a word as a whole.
7. Tendency to guess wildly at words. The pupil pays attention to specific letters and guesses wildly at the rest (*horse* becomes *house*). The pupil's rendition of a word is often phonetically unrelated to the desired response. The spelling of words may be odd.

8. Arrhythmical reading that is replete with word-recognition errors. The pupil shows more vowel, consonant, reversal, omission, addition, substitution, perservation, and repetition errors.

Obviously, the word-identification program must be designed to help pupils who show any of the problems listed above.

In assessing and evaluating pupil inadequacies in word-identification, it is important that the teacher determine whether children have the same difficulty in pronouncing words in isolation as in identifying them in context. Lyon (1984) found that word recognition is faster in context than in isolation, especially for poor readers.

OUTLINE OF PART V

Part V consists of two chapters, each designed to provide for the attainment of one of the major goals of reading instruction, that of competency in identifying words. These chapters individually and collectively have as their major purposes the development of a sight or recognition vocabulary; the development of accuracy, automaticity and fluency in identifying words and of recoding words; the teaching of within-word cues; and learning how to break the alphabetic code.

Chapter 8, "Developing Instant Recognition of Letters and Words: The Integrated Reading Method", has as its purpose the development of what is commonly referred to as a sight vocabulary but which might more correctly be termed an instant recognition vocabulary. It teaches the learner how to encode printed letters and words. The chapter initially focuses on the letters of the alphabet. It discusses letter discrimination, letter reversal, letter naming and writing, and especially the significance of letters and letter sequence in the word-identification process. The second part of the chapter deals with word identification and with the use of the Integrated Reading Method in developing word identification. It is designed to help pupils to become independent and automatic in the process of naming the configuration or in recoding. It outlines the teaching of the within-word cues, of the rules mapping letters to phonemes or the grapheme-phoneme correspondences, and of the coding principles of the English writing system. It teaches the pupil to identify words as a total configuration or gestalt but also as composed of letters whose sequence gives the word its ideosyncratic identity and symbolizes the sequence of sounds that represent the total word.

The first part of chapter 9 "Development of Grapheme-Phoneme Correspondence Knowledge and of Structural or Morphemic Analysis Skills" focuses on phonics or the grapheme-phoneme correspondences, on spelling patterns, on phonograms, and identification by analogy. It provides the information needed to break the alphabetic code, to convert the visual sequence of letters into the appropriate sequence of sounds, and to become proficient in the recoding process. The second part of chapter 9 develops an understanding of the morphemes. It is based on the observation that deficiencies in sight vocabulary and the pupil's miscues in reading words are often the direct consequence of an inability to handle morphemic cues, particularly inflectional endings and inflectional changes, contractions, compound words, prefixes and suffixes, syllabication, and accent. The morphemes, which affect both a word's structure and meaning, are another facet of the graphic or within-word cue system (and indeed of the meaning cue system) that help readers both to identify words and to associate meaning with them.

Figure Part V-1 graphs the content of chapter 9:

Figure Part V-1: The Word Identification and Word Recognition Process

The Grapheme-Phoneme Correspondences		Strucural and Morphemic Analysis Skills
Consonants	*Vowels*	
Beginning, middle, and ending single consonant grapheme-phoneme correspondences	*Single short vowel correspondences*	*Inflectional endings (s, 's, s', es, en, ess, ing, ed, er, est)*
Rhyming and the phonograms.	Single long vowel correspondences	*Inflectional changes (city-cities, wife-wives)*
Beginning and ending consonant blends	*Long* vowel–*Silent e.*	*Compound words*
Consonant digraphs a. *ch, sh, th, th,* 　*wh, ng, zh* b. *gh, ph* c. Doubling of same consonant (*bb, dd, ff, gg,* etc.) d. Silent letter combinations: (*mb, ck, gm, kn, wr,* etc.)	*Double vowel correspondences: ai, ay, ee, ea, oa,* etc. *Modified Vowels: au, aw, eu, ew.* *Diphthongs: oi* and *ou*	*Contractions* *Roots, prefixes, and suffixes* *Hyphenated words* *Syllabication*
Three letter blends (*chr, phr, scr, spr*) *Trigraphs (chm, cht, ght, tch)*	*R-controlled vowels*	*Accentuation*

If reading is a matter of making global and focal predictions while reading and if this depends on making use of one's personal schemata and of the meaning and within-word cues, it necessarily follows that teachers of reading need to expand the pupil's schemata, especially in the area of the within-word cues.

Chapters 8 and 9 thus focus on the within-word cues, expanding both the pupil's declarative knowledge (the *what*) and his procedural knowledge (the *how*): *What* the pupil needs to be taught to become an efficient identifier and recoder of words and *how* the information is to be taught.

Chapter 8
Developing Instant Recognition of Letters and Words: Using the Integrated Reading Method

I. Introduction
II. Developing Instant Recognition and Naming of Letters
    A. Developing Letter Discrimination and Recognition
    B. Letter Orientation and the Problem of Reversing
        1. Causes of Reversal Behavior
        2. Correction of Reversal Difficulties
    C. Teaching Letter Naming
    D. Writing the Letters
    E. Sounding the Letters
    F. Letter Sequence and Word Identification
III. Developing Instant Recognition and Naming of Words
IV. Stages of Word Identification
V. The Steps of the Integrated Reading Method
    A. The Pupil Sees the Word
        1. Parallel Processing of the Letters
        2. Instructional Directives
    B. The Pupil Hears the Word Spoken
    C. The Pupil Pronounces the Word
    D. The Unknown Word Is Contrasted With a Known Word
        1. The Coding System
        2. Phonological Awareness
        3. Developing the Spelling-Sound Correspondence Rules: Grapheme-Phoneme Relationships
        4. The Minimum-Difference Strategy
        5. Adjunct Strategies
            a. Teaching of Spelling Patterns
            b. Teaching the Phonograms
    E. The Pupil Spells the Word Orally
    F. The Pupil Traces and Writes the Word From Memory
    G. The Teacher Presents the Word in Another Sentence Context
    H. The Target Word is Practiced and Rehearsed
V. Whole Word or Analytical Phonics Versus Synthetic Phonics
VI. Summary

CHAPTER 8
Developing Instant Recognition of Letters and Words: Using the Integrated Reading Method

The introduction to Part V of this text suggested that the major goal of Part V is teaching the pupil a sight or instant recognition vocabulary. It would be fortunate indeed if all children learning to read could identify all words in sentences by using meaning cues or that they came to the reading task with a schema enriched with a total understanding of the within-word cues. Unfortunately, such is not the case. Children need to be specifically taught to identify words, and chapter 8 presents the Integrated Method as a model to accomplish this goal.

The issue in chapter 8 is different from that in chapter 5. In chapter 5, the concern was with the strategies the pupil could use to predict an unknown word, including the nonvisual information, the meaning cues and the within-word cues or a combination thereof. In this chapter, the issue is: What can the pupil do and indeed what can the teacher do if the pupil's knowledge of the meaning and within-word cues is not adequate to the task? How can the pupil be helped to identify, sound, and to remember the word? Chapter 8 thus focuses on the specific task of teaching children how to identify or to encode total words, how to remember them, and how to sound or name them.

We begin our analysis by examining the problems of letter discrimination and of letter naming. Most children come to school with substantial information about letters. They frequently can discriminate one letter from another and can name them. Unfortunately, there are some who cannot do this and need to be taught.

DEVELOPING INSTANT RECOGNITION AND NAMING OF LETTERS

Differentiation and identification of the shapes of single letters and naming of the letters are necessary prerequisites for reading efficiency. The ability to recognize, discriminate, and name the letters is one of the best predictors of first-grade reading achievement, and the lack of that knowledge almost certainly assures poor word recognition and low reading achievement (Finn, 1985).

Developing Letter Discrimination and Recognition

There are many data to support the thesis that letter recognition is an important reading process. When recoding is difficult, as it often is for the beginning and the poor reader, the reader frequently resorts to serial letter-by-letter processing. Even mature readers, although they are capable of perceiving more complex forms or gestalten, also at times have to analyze words into their parts. Children pay particular attention to the parts of words when they are required to discriminate between similar-appearing words. Four- and five-year-old children and poor readers, who have greater difficulty with physically confusable or similar words (Fredericksen, 1979; Steinheiser & Guthrie, 1977), generally tend to identify words by certain key letters, letter arrangements, or other outstanding characteristics.

Eye-movement studies also indicate that children rarely see a total word per fixation. In the first grade not more than one-half of a word is usually seen. This means that the child must look at the parts of words, retain them in memory, and combine them mentally to form the total word. Furthermore, it takes the reader longer to process long words than short words, with the reader spending about 30 milliseconds on a word for each additional letter (Carpenter & Just, 1981).

Marchbanks and Levin (1965), in a study involving 50 kindergarten children and 50 first-grade children, found that specific letters were much more important in determining recognition than was the overall shape of the word. The initial letter was the most salient cue, next came the final letter, and finally the internal letters. The least-used cue was the word shape. Carpenter and Just (1981), Just and Carpenter (1987), Marsh et al. (1981), and Calfee and Pointkowski (1981) found that children generally identify words through the letters or information given at the beginning of the word. Disabled readers have special difficulty with the medial and final segments of words and with vowels (Shankweiler & Liberman, 1972) which usually are placed in the middle of words.

Clearly, the mature reader reacts to the total word in recognition and in meaningful interpretation, but children may not do so in learning to identify the word. The unit of recognition is not necessarily the unit of identification. And, as we shall see later, even though the reader needs to develop instant recognition of words as a total configuration or gestalt, recognition of individual letters, especially of the sequence of letters in words, plays a key role in attaining success in reading.

A key question still remains. How does the child recognize and discriminate the form of each of the 26 letters? What determines whether two letters are equivalent or different? Smith (1988) suggests that letter identification and indeed word identification are special problems of pattern recognition. Both involve the discrimination and categorization of visual information. Smith (1988) and Rayner and Pollatsek (1989) all favor a feature-detection or feature-identification analysis model of letter or word identification over a template-matching model. The latter suggests that we have stored in our brains a representation of every pattern that we can recognize. This view is rejected because any slight variation of the letter A (such as lower case vs. upper case, cursive vs. manuscript), for example, would result in nonrecognition of the symbol. The starting point for feature-detection theory (Rayner & Pollatsek, 1989) is the recognition that letters have many common elements (i.e., they consist of horizontal, vertical, oblique, and curved lines), but each letter also has components different from every other letter. Feature detection begins with the analysis of these component elements of letters.

The consensus today is that letter recognition (of *h*, for example) involves discrimination of the distinguishing or criterial features (Rayner & Pollatsek, 1989) that differentiate one letter from another. The perceiver in identifying a letter develops a list of features for that letter and compares this list of features with a list stored in memory.

Letters are clearly conglomerates of features, consisting of lines, angles, circles, and semi-circles. Montgomery (1977) notes that 23 letters of the alphabet can be formed using small circles (o) short sticks (i), long sticks (l), and looped sticks (r). Blair (1977) notes that lower-case letters can be grouped on the basis of size and shape into six groups: stick letters (i,l,t), round letters (o,a,c,e), tall letters (b,d,h,f,k), tail letters (g,p,q,j), and slant letters (v,w,x,y,z). In general, criterial differences are the short, long, and looped sticks, the height and slant of the letters, or the tail on some letters. Gibson (1969) notes that the distinguishing letter features of capital letters include among others straight lines: horizontal (A), vertical (B), diagonal (K); curved lines: closed (D), open vertically (J), open horizontally (G); and intersection: (A) (E).

However, it is not enough for the learner to know that a letter has long or short sticks or circles. The perceiver must also know which features are criterial for specific categories, which permit the placement of the letter into a distinctive category (Smith, 1988), and which differentiate one letter from another. Thus, the prime concerns in letter identification are how to segregate visual configurations into categories and to determine what the criterial sets of features for a given category are.

Each of the 26 letters of the alphabet has a specific "feature list" in Smith's (p. 107) terminology. The feature list permits the allocation of visual information to specific categories. Smith calls any set of features that meet the specifications of a particular category a "criterial set." Alternative criterial sets of features which specify the same category are termed "functionally equivalent" (e.g., *a, A*). Letters which possess certain criterial or distinctive attributes are placed into different categories and are perceived to be different. When letters share many features (e.g., *b, d, p, q*), or when they differ in only one feature, they are described as similar and are frequently confused with each other. Letters that are rarely confused with each other are assumed to have very few features in common (Smith, 1988). Dunn-Rankin (1968) found that typical confusion clusters are (a, e, n, o, u), (t, f, i), and (h, m, n).

Smith (1988) does not define what a feature is because: "Not enough is known about the structure of the human visual system to say exactly what is the featural information that the system looks for" (p. 113). Interestingly feature analysis, that is, scrutinizing a stimulus pattern, a letter or word for features in order to recognize clearly, involves bottom-up processing (Woolfolk, 1990).

Smith (1988) observes that "Presenting *h* to children 50 times and telling them it is "*h*" because it has an ascender will not help them to discriminate the letter. The presentation of *h* and other letters in pairs and groups together with the feedback that they are *not* functionally equivalent is the kind of information required for the visual system and the brain to find out very quickly what the distinctive features really are" (p. 14). Although the significant difference between *h* and *n* may be the ascender in *h*, it is "an oversimplification to say that the ascender is the actual feature" (p. 14). Smith (1988) believes it is the perceiver who determines what is a significant or criterial difference and what is functionally equivalent. Smith "trusts" the child's ability to locate the information required, provided the child has the opportunity to make comparisons and to discover what the significant differences are. He adds: "Remember, the primary problem of identification is to distinguish the presented configuration from all those to which it might be equivalent but is not" (p. 103). Lovitt (1984) suggests a sequence for introducing the lower case letters, using frequency and learnability of the letters as the criterion (Table 8-1).

Another criterion for letter introduction may be the socioeconomic status of the learner. Children from homes at a lower socioeconomic level seem to be able to learn the capital letters more rapidly than the lower- case letters (Wheelock & Silvaroli, 1967). The letters of decreasing difficulty for

TABLE 8-1: Sequence for Introducing Letters

	a	m	t	s	i	f	d	r	o	g	l	h	u	c
Frequence	M	H	H	H	H	M	H	M	M	M	H	M	M	H
Learning	E	E	D	E	M	E	D	M	M	M	M	M	D	M
Frequence	M	H	M	M	L	M	L	L	L	L	L	L		
Learnability	M	M	M	E	M	M	D	D	D	D	D	D		
	b	n	k	v	e	p	w	j	y	x	q	z		

Key: Frequency: H (high), M (medium), L (low)
   Learnability: E (easy), M (medium), D (difficult).
From Lovitt, 1984, p. 13.

first-grade children of lower socioeconomic homes are: *l, q, g, d, t, b, a, j, u, v, n, y, r, f, w, i, m, p, k, e, x, c, z, s,* and *o*, with children confusing the *l* most frequently (76%) and the *o* the least frequently (7%).

Suggestions (Dechant, 1981, 1982) for teaching letter discrimination include: (a) teaching of letter differences rather than similarities, (b) use of color, and (c) use of kinesthetic techniques. The teacher needs to point out to the learner the specific features (e.g., tall-short, open-closed, curved-straight) that distinguish one letter from another. The pupil must be relatively more skilled in noting the differences than in noting the similarities. The pupil must learn what to look for. Matching of a symbol to its duplicate while both forms are visible (i.e., simultaneous discrimination) is not as useful in developing a visual memory for a symbol as is locating an example of the symbol after the stimulus card has been removed (i.e., successive discrimination).

The use of color to make the letter stand out from the word is particularly effective in developing letter discrimination. If the target word is *hat*, and the *h* has not been mastered, color the *h*. Jones (1965) found that color was a definite aid to visual perception among kindergarten children. Egeland (1975) suggests coloring in red the parts of two letters that are different and then gradually fading out the color cue. Copple (1975) recommends the use of transparent overlays: placing an *f* over a *b* immediately reveals the difference. Kinesthetic techniques, such as cutting out letters, tracing letters, writing letters in clay or sand, or copying letters, are useful in teaching letter discrimination or in reinforcing discrimination.

Letter Orientation and the Problem of Reversing

Another concern in letter and word discrimination is the orientation of letters and words. This is a new concept for young children. They have not been taught to observe directions in their everyday perceptions. A car looks like a car whether the eye movement is from left to right or from right to left. However, in reading a letter or word this is not so. In the letters, *b* and *d*, the orientation makes the difference. The letters, s-a-w, read from left to right say /*saw*/, but read from right to left say /*was*/. Thus, one of the first requirements in learning to read is the learning of new habits of perception. Children must learn to read through words by processing from left to right. They must learn that the order of the letters in a word symbolizes the time order in which the sounds are made.

Various stimuli can become a sign or a symbol for the same referent. If the stimulus is incompletely differentiated, it will be confused with similar stimuli. In reading, numerous errors arise because of this simple fact. The child who reverses, who sees *b* as *d* and who sees *was* and reads *saw*, makes such an error. He has confused the sign. Reversals frequently may be simply stimuli that are not completely differentiated from all others. The development of the right-left direction sense and the ability to differentiate right from left develops steadily between the ages of 5 and 9, being most rapid at ages 6 and 7. The right-left discrimination on a person facing the examinee is a separate skill that develops between 8 and 11 and is probably not developed completely until age 12.

The term commonly used to indicate that the pupil is making the wrong directional attack on letters or words is reversing. Reversals (or strephosymbolia, twisted symbols, a term originated by Orton, 1928), is the tendency to reverse letters, parts of words, or even whole words. Reversals of letters showing right-left symmetry (*p* and *q* and *b* and *d*) are called static reversals. When the sequence of letters is reversed and a new word is formed (*was* for *saw*), the reversal is termed a kinetic reversal. Other types of reversals involve various transpositions of letters (animal-aminal). There are numerous kinds of transposition (initial letter to an internal position, terminal letter to an initial position, internal letter to a different internal position, etc.). The parts of phrases and compound words may also be transposed as when "in the house" becomes "house in the", or "barnyard" becomes "yardbarn." Finally, letters within words may be inverted while reading: *way* becomes *may*; *help* becomes *yelp*; or *n* is confused with *u*. It is interesting to note that only in the cases of static reversals (*b-d*) is the second letter a mirror image of the first. "No" is not a mirror image of "on." Thus, in reversals other than static reversals, the difficulty is not one of letter orientation, but rather may be one of letter sequence.

Causes of Reversal Behavior

Numerous causes have been adduced to explain reversals. Orton (1928) suggested that reversal behavior is caused by defective neurological organization or inadequate, mixed, or left cerebral dominance. Reversals are said to be indicative of perceptual disorders that reflect impaired neurological processes or developmental deficits or delays. Orton inferred that in the case of confused dominance the child on one occasion would attack the written word with a left and, at another time, with a right orientation. Orton suggested that a person looking at the word *saw* develops an engram for the word in the dominant brain hemisphere (usually the left) and a mirror image for the word in the nondominant or right hemisphere. Orton further believed that, if the left hemisphere of right handers did not become dominant before the child begins to read, the result is the coexistence of mirror images in the left and right hemisphere, and this interhemispheric rivalry in turn leads to reversals, or to reading of the mirror image of the letter or word.

Vellutino (1979; 1980, 1987) rejects Orton's hypothesis and observes that errors such as calling *was* /saw/ are the result of difficulties in visual-verbal learning and in storing and retrieving the names of printed words rather than of visual misperception, dysfunction in the visual-spacial system, or difficulty in maintaining proper directionality. Vellutino suggests that reversal behavior is a symptom of a reading disorder rather than the cause of the disorder. Vellutino adds that reversal errors account for no more than 20% to 25% of the reading errors of severely disabled or dyslexic readers. We might add that this is not an insignificant number.

Other explanations of reversal behavior are:

1. Inadequate maturation. During the early school years, reversals have been considered to be normal phenomena. Among kindergarten children the incidence of reversals is as high as 90%. It drops sharply between the ages of 7 and 7 and is about 50% by the end of that period. Thus, in most instances reversals can be explained developmentally. It is quite likely that some children reverse because they are taught letter and word discrimination before they are ready.
2. Unfamiliarity with the concept of directionality as it relates to letter and word discrimination. The pupil has inadequate direction sense and has not learned that directionality is a distinguishing feature in letter perception (Moyer & Newcomer, 1977). The pupil cannot or does not use directional cues in identifying letters and words.
3. Uncertainty about the phonemic value of a letter permits the following letter, about which there is no uncertainty, to be decoded ahead of it (Stott, 1973). This happens especially when a consonant follows a vowel (e.g., *at*), since consonants are better known.

Correction of Reversal Difficulties

We (Dechant, 1982) have identified 15 strategies for dealing with reversal behavior. Smith (1988) suggests that children who reverse in reading must be reading words or sentences which are essentially meaningless: "No one who is reading for sense could confuse words like *big* and *dig*, or *was* and *saw*, in a meaningful context" (p. 82). The natural inference is that all remediation activities should involve letters and words in context, not in isolation. Smith adds: "There is only one possible way of making learning to distinguish *b* from *d* even more difficult and that is to *show* them one at a time. This removes every relational clue, and puts the learner in a situation most likely to confound even experienced readers" (p. 83).

Teaching Letter Naming

To this point we have discussed letter discrimination and the importance of moving from left to right in making letter discriminations. Another important step in letter discrimination is naming the letter.

Naming of the letters is distinct from letter discrimination. Smith (1988) observes that we "comprehend" a letter when we can say its name. It then takes on meaning. He suggests that the association of a name with a visual configuration is relatively easy and adds that the association of a name with a category (e.g., letters) is "neither necessary nor primary in the discrimination process" (p. 110).

Knowledge of letter names is one of the best predictors of the child's readiness for reading (Barrett, 1965a, 1965b, 1967; Ehri, 1983) and for reading achievement in grades one and two (Chall, 1967, 1983). Chall found that letter-name knowledge correlates more highly with reading than does intelligence. Adams (1990) states that letter-naming ability, together with phonological awareness, rhyming, and segmenting ability, are the best predictors of success in beginning reading.

Barrett (1965a, 1965b) found that being able to discriminate, recognize, and name letters (and numbers) was the best single predictor of first-grade reading achievement, but pattern copying and word matching were also strongly related. Visual discrimination of letters and words had a slightly higher value than visual discrimination of geometric designs and pictures. Auditory discrimination, language facility, and story sense also contributed to the prediction of first-grade reading achievement. In a later study, Barrett (1967) found that recognition of letters had the highest correlation with beginning reading achievement; discrimination of the beginning sounds of words had the next highest correlation; and ending sounds, shape completion, ability to copy a sentence, language facility and story sense, and discrimination of vowel sounds in words were also positively related.

Walsh, Price, and Gillingham (1988) found that letter-naming facility or letter-naming speed and ease was strongly associated with subsequent progress in reading in kindergarten children, but not so for second-grade children. The obtained correlations for two kindergarten classes were .80 and .89. Letter naming appears to be critical at the kindergarten level, but its effect on reading achievement weakens with advancing age and experience. Groff (1984), even though the preponderance of the research suggests otherwise, casts some doubt on whether teaching of the names of the letters does in fact have a positive impact on learning to read.

Studies indicate that lack of ability to name the letters of the alphabet with ease and accuracy is a clear hindrance to beginning reading and may be predictive of reading failure (Lesgold & Curtis, 1981). Disabled readers do in fact have greater difficulty in naming letters (Denckla & Ruddell, 1976).

The value of letter naming is that it is a way of labeling symbols, making it easier to discriminate (Durkin, 1970) and to remember them (Robeck, 1972; Robeck & Wilson, 1974; Samuels, 1972, 1973). Facility with letter naming eases the process of learning to read by vesting the letters with immediate familiarity; it facilitates their storage in long-term memory (Walsh, Price, & Gillingham, 1988); it gives children referents with which to associate phonemes (Ehri, 1984, 1987, 1989). Letter naming may be the first stage in learning to recode. Letter naming involves processes which, if slow and awkward, obstruct the transitions through which beginning readers must pass. Walsh, Price, and Gillingham (1988) note that facility in letter naming can be likened to a bridge that perhaps could be burned after crossing, but which nonetheless needs to be built before crossing.

Ability to name the letters may indicate higher intelligence, higher associative learning ability, higher auditory comprehension, favored socioeconomic status, greater maturation, and increased cognitive ability. Certainly, the child who is able to name letters can discriminate between variant letter shapes and has associated a meaning with the letter (Walcutt, Lamport, & McCracken, 1974; Smith, 1988,). Grapheme-phoneme knowledge is more significant than is grapheme-name knowledge (Jenkins, Bausell, & Jenkins, 1972), but letter-name knowledge and phonics knowledge are highly correlated (Groff, 1984). Children who know the alphabet tend to be good readers, but teaching letter names will not of itself turn a poor reader into a good one (Smith, 1977).

Writing the Letters

The pupil also must learn to write the letters of the alphabet in both manuscript and cursive form. The ability to write the letters dictated is an important indicator of first-grade reading achievement. At present, manuscript, script, or printscript is the first mode of writing taught to the child.

It was introduced into this country in 1921 by Marjorie Wise. It consists of sans serif letters, that is, letters without ornamentation. The chief reason for using manuscript writing first is that children do not experience as much difficulty with the straight vertical lines, circles, and part circles used in manuscript writing as with the more complex forms used in cursive writing. In manuscript writing the letters are not joined, and the form of the letters is like that met in reading. This permits children to compare what they write with what they read.

Sounding the Letters

Individual letters cannot be sounded out like words; their appearance has a purely arbitrary relationship to the way they are pronounced. We defer additional discussion of this question to later in the chapter.

Letter Sequence and Word Identification

The ultimate concern of all letter identification is word identification. It is here that the letter sequence in words becomes an important issue. The research clearly supports the importance of identifying the visual sequence. A frequent characteristic of disabled readers is that they have greater difficulty than do good readers with the sequence in words.

It is our contention that beginning readers really "see" the word's configuration clearly only when they can "see" or perceive the elements or features that individualize the configuration or word; hence, when they have a perception of the word's structure. The most basic structural elements or featural aspects that distinguish one word from another are the letters or graphemes, but these appear in a definite order in words. It is thus the sequence of the letters that individualizes each word's visual configuration, giving it idiosyncratic identity. It is the sequence of letters that individualizes and gives featural identity to the configurations of *eat*, *ate*, and *tea*, which are composed of the same letters. The basic structural unit, or pattern or gestalt in words, thus, is not the configuration per se; it is the word's configuration as it is individualized by the sequence of letters and, as we shall see later, by the phoneme-grapheme interrelationships. When pupils learn a gestalt for a word that is based on the perception of these interrelationships, they learn a code that is applicable to other words.

Good readers are able to keep in mind the total configuration or the total language pattern while at the same time attending to parts of the word (Goins, 1950, 1958). They can shift from whole to part and from detail to whole. They recognize the importance of the relationships of the letters to one another within the total word. They know how words are structured and that the arrangement of the letters in a word controls the way the letters function. Adams (1990) notes that even skilled readers look at almost every word and at most of the letters of each word.

In summary, pupils, from the beginning, need to see the word both as a unit and as made of parts that individualize that unit. Montgomery (1977) observes that the essence of pattern recognition lies in paying attention to detail, not in isolation, but in relation to the whole structure.

DEVELOPING INSTANT RECOGNITION AND NAMING OF WORDS

The remainder of this chapter deals with the development of a sight vocabulary. The word is the largest linguistic unit that lends itself to instant recognition. Sentences rarely are recognized as a unit. The history of the teaching of reading is replete with various methods used to help the child to identify and recognize the printed symbol. We present in this chapter the Integrated Reading Method, termed by us "the eclectic method" in 1961, as an option in helping children to identify words fluently, accurately, and with ease. The Integrated Reading Method (IRM) is an amalgamation of the configuration, linguistic, and kinesthetic methods. It is an eclectic, multisensory, and multifaceted approach suitable to the needs of different readers, both developmental and remedial.

The IRM is an analytical method of teaching word identification which combines the strengths of the word and sentence methods. It begins with a focus on meaningful language patterns and the reading of total language structures and emphasizes that the basic unit of reading is the sentence. However, it also accepts the view formulated in linguistic methods that for most children, especially beginning readers and poor readers, the teaching of reading has to come down to the level of individual word identification and the association of letter and sound patterns.

From the sentence method (Huey, 1912) the IRM brings the emphasis on total language and meaning units, that is, on the sentence as the basic unit of reading. Sentence advocates observe that meaning comes only through understanding total language structures exemplified in a sentence. Undoubtedly, the sentence (or indeed the story) is the basic unit of reading, but the word is just as surely the basic unit of identification and recognition. Meaningful reading occurs only when the reader comprehends the total sentence unit. However, the word is the largest linguistic unit that readily lends itself to identification. The sentence methods best illustrate how one reads rather than how one identifies words.

From the analytical or whole-word method the IRM brings three aspects:

1. The usefulness of learning the word as a total unit. This is the emphasis of the sight-configuration method.

2. The teaching of a whole-word or analytical phonics. This is the emphasis in linguistic methods.
3. The importance of having the pupil trace and write the word. This emphasis comes from the kinesthetic-tactile methods. Fernald (1943) originated the kinesthetic or VAKT (visual, auditory, kinesthetic, tactile) method.

From the synthetic alphabet method and from the linguistic methods the IRM brings the spelling of the word: *c-a-t* (sē-ā-tē) is matched with /kăt/. The *New England Primer* in 1690 and the *Webster American Spelling Book* in 1793 were based on the alphabet method. From the syllable method (also a synthetic method) the IRM brings the teaching of the phonogram units. From the linguistic method comes the importance of teaching children to break the alphabetic code or to develop a coding system. Bloomfield and Barnhart (Bloomfield, 1942; Bloomfield & Barnhart, 1961), and Fries (1963) presented a linguistic approach whose central thesis was that the major task facing the child is the mastery of the graphic system that reflects the spoken language system. These early linguists defined reading as the act of turning the graphic shape back to speech. Bloomfield differentiated between the act of reading (recognition of grapheme-phoneme correspondences) and the goal of reading (comprehension). He separated the problem of the study of word form from the study of word meaning. He described reading as recoding printed symbols into sound and then extracting meaning from sound. Linguists pointed out that there is an inseparable relationship between the words as they are printed and the sounds for which the letters are conventional signs, and that converting letters to meaning requires a concentration upon letter and sound to bring about an automatic association between them as rapidly as possible.

IRM also emphasizes and incorporates the use of all the word-identification cues: the meaning cues and the within-word or structural cues, or in other words, the graphic, the grapho-phonological, the lexical, the semantic, and the syntactic information. IRM is actually a meshing of top-down and bottom-up approaches in reading; of moving from whole to part and back to whole. It thus follows the interactive mode. It introduces the pupil to the word in the context of total language or meaning-bearing units (stories, paragraphs, and sentences), moves toward a bottom-up, subskills approach, isolating the word to be identified, and ends with the word back in the sentence or paragraph context. In addition, it requires pupils, especially when reading expository text, to use the target word in the semantic and syntactic context in which it was originally placed.

STAGES OF WORD IDENTIFICATION

As already noted, the Integrated Reading Method is based on a study of the various reading methods that gained popularity over the course of our history, but it also is based on what teachers and researchers know about the stages of reading development in children. Marsh et al. (1981), in their four-stage analysis of initial reading, suggest that the first two stages of word identification involve a simple rote association between the word and the name of the word. In stage 1 the learner is a context-dependent learner. Since at this stage the learner's knowledge of the within-word cues is essentially nil, the child must rely on context and particularly on his nonvisual information or world knowledge. If the unknown word is presented in a sentence or story, the child will guess at the word using prior context, some arbitrary characteristic of the word, or perhaps even the initial letter of the word as a guide. Thus young children will have little difficulty reading the word *Stop* on a stop sign but cannot read it in isolation. When the word is presented out of context the child will respond with wild guesses: *boy* becomes *brother*.

Marsh et al. (1981) refer to this stage as the linguistic guessing stage. The errors that the child makes at this stage are not representative of the graphic cues, with the possible exception of a letter that the target word and the substitute word might have in common. This is especially so if the similar letters occur at the beginning of each word. Thus, beginning readers are in fact attending to visually distinctive cues and they do focus initially on individual letters, especially the beginning letter. Ehri and Wilce (1985) argue that the importance of the beginning letter is really due to phonetic rather than visual characteristics.

In stage two the child responds to the unknown isolated word on the basis of its shared graphemic or letter cues with a known word (Marsh et al. 1981). At this stage, the child can read a few words out of context and may have mastered letter names. In contrast to stage 1, in which the child may be relying chiefly on context and perhaps on the initial letter of words, in stage 2 the child may use, in addition, word shape, word length, and the final letter of the word to identify the word. The errors that the pupil makes when reading words in isolation are the result of the pupil's attempt at analysis of the target word. They thus tend to be consistent with the graphic cues, especially the initial letter, or with the graphemic features. However, the child uses graphemic cues only to the extent that they are necessary to discriminate one printed word from another (Rayner & Pollatsek, 1989). Thus, as pupils grow older, they rely more on word-shape or letter-feature information (Rayner and Pollatsek, 1989), that is, the featural aspects of words. Frith (1985) notes that most five- and six-year-olds are at the logographic stage: they identify words on the basis of salient graphic cues or by guessing.

Marsh et al.'s steps 3 and 4 involve sequential recoding and hierarchical recoding. Step 3 is the beginning of an appreciation of the alphabetic principle. Whereas in step 2 the initial letter is salient because of its visual distinctiveness, the pupil at some point begins to grasp in some small measure the orthographic regularity of the alphabetic principle (Rayner & Pollatsek, 1989, p. 376). Kindergarten and beginning first-grade children generally are not able to use orthographic structure in word identification, but towards the end of first grade and certainly beyond second grade children are able to do so. Sensitivity to orthographic cues thus evolves during second grade (in some learners it is clearly earlier). This means that the learner is gradually moving away from relying totally on the first letter, is paying attention to the total word, and is learning to process letters in parallel. The child is learning to process units larger than a single letter. He is learning, either through explicit teaching or by learning it himself, that letters may be sounded. The child learns the rules which allow for recoding of novel words. The child learns to process a series of letters and to relate this series to a series of sounds (i.e., sequential recoding) in a left-to-right sequence. The child begins the process of letter-sound analyzing.

The beginning reader, according to Glushko (1981), identifies a word such as *third* by visual orthographic units or by analogy to another word such as *bird* (Mason et al. suggest that identification by analogy occurs much later). Glushko notes that the reader directly accesses the mental lexicon via visual-orthographic units (e.g., word families, or phonograms such as *ird*) without the use of grapheme-phoneme rules. The word in this model is sounded or recoded auditorily after lexical access, hence a postlexical process. Postlexical phonological coding is clearly necessary in reading aloud, but, as we noted in chapter 1, it is also a part of silent reading "as readers 'check' auditory representations of words read analogically" (Foorman & Liberman, 1989, p. 349). Foorman and Liberman also point out that visual-orthographic awareness demands a level of abstraction beyond that of most six-year-olds. They note that orthographic cues are operative when the reader can analyze the word into orthographic units with optional phonological recoding.

Stage 4 is the stage of refinement of phonic knowledge (i.e., understanding of the grapheme-phoneme correspondence rules and identification by analogy). It is the stage in which the child processes letters and words as do adults. It happens by about fourth grade, between the ages of 8 and 10.

Foorman and Liberman (1989) observe that phonics rules are grapheme-phoneme correspondence rules that stress the regularities of the English alphabet (e.g., *c* represents /k/ before *a, o, u)*. The purpose of phonics instruction is to teach the correspondence rules as "an aid to accessing knowledge about words," and application of these rules results in the prelexical phonological representation or code of which we spoke in chapter 1. Only after the prelexical codes are used to assign phonemes to graphemes, after these phonemes are then synthesized into a sound representation, and finally after the learner forms a correspondence between the sound representation and a semantic unit in the mental lexicon does meaningful recoding occur.

Steps 3 and 4 involve a relative long period of time: from first to fourth or fifth grade. Steps 3 and 4 are initiated at least partially because of the increasing number of words with which the learner has to cope. The significant point is that in the process of learning to identify words there is a gradual development from focusing on a single characteristic of a word (i.e., perhaps the initial letter) to attending to all the letters in sequence and in parallel.

Studies show that detailed training on specific grapheme-phoneme correspondences helps children to identify words (Rayner & Pollatsek, 1989), and that by fourth or fifth grade the most important correspondences have been mastered by most children.

Fourth graders are more flexible in their approach than are younger children, using all the strategies (visual cues such as shape and length, graphemic cues, orthographic cues, and phonic cues) as the situation dictates. Rayner and Pollatsek (1989) note that towards the end of first grade the eye is ahead of the voice in oral reading. They add:

> Characteristics of the timing or discrepancy between the eyes and the voice make it highly likely that the oral response is a product of the lexicon (because the word has already been processed by the eyes and is likely stored in short term memory) rather than the means of accessing the lexicon. Thus the errors made by children who have entered stages 3 and 4 could well be memory rather than encoding errors. (p. 364)

Even though the grapheme-phoneme correspondence rules are an important aid to the reader, the child must, when reading totally irregular words, at times learn word-specific associations between the printed word and its pronunciation (Rayner & Pollatsek, 1989). If the learner, at least initially, accesses meaning or the mental lexicon through the use of the visual, graphemic, and context cues, then phonological coding is clearly not necessary (Backman et al., 1984; Barron, 1986) for accessing the mental lexicon, and the learner only gradually adds the phonological route to meaning to the already learned direct visual-access route. However, Rayner and Pollatsek (1989) suggest that the best hypothesis is that both beginning and skilled readers can use graphemic and phonological information to access meaning. Beginning readers will be less proficient in the use of the phonological route. Lomax and McGee (1987) present a five-step model that parallels the model we have just discussed. Their model emphasizes:

1. Understanding of the functions of print: awareness of oral and written language units, awareness that print can represent speech, objects, or meaning, awareness that print is different from pictures and consists of letters, words, and sentences. Metalinguistic awareness including print awareness, concepts about

print in books (i.e., letters, words, sentences), and sense of story structure is today receiving greater attention from reading specialists (Alexander, 1988). Implied in this first component is that children need to recognize the sign or referent potential of print.
2. Graphic awareness: Awareness of the distinctive features in letters and words and of their orientation. Graphic awareness emphasizes the role of visual discrimination in sight-word recognition. Children need to learn to recognize words as unique visual and graphic patterns.
3. Phonemic awareness: awareness that words consist of phonemes and the ability to segment words into phonemes. The reader needs to perceive written words as a sequence of letters and spoken words as sequences of sound. He needs to recognize that print is encoded speech. A prerequisite skill for phonemic awareness is auditory discrimination.
4. Grapheme-phoneme correspondence knowledge: knowledge of the letters (including the ability to name them) and of the sounds associated with them; using this knowledge in blending and in recoding unknown words.
5. Word reading: i.e., the ability to read isolated words.

THE STEPS OF THE INTEGRATED READING METHOD

The IRM consists of the following steps:

1. Present the target word (preferably a word which the pupil has already heard and spoken and for which the pupil has meaning) in either manuscript or cursive form in a sentence on the chalkboard. Read the sentence, underline, frame or color the word to be taught, and write it in isolation on the chalkboard.
2. Pronounce the word making sure that the children look at the word as it is pronounced.
3. Have pupils pronounce the word, again making sure that they look at the word when it is pronounced.
4. Present another word, a word that the pupil knows and which exemplifies either the same spelling pattern as the target word or at least is a contrastive word which is only minimally different (perhaps a different beginning consonant) from the first word, and pronounce it. Align this second word under the first word:

    MAN   OVER
    RAN   EVER

5. Have pupils spell the target word orally, pointing to each letter as they say the name of the letter, and have them say the word.
6. Have pupils trace the target word with their forefinger or pencil, making certain that they pronounce the word syllable by syllable while tracing it.
7. Have pupils write the target word from memory, again making certain that they say the word while writing it.
8. Again explain the meaning of the target word and present the word in another written sentence context on the chalkboard and/or on the back of a 4" × 6" inch card. Then: (a) read the sentence to the pupils, (b) have pupils read the sentence aloud, and (c) have pupils identify and underline, frame or trace in color the target word that is being taught, and have them state the meaning of the word.
9. Present the target word again in isolation and have pupils pronounce it.

The teacher must constantly evaluate whether each of the steps of the IRM is necessary for a given child. However, the teacher should not capriciously omit any of the steps. It is reasonable to expect that as children march up the educational ladder and as they become more proficient in reading and comprehension, spelling, tracing, and writing, and indeed recoding of the word will become less important. Teaching of recoding is relatively more important early; it is less emphasized later when children have learned how to read. Recoding is meant to lead to decoding. Reading must become automated so decoding may become more proficient. And, as decoding becomes more efficient, the pupil will focus less and less on recoding.

The IRM is to be used only when the pupil cannot identify the word in sentence context after having used the predicting strategies identified in chapter 5. It is when pupils have applied the meaning and within-word cues that have previously become a part of their personal schemata to identify the word and when this process has failed (principally because pupils cannot use meaning cues or because there are major gaps in their knowledge of the within-word, phonic, and morphemic cues) that the teacher may have to resort to the Integrated Reading Method. It is when the pupil's schemata have gaps in respect to the within-word cues that the method is especially effective.

Even though we suggest that the word to be identified should flow from a meaningful sentence context, there is some difference of opinion as to whether pupils learn best to identify words in context or in isolation.

Rash, Johnson, and Gleadow (1984) report that kindergarten children who were taught words in sentences learned them with significantly fewer trials than did children who were taught the same words in isolation. Nemko (1984) obtained the opposite results. Pupils trained in isolation gave more correct responses than did those trained in context. Ehri and Roberts (1979) and Ehri and Wilce (1979, 1980) found that teaching words in context resulted in slower learning of the graphic and phonic features of words. Likewise, Singer, Samuels, and Spiroff (1973–1974) found that word-identification efficiency was greater when words were taught in isolation than in context or with a picture or both.

There is significant research (Cunningham, 1980; McNinch, 1981; Merlin & Rogers, 1981) indicating that children are best served when they first learn words in oral context and when the word is then presented in isolation, then in written context, and finally again in isolation (Jolly, 1981). IRM presents words first in context, then in isolation, again in context, and again in isolation. Wiesendanger and Bader (1987) indeed found significant progress in primary-grade children when words were taught in the manner indicated by Jolly, but those children made the greatest gains who were taught the target words and the similar-appearing words (e.g., *when* and *where* or *then* and *their*) separately and when the words with clear featural differences were then contrasted with one another. Lowest gains occurred when the similar words were taught simultaneously; the second highest gains occurred in the group where only the target word was taught. In a way, we agree with all of these contentions. The pupil must clearly identify the word as an idiosyncratic form and this is probably done best when the word is singled out for specific attention, but the pupil must also learn to use meaning cues to decipher the word, and these are best offered in total sentence structures.

The word which the pupil cannot handle in print should be within the pupil's vocabulary, and thus is a word for which the pupil has already developed a meaning. If this is not the case, then the pupil must be helped to acquire a meaning for the word. Teaching of meaning at this level should begin with the association of meaning with the sound of the word. Thus, if the sentence in Step 1 is "Jim hit the ball over the fence," and if the word that the child needs to learn to identify is *over*, the teacher should use the word *over* orally in various contexts to assure that the pupil has aural-oral meaning for the word before introducing the pupil to the written sentence.

The target word should be a high-utility word and should flow out of the pupil's language experience story, from a basal reader story, from a trade book, from a basic word list such as the *Dolch Basic Sight Word List*, or from other reading to which the child is introduced. As in the Fernald Method (Fernald, 1943), sometimes the word may simply be one that the pupil wants to learn.

The discussion that follows examines the rationale for each of the steps of the IRM and presents evidence for including each step in word-identification method.

The Pupil Sees the Word

Step 1: Present the target word (preferably a word which the pupil has already heard and spoken and for which the pupil has meaning) in either manuscript or cursive form in a sentence on the chalkboard. Read the sentence, underline, frame or color the word to be taught, and write the word on the blackboard.

Remember that the primary purpose of the IRM is to help the pupil who has difficulty identifying and remembering a word and associating a sound with the word: when the pupil cannot, for illustration, identify and recode the word *over* in the sentence "The boy hit the ball over the fence." The sentence that contains the target word should be written on the chalkboard (in one-to-one or small-group teaching it may be written by the teacher or the pupil on the back of a 4" × 6" inch card). The pupil should be shown that the word to be learned is *over*. The word *over* should be written in isolation on the blackboard and may be written on the front of the card.

Step 1 of the IRM gets at the first two aspects of word identification, namely, the visual discrimination of the word and the development of a visual memory for the word. Word identification requires the pupil to visually identify the total configuration that is a word, to develop a gestalt for the word, to experience the "flash" global identification of the word as a whole, and to process the letters simultaneously in parallel so as to identify the whole word. Unquestionably, many beginners and disabled readers, and even college students (Haber et al., 1983), use the word's configuration, its shape and length, to identify it. They cannot analyze the word into its parts or cannot develop a memory for the sequences of letters in the word. For them, the configuration of the word may be the only useable clue.

The configuration cues are the word's length (words like *grandmother, elephant, Christmas, Halloween*, are readily identifiable by their length), and its shape, configuration, or physiognomy (ascending and descending letters identify a word and give it shape). Children are born with the ability to discriminate shapes, and teaching should make use of this prior knowledge. On the other hand, there is little justification for having children match words with shapes or having children "guess" what words a particular configuration represents. The shape and length of the words are not the features that constitute a significant difference in and between words.

Furthermore, identifying a word by length and shape or by configuration cues alone has additional deficiencies: it is not a reliable strategy in the identification of other words, forcing the pupil to learn each word as a totally independent squiggle, and it does not help the pupil to discriminate between similar-appearing configurations such as *people* and *purple*, both of which have the same arrangement of one ascending and two descending letters. Obviously, it is impossible to discriminate between the two words on the basis of configuration alone. And, even after identifying a word's shape or length, one is hard put to use this knowledge in identifying other words. The word's shape, as such, has relatively little transfer value. Asking children to recognize words solely by length and shape ignores the fact that printed words are symbols of sound and that letters are symbols of sound (Terman & Walcutt, 1958). Terman and Walcutt (1958) note that for children who do not know the alphabet as printed letters and as symbols of sound, the word on the page is a totally new squiggle.

Liberman (1985) decries the emphasis on whole-word learning, nonanalytic memorization of visual configurations, and guessing from context. He observes: "Such a method . . . must effectively delay or even prevent a child's understanding of the structure of the language and of how the orthography describes it, and it may well leave him functionally illiterate, unable to read new words that he has not already seen and memorized" (pp. 100–101).

As children are exposed to an increasingly greater number of words and to more similar-appearing words, identification by shape and length becomes even less useful. Young children and poor readers generally, being prone to attend to certain key letters, letter arrangements, or "outstanding" characteristics, are helped little when they meet other words with similar characteristics. Many poor readers are such because they were taught only to recognize words by configuration. The memory load that is created by having to learn hundreds of new and ever less discriminable words becomes quickly excessive and partially contributes to the reading difficulties that one sees so frequently among third and fourth graders. As the differences between configurations become ever finer, with letters curving left and right (*b-d*) and upward and downward (*n-u*), some children become confused, lose confidence, and turn against reading. The memory of disabled readers in particular is easily overloaded (Miles, 1983). The disabled reader, perhaps more so than any other reader, must be freed from having to memorize thousands of words as independent squiggles.

Parallel Processing of the Letters

The real questions are: "How does the reader differentiate between *people* and *purple*? How do the configurations of these words become differentiated? What accounts for each word's significant variation from every other word?" Even more to the point: How are wholes recognized? What do readers know when they know what a word looks like (Smith, 1988)? Undoubtedly, readers can and do sometimes identify words letter-by-letter. Rayner and Pollatsek (1989) observe, "In an alphabetic language, it seems obvious that letters must be natural units in the perception of words" (p. 75). They add, however, that skilled readers may bypass letter identification entirely. Smith (1988) observes, "It is only when words cannot be identified immediately that the prior identification of letters becomes relevant at all" (p. 148). Smith suggests that the question is not whether readers can identify words letter-by-letter, but rather whether skilled readers normally do so. Smith suggests that skilled readers identify words pretty much the same way as they identify a picture: they recognize the word as a visual pattern through visual features. In this chapter we are more concerned with the way beginning readers and poor word identifiers learn to identify words rather than with how skilled readers do so.

That letter-by-letter identification is not the way words are normally identified and that letters in words are processed in parallel rather than sequentially is supported by research (Rayner & Pollatsek, 1989). Cattell (1885a, 1885b) and Erdmann and Dodge (1889) years ago found that words are as readily identifiable as are letters, and Reicher (1969) discovered that letters in words or in context are actually identified more accurately than are letters in isolation. Smith (1988) asserts that words are generally identified as "wholes," with the reader using the same kind of strategy as in identifying letters. He adds that "the word is identified by the distribution of features across its entire configuration" (p. 122). He proposes a feature-analytic model like that discussed in the previous section.

The obvious question is: What are the features of words? Smith argues that they are the same as for letters, because words consist of letters, but the feature list of words requires an additional dimension: the analysis of word configurations involves "the position of features [i.e., letters] within a sequence" (Smith, 1988, p. 121).

Smith (1988), while noting that readers are very sensitive to the predictability of letter sequences (i.e., they are quite proficient in predicting what letters can or cannot follow other letters), nonetheless maintains that words are not identified by letters but by features. He argues that one cannot identify a word and its letters simultaneously. However, the evidence shows rather forcefully that pupils, especially beginning readers, do learn to identify and to remember words by focusing on the word's orthographic structure. Thousands of children in our early history learned to read using a spelling approach.

We (Dechant 1964, 1971, 1982; Dechant & Smith, 1961, 1977) have maintained that it is the sequence of letters (it might be more correct to say the sequence of letter features) that give the word its featural identity and its idiosyncratic form. Words are constructed alphabetically, and the order of the letters identifies the word and symbolizes its sounding. Smith (1988) appears to support this view when he notes that the knowledge of the way in which letters are grouped into words, or orthographic information, is a part of the fluent reader's cognitive structure. He adds: "It is an alternative nonvisual source of information to the featural or visual information that the eyes pick up from the page. To the extent that both of these sources of information reduce the number of alternatives that a particular letter might be there is redundancy" (p. 124). Smith terms such duplication of information sequential redundancy: i.e., "the occurrence of particular alternatives in one part of a sequence limits the range of alternatives that can occur anywhere else in the sequence" (p. 124). Thus, the letter *t* can be followed only by *h, r, a, e, i, o, u,* and *y*.

Instructional Directives

What instructional directives can one derive from these data? It seems that good teaching of word discrimination includes calling attention to the salient features that distinguish each word from every other word, emphasizing contrasting shapes and the visual features of words, noting similarities and differences, teaching children what a word is not, calling attention to the letter sequences that give the word its identity and its individual and idiosyncratic form, discriminating between similar-appearing words, teaching the pupil to perceive the word both as a whole and as consisting of parts, and emphasizing the importance of letter and word orientation.

In distinguishing the word *John*, good cues may be the length of the word, the two upright strokes, or the shape of the fishhook at the beginning, but these cues lack transferability. They do not help the reader to identify other words. They work as long as the pupil does not have to say what the word *John* is not. If the cue is the *J*, the pupil cannot discriminate *John* from *Jack*. Smith notes that "until children can understand what they have to distinguish *John* from, they will never acquire an appropriate set of distinctive features for identifying that word" (1988, p. 128). They have to see a representative sample of words that are not *John* in order to find out in what respects *John* is different. Pupils must be relatively more skilled in noting the differences among words than in noting the similarities. They must learn to distinguish *John* from all the other configurations with which it is not functionally equivalent. "Attempting to teach 'one word at a time' — writing a word on a variety of different surfaces and occasions and insisting 'This is *John*; this is *John* — will not help children to learn the word because they will never learn how *John* may be distinguished from any other word" (Smith, 1988, p. 129).

In beginning reading, it is imperative that pupils be taught to look at the word, to scan the word, to scrutinize the word from left to right, and to inspect it with great care. They must learn to attend visually to the graphic cues and to perceive the importance of particular details in letter shapes. Often the poor reader's failure to identify a letter or word is simply a matter of inattention. Maximizing the pupil's attention is an essential factor in word identification. Selective attending makes the difference between the poor reader's perception of a multiplicity of irregular marks arranged in horizontal lines on a page and the good reader's recognition of combinations of letters composing familiar and meaning-associated patterns.

Underlining the word, framing it, coloring it, and having the pupil locate the word in a sentence, all serve to draw attention to the word. Color can heighten attention to the salient features and allow a word to be learned stand apart from the remainder of the sentence. Perceptual processing is facilitated when the figure, or the stimuli to be attended to, is enhanced and background is reduced. Color has the effect of enhancing the figure. Other techniques useful in dealing with difficulties in figure-ground perception are the use of wider space between words and between lines of print, permitting the child to point at the word, which helps the child focus on the word and to stay on line, or the use of a card with a window cut out of it to track the word.

Smith (1988) notes that:

1. Children do not learn best to identify words through simple repetitious presentation of the word.
2. Children do not need to be told interminably what a word is; they have to be able to see what it is not.
3. Children learn best by acquaintance with a wide variety of nonequivalent alternatives (*cat, fat, hat*, etc.). Through this children learn to discriminate distinctive features, to establish feature lists, to recognize functional equivalences, and to develop a pool of knowledge about the redundancy of words.

The Pupil Hears the Word Spoken

Step 2: Pronounce the word, making sure that children look at the word as it is pronounced.

Step 1 has the pupil see or visually scrutinize the word and Step 2 has the pupil hear the word. Steps 1 and 2 combine the visual and auditory modalities, associating the visual sequence with the auditory sequence. Hearing the word has a direct effect on visual identification of and especially on memory for the printed word. Doehring (1976) found that young children master reading with a great deal of help from acoustic intermediaries, and Rose (1969) reported that the fade-out of the visually acquired stimulus is rapid if it is not recoded in acoustic form. Vellutino (1987) reports that poor readers have trouble storing, remembering, and retrieving words they hear.

Step 2 is quite simple. The teacher is simply providing a name for the visual configuration. But, even so, this step should not proceed without care. Too many times, children are presumed to be looking at the word (they hear the word spoken by the teacher and even repeat the word), when in fact they are not looking at the word and are simply using their short-term auditory memory to repeat the word. With older children, it may be desirable to have the pupil attempt a pronunciation before the teacher pronounces the word.

Step 2 is not the answer to full identification of the word. Thus, Betts, as early as 1961, noted that when the sight configuration method is stripped of its pedaguese, it is merely a "tell-the-child-the-word" procedure. Naming the word for the pupil is a constant temptation for the teacher when the pupil stumbles and fumbles over print, but it is not the solution to the pupil's problem.

The Pupil Pronounces the Word

Step 3: Have pupils pronounce the word, again, making sure that they look at the word as it is pronounced.

Step 3 has the pupil pronounce and name the word. Naming involves programming and executing a complex sequence of motor activities, which if not entirely subsequent to word recognition (Gough, 1984,), are clearly different from word recognition. It is only recently that researchers have recognized that the articulatory motor responses made in programming a speech sound are involved in perceiving that sound (Samuels & Kamil, 1984) and in committing it to phonological memory. Ehri (1989) suggests that a way to improve pupils' ability to detect consistent sounds in words is to teach them to monitor articulatory (and acoustic cues): to monitor what their mouths are doing to pronounce words.

Sounding of the word (and even subvocalizing when reading silently) allows the reader to use the articulatory loop to extend memory through verbal rehearsal. Saying the word or thinking the pronunciation keeps the parts of words in short-term memory longer than does simple visual processing (Adams, 1990). It is why we read aloud when we get tired, the text gets difficult, or we are subjected to distraction. Sounding out words forces children to attend to all the letters in a left-to-right sequence.

Step 3 completes the initial processing of the word: the pupil now has seen the word and developed an image of the word; has heard the word spoken or named, and has spoken the word. The pupil has practiced a visual-auditory-articulatory association for the word.

The emphasis in steps 1-3 is thus on the development of visual discrimination and identification of and memory for the printed symbol and matching of a visual sequence (the written word) with an auditory sequence (the spoken word). If children are to be successful word identifiers, they generally need to be able to integrate data from one sense modality with that of another, to associate the letter shapes with the phonemes, to make a visual-auditory match, or to recode.

Steps 1, 2, and 3 help the pupil to develop a basic sight vocabulary. Most children can and do learn words "by sight." Many believe that having children learn perhaps 50 or so words by sight "lays the foundation for their systematic learning of word identification skills" (Mason & Au, 1986, p. 62) and allows children to do some reading of connected text almost immediately.

Sight-word teaching in the beginning stages of reading instruction should be guided by the following principles (Swaby, 1984):

1. Teach no more than five words per instructional period.
2. Adjust instruction to the learning rates of the child.
3. Teach words within a total language context: as part of a sentence.
4. Teach sight vocabulary to an automatic level.
5. Emphasize the most useful words, those that are most essential to the meaning of the selection, those that occur most frequently, and those that have highly generalizable segments.
6. Provide intensive practice.

If the teaching of word identification were to stop with steps 1, 2, and 3, and unfortunately it often does, pupils at most would learn to use the configuration cues of length and shape, to develop a visual memory of the word, and to associate a visual sequence with an auditory sequence. The pupil would learn that *over* says /ōvər/ through a simple association and memory technique, namely, that of associating the whole word configuration *over* with the whole-word auditory response /ōvər/. That is all that having the teacher name the configuration can teach. If the aim of freeing children from having to memorize thousands of independent squiggles has any significance, then something more is needed than is provided in steps 1, 2, and 3. Basic goals in word identification instruction have to be independence and self-direction in the word-identification process.

Despite the fact that steps 1, 2, and 3 are simply not enough, they do allow for storage and retrieval of the word from memory, and they permit the learner to process the word further, even after it no longer is in the attentional field of the learner.

The Unknown Word Is Contrasted With a Known Word

Step 4: Present another word, a word that the pupil knows and that exemplifies, if possible, the same spelling pattern as the target word and pronounce it. Align this second word under the first word on the blackboard. The second word should be a contrastive word that is only minimally different (perhaps a different beginning consonant) from the first word.

Step 4 continues to develop visual discrimination of and memory for the word, but emphasizes particularly the association of sound with the visual symbol. This step's major function is that of teaching the pupil why the sound is represented in and by the visual symbol. A basic position taken in this text is that learners need to master the alphabetic principle, which is learned through phonological recoding. As we noted in chapter 1, phonological coding may occur either before or after lexical access.

For some, especially poor readers and beginning readers, reading is often a matter of translating writing into speech. Such processing is termed mediated processing or phonological mediation, and it is known as the phonological encoding hypothesis (first suggested by Rubenstein, 1971). However, other readers, particularly mature readers, often decode directly from graphemes to meaning, thus taking the direct visual access route to the internal lexicon. Swanson (1984) asserts that with such readers phonological coding of the word occurs after lexical access and that it holds accessed words in working memory while subsequent words are processed and the meaning of the sentence is determined. Phonological coding is thus a holding mechanism until integration mechanisms work out the meaning of the passage.

There are clearly readers, especially those who are just starting reading, who use word-specific association (i.e., memorized associations between individual, whole printed words and their pronunciations (Baron & Treiman, 1980; Treiman & Baron, 1983). Such pupils will have learned only what is taught in steps 1–3. They may even learn to recode through incidental learning. However, most learners need to be taught to relate spelling to sound (i.e., and to use phonological mediation, phonological recoding, or a phonological code that mediates semantic access.

Step 4 is designed especially to help those readers who either do or who must use the phonological route to meaning. The strategy in Step 4 is:

1. To teach the pupil a coding system for identifying words, a phonological code that helps the pupil to identify words quickly and easily. Step 4 presents a systematic approach for developing the ability to convert or recode the graphic symbol into the sound symbol or for "seeing" the pronunciation in the printed form. It teaches the pupil how to become self-directive in recoding. It teaches how to break the alphabetic code. It develops an insight, instead of simple association and memory into why words are pronounced the way they are. It teaches the pupil how to "unlock" the sound of the word. It teaches the pupil why over says /ōvər/ and why cat says /kăt/. The pupil learns that in the word cat the

c, which can represent /k/, /s/, /sh/, /ch/, represents /k/ because it precedes *a* in the syllable; and the pupil learns that the *a*, which can represent /ā/, /ă/, /â/, or /ä/, represents /ă/ in the word *cat* because it is a single vowel followed by a single consonant in the same syllable.
2. To provide for the systematic teaching of the within-word cues (i.e., grapheme-phoneme correspondences, phonograms, spelling patterns, identification by analogy, and morphemic cues) thereby improving the predictive efficiency of which we spoke in chapter 5.
3. To help make the pupil's responses to the spelling patterns in words so automatic that the graphic shapes and the sounding of those shapes sink below the level of threshold of attention, leaving only a consciousness of schematic, semantic, and syntactic meaning.
4. To develop the pupil's sensitivity to the orthographic structure of words (this usually develops in second grade) and to develop the automatic semantic activation from the word itself of which we wrote in chapter 5.

The Coding System

The phonological code is nothing more than a system that permits children to recode words or to use the internal composition of the word (the letters that compose it) to name it. It is a system that permits readers to recode new words fluently, with ease, with accuracy and independence, and that has wider applicability in word recognition than does the rote identification of individual configurations. It provides the pupil with the ability to identify and recode words not previously seen.

Words are constructed alphabetically, and readers can learn to figure out or to sound out the name of a new configuration from the letters of the words and from the letter sequence. Readers can learn to recode without having to be told what the word is. To do so they must learn to break the alphabetic code, and when they have learned this, they have learned a system for identifying words. English is founded on an alphabetic base, and beginning readers will progress in recoding only as they gain an understanding of this principle (Calfee, 1982). The discovery of the alphabetic principle is in many ways the key to successfully learning to read (Rayner & Pollatsek, 1989). Ehri (1979) observed that if the light were not so gradual in dawning, the relationship between print and speech might be one of the most remarkable discoveries of childhood.

There are problems in understanding the alphabetic principle. Young children have an imperfect idea of what phonemes are (Rayner & Pollatsek,

1989). Phonemes are abstractions. The phoneme /d/ is an abstraction because its perception and production are highly dependent upon the vowels that precede it and that follow it. A second difficulty is that our alphabet does not code each of the vowel phonemes or indeed the consonant phonemes with a unique symbol.

If the pupil needs to learn to break the alphabetic code, it is appropriate to ask how this is done. We earlier in this chapter and in the previous chapter noted the importance of having the pupil identify the sequence of letters. Steps 2 and 3 teach the pupil that a sequence of letters represents or stands for a sequence of sounds. However, these steps simply develop a rote association between the visual and the auditory sequence. They emphasize rote learning rather than insightful learning. Step 4 goes beyond that. It teaches the pupil how to figure out the sequence of sounds from the sequence of letters.

Teaching needs to focus children's attention on the sequential and positional visual-orthographic constraints on letters in printed words and on the relation of the visual-orthographic information to the phonological information already represented in the internal lexicon. The reader who can identify and turn a sequence of letters into a sequence of sounds using his knowledge of the grapheme-phoneme correspondences and of the morphemic cues has indeed developed a coding system. The pupil who can convert the letter sequence *people* into the sound sequence /pēpəl/ has learned to individualize and to discriminate the configuration people and has learned to use the letters as cues to the sounding of the configuration. But, he has also learned something more. He has learned a coding system based on the probabilities that characterize the written/spoken or printed/sound relationships of the English language. He has learned that the visual/auditory association follows certain internal (i.e., within the word) consistencies or probabilities. In unlocking the pronunciation of the symbol *phlogiston*, it is almost certain that most readers will pronounce the word as /flŏg/ ĭs /tən/ or /flō/ jĭs /tən/. It is the sequence of letters and the knowledge of the grapheme-phoneme interrelationships, in other words the code the pupil has learned, that permits this. It is especially significant that the *ph* is converted to /f/, but also that the word can be divided in two different ways, resulting in the assignment of different values to the vowels.

Three-year-olds are using a coding system, the "transitional probabilities" (Bruner, 1957a) or the "conditional redundancies of English orthography" (Gibson & Levin, 1975) that characterize the English language when they use regular endings to create words such as *selled, runned*, or *mans* for the irregular *sold, ran*, or *men*, and so do the first graders who read *come* as /kōm/. The child who says "I wented to see the sheeps and I falled down" has detected subtle rules for past tense and plurals (Hart, 1983). Because these children are dealing with irregularities they make errors. Thus, the letter sequence is not an exact indication of the pronunciation of a word, but the system is a valuable cue in 85% of the cases.

Phonological Awareness

Two principles guide our discussion of strategies in developing a coding system:

1. The young learner needs to develop phonological awareness: it is an enabling skill for acquiring phonics knowledge.
2. Children develop phonological awareness, and indeed phonics knowledge, as a consequence of reading, but both phonological awareness and grapheme knowledge must also be developed through direct instruction.

Coding, or the ability to recode, depends on phonological awareness. Phonological awareness is the awareness of the relationship between the printed word and the sound representation of the word. It is central to learning the alphabetic principle (Rayner & Pollatsek, 1989). Phonological awareness (Ehri, 1989) includes phonemic segmentation (segmentation of a spoken word into its component phonemes – "What are the three phonemes in fish?"); blending sequences of separately articulated phonemes to form a syllable or word ("What word is this, /f/, /i/, /sh/?"); detecting rhyming and alliteration; and deleting or substituting sounds in words ("Say /meat/ and then say it with /f/ instead of /m/").

The relationship between phonological awareness and success in learning to read is well documented (e.g., Pratt & Brady, 1988; Manis, 1985; Share et al., 1984; Stanovich, Cunningham, & Feeman, 1984). Indeed, there is growing evidence of a causal connection between these two processes (e.g., Bradley & Bryant, 1983; Fox & Routh, 1984; Juel, Griffith, & Gough, 1986; Gough & Tunmer, 1986; Maclean, Bryant, & Bradley, 1987; Torneus, 1984; Tunmer & Nesdale, 1985; Wagner & Torgesen, 1987; Adams, 1990). There is also support for the positive effects of early training in phonological awareness (e.g., Content et al., 1986; Torneus, 1984). Nicholson (1986) notes that early teaching of phonemic awareness produces the ability to sound out words. The research further indicates that learning to read an alphabetic language system such as ours allows phonological awareness to develop (Read et al., 1986).

Phonological awareness does not develop spontaneously; it is developed through direct teaching and as a by-product of learning to read. Perfetti et al. (1987) concluded from their study that the ability to blend phonemes plays a causal role in the acquisition of reading, which in turn effectuates the development of the awareness that words can be segmented into phonemes. Conversely, studies (Catts, 1986; Torgesen, 1985) show that the reading disabled often have difficulty processing the phonological aspects of language. They lack phonological awareness; they cannot handle phoneme and syllable segmentation tasks and rhyming (Vellutino & Scanlon, 1987); they have problems in naming or encoding the verbal stimuli phonologically or in using the phonological-based codes to store verbal information; and they have difficulty retrieving the phonological codes from memory which allows for naming of visually presented stimuli (Catts, 1986). Maclean, Bryant, and Bradley (1987) found that knowledge of nursery rhymes among 3-year-olds was a significant predictor of later prereading skills.

The research clearly supports the view that phonological processing deficits disrupt the reader's ability to acquire recoding skills. Stanovich (1988) observes that most researchers have located the proximal locus of severe reading disability or dyslexia at the word-recognition level and have identified the locus of reading deficits in word recognition at the phonological-processing level. Siegel (1989) observes that virtually all children with reading disability have problems with phonological processes. Stanovich (1988) adds that there is increasing evidence that the linkage of phonological ability to reading is a causal one. He notes that the phonological insensitivity makes the learning of grapheme-to-phoneme correspondence very difficult. Mann (1989) observes that disabled readers consistently show two areas of deficiency: lack of phonological awareness and difficulties in phonological processing.

Olson et al. (1989) found that phonological coding (measured by speed and accuracy in reading non-words or nonsense words aloud) and sequential language skills (i.e., recognition of rhyming and phoneme segmentation) were substantially lower for reading-disabled children irrespective of IQ scores, and that the phonological deficit was highly heritable. However, they add that in the "garden-variety" poor reader, phonological coding may be developmentally delayed rather than the result of a genetic deficiency. Foorman and Liberman (1989) found that of 80 first graders, those identified as good readers shifted in the beginning of first grade from a logographic to an alphabetic strategy (i.e., they used grapheme-phoneme correspondences). They applied prelexical grapheme-phoneme correspondence rules, whereas poor readers used visual rather than phonological coding and relied on visual-orthographic knowledge. The poor readers were at the logographic level; the good readers at the alphabetic phonological reading level.

Ehri (1989) blames inadequate instruction for the reader's deficiency in both reading and phonological coding and notes that remediation of a phonemic awareness deficiency should combine phonological training with spelling training. Children need to be taught how to symbolize sounds with letters. However, Bradley and Bryant (1983, 1985) caution that phonological awareness leads to success in beginning reading only to the extent that sounds are represented orthographically. They observe that phonological awareness is a product of, not a prerequisite to, learning to read.

Developing the Spelling-Sound Correspondence Rules: Grapheme-Phoneme Relationships

The best way of developing the alphabetic code appears to be through learning of the phoneme-grapheme interrelationships, or phonics. In chapter 9 we shall identify which grapheme-phoneme correspondences need to be taught and which of the correspondences the pupil needs to learn. Here our focus is the role of phonics in the acquisition of a coding system and more generally in becoming a skilled reader.

Learning of the spelling/sound correspondences rules maximizes the transfer of learning. It teaches the pupil to be a better focal predictor. A basic contribution of phonics instruction is that it forces pupils to look at the parts of the word, to visually study the word, and to identify where the significant difference in a word is. Thus, phonics may lead to a somewhat different perception or gestalt than if the word were perceived strictly by concentrating on the configuration alone. Through phonics pupils learn to scrutinize the configuration more accurately and thus develop the habit of being unsatisfied with a general, overall view of a word.

That knowledge of phonics and phonemic analysis training are valuable in the reading program is well established (Marsh et al., 1981; Williams, 1984). Chall (1987) notes that the research in the last 70 years overwhelmingly indicates that direct instruction in phonics contributes to the development of better recoding, word recognition, and comprehension. Adams (1990) points out that skilled readers usually recode printed words into their spoken images. McCusker et al. (1981) found that phonological recoding is generally required when the reader has not previously seen the word. They note that the phonological codes play a critical role in storing information in working memory, and as already mentioned, in reading, a memory for visually presented sequence of letters becomes very significant (Bradley, 1983). Earlier we noted that children, before becoming proficient readers, need to become skilled in sequential and hierarchical coding (Marsh et al., 1981). Conversely, disabled readers have a lot of difficulty with phonics, cannot use the phonetic code to unlock unknown words (Kochnower et al., 1983), have major difficulty with the graphemic and phonemic factors, cannot analyze whole word sounds into phonemes (phoneme segmentation), are deficient in naming, and are less able to construct and use a phonetic code (Stanovich, 1988).

The Minimum-Difference Strategy

The primary strategy of Step 4 is use of minimum difference, minimum variation, or contrast. Step 4 recommends, when possible, that the target word be contrasted with another word that the pupil already knows. It is beneficial to color the two contrasting letters that differentiate the one word from the other. Color calls attention to the grapheme-phoneme correspondence being taught. Contrasting of the words focuses the pupil's attention on the salient features of words and enhances the teaching of recoding and of the grapheme-phoneme correspondences. Thus, the pupil, instead of learning simply to deal with *over* and with *cat,*, might be introduced to *ever* which is only minimally different from *over* or to *bat* which is only minimally different from *cat*. The pupil needs to learn to respond to the contrastive features or letters that identify and differentiate whole-word patterns (e.g., *bat* from *cat*). Fries (1963) notes that the understanding of the difference that any particular letter makes in the spelling pattern is developed through the experience of pronouncing a variety of contrastive word pairs with minimum differences in their spelling patterns, for example, *bat-at; bat-fat; bat-pat*. Smith (1988) observes that children learn best by being exposed to a wide variety of nonequivalent alternatives.

The critical element in reading is not the perception of sameness, even though pupils should be able to see the similarities in words. Rather, the pupil in reading needs to discriminate every word from every other word. This is precisely the import of the minimum contrast technique. Presenting *bat* 50 times in a variety of ways and in a variety of contexts, and telling the pupils it is /băt/ does not help to discriminate the word. Smith (1978, 1988) notes that attempting to teach one word at a time, writing the word on a variety of surfaces, and repeatedly reminding the pupil /thĭs ĭs băt/, will not teach the pupil to identify and discriminate the word. Good cues in discriminating *bat* may be the shortness of the word and the two ascending letters, but these cues lack transferability, and they certainly will not help the pupil to discriminate *bat* from similar-appearing words such as *fat* and *hat*. Pupils learn what they need to learn only when *fat* and *bat* are contrasted (when it becomes clear that the words are not functionally equivalent and that they differ from every other word because they contain at least one grapheme-phoneme difference); in other words, only when pupils are exposed to other contrastive words that are not bat. Thus, the pupil is taught not only what the word is but also what it is not. Smith (1971, 1978, 1988) notes that until pupils are shown what to distinguish a word from, they will not acquire an appropriate set of distinctive features for identifying that word. They have to see a representative sample of words that are not bat in order to find out in what respects bat is different. They need to learn what to look for.

Nulman and Gerber (1984) report improved performance in spelling following the use of a method similar to the one suggested here, which contrasted imitated and modeled spellings of words. Pairing of incorrect and correct spellings (and by inference, pairing of contrastive words in developing recognition and recoding of a word) has the effect of focusing attention, prompts learners to apply different kinds of phonological and orthographic information implicit in the English writing system, helps them to attend to and remember the differences between the target word and the contrastive word, teaches phonemic segmentation and grapheme-phoneme correspondence rules, and helps pupils to reduce uncertainty through the use of their admittedly limited orthographic information.

Contrasting of words develops an attack strategy and self-management in word identification. It focuses on the portion of the word about which there is a high degree of uncertainty. It teaches the pupil to generate alternative recodings (for example *c* as /k/ or /s/: cat-kat; city-site), to use phonograms and spelling patterns to recode the word, and to use identification by analogy. It induces a problem-solving "set," teaching the pupil to carefully scrutinize the word, the organization of the letters within the word, and the sequence of the letters within the word.

It is, of course, impossible to find a suitable contrastive word for every word. Not all English words follow basic alphabetic principles, and thus it is not always possible to contrast the word with another word. It is, nevertheless, relatively easy to use the principle of contrast to teach the grapheme-phoneme correspondences and the morphemic skills. The alphabetic principle is learned best when initial teaching emphasizes only the beginning consonant in a pair of contrastive words, then only the middle vowel, and finally only the ending consonant. Thus, if the intent is to teach initial-consonant discrimination, only the beginning consonant should be varied in the pair of contrasting words (cat-fat). If the intent is to teach the morphemic skills, words might be contrasted by writing, one above the other: port and ports, deport and deports, play and plays, played and playing.

Adjunct Strategies

Significant adjuncts to Step 4 for developing a code based on a knowledge of the grapheme-phoneme correspondences, in addition the principle of minimum difference and the use of color, are the following:

1. Teaching the basic spelling patterns: cvc, vc, cvc$\not{e}$, cv$\not{y}$c: This aids in the teaching of the vowel grapheme-phoneme correspondences. Applied to syllable units, knowledge of the spelling patterns and of their effect on vowel sounding permits the pupil to achieve a

high degree of success in sounding vowels. It helps to reduce uncertainty in prediction.
2. Teaching the phonograms: This aids in the development of automaticity in recoding.
3. Teaching identification by analogy (see chapter 5).

Teaching of Spelling Patterns Organizing teaching around the basic spelling patterns (*vc, cvc, cvcé,* and *cvýc*) develops recoding of the word, introduces the vowel grapheme-phoneme correspondences, and develops a knowledge of word structure:

cvc:	cat	cot	cat	cv:	go	he	be
	bat	cut	cab		so	me	by

vc:	at	in	if	cvcé:	fire	cvýc:	boat
	it	on	in		hire		goat

Expansion of spelling-pattern principles to two and three syllable words involves breaking of words into their basic spelling-pattern units and then applying basic spelling-pattern principles to these units. For example:

cvc/cvc	cv/cvcé	cvc/vcc	cv/cvc
big/top	re/vive	spel/ling	pu/pil

cvvcc/vcc	vc/cvcé	cv/cvc
teach/ing	lo/cate	ba/sic

The recoding process is affected directly by the complexity of the letter/sound correspondences. To recode two- or three-syllable words, the word must first be divided into morphemic units (international becomes intermation-al), then parsed into syllables, and finally into spelling/sound units.

Teaching the Phonograms

Teaching the phonograms helps pupils to simplify sounding of thousands of words. Learning word differences and language patterns is further simplified for pupils when they are taught that within many spelling patterns there exists a phonogram unit that repeats itself in thousands of words. Thus the cvcé spelling pattern contains the vcé phonogram: For example:

ire	ame	one
fire	came	bone
hire	fame	cone
tire	game	lone

Research shows that focusing on word families or phonograms facilitates word recognition. The word phonogram is used here to refer to any combination of symbols representing a syllable (um = /ŭm/; ad = /ăd/) that begins with a sounded vowel and that ends in a sounded consonant (e.g., *ile* is thus a phonogram). Groff (1971, 1981) suggests that the phonogram is the natural unit for the beginner and that it is the most useful unit in learning how to decode words. Glass and Burton (1973) found that most pupils in their study (second and fifth graders) used a sound-cluster approach in decoding words. Glass (1967, 1973a, 1973b) identified 119 common sound clusters. Swenson (1975) found that in matching consonant-vowel-consonant (cvc) trigrams, first-grade average readers attended more to the vc combinations than to single letters, while poor readers relied on the first letter only. Gibson (1970) notes that letter clustering is an important strategy for developing reading, but adds that disabled readers are not able to use syllable groupings and intra-word redundancies as effectively as do skilled readers. Indeed, syllable awareness is often lacking in preliterate children who are likely to become poor readers. Santa (1977) notes that good word identifiers, in contrast to young children and disabled readers, abstract higher-order spelling patterns from words (cvc, cvce, cvcc) and then apply these orthographic spelling redundancies to unfamiliar words. Just and Carpenter (1987) observe that learning to recognize and pronounce a phonogram unit may help a child to acquire a visual representation of the unit. Bradley (1983) notes that detecting visual similarities and differences in written words will not help readers if they are unable to name the visual sequence that represents the word. He suggests that if readers cannot label the pattern, they cannot generalize from a pattern that they recognize to one that they do not, as, for example, from *and* to *hand* (Bradley, et al., 1979). Smith (1988) notes that "uncertainty about the sound of a particular letter diminishes as letters are considered not in isolation but as a part of letter clusters on spelling patterns" (p. 143). Adams (1990) notes that the skilled reader's rapid recognition and recoding of words is a direct outcome of his or her knowledge of the spelling patterns rather than of the application of phonic rules.

The Pupil Spells the Word Orally

Step 5: Have pupils spell the target word orally, pointing to each letter as they say the name of the letter, and have them say the word.

Steps 5, 6, and 7, involving spelling, tracing, and writing the word from memory, are included in the IRM because they help particularly those learners who have significant difficulty in discriminating words and in developing a memory for them.

Pupils should spell the word orally with the word to be learned in front of them and should say the word after they have spelled it: thus, c (sĕ)–a (ā)–t (tē) is /kăt/. Even though the pupil will later be required to write the word from memory (step 7), there is value here in having the pupil spell the word orally from memory without benefit of the printed word. The teacher may tell the pupil: (a) "Spell the word kăt" or (b) "Spell the name of the animal pictured on this card" (showing a card with a picture of a cat on it).

Learning to read and to spell are complementary processes (C. Chomsky, 1979; Henderson & Beers, 1980; Moffett & Wagner, 1976; F. Smith, 1982). Chomsky (1979) suggests that one of the better ways for the beginning reader to gain experience with alphabetic representation and with the phonetic makeup of words is writing in one's own invented spelling or according to the way words sound. Adams (1990) notes that encouraging beginning readers to use invented spelling benefits them more in spelling and word recognition than does encouraging the use of conventional spelling.

Bradley and Bryant (1985, 1989) found that a combination of phonological awareness and spelling instruction (involving teaching of the letters, dissecting words into constituent phonemes, teaching the correspondences between letters and sounds, and teaching children how letters are blended to form pronunciations) facilitated children's word reading. Ehri (1989) and Ehri and Wilce (1985, 1987a, 1987b) found that as children move into word reading, they learn to read words by remembering associations between letters in spellings and sounds detected in pronunciations of words. They learn through making phonetic sense of letters that they see in their spellings of words, through connecting letters to sounds in pronunciations, and through storing the connections in memory. In addition, there is a close relationship between reading deficiency and spelling difficulties, with the pupil often being more deficient in spelling than in reading (Newton et al., 1979; Rabinovitch, 1968; Yule & Rutter, 1976). There is indeed a form of acquired reading disability (spelling dyslexia or alexia without agraphia) in which the pupil is unable to read except by spelling out each letter of the word. Apparently, some children must learn to read in similar fashion (Prior & McCorriston, 1983). The advantages of spelling are:

1. Spelling of the word forces the pupil to visually scrutinize the word, and to focus on the distinctive characteristics of the word. Rather than emphasizing only the word's configuration in developing a visual memory for the word, the teacher will accomplish more by helping readers to note the differences between words and by calling attention to the salient characteristics of words, which surely include the letters themselves.

2. Spelling in addition focuses on the sequence of letters and develops a sequential memory of the letters of the word, thus preparing the pupil to make a visual-auditory match, or to match a visual with an auditory sequence. The crucial difference between *ate, eat,* and *tea* is the sequence of letters. Phonics deficits, in particular, are often due to difficulties in sequencing phonemes rather than to lack of knowledge of single grapheme-phoneme correspondences. Spelling thus is beneficial in developing a coding system. It develops left-to-right direction in visual identification. Spelling, including sounding of the word, and as we will note later, writing of it, forces children to attend to all the letters in a left-to-right sequence. Spelling develops an auditory memory for the word; it improves spelling of the word; it teaches that each word has an individual, idiosyncratic graphic representation and that the sequence of letters gives it its identity.
3. Spelling also influences the attainment of meaning. English spelling in general represents meaning more than sound: words that look alike tend to share the same sense (Smith, 1988).

A simple activity (Lovitt, 1984) for using spelling to develop a sight word vocabulary involves having pupils cut the word (e.g., bake) into letters (lettered blocks might be used) and have them arrange the letters in proper order. If the pupil spells the word correctly, the letters are put into an envelope and the word that has been learned is written on the envelope.

The Pupil Traces and Writes the Word From Memory

Step 6: Have pupils trace the target word with their forefinger, pencil, crayon or fiber-tipped pen making certain that they pronounce the word syllable by syllable while tracing it.

Step 7: Have pupils write the word from memory, again making certain that pupils say the word while writing it.

Steps 6 and 7 require children to trace the word and ultimately to write it from memory. In the Fernald method (Fernald, 1943) pupils place their finger on the paper and trace the word again and again until they can write the word from memory, always saying the total word syllable by syllable while tracing.

The teacher may write the word on a 4" × 12" inch strip of paper, or on the chalkboard, saying the word before writing it and again saying it syllable by syllable as she is writing it. The t's are crossed and the i's are dotted when the teacher pronounces the word a second time. The word to be traced, whether written in manuscript or cursive form, needs to be written in a large enough form so that the pupil can use fingers or felt pen (using a pencil, crayon, or fiber-tipped pen has about equal effect) to trace it.

There are unfortunately young children and poor readers who can use neither whole-word (i.e., the shape and length of the word) nor letter-by-letter identification. They perceive clearly neither the total configuration nor the details of the word. For the former, the word is a jumble of lines; nothing stands out; the figure and ground are fused and the page looks like an undifferentiated mass. The latter have not acquired an understanding of the importance of particular details in letter shapes and of their relationship to one another within the total word; they treat words as solid wholes defying analysis.

Furthermore, there are children who have great difficulty in associating a visual sequence with an auditory sequence, in making a visual-auditory match, or in naming a visual sequence of letters. They have special problems with recoding of the word, even though they do not have either visual or auditory sensory deficits. Poor readers indeed often have greater difficulty with visual-auditory or cross modal tasks (Bradley, 1983).

It is with these children (i.e., those who cannot develop a visual discrimination and memory for the word or who have difficulty with the recoding process, and indeed with those who are totally deficient in phonics and who cannot blend reliably) that tracing and writing from memory have special significance. Such children learn only when they see the word, trace and write the word, and then say the word.

The use of tracing (the tactile component) and of writing from memory (the kinesthetic component) in developing visual identification for a word and in effecting a visual-auditory connection has a long history. The VAKT method of Fernald (1943) and the methods of Strauss and Lehtinen (1947), and of Gillingham and Stillmann (1960, 1973) are well-known.

When children have special difficulty in developing a visual image or memory for a word or when the visual-auditory association is disrupted, teaching for the pupil may involve the following steps:

1. Teach the pupil to recognize and name the letters of the alphabet.
2. Teach the pupil to spell words letter by letter.
3. Teach the pupil to associate the spelling of the word with its phonemic equivalents (kŭh-ă-tŭh).
4. Teach the pupil to associate the intact phonemic sounds (kŭh-ă-tŭh) with letters that are traced or felt by hand. This is the auditory-tactile association.
5. Teach the pupil to read the word with the aid of tactile letters.
6. Teach the pupil to read the word without the aid of tactile letters.

Tracing and writing help to stamp in the visual image. The normal sequence in kinesthetic identification of a word is tracing of the target word, matching the word with one of four possible choices (cat = bat, hat, rat, or cat), drawing the word from a dotted outline form, copying the word with a sample of the word available for comparison, and writing the word from memory. Cooper (1947) had pupils trace the word in a shallow sand or salt tray (e.g., the lid of a shoe box). Painting of the bottom of the tray is helpful. Tracing does not stop until the pupil can write the word from memory.

Traynelis-Yurek (1985), in a study of five children in remedial programs, found that children learned new words better when tracing words with the non-preferred hand. This study confirms neurological findings that most individuals show better mental processing of touch with the nondominant hand, presumably because tactile imput is processed primarily in the right hemisphere of the brain.

Niensted (1968) adapted the Fernald method to group use with high-school juniors. The method involves teacher-prepared duplicated manuscripts to be traced by the students as the graphemes are pronounced, followed by an underlining of the syllables and a reading of the passages, using meaningful phrasing.

In rare instances (because some children's nervous system may be overloaded, by using all the senses simultaneously, thus inhibiting attention and motivation and perhaps causing fatigue) it may help to block one or more of the senses such as by plugging the child's ears while presenting the word visually, tactually, or kinesthetically, or by blindfolding the pupil and letting him hear, trace, and write the word (Blau & Blau, 1968, 1969).

Another approach is to write the target word on the board and have the children look at it and form a mental picture of it. Have them close their eyes and visualize the word. Then let them open their eyes, check the word on the blackboard, and see whether the word is like their mental picture of the word. Erase the word from the board and have them write the word on the board again. Let the children compare their written word with the one on the board. If the word is incorrect, repeat the procedure until the children can write it from memory (Lovitt, 1984).

Step 6, tracing, may be omitted if the pupil masters word identification relatively easily, but should always be strongly considered with the severely disabled reader (Hulme, 1981a, 1981b). The average tracing period is about two months, ranging from one to about eight months. Recent studies (Carbo, 1980, 1983; Weinberg, 1983; Wheeler, 1983) found that underachieving primary children learn better through tactual and kinesthetic modalities than through visual and auditory methods. Carbo (1983) observes that the research clearly indicates that poor readers tend to be tactile-kinesthetic learners. Gardiner (1986) also reported greater progress among fourth-grade underachievers when taught by a kinesthetic approach than when taught by a combined auditory-visual method. Tracing and writing are effective, even with good readers, in teaching discrimination of similar or look-alike words, in teaching words with irregular phoneme-grapheme correspondences, in teaching function words such as but, if, the, and their, and when the pupil has not learned to identify the letters of the alphabet. With most pupils, tracing may not be necessary, but writing the word from memory should always be a part of the reading method. Miles (1983) cautions that writing a word many times is unlikely to be effective with severely disabled readers unless the pupil is taught about the ways in which specific sounds are symbolized graphically.

The kinesthetic-tactile aspect is time consuming, but it emphasizes careful scrutiny and study of the word; it enforces consistent left-to-right direction in reading; and the sensory impressions created by tracing and writing, reinforce the visual impression. Some suggest that enforced attention to details in sequence rather than the tactile-kinesthetic sensation is the significant aid to learning. The tracing-writing method also helps children to overcome reversal and transposition tendencies, strengthens and even ensures the visual-auditory association for letters and words through the kinesthetic linkage, develops and strengthens sequential memory, and develops the syllabic basis for building an extensive reading vocabulary (Ansara, 1982). Furthermore, it allows for immediate notation and correction of errors and for observation of progress at each stage.

The Teacher Presents the Word in Another Sentence Context

Step 8: Again explain the meaning of the target word and present the word in another written sentence context (on the chalkboard, on chart paper, and/or on the back of the 4" × 6" inch card), then: (a) read the sentence to the pupils; (b) have pupils read the sentence aloud; and (c) have pupils identify and underline, frame, or trace in color the target word and have them state the meaning of the word.

It is a common finding that teachers frequently do not introduce the word in context or in a written sentence (Durkin, 1984b). Step 8 brings the target word back to the semantic and syntactic context, to the sentence or story context, into which it was originally placed. The sentence may at times be formulated and written by the teacher; at other times the pupil is asked to formulate and write the sentence. When working with groups, the teacher might print the sentence on a ditto master, quickly duplicate it, and give the child his own copy or use a microcomputer printer to produce a copy for each child. This copy could then be taken home and read to the parents.

Meaning always has to be primary in reading. The pupil must realize that print says something. Writing and print have as their chief function the recall of entire language patterns, especially sentence-level utterances. The teacher should be satisfied only when children's oral reading of a sentence indicates, through the features of pitch, sequence, and stress, that they in fact understand the total meaning. The very least the teacher should accept in the beginning is that children read the sentence as they would "talk" it to a friend. Many readers, especially beginning and poor readers, exhibit a marked lack of fluency. Their reading lacks accuracy, speed, and expression (Rasinski, 1989). Despite the importance of fluency for proficient reading, it is an oft-neglected goal of reading instruction (Allington, 1983).

With nonfluent readers, especially beginning and poor readers, it is strongly recommended that the teacher use such techniques as choral reading, the neurological impress method, the imitative method, the repeated-readings method with or without a model, the multiple oral rereading method (Moyer, 1983), the simultaneous listening and reading or read-along method, paired reading, or cooperative pair work (Koskinen & Blum, 1986; Topping, 1989) to develop automaticity in word recoding and fluency in reading.

The oral neurological-impress method (Heckelman, 1966, 1969) is a system of unison reading whereby the pupil and the teacher read aloud, but the teacher reads slightly faster and louder than the pupil. The material should initially be on the pupil's independent level. Practice may be limited to 15 minutes a day. This approach is especially effective with those who are phonics-bound or with children who have had intensive phonics training but still are not reading fluently. Langford (1974) and Bos (1982) found the method to be effective with severely disabled readers. Henk (1983) recommended that the neurological impress method replace the silent reading step in the DRA. Hollingsworth (1978) found that the neurological impress method was effective with fourth to sixth grade remedial reading pupils when used with as many as 10 pupils at a time. The pupils' comprehension scores increased. As the pupil becomes more proficient the teacher may reduce the volume of her voice and may even lag slightly behind the pupil. Moving the finger across the page of print while saying the words is continued throughout the program. A variation of the neurological impress method is to have a poor reader read with an average reader who can read the material fluently with both pupils sitting side by side and reading from one book (Eldredge & Butterfield, 1986).

Other similar approaches are the imitative method (the pupil listens to the teacher reading a passage and then tries to imitate the teacher), simultaneous listening and reading or tape-assisted reading (the pupil follows along on the pages while listening to an audiotape of the passage or book), and the repeated-readings method (Dahl & Samuels, 1975; Kann, 1983; Dowhower, 1987, 1989; Samuels, 1979, 1985, 1988) which requires children to read a passage on their instructional level again and again until they can read it fluently without error, or reading in phrases (Allington, 1983; Gregory, 1986). C. Chomsky (1976, 1978) and Aulls and Gelbart (1980) found significant improvement in comprehension when students listen to tapes while simultaneously following along in a book, rehearsing to the point of memorization, and rereading the story until oral fluency is reached.

Dowhower (1987, 1989) found that repeated-reading practice, whether assisted as by use of an audio-taped model or unassisted, improves rate, word-recognition accuracy, comprehension, prosodic reading (i.e., segmenting text into meaningful phrases), and reduces miscues. Practice on a single passage was found to be not as effective as practice on a series of passages, and prosodic reading was most facilitated by a read-along procedure. Dowhower's studies showed that fluency, rate, and comprehension gains tend to transfer to the reading of novel or unpracticed passages. Dowhower also observes that repeated reading helps children who are processing text on a word-by-word level, can be incorporated into any reading approach, and helps particularly those who make few oral reading errors but are reading fewer than 45 words per minute (WPM) (Dowhower, 1987).

Dowhower recommends that passages be kept short (50 to 300 words in length); that pupils should attain an 85% accuracy in word recognition before practice is begun; that practice passages be kept at the same level of difficulty until progress occurs; that unassisted repeated reading be used when the pupil reaches 60 WPM; that a mastery-level-for-speed goal, perhaps 85 to 100 WPM, be set for word-by-word or remedial readers; and that a mastery goal of three to five readings be set for children with relatively high rates of speed and accuracy.

Reitsma (1988) found guided reading (in which children had to read on their own and had to correct all errors themselves with teacher feedback) and speech-select (in which children practiced independently but had the opportunity to ask for pronunciation of any unknown word through computer-based speech) both improved reading fluency. Koskinen and Blum (1986), after noting that skill and fluency in reading develop as pupils practice reading, note that paired repeated reading (a combination of paired reading and of the repeated readings method) is a significant contributor to oral reading fluency and to comprehension. They recommend the strategy be used during the independent follow-up to reading instruction.

The Target Word is Practiced and Rehearsed

Step 9: Present the target word again in isolation and have pupils pronounce it.

This final step of the IRM is designed to assure the automaticity in recoding of which Samuels (LaBerge & Samuels, 1974; Samuels, 1987; Samuels & Kamil, 1984) speaks and which is needed for the automatic semantic activation of which we spoke in chapter 5. Skilled readers are readers who have developed automaticity in recoding. It is not enough that pupils have mastered grapheme-phoneme correspondences or that they can blend sounds. Their knowledge must go beyond accuracy to automaticity (LaBerge & Samuels, 1976, 1985; Samuels, 1988), and to the point of overlearning. Efficiency in comprehension is dependent upon speed decoding.

Rayner and Pollatsek (1989) note that automaticity means rapid and effortless reading, lack of awareness of the process, and lack of conscious control by the reader. It means the ability to process the printed word so efficiently and so rapidly that during each fixation the reader has some 130 to 140 msec. for cognitive processing. Samuels (1987) asserts that automaticity in recoding simply means that the word-recognition task requires little attention. There is no shortage of published materials that encourage and promote quick recoding of words and the development of visual memory for a word configuration. Such materials involve the use of flash or picture-word cards, teacher-made tachistoscopes, word-identification games of all kinds, (e.g., bingo games), programmed materials, computer programs, and so forth.

Step 9 involves using the word in meaningful contexts, using the word in spelling and writing lessons, using both color and the linguistic principle of minimal difference to teach pupils where the significant difference between words is, and having children see, discuss, use, define, and write the word.

WHOLE WORD OR ANALYTICAL PHONICS VERSUS SYNTHETIC PHONICS

The recommended program for phonics instruction in this text and in the Integrated Reading Method is analytical or whole-word phonics. Thus, the target word is a whole word, and the pupil is encouraged to scan through the word, match the visual sequence with the auditory sequence, and sound the total word. In analytical phonics the pupil is taught the *b*/b/ correspondence in the context of the total word. *B* does not say /bŭh/; it represents the sound heard at the beginning of words such as box, boy, and big. However, teaching /b/ as /bŭh/ may be a necessary crutch in the beginning, and Wallach and Wallach (1982) note that it does not hamper learning. Bannatyne (1973) observes that it is impossible to blend *l-i-t*, if *l* is sounded /lŭh/.

Clearly, there are children who benefit from a synthetic, letter-by-letter phonics method. The Integrated Reading Method allows for a synthetic phonic approach. The synthetic phonics method was originated by Ickelsamer in 1534 and was introduced in America in 1782 by Noah Webster. Some children may need to focus on the individual letters (*c-a-t*) and their auditory equivalents (kŭh- ă-tŭh), and only then on the total word. Jorm and Share (1983) go so far as to observe that the evidence from classroom and laboratory research favors beginning instruction that emphasizes the acquisition of the alphabetic code (on this point the observations made earlier concur), but they suggest further that the favored programs are those synthetic phonics programs in which letter/sound correspondences are taught together with blending of the separate sounds into phonograms and words, and together with phonological awareness skills such as segmenting of words into phonemes.

In synthetic programs the teacher initially concentrates on the teaching of the symbol-sound associations of perhaps three to five consonants (*b, d, m, p, t*) and one vowel. One by one the consonants are joined with each of the other vowels. Each phoneme should be correlated with a key word. The key words for vowels may take two forms. The vowel sound may occur at the beginning of the key word (/ă/ — apple, at; / ĕ/ — elephant, Eskimo; / ĭ/ — Indian, igloo, it; /ŏ/ — ostrich, octopus, on; /ŭ/ — umbrella, up), or the vowel may be taught using a key word in which the vowels occurs in the middle of the word as in cat, bed, fish, top, and duck.

A key skill required in synthetic phonics is the ability to segment sounds. Sound segmentation, which is a subset of phonological awareness, requires the recognition that words spoken orally can be divided into smaller units or sounds (Richek, List & Lerner, 1982). Wallach and Wallach (1982) found that instruction in segmentation increased the reading ability of remedial readers. Liberman et al. (1985) cite a dozen studies affirming that the ability to segment speech into its constituent sound units is a strong predictor of reading ability.

Another phonological awareness skill is that of blending (also called auditory synthesis, sequential decoding, and oral sequencing) which is the synthesis of the individual phonemes to form a total word. Ramsey (1972) reports that 40% of the errors made by second graders on a test of unfamiliar words resulted from difficulties in blending. Auditory blending is particularly important in grades 1 and 2 when pupils are learning to read, when reading is taught by a synthetic phonic method, and when the pupil must analyze words into syllables to arrive at the pronunciation of a word. It appears to have less bearing on reading achievement after the fundamentals of reading have been mastered. Poor readers usually can blend heard sounds, but they cannot blend them when they must first begin with the letters, produce the sounds that the letters represent, and then blend them.

Blending may take four forms:

1. Sounding and blending of each letter: cat = /kŭh-ă-tŭh/. This is letter-by-letter sounding.
2. Sounding of the beginning consonant and the following vowel and blending these with the final consonant: ca-t, /kă/-/t/.
3. Sounding of the initial consonant and joining it to the vowel and ending consonant (the phonogram): c-at, /k/-/ăt/.
4. Sounding of the beginning consonant and following vowel /kă/, sounding of the vowel and the final consonant /ăt/, and then blending them /kă/ăt/ to form the word cat /kăt/.

Each of these approaches has its problems. Letter-by-letter sounding and blending (b/a/t) often results in a distortion of the individual sounds. When pupils are asked to blend a beginning consonant with a phonogram /b/ăt/, they tend to develop the habit of looking first at the end of the word. This may cause difficulties for pupils who reverse. Joining the vowel to the beginning consonant /bă/t/ makes it difficult to know whether to give the vowel its long or short sound. It seems preferable to blend the beginning consonant with the phonogram. There are two ways of teaching the phonogram.: either by blending /ă/ and /t/ or by teaching these as a unit /ăt/. The latter, in many instances, is easier than teaching the blending of /b/-/ă/-/t/.

The teacher develops the blending skill by:

1. Having the pupil form the mouth in preparation for saying the initial consonant, but then say the following vowel instead: /b/ē/. This technique is especially effective when the initial consonant is unvoiced and when the syllable ends in a vowel.
2. Having the pupil join the beginning consonant to the ending phonogram. In this technique the single syllable is divided into two parts: the beginning consonant and the ending phonogram.
3. Using an auditory method, with the teacher pronouncing the word in parts /sh/-/ēt/ and the pupil being required to combine the parts to form the whole word /shēt/. Pupils do not see the printed word in this approach.
4. Using an auditory-visual method, with the teacher using manipulatives to point out how sounds and letters may be substituted for one another to make new words. The teacher shows the pupil a card with the word feet on it and says: "This word is /fēt/. Now I am going to make the word. . . ." With this, the teacher folds down a flap on which is written *sh* so as to make the word *sheet*. If the pupil can pronounce the word, it is assumed he can blend *sh* in the initial position. Haddock (1978) found that the auditory-visual method was more effective than the auditory method.

SUMMARY

The emphasis of chapter 8 is the development of a sight or recognition vocabulary, without which the pupil cannot group words into thought units and without which the pupil cannot use context and meaning cues effectively. The chapter is designed to help the learner to master recognizing and encoding of the printed word; to develop automaticity in recoding the printed symbol; to teach the importance of the orthographic structure of words; and to outline how the within-word cues, the rules mapping letters to phonemes, and the coding principles of the English writing system are to be taught.

It is not IRM nor the nine steps that comprise it that are the significant or critical elements. It is rather a question of how best to develop a sight vocabulary: namely, how one best teaches visual discrimination of the symbol, memory for the symbol, recoding of the symbol, and association of meaning with the symbol. The IRM programs for each of these. It especially focuses on the development of a knowledge of the within-word cues, knowledge which becomes a part of the pupil's schemata and which will help her to identify words independently and accurately.

Step 4 of IRM is the crucial step. It is at that point that the pupil should learn the strategies that will make her self-directive in the word-identification and the word-naming process. It is at that point that the pupil should learn the grapheme-phoneme correspondences. We feel these are best learned through an analytic-synthetic method, but for some children the teacher may need to use a synthetic-analytic method, beginning with word parts and proceeding to the total word.

Chapter 9
Development of Grapheme-Phoneme Correspondence Knowledge and of the Structural or Morphemic Analysis Skills

I. Introduction
II. Development of Grapheme-Phoneme Correspondence Knowledge
   A. Oral Reading Errors and Phonics
   B. Terminology
   C. Definition of Phonics
   D. Consonant Correspondences
      1. Beginning Consonant Correspondences
      2. Middle and End Consonant Correspondences
      3. Rhyming and the Phonograms
      4. Beginning and Ending Consonant Clusters
      5. Teaching Consonant Correspondences
   E. Vowel Grapheme-Phoneme Correspondences
      1. Short Vowel Correspondences
      2. Long or Glided Vowel Correspondences
      3. Modified Vowel Correspondences
      4. Diphthongs
      5. *R*-Controlled Vowels
      6. Teaching Vowel Correspondences
III. Development of Structural or Morphemic Analysis Knowledge
   A. Morphology and Morphemes
   B. Teaching the Inflectional Endings
   C. Teaching the Inflectional Changes
   D. Teaching Compound Words
   E. Teaching Contractions
   F. Teaching Roots, Prefixes, and Suffixes
   G. Teaching Hyphenated Words
   H. Developing Syllabication Skills
      1. Development in Syllabication
      2. Syllabication Rules
   I. Developing Accentuation Skills
   J. Exercises and Activities
IV Summary

CHAPTER 9
Development of Grapheme-Phoneme Correspondence Knowledge and of the Structural or Morphemic Analysis Skills

Chapter 5 discussed the predictive nature of the reading process and concluded that efficiency of prediction, especially of focal prediction, depends to a great degree upon the reader's knowledge of and ability to use the within-word cues, and upon developing automatic semantic activation.

Chapter 8 identified the role of the grapheme-phoneme correspondences rules in identifying and naming words when the pupil cannot predict the word in context. It offered numerous suggestions (such as spelling the word, tracing and writing the word, calling the pupil's attention to the salient features of words, teaching the pupil what a word is not, identifying where the significant differences between words lie, and scrutinizing through the word from left to right) for helping the pupil to develop a visual discrimination of and a visual memory for the symbol, but it also noted that if only configuration, picture cues and naming the word are used, the pupil is short-changed. Chapter 8 thus emphasized that the pupil needs to develop a code for sounding and naming words with accuracy and with automaticity. As we (Dechant, 1964) observed some years ago:

> In reading, good teaching seems to mean that the teacher must devise techniques of instruction which help the pupil to construct a generic code or coding system that has wider applicability in reading than would the rote identification of individual words and which permits the pupil to analyze new words without having to learn a new configuration each time. (p. 195)

We believe that such a code can only be developed by teaching children the grapheme-phoneme correspondences and developing their morphemic cue knowledge.

DEVELOPMENT OF GRAPHEME-PHONEME CORRESPONDENCE KNOWLEDGE

We have thus divided the chapter into two basic segments. The first deals with grapheme-phoneme information, the second, with morphemic knowledge.

The first section is intended to identify the grapheme-phoneme information that the teacher of reading should possess and that the teacher, at least to some extent, needs to share with children learning to read. This information needs to become part of their nonvisual information or schematic structure. It should include an understanding of the use of the within-word cues, particularly the phonic cues or the grapheme-phoneme correspondences, identification by analogy cues, and use of phonogram cues in word identification. Children need to be taught to become self-directive in the sounding and naming of the visual configuration.

That recoding is a valuable asset for the reader to possess is no longer an issue (Groff, 1986). Carnine (1977) found that transfer to unknown words, even to irregular words, is better when the pupil is taught phonics. Rosso and Emans (1981) found that knowledge of phonic generalizations helps children to recode unrecognized words, even if the pupil cannot state the phonics rule. Bradley (1983) found that recoding of the word is in itself effective in developing a memory for a visually presented sequence of letters. Venezky (1983) notes that recoding at a minimum helps the beginning reader to validate the word identification made by sight and through context.

MacLean (1988) notes that phonics plays an important role especially in early reading instruction. It is a catalyst which triggers the process of learning to read. It helps readers to identify unfamiliar words. He notes that the process of learning to identify unfamiliar words is clearly distinct from the recognition of familiar words. Furthermore, phonics instruction increases children's phonemic awareness or awareness of grapheme-phoneme interrelationships (Bradley & Bryant, 1985; Share et al., 1984). It enables learners to match written with spoken words and teaches pupils to match the visual sequence of letters with the auditory sequence of sounds. It thus helps readers to get at the thousands of word meanings that they have already acquired, but for which they have not learned to recognize and sound the graphic equivalent.

Children who fail the word-identification task have a sight-word deficiency. They cannot remember the visual sequence of letters that form a word, visually discriminate the word as a gestalt, or deal with the orthographic structure of words. They cannot name the word, deal with the phonologic information contained in the printed word, or make a visual sequence–auditory sequence match. A major reason for their deficiency is that they have not developed an understanding of the grapheme-phoneme correspondences. They have not learned to recode.

Oral Reading Errors and Phonics

The sight-word deficiency is often symptomatically expressed as by oral reading errors or miscues. These errors are obviously detectable only when the pupil is reading orally. Oral reading errors occur because the reader cannot perform the third function of the word-identification process, namely that of associating sound with the graphic symbol, that of sounding or naming the word, or that of recoding. The oral reading miscues that result when the pupil cannot name the word are usually of the following types: omissions of a word or part of a word, including refusal to attempt to sound the word; additions or insertions; substitutions, including mispronunciations, contraction errors, and misplaced accent; repetitions or regressions; hesitations; and reversals. The analysis of the oral reading errors (Dechant, 1981; 1982; Goodman, 1969; Goodman & Burke, 1972) is a subject of interest in its own right. For our purposes, it is enough to note that the teacher of reading needs to give children the opportunity to read orally. She needs to diagnose the pupil's difficulties in reading words, both in isolation and in context, and to identify the location (beginning, middle, or end of the syllable) or portion of the syllable in which the errors are concentrated. Even a casual analysis reveals that the basic deficiency that explains the oral reading errors of children is either a deficiency in grapheme-phoneme knowledge or in morphemic analysis knowledge. If this is so, then it follows that pupils must be taught the grapheme-phoneme correspondences and the morphemic analysis skills. The simple fact is that pupils cannot become independent and self-directive in the word-identification process, in identifying and recoding, and in predicting themselves through text unless they learn the grapheme-phoneme correspondences and the morphemic analysis skills.

The pupil may acquire phonic information through direct instruction or incidentally as a consequence of reading. Direct instruction seems to be more effective than incidental instruction. Unfortunately, the pupil is often left to acquire the information incidentally because the pupil's teacher does not possess this information. The question, "Why is it necessary to teach phonics?" should no longer mystify. Phonics teaches children to see /kăt/ in *cat*; to see why *cat* is /kăt/. It develops an insight. It teaches children that the visual/auditory associations follow certain within-word consistencies or probabilities.

Terminology

Before taking up the specifics of phonics instruction, examine a few terms. The terms that are of interest here are phonology, phonetics, phonemics, phonemes, morphology, graphemes, morphemes, orthography, alphabet, letters, and syntax.

1. *Phonology* is the study of speech sounds; it includes the study of both phonetics and phonemics.
2. *Phonetics* is the study of speech production; it is the study of the sounds or phones used in speech, including their pronunciations, the symbolization of the sounds, and the action of the larynx, tongue, and lips in sound production. Phonetics studies phonetic alphabets which represent graphically the actual pronunciations of linguistic forms. Phonetics furthermore deals with the variant pronunciations in different regions of a country and with the perception of speech by the hearing mechanism. Applied phonetics includes: (a) correction of defective speech; (b) teaching of "standard" speech in a given region; and (c) devising symbols to represent speech sounds.
3. *Phonemics* is the study of how sounds function to convey differences of meaning; it is the study of the speech sounds that are used in a language. It is thus a study of phonemes. Phonemic analysis deals only with those sounds that are significant in the language (the phonemes) and ignores the nonsignificant differences (the allophones). The *p* sound in *pet, spot, suppose*, and *top* is slightly different in each instance, but the difference is considered to be nonsignificant.

    Basically two kinds of sound are produced by the human speech mechanism. Phones are speech sounds of any kind. Young children always produce a far greater number of sounds than they later use in the language. Phonemes are speech sounds that are a part of the language. Thus, all phonemes are phones, but not all phones are phonemes.
4. The *phonemes*, of which there are 45 in the English language, have one prime purpose in language. They are the smallest units of sound that can differentiate one utterance from another. For example, a single letter, representing a simple sound, completely changes the meaning in the sentences, "A stitch in time saves none" and "There's no business like shoe business."
5. *Morphology* is the study of the meanings of language and of word form and word structure. Morphology and syntax compose the grammar of language.
6. The *grapheme* is the smallest unit of printed word structure that represents a phoneme. The *morpheme* is the smallest unit of word structure that has meaning. A grapheme is a class of closely related graphs (letters or combinations of letters, for example *sh*) consti-

tuting the smallest unit of writing that distinguishes one printed word from another. The grapheme as such has no meaning. The writing of graphemes in proper order to form morphemes is *orthography* or spelling. The set of graphic shapes that represent the phonemes of the language is the *alphabet*.

The grapheme is described as the counterpart of a phoneme. This distinguishes it from a letter. There are 26 letters in the alphabet, but there are many more graphemes. The word *cat* has three letters and three graphemes; the word *that* has four letters, but only three graphemes. The combination *th* is one grapheme. The word *brag* has four letters and four graphemes; the *b* and *r* in *br* do not lose their individual identity. *Th* is a digraph, but *br* is a blend. Graphemes are single letters or letter combinations that represent a single phoneme.

7. *Syntax* is the manner in which words are grouped into utterances or sentences. An utterance is a series of words that is spoken at one time.

Definition of Phonics

Phonics is the study of the phoneme-grapheme correspondences; it is the study of the speech equivalents of printed symbols and the use of the knowledge gained to identify and pronounce printed words. It develops an understanding of the correspondences between the English language spelling system and the English sounding system. It is the study of the letter-sound relationships or of the relationships of the graphemes to the phonemes. Phonics instruction represents the various teaching practices that aim to develop the pupil's ability to sound out a word by matching the letters by which a word is spelled with the specific sounds which these letters represent. Phonic analysis is the actual process of sounding out letters or letter combinations to arrive at the pronunciation of the word.

Success in learning the phoneme-grapheme correspondences depends upon: the identification and discrimination of one sound from another, and the visual discrimination of the letters that represent language sounds. Before beginning phonics instruction, children should be able to see differences in printed letters and words, and they should have learned to differentiate the separate sounds in spoken words. The teaching task that remains after mastery of visual and auditory discrimination is one of developing an association, or correspondence, between the grapheme and the phoneme.

Chapter 9 does not imply that reading is simply the recognition of the symbol-sound correspondences to the point where the reader responds to the letters and words with appropriate speech. The pupil must learn to crack the graphic code (the letter-sound relationships), but reading should not be equated with cracking the code. Reading is more than simply pronouncing. The issue is not whether one can comprehend the meaning of a word before sounding it. Obviously, one can. However, especially in beginning reading, the naming of a word normally occurs before the meaning is associated with the word.

We summarize here what Smith (1988) has to say about phonics because he is generally considered to provide a top-down, whole-language emphasis, which some incorrectly interpret to mean "no phonics." He notes that phonic rules have many exceptions and can only be considered as probabilistic guides to the way words are pronounced. Smith notes that children master phonics as a result of learning to read rather than as a prerequisite for reading. He acknowledges that fluent readers can use their knowledge of spelling-sound correspondences to help identify unfamiliar words, and adds that the existence of such correspondences should not be concealed from children learning to read. Smith concludes that any of the strategies, including the grapheme-phoneme correspondence rules, "are likely to be inadequate when used alone" (p. 146). He adds that while all the word identification strategies "will reduce uncertainty, none is likely to eliminate all alternatives by itself ... to ignore alternative means of reducing uncertainty is to ignore redundancy which is a central part of all aspects of language" (p. 146), and with this we agree. Unfortunately, too often grapheme-phoneme information is the alternative means that is ignored by the teacher in her teaching and by the pupil in his reading. Smith views phonic rules as sentinels: they protect the reader against making impossible hypotheses.

Consonant Correspondences

The content of phonics consists of consonant grapheme-phoneme correspondences and of the vowel grapheme-phoneme correspondences. The presentation that follows begins with the consonant correspondences. This first section identifies what needs to be taught, or, perhaps more importantly, what the teacher needs to know. Later sections deal with the how of teaching the phonic skills. Examine first the content represented by the consonant correspondences. This content is presented under four major headings: beginning consonant correspondences, end consonant correspondences, rhyming and the phonograms, and beginning and ending consonant clusters.

Beginning Consonant Correspondences

Pupils need to learn what is meant when the teacher says, "This word begins with an *m, t, h, p,* or *n* sound." Pupils must learn to deal with beginning consonant substitution. They need to learn what changing the

TABLE 9-1: The Consonant Sounds of the Language

Plosives		Fricatives		Nasals	Semivowels	
Voiced	Unvoiced	Voiced	Unvoiced	Voiced	Voiced	Unvoiced
/b/	/p/	/th̸/	/th/	/m/	/r/	/h/
/d/	/t/	/v/	/f/	/n/	/l/	/hw/
/g/	/k/	/z/	/s/	/ng/	/y/	
		/zh/	/sh/		/w/	
		/j/	/ch/			

*Sounds are voiced if they are accompanied by vibration of the vocal cords; they are unvoiced if there is no vibration of the vocal cords. Voiced sounds can generally be vocalized only in connection with a vowel sound: for example: *b-/be/*; *m, n,* and *ng* are exceptions. The sound represented by *f,* on the other hand, can be made with the upper teeth and the lower lip without using the vocal cords; it is, therefore, termed an unvoiced sound, and the consonant *f* is an unvoiced consonant. Smith (1988, p. 136) notes that "There is only one way to tell whether *th* should be pronounced as in /this/ or as in /thank/, and that is to remember every instance."

initial consonant does to the sound and the meaning of a word. The pertinent data about beginning consonant correspondences are:

I. There are 21 consonant letters and 25 consonant sounds or phonemes in the English Language. Table 9-1 identifies these consonant sounds, indicating also which of the sounds are voiced or unvoiced.

There are 45 distinct phonemes in the language (25 consonant and 20 vowel phonemes), combining in varying ways with graphemes to form some 250 grapheme-phoneme correspondences. Of the 21 consonant letters, only three (the *c, q,* and *x*) do not represent a distinct phoneme.

II. There are five letter combinations, *ch, sh, th, ng,* and *wh,* that represent six additional phonemes: *ch* =/ch/; *sh* =/sh/; *th* = unvoiced as in *ether* and voiced /th̸/ as in *either*; wh =/hw/; and ng =/ng/.

III. One consonant phoneme, /zh/, can be represented only by another letter or letters: by *g* (garage), by *s* (measure), or by *z* (azure). *Zh* as a grapheme does not occur in the printed words of the English language, although it appears in words borrowed from others (e.g., Zhivago).

IV. The consonant letters *b, f,* (except in *of*), *h, j, k, l, m, p, r, v, w,* and *y* represent only one sound.

V. The other consonant letters may represent more than one phoneme:
c = /k/ cat; /s/ city/; /sh/ vicious; /ch/ cello
d = /d/ dog; /j/ soldier; /t/ helped
g = /g/ go; /j/ giant; /zh/ garage
n = /n/ not; /ng/ finger or bank

q(u) = /kw/ quit; /k/ liquor; /k-w/ liquid
s = /s/ see; /z/ his; /sh/ sure, nauseous; /zh/ treasure
t = /t/ top; /ch/ picture; /sh/ nation
x = /ks/ box; /gz/ exact; /z/ xylophone; /ksh/ anxious; /gzh/ luxurious
z = /z/ zoo; /s/ waltz; /zh/ azure

Even though many of the variant sounds occur only in the middle or end of a word, they are all covered in this section.

VI. The difficulties of some readers result from their inability to discriminate certain sounds, and from the fact that not all sounds are equally easy to articulate. There is an order of primitivity of sounds. Sounds generally are produced by children in the following sequence: /m/, /p/, /b/, /t/, /d/, /n/, /h/, /w/, /f/, /v/, /k/, /g/, /th/, /sh/, /zh/, /ch/, /j/, /s/, /z/, /r/, and /l/. Most articulatory errors made by primary children involve /f/, /l/, /r/, /s/, /sh/, /k/, /th/, and /ch/. In phonic instruction the /k/, /q/, /v/, /x/, /y/, and /z/ might well be taught last.

VII. Additional difficulties may occur because not all letters are equally easy to identify. The most frequently confused pairs of letters in rank order by non-reading kindergarteners are: *p-g, d-p, d-b, b-p, h-u, i-l, k-y, t-u, c-e, d-h, h-n, h-y, j-k*, and *n-u*.

VIII. It is not enough for the pupil to know that the *c* may represent /k/, /s/, /sh/, or /ch/. The pupil also needs to learn when the variant sounds of certain letters occur. For example:

A. The letter c represents /k/, /s/, /sh/, /ch/:
   1. *C* represents /k/ before *a* (except in *façade*), *o*, and *u* (cat, cot, cut), when followed by a consonant (clap, clip, crop), or at the end of a syllable (arc, havoc, zodiac). The /k/ sound of *c* occurs 74% of the time.
   2. *C* represents /s/ before *e, i*, and *y*. The /s/ sound of *c* occurs 22% of the time.
   3. *C* represents /sh/ when *c* occurs in the middle or end syllable of a word and is followed by *i* as in vicious, electrician, social, ancient, precious, or by *e* (ocean); it represents /ch/ in Italian words such as cello and concerto.

B. The letter d represents /d/, /j/, /t/:
   1. In combination with *u, d* often represents /j/ as in graduate, gradual, individual, etc.; it also represents /d/: dual, duet, etc.
   2. In combination with *i*, the *d* may say /j/ as in soldier and cordial; and /d/ as in dial, diet, etc.
   3. In the ending *ed* the *d* represents /t/ when *ed* follows an unvoiced consonant (puffed, packed, dipped, wished).

C. The letter g represents /g/, /j/, /zh/:
   1. *G* represents /g/ before *a, o*, and *u* (gave, go, gun), when it

ends a syllable (tag, rag), and when it is followed by a consonant (glad, gradual).
2. G represents /j/ before *e, i,* and *y,* except in such words as: get, give, girl, tiger, gift, geese, gear, geyser, giddy, gild, gill, and finger.
3. G represents /zh/ in words borrowed from the French (fuselage, beige, corsage, cortege, barrage, sabotage, espionage, camouflage, rouge, garage, mirage).
4. The *gu* combination represents /g/: guard, guess, guest, guide, guilt, guinea, guarantee, guitar. The *gu* in penguin represents /gw/.
5. *Gue* represents /g/ as in vague, league, fatigue, intrigue.
6. Words of one syllable ending with the sound of /j/ are usually spelled with the *dge* ending if the sound is immediately preceded by a short vowel sound (edge, fudge), and with the *ge* ending if the sound is immediately preceded by a long vowel sound or a consonant (cage, change).

D. The letter k:
   1. *Ck* at the end of a word preceded by a short vowel represents /k/: back, click.
   2. *Nk* is commonly pronounced *ngk*: *ank* is /ăngk/ as in bank, drank; *ink* is /ĭngk/ as in blink, drink; *unk* is /ŭngk/ as in flunk, junk; *onk* is /ŏngk/ as in honk or /ŭngk/ as in monk.

E. The letter n represents /n/ or /ng/:
   1. *N* represents /ng/ before *k* (bank, drink) or when it precedes a *c* pronounced /k/ as in uncle.
   2. *N* represents /ng/ before *g* pronounced /g/ as in single, finger, linger, but not in singer.

F. The letter q represents /k/, /kw/, or /k-w/:
   1. *Q* occurs only in the combination *qu* and usually represents /kw/: quit.
   2. *Qu* represents simply /k/ in some words: liquor, conquer.
   3. *Qu* represents /k-w/ in liquid.
   4. *Que* at the end of a word is simply a /k/ sound: unique, critique, picturesque, plaque.

G. The letter s represents /s/, /z/, /sh/, /zh/:
   1. *S* represents /s/:
      a. At the beginning of a word or syllable: sell, sunset.
      b. As the initial letter of a consonant blend: best, task, spring. Some letter clusters can be both blends (switch) and digraphs (sword). The consonant digraph *sh* is pronounced /sh/.
      c. In conjunction with another *s* at the end of a word: dress, miss, fuss, recess; the *ss* in the middle of a word may be /sh/: tissue.

d. After unvoiced consonants: puffs, ducks, maps, cats, myths.
   2. *S* represents /z/:
      a. After voiced consonants: for example /b/ (cobs), /d/ (lids), /g/ (gags), /l/ (pills), /m/ (hams), /h/ (vans), /ng/ (rings), /r/ (cars), /v/ (lives), voiced /th/ (lathes).
      b. After long vowel sounds (flies).
      c. When the *s* occurs between two vowels (closet). Words ending in *se* may have the sounds of /s/ as in house or of /z/ as in arose or house (to house something).
      d. At the end of some one-syllable words (as, has, was, is, his).
   3. *S* represents /sh/ in words such as sure, sugar, mansion, and when double *s* is followed by a vowel: (issue, tissue, pressure, fissure).
   4. *S* represents /zh/ in words such as: vision, measure, treasure, pleasure, usury, composure, exposure, fusion, etc.
H. The letter t represents /t/, /ch/, /sh/:
   1. *T* represents *ch*, when followed by *ure* (pictures, pasture).
   2. *T* represents /sh/ or /ch/ in the combinations *ti* as in nation or question or *te* as in righteous.
I. The letter x represents /ks/, /gz/, /z/, /ksh/, /gzh/:
   1. *X* does not represent a separate and distinct phoneme. It most commonly represents /ks/ as in ax, box, fix, fox.
   2. *X* represents /z/ at the beginning of a word (Xerox, xylophone).
   3. *X* represents /gz/ in an unstressed syllable that precedes a vowel sound (exact, exist). When the accent is on the vowel preceding the *x* (exit), the *x* represents /ks/.
   4. *X* may also represent /ksh/ anxious or /gzh/ luxurious.
J. The letter z represents /z/, /s/, /zh/:
   1. *Z* represents /s/ in one word, waltz.
   2. *Z* represents /zh/ in words such as azure, seizure, etc.

The consonant grapheme-phoneme correspondences should be introduced to children slowly and perhaps in five segments; the order may well be: (a) *b, c* (hard sound), *d, g* (hard sound), *h, j, m, n, p, t, w*; (b) *f, l, r, s*; (c) *c* as /s/, *g* as /j/; (d) *k* and *q*; and (e) *v, x, y,* and *z*.

Middle and End Consonant Correspondences

In whole-word or analytic phonics the pupil has to deal visually with the beginning consonant, the median vowel, and the ending consonant from the beginning. The following statements summarize basic knowledge about end consonant correspondences:

1. Consonants generally represent the same sound at the end of the word as at the beginning of the word.
2. Some of the variant sounds of the consonants occur only in the middle or at the end of a word: d = /t/, helped; d = /j/, individual; n = /ng/, bank; t = /ch/, picture; z = /ks/, box, etc.
3. *S* at the end of a word represents /z/: (a) in some one-syllable words: his, is, was, as, has, (b) after voiced consonants (lathes), and (c) after long vowels (flies).
4. The *es* ending represents /s/ after unvoiced sounds (takes); it represents /z/ after voiced sounds (halves, gauges); and it represents /z/ after the sibilants (*s, ss, ch, sh, z*): loses, churches, Grace's.
5. The letters *f, l,* and *s* are frequently doubled at the end of a word: cuff, less, call. There are many exceptions: has, is, if, etc.
6. Some other consonants occasionally are also doubled at the end of a word: ebb, add, egg, mumm, err, mitt, fuzz. The consonants *c, h, j, k, g, v, w, x,* and *y* are never doubled at the end of a word. When *cc* and *gg* are followed by *e, i,* or *y,* they represent two distinct sounds: success, suggest.

Rhyming and the Phonograms

Phonogram knowledge is important in dealing effectively with the grapheme-phoneme correspondences. Phonograms are closed syllables or units of sounds that begin with a vowel and that end with a sounded consonant: *et, ile,* etc. They are particularly helpful in that the phonogram unit (e.g., *an*) has a high degree of consistency across a word. Thus *an* represents the same sound in the beginning (animal), middle (advancing), and end of a word (man). A few additional observations follow:

1. After children have learned to listen to the ending /t/ sound, they should learn that words, that have the same vowel and consonant sound (for example, *at*) in the ending syllable, are rhyming words: that, bat, cat, fat.
2. The pupil also needs to learn to identify the basic phonograms. The pupil needs to see that words ending in a consonant sound like cat and mile contain the respective phonograms (or word families) *at* and *ile.*
3. The sounding of vowels is regulated in most cases by the letter pattern that follows the vowel, and since the phonogram (*if, ite,*

ate, ike) has the vowel plus its following letter pattern, the reader can quickly learn to see the entire pattern as a unit. Experience teaches that pupils taught to analyze words into phonograms quickly read sound-symbol patterns and are safely past letter-by-letter perception.

Teachers should put special effort into the teaching of the phonogram. Pupils taught to analyze monosyllable words into a consonant-plus phonogram pattern (b-at) often learn sound-syllable patterns with relative ease, thus being freed from letter-by-letter perception.

Rubin (1982) and Ringler and Weber (1984) have identified the steps for teaching phonograms:

1. Introduce the unfamiliar word: e.g., chalk.
2. Focus the pupil's attention on the *alk* phonogram and show the pupil that he has previously met the phonogram in walk and talk.
3. Read a list of words, some of which contain the *alk* phonogram and hence rhyme and some of which do not. Have pupils identify the words that rhyme.
4. Write the word chalk on the blackboard and underline the *alk* phonogram.
5. Teach the pupil to substitute *ch* for *w* or *t*.
6. Have the pupil substitute different initial consonants and blends for the consonant *ch* to form new words.
7. Teach the pupil to blend *ch* with *alk* to arrive at chalk.
8. Have the students practice reading of the *alk* phonogram by reading sentences and paragraphs containing *alk* words.

A useful device is a simple word wheel with the most frequently used phonograms printed on the outer edge of the larger wheel and the single and double consonants printed on a superimposed smaller wheel. As the smaller wheel is turned, the pupil is required to sound the word created and to use it in a sentence.

Children in the primary grades should be required to develop their own phonogram book. As words are introduced in reading, children should learn that each word that ends in a pronounced consonant contains a phonogram. The pupil should initially be introduced to the phonograms exemplifying the vc spelling pattern; gradually this is expanded to include the vc¢ pattern (e.g., mile) and the cvvc pattern (e.g., boat). Not only do pupils learn how words are structured, but they also learn the basic spelling patterns and vowel rules. Thus, using a looseleaf notebook, the teacher helps children to focus on the *ad* phonogram when children are first introduced to it in the word bad. The phonogram page for *ad* starts with the word bad, but gradually is expanded to include dad, had, lad, mad, pad, sad, clad, glad, Chad, etc. Knafle (1973) found that color or underlining may be effectively used as cues to enhance children's learning of pattern similarities such as cat, mat, fat. Color cues and underlining appear to aid children in detecting structure. Table 9-2 identifies common phonograms.

Beginning and Ending Consonant Clusters

Children also need to learn to deal with the consonant clusters. These include consonant blends (two or three letter combinations representing two or three distinct sounds: *s*cold, *scr*ipt), consonant digraphs (two-letter combinations representing one sound: *sh*ip, gra*ph*), and consonant trigraphs (three letter combinations representing one sound: ya*cht*). Information about beginning and ending consonant clusters includes the following:

I. The term, consonant clusters, includes:
  A. Beginning consonant blends
     bl /bl/ as in blue *sc* /sk/ as in scold
     br /br/ as in bring *sk* /sk/ as in skate
     cl /kl/ as in clean *sl* /sl/ as in sleep
     cr /kr/ as in cream *sm* /sm/ as in smoke
     dr /dr/ as in dress *sn* /sn/ as in snow
     dw /dw/ as in dwarf *sp* /sp/ as in spoon
     fl /fl/ as in flag *squ* /skw/ as in squat
     fr /fr/ as in free *st* /st/ as in stand
     gl /gl/ as in glass *sw* /sw/ as in swing
     gr /gr/ as in grass *tr* /tr/ as in tree
     pl /pl/ as in play *tw* /tw/ as in twig
     pr /pr/ as in pride
  B. End consonant blends
     ct (act)   lp (alp)   rb (garb)   rt (art)
     ft (raft)   lt (fault)   rc (arc)   sc (disc)
     lb (bulb)   mp (pump)   rd (lard)   sk (desk)
     lc (talc)   nd (band)   rf (dwarf)   sm (spasm)
     ld (bald)   nk (bank)   rl (snarl)   sp (clasp)
     lf (elf)   ns (lens)   rm (arm)   st (nest)
     lk (elk)   nt (ant)   rn (barn)
     lm (elm)   pt (apt)   rp (harp)
  C. Beginning and ending consonant digraphs
    1. Consonant digraphs that represent a distinct phoneme:
       a. ch = /ch/ church; /j/ spinach; /sh/ chef; /k/ Christmas; /ch/ may be spelled *ch* (child), *tch* (watch), *te* (righteous), *ti* (question), or *tu* (future).

TABLE 9-2: The Phonograms

ab	as	end	ire	ome /ŭm/	ox
ace	ase	ent	irt	ome /ōm/	ub
ack	ash	ep	is	on	ube
act	ask	ern	ise	one /ōn/	uch
ad	ass	erse	ish	ong	uck
ade	ast	esk	isk	ood /ù/ /ü/	ud
aff	aste (paste)	ess	iss	oof	ude
aft	at	est	ist	ook	udge
ag	atch	et	it	ool	uff
age	ate	etch	itch	oom	ug
aid	aught	ex	ite	oon	uge
ail	ave	ib	ith	oop	ule
aim	awn	ibe	ive	oor	ull /ŭl/
ain	ax	ice	ix	oot	ull /ùl/
air	aze	ick	ize	op	ult
aise	each	id	izz	ope	um
ait	ead	ide	oach	or	umb
ake	eak	ief	oad	orb	ume
ale	eal	ield	oak	orch	ump
alk	eam	ite	oal	ord	un
all	ean	iff	oam	ore	unch
alt	eap	ift	oan	ork	und
am	ear	ig	oap	orn	une
ame	ease	igh	oar	orse	ung
amp	east	ight	oast	ort	unk
an	eat	ike	oat	ose /lose/ /hose/	unt
ance	eb	ild	ob	oss	up
anch (ranch)	eck	ilk	obe	ost	ur
and	ed	ile	ock	ot	ure
ane	eed	ilk	od	otch	urn
ang	eel	ill	ode	ote	urse
ange	eem	ilt	odge	oth	urt
ank	een	im	off	oud	us
ant	eep	ime	oft	ough	use
ap	eer	in	og	ought	ush /pùsh/
ape	eet	ince	oid	ould	usk
ar	eg	ind	oil	ounce	uss
ard	eigh	ine	oin	ound	ust
are (âr)	eight	ing	oke	our	utch
arge (barge)	ell	inge	old	ouse	ut
ark	elm	ink	ole	out	ute
arm	elp	int /ĭnt/	oll	outh	uzz
arn	elt	ip	olt	ove /ŭ/ /ō/	
arp	em	ipe	om	owl	
art	en	ird	omb	own	

b. sh = /sh/ ship, fish; /sh/ may be spelled *ce* (ocean), *ch* machine, *c* (special), *psh* (pshaw), *s* (sure), *sch* (schist), *sc* (conscience), *se* (nauseous), *sh* (she), *si* (tension), *ss* (issue), and *ti* (nation).
c. th = /th/ either; /th/ ether; /t/ Thomas.
d. wh = /hw/ wheel; /h/ who; /w/ whale.
e. ng = /ng/ sing; /ng-g/ finger; /nj/ strange; /ng/ may be spelled *n* (ink), *ng* (long) or *ngue* (tongue).

2. The consonant digraphs, *gh* and *ph*, that do not represent a distinct phoneme:
    a. gh = /g/ ghost; /f/ enough
    b. ph = /g/ graph; /v/ Stephen; /p/ diphthong

3. Consonants that are doubled:
bb (rabbit), *cc* (account, raccoon), *dd* (add), *ff* (cuff), *gg* (egg), *ll* (call), *mm* (common), *nn* (inn), *pp* (happy), *rr* (purr), *ss* (hiss), *tt* (mitt), *vv* (flivver), *zz* (buzzer). When a double consonant occurs in a word, usually only one is pronounced. Note that *ss* in *tissue, issue* is /sh/; *gg* in *exaggerate* is /j/; and that when *cc* and *gg* are followed by *e, i,* or *y*, they may represent two distinct sounds: *success, suggest*.

4. Consonant combinations in which one letter is said to be silent:
    a. Silent *b*: bo*m*b, climb, crumb, dumb, lamb, limb, numb, thumb, tomb; de*b*t, debtor, doubt, subtle, *bd*ellium.
    b. Silent *c*: ba*ck*, sack, etc.; a*s*cend, ascent, descent, scene, scent, scepter, muscle, science, scissor; indi*ct*, victuals; *cz*ar.
    c. Silent *d*: (*dge* becomes /j/: edge, fudge) han*d*kerchief, We*d*nesday, han*d*some; a*d*just.
    d. Silent *g*: diaphra*g*m, paradigm; ali*g*n, campaign, design, foreign, gnat, gnaw, sign.
    e. Silent *h*: ag*h*ast, ghost; enough, laugh; exhaust, exhibit; hemor*rh*age, rhesus, rhetoric, rhinestone, rhinoceros;, rheumatism, rhubarb, rhyme, myrrh, rhythmic; she*ph*ard; *Th*omas, Thompson, Theresa, Thames, Thailand; ve*h*ement, vehicle, ah, heir, honest, hour, oh, etc.
    f. Silent *k*: *k*nee, knife, know, etc.
    g. Silent *l*: a*l*m, alms, balmy, palm, calm, psalm, salmon; ba*l*k, calk, polka, chalk, folk, walk, talk, yolk; ca*lf*, half; so*l*der, could, would, should.
    h. Silent *m*: *m*nenomic.

i. Silent *n*: autu*mn*, colu*mn*, hy*mn*, etc.
j. Silent *p*: cu*p*board; *p*neumonia, pneumatic; cor*ps*, psalm, pseudo, psychiatry, pshaw, psychic; ras*p*berry; *p*tomaine.
k. Silent *s*: is*l*e, aisle, Carlisle, island; Arkansas, bas-relief, debris, cor*ps*, Illinois, Louisville, rendezvous, St. Louis, viscount; *sc* becomes /z/ discern; *ss* becomes /z/ scissors.
l. Silent *t*: cas*t*le, chestnut, Christmas, fasten, hasten, hustle, listen, mustn't, thistle, whistle, nestle, rustle, etc.; mort-age; o*f*ten, soften.
m. Silent *w*: *w*reck, wrapper, wren, wrinkle, wrist, write, wrong, awry, wrap; ans*w*er, sword; bo*w*ler, bowl; o*w*n, owner; *t*wo, toward; *w*ho, *w*hom; and in the *ow* ending (snow, blow).
n. of the above digraph combinations those that occur most frequently are: *bt, dg, dj, gh, gn, kn, lm, lk, mb, mn, rh, ps, tch, wh,* and *wr* (Burmeister, 1971; 1983, p. 658).

D. Three-letter blends
 chr /kr/ Christ, chrome, Christmas
 phr /fr/ phrase, phrenology
 sch /sk/ scheme, school
 scr /skr/ screech, screen, scroll, script
 shr /shr/ shrank, shred, shrewd, shriek, shrill, shrimp, shrink, shrub, shrug
 spl /spl/ splash, splice, splint, split, splotch, splurge
 spr /spr/ sprain, sprang, spray, spread, spring, sprint, sprout, spruce, sprung
 str /str/ straw, street, string, strong

E. Consonant trigraphs
 chm /m/ drachm   sch /s/ schism
 cht /t/ yacht   sch /sh/ schist
 ght /t/ thought   tch /ch/ match
 rps /r/ corps

II. The letters *ch, sh, th, wh,* and *ng* each may represent a sound or phoneme different from any other consonant sound: thus, /ch/, /sh/, /th/, /th/, /hw/, and /ng/.

III. The /zh/ sound is not written as *zh* except in borrowed words such as Zhivago. It may be represented by *g* (garage), by *s* (division), or by *z* (azure).

IV. *Ch* represents /j/ in spinach or Greenwich; it represents /sh/ in words borrowed from the French: cache, chagrin, Chicago, creche, gauche, machine, chauffeur, chic, parachute, chaperon, brochure, charlatan, echelon, chiffon, chevron, machinery, and mustache. By far, the most frequent sound of *ch* is /ch/.

V. *Ch* as /k/ occurs in words derived for the Greek and Hebrew such as chasm, chorus, Christ, chrism, Christmas, chrome, scheme, ache, chemist, chloride, choral, technic, technique, orchid, school, echo, chaos, chord, orchestra, anchor, character, architect, archives, catechism, cholesterol, chronic, hierarchy, oligarchy.
VI. *Sh* always represents /sh/.
VII. *Th* represents the following sounds:
  A. Unvoiced /th/ as in ether:
    1. When *th* occurs at the end of a word (bath), except smooth.
    2. In the combination *ths* when it is preceded by a short vowel sound (deaths) or by a consonant (months).
    3. When initial *th* occurs in a content word: thin, think, thumb.
  B. Voiced /th/ as in either:
    1. In the plural of some words (mouths).
    2. When *th* is at the beginning of function words (the, them, there, that, those, this, thither).
    3. In *the* endings (bathe).
    4. In with and smooth.
  C. /t/: In proper names: Thomas, Esther, etc.
VIII. *Wh* is pronounced /hw/ as in wheel, or simply /h/ before o: who, whom, whole, wholly, whoop, whose; it may also represent *w* as in whale.
IX. *Ng* represents /ng/: sing, rang, long. The combination ng is not always a digraph. In plurisyllables such as linger, finger, and stronger, but not in singer, the *ng* represents /ng-g/. In words like strange, the *ng* represents /nj/.
X. *Gh* represents a previously learned consonant sound: either /g/ ghost or /f/ enough. *Gh* often is silent: eight, freight, neighbor, sleigh, straight, weigh, weight, etc.
XI. *Ph* represents either /f/: phase, /v/: Stephen, or /p/: diphtheria.

Teaching Consonant Correspondences

The following strategies, involving the development of sight words and the concomitant teaching of all consonant grapheme-phoneme correspondences (beginning and ending single consonants, consonant blends, and consonant digraphs and trigraphs), have application in all such teaching:
  I. Develop an auditory discrimination for the target word (e.g., bat, hat, etc.): let the pupil hear and learn to detect differences among words at the beginning, middle, and end of the word, but, when teaching beginning consonants, emphasize the beginning consonant.
  II. Develop a visual discrimination for the word to be learned, capitalizing upon the pupil's discrimination of the individual letters, and right from the beginning teach the child the importance of directio-

nality, of orientation of letters and words, and of sequences in reading. In this initial teaching:
  A. Help the pupil to develop a mental image of the word.
  B. Teach the child that each word has a name and a meaning.
  C. Pay special attention to words that are similar in appearance or that are easily reversed.
III. Using the principle of minimum difference, have the pupil initially discriminate between words whose only difference is at the beginning (bat-hat) of a word. Teach children that bat is not hat. Start teaching the grapheme-phoneme correspondences with known words and preferably with words in which there is only one grapheme-phoneme difference (bat, cat, fat, rat, etc.).
IV. Print each word to be learned on the blackboard and carefully follow the steps of the Integrated Reading Method (see chapter 8), emphasizing particularly the following:
  A. Have the pupil carefully scrutinize the word from left to right and call the pupil's attention to the sequence of letters within the word.
  B. Have the pupil both hear and say the word.
  C. Contrast the word with another word that has the same spelling pattern: bat-rat. Groff (1971) recommends that *t* be contrasted with *s*, *l* with *c*, *f* with *m*, *b* with *r*, *h* with *w*, *p* with *v*, *d* with *n*, *k* with *g*, *j* with *z*, and *g* with *x*.
    1. Color the grapheme for which a phoneme association is to be learned: for example, color the *b* in bell. This calls attention to what is being taught and shows how words differ.
    2. Print the letter *b* in color on the chalkboard, give its name, and write out other words beginning with the *b* sound. Have pupils name things in the room that begin with /b/.
    3. Associate the letter *b* with the key picture, perhaps with the picture of a bell. Refer to the *b* sound as the "bell" sound.
    4. Teach pupils to associate the *b* sound with both the capital and lower case letter *b*. Pupils may be shown that a word like Ben, which begins with a capital letter, is sounded in the beginning just like the word bug. It is helpful to show pupils that if a personal name begins with *b*, the capital *B* must be used.
  D. Teach the basic phonogram that the word contains, emphasizing the vc, vcc, vc$\cancel{e}$, v$\cancel{y}$c, and v$\cancel{y}$cc phonograms in that order.
  E. Have the pupil spell, trace, and write the word.
  F. Have the pupil identify the word in a sentence context and in isolation.
V. Teach pupils that changing the consonant at the beginning of the word alters both meaning and the pronunciation: bat-hat.

VI. Refer to one of the multiple published phonic workbooks to develop automaticity in recoding.

Essentially the same process should be used in teaching beginning and ending single consonants and beginning and ending consonant blends, consonant digraphs, and trigraphs. Computers and computer programs are readily available for teaching consonant grapheme-phoneme correspondences. Computer reading software is generally of a drill and practice type and is devoted almost always to the teaching of specific skills. Rude (1986) notes that microcomputers, with the use of high-quality software, can indeed augment a teacher's instructional efforts by providing activities to reinforce previously taught skills (Rude, 1986). Miller (1989), while suggesting that technology can change or expand our visions of teaching and learning, observes that it is puzzling that many teachers who decry the use of drill put undue emphasis on microcomputer programs. Computer-based programs fit an educational context of skill teaching, repetitious exercises, and tightly controlled instructional sequences. Educational tracking, constant testing, and immediate feedback of results are valued in such programs. Smith (1988) observes, "There is no evidence that such computer programs have succeeded in making children literate, and no convincing theories that they could succeed" (p. 207). He, however, adds: "This does not mean that computers have no place in the literacy classroom" (p. 207).

Vowel Grapheme-Phoneme Correspondences

Children from the beginning must learn to break the alphabetic code; this means they must be able to deal with both consonants and vowels. Pupils must become fluent with the short vowel sounds that they hear in words like bat, net, pin, cot and hut, but they also need to learn the long *a* sound as in age; the long *e* sound as in be; the long *i* sound as in bite; the long *o* sound as in go; the special *o* sounds as in off and in orb; and the long *u* sound as in use and rule. Almost invariably poor readers are deficient in vowel grapheme-phoneme knowledge. They cannot deal with the open vowel pattern as in he or me, with the vowel with final *e* pattern as in fine, and with the double vowel pattern in such words as a*i*d, pl*a*y, cr*ea*m, b*ee*, s*ei*ze, k*e*y, p*i*e, b*oa*t, f*oe*, s*ou*l, and sh*o*w, where the first vowel letter represents its long sound and the second vowel letter is not pronounced. The modified vowel patterns (ch*ai*r, *au*ght, l*a*w, p*ea*r, f*ea*r, ch*ee*r, f*a*ll, w*ei*rd, b*a*rley, b*oa*rd, j*ou*rnal) give the pupil even more trouble.

In summary, seven basic vowel patterns must be mastered:

1. The single-vowel letter pattern as in bat or at. This is a clue to the short-vowel sound.

2. The open-vowel pattern as in be or me (long-vowel clue).
3. The vowel letter with a final e pattern as in rope or use (long-vowel clue).
4. The double-vowel letter pattern as in rain (long-vowel clue).
5. The diphthongs: oi and ou.
6. The modified vowel pattern as in au or aw and in eu or ew.
7. The r-controlled vowel as in car, care, war, her, first, word, hurt, cure, sure, etc.

Information about the vowel correspondences that must be learned by pupils, if they are to develop a code for identifying words, is presented under five headings: (a) short vowel correspondences, (b) long vowel correspondences, (c) modified vowel correspondences, (d) diphthongs, and (e) r-controlled vowels.

Short Vowel Correspondences

The pertinent information about short or ungilded vowels is:

I. There are 5 vowel letters (a, e, i, o, u) or perhaps 7 (y and w function as semivowels), and 20 vowel phonemes.
II. Each of the five basic vowel letters represents distinct phonemes, but in combination with other vowels may represent other distinct phonemes.
III. The 20 vowel phonemes are:

a	e	i and y*
/ă/ hat	/ĕ/ bed	/ĭ/ bit, crypt
/ā/ fade	/ē/ be	/ī/ bite, cry
/ä/ car	/è/ /ûr/ term	
/â/ care		

o	u	
/ŏ/ lot	/ŭ/ hut	/oi/ toil, boy
/ō/ so	/ū/ /yü/ /yo͞o/ use	/ou/ /aù/ house, now
/ò/ off, orb	/ü/ /o͞o/ rule	/ə/ ago
	/ù/ /o͝o/ pull, sure	
	/yù/ /yo͝o/ cure	

---

*Y at the beginning of a word or syllable is a consonant; as a vowel, it represents ī, or ĭ, or ē. In one syllable words ending in y preceded by a consonant (e.g., by, cry) the y represents a long i; at the end of polysyllabic words (ably, baby), the y represents long e. Y in the middle of a word or syllable usually represents the short i: hymn, gym, cymbal, synonym.

IV. A single vowel letter followed by a single consonant (except by *r*) at the beginning or in the middle of a syllable or a one syllable word or in a VC or VCV spelling pattern usually represents its short or unglided sound (am, an, at, if, in, it, up, top). This is vowel rule I. Most vowels in monosyllabic words follow this rule.

V. The short vowel rule also generally applies when the syllable or monosyllabic word ends in a double consonant (the spelling pattern of cvcc or vcc): ba*ck*, fa*ct*, ra*ft*, la*mp*, ba*nd*, ta*nk*, cha*nt*, ta*sk*, la*st*, de*ck*, e*lm*, he*mp*, be*nd*, le*nt*, de*sk*, we*st*, mi*lk*, ti*lt*, si*nk*, hi*nt* ri*sk*, fi*st*, so*ck*, du*ck*, cu*lt*, ju*mp*, fu*nd*, su*ng*, su*nk*. Common exceptions to the above are: a*ll*, *igh*, *ind*, *ild*, *old*, *ill*, *olt*, *ost*; the frequent *r* combinations such as p*ark*, w*ard*, w*arm*, h*erd*, f*ork*, b*orn*, w*ord*, h*urt*; and the phonograms in such words as p*int*, c*limb*, gr*oss*, b*oth*, c*omb*, d*on't*, w*on't*. These should be taught as phonograms. Examples of each are:

   A. /ȯ/ with *all*: ball, call, fall: the /ȯ/ sound of *a* also occurs when *a* is followed by a single *l* (talk, walk, salt, halt, walnut, walrus, waltz).
   B. Long *i* with *igh*: bright, fight, high, nigh, sigh, etc.
   with *ind*: bind, blind, find, grind, hind, kind, mind, rind, wind, etc.; note wĭnd.
   with *ild*: child, mild, wild.
   C. Long *o* with *old*: cold, fold, gold, hold, old, etc.
   with *oll*: knoll, poll, roll, toll, scroll, stroll, etc.; note, doll.
   with *olt*: bolt, colt, jolt.
   with *ost*: ghost, most, post.

In some combinations (*oth*, *oss*, *ost*, *off*, *oft*) the *o* generally takes on the ȯ sound:
   broth, cloth, moth, but also bōth.
   boss, cross, gloss, loss, moss, but also grōss.
   cost, frost, lost, but also ghōst, mōst, and pōst.
   off, scoff, oft, soft, and loft.

In gong, long, prong, throng, strong, song, and tongs, the *o* may represent either *ȯ* or short *o*.

VI. Vowel variations that do not follow vowel rule I and that the pupil must be introduced to early are:
   A. The ŏ or ȯ sound of words in og: fog, hog, log, cog, dog.
   B. The short u sound of o: son, ton, won, one, come, done, glove, love, none, shove, some, above, among, cover, dozen, money, etc. Note that in most instances the *o* is followed by *m*, *n*, *p*, *t*, or *v*.

C. The short o sound of a: The *a* often represents a short *o* sound when it follows *w*. The following words illustrate this use: swamp, swan, swap, swat, wand, want (also wȯnt), wash, (also wȯsh, wasp (also wȯsp), watch (also wȯtch), what (also hwŭt). The short ă sound of *a*, following *w*, also occurs: wacky, wag, wagon, wax, etc.
D. The variant sounds of the vowel when it is followed by r:
   1. The ä sound: bar, cat, jar, scar, etc.
   2. The ȯ sound of *a* when *ar* follows *w*: war, ward, wart, dwarf, warp, etc.
   3. The /ė/ or /û/ sound of *e* (her), of *i* (fir), of *o* (word), or of *u* (fur).
   4. The /ȯ/ sound of *o* (for).
E. The schwa: In a two-syllable word the vowel sound in the unstressed syllable often is a softened sound and is represented by the symbol "ə". It is termed the schwa sound. Illustrative words are: ab*o*ut, tak*e*n, Apr*i*l, circ*u*s, pig*eo*n, lem*o*n, vill*ai*n, porp*oi*se, vic*iou*s, etc.

Long or Glided Vowel Correspondences

The information summarized under this general heading includes the single vowel letter–phoneme correspondence (e.g., m*e*), the vowel in cvc∉ and cvy̸c spelling patterns (f*i*re or c*o*at), and vowel combinations that present a great variation in pronunciation and with which only the context may provide the cue for correct pronunciation.

   I. The vowel letter receives its long sound when a single vowel letter comes at the end of a one-syllable word or when it is placed in a cv spelling pattern: be, he, she, me, we, go, no, so, by, cry, fly, fry, my, sky, sly, spy, try, why. Note ha, do, to, too, two, and who. The second vowel rule thus reads: A single vowel letter at the end of a syllable or one-syllable word or in a cv or ccv spelling pattern usually represents a long sound.
   II. In one-syllable words in which there are two vowel letters, the second one being a silent *e* preceded by a single consonant letter or a cvc∉ spelling pattern, the initial vowel letter represents a long vowel sound: hate, fire, stove, use. Common exceptions to Vowel Rule III are: are, come, done, give, gone, have, lose, love, move, none, one, prove, some, sure, there, were, where, and whose.
   The cvc∉ rule has a 93% predictability (Gates & Lowry, 1983) if

expanded to say that the first vowel is either long (fir*e*) or a short *i* sound (active). Exceptions to the rule are words ending in *some* (handsome), in *ove* (dōv*e*, dŭv), move (mōōv), and some words ending in a vowel plus *re* (dare, here).
III. Many two-syllable words do not follow Vowel Rule III stated in #2. Examples include: *ace* (furnace, palace, preface); *age* (cabbage, cottage, courage); *ege* (college, privilege); *ige* (prestige); *ase* (purchase); *ate* (chocolate, climate); *ice* (office, practice); *ile* (automobile); *ine* (engine, famine); *ise* (promise); *ite* (favorite); *ive* (active, motive); *ome* (become); *ose* (purpose); *uce* (lettuce).
IV. A common exception to the cvc*e* rule is the *â* sound of *a* in the *are* ending: *care, dare, fare, glare, flare, rare, scare, spare*, etc. This /â/ sound is a more open sound than the long *a* sound and occurs commonly in accented syllables or in conjunction with the *r* sound. In words like *here, mere* (but note *were, there, where*), and in such words as *fear* and *cheer* the sound of the *e* is represented by /Ĭ/. The chief exception to the *are* (âr) ending is the word *are*.
V. There are two distinct long *u* sounds: *use* and *rule*. The sound in *use* is a *yü* or *yōō* sound; that in *rule* is, simply an *ü* or a *ōō* sound. The sound in *use* occurs also in such words as beauty, feud, few, cue, you, etc. The sound in *rule* (also in threw, move, shoe, food, group, through, blue) occurs commonly after *r* and *l*, especially when these consonants are preceded by another consonant (brute). The sound in *use* is symbolized by /ū/, /yü/, or /yōō/; the sound in *rule*, by /ü/ or /ōō/.
VI. There are also two *u*/ōō sounds; *sure* and *cure*. The sound in sure is simply the ōō sound; in cure, it is the *yü* or *yōō* sound.
VII. In certain adjacent combinations, especially *ai, ay, ea, ee, oa, oe, ow, ue*, and *ui*, in a cvvc spelling pattern, the second letter may be silent and the first letter represents the long vowel sound. Examples of the cvvc pattern or of the fourth vowel rule are:
  A. The *ai* combination has the long /ā/ sound about 75%[*] of the time, (aid, bait); in 16% of the cases, it is followed by *r* and is pronounced /â/ as in air, chair, fair, flair, hair, pair, and stair. The other pronunciations should be learned as sight words: aisle, said, again. In mountain, villain, fountain, curtain, chieftain, certain, captain, bargain, etc., the *ai* becomes a schwa.
  B. The *ay* combinations as in play, ray and hay represents the /ā/ sound about 95% of the time. Common exceptions are aye, says, yesterday, and kayak.

---

[*]Percentages reported are from Burmeister (1968a, 1968b; 1983).

C. The *ee* combination as in bee or beet represents /ē/ about 86% of the time. As already noted, in words like cheer, deer, jeer, peer, sheer, sneer, steer, and veer, the double *e* represents /ĭ/ 13% of the time. A common exception is been.
D. The *ea* combination is more inconsistent. In attacking words with the *ea* combination, the pupil's best guess is the long *e* sound (beach, bean, clean). It occurs about 50% of the time. The next most common usage (28%) is that of the short *e* /ĕ/ as in bread, dead, deaf, and head. The pupil must learn that great, break, and steak are pronounced as /grāt/, /brāk/, and /stāk/. The ending *ear* may be pronounced four ways: as /ĭr/ in beard, dear, ear (9%); as /â/ in pear, bear, wear; as /ė/ or /ûr/ in earth, earn, pearl, and as /ä/ in heart. Other exceptions are guinea and sergeant.
E. The *oa* combination as in coat or boat is sounded like a long *o* about 94% of the time. The *oa*, pronounced as in broad, /ȯ/ occurs the remaining 6% of the time. Common examples are words in which the *oa* is followed by *r*: roar, oar, soar, and board.
F. The *oe* combination is pronounced as long *o* (foe, hoe) 60% of the time; as lone *e* (Phoebe) 23% of the time, and as /o͞o/ or /ü/ in such words as shoe, snowshoe, canoe, and horseshoe, about 19% of the time. Common exceptions are does and words that separate the *o* from the *e*: poet, poem.
G. The *ow* combination is listed here because in about 50% of the cases it follows Vowel Rule IV. Thus, in snow, blow, and glow, the *w* is not pronounced, and the *o* is given its long sound. In the remaining cases, it is pronounced as /ou/ or /aù/ (town, gown). Knowledge is an exception.
H. The *ue* combination generally represents one of the long *u* sounds:
  1. *ue* as /yü/: cue, due, hue, inbue, statue, tissue: 63%.
  2. *ue* as /ü/ blue, clue, flue, glue, rue, slue, true, accrue, construe, gruesome, sue: 37%.
I. The *ui* combination also represents for the most part one of the long *u* sounds:
  1. *ui* as /yü/: nuisance, suit: 24% of the time.
  2. *ui* as /ü/: bruise, cruise, juice, fruit, recruit: 29%.
  3. *ui* can also represent /ĭ/: build, built, guilt: 47%. Suite is an exception.

VIII. When a single vowel letter or a group of vowel letters in a word can represent one of two or three sounds, and if the position and number of the vowel letters or the spelling pattern do not indicate which vowel sound is to be applied, word meaning or context must be used as a clue to pronunciation. If the relationship between a vowel letter and a vowel sound is one that occurs in only a few words, the words are best taught through configuration cues, spelling, tracing, and writing rather than through phonic cues.

The following gives examples where context plays a major role. It also contains vowel combinations (*ei, ie, oo, ou*) that sometimes follow the cvvc principle, but where the variants are so numerous that context often is the only clue as to what the word is:

A. Sounds of *a*: /ĕ/ as in any; /ĭ/ as in senate; /ä/ as in mama.
B. Sounds of *e*: /ĭ/ as in pretty; /ō/ as in sew; /ä/ as in sergeant.
C. Sounds of *i*:
   1. /ē/ as in ski, broccoli, police, spaghetti, machine, unique, fatigue, etc.
   2. /y/ as in familiar, genius, behavior, junior, senior, Indian, brilliant, valiant, onion.
D. Sounds of *o*: /ĭ/ as in *women*; /ù/ or /ŏŏ/ as in *wolf*; /ü/ or /o͞o/ as in *do, to, who*.
E. Sounds of *u*: /ĕ/ as in bury; /ĭ/ as in *busy*; /ù/ or /ŏŏ/ as in *bull, full, pull, put*.
F. Sounds of *ei* and *ey*: A common pronunciation (40%) for *ei* is that of a long *a*: beige, reign, rein, seine, vein, eight, sleight, etc. In words like heir and their, the *ei* is *â*: 6%.

   In some instances (26%) *ei* is simply pronounced as long *e*, the second vowel letter being silent: ceiling, deceive, receive, perceive, leisure, seize, either, neither.

   The *ei* may be pronounced as long *i* as in height (11%), short *e* (1%) as in heifer, and short *i* as in forfeit, sovereign, foreign and in weird (15%). The *ey* is pronounced /ē/ in honey, kidney, key (67%). It is pronounced as long *a* in hey, obey, prey, they (20%). This latter sound is common in monosyllables and when *ey* occurs in a stressed syllable ending a word: obey, convey, *Ey* also occurs as long *ī*: eye.
G. Sounds of *ie*: *ie* may be a long *e* (55%), a short *i* (11%), a long *i* (17%), or a short *e* (3%)
   1. Long *e*: brief, field, frieze, grieve, niece, shriek, siege, etc., and in two-syllable words ending in *ie*: cookie, collie, prairie, brownie, lassie, etc.
   2. Long *i*: die, fried, lie, pie, tried, etc.
   3. Short *e*: friend.
   4. Short *i*: sieve, cashier.
H. Sounds of *oo*:
   1. *Oo* as /ü/ or /o͞o/: boot, broom, cool, food, fool, etc.: 59%.
   2. *Oo* as /ù/ or /ŏŏ/: book, foot, good, wood, wool: 36%; spook is an exception.

3. *Oo* as /ȯ/: door, floor: 3%.
4. *Oo* as /ŭ/: blood, flood: 2%.

I. Sounds of *ou*:
   1. *Ou* as /ou/ or /aù/: blouse, bough, bounce, bound, etc.: 35%.
   2. *Ou* as /ō/: soul, though, although, doughnut, thorough, etc.: 6%.
   3. *Ou* as /ü/ or /o͞o/ or as /ū/ (yü or yo͞o): group, route, soup, through, wound, you, youth, etc.: 7%.
   4. *Ou* as /ŭ/: cousin, country, couple, double, enough, tough, rough, touch, trouble, young, etc.: 4%.
   5. *Ou* as /ȯ/: bought, brought, cough, fought, ought, sought, thought, wrought, etc. Also, in four, mourn, pour, etc.
   6. *Ou* as /ù/: could, should, tour, would, your: 3%.
   7. *Ou* as /ə/: vigorous, rigorous: 41%.
   8. *Our* as /ėr/ or /ûr/: adjourn, journal, journey, flourish: 3%.

J. Other rare vowel combinations include:
   1. *ae* as /ē/ (algae) or /ĕ/ (aesthetic).
   2. *ao* as in extraordinary.
   3. *eo* as /ĕ/ (leopard), /ɛ/ (people), /ə/ (pigeon).
   4. *ia* as /ə/ (carriage or parliament).
   5. *uo* as /ù/ or /o͞o/ (buoyant).
   6. *uy* as /ī/ (buy).

Modified Vowel Correspondences

Some vowel combinations characteristically represent a sound distinct from that represented by either of the vowel letters: for example, *au*, *aw*, *ew*, or they may follow the principle of silentness, but it is the first vowel that is silent: *eu*.

1. Sounds of *au* and *aw*:

   The combination *au* is pronounced /ȯ/ (ought) about 94% of the time: the principal exceptions are draught, gauge, aunt, chauffeur, and laugh. *Aw* is pronounced as /ȯ/ (law) 100% of the time when it occurs at the end of the word or syllable or is followed by *k*, *l*, or *n*. The /ȯ/ sound is represented by *au* or *aw* in the beginning and the middle of the word (August, awe, cause, crawl), but at the end of a word it is always *aw* (law).

   Au as /ȯ/: aught, caught, cause, fault, haul, pause, etc.

   Aw as /ȯ/: claw, crawl, dawn, draw, hawk, jaw, law, etc.

2. Sounds of *eu* and *ew*:
   a. *eu* as /ū/ or /yü/: feud, neutral, Europe: 73%.
   b. *eu* as /ü/ or /o͞o/: maneuver, sleuth: 10%.

c. *eu* as /ė/ or /û/: amateur: 15%.
d. *eu* as /ù/ or /o͞o/: pleurisy: 3%.
e. *ew* as /ū/ or /yü/: few, new, pew, stew, view, etc.
f. *ew* as /ü/ or /o͞o/: blew, crew, drew, flew, grew, Jew, threw, jewel.
e. *ew* as /ō/: sew

Diphthongs

Diphthongs are digraphs that represent a gliding monosyllabic speech sound. They are two succeeding vowel sounds that are joined in a single syllable under a single stress. The sound is distinct from that represented by either of the single letters. The most common such combinations are *oi, oy, ou* (house), and *ow* (brow).

1. The sound of *oi*, as in boil, broil, choice, coil, coin, droit, foil, etc., occurs about 98% of the time. Common exceptions are choir and porpoise.
2. The sound of *oy* as /oi/, as in boy, joy, toy, occurs about 98% of the time. An exception is coyote.
3. The diphthongal sound of *ou* occurs in such words as: cloud, couch, count, flour, found, ground, hour, house, loud, mouse, etc.
4. The diphthongal sound of *ow* occurs about 50% of the time, particularly at the end of words: bow, brow, brown, clown, cow, etc.

R-Controlled Vowels

The vowel letters followed by *r* are often modified by the *r* and result in a new sound. The vowel represents neither a long nor a short sound. The variant sounds of the combination of a vowel and *r* are:

/är/   As in car, park, etc.
/âr/   In the cvce̸ spelling pattern (care, flare); and in words like there, where, very, chair, pear, etc.
/ăr/   In some words when the *r* is followed by a vowel (charity, paradise, parachute) and when the *r* is followed by a second *r* (barrel, sparrow).
/òr/   When the *ar* follows *w* (ward, war, warn), and in the *or* combinations: for, fork, born, corn, etc.
/ər/   In unaccented syllables the *ar* (liar, dollar, westward), *er* (hotter, baker), *ir* (elixir), *or* (doctor); and *ur* (murmur) represent the schwa + *r* sound. The schwa also occurs when the *a* is the final letter in an unaccented syllable and is followed by *r* (Maroon, cataract).

/ėr/ or /ŭr/ When *er* (her, revert), *ir* (first), *or* (word, work, worm, etc., where *or* follows *w*) and *ur* (hurt) occur in an accented syllable. The sound is also /ėr/ in an unaccented syllable when *er* is followed by a consonant (adverb) and in such words as pearl and journal.

/ĕr/ When the *er* is followed by a vowel (America, peril, merit), in the suffix *ary* (stationary, sanitary), and when the *r* following *e* is doubled (merry, error, derrick).

/ĭr/ In the cvc¢ spelling pattern (here), in other words where the long *e* sound is followed by *r* as in weird, fear, cheer, etc., when the *ir* is followed by a vowel (virile, spirit, miracle), or when the r is doubled (mirror).

/ĭr/ In the cvc¢ spelling pattern (fire).
/ɔr/ In the cvc¢ spelling pattern (more, store).
/ŏr/ When the *or* is followed by a vowel (quorum) or the *r* is doubled (borrow, sorry).
/yù/ or /yo͞o/ As in cure.
/ùr/ As in sure, jury.

Sometimes the *r* is separated from the vowel preceding it and has no effect on its pronunciation: arise, around, arena, spiral, Irish, hero, irate, siren, uranium, pirate, furious, wiry, glory, tyrant, story, etc.

Teaching Vowel Correspondences

The most natural sequence in teaching the vowel correspondences seems to be: teaching the meaning of vowel, teaching the short-vowel correspondences, teaching the long-vowel correspondences, teaching the pupil to discriminate between short- and long-vowel correspondences, teaching the effect of adding an *e* to a syllable containing a short vowel sound in the middle position (hat, hate), teaching the sounds of two adjacent vowel letters, teaching the diphthongs, teaching the modified vowel patterns *au*, *aw*, *eu*, *ew*, and teaching the *r*-controlled vowels.

Consider now a few principles that might guide teaching of these vowel correspondences:

1. Teach children to project the short vowel sound onto the word as their first attempt at recoding the word. If the word thus formed does not sound like a word that they already know or if it does not make sense in the context, then another attempt must be made.

2. Teach vowel rules inductively (by having the pupil experience numerous examples and non-examples) and deductively (by having the pupil apply the generalization to both examples and non-examples of the generalizations). The pupil learns

vowel generalizations or rules best by frequent experiences with words that exemplify the rule. These experiences should be consistent. Thus, exceptions should be learned as sight words. Only those rules which have wide applicability are worth teaching.
3. Teach experientially and inductively the principles of:
   a. Variability: The pronunciation of the written vowel may change from one word to another or the same vowel letter can represent more than one sound. The letter *e* may represent /ĕ/ as in bed or /ē/ as in he.
   b. Position: The sound represented by the vowel letter changes depending upon its position in the word: e.g., bat, me.
   c. Silentness: Some vowels letters in words are not pronounced: e.g., boat. fire, boat.
   d. Context: Word meaning or context may be the only useful cue to a word's pronunciation.
4. Help pupils to master the basic spelling patterns (cvc, cv, cvc̸e, and cvy̸c) and teach them that sounding of the vowels is generally determined by the spelling pattern of which it is a part. Thus, the pupil should be taught the grapheme-phoneme correspondence (for example, *a* /ă/) in the context of a total word, beginning with the vc and cvc spelling patterns. The pupil needs to learn the five basic spelling patterns and the parallel vowel patterns:
   vc (at): closed syllable, short vowel pattern.
   cvc (bat): closed syllable, short vowel pattern.
   cv (go): open syllable, long vowel pattern.
   cvc̸e (fire): vowel plus *e*, long vowel pattern.
   cvy̸c (coat): double vowel, long vowel pattern.
5. Teach the short and long vowels separately, with sufficient intervening instruction to ensure that the short-vowel correspondence is mastered before the long-vowel correspondence is introduced (Venezky, 1983). Underline or color the letter in the grapheme-phoneme correspondence being taught.
6. Teach exceptions as "sight" words. Children should learn to use the context as a clue to pronunciation. Teaching of the phonograms and of identification by analogy can help the pupil with words that do not fit grapheme-phoneme rules.
7. Develop a knowledge of the phonograms, beginning with vc (*ĕt*) or vcc (*ĕnt*) pattern and gradually expanding to the vc̸e (*īre*) and vvc (*ō̸at*) patterns, and include the study of irregular combinations: e.g., the *är* phonogram (*car, far*), the *ȯl* phonogram (*call, fall*), etc.

8. Develop the identification by analogy strategy: e.g., teach the pupil to identify mast by getting the *m* from milk which the pupil knows and the *ast* phonogram from the word last which he also knows and combine them to form mast.
9. Teach generalizations inductively by presenting numerous examples of the grapheme-phoneme rule, but also teach generalizations formally: teach the pupil that when there is only one vowel letter in a word (as in words like at and bat), or when the word is placed in a vc or cvc spelling pattern, and when that vowel letter is followed by a single consonant letter (at or bat), then the vowel usually represents its short vowel sound.
10. Teach the pupil that the short-vowel generalization generally applies also when the vowel is followed by a double consonant. Thus: back, lamp, sang, bend, desk, west, fish, etc., and that the short-vowel rule should be applied to the accented syllable in multisyllabic words: bonnet, bobbin, bandit, cabin.
11. Teach the pupil to verbalize the principle of position (the sound represented by the vowel letter in the word changes depending upon the position of the vowel letter in the word) and to verbalize the first vowel rule: A single vowel letter at the beginning or in the middle of a one syllable word usually represents that letter's short sound; a single vowel letter at the end of a syllable (e.g., go, she) usually represents its long sound, etc.
12. Teach pupils the major exceptions to the short vowel rule. For example:
    a. The *ò* sound in fog, hog.
    b. The *ä* sound of *a* (car, far, star).
    c. The *ŭ* sound of *o* (son, won).
    d. The *ŏ* sound of *a* following *w* (swamp, swap, wand)
    e. The *ò* sound of *a* (dwarf, war, warm).
    f. The schwa sound.
13. Teach the pupil the cvcĕ spelling pattern and the sounding of the first vowel; teach the cv spelling pattern or the open syllable rule (go, she, we, me, fly, sky, try, etc.) and have pupils apply the rule to two-syllable words: c*e*ment, b*a*con; teach pupils to distinguish between the two long *u* sounds: for example, in use, and rule; teach pupils the generalization that covers cvvc spelling patterns; and teach pupils the modified vowels patterns (*au, aw, eu, ew*), the diphthongs (*oi, ou, ow*), and the r-controlled vowels.

14. Teach pupils to read phonograms containing a long vowel sound: for example, *ite, eat, ike, ail, oil, ight, ind, ild, old, olt,* etc. and have pupils form words using the phonograms: *ike*: bike, dike, hike, like, mike, pike.
15. Teach pupils the short /i/ and long /i/ sound of *y*; cry, fly, my, crypt, myth.
16. Have pupils select from a list of *ow* words those words that have the *ō* sound and those that have the diphthongal sound of *ow*.
17. Teach the *r*-controlled vowels in lists such as:
    a. her, birth, turn, dirt, first, etc.
    b. car, farm, park, far, yard, etc.
    c. for, short, corn, etc.
    d. more, shore, store, etc.
    e. share, care, fair, there, etc.

DEVELOPMENT OF STRUCTURAL OR MORPHEMIC ANALYSIS KNOWLEDGE

A basic reason for the reader's deficiencies in sight vocabulary (other than lack of knowledge of grapheme-phoneme correspondences) is weakness in structural or morphemic analysis skills. The pupil is unable to use the meaning elements in words, in other words, the free and bound morphemes to identify the word. Such a reader often cannot analyze the structure of a long, unknown word into its meaning parts, and thus may not be able to identify the word. Morphemic analysis helps the pupil to get to the pronunciation by breaking the word into its meaning parts, sounding the parts (root, inflectional endings, prefixes, suffixes, etc.), and blending the parts to arrive at the total word. The content to be taught in the area of morphemic analysis includes an understanding of morphemes, of inflectional endings, (such as *s es, ed,* and *ing*), inflectional changes (such as changing *y* to *i*, dropping the final *e*, doubling the final consonant, changing *d* to *t*, etc.), compound words, contractions with *t*, derived words consisting of roots, prefixes, and suffixes, hyphenated words, syllabication, and accentuation. Teaching of morphemic skills should provide knowledge of and ability in the use of morphemic cues in the identification and comprehension of words. Examine first what is meant by morphology and morpheme.

Morphology and Morphemes

Morphology permits the introduction of minute changes into the word to produce a special meaning. It is the study of word structure and word meaning. Morphemic analysis is an analysis of the word into its morphemes. Morphemes are an important facet of the graphic and within-word cue system, and they have the added advantage of being also an important meaning cue system. They are the smallest units of language structure that can convey meaning. The smallest unit of word structure is the letter or grapheme.

Morphemes are either free or bound. A morpheme is free when it can stand alone in a sentence; it has lexical meaning; it is a word. Every new meaning of a word creates a new morpheme. The word "book" is one morpheme when it denotes a bound set of printed pages; it is a different morpheme when the word designates the function of an arresting officer (Smith & Barrett, 1974). A bound morpheme cannot stand alone in a sentence. It has lexical meaning if it has a meaning of its own (e.g., prefixes and suffixes have such meaning), and it has relational meaning if it has a grammatical meaning. For example, in the sentence, "The United States exports wheat to Russia," the *ex* in *exports* has lexical meaning. It has meaning in and of itself; the *s* at the end of the word has no meaning of itself. It has meaning only to the extent that it makes the verb a third person singular. It is said to have relational or grammatical meaning. The *s* may take on a relational meaning also when it changes a noun from the singular to the plural or when it denotes the possessive case. The bound morphemes are always attached or affixed to a free morpheme (e.g., *un-do; hit-s*). Prefixes and suffixes are bound morphemes. Thousands of words consist of a root and affixes (a combination of free and bound morphemes), or possibly two roots (a combination of two free morphemes). Figure 9-1 shows the interrelationship between the various morphemes. Knowledge of morphemes is developed by (Burmeister, 1983):

1. Familiarizing children first with the concept of free morphemes.
2. Teaching children the inflectional suffixes: run*s*, boy*s*, runn*ing*, walk*ed*, etc.
3. Having children combine two free morphemes to form a compound word (kindergarten and first grade): *sand-box* = *sandbox*

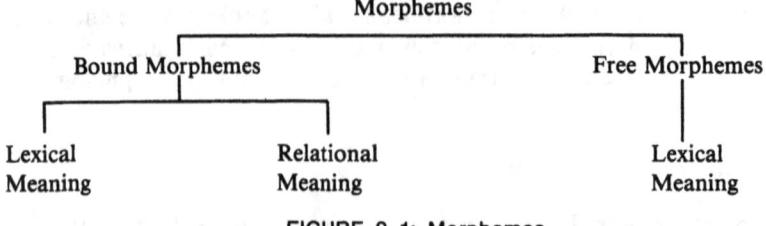

FIGURE 9-1: Morphemes

4. Having children experience bound morphemes by presenting them with free morphemes that they already know (late second grade): *un-kind; re-open; kind-ness*.
5. Introducing words composed of two morphemes (fourth grade): *geo-graphy = geography; geo-logy = geology*.

Morpheme knowledge, as indicated earlier, consists of an understanding of eight different ways of forming and changing the structure and meanings of words.

Teaching the Inflectional Endings

The inflectional endings are *s, es, en, 's, s', ess, ing, ed, er*, and *est*. They change the root word and the resultant variant of the word differs from the root according to:

	a.	Number or plural (cat*s*, fish*es*, ox*en*)
Nouns	b.	Possession (Mary'*s*, cats')
	c.	Gender (steward*ess*)
	d.	Makes a verb a noun (bak*er*)
Verbs	e.	Voice or tense (hit*s*, take*s*, is hitt*ing*, batt*ed*, tak*en*)
	f.	Makes a noun a verb (strength*en*)
	g.	Comparison or comparative (cold*er*)
Adjectives	h.	Superlative (cold*est*)
	i.	Makes a noun an adjective (wool*en*)

Inflected variants or endings indicate a grammatical or syntactic change but not a change in the basic meaning of the word; suffixes change the grammatical category or word class (i.e., they identify the word as a part of speech) and often change the word's meaning (Ringler & Weber, 1984).

The earliest morphemic skill to be taught is the analysis of the inflectional ending *s*. *S* creates new words simply by being added to a root: *cat-cats; hit-hits; Mary-Mary's*. All these uses of *s* are normally acquired in first grade: plural *s* at the preprimer level; third person *s* at the primer level; and apostrophe *s* at the end of the first grade.

The knowledge of the functions of *ing* is normally acquired at the primer level. There are numerous spelling rules associated with adding an inflected ending or a suffix beginning with a vowel to a word.

A knowledge of the function of *ed* is usually acquired at the primer level. The pupil needs to learn that: (a) The *e* in *ed* is silent (begg*ed*) except after *d* and *t* (nod*ded*) and the vowel in the root word, if it represents a long vowel sound, retains its long sound (cheat*ed*); and (b) the *d* is pronounced as /t/

after the voiceless consonants such as *f* (puffed), *k* (peeked), *p* (dipped), *sh* (wished), but not after *t*; it is pronounced as /d/ after the voiced consonants (begged, canned). *Er* (hotter), the comparative, is introduced at the primer level; *est*, at the first-reader level.

Even though the pupil needs to learn how to form new words and meanings by adding inflectional endings, the reading of these endings should be especially emphasized. Thus, the pupil needs to learn that:

1. The *s* at the end of a word can represent /s/ or /z/. When to read it as /z/ needs to be taught.
2. When *ing* is added to a word, and when this results in the doubling of the preceding consonant (omi*tt*ing), the second consonant is silent, except in compounds (bookkeeper).
3. When *ed* is added to a word, the *ed* may represent /d/, /t/, or /əd/ (begged, helped, hunted).
4. *Es* at the end of a word (fishes, foxes, churches) is read /əz/ or /əs/.
5. *Er*, when used as an inflectional ending, says /ər/.

Teaching the Inflectional Changes

Inflectional changes take many forms. They may present the following spelling and reading difficulties:

1. Drop final *e* before adding a suffix or an inflectional ending beginning with a vowel: bake—baking, baked, baker. Note particularly the sounding of the initial vowel. A few words also drop the *e* when the suffix begins with a consonant (e.g., duly, truly). Note that words ending in *ce* and *ge* (e.g., changeable, courageous, noticeable) retain the *e*.
2. Change *y* to *i* when adding a suffix or an inflectional ending beginning with a vowel: busy—busier, busiest; happy—happier, happiest.
3. Retain the *y* when the suffix is *ing*: copy—copying.
4. Do not change the *y* to *i* when the *y* is preceded by a vowel: played, staying.
5. Form the plural of a word ending in *y* by changing the *y* to *i* and adding es: city—cities; baby—babies.
6. Change the *f* (loaf, wife) to *v* in plurals (loaves, wives) and add *es*.
7. Inflectional changes (such as *y* to *i* and dropping final e) are introduced at the first-reader level; changing *f* to *v* is taught at the second-reader level.

Teaching Compound Words

The ability to see two words (bat - boy) in a longer word (batboy) is helpful in pronouncing the word. Often the pupil knows one of the words and can use picture reading, contextual clues, or phonetic cues to identify the other. The pupil needs to see:

1. That compounds consist of two simpler words.
2. That compounds have at least two sounded vowels.
3. That the meanings of compounds often are a synthesis of the two words making up the compound: campfire, cornstalk, cowboy, earthquake, eyelash, etc. With such words the pupil should learn to combine the meanings of the two words making up the compound.
4. That sometimes two words making up the compound create a meaning totally unrelated to the parts: township, forget, pullman, hamlet, brainstorm, etc. With such words the pupil should be taught to use the context to figure out the meaning of the compound or should consult the dictionary, if context analysis is inadequate.
5. That compounds may be formed from (Just and Carpenter, 1987, p. 122): (a) noun-noun: pancake, airplane; (b) verb-noun: crybaby; (c) adjective-noun: strongman, softball; (d) adjective-adjective: highborn, high-strung; and (e) noun-verb: spoonfed
6. That sometimes compounds are written as two words: ice cream, living room, post office, oil painting, moth-eaten, high-strung, etc. The hyphen may be added in some words, but may be omitted in others.

Teaching Contractions

The use of the apostrophe in contractions is introduced after the use of the apostrophe to identify the possessive case, but still in first grade. In teaching the contractions, grouping of the contractions can be quite helpful. Table 9-3 illustrates the various combinations.

As with inflectional endings the reading of the contractions needs to be taught: for example, they'll-/thāl/, you'll-/ūl/, here's-/hĭrz/, there's-/thârz/, or you're-/yùr/.

Teaching Roots, Prefixes, and Suffixes

Being able to break a word into its root, prefix, and suffix is another valuable aid in developing meaning for a word. Children need to be taught

TABLE 9-3: Contractions*

With "Not"	With "Will"	With "Would" or "Had"	With "Am," "Is," "Has," "Are"	With "Us"	With "Have"
ain't	he'll	anybody'd	I'm (am)	let's	I've
aren't	I'll	he'd	he's (is or has)		they've
can't	she'll	I'd	here's (is or has)		we've
couldn't	there'll	she'd	it's (is or has)		you've
didn't	we'll	they'd	she's (is or has)		
don't	who'll	we'd	that's (is or has)		
hadn't	you'll	who'd	there's (is or has)		
hasn't	it'll	you'd	what's (is or has)		
haven't	they'll		where's (is or has)		
weren't	that'll		who's (is or has)		
won't			they're (are)		
wouldn't			we're (are)		
isn't			you're (are)		
shouldn't					
doesn't					
wasn't					
mustn't					

*Adapted from Richek, List, and Lerner, 1982.

to decompose a word into its parts: its root, its prefixes, and its suffixes. "Derived" words are different from inflected words. Derived words are formed by adding either a prefix or a suffix or both to the root. Prefixes are morphemes placed in front of the root; suffixes are morphemes placed after the root word.

Most two- and three-syllable words are composed of a root, prefix, and/or suffix. The root, prefix, and suffix have their own individual meanings: the root is the main part of the word and is the reservoir of meaning; the prefix changes the meaning of a word much as an adjective changes the meaning of a noun (for example, *circumnavigate* is a specific type of sailing—a sailing around); and the suffix identifies the part of speech of the word (bad*ly* - adverb; condit*ion* - noun). Seven combinations of roots, prefixes, and suffixes are possible:

a. Root by itself as in stand (root word/free morpheme).
b. Prefix + root as in prefix (prefix plus free morpheme).
c. Root + suffix as in badly (free morpheme plus suffix).
d. Prefix + root + suffix as in interchangeable (prefix plus root word plus suffix)
e. Root + root as in cowboy (compound word: two free morphemes).
f. Bound morpheme + bound morpheme as in geography, telegraphy.
g. Root + inflectional ending as in printed (free morpheme plus inflectional ending.)

DEVELOPMENT OF CORRESPONDENCE KNOWLEDGE

The basic roots, prefixes, and suffixes have been listed by Dechant (1973, 1981, 1982) and by White, Sowell, and Yanagihara (1989). Some are reproduced in Tables 9-4 and 9-5. The Greek and Latin roots, prefixes, and suffixes have the greatest utility. We offer only a few samples here in Tables 9-6 and 9-7.

It is probably best to begin the teaching of affixes by teaching suffixes before prefixes. This permits the child, moving left to right, to encounter the root word first. It is customary to teach roots by asking the pupil what the root word in an affixed word is. Thus, in interchanged, the root word is *change*, but note that in anthropology, geology, and philosophy, the root word is the word itself. The aforementioned approach has relatively little value in this situation. The pupil needs to learn that anthropology consists of two roots (*anthropos* and *logos*) and therefore means the study of man; geology is formed from *geos* and *logos* and therefore means study of the earth; philosophy consists of *philos* and *sophos* and therefore means a love of wisdom.

Teaching Hyphenated Words

Learning hyphenation skills occurs generally at the fourth-grade level. Whenever a compound word is used as a modifier and occurs before the word that it modifies, it is hyphenated: living-room furniture, high-school dance. The hyphen also is used with *self* (self-denial, self-confidence, self-control) when *self* precedes the word, and with compound numbers from 21 to 99 (twenty-six men). Hyphenation presents no additional reading problems. It does present spelling problems.

Developing Syllabication Skills

Syllabication must receive attention at all levels of reading instruction. For most pupils, learning in this area is greatest during the intermediate grades.

TABLE 9-4: Sample Prefixes and Suffixes

Prefix	*Meaning*	*Examples*
ex, e, ef, es	out of	exit, exhale, extract
re	back, again	recede, reanimate
trans	across	transgress, transcend

Suffix	*Meaning*	*Examples*
ful	full of	graceful, blissful
fy	to make	glorify, falsify
less	without	motionless
ness	state, quality of, degree of	preparedness, blindness

TABLE 9-5: Suffixes Grouped by Part of Speech

Noun Suffixes		Adjective Suffixes		Verb Suffixes	Adverb Suffixes
ness	ship	able	ary	ize	ly
ment	or, er, ar	ible	ory	ate	wise
ance	ism	al	ant	fy	ways
tion	ist	ful	ent		ward
ant	age	ive	an		
ion	al	ous	ate		
sion	ent	ious	ative		
ation	arium	ic			
ity	ary	ish			
cy	ery	less			
ty	ian				
ence	ude				
hood					

TABLE 9-6: Sample Latin Roots

Latin Word	Meaning	Related English Words
facere, facio, feci, factum	to do, make	fact, factory, factor
legere, lego, legi, lectum	to choose, collect, gather, read	elect, lector
Mittere, mitto, misi, missum	to send	mission, remit, admit
portare, porto, portavi, portatum	to carry	export, import, report
scribere, scribo, scripsi, scriptum	to write	script, manuscript, inscription
videre, video, vidi, visum	to see	vision, visible, visit

TABLE 9-7: Sample Greek Roots

Greek Word	Meaning	Related English Words
graphein, grapho, gegrapha	to write, inscribe	graph, monograph
bios	life	biography, biology
geos	earth, land	geologist, geometry
logos	word, thought, study	geology, biology

Lexicographers divide words by structure and linguists divide them by pronunciation. Linguists have argued that the syllable is a phonological unit, not a graphemic unit. A spoken syllable is defined as a unit of pronunciation or as an uninterrupted unit of speech, containing one vowel phoneme or sound, that is pronounced with one impulse. Rayner and

Pollatsek (1989) define a syllable as an "acoustic unit whose duration can be measured and which is relatively invariant in different contexts" (p. 331).

The spoken syllable does not always correspond exactly to the written or printed syllable. Printing conventions for the division of words at the end of a line have not always followed the pattern of speech syllables. However, speech syllables and printed syllables do correspond with enough regularity that the printed syllable can be used in dividing words into parts, which can be readily analyzed and blended to pronounce words. Thus, a printed syllable will be considered as the sequence of letters more or less approximating the syllable of speech.

Syllables are of two kinds: closed syllables and open syllables. A closed syllable is one that ends with a sounded consonant: cat, basis, and magnetic. The vowel in a closed syllable usually represents a short vowel sound. An open syllable is one that ends in a sounded vowel: cry, by. The vowel in an open syllable is usually a long vowel.

Development in Syllabication

Development in syllabication skills involves the following steps:
1. The pupil, even at the first-grade level, must be trained to hear the distinct vowel sounds in words.
2. The pupil must learn that the number of vowel sounds, or vowels heard, not the number of vowel letters seen, identifies the number of syllables in spoken words. A vowel itself may form a syllable: *a-corn, i-de-a, vi-o-let,* etc.
3. Pupils must learn to identify the number of syllables in printed words. Teaching of syllabications begins when the pupil is introduced to *ing, ed,* and simple compounds, hence in first grade. Early in the grades the pupil needs to learn that some words ending in *ed* have only one syllable (*cooked*); others have two syllables (*landed*).
4. The pupil must learn to accent the proper syllable. Accentuation should be taught only after the pupil has mastered steps one through three and after the pupil has learned something about prefixes and suffixes. These latter rarely are accented (*in*tend, fish*ing*).
5. Children must learn to apply phonic skills, especially spelling-pattern principles, to the separate syllables in words. Thus, the pupil should learn that the sound of the letter *a* in *rabbit* is short because it occurs in a cvc spelling pattern.
6. The pupil must learn to mark syllable division, and must learn to syllabicate two- and three-syllable words. These skills should be learned in grade 3. Helping pupils to pronounce polysyllabic

words involves (Early and Sawyer, 1984):
  a. Teaching pupils that many words (e.g., compounds) consist of two simpler words.
  b. Teaching pupils that many words contain a root plus prefixes and suffixes.
  c. Teaching pupils that some words are neither compounds nor roots plus prefixes and affixes, but must be pronounced syllable by syllable (e.g., anecdote).
  d. Teaching pupils that some words must be looked up in the dictionary.
7. The pupil should learn to constantly check whether the word read makes sense in the sentence.
8. The pupil must learn the basic syllabication generalizations and some of the exceptions.

Syllabication Rules

Even though it may be argued that syllabication teaching is somewhat useless, since syllabication generally occurs after the word is sounded (Glass, 1967), there seems to be a genuine value in knowing how to syllabicate. Good readers know how to divide words. The following generalizations do help the reader:

I. Rule 1: Double consonant rule (vc/ cv): when two consonant letters follow a vowel letter, as in, after, kitten, pencil, summer, and butter, the word is divided between the two consonants, and the first syllable ends with the first consonant. In instances of this kind the second consonant is silent when the consonants are the same, except in compounds: bookkeeper. Since the first vowel is a single vowel followed by a consonant, and is thus a cvc spelling pattern, it is given its short sound. Not all double consonant letters are divided. Consonant blends (although there are many exceptions) and digraphs generally fall into this category (gam-bler, mi-grate, di-graph, re-think).

II. Rule 2: Single consonant rule (v/ cv): when only one consonant letter, consonant blend, or digraph follows a vowel letter, as in paper, bacon, prefer, begun, and reshape, the word is usually divided after the first vowel letter, and the consonant, or consonant blend or digraph, begins the second syllable. The first vowel letter, in that it ends a syllable and is in a cv or cvv spelling pattern, is usually given its long sound (si-lent, no-mad, ba-sin, da-tum, mi-nus, to-tal, ha-zel, si-nus, fa-tal, ce-ment, di-graph, re-shape). Whenever an *x* falls

between two vowel letters (exit, exact, oxen), the *x* is sounded with the first vowel letter.
III. Exceptions
   A. Not all words follow the rules. For example, planet, solid, robin, travel, study, record, river, primer, cabin, tropic, present, timid, habit, pity, body, quiver, copy, lily, bigot, honor, venom, olive, legend, lemon, valid, limit, dragon, wagon, digit, solid, cherish, volume, lizard, snivel, cherub, and profit join the consonant to the first vowel. Record, primer, and present may be divided according to both rules, depending upon their meaning in the sentence. Such words follow a vc/v principle. Usually in vc/c words, the first vowel is accented and the vowel tends to be short.
   B. The suffix *ed* is a syllable only when it follows *d* or *t*: bunted, handed.
   C. Whenever *le* ends a word and is preceded by a consonant (i.e., in vc/cle or v/cle words) the last syllable consists of the consonant and the *le*: mid-dle, peo-ple, a-ble, ta-ble. When *le* is preceded by *ck*, *le* is a separate syllable: freck-le, buck-le. When *gle* is preceded by *n*, as in jingle, mingle, single, tangle, it is pronounced as *ng-gəl*. The *le* in *ble*, *tle*, *dle*, says the /əl/.
   D. In *tle* the *t* sometimes is silent and at times may be pronounced. Thus, in battle, brittle, mantle, cattle, little, rattle, and tattle, the *t* is pronounced; in castle, hustle, jostle, and rustle, (words in which the *tle* follows the letter *s*) it is silent.
   E. Sometimes it is necessary to divide between two vowels: cre-ate, archa-ic, cere-al, be-ing, muse-um, cli-ent, o-asis, po-em, go-ing, zo-ology, fu-el, flu-id, etc.
   F. In a compound word the division comes between the two words making up the compound: post-man.
   G. Prefixes and suffixes are usually set apart from the rest of the word: trans-port, go-ing.

Developing Accentuation Skills

Accentuation is usually taught only after the pupil has learned to hear the number of syllables in spoken and written words. This generally occurs in second grade. In third grade the use of stress marks should be taught and some basic generalizations should be introduced. The following statements summarize the knowledge base that the pupil needs to acquire:

1. Words of two or more syllables are usually pronounced with more stress on one syllable. This is the accent. The accent mark (') in dictionaries is usually after the syllable that receives the stress.

2. Basic generalizations that the pupil should learn are:
   a. Generally words of two syllables, in which two consonants follow the first vowel, accent the first syllable: thus, after, kitten, puppet, and butter. This occurs also in (bacon, pilot), but there are many exceptions: prefer, begin.
   b. When a two-syllable word contains two vowels in the second syllable but only one is pronounced, the second syllable generally is accented: abide, abode, delay, and proceed. Usually the last syllable contains a long vowel sound.
3. Compound words usually carry the primary accent on (or within) the first word: bellhop, bulldog, carhop, dishpan, godson, pigpen. There are many exceptions to this rule: another, forget, upon.
4. Syllables beginning with a consonant followed by *le* (circle, rabble) are not accented. The vowel letter in the unstressed syllable represents the schwa sound.
5. In three-syllable words, in which the root word's second syllable ends in a silent *e* and is accented (advise, excite, translate), the accent is often on the second syllable: advisor, excited, translated. Other three-syllable words have their accent on the first syllable: piloted, traveled, shivered.
6. Root-word syllables, when preceded by prefixes or followed by suffixes, usually are accented: amuse, amusement. Prefixes and suffixes are rarely accented.
7. Words ending in *ion, ity, ic, ical, ian,* or *ious* have the accent immediately before these suffixes: consternation, athletic, immersion, harmonious, humidity, psychological, historian.
8. Words of three or more syllables ending in a silent *e* usually accent the third-to-last syllable: graduate, accommodate, anticipate.
9. Homographs or words with identical spellings receive their accent from the context in which they are used: con' tract and con tract'.
10. Words of three or more syllables (fragmentation) often have secondary or even tertiary accents: lo' co mo' tive.
11. Words that can be used both as nouns and as verbs generally accent the second syllable when used as verbs (present') and the first syllable when used as nouns (pres' ent).

In introducing pupils to accent and syllabication, the teacher needs to use words that the pupils know. Repeated exercise with actual words will help pupils obtain a functional knowledge of the generalizations stated above.

Exercises and Activities

Numerous basal-reader workbooks, other skill-development books, and computer programs are available. These both teach and provide the practice needed to develop automaticity in sounding the morphemic elements and in developing meaning for them.

SUMMARY

Chapter 9 outlines the knowledge that pupils need to have to break the alphabetic code and to develop a sight vocabulary. It provides the pupil with a knowledge of the within-word cues. It develops primarily the recoding process; it develops automaticity in recoding; it expands the pupil's predictive ability by helping the pupil to recode most of the words; it aids the pupil even in developing a memory for the visual configuration; it triggers the process of learning to read; and it teaches the pupil that the writer's message reveals itself at least partially through the grapho-phonic cues, through the orthographic and internal structure of words, and through the sound information contained in that structure. The second half of chapter 9 addressed another of the within-word cues: namely, the structural or morphemic cues. The morphemes affect a word structurally and semantically. The semantic or meaning aspects will receive more attention in chapter 11. Chapter 9 focused on how the morphemic cues affect the word's structure and on the role they play in giving a word its idiosyncratic shape and form.

PART VI
The Comprehension Process

Part VI is about the comprehension process, not as a separate but as an integrated process. It is really about comprehending (McNeil, 1984, 1987) rather than about comprehension. Davis (1944; 1972) early noted that underlying comprehension are two general mental abilities: ability to remember word meanings (lexical access or word knowledge) and ability to reason with words. Comprehension or thinking with words begins with the association of meaning with individual words, but extends to reasoning with successive words (with phrases, sentences, paragraphs, and total text), to interpreting words in their contextual setting, to reasoning one's way through smaller idea segments, to grasping the meaning of a larger unitary idea, and to comprehending on qualitatively different levels (literal, inferential, evaluative, etc.). Comprehension is thinking on the highest level. It is a cognitive process. It requires inference, verifying, correcting, and confirming of expectancies about the text.

It is also clear that if adequate communication between writer and reader, and hence comprehension, is to occur in reading (and reading has not much value if it does not), the reader must have some commonality of experience with the writer, must have developed an adequate background of world experience, must have adequate topical knowledge, and must become familiar with the writer's ways of expressing meaning. To comprehend, readers need also basic language skills, an understanding of language patterns, the ability to recognize the structural elements composing a sentence, and the ability to perceive the syntactic interrelationships of these elements.

Good comprehenders treat the sentence as a unit of meaning. They read in phrase-like units, and are flexible in their pattern of reading, varying their eye movements, and changing the size of the processing unit. They regress only after they are unsuccessful in grasping the meaning of a larger segment of text. They pay most attention to the information relevant to their purpose, ignore useless information, read in the largest unit appropriate to the task, and process the least amount of visual information possible. They use a scan-for-meaning pattern. They concentrate most of their processing capacity on the extraction of meaning, rather than analyzing the passage in a word-by-word manner (Hochberg, 1970).

DESCRIPTIONS OF COMPREHENSION

Descriptions of reading comprehension abound. Gibson and Levin (1975) note that we comprehend "the meaning of a word, the meaning of a sentence, or the meaning of a passage of discourse when we apprehend the intention of the writer and succeed in relating his message to the larger context of our own system of knowledge" (p. 400). Johnson (1982) pointed out that comprehension is building bridges from the new to the known; it is relating what one attends to in the world around us or to what one already has in his head. Goodman (1984) observes that making sense of print is what reading is all about. Anderson and Pearson (1984) view comprehension as a process by which the reader constructs meaning by interacting with the text. They note: "To say that one has comprehended a text is to say that she has found a mental "home" for the information in the text, or else that she has modified an existing mental home in order to accommodate that new information" (p. 225).

Cooper (1986) observes: "The interaction between the reader and the text is the foundation of comprehension. In the process of comprehending, the reader relates the information presented by the author to information stored in his or her mind (memory); this process of relating new information to old information is the process of comprehending" (p. 3). Later, Cooper comments that "comprehension is the process of constructing meaning by taking the relevant ideas from the text and relating them to ideas you already have; this is the process of the reader interacting with the text" (p. 5). Comprehension is a process by which the reader constructs meaning by using the clues in the text and by relating these cues to one's existing schemata (Cooper, 1986). Early and Sawyer (1984) note that "reading as reasoning is more than *seeking* meaning. Connecting meanings with words the writer uses, the reader draws on prior knowledge (his or her personal schema) to compose meanings suggested by the text. The closer the writer's intentions and experiences are to the reader's purposes and prior knowledge the more closely the reader's "composed meanings" will match the writer's intended message" (p. 373).

Perfetti (1985) observes that comprehension is a set of interrelated processes by which "the reader builds a representation of text meaning" (p. 4). Smith (1988) defines comprehension as identification and apprehension of meaning and as "making sense of print" (p. 54). He defines it as "the reduction of the reader's uncertainty" (p. 154) and adds that "when uncertainty reduction is taking place, there must be some comprehension" (p. 53).

In summary, comprehension is perceived by these researchers and writers as a process; it is a process of information search involving interaction between reader and text, of actively constructing a meaningful representation of the writer's written message, and of building a representation of text meaning. It is a process of making sense out of print. Good and successful comprehenders relate the text to the larger context of their own system of knowledge; relate what is in print to what is in their head; and use the text as a blueprint for meaning. The reader's schema is primary in these formulations.

Comprehension thus depends upon two kinds of information: the current information received from the text by the receptor systems and the stored information that is available in memory. Readers extract meaning from what they read on the basis of the visual information (the surface structure of the language), but also on the basis of the deep structure and the knowledge and experiences contained within their brain.

BASIC COMPREHENSION PROCESSES AND SUBPROCESSES

Chapter 7 suggested that comprehension occurs when pupils attend to and are interested in the material, when pupils have a purpose for reading, when they relate the material to their personal schemata, when the teacher provides pupils with the background for reading the materials, when they make inferences, activate appropriate concepts, relate new information to old, and create mental images, when readers use a hypothesizing-confirming/rejecting strategy, when the teacher and pupil use a question strategy, when pupils monitor their prediction and comprehension (they know when they are comprehending and when they are not), and when readers are taught to read the material fluently with proper phrasing and rhythm and with proper sentence sense.

The teacher can help pupils by getting their attention, by making sure that they have attained adequate intellectual and conceptual maturity to comprehend, by providing the experiences needed for meaningful reading, by providing adequate intellectual stimulation and practice in concept formation and in the use of language, and by providing opportunities for wide reading. The pupil is aided when the teacher helps the pupil to make use of context cues (this is especially important if the pupil has difficulty naming concepts), models the kinds of strategies a reader should use during reading, and points out specifically what needs to be done to cope with a particular comprehension problem (Davey, 1983).

Comprehension itself is an inference; it is a mental construct; it cannot be observed directly. We do not observe the comprehending; we observe the products of comprehension or the behaviors that result after comprehension has occurred. Davis (1968, 1972), using statistical analysis, concluded that reading comprehension is a composite of at least five underlying mental skills:

1. Remembering and recalling word meanings.
2. Finding answers to questions answered explicitly in the passage.
3. Drawing inferences from the content; reasoning with the content.
4. Recognizing a writer's purpose, attitude, tone, and mood.
5. Following the structure of a passage.

Davis, nonetheless, rejected the notion of comprehension as a body of separate, independent skills.

Vacca and Jones (1976) suggested that reading may be symbolized as $R > S_1 + S_3 + S_n$, meaning that reading is greater than the sum of the teachable skills. Comprehension is thus perceived as a process in which the subskills are integrated into a unitary and single process. Vacca and Vacca (1986) note, "Although it's likely that a composite of comprehension skills does exist, it's just as likely that the interaction among these skills is what [really] matters" (p. 19). Perfetti and Lesgold (1979) suggest that the processes and subprocesses or components of reading comprehension are not functionally independent, but rather that they are mutually facilitative. The processes and subprocesses can indeed be isolated, but they must also be interrelated. Poor comprehenders are clearly individuals who have not integrated the subskills.

Chapters 8 and 9 stressed that reading is a word-recognition process. It should be obvious from the content in chapters 8 and 9 that comprehension will not be very effective if the reader has not mastered word identification and recognition. Comprehension does depend upon fluent and accurate word recognition. But, it is just as obvious that speed and automaticity in recoding, in and of themselves, are not reading and they do not compensate for comprehension. Word recognition is necessary for comprehension to occur, but word calling does not guarantee good comprehension.

Part VI (chapters 10–12) focuses on reading as a comprehension process. Chapters 10, 11, and 12 deal with the essence of reading. They describe comprehension as a process of: (a) lexical access (the encoding of meaning of a single word), (b) semantic encoding (the encoding of meaning that is appropriate to the context), (c) the assembly and integration of propositions (understanding of phrases and sentences); and (d) text modeling (the development of an understanding of total text). The model presented here relies heavily on Perfetti (1985), Irwin (1986a, b), Just and Carpenter (1987), and on the writer's own perception of what comprehension involves. Figure Part VI-1 identifies these basic processes of comprehension.

Figure Part VI-1 illustrates that comprehension of total text depends on several levels of representation: the perceptual processes used to identify or encode words; the lexical processes used to access word meaning; the semantic encoding processes which lead to the encoding of the meaning that fits the context; the semantic and syntactic contextual processes used to organize word meaning into larger units such as phrases, clauses, and sentences; the referential processes which relate words to objects, events, or ideas; predictive processes which allow the reader to predict himself through print; schema activation or the schematic processes (i.e., previous knowledge or schemata, one's knowledge of the world in general and knowledge of language); the integrative or coherence processes which connect words within sentences and sentences with other sentences; inference processes which relate the text to the reader's world knowledge; and metacognitive processes or knowing whether the words and sentences make sense. These processes conjointly permit the reader to construct a representation of the total text (Just & Carpenter, 1987).

To understand the total text, readers must not only make sense out of each sentence in itself, but they must also determine its relations to preceding and subsequent portions of the text. They must determine the relationships among the events, objects, and facts described by the text and must construct a representation that integrates the information (Just & Carpenter, 1987). In processing text, readers thus combine the explicit propositions or ideas within the text with their previous knowledge or schemata, both of matters of the world and of word meanings, to produce a text model.

Each of the processes and subprocesses identified in Figure Part IV-1 are discussed in greater detail in the chapters that follow. In addition, we recommend that you refer back to Figure 1-3, which provides an expanded version of the comprehension processes.

The processes that operate during comprehension proceed simultaneously, constantly interacting with each other. Just and Carpenter (1987) note that all comprehension processes, many of which are automatic, can occur at the same time or in parallel and are integrated in the working

Figure Part VI-1 The Comprehension Process

Development of Meaning for Individual Words

Lexical Access (Encoding the meaning of a single word: the word concept)

Semantic Access (Encoding the meaning that is appropriate to the context).

Referential Process (The reader must identify the referent. Words have referents; they represent something; the referent for the word *book* is the object, book.)

Schematic Processes (The word in text elicits a representation of the referent and the representation of the referent or meaning is stored in the mind in the form of schemata. The representation of the referent, (i.e., of book) is stored in the brain as a schema. Comprehension occurs when words, sentences, and paragraphs are matched with slots in the reader's schemata. The reader interprets text in terms of what he knows.)

Semantic and Syntactic Context (Comprehension is a matter of processing the semantic and syntactic context. Context effects occur because of what is stored in the mind of the reader and because of what is on the printed page. The text-context and the with-mind context provide cues to the meaning of what is on the page.

Inferencing and Predicting Processes (Readers often must infer and interpret what is on the printed page in terms of what they bring to the reading task, and from context cues.)

Monitoring of Comprehension or Metacognitive Processes (Readers must constantly monitor the text to see whether it makes sense, and if it does not, must use appropriate fixup strategies.)

Development of Meaning for Units of Increasing Size (Reasoning with Words)

Assembly and Integration of Propositions (Encoding the meaning of phrases and sentences). It includes:

Assembly of Propositions (Assembly of the individual idea units in a phrase or sentence.)

Chunking (Grouping of the words into meaningful phrases or thought units)

Microselection (Identification of the idea units that need to be remembered, especially of the main idea in sentences.)

Integration or Linking of Propositions into a Cohesive Whole (Integrative processing is necessary in understanding sentences and in inferring the relationships between sentences. Propositions held in short-term memory must be assembled or integrated in long-term memory. Integrative processing links present text to earlier text: e.g., pronouns usually refer to earlier text.)

Text Modeling (Encoding the meaning or developing a representation of paragraphs and extended text). It includes:

Understanding of Text's Coherence and Organization (Understanding of textual unity, including cohesion and organization, leading to a summary. Cohesion is the connectedness between sentences and total text; organization refers to interparagraph organization. It includes an understanding of story grammar and of the organization pattern in expository materials, and identification of the cues that signal organization.)

memory. They occur in an unspecified order and are interactive. Just and Carpenter (1987) also believe that comprehension is immediate. "The cognitive system attempts the multiple levels of interpretation as soon as it gets access to the words" (p. 16), but this does not imply that comprehension is immediately successful or that the reader comprehends everything at once. The text can force postponement of interpretation by withholding essential information. Eye-movement data support such an interpretation. The reader spends more time on those words that are long, infrequent, or syntactically anomalous (Just & Carpenter, 1980).

The effectiveness of the comprehension processes in any given situation depends upon the reader, the text that is being read, the purpose for reading, the situation in which reading occurs, and so forth. Mackworth (1971, 1972) so aptly observed that reading can only be defined in terms of who is reading what, in what state, and for what reasons.

Part VI consists of three chapters: Chapter 10, "Lexical Access and Semantic Encoding: Strategies for the Development of Meaning for Individual Words," is the first of three chapters that deal with the comprehension process. It is specifically concerned with strategies for developing meaning for words: with lexical access (i.e., encoding the meaning of single words) and with semantic encoding (i.e., encoding the meaning that is appropriate to the context). It focuses on the development of meaning for single words, both in isolation and in context. It is most concerned with the semantic content of words and with the problems related to the association of meaning with individual words. Chapter 11, "Assembly and Integration of Propositions and Text Modeling: Strategies for the Development of Meaning for Units of Increasing Size: Phrases, Sentences, Paragraphs, and Total Text," deals with the assembly and integration of propositions (i.e., with the comprehension of phrases and sentences) and with text modeling (i.e., with the comprehension of paragraphs and extended text). It is concerned with reasoning with words and with word meanings; with reasoning one's way through idea segments; and with the grasp of meaning of a larger unitary idea. The reader must chunk idea units and words into meaningful phrases, sentences, and paragraphs, and total text. Chapter 12, "Strategies for the Development of the Higher Levels of Comprehending," examines the higher levels of comprehending (i.e., literal, inferential, organizational, evaluative, appreciative, and integrative). Text modeling requires these higher-level comprehension skills. Readers are constantly building a representation of text. When they tap a representation of text that is explicitly stated in the text, they are said to be processing the information on a literal level. When readers convert ideas into a coherent whole, when they organize individual idea units into a summary, and when they attain inter-sentence and inter-paragraph integration, they are processing the text information on an organizational level. When readers read between the lines, predicting their way through print, integrating the explicit information in the text with prior knowledge and building a representation of text, they are processing the text on an inferential level.

Figure Part VI-2 represents the organization of part 6, but also indicates that comprehending units of increasing involves new and distinctive processes at each level of development.

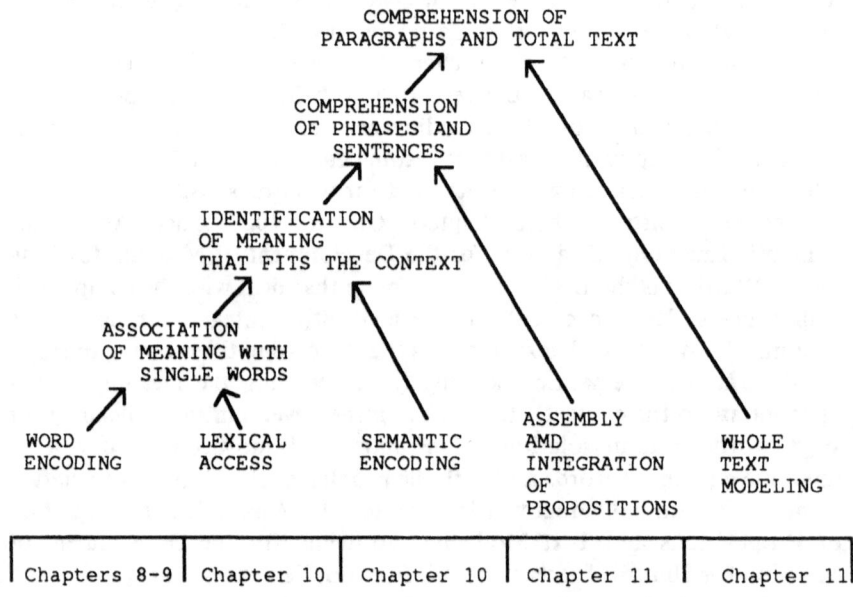

Figure Part VI-2

Chapter 10
Lexical Access and Semantic Encoding: Strategies for the Development of Meaning for Individual Words

    I. Introduction
   II. Lexical Access
       A. Referential Processes
       B. Schematic Processes
       C. Semantic and Syntactic Context
       D. Inferencing and Predicting Processes
       E. Metacognitive Processes
  III. Pupil Differences in Lexical Access
  IV. Conceptualization and Word Meaning
   V. Causes of Word Meaning Difficulties
 VI. General Strategies for Developing Word Meaning
       A. Providing Direct and Vicarious Experience
       B. Teaching Meaning as an Association Process
       C. Teaching Words in Semantically and Topically Related Sets
          1. Semantic Association
          2. Semantic Mapping
          3. Semantic Feature Analysis
       D. Teaching Pupils to Infer Meaning From Context Cues
          1. Typographical or Format Aids
          2. Structural Cues
          3. Illustrations
          4. Semantic Context Cues
          5. Syntactic Context Cues and Presentation Cues
          6. Analogy Cues
          7. Context Plus Phonic or Morphemic Cues
          8. Use of the Cloze Technique
 VII. Semantic Encoding
VIII. Additional Strategies for Developing Word Meaning
       E. Teaching Pupils to Use Morphemic Units as Cues to Meaning
       F. Teaching the Meaning of Homonyms
       G. Teaching Pupils to Use and Interpret High-Imagery Words

    H. Teaching Special Vocabularies
    I. Teaching the Etymology of Words
    J. Teaching Space, Numerical, and Time Concepts
    K. Teaching the Interpretation of Figurative and Idiomatic Expressions
        1. Figures of Resemblance
        2. Figures of Contrast or Satire
        3. Figures of Exaggeration
    L. Teaching the Use of the Dictionary as a Guide to Meaning
IX. Summary

CHAPTER 10
Lexical Access and Semantic Encoding: Strategies for the Development of Meaning for Individual Words

As noted in chapter 1 and in the introduction to this section, the reader cannot develop a meaningful representation of the writer's written message without lexical access or the encoding of the meaning of single words and without semantic meaning or the encoding of the meaning that is appropriate to the context. Chapter 10 concerns itself with these two processes of comprehension.

Our initial concern in this chapter is lexical access. Downey and Leong (1982) note that, for readers to take meaning to and from the printed page, they must first have recourse to their lexicon or mental dictionary so they can extract meaning for the printed word from their long-term semantic memory. They must associate words with familiar concepts represented in their memory. The association of meaning with words is critical because the validity of the reader's predictions and comprehension of the text depends on it. Sternberg (1987) notes that "one's level of vocabulary is highly predictive, if not determinative, of one's level of reading comprehension" (p. 90). Research has consistently shown that comprehension is a direct function of (a) the number of words that readers know or that they have stored in semantic memory, and (b) the number and quality of meanings that they have associated with these words.

Comprehension of what is read is clearly limited by the inefficient operation of lexical access. Reading for meaning begins with the association of meaning with individual words. Readers are clearly aided in comprehension if they know or if they learn the meanings of the unfamiliar words that the text contains (Carnine, et al., 1984). Conversely, if a text contains many unfamiliar words, the reader's comprehension is at risk.

Comprehension is impeded by not knowing enough of the words. When words are not known, the reader's text representation tends to be incomplete (Perfetti, 1985).

Children come to school and to each classroom experience with a vast reservoir of meanings. Words are labels for the meanings in the mental lexicon. This reservoir of meanings and words is part of their schemata. However, the child's mental lexicon is usually much smaller than it might be. It is up to the teacher to help pupils expand their world of meaning. The expansion of the pupil's schemata, of which we spoke in chapter 4, requires the development of meaning for additional words (expansion in breadth) and the broadening of the meanings (expansion in depth) that the pupil already possesses. Schemata and vocabulary are both important to comprehension. Vocabulary and schemata must interact for comprehension to take place (May, 1986).

The association of meaning or experience with a word is indeed the most elemental form of comprehension, but it is an absolute necessity in learning to comprehend and in reading with meaning. It is what builds a referent for a word. It is highly related to reading achievement in the elementary and secondary school years. Davis (1944, 1972) found in his research that word meaning emerged as the most differentiated comprehension skill. Research (Anderson & Freebody, 1981; Carnine, Kameenui, & Coyle, 1984; Mezynski, 1983) almost universally draws a close relationship between knowledge of word meanings and reading comprehension. For this reason, vocabulary training is an effective means of improving comprehension. Beck, Perfetti, and McKeown (1982) found that construction of passage meaning is easier when individual word meanings are understood. Only if pupils know words can they chunk information into meaningful units (Pearson, 1975, calls these semantic chunks), into phrases, sentences, and thought units, or into memory storage units that facilitate the synthesizing process of cementing ideas together (Peters, 1977). The simple fact is that having an ample reservoir of word meanings helps the reader to read sentences and paragraphs. Expanding the pupil's word meaning is one of the best ways of helping the pupil develop the knowledge base required for reading. And, teaching of word meanings is best when it relates the word to familiar concepts in context.

LEXICAL ACCESS

Lexical access, or the encoding of the meaning of single words, is the association of the reader's concepts and meanings with the printed word. It is the development of meaning for individual words. It includes the literal or denotative meanings of words and the alternate and connotative meanings of words. The words represent individual idea units which are stored in the reader's long-term memory and from which total text modeling develops.

There are major interrelating processes that are activated immediately with word identification or word encoding and with lexical access. These are the referential and schematic processes, the semantic and syntactic context, the inferencing or predicting processes, and the metacognitive processes. As the reader moves from simple words (the concern of chapter 10) to phrases, sentences, paragraphs, and total text (the concern of chapter 11), the role of each of these processes in the development of a representation of text becomes progressively greater.

Referential Processes

It is at the lexical level (but really no less so at the semantic encoding, assembly and integration of propositions, and text modeling levels) that the referential processes are especially important. Meaning for words arises from the way in which words are used in relation to the extralinguistic world of objects, ideas, events, and direct and vicarious experiences (Crystal, 1976): that is, in relation to the referent of the word. Words have no meaning of their own; they refer to, represent, or stand for something; the something is the word's referent. The referent for *cat* may be the furry little animal that the child has as a pet. It is the referent that gives the word cat its meaning. Referents are the complex of experiences that the reader has associated with words, which he has stored in the mind as schemata, which constitute the semantic field, and which are important in making inferences about and in comprehending text (McNeil, 1987).

Schematic Processes

Just and Carpenter (1987) note that the central information about a word or the representation of the referent, which is stored in the mental lexicon, is the representation of the associated concept, the schema, including its properties and its relation to other concepts. This information is termed the word meaning or word-concept. The semantic features of a word are usually represented as a network of nodes (i.e., concepts and features) that are interconnected by links.

In the illustration that follows, animal is superordinate to bird and bird is superordinate to canary and robin.

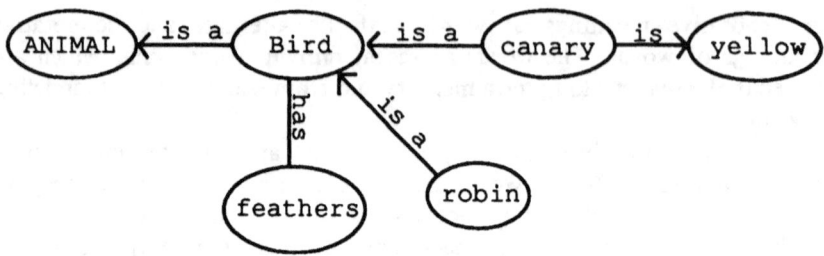

Labels on the links indicate the nature of the relation between the nodes they connect. Concepts are linked to their superordinates by an "is a" relation. Properties of the concepts are linked by "has," "is," or "can" relations. Just and Carpenter (1987) note that the concept or schema, *kitchen*, thus has slots for appliances, for users (e.g., family member, friend, hired cook), and for activities (e.g., cooking, eating, washing dishes). It is related to the schema *house*, which may be the superordinate concept, but also to dining room, to which it is coordinate. A characteristic of the lexical network is that activation of one node can produce activation of other nodes to which it is linked in the network (Just & Carpenter, 1987).

A significant point made in chapter 4 is that good readers interpret text with respect to what they know; they activate their prior knowledge in developing a representation of the total text. Schematic processes, which we have referred to as the within-mind context, thus play a critical role in the processing and comprehension of text, and not merely in the retrieval of information or the recall of text. They are the scaffolding with which the reader constructs the meaning of text. Schematic processes are important simply because the text must be interpreted with respect to one's personal schemata. Processing of text requires the reader to combine the explicit propositions in text with his own schemata to build a representation of text. The reader's personal schemata are often more important in the comprehension of text than is the text itself. The reader's schemata interact with the textual cues to create meaning. As we shall see later, a story schema, with slots for setting, plot, resolution, and theme, greatly aids the reader in comprehending and recalling stories, in understanding the temporal and causal relations among the story parts, and in organizing information from a story.

Semantic and Syntactic Context

Writers, researchers, and teachers have all noted the importance of the semantic and syntactic context in lexical access, in semantic encoding, and in the comprehension of extended text. Comprehension is a matter of processing the semantic and syntactic context and of determining a word's semantic and syntactic status.

The semantic context functions as a cue to the meaning of a single word presented in context, but it has an even greater role in making predictions about subsequent information and in organizing word meanings into the meanings of larger and higher-order units such as phrases, sentences, and extended text (Baker & Brown, 1984b). The semantic context contains the experiential content of meaning. It identifies the referent. It is the organization of the semantic information within one's schemata. The syntactic context (i.e., the order in which the words appear) or the encoding of a syntactic pattern also triggers activation of a word in memory. The semantic and syntactic contexts are operative when the reader uses the within-text context, the specific words chosen, the typographical aids, definitions, synonyms, and the word order, punctuation, and other stylistic devices to construct the message that the writer intended and which existed in her mind as she was writing.

Inferencing and Predicting Processes

As in the case of the schematic processes and of the semantic and syntactic context, inference processes are also used to encode the meaning of single words presented in context, but their role is also a continuous one through the total-text modeling process. Comprehension occurs when words, sentences, and paragraphs are matched with slots in the reader's schemata (McNeil, 1987, p. 36). Often the slots are filled by explicit information or by information that is directly or explicitly stated in the text; at other times, they must be filled by inferences or by information implicitly stated in the text. Since the writer's message can never be totally explicit, readers, of necessity, must infer and interpret what is on the printed page in terms of what they bring to the reading task.

Perfetti (1985) notes that text recalls often reflect a combination of what the reader knows and what is readily inferred. Thus in reading "The room was warm and stuffy, so they opened the window," the pupil may recall *hot* instead of *warm*. If the general context is a doctor's office, the reader may recall *office* instead of *room*. If Joe and his daughter were in the room, the reader likely will recall *Joe* instead of *they*, since it is likely that an adult opened the window. Perfetti adds that it is probable that all these inferential changes are governed by a single comprehension principle: in processing a text, the explicit propositions are combined with the reader's nonvisual information or schemata to produce a text model. This knowledge includes what the reader knows about word meanings as well as what he knows about other matters of the world.

Inferencing processes are used in encoding the meaning of single words and of phrases in context and to infer the connection between phrases and sentences. They are used in deducing the antecedents of anaphora or pronouns and in inferring the links between sentences when these are not explicit but implied. They are used in interpreting a sentence such as, "She was a viscountess, but he was only a baron" (The word *only* permits the reader to infer that viscountesses rank higher than barons (Carroll, 1969; McNeil, 1987). Inferencing processes are used in filling gaps in the text or in making slot-filling inferences in one's schemata. And, they are used in making inferences about how the narrative will end or what an appropriate title for the story might be.

Pupils with inadequate schemata or who cannot use semantic and syntactic context cues will have great difficulty in inferring or predicting. They cannot fill in the missing information. They cannot use the hypothesizing–confirming/rejecting strategy of which we spoke in chapter 5. Inferencing is the application of schemata to text which has left out some information, but if readers do not have the schemata, they have nothing to apply.

Metacognitive Processes

Monitoring strategies (Weinstein, 1987) include reflecting on one's own thinking processes, establishing learning goals, assessing the degree to which the goals are being attained, knowing whether one is being successful in making sense out of the text, and modifying strategies or knowing what to do if comprehension is not occurring. The metacognitive processes include the knowledge, "This word or sentence makes sense; it fits my schema," or "It doesn't make sense. I have to evaluate my schemata. I need to reread. I need to read further." You may want to reread the section in chapter 7 on the metacognitive processes.

Lexical access is a significant first step in comprehending text. Success in lexical access depends on the ongoing interaction of the referential and schematic processes, of the semantic and syntactic context, of the inferencing and predicting processes, and of the metacognitive processes.

PUPIL DIFFERENCES IN LEXICAL ACCESS

Good readers exhibit their advantage in lexical access over poor readers in many ways. They remember words better, have larger vocabularies, and their semantic entries tend to have more semantic detail than do those of poor readers. They have more specific-concept knowledge (vocabulary) and more general concept-knowledge knowledge (schemata) (Perfetti, 1985).

They have more breadth (i.e., the number of semantic entries or the number of nodes is greater) and more depth (i.e., the number and type of links are greater). Knowing more words or having breadth in vocabulary permits contextual processes to operate; knowing more about some words or having greater depth permits precise representation or modeling of text.

Good readers are more adept at relating the words on the printed page to their referent or to the actual object, event, or experience which gives the word meaning. They are better able to convert the information from the referent into a representation or a schema. They are better in determining the word's semantic and syntactic status.

Good readers, especially if they are highly verbal, are better at inferring the meaning of unfamiliar words in context, at inferring the one meaning of multiple meanings that fits the context, at filling in the gaps in the text, in applying schemata to text which has left out some information, and in using morphological and semantic context cues (i.e., they know what an unknown word refers to in a given context) (Perfetti, 1985; Sternberg, Powell, & Kaye, 1983). Inferencing is particularly important in semantic encoding. The ability to use semantic encoding means knowing what the referent of an unknown word is in a specifically constrained context. Good readers are more adept than young children and poor readers in processing text. They are better in combining the explicit propositions (i.e., specific concept knowledge) or words in text with their general-concept knowledge or schemata to produce a text model. Text recalls reflect a combination of what the reader knows and what is readily inferred.

Good readers also have a word identification or word encoding advantage. The ability to comprehend depends upon the reader's ability to access the semantic information contained in words that were acquired through experience and conceptualization, but it also depends upon mastery of perception skills, on efficient recoding (Fredericksen, 1978), and on efficient storage of words in memory (Ansara, 1982). It is another reason why skilled readers have an advantage over unskilled readers and why pupils must develop fluency and automaticity in identifying words.

Conversely, poor readers (and young children) often have inadequate world knowledge; cannot activate word meanings; are slower in processing linguistic codes; tend to take everything literally (metaphors and idioms go right over their heads); are oblivious to the fact that they do not understand (i.e., they are not good at monitoring their own comprehension processes); and often focus on reading as a recoding process and not as a meaning-gathering process (they often are unaware that they must make sense of the text) (Rayner & Pollatsek, 1989). The differences between skilled and unskilled readers increase on longer words, low-frequency words, and pseudo words (Perfetti, 1985).

CONCEPTUALIZATON AND WORD MEANING

All the strategies discussed later in this chapter for developing meaning are secondary to the ability to develop concepts, or to build schemata. Success in reading, and certainly success in developing meaning for words and in developing the higher-level comprehension skills, depends significantly upon the pupil's ability to think on an abstract level. This process is called conceptualization and the end result is a concept. A word is the verbal expression of a concept.

Pupils go through stages as they develop concepts. They grow in conceptualization. Concise and specific concepts develop first. The child learns to discriminate one object from another. With repeated experience with similar objects, children acquire new layers of meaning and their perceptions become increasingly wider, richer, more diversified, and more complex. Perception and growth in meaning is unidirectional (always growing richer) and irreversible. The pupil proceeds from simple experience and from simple sensation and perception to concept via abstraction and finally arrives at categorization and generalization.

Rosner et al. (1981) found that a major deficit affecting learning-disabled children is difficulty in perception and concept formation. Such children are unable to engage in any kind of inferential reading. When children cannot think on an abstract level, when they cannot form concepts, or when symbolic thinking is defective, they cannot understand sentences and memory may also be detrimentally affected. Conversely, the greater the number of concepts that readers have formed and have associated with and fixed through words, the better tends to be their understanding of what is read.

From a diagnostic point of view, it is important, then, for teachers to find at what level of conceptualization the pupil is. Comprehension difficulties are directly related to the child's lack of adequate conceptualization abilities. Many of the disabled reader's reading difficulties, especially substitutions in reading that do not make sense, or that do not fit the semantic and syntactic context, can be traced in immaturity in conceptualization.

It is unrealistic to expect reading comprehension to exceed the conceptual level of the learner, or to expect children to possess word meanings beyond their ability to perceive. It is unrealistic to expect pupils to be able to deal with abstract concepts and the symbols that represent them if they have not attained an adequate level of conceptualization. Reading comprehension thus must await conceptual development. Just and Carpenter (1987) note that the development in vocabulary or schemata formation goes hand in hand with the development of conceptual knowledge, and that vocabulary acquisition is a form of concept learning.

Concept development activities that develop vocabulary and word meaning include:

1. Provide experience with the concrete reality, for example, seeing a globe.
2. Have pupils label the concept: The round object that represents the earth is named a globe.
3. Have pupils identify a concept's relevant attributes, its unchanging core of experience, or its invariant characteristic: A globe is spherical and it represents the earth; an airplane is an aircraft with fixed wings and that is driven by a screw propeller or a rearward jet.
4. Have pupils identify the concept's irrelevant attributes: The size or composition of the globe is an irrelevant attribute.
5. Have pupils contrast the concept with a non-example (a wall map is not an example of a globe; it is nonspherical).
6. Have pupils identify the relationship that the concept has to other concepts. (Globe and map both represent the earth.)
7. Provide opportunities for application of the concept.
8. Use word maps to explain the concept further.

Peters (1977) notes that too often today in teaching word meanings only a general definition for the word is given and perhaps one example. Memorization of definitions is simply inadequate to develop a meaning vocabulary. Vocabulary teaching is more effective when pupils are directly involved in constructing meaning rather than memorizing definitions or synonyms (Beck, Perfetti, & McKeown, 1982). Pupils need practice in using words in many and varied situations, in conversation and in writing, and in situations in which words are experienced directly and concretely. There is no substitute for direct experience. Concrete examples, role-playing simulations, and even the use of pictures are more effective than abstract definitions. Peters suggests that activities such as the following might be employed:

1. Given the name (e.g., desert) of an attribute, the pupil should be able to select an example of the attribute or to give a characteristic of the attribute (an area where the temperature varies greatly from day to night; great temperature variation is an attribute of a desert).
2. Given the relevant and irrelevant attributes of a concept, the pupil should be able to list and classify the attributes as either relevant or irrelevant.

3. Given an example of the concept, the pupil should be able to select another example of the concept or select the name of the concept.

Schwartz and Raphael (1985) and Duffelmeier (1988) recommend the use of word maps to teach definitions, emphasizing (a) the concept or general class to which the word belongs (what is it?), (b) the primary properties of the concept (what is it like?), and (c) examples of the concept. The center of the word map is the place to record what the main concept is; in the topmost box is written a more generic word that answers "What is it?" The "What is it like?" boxes may contain such observations as: sandwiches are served on a bun and may be served with catsup, pickles, relish, mustard, and onions.

CONCEPTUAL FRAMEWORK

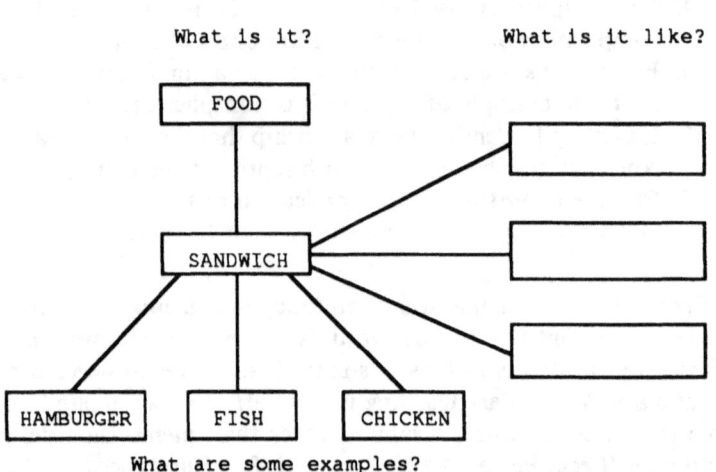

Mason and Au (1986) and Roth, Smith, and Anderson (1984) suggest that the development of conceptual frameworks is enhanced when:

1. Students practice talking about ideas, when they discuss them with others, and when the teacher provides corrective feedback.
2. Students engage in experiments and hands-on activities.
3. Students are involved in small group problem-solving sessions.
4. Students engage in expository writing experiences that require them to explain the concepts in applied situations.
5. Students create concept maps.

CAUSES OF WORD MEANING DIFFICULTIES

Developing word meaning is obviously one of the reading teacher's most important tasks. Even though pupils appear to possess the meanings needed for the comprehension of the reading materials available to them, the teacher constantly must expand the pupil's semantic meanings and check upon the adequacies of the pupil's present meanings. Fortunately, it appears that children have a far greater knowledge of the literal meaning of words than is usually credited to them. First graders generally have a speaking vocabulary of over 2,500 words and possibly a recognition vocabulary of up to 20,000 words. Certainly, no teacher ever taught children even most of the words that they know. Unfortunately, few pupils have had sufficient experience to appreciate all the connotations or multiple meanings of a word. They have not developed precision in meaning. This knowledge comes only through extensive experience.

The difficulties that pupils experience in dealing with words are essentially of three types:

1. The pupil knows the meaning, but cannot identify the word. For example, in "The boy hit the ball over the fence," the word over is in the pupil's aural-oral vocabulary, but the pupil cannot decipher the printed form. This is not a problem of meaning. It is a word-identification problem.
2. The pupil cannot identify the word and does not know the meaning. For example, in "Bill was taciturn," the word taciturn is not in the pupil's aural-oral vocabulary.
3. The pupil can identify the word but does not know the meaning, as with "run" in "The bankruptcy caused a run on the bank." This is a problem of multiple meanings.

Numerous causes or reasons may be given to explain children's difficulties with word meaning. A major cause is the simple fact that the associations that can be made with the word are exceedingly complex. Words may have denotative and connotative meanings. Denotative meaning is the literal meaning; the denotation or referent for the word *cloud* is the cloud itself. Connotative meanings are based on the individual's personal store of unique experiences and perceptions; they involve idiosyncratic meanings of words rather than commonly shared meanings (Ringler & Weber, 1984). Connotative meanings often represent the emotionalized meaning of a word: thus, the word *red*, when it is used to refer to a person with communistic leanings, is being given a connotative meaning. It is also being used in a connotative sense in the sentence, "When I see her, I see red."

Another complication is that words may have more than one meaning. Generally, the more frequently a word is used, the more meanings it tends to have. The number of meanings actually elicited by a word depends on the number and quality of experiences that the reader has associated with the word. Each new level of meaning requires a corresponding broadening of experiences with objective reality. Words with multiple meanings are called homographs.

Two words may have the same or similar meanings: e.g., small, microscopic, minuscule, tiny, diminutive, and lilliputian; or great, big, monstrous, enormous, immense, stupendous, huge, super, large, tremendous, gigantic, colossal, mammoth, vast, and gargantuan. Two words, though pronounced alike, may have different spellings and meanings: blue-blew. Such words are referred to as homonyms or homophones.

The same graphic image may have different pronunciation and meanings: wĭnd-wīnd. Such words are termed heteronyms or homographs. Heteronyms are words of like spelling whose pronunciation and meaning change, dependent upon their use in the sentence or the context. Thus;, The *wind* did all kinds of damage. I forgot to *wind* my watch. Examples of heteronyms are: abstract, annex, august, bass, bow, buffet, close, combine, compact, conduct, console, consort, content, contract, convert, convict, desert, digest, dove, entrance, excuse, exploit, extract, incense, intern, invalid, lead (lēd or lĕd), live, minute, object, perfect, permit, present, primer, produce, project, protest, read, rebel, record, refuse, relay, row, sow, subject, suspect, upset, wind, and wound. For a more extensive list see Johnston (1988).

Words may also be used in a specific or generic or abstract sense. The word *dot* may allow for only slight variations of meaning. It refers to something very concrete. The word *democracy* has an invariant meaning base, but it also allows for a multitude of differing interpretations. Words often have meanings peculiar to a given content area (e.g., *cold war* in history). Words may have different syntactic functions (e.g., The *best* is not good enough; He is the *best* worker.) and have differing inflectional endings (*cat's, cats*). The word *cat's* is indeed different from the word *cat* and has an added meaning dimension. The syntax determines which of the semantic meanings is the appropriate one. Children generally have difficulty in learning context-dependent words (past tense verbs, prepositions and conjunctions), but learn context-free words (nouns and adjectives) with greater ease. Function words (e.g., prepositions) are always more difficult to learn than are content words (e.g., nouns).

Words often are used in their metaphorical rather than their literal sense. The problems of associating meaning with symbols is often aggravated when words, placed within an idiomatic expression or as a part of a figure of speech, take on a completely different meaning: e.g., facing the music, breaking the ice with someone, leaving no stone unturned. Many words, especially words that stand for time, space, and quantitative concepts (e.g., beyond, deep, some, most, never, different) and conjunctions and prepositions, do not have clear and definite referents.

Acronyms, abbreviations, palindromes, paronyms, eponyms, and metonyms add to the lexical access problem. Acronyms are words formed from the initial letters of words (WAC-Woman's Army Corps, RADAR, AWOL, NAACP, etc.) Palindromes are words that read the same either forwards or backwards (radar, kayak, mom, dad, noon, pop, level, deed, peep, ere, did, eve, tot, dud, toot). Paronyms are words with the same root: wise, wisdom. Eponyms are words that derive from a place, object, or nation (*spoonerism*, after Rev. Spooner, *Romulus* as the eponym of Rome.) Metonyms are created by the substitution of an attribute or characteristic for the total ("The Crown" to represent the king; the use of "pen" to represent the power of literature in "The pen is mightier than the sword"). Additional causes of word-meaning difficulties are:

1. Low intelligence, low learning efficiency, inadequate conceptual development, or lack of intellectual stimulation: Some children think on a concrete rather than on an abstract level. Children with low levels of abstract reasoning ability often cannot use contextual signals to understand what they are reading. Others simply have not been stimulated to acquire new meanings.

2. Retardation in language, speech defects, or linguistic background: Pupils sometimes are deficient in word meanings because they were slow in learning to talk or did not have adequate practice in the use of language. Speech defects also may impede the development of meaning. Dialect and bilingual background may both be a problem.

3. Ignoring or inability to use the context cues: The specific meaning elicited by a word is a function of the context in which the word occurs, both the within-text and the within-mind context.

4. Difficulty level of the materials: The materials to be read are simply too difficult for the pupil to use the context to ascertain the word's meanings.

5. Inadequacies in word recognition: Poor readers often understand the material when it is read to them but not when they read it. Poor comprehenders tend to have extraordinary difficulty recoding unfamiliar words. This hinders the attainment of meanings.

6. Impulsivity: The pupil latches on to the first meaning that comes to mind. Impulsive readers tend to have difficulty with words having multiple meanings.

7. Lack of adequate experiences: Few pupils have had sufficient experience to appreciate all the connotations or multiple meanings of a word. The reader's schema thus is often inadequate. Association of meaning with a symbol cannot occur unless the person has had some experience, whether real or vicarious, with that something for which the symbol stands. The

word, *apple*, for example, has no meaning to the child who has never had either a first-hand or vicarious experience with an apple. Children must first have an experience with an apple if they are to be able to read the word apple.

8. Very little reading: Wide reading is an optimum vocabulary builder.

9. Lack of or inadequate maturation: Pupils acquire meanings as they mature.

10. Poor sensory mechanisms, such as defective vision and hearing, prohibiting the pupil from acquiring experience.

11. Infrequent occurrence of the words: Words often are described as "hard" simply because they are used very infrequently. For example, the words *protean, antimacassar, jejune, tureen, patina, medicant, thermotasix, arachnids* (Early & Sawer, 1984) are difficult, not because of their abstractness or meaning, but rather because they are used so infrequently.

12. Cultural and socioeconomic variances: The meanings that the pupil can take to a word, in fact, whether the pupil will have learned a meaning for the word at all, are often culturally based. Certainly, children from upper socioeconomic levels have a "hidden curriculum," a world of meanings that allows them to react better to printed words.

GENERAL STRATEGIES FOR DEVELOPING WORD MEANING

A few simple principles that guide all vocabulary instruction, concern us first. Teachers should help children in learning:

1. The word's primary, basic, literal, and denotative meaning. Research data (Mason, Kniseley, & Kendall, 1979) clearly show that children are more likely to react to the primary meaning of a word regardless of the context of a sentence.
2. The word's secondary or alternate meanings. Children must be taught that words may have more than one meaning, and that they need to learn the more frequently used meanings.
3. The word's contextually supported meaning, the one meaning of the multiple meanings that fit the context. This is semantic encoding and it is a skill that needs to be taught.

In developing meaning for words teachers have many options. The remainder of this chapter focuses on some of these options, beginning with the role of direct and indirect or vicarious experience. The chapter describes the association of meaning with words as a function of: (a) teaching words in semantically and topically related sets (i.e., semantic association, semantic mapping, and semantic feature analysis); (b) teaching pupils to infer meaning from context clues; (c) teaching pupils to use morphemic units as cues to meaning; (d) teaching the meaning of homonyms, high-imagery words, special vocabularies, etymology, and the interpretating of figurative and idiomatic expressions; and (e) using the dictionary as a guide to meaning.

Providing Direct and Vicarious Experience

We noted earlier that basic to all vocabulary instruction is the development of concepts or schemata and the naming of these concepts. Words are the names of concepts and schemata. Both conceptualization and development of vocabulary depend upon experience, either direct or indirect.

The direct experience, observation, or participation approach consists of activities such as: a "bring and tell" activity which requires children to bring objects to school and talk about them; classroom demonstrations, models, exhibits; science activities such as collecting shells and rocks or caring for an aquarium or for plants; and field trips to farms, food markets, factories, trains, museums, circuses, newspapers, planetariums, zoos, fire departments, bakeries, airplanes, post offices, school buildings, libraries, and stores. Concepts develop from experience, and their richness and scope are in direct proportion to the richness and breadth of the individual's experience. Pupils learn concepts and the words that represent them best through direct, purposeful experiences. Learning is much more intense and meaningful when it is first hand (Vacca & Vacca, 1986). Experience plays a key role in vocabulary development. The most significant reason for differences in learning among children is the differential in experience (Dechant, 1970).

The indirect or vicarious experience approach may be needed because direct experience is not always possible. It may take three forms:

I. Direct instruction in vocabulary: Teaching the use of morphemic cues, context cues, dictionary skills, study of word lists, word parts, word origins, etc., using words in written sentences, reading them orally, and using words in discussion. Studies (Vaughan, Crawley & Mountain, 1979; Nagy, Hermann & Anderson, 1985) generally show that direct instruction in vocabulary is superior to incidental instruction. Dupuis and Snyder (1983) suggest that direct, systematic vocabulary instruction leads to easier recall and is associated with frequent use of the words in different and in varied ways. Words are learned best when they are taught in depth through frequent encounters and through the use of manipulative activities.
II. Incidental experience approach involving the use of:
    A. Labeling: By labeling of objects, materials, and apparatuses used in the classroom; by using signs such as "put milk bottles here,"

"Grocery Store," etc.; and labeling collections such as insects, leaves, rocks, and shells.
B. Teaching children to read pictures: By teaching children to read pictures in books and by using pictures to teach the multiple meanings of words, to develop meanings for prepositions, to understand the meanings of opposites, and to develop an understanding of sequence.
C. Engaging children in conversation and storytelling: By using language activities (such as having children tell a story about a picture, describe a piece of art, tell of experiences at the lake, identify the sequence of events in a story) or by using word games.
D. Using description, riddle, or rhyme games: By having the child identify what has been described in what the teacher read; reading riddles to children and having them identify the subject of the riddles; or having children identify the correct word, using the rhyming principle to do so. Illustrative examples are:
  1. *Riddle*
     I'm a desert animal
     I don't run dry
     I can carry a seven-day water supply.
     What am I?
  2. *Rhyme*
     Johnny jumped over the wall
     Only to have a terrible . . . .
E. Using audio-visual aids: By using slides, filmstrips, television, and disk and tape recordings to illustrate words (e.g., satellite, rocket, pyramid, cactus, coyote) for which the pupil has not had a first-hand experience; using charts, maps, diagrams, and graphs; and using film readers which permit the child to see and hear the film and to follow the same context in a correlated reader.
F. Using dramatization, marionette and puppet shows, pageants, and operettas: Activities such as these are especially useful in developing meaning for abstract terms such as love, courage, cooperation, friendship, sportsmanship, and appreciation.
G. Helping children construct and use picture dictionaries: Children profit greatly from this activity.
H. Having children respond to oral and written directions: By posting directions on the bulletin board or blackboard or by requiring children to carry out oral directions (Get your colors, Pam). Two games, the "Do This" and the "Yes and No" game, are suitable activities. Each game requires a set of cards. One set gives directions and the other asks questions. The child selects a card, reads it aloud, and carries out the desired directions or answers

the question. "Do This" cards contain statements such as: "Stand up and point to the left," "Point to the sky," "Clap your hands," or "Give the number that follows five." "Yes and No" cards contain statements like the following: "Can a dog fly?" "Can birds sing?" "Are cats bigger than lambs?" If the responses to the directions and questions show that the child does not possess the concept involved, the card is put on the bottom of the pack. If the response is adequate, the child keeps the card. The child with the most cards wins the game.

III. Wide or extensive reading: Reading, in and of itself, is a valuable aid in acquiring word meanings and in developing one's vocabulary. Nagy and Anderson (1982, 1984) and Nagy, Herrmann, and Anderson (1985) observe that after third grade a major factor in vocabulary acquisition is the amount of independent reading done by pupils. Research clearly shows that the greater the amount of time pupils spend on a task (Rosenshine, 1979), the greater the number of books read, the greater the number of words taught, the better tends to be the pupil's performance on the task.

The teacher needs to be ever mindful that each new level of meaning requires a corresponding broadening of experience with objective reality. Moreover, the quality of meaning is greatly influenced by the quantity and quality of previously acquired meanings and concepts. Thus, meaning must be built upon the child's previous background of experience. Concepts and the development of meaning for words clearly depend on direct and indirect experience. Each of the strategies that follow are illustrative of direct instruction in vocabulary.

Teaching Meaning as an Associative Process

As just noted, meaning can be associated with the printed word only by associating the word with an experience, whether real or vicarious, or by associating it with another symbol (e.g., the spoken word) that has meaning for the child. For most children the latter is a natural process. Children are asked to look at the word "cat", and are told that it is pronounced /kăt/. It is assumed that they will then take the meaning to the printed word that they had previously associated only with the heard or spoken word. It is here that phonic cues aid meaning. If the pupil can pronounce the word, using phonic cues, and if the word so pronounced is in the pupil's aural-oral vocabulary, the pupil can then take meaning to the printed symbols.

Generally, children have already developed most of the meanings that they encounter in their early reading experiences. This is particularly so when they are introduced to reading through the language-experience approach. They also have associated these meanings or experiences with a heard or spoken symbol. Teaching these children to associate meanings with words then means that the teacher must get them to identify the visual symbol and to link it with the meaning that has already been associated with a spoken symbol. Lexical access thus may be made through the sound of the word. The printed word can activate the sound of the word which produces direct access to meaning.

Teaching Words in Semantically and Topically Related Sets

Development of vocabulary may also take the form of semantic association, semantic mapping, and semantic feature analysis (Johnson, 1983). Beck (1984) and Pearson (1985) emphasize ownership of a word or really knowing a word. Ownership requires the kind of semantic elaboration that occurs in semantic mapping and semantic feature analysis.

Semantic Association

In semantic associations pupils are asked to group a list of words about a more general concept. For the concept conveyances, words that might be so grouped include:

airplane	dogcart	monoplane	space shuttle
aquaplane	dogsled	moped	stage coach
amphibious vehicle	donkey	motorcycle	stroller
balloon	dromedary	mule	submarine
bark	droshky	ostrich	subway
barouche	dune buggy	oxen	tank
blimp	elephant	pack animal	taxi
boat (row, motor, sail)	elevator	parachute	three-wheeler
bobsled	escalator	phaeton	tractor
buckboard	ferry	pickup	train
buffalo	gig	pogo stick	tricycle
buggy	glider	power mower	trolley car
bus	golf-cart	ricksha	truck
camel	gondola	rocket	U F O
canoe	hang glider	roller skates	unicycle
car	helicopter	sedan chair	van
caravel	horse	ship	wagon
carriage	hot air balloon	skateboard	water skis
cart	jeep	ski	wheel barrow
chaise	jet	sled	wheel chair
chariot	jet ski	sleigh	wind surfer
conestoga wagon	kayak	snow skis	yacht
cutter	litter	space ship	

LEXICAL ACCESS AND SEMANTIC ENCODING   367

The teacher may then lead a discussion on the meanings and uses of the words, especially of those words that are new to any of the pupils. This encourages reexamination of old knowledge and provides for the acquisition of new knowledge. It emphasizes what a list of words have in common: they all identify conveyances.

Semantic Mapping

	Conveyances	
"On Water" *Conveyances*	*"In The Air"* *Conveyances*	*"On Land"* *Conveyances*
Boat	Airplane	Buckboard
Canoe	Balloon	Buggy
Ferry	Blimp	Buffalo
Gondola	Glider	Bus
Ship	Hang Glider	Car
Submarine	Helicopter	Carriage
Water Skis	Jet	Cart
Yacht	Parachute	Chariot

In semantic mapping the pupil is required to group the words on the basis of categories. Categories that come immediately to mind are: air conveyances, land conveyances, and water conveyances; but also wind, mechanical, animal, or people-powered conveyances; steam, gas, diesel, propane, alcohol, or coal-powered conveyances; or simply fast and slow conveyances.

Hofler (1981) recommends the use of word lines to depict the relationship between words in a single category, such as size, degree or intensity, or relationship (e.g., antonym, synonym).

SIZE

miniscule	minute	tiny	little	medium	large	huge	gigantic	behemoth	colossal

Additional classification activities are:

1. Branching trees: The most common form of classification takes the form of a word tree representing the class-example relationship:

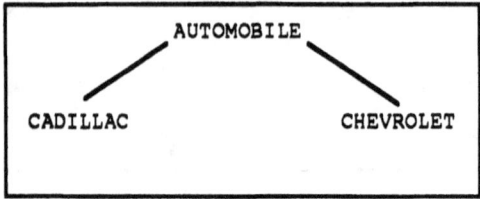

2. Abstraction ladder: In the abstraction ladder a general category (e.g., transportation) is transformed into increasingly specific categories:

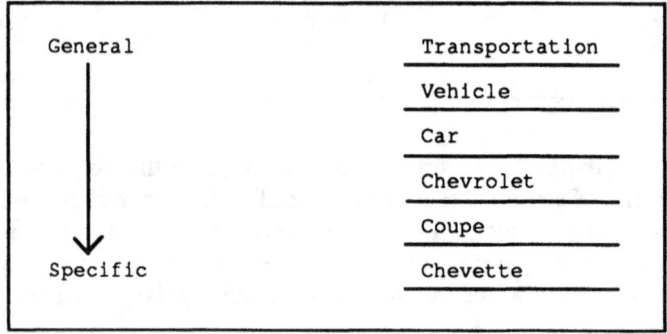

3. Require pupils to classify things one might find on a street; things found on a farm; things to eat; things to ride in; things that are animals, plants, fruits, birds, countries, clothing, colors, or insects; or things that fly, run, or float.
4. Have pupils rank a series of words of similar meaning (such as loathe, hate, despise, abhor, dislike, annoyed with) on the basis of one feature (such as intensity). Other examples are: lying, dishonest, untruthful, deceitful, tricky, shady, underhanded; nullify, negate, abolish, annul, void, invalidate, cancel, repeal, revoke, rescind (Burmeister, 1983); or difficult, hard, perplexing, arduous, laborious, troublesome, callous, unyielding, firm, rigid, unfeeling, stubborn, inflexible, adamant, unbending, resistant, unmerciful, demanding, harsh, severe, stern (Early & Sawyer, 1984). Such words can be grouped both as to meaning categories and as to intensity within a specific meaning category.

5. Have pupils select from a list of words the one word that does not belong with the others: loathe, hate, love, dislike.

Categorizing or grouping aids in recall. It permits greater amounts of material to be transferred into long-term memory (Vaughan, Crawley & Mountain, 1979).

Semantic Feature Analysis

Semantic feature analysis is designed to identify the differences between the list of words. It begins with a listing of characteristics and ends by illustrating that all words are in reality different from one another. All words have slightly different meanings. There is probably no such thing as a synonym for another word. The term synonym stands for "something like" not for "the same as." Semantic analysis helps to illustrate this. It involves the following steps (Johnson, 1983):

1. Select a category (conveyances).
2. Have pupils suggest and list, in a column, some words within the category (cat, truck, bus, train, bicycle, boat, ship, gondola, airplane, helicopter, etc.).
3. Have pupils suggest and list in a row the features shared by some of the words and list these across the top of the blackboard or a grid sheet (wheels, wooden, enclosed, open, engine, man-powered, animal-powered, legs and feet, wings, propeller, pedals, steering wheel, handle bars, sails, tires, etc.)

OBJECT	FEATURE										
car											
truck											
bus											
bicycle											

4. Have pupils indicate by a plus (+) or a minus (−) whether a given conveyance possesses the attribute. With young children it may be desirable to use smiling or sad faces instead of pluses and minuses.

FEATURE

OBJECT	wheels	tires	engine	handlebars	wings	sails	pedals
car	+	+	+	−	−	−	−
truck	+	+	+	−	−	−	−
bus	+	+	+	−	−	−	−
train	+	−	+	−	−	−	−
boat	−	−	+	−	−	+	−

5. Have pupils expand the list of conveyances and suggest more attributes than those listed.
6. Have pupils complete the expanded matrix with pluses and minuses.
7. Help pupils realize that if enough attributes are considered no two words have the identical pattern of pluses and minuses; hence, no two words have identical meanings. Each word is truly unique.

The variant emphasis in the three forms of vocabulary building are summarized as follows: (a) semantic association emphasizes the identification of variant samples of a category (car, truck, boat, airplane) and stresses what words have in common (all are conveyances); (b) semantic mapping groups the samples into categories (land conveyances, water conveyances, air conveyances); and (c) semantic feature analysis emphasizes the differences between the samples: how is a car different from a truck, a boat, or an airplane? These three instructional strategies help pupils get at relations between concepts by noting commonality, by classifying, and by noting differences. They help pupils to process what is read, to integrate it with prior knowledge, and to expand their personal schema.

Teaching Pupils to Infer Meaning From Context Cues

Another frequently used strategy that enhances pupils' vocabulary growth is teaching them to infer meaning from context cues. This strategy aids growth in vocabulary and word meaning in two principal ways. First, it aids lexical access by helping the pupil to identify the literal and denotative meaning of a word for which the pupil has no meaning: thus, the context helps the pupil to identify the unknown meaning of the word *taciturn* in "Bill was very talkative, but Mary was taciturn." Second, it aids semantic encoding by helping the pupil to encode the one meaning of multiple meanings that fits the context (Perfetti, 1985).

Word study must deal with new words as they are met in context. We suggest that you review the discussion in chapter 5, even though the main concern there is the identification of words in a sentence context. Let us make a few brief observations:

1. Meaning cues consist of picture cues, morphemic cues, semantic cues (both within-text and within-mind cues), and syntactic cues. The major meaning cue is the reader's nonvisual information or schemata.
2. Meaning cues are cues that readers use when they anticipate what word, in terms of meaning, best completes the meaning of a sentence. Getting meaning from context (or from meaning cues) involves using information surrounding a troublesome word to help reveal its meaning (Vacca & Vacca, 1986, 1989).
3. Meaning cues, especially schematic, semantic, and syntactic context cues, facilitate word identification (the concern in chapter 5), but also lexical access and semantic encoding (the concern in chapter 10).
4. In the beginning, the teacher should be careful that context cues are not overemphasized and that the reading exercise does not contain too many strange words. Skill in using the context needs constant refinement. Some pupils rely too much on the context. As noted in chapter 5, context cues are seldom adequate alone. In some instances, context may even lead to confusion or error because the reading material is too difficult, it contains too many difficult words, or the reader is not familiar with the subject matter. When pupils rely too much on context, their reading often

makes sense, but sometimes it is not the meaning intended by the writer. Their reading is often quite inaccurate. They skip over words or add new words, but their most frequent error is that of substituting what they think the story should say.
5. The syntax is often such that only a given type of word (adjective, adverb, verb) is likely to fit into a particular slot in the sentence. The particular meaning which the reader brings to the word is influenced by the sentence context in which the word is placed.
6. Full comprehension occurs only when the meanings of all the words are interrelated.

It is a truism that readers will not become proficient in meaning without repeated encounters with words in context, without learning to identify the meaning that fits the context, and without using their personal schemata to predict the meaning that best fits the context. Inferring meaning from context involves use of the cues in text and of the reader's nonvisual information to develop a representation of the text. The lexical, syntactic, semantic, schematic, referential, inferential, and metacognitive processes all help pupils to learn unknown words (Just & Carpenter, 1987).

However, the research we cited in chapter 5, led us to conclude with Jenkins, Matlock, and Slocum (1989) that even though readers *can* learn word meanings from context, the probability that they actually *will* learn word meaning from context is low. This is particularly so if readers are not given formal instruction in the use of context cues. Jenkins, Stein, and Wysocki (1984) found that, even with extraordinary rich contexts, only a modest increase in knowledge of target words occurs. Stein and Jenkins (1989) found that fourth-grade pupils could supply definitions in context for only 15% of the words. Jenkins, Matlock, and Slocum (1989) conclude from their study of fifth graders that direct instruction in individual or specific meanings increased vocabulary, is superior in developing meaning vocabulary compared to teaching based on deriving meaning from context, and enhances the ability to learn new words independently. Gains in direct teaching were proportional to the amount of practice. The remainder of this section rests on the assumption that direct instruction of meaning and instruction in deriving meanings from context should both be stressed.

To assure that children will be successful in utilizing context cues in developing meaning for words, the teacher should constantly broaden their experiences (thus increasing their store of meaning), make certain that the material being read is not too difficult, help pupils to develop adequate word-recognition skills and sight vocabulary (especially of the core words), encourage wide reading, and provide systematized instruction in the use of context cues. Pupils should be encouraged to say "blank" to themselves when they meet an unknown word, but to continue to read with the expectation that they might be able to figure out the word using the additional context. If context cues do not offer an appropriate word, the pupil should learn to verify his or her prediction by using other word-analysis skills.

Context offers the reader many types of clues to word meaning. It may help to define the word, relate it to previous experiences, associate it with a word whose meaning is known, provide a synonym, and indicate the mood and the tone the writer attaches to the word. Typographical aids, definitions, examples, and synonyms are all helpful precisely because they make it easier to infer meaning from context. The major types of contextual aids or context cues useful in interpreting what one is reading are:

1. *TYPOGRAPHICAL OR FORMAT AIDS*: These are ellipses, quotation marks, parenthesized definitions, dashes, boldface type, capital letters, footnotes, glossary references, size and type of print, boldness of print, and italics. Parentheses, dashes, and commas often signal that the author has provided a synonym, description, definition, or explanation of a preceding word. Quotation marks may be used to highlight an unusual use of a particular word (Ringler and Weber, 1984, p. 121). Italic type may be used to show that a word should be given extra stress (Do you *really* want another piece of chicken?), to show that a word is being named (Use your dictionary to look up the word *encyclopedia*), to identify a word as a foreign word (Dr. Roger's *Chateau* had 10,000 square feet of living space), or to identify the title of a book or play. Capital letters may be used to indicate strong emotion or feeling (As Johnny started down the icy steps, his mom called out, "BE CAREFUL.") or to indicate that the words are printed on a sign (The home was clearly marked by the words, PARKVIEW FARM, printed on a large sign at the entrance).
2. *COMPARISON AND CONTRAST CUES*: A comparison cue is present when the unknown word is compared to one that is known: "Like her sleepy brother, Jenny felt *drowsy*." The contrast cue contains words like *in contrast, conversely, however, but, rather,* etc. These indicate that a contrasting idea is about to be presented: John and Jenny broke the glass, *but* neither one would admit it.
3. *PICTORIAL AND GRAPHIC REPRESENTATIONS OR ILLUSTRATIONS*: These are accompanying pictures, diagrams, charts, graphs, and maps.
4. *SEMANTIC CONTEXT CUES*: Semantic context cues may take the form of definitions, synonyms, inferences contrast or antonyms, summarizing words, and so forth.

*DEFINITION CUE: The unknown word is equated to a more familiar or known word or the descriptive context defines the unknown word. "A *stalactite* is an icicle-like formation hanging from the roof of the cave that is created when limewater drips from the cave ceiling."

*SYNONYM CUE: The unknown word is paired to a familiar synonym or to a closely related word. Mary and Bill are sister and brother; they are *siblings*.

*EXPERIENCE OR INFERENCE CUE: The reader uses past experience to decode the meaning. "It was so *frigid* outside that I quickly buttoned up my coat."

*CONTRAST OR ANTONYM CUE: The unknown word is contrasted with an antonym or phrase that is opposite in meaning. "The water in the pool was not deep. It was *shallow*." Antonyms are words opposite in meaning to other words. Antonym pairs useful in such an antonym practice include (Auckerman and Auckerman, 1981, p. 268): black-white, morning-night, first-last, up-down, rich-poor, same-different, fast-slow, on-off, stop-go, front-back, empty-full, open-shut, soft-hard, girls-boys, east-west, late-early, light-dark, weak-strong, sick-well, summer-winter, good-bad, left-right, more-less, north-south, happy-sad, hot-cold, above-below, near-far, big-little, save-spend, stand-sit, easy-difficult, succeed-fail, asleep-awake, etc.

*SUMMARY CUE: The unknown word summarizes several previously-stated ideas, meanings, or details. "John had not eaten for two days. He had walked for miles. He was sure he had lost ten pounds. By the time he reached home, he was *emaciated*."

*EXAMPLE CUE: The meaning of an unknown word is revealed by providing additional information in the form of appositives, phrases, or clauses: "*Rodents*, such as mice, rats, and beavers, are known for their gnawing and biting." Illustrating a word by a direct description, modifier, or restatement is the same technique as using an example.

*COMMON EXPRESSION: The meaning is ascertained by the use of the word in a familiar language pattern. "See ya later, *alligator*." "Justin was as *quiet as a mouse*."

*MOOD CUE: The tone or mood of the sentence suggests the meaning of the word. "The old cellar was dim and cool and quiet. After being out in the hot sun all day, I had a feeling of *relief* when I went down"(Breen, 1988, p. 108).

5. SYNTACTIC CONTEXT CUES: These include the position of words in the sentence, the general organization of a selection, the use of appositive phrases and clauses, use of non-restrictive clauses, or the use of figures of speech. The order of presentation

is especially significant: *"The boy with the broken arm sat in the chair"* or *"The boy sat in the chair with the broken arm."* Syntactic cues exist in the flow of language and help the reader to anticipate certain words which must come next in a sentence or paragraph. Activities may include some such as the following:

*Jenny gave her cat some milk to____. Only a verb can complete the sentence. The word *to* should cause the pupil to look for a verb.

*John waved frantically to get the policeman to stop. Only an adverb can follow the verb *waved*.

6. *ANALOGY CUES*: The cue to selection of the correct word is the analogy within the sentence. Analogies help the reader to bridge what is known with what is new. Hayes and Tierney (1983) note that analogies activate the background knowledge needed for understanding text. Analogies trigger critical thinking about relationships; they are comparisons of two similar relationships. The relationships expressed by analogies include antonyms, synonyms, part-to-whole, number, process, degree, characteristic, function, origin, homonyms, classification, etc. A simple analogy is (Vacca, 1981, pp. 248-249; Vacca and Vacca, 1986, p. 316): Eating : People :: photosynthesis :____ Translated this means: Eating is to people as photosynthesis is to plants; or people can't survive without eating and plants can't survive without photosynthesis; or both eating and photosynthesis are essential life-sustaining processes. Other sample analogies are:

   *Part to whole: Clutch: transmission :: key : ____ (starter, engine, exhaust).

   *Synonym: Bourgeoisie : middle class :: proletariat : ____ (upper class, lower class, royalty).

   *Antonym: Pinch : handful :: sip : ____ (gulp, taste).

7. *CONTEXT PLUS PHONIC OR MORPHEMIC CUES*: Pupils should be taught to use context cues together with phonic and/or morphemic cues. Exercises such as the following are helpful:

   *Teach children to use sentence meaning plus partial pronunciation to unlock words. In the sentence, "Jimmy fell—the stairs," the context helps to identify any number of meanings that will meet meaning and syntax requirements: e.g., *off, up, against, into, down*, etc.. The child who knows that the missing word begins with the letter *d* (and hence with the /d/ sound) can select the one word that meets meaning, syntax, and sound criteria. Using both

meaning and phonic analysis the pupil can be more certain that the missing word is *down*.

Have children listen to sentences read to them by the teacher, in which the final word is omitted. The pupils may be told that the words should begin with a specific sound such as /b/. Sample sentences are:

   a. I went swimming in a _____ (brook).
   b. In the birdhouse I saw a _____ (bird).

8. *USE THE CLOZE TECHNIQUE*: The cloze technique, developed by Wilson Taylor (1953), is an effective instructional tool, helpful in zeroing in on the use of contextual cues as aids in word recognition and comprehension. The term *Cloze* describes the tendency of the individual to anticipate what will complete an unfinished pattern (Zintz, 1977). In reading, successful anticipation depends on the ability of the readers to use the context to identify the word that will complete a passage. It is assumed that the better the readers are at understanding the passage, the more likely it is that they will be correct in guessing the missing word. Cloze passages usually have every fifth word deleted: the pupil is expected to fill in the missing word. A low score indicates that the pupil cannot utilize context cues and the redundancy of the language to gain help in reading with meaning.

SEMANTIC ENCODING

To this point our focus has been on lexical access. Semantic encoding presents slightly different problems. Even though we have generally indicated the comparability of lexical access and semantic encoding, semantic encoding, the ability to select the contextually appropriate meaning, is operable only when the word has multiple meanings and the reader uses the context to select the one meaning from many that fits that context. It is different from lexical access. It is an instance of lexical ambiguity. The ability to use semantic encoding involves knowing what the referent of an unknown word is in a specifically constrained context. It is a key skill in reading; it is an ability that is part of the definition of reading ability and that contributes directly to reading comprehension scores (Perfetti, 1985). Semantic encoding depends upon: (a) the availability of the word's meanings in memory or in the mental lexicon, (b) the activation of the reader's schemata; (c) the ability to use the semantic and syntactic cues in text (i.e., the typographical or format cues, structure cues, pictorial and graphic cues, syntactic context cues, etc.), (d) the ability to use the morphemic cues; and (e) inferencing.

Words, even at the word-identification and lexical-access level, can be activated in memory from context, and the activation of a word characteristically spreads to semantically related words. This means that a given word's activation might well occur as a result of context prior to any information whatsoever from the word itself (Perfetti, 1985). The spreading semantic activation simply means that the identification of words is facilitated by context. Chapter 5 explained the role of the meaning cues in word identification. Words obviously can be accessed in memory through semantic processes as well as on the basis of featural information, and indeed, semantic activation can compensate for insufficient letter and feature activation.

Context also can help the reader to determine the specific meaning of multiple meanings of a word; it helps the reader to identify the meaning intended. Context effects are particularly operative in semantic encoding, or when the reader has to identify the one meaning of multiple meanings that fits the context. Artley (1975) notes that it is the context, in which the word is embedded, that gives it its unique flavor. Frequently, the context is such that the reader can readily identify the target word and its meaning (e.g., Mary can *run* like a deer). However, the reader often finds himself in the situation where he can identify and name the word, but cannot interpret the meaning (e.g., The bankruptcy caused a *run* on the bank). *Run* happens to be a word that may have 109 meanings, and in the sentence given it obviously means something other than "to move swiftly." If the phrase "run on the bank" appears in a larger context (such as; "The rumor of bankruptcy of the Merchants State Bank caused a run on the bank. Housewives, farmers, and even businessmen were rushing in and out of the bank withdrawing their money"), the pupil's experience with banks may help the pupil ascertain the meaning of the word *run* in this specific context.

We are dealing here with the validity of the reader's perceptions, of his prediction, and of his comprehension. Clearly, the validity of perception is its predictive value as a guide for action (Herrick, 1956). The meaning of "to move swiftly" that may be aroused by the word "run" may be adequate in one response situation; in another situation, such a response to the word would not be validated in action. The word might then more appropriately suggest the concept "people withdrawing their money." Readers call upon their personal schema and generally assume that the meaning that was most successful in the past is more likely to be correct now. They interpret the sensory data on the basis of their past experience. When they find their prediction to be in error, they must change their interpretation, even though the retinal image has not changed. When one has a great deal of relevant and consistent experience to relate to stimulus patterns, the probability of the success of one's prediction as a guide to action is high. When experience is limited or inconsistent, the reverse holds true.

Rayner and Pollatsek (1989) suggest that if the prior context is strong and unambiguous, only one meaning is assessed. However, if this is not the case, additional meanings of the lexically ambiguous word are automatically assessed. Some are quickly inhibited, either by the much more dominant (i.e., most frequently encountered) meaning or by a prior context. If none of the alternate meanings are inhibited, than all meanings presumably are consciously processed and put into short-term memory to await disambiguation.

Perfetti (1985) suggests that when the pupil encounters a word with multiple meanings in context, all known meanings are activated at least briefly in memory, but the contextually appropriate meaning will win out. The more frequent meaning of the word tends to receive the initial and the longer activation. Context biases one meaning more heavily than another. It receives greater activation and is selected for encoding. Semantic encoding is thus determined by the context. Rayner and Pollatsek (1989) note that the selection of the appropriate meaning of the lexically ambiguous words appears to occur only after the meanings of all (or at least most) have been assessed. They make the additional observations that:

1. When the prior context is weak or nonexistent, that is, when the context does not reduce ambiguity, gaze durations on the ambiguous word are longer.
2. The two main processes appear to be dominance (i.e., frequency with which the word is encountered) and prior context.
3. The dominant word at times inhibits the contextually appropriate meaning. If it does not make sense, a second access of the lexical item is required.

Good readers have larger vocabularies than poor readers, are more skillful in inferring the meaning of unknown words, and are more proficient in acquiring the subtle distinctions that are associated with particular contexts. Thus sometimes the words *under* and *beneath* can be interchanged, but they cannot be in the following examples: "It was *under* the McKinley administration. . . ." and "He considered it *beneath* him to sweep the floor" (Just & Carpenter, 1987, pp. 110–111).

Multiple meanings for words are a continuous problem for the reader and often put comprehension at risk. The word polysemy is used to refer to the different meanings and uses of words, and the term "polysemous words" refers to words with multiple meanings. As already noted, the word *run*, for example, according to the *American College Dictionary*, has 109 distinct meanings; the word *take* has 76 meanings; and the word *round* has 83 different meanings. *Run* can mean to move swiftly, to go back and forth (The boat runs between Georgia and New York), to run in an election, to win a race (The horse ran first), to run into debt, to run (trace) a story back to its source, to run (smuggle) contraband, and to run a store.

ADDITIONAL STRATEGIES FOR DEVELOPING WORD MEANING

To this point we have noted that vocabulary development can be enhanced by concept-development activities, by teaching words in semantically and topically related sets, and by teaching pupils to infer meaning from context cues, including the use of the cloze technique. We also discussed the special problem presented to reader by words with multiple meanings. Another effective classroom strategy is to teach pupils to use morphemic elements as cues to meaning.

Teaching Pupils to Use Morphemic Units as Cues to Meaning

Studying a word's structure and the meaning of its variant parts is a useful strategy in the development of meanings for words. Morphemes are the meaning units of words and, of course, they also affect the word's structure. Sternberg et al. (1983) refer to semantic and syntactic elements within and among sentences as external cues and to the morphological elements within words, such as prefixes and suffixes, as internal cues to meaning. Words take on new meaning and structure because they carry inflectional endings (cats, cat's, hits, bigger, biggest, landed), have undergone inflectional changes (loaves), are compound words, are contracted words (can't), change their accent (sub/ject' or sub'/ject), are affixed words, or are multiple syllable words.

You may want to refer back to chapter 9, where morphemes were discussed more fully.

Teaching the Meaning of Homonyms:

Pupils are also aided in the study of vocabulary by a study of the homonyms. Homonyms or homophones are words that sound alike but have different spellings and meanings: for example, ate-eight, cell-sell, two-to-too. They frequently lead to recognition and meaning difficulties. To illustrate their difference, the teacher must use them in various contexts.

The term homophone is sometimes restricted to words that sound alike, but that are spelled differently and that have different meanings (red, read). The term homonym, is also used for words that are pronounced the same and have different meanings, but that are also spelled the same: bat (baseball bat) and bat (animal). The term homograph may also be used for such words. Homograph is likewise used to identify words that are spelled the same but have different pronunciations and different meanings: lead (dense metal) and lead (verb). Such words are also termed heteronyms (Rubin, 1982).

Labov (1966) notes that dialect can increase the number of homonyms in the spoken language, leading to confusion in interpretation of the written language and the need to put extraordinary reliance on context. The omission of the /r/ in *guard* makes homonyms of *guard* and *god*; omission of the /l/ in *toll* makes homonyms of *toll* and *toe*. Some common homonyms are (see Fry et al., 1985):

ate-eight	four-for	red-read
be-bee	here-hear	see-sea
blue-blew	hour-our	sun-son
cent-sent-scent	no-know	to-too-two

Teaching Pupils to Use and Interpret High-Imagery Words

Pupils are also aided in the apprehension of meaning when they are taught to use and interpret high imagery words (e.g., glistening, billowing, swirling) and to analyze the sense appeal of words (Paivio, 1983; Sheikh, 1983). Exercises such as the following develop this ability:

1. The bumpy highway caused the car to *creak* and *rattle*, but we went merrily on our way.
   Creak appeals to the sense(s) of _____ (touch, sight, sound, taste, smell).
   Rattle appeals to the sense(s) of _____ (touch, sight, sound, taste, smell).
2. Icicles, hanging from the roof of our battered cabin, *dripped* and *peppered* the snow beneath *with holes* where melted water fell.
   The pupil is required to indicate which senses the words *dripped, peppered with holes*, and *melted* appeal to.

Sample words useful in teaching the difference in sense appeal of words are:

Touch	*Sight*	*Sound*	*Taste*	*Smell*
frozen	dark	buzzing	bitter	burning
hot	pale	creaking	peppery	fresh
rough	snowy	hissing	salty	smoking
sandy	trembling	whining	sweet	stuffy

Wolpert (1972) found that high-imagery words are learned significantly more easily than low-imagery words, and that imagery value had a substantially greater effect on learning than did word length or shape. Hargis and Gickling (1978) found that high-imagery words are more readily learned as sight words and remain in memory storage longer.

Teaching Special Vocabularies

Knowledge of special vocabularies is particularly important in the content areas. Special vocabularies are of three types (Dillner & Olson, 1977; Vacca, 1981): (a) Special vocabularies or words that are common to all content areas but that take on a special meaning in a given content area (e.g., root); (b) technical vocabularies or words that are peculiar to a given content area (e.g., polygon); and (c) symbols that are used in a given content area (e.g., NATO, UNESCO).

Burmeister (1983) notes that the word *root* may mean root of the word (Language Arts), square root (Arithmetic), the root of the plant (Science), or the root of the matter (Social Studies). Every subject matter field has its own unique language to represent its important concepts.

Teaching the Etymology of Words

Pupils are also helped to expand their word meanings through the study of the origin of words and how words change. The following exercises are helpful:

1. Study and teach the surnames of children in the class. For example, names like Baker, Butler, Binder, Bishop, Cook, Brewer, Dechant, and Dreher identify occupations. Other surnames represent objects, for example, Ball and Bell. Some surnames identify certain characteristics of an object or person: thus, Belle, Breit, Fair, and Good. Some identify colors: Black, Braun, Brown, Gray, Green, Roth, Schwartz, and White, and some are animal names: Beaver, Bee, Bird, Crow, and Ochs.
2. Teach the foreign origin of words. The Dutch, the French, the Germans, and the Italians have given us many words. The following are just a few: (Italian) soprano, piccolo, piano, contralto; (French) carburetor, chauffeur, coupe, beau, chateau, trousseau, chamois, machine, boudoir, bouquet, barrage, croquet, sachet, ballet, marionette, quiche, omelet, mayonnaise, and cologne; and (German) kindergarten, waltz, sauerkraut, and wiener. Words of Latin and Greek origin are so numerous that a list is not particularly helpful. Carafe, algebra, candy, sugar, and

coffee are Arabic in origin; schlemiel, schlep, and shtick are Yiddish; macho, potato, maize, llama, and patio are Spanish; moccasin, toboggan, raccoon, chipmunk, tepee, and yucca are American Indian; kayak and igloo are Eskimo in origin; and sputnik and babushka are Russian.
3. Teach new words in the language. Sample words are: amtrac, audiphile, bazooka, chopper-copper, cloverleaf, deicer, fat cat, freebies, greenroom, bottom line, ballpark figure, cheap shot, etc.
4. Teach words that result from a blending of two other words: smog (smoke + fog); brunch (breakfast + lunch); motel (motor + hotel); moped (motor + pedal); motorcross (motor + cross country); motorcade (motor and cavalcade); and twirl (twist and whirl).
5. Teach common phrases that have been borrowed from other languages: for examples, a la mode, a prior, a posteriori, ad infinitum, ad volorem, alma mater, coup d'etat, e pluribus unum, esprit de corps, ex cathedra, ex officio, ex post facto, in loco parentis, in memoriam, ipso facto, laissez-faire, modus operandi, non sequitur, par excellence, per diem, pro rata, sine quo non, status quo, tabula rasa, tempus fugit, vice versa, viv-a-vis, etc. (Zintz & Maggart, 1984).
6. Have pupils study acronyms, words formed from the first letter or letters of words. Examples are:

CORE	SCUBA	NATO	VIP
DDT	RADAR	UFO	RSVP
EEG	UNESCO	ZIP	COD
ERA	IOU	POW	MIA
EKG	NASA	TLC	ESP
IQ	AWOL	KKK	MPH
LSD	TGIF	UNICEF	NOW
NASA	NAACP	SWAT	
ZIP	CARE	TV	
ROTC	COBOL	WAC	

Teaching Space, Numerical, and Time Concepts

In our language there are many words or concepts that do not have clear and definite reference points. Among these are space concepts and some quantitative and time concepts. Teaching of word meaning should focus more attention on such words.

Space words or concepts include: bottom, under, beside, in front, toward-away, beyond, up-down, round, flat, straight, join, moving-still, deep-shallow, top, through, away from, next to, inside, middle, farthest, over, around, between, nearest, corner, behind, side, under, below, forward, right, above, separated, left, in order. Quantitative words or concepts to be taught include big-small, tall-short, wide, fat-narrow, thin, some, not many, few, widest, most, whole, second, several, almost, half, as many, not first or last, medium-sized, zero, every, pair, equal, third, least. Time words or concepts that need to be taught include follow, fast-slow, now, early-late, past, start, begin-stop-finish, after, beginning, never, always. The pupil must also learn such concept words as different, other, alike, matches, skip, open-closed, soft-hard, easy-hard, dark-light, loud, light-heavy, with-without.

A suggested sequence for teaching these basic concepts is:

1. Present the concept through the use of concrete materials and use it in several concrete situations.
2. Specifically label the concept.
3. Illustrate the concept in a photo, picture, or drawing. Using the word in a phrase with an accompanying picture is especially helpful.
4. Use the concept in a sentence.
5. Show that an object can, for example, be both far and near, dependent upon the referent object.
6. Focus attention on opposites: left-right, top-bottom.
7. Focus on degree: far, farther, farthest.

Teaching the Interpretation of Figurative and Idiomatic Expressions

Figurative uses of language are a potential source of comprehension difficulty across the total spectrum of language (Ortony, 1984): at the word level, understanding of a metaphor; at the phrase level, understanding of clichés and idiomatic expressions; at the sentence level, understanding of a proverb; and at the total-text level, understanding of a fable or allegory. Numerous idiomatic expressions cause meaning problems: for example, Jack-of-all-trades, devil-may-care attitude, penny-wise and pound-foolish, to be down and out, going to the root of the matter, be in hot water, don't cry over spilt milk, cost a pretty penny, burn the candle at both ends, blow off steam, to play with fire, get down to brass tacks, have an ax to grind, cook someone's goose, talk through one's hat, sit on the fence, put through the mill. Developing figurative-meaning skills consists of (a) familiarizing the pupil with the figures of speech (allegory, onomatopoeia, metaphor, personification, simile, metonymy, antithesis, epigram, irony, apostrophe, hyperbole, euphemism, synecdoche), and (b) activities to apply this understanding in reading.

The major figures of speech are:

Figures of Resemblance

An *allegory* is a prolonged metaphor—a story that is in total a comparison (as in *The Pilgrim's Process* or in *The Grasshopper and the Ant*.) *Onomatopoeia* is the use of words whose sounds suggest the meaning (buzz, bowwow, splash, crackle, "the murmurous haunt of flies"). A *metaphor* is an analogy or expression of comparison which, unlike the simile, does not use *as* or *like* ("You're a clumsy ox"). It is either a directly stated or an implied comparison. Other examples are: Mary is a walking encyclopedia; she's a regular adding machine; Jenny is a fountain of kindness. *Personification* is the endowment of an inanimate object or abstract idea with personal attributes ("The leaves danced in the wind"; "The flames ate hungrily at the wooden foundation"). A *simile* compares two object or actions and usually joins then with *as* or *like* as light as a feather, as strong as an ox, as busy as a bee, as happy as a lark, as sly as a fox, as hungry as a bear, as meek as a lamb, drank like a fish, waddled like a duck, worked like a horse, car goes like the wind). *Metonymy* is the use of one word for another, the first word being suggestive of the other ("The woman keeps a good table"; "The pen (power of literature) is mightier than the sword (force)"; "The White House announced a new arms control policy"). *Allusion* is an indirect reference to a person, whether real or mythical, a place, or thing (He is a modern David).

Figures of Contrast or Satire

Antithesis is a strong contrasting of ideas ("Man proposes, God disposes"; "Give me liberty or give me death"). An *epigram* is a short, terse, satirical, or witty statement. In *irony,* the implied evaluation is the opposite of that stated. It is a subtle sarcasm (Thanks for being so prompt). *Apostrophe* is the addressing of the dead as living, or the absent as present ("Arise dead sons of the land and sweep the enemy from our shore"). *Oxymoron* is a seeming self-contradiction; two incongruous words are used together: hot bed of apathy; benign neglect; cruel kindness.

Figures of Exaggeration

Hyperbole is an exaggeration ("His eyes opened wide as saucers"; "The story is as old as time"). *Euphemism* is the substitution of an inoffensive expression for one that may be considered unpleasant (mortician for undertaker; underachiever for disabled reader; plump for fat). *Synecdoche* is the use of the part for the whole ("Five hundred hands worked on the job,"; "My set of wheels takes me where I want to go").

Sample activities that help pupils to read words used in a figurative sense include:

1. Have pupil define the underlined words in sentences such as:
   a. I was *tickled to death*.
   b. Garden flowers *laughed* merrily.
   c. The squirrel *froze* in its tracks.
2. Illustrate figurative language with pictures (Groesbeck, 1961). Have pupils look at the illustrations and select the one that best describes the meaning of the sentence.

1. Boats were dancing up and down on the waves.

3. Have children illustrate the literal and figurative meaning of phrases and sentences such as:
   a. a fish bowl
   b. a sleeping bag
   c. I bought two seats for the play.
   d. We zipped up our cottage and headed for home.
4. Have the pupil identify the figure of speech used and have them write out the meaning of sentences containing various figures of speech.
   a. I laughed until I thought I would die. (Hyperbole)
   b. Her face turned as red as a beet. (Simile)
   c. The summer months sure fly by. (Personification)
   d. "Zzzing! Yowww!" howled the saw. (Onomatopoeia and Personification)

If the pupil is to be successful in interpreting metaphors and similies, the pupil must identify the critical attribute that is shared by two items (Readence et al., 1983). For illustration, in the metaphor "The cat walks across our furniture like a cheetah," it is the fact that both cats and cheetahs do not have retractible claws and thus damage furniture that explains the metaphor. The metaphor, "The smoke from the forest was pea soup," is interpretable only if the reader knows that pea soup is thick. The reader must have a schema for each of the items that are being compared.

Teaching the Use of the Dictionary as a Guide to Meaning

The meaning of some words may best be learned by looking the word up in the dictionary. Picture dictionaries can be used as early as the primer level of first grade and simple glossaries can be introduced at the third-grade level. Commercial dictionaries can be introduced at the fourth-grade level.

SUMMARY

Chapter 10 has dealt with the association of meaning with individual words. In Chapter 7 the development of word meanings was identified as an important phase of Step 1 of the Directed Reading Activity and in the expansion of the pupil's schema. Chapter 10 identifies what needs to be taught, how teaching of word meaning is best done, and what strategies are most effective. It suggests that the reader cannot comprehend without knowing the meaning of and for words, but also notes that this does not assure comprehension. Word meaning or lexical access is a prerequisite for reading comprehension, but in and of itself it is insufficient to effect comprehension of total discourse. The reader may well know individual word meanings, but may not be able to read phrases, sentences, and paragraphs.

Chapter 11
Assembly and Integration of Propositions and Text Modeling: Strategies for the Development of Meaning for Units of Increasing Size: Phrases, Sentences, Paragraphs, and Total Text

    I. Introduction
   II. Assembly and Integration of Propositions
       A. Assembly of Propositions
       B. Chunking
       C. Microselection
       D. Integration of Propositions
  III. Phrase Reading
       A. Strategies for Developing Phrase Reading
          1. Objectives
          2. Techniques
  IV. Sentence Reading
       A. What the Pupil Needs to Know and What the Teacher Needs to Teach
       B. Reading the Syntactic Structure
       C. Reading the Punctuation
       D. Comprehending Anaphora and Ellipses
   V. Text Modeling Processes
       A. Integration of Propositions: Local Coherence or Cohesion
       B. Understanding the Text's Global Coherence or Organization
  VI. Paragraph and Total-Text Reading
       A. Subskills of Paragraph Comprehension
       B. Reading for the Main Idea
       C. Reading for Details: Simple Listing, Sequence, and Directions
       D. Comprehending Paragraph Organization
       E. Cues Signaling Paragraph and Whole-Text Organization
 VII. Summary

CHAPTER 11

Assembly and Integration of Propositions and Text Modeling: Strategies for the Development of Meaning for Units of Increasing Size: Phrases, Sentences, Paragraphs, and Total Text

The previous chapter's concern was lexical access and semantic encoding, or the association of meaning with a single word, which is the most elemental form of comprehension. This chapter goes beyond this, exploring the problems of reading when the reader has to grasp the meaning of a larger unitary idea, to organize meaning into thought units, and to comprehend units of increasing size, namely such higher-order structures as phrases, clauses, sentences, paragraphs, and total text. Smith and Dechant (1961; Dechant & Smith, 1977) note that the good reader is not limited to word-by-word reading. The good reader can reason with words, with verbal concepts, and with sentences (Just & Carpenter, 1987).

Irwin (1986a) rightly observes that for full comprehension the pupil must understand the individual words, the meaning of the single sentence, how one sentence relates to another, and how the whole text fits together. The reader must chunk words into meaningful phrases and must select from those phrases the ideas that are to be remembered; must understand and selectively recall ideas in individual sentences; must infer relationships between phrases and sentences; and must connect the individual ideas into a coherent whole by inferring relationships among individual sentences and by summarizing the passage.

Possession of word meaning, or the ability to access semantic information, without which readers cannot label their own schemata, does not by itself make a reader. The meaning of a sentence is not obtained by piling up, as it were, the meanings of individual words. Comprehension is not simply a process of recoding and decoding the individual words, and then stringing them together like beads, to come up with the full meaning of a sentence.

Reading requires reasoning with words and an interpretation of the interrelationships between words. Poor readers who have become word readers have fallen into the error of not "reading" the phrase or sentence units that give meaning to the word. The sentence circumscribes the word, giving it the distinct meaning intended by the speaker or writer. The sentence is the meaning-bearing language pattern, and disabled readers often fail to achieve total comprehension because they do not read language structures as wholes. They do not realize that there are aspects of meaning which are not in the individual written word.

ASSEMBLY AND INTEGRATION OF PROPOSITIONS

The third subset (the first two are lexical access and semantic encoding) of comprehension is the assembly and integration of propositions. A text is nothing more than an ordered sequence of propositions, and comprehension is nothing more than relating ideas encoded in propositions. Assembly and integration of propositions are responsible for phrase and sentence comprehension and involve four steps:

1. Assembly of propositions or of the individual idea units or meaning units in a phrase or sentence.
2. Chunking or the grouping of words into meaningful phrases, syntactic units, or thought units.
3. Microselection or the identification of idea units that need to be remembered. Kintsch and Van Dijk (1978) observe that good readers select what is important in each sentence and retain only that information in memory.
4. Integration of propositions or the linking of successively occurring propositions or idea units within and across sentences into a cohesive whole.

We examine these four aspects here, because each of them is involved in phrase, sentence, paragraph, and total-text reading.

Assembly of Propositions

A proposition is the meaning information that the reader assembles from a phrase or a sentence. Propositions are the abstract, elementary meaning or idea units that comprise the meaning of a sentence (Perfetti, 1985). They are symbolic structures that include a predicate and one or more arguments (Just & Carpenter, 1987). They are the smallest unit of knowledge that can be true or false: thus "John is" is a proposition. The sentence, "Bernard carved a melon," represents three propositions: the *action* is carving; the *agent* is Bernard; and the *object* is the melon which is being carved (Just & Carpenter, 1987; Woolfolk, 1990). Just and Carpenter note that by conjoining propositions and embedding them, one inside another, it is possible to construct representations of entire text. The point of emphasis here is that information is internally represented in a propositional format. The use of the concept of proposition to represent the content of a text was developed by Kintsch (1977) and van Dijk (Kintsch & Van Dijk, 1978). They conceptualized that the meaning of total text can be represented as an interconnected structure of propositions.

Chunking

Irwin (1986a) suggests that the reader's initial processing of a sentence involves the grouping of words into meaningful phrases and terms it chunking. Chunking involves an understanding of syntax and its use in written language. Chunking is the assembly of words into meaningful syntactical (and semantic) units (Irwin, 1986a). Harris and Sipay (1985) observe that grouping words into thought units or phrases facilitates comprehension by placing less strain on the reader's information-processing capacity.

Syntax helps a reader decode a linear string of words into a more complex, interrelated structure. The syntactic organization holds the words of a sentence together in the working memory in their appropriate groupings while the meaning of the sentence is being processed (Just & Carpenter, 1987). Syntactic analysis identifies the grammatical relations among the constituents of a sentence. Thus, the constituents of and the relations between the constituents of the sentence, "The delighted teacher uncorked the champagne," may be represented as (Just & Carpenter, 1987, p. 132):

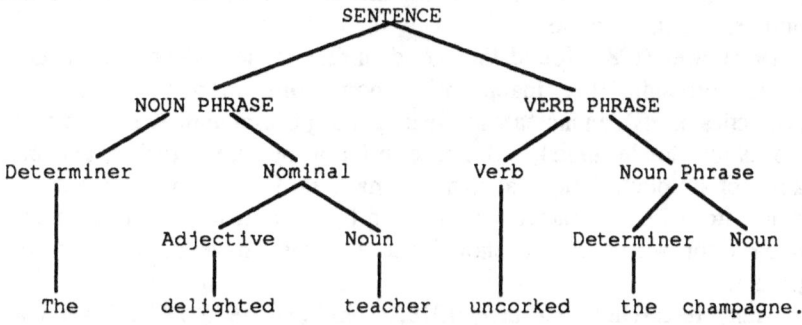

Microselection

Another phase of the assembly and integration of propositions is microselection (Irwin, 1986a). Good readers identify the important idea units or propositions that need to be committed to memory. Microselection is analogous to identifying the main idea in a sentence. Paraphrasing activities aid the pupil in microselection.

Integration of Propositions

Obviously the successively occurring propositions in phrases and sentences must be related or linked to each other. They must be "integrated." This is a distinct process whose discussion we will defer until we examine text modeling later in the chapter.

PHRASE READING

Phrase reading involves each of the comprehension processes identified in this and the previous chapter. It involves lexical access, semantic encoding, assembly of propositions, chunking, microselection, and integration of propositions. Good readers are able to organize what they have read into meaningful phrase and even sentence units. Good comprehenders know the boundaries between meaningful phrases (Irwin, 1986a); they can organize the sentences into grammatical and semantic units; they chunk the phrase units appropriately; they react to words and their modifiers or to the phrase or clause as a unit; they read in thought units; they understand the cues that signal noun, verb, and prepositional phrases; and they are proficient in seeing meaningful relationships among the words that they read. Thus, in the sentence, "The red balloon slowly disappeared into the blue sky," the word slowly is chunked with disappeared (Irwin, 1986a). To do this type of processing the reader must know the meaning of words and have a basic understanding of syntax.

Dowhower (1987) found that good phrase readers show a decrease in pausal intrusions (i.e., inappropriate hesitations within words or within syntactical units), an increase in the length of phrasal units (i.e., they chunk words into longer units), a decrease in inappropriate phrasing, and more appropriate pitch changes at terminal markers. Poor readers, on the other hand, are often characterized by word-by-word reading. Their memory images for words are so short-lived that they have difficulty reading phrases.

Many researchers (Cromer, 1970; Golinkoff, 1975–1976; Mason and Kendall, 1978; Stevens, 1981) look upon phrases as the natural unit of reading. Linguists today emphasize phrase-structure grammars rather than the transformational grammar of Chomsky. In phrase-structure grammars, the phrase structure is a metaphor used to represent the basic information in the reader's head when the syntax of a sentence has been comprehended. However, national educational surveys indicate that pupils (9, 13, and 17 year's of age) have more difficulty identifying the meaning of a specific word group than with identifying the overall meaning of a passage (National Assessment of Educational Progress, 1973, 1975, 1982, 1984, 1985, 1986.)

Phrase reading should be stressed by the end of first grade. If children cannot phrase properly, if emphasis on words is wrong, or if the pitch and intonation are improper, the child will probably not read with full meaning the sentence or total-language structure, and comprehension is likely to suffer. Phrase reading attempts to get the pupil away from word-by-word reading. The latter usually results from slowness and inaccuracy in word recognition. Readers who have word-identification difficulties will have difficulty in chunking (Irwin, 1986a) Thus, the materials used to develop phrase-reading ability should present few or no difficulties in word recognition, sight vocabulary, or word meaning for the learner and should be written on the pupil's independent reading level. Cromer (1970) found that the performance of readers who are poor in comprehension but who had adequate word recognition skills was significantly increased by the grouping of words within a sentence into separate phrase units, whereas this imposed visual-spatial change did not significantly improve the comprehension of readers who still lacked the recoding skills necessary to translate the written word into a verbal component.

Weiss (1983) found that dividing a reading text into phrases or marking phrase boundaries in text with penciled slash or vertical lines raised fourth-and seventh-grade pupils' comprehension about one level and aided fluency in reading. Amble (1967) found that children's phrase-reading ability can be improved and that the improvement was lasting. O'Shea and Sindelar (1983) found that slow but accurate readers improved by segmenting text into phrases; K. Stevens (1981) had similar results with high-school sophomores. Irwin (1986a) suggests that phrase reading or chunking fluency develops best when pupils are given adequate opportunities to practice reading fluently.

Strategies for Developing Phrase Reading

Objectives

Pupils should be taught to read in thought units, to identify and comprehend phrases within sentence units, to pay attention to oral cues such as pitch and pauses and in silent reading to punctuation and pauses, to read and comprehend idiomatic expressions and proverbs, and to develop flexibility in reading.

Techniques

1. Develop the pupil's word-identification skills and sight vocabulary; develop the pupil's memory images for words.
2. Model phrase reading or thought-unit reading for children by reading orally to them, stressing individual phrase units.
3. Teach pupils to attend to oral cues to phrasing such as pitch, intonation, inflections, and pauses.
4. Engage pupils in dramatic reading of a play or poem.
5. Teach pupils to use punctuation as cues to phrasing.
6. Use tachistoscopic phrase activities.
7. Use choral reading.
8. Have pupils read in unison with the teacher.
9. Enlarge the pupil's eye-voice span and the recognition span.
10. Have pupils group scrambled words into appropriate phrases.
11. Have pupils rearrange scrambled phrases into correct sentence order.
12. Have pupils listen to tape recordings of reading properly phrased.
13. Use the imitative method, the neurological impress method, the repeated readings method, the simultaneous listening and reading method, and the paired reading method to develop fluency in reading.
14. Have pupils segment sentences into phrases or thought units.
15. Have pupils identify phrases in sentences by inserting slash marks between phrasal units in sentences (The mailman/left us/a most welcome package/ this morning) or by coloring, underlining, or encircling the phrase units of a sentence.
16. Have pupils match simple phrases (e.g., a big meal) and especially idiomatic phrases and proverbs (e.g., to blow one's stack) with a single word or with a more easily understood phrase:
    - ____ a. big meal
    - ____ b. away from everybody
    - ____ c. to cut down
    - ____ d. to blow one's stack
    - 1. chop
    - 2. feast
    - 3. alone
    - 4. angry

The reader should refer back to the section "Teaching the Interpretation of Figurative and Idiomatic Expressions" in chapter 10 for an extensive list of idiomatic expressions and for additional activities to develop phrase reading.

SENTENCE READING

Rayner and Pollatsek (1989) point out that sentences can be understood on many levels: by their syntax or by their subunits such as phrases; by understanding the functions of the components of a sentence: the agent, the action, the recipient of the action; or by understanding what the writer intended to convey. We have already described these functions. Our focus here is on reading units larger than single words or phrases; it is on the reading of sentences. Huey (1912) wrote that language begins with the sentence. The sentence is the basic meaning-bearing pattern. Comprehension of printed materials requires the perception of complete language structures such as the sentence. To process sentences readers must know the meaning of word, have a basic understanding of syntax, use redundancy cues to work out the meaning of a sentence, and heed both semantic and syntactic signals. Difficulties in comprehending sentences thus may be semantic or syntactic in nature. Many of the semantic difficulties were identified in chapter 10. The syntactic difficulties are of major concern here. Caramazza and Berndt (1978) observe that lexical meanings are relatively fixed representations, but sentence meanings (what some term semantic meanings) are novel, complex representations, constructed by combining the meanings of single lexical items into a coherent whole.

What the Pupil Needs to Learn and What the Teacher Needs to Teach

This section of the chapter summarizes the subskills that are crucial to the understanding of sentences. It identifies also the coherent linkages that connect parts of a sentence and one sentence with another. It summarizes what needs to be taught so as to help the pupil to develop sentence comprehension. The teacher needs to:

1. Expand the pupil's vocabulary and word-meaning skills and develop the ability to integrate individual word meanings within sentences.
2. Teach the pupil to read in phrase units and to comprehend phrase units.
3. Develop the pupil's sentence sense: sentence sense is the ability to process language and syntactic structures. Disabled readers often lack the syntactic skills or the sentence sense required for good comprehension. Inability to use sentence language in conversation is a major cause of reading disability. (Lefevre, 1964).
4. Have pupils identify and understand basic sentence patterns (e.g., NV, NVN, NVNN, NLadv, NLVN, NLVadj., etc.).

5. Familiarize students with the roles of function words, markers, or so-called empty words. They are cues to written language patterns and are frequently identified as noun markers ("my house," any, this, a , the, some, etc.), verb markers ("am coming," are, is, was, have, do, will, shall, can, may, ought, etc.), clause markers (now, like, until, if, although, since, before, however, etc.), negatives (no, not, never, nor, none, etc.), qualifiers (very, too, much), and question markers (when, where, who, which, why, how, what, etc.) (Heilman, Blair, and Rupley, 1986).
6. Have pupils identify the who, what, when, where, and how of a sentence and to recognize and use the information signals indicating where something is done (e.g., over, in, on, in front of, etc.), when something is done (e.g., before, after, later, while, now, etc.), and how something is done (e.g., carefully) (Hittelman, 1988).
7. Help pupils identify whether the sentence tells or asks, whether it is a declarative sentence, or whether it is a question or interrogative sentence.
8. Have pupils identify, comprehend, and remember the main idea or the main idea units of a sentence. This involves, as we noted earlier, microselection or the identification of the important points to remember.
9. Teach pupils that in reading it often is the punctuation, especially the period, question mark, comma, colon, dash, quotation marks, and apostrophe, that is the cue to syntactical variations and ultimately to variations in meaning. Readers must learn to use the writer's punctuation as a cue to meaning.
10. Help pupils to use the inter-word syntactical cues such as word order as cues to sentence meaning (e.g., "The boy with the broken arm sat in the chair" versus "The boy sat in the chair with the broken arm)".
11. Help pupils identify the referents for anaphora and ellipses.
12. Teach pupils the use of morphological inflections in words or of the intra- word cues signaling tense (s, ing, ed), number (s, es, en), possession ('s, s'), gender (ess), comparative (er), superlative (est), and of prefixes, suffixes, contractions, accents, etc., as cues to meaning.
13. Develop the awareness that the suprasegmentals of stress, changes of pitch and intonation, juncture, and the rhythms of the sentence convey phonemic differences and change meanings; and that they are implicitly encoded in the sentence that the pupil reads and that these intra-sentence cues or grammatical inflections are designed to help the pupil to phrase properly, to improve the grasp of

meaning, and to improve the communication between writer and reader. Poor readers do not apprehend the relationships between the spoken and written language patterns. They cannot translate the printed text with its carefully chosen word order and function words into the intonation pattern of the writer. As a result, when they read aloud they read with an improper pitch and intonation, with resultant diminished grasp of meaning and diminished communication of meaning between writer and reader. Until the reader translates correctly the printed text into the intonation pattern of the writer, he may not be getting the meaning intended (Dechant, 1964). It is important that the reader read the sentence the way the writer would have read it (i.e., with proper stress, intonation, juncture, and rhythm).

14. Develop the awareness of how sentences can be joined or connected (e.g., and, moreover, furthermore, in addition, too, also) and how they can be separated (e.g., but, neither-nor, etc.). The reader must learn how to link and integrate propositions or idea units in long-term memory. This is a process of linking one proposition with another within a sentence and of one sentence with another, thereby creating textual unity. Sentences need to be understood in the light of previous and subsequent sentences.

15. Develop an understanding of the surface and deep structure of language. Sentences have a surface structure (i.e., what is on the printed page) and a deep structure (i.e., what the sentence means). Two sentences may have similar surface structures but different meanings or the surface structures may be different, but the meanings are the same. Thus, the two sentences, "Jim gave Pam a book" or "Pam was given a book by Jim," are different in surface structure but similar in meaning. In other instances the surface structures are similar, but the meanings or deep structure are said to require a transformation. The closer the match between the surface and deep structures the easier the sentence is to understand (McNeil, 1987).

16. Develop sensitivity to common transformations of basic or kernel sentences such as from the declarative to the passive (The boy was given a watch), in which the object of an action is put in the syntactic subject position, from statements of fact to negative sentences, or from declarative sentences to imperative sentences or questions. Rayner and Pollatsek (1989) point out that negative sentences are harder to process than are positive sentences.

17. Teach pupils that sentences may begin with "It" or "There" (There are six girls in the classroom); that sentences may have an unexpected sentence order (He sat after he stood); that sentences

may have information deleted (John saw Mary and he said hello); or that sentences' logical composition may be out of the ordinary (I won't do that unless you do) (Richek, List, & Lerner, 1982).

18. Teach pupils that in some sentences the subordinate or dependent clause follows the main clause (The girl saw the boy who caught the fish) or it may be embedded in the main clause (The sketch that John drew was published in the Sunday edition of the newspaper). Restrictive clauses (e.g., The man who called my name was my brother) and nonrestrictive clauses or appositive clauses with commas (My brother, who is a lawyer, visited us today) both cause comprehension difficulties. Kachuck (1981) reports that Bormuth and associates found that 33% of the fourth graders they studied made errors in processing singly embedded restrictive clauses when reading paragraphs.

19. Teach pupils to interpret infinitives or clauses used as subjects ("To work is good." "What you think is your business."), and to interpret absolute constructions (There being nothing left to do, let's get out of here).

20. Develop an understanding of the effect that compounding (of subjects, predicates, objects, and sentences), modification (by adding adjectives, adverbs, adverbial and adjectival phrases and clauses), and the use of appositives have upon the meaning of a sentence (Hittelman, 1983, 1988) and then have pupils decipher the meanings of such sentences. Compounding results when subjects, predicates, direct objects, or sentences are combined: "John and Jenny sat and waited for the train." Modification results when adjectives, adverbs, qualifiers, and adjective and adverbial phrases and clauses are added: "The Brave young boy, who had just saved his sister's life, was praised by all." Apposition occurs when words, phrases or clauses are used to restate a preceding noun: "John, the captain of the team, was honored by his teammates."

21. Teach pupils to interpret logical, coordinate and subordinate connectives and function words (correlative conjunctions such as either-or or neither-nor, conjunctive adverbs such as hence, so, or nevertheless, subordinating conjunctions such as although, even though, whereas and other function words such as noun determiners (who, which, where), qualifiers (very, too, much), prepositions, question markers, verb auxiliaries or verb markers (am, are, is, have, do, will, shall, etc.) and negatives (no, not, never, nor, etc.) and to use them as cues to meaning. Function words have no real-world referents and thus do not have meaning in isolation.

22. Develop the ability to break complex and compound sentences into their simple parts or kernel sentences (Richek, List & Lerner, 1982): "Spiders, animals that many people dislike, are not actually insects, but often are mistaken for them." Here the kernel sentences are: (a) Spiders are not actually insects; (b) Most people dislike spiders; and (c) Many people mistake spiders for insects.

Sentences appear as simple, complex, and compound sentences. The longer the sentence, the more difficult it usually is to comprehend. Complex and compound sentences present special difficulties because they contain dependent clauses, greater variations in word order, and greater use of connectives and function words; the punctuation tends to be more complex; and there is a greater use of pronouns. Sentence length in words and syllables may be related to reading difficulties, but it is usually the syntactic and semantic complexity of the sentence rather than its length that causes comprehension difficulties.

Teaching children to read sentence should at a minimum emphasize identifying the main ideas of sentences; reading sentence structure, especially sentence patterns; paying attention to the integrative processing triggering mechanisms, especially anaphora, connectives, punctuation, and slot-filling inferences; and interpreting passive sentences and sentences with relative clauses. We single out a few of these for further discussion.

Reading the Syntactic Structure

The syntactic structure of the sentence serves as a cue to the fuller meaning of what is written. Written English presents special difficulties in this regard. It is less redundant than oral English, often containing logical and subordinate connectives, thus increasing sentence complexity.

For the most part, children do not have major problems in learning the grammatical and syntactic structure of their language. Although some growth in syntactic knowledge and the ability to deal with the lexical and deep structure tasks continues to age 10 (Chomsky, 1969) and may not be fully developed until about the age of 12, most five-and six-year-old children (and indeed two-year-olds) know the mechanics of grammar in a practical way. They have learned the structural features of their language. They can use syntax cues to arrive at the meanings of words. They can form sentences or utterances, handle subjects and predicates, and punctuate their spoken sentences by pauses and inflections. Without the benefit of formal instruction, they apply the rules of grammar in their speech. However, learning-disabled 12-year-old children seem to operate on the 7-to 8-year-old level in ability to interpret lexical tasks; they operate on the 5 -to

6-year-old level in dealing with syntactic aspects (Wigg, Semel & Abele, 1981).

Language learning appears to be largely instinctive. The process of first language learning occurs in a rapid, smooth and predictable sequence. The child seems to be equipped biologically both to use and to learn language (Smith, 1971). Children develop the rules rapidly between the age of 18 months and 4 years. The pattern of development of these rules is so systematic and invariant that it is believed that children have an innate predisposition or capacity for discovering the rules and structures of language (Chomsky, 1969).

Grammar and syntax serve a very useful function in comprehending both oral and written language. Readers do a better job of decoding if they understand language structures. Language structures communicate meanings, and the better the reader's knowledge of language structure, the less need the reader has for visual information. Good readers are such because they use the language structure, the syntax, the word order, the inflectional endings and the punctuation to redundantly define the meaning of symbols. Good readers can deal with both surface and deep structure. They have a firm knowledge of syntax (rules in ordering words in sentences) and of semantics (knowledge of word meanings); they are able to process sentences (Frasure & Entwisle, 1973) more efficiently than poor readers and thus are better comprehenders. They concentrate most of their processing ability on the extraction of meanings, using both semantic and syntactic context in reading, and employ an analysis-by-synthesis strategy of reading for meaning. They sample the text to validate linguistic expectancies of the information content of the text rather than analyzing the passage in a word-by-word manner (Hochberg, 1970).

Reading the Punctuation

Punctuation is an inter-word syntactical cue or a facet of sentence structure that affects meaning. It is one of the linguistic devices that tie together the parts of sentences. Punctuation is frequently looked upon merely as a discipline in writing. Yet, the writer punctuates not for himself, but for the reader. Punctuation is not only a set of rules to be learned, but also a way to facilitate the grasp of meaning. Knowledge of punctuation assists the reader in determining the correct pauses, pitch, stress, and intonation in a sentence and thereby aids the comprehension process (Leu & Kinzer, 1987). It helps the reader to phrase properly when reading.

Exercises useful in teaching reading of the punctuation may take multiple forms: teaching the functional differences between the period and the question mark (e.g., Mary has a kitten. Does Mary have a kitten?); teaching how a misplaced comma may falsify the intended meaning of a sentence (e.g., The school, kitchen, and cafeteria are off-limits during regular school hours.); having children see the effect of adding or deleting a comma (e.g., Jenny, my granddaughter, works at the hospital. Jenny, my granddaughter works at the hospital); teaching pupils that the colon indicates that something will follow; or that the dash indicates that the reader should pause when reading.

Comprehending Anaphora and Ellipses

Understanding of anaphora and of their relation to their antecedent is critical to understanding of sentences, paragraphs, and total text. Anaphora, although having no fixed semantic interpretation of their own, derive their meaning from a previous sentence or an earlier part of the sentence, paragraph, or passage in which they occur. They are cohesive ties, a type of redundancy that links one phrase, clause, or sentence with another. They serve as signals for the connectedness between phrases and sentences and transfer meaning from one phrase or sentence to the next. They carry meaning across phrases, clauses, sentences, and paragraphs. They function like a linguistic mortar to connect together the ideas in a text. Anaphora relate back to preceding words, phrases, or sentences; cataphora relate forward. In cataphoric relationships the reference terms (i.e., the pronoun) precedes the referent. A major problem in comprehending written text is that of identifying the intended or antecedent referent. Barnitz (1986) observes that anaphora resolution, or the process of determining the intended referent of an anaphoric form, is an important property of the language/reading comprehension process.

Certain conventions guide the choice of pronouns in writing and help to identify the antecedent in reading. Common examples are gender cues, number cues, and parallelism cues.

1. Gender: He cannot refer to a woman.
2. Number: Generally the pronoun will preserve the number of the noun, but there are exceptions. Thus: "Every week the teacher gives her best pupil a prize. She buys them in the supermarket." (Rayner & Pollatsek, 1989, p. 269).
3. Parallelism of form: "John lent Jim his car. He also lent him his TV." (Rayner & Pollatsek, 1989, p. 269).

Sometimes, the referents for anaphora are found in the same sentence; at other times, they may be found in a preceding or (with cataphora) in a subsequent sentence. Often the referents for anaphora are only suggested in the text. This requires readers to use their personal schemata and the text schema to infer the referent. The more linking inferences the text requires, the heavier is the reader's processing load. Children learn to process anaphora or cohesive ties at about the age of 9 or 10.

There are several types of anaphora or cohesive ties that signal the reader to relate the present text with earlier text, thus creating text unity. Halliday and Hassan (1976) identify five elements that bond utterances or that create cohesion:

1. Reference or Referential Ties: (a) pronominal pronouns (e.g., I, my, we, he, his, hers), (b) definite article (*the*), and (c) demonstrative pronouns (such as this, these, or that and those), or locational or locative pronouns (such as here or there).
2. Lexical ties: (a) reiteration (repetition, synonymy, superordinate or class-inclusive anaphora, or general word) and (b) collocation.
3. Substitution ties: (a) nominal (noun phrase), (b) verbal (verb phrase), and (c) clausal (clause phrase).
4. Ties of ellipsis: (a) nominal (deleted noun), (b) verbal (deleted verb phrase), and (c) clausal (deleted clause).
5. Conjunction ties or connectives: (a) cohesive conjunctive—additive ("and" type), adversative ("but" type), temporal (such as *now* and *then*)—(b) continuative.

Baumann and Stevenson (1986a, b) present a slightly different categorization:

1. Noun substitutes: includes pronouns (personal, demonstrative, relative, interrogative, indefinite, reciprocal—who, which, what, whom, whose, some, any, none, etc.); locative pronouns (here, there); temporal anaphora (now, then, before, after, later, earlier, sooner, etc.); synonym anaphora; superordinate anaphora; arithmetic anaphora (one, some, all, none, few, many, several, couple, two, both, latter, former); and deleted nouns.
2. Verb substitutes: includes inclusive anaphora (do, does, do so, don't, so is, so has: "I don't know these people, but you do"), deleted verb ("Mom likes peaches. Dad does not."), and predicate adjective ("Jim is sick. Jane is not.").
3. Clausal substitutes: either inclusive anaphora (so, not: "Will Bill come today. I think not.") or deleted clause ("Who broke the window? Harry.").

Reference ties connect a pronoun, article, or demonstrative adverb to a previous noun or phrase. They involve a relationship between a term and its referent. In pronominal anaphora the antecedent is replaced by a personal pronoun such as I, me, we, us, you, he, him, they; in demonstrative anaphora, the antecedent is replaced by a demonstrative pronoun such as this, that, these, or those; in locational pronouns, the antecedent is replaced by words like here or there: "Bill and Mary went to London. We also went there." An example of a comparative tie is: "You gave Jim three dollars. Why didn't you give me the same?"

The conjunction ties are connectives that relate sentences. They suggest a logical relationship between items, but they do not have referents. They indicate the manner of connection. The conjunctive ties may be additive (and, furthermore, thus, etc.), adversative (but, however, yet, instead), causal (because, if..then, or so), or temporal (then, before, next, second). For example (Arnold, 1988):

1. Robert threw the ball to Janet. And she threw it back (additive).
2. Robert threw the ball to Janet. But, it sailed over her head (adversative).
3. Margaret never did her homework. So her grades were poor (causal).
4. Phillip put on his sock. Then he saw a big hole in it (temporal).

Lexical ties are of two types: reiteration and collocation. Reiteration ties involve the repetition of the word that ties ideas together (e.g., Pam's dog is very old. The dog walks slowly these days); the use of a superordinate synonym (the animal walks slowly these days); a co-ordinate synonym (The canine walks slowly these days), or a subordinate synonym (Blackie walks slowly these days); or the use of a more general referent (The poor thing walks slowly these days) (Arnold, 1988). Collocation ties are ties that tend to occur together; collocation is the concurrence of words that regularly go together in language (e.g., "Jennie brought a knife and fork. Will you bring a spoon?")

Substitution ties involve the use or substitution of more inclusive terms such as "these reasons" or "these problems" for a previously mentioned noun phrase, verb phrase, or clause. The focus is on what is being replaced: a noun, verb, phrase, or clause. Examples of a nominal substitution, verbal substitution, and clausal substitution are (Arnold, 1988):

1. "John found three wooden boxes to build a fort. Gregory found two cardboard ones." (nominal)
2. "Has Rose cleaned the kitchen yet? She did this Morning." (verbal)
3. "Has she had lunch?" "I hope not." (clausal)

Ellipsis is the total omission of a word or phrase (Durkin, 1981) or of a part of the message, but the message can be inferred. An example of an ellipsis is: "Would you like a candy bar? I have two." Like substitution, ellipses may occur on the nominal (word) level, on the verbal level, or on the clausal level. Each of the examples that follow identifies a different type of anaphora or ellipses.

1. Pronouns: The pronoun or reference ties refers to a previously mentioned noun:
   Pam will be back soon. SHE stepped out of the office about ten minutes ago. She refers to ____ (Pam).
2. Demonstrative adverbs (adverb referents): here, there.
   a. I've shoveled the snow and scraped the ice. Park HERE.
   For proper interpretation of this sentence the reader must know that he is to park on that place or ground where the snow and ice have been removed.
   b. If Chad goes to the store today, you'll likely see him THERE. There refers to in the store.
3. Deleted nouns: Few, many, several, one, others, some, all. Deleted nouns is a form of substitution where words like few, many, several, one, others, or some are substituted (these are nominal substitution ties) for a previously mentioned noun or noun phrase. In each of the following sentences, the question is what word as left out or deleted?
   a. Jenny's pen is out of ink. SHE needs a new ONE. She refers to ____ and one refers to ____.
   b. The food was left out in the sun, and SOME was spoiled (Ringler and Weber, 1984, p. 241). Some refers to ____.
   c. All the children heard a loud noise. SEVERAL said it was a falling rock. OTHERS thought it was a roaring river. A FEW started to run away (Ringler & Weber, 1984, p. 242). Several refers to ____; Others refers to ____; and few refers to ____.
4. Deleted verb, verb phrase or clause: so does, do so, will also, will too, does not, will not, cannot, would not, as does, as did, as will. These are examples of verbal substitutions.
   a. John read the newspaper. SO DID Justin. Jenny, however, refused to DO SO. So did refers to ____; do so refers to ____.
   b. Since nobody volunteered to do the dishes, Grandma DID THEM. (Durkin, 1981). Did them refers to ____.
   c. Tom washed the windows. He did IT very quickly. It refers to ____. (This is a clausal substitution).
5. Deleted adjective: so is, is also, is too, as is, was too, are too, is not.
   a. John is a fine basketball player. SO IS Chad. So is refers to .
   b. John is a very responsible young man. Jim IS NOT. Is not refers to ____.

6. Arithmetic anaphora: the former, the latter, the first, the second, the two, etc.
   a. Jack and Mary were playing on the swing and the TWO of them got hurt. The two refers to _____ .
7. Class-inclusive or superordinate anaphora. The substituted word is a class word encompassing the referent.
   a. The rose was bright red. The FLOWER was just picked (Ringler & Weber, 1984, p. 235). The flower refers to _____ .
   b. Will you feed Bozo and Junior? REPTILES also have to eat. Reptiles refers to _____ .
8. Inclusive anaphora: this, that, these, those, the idea, the concept; the substituted words refer back to a whole phrase, clause, or multiple clauses, or sentences.
   a. Children go through different stages of development, as they increase in age. THIS is important in understanding children. This refers to _____ .
   b. No matter where the twins went, they always went together. That's why IT was a mystery why only one came. It refers to _____ .

Children comprehend anaphoric forms and understand the referents with differing levels of proficiency. Barnitz (1979, 1980) found that when the referent is a noun or phrase (e.g., John and his father wanted to buy a large train set because it was on sale), the anaphora are easier to process than when the referent is a clause or sentence (e.g., Mary says she rides her skateboard in the busy street, but Marvin does not believe it; Chad and John went swimming. They enjoyed it). When the referent precedes the anaphor (as in the two examples above), the anaphor is easier to process than when it follows (e.g., Because it was on sale, John and his father wanted to buy a large train set).

The article *the* is also an anaphoric reference. Difficulties in interpreting it correctly are illustrated in the following sentences: "The teacher, an expert in astronomy, received an award for service to the community" and "The teacher and THE expert in astronomy received an award for service to the community." In the first sentence, "teacher" and "expert in astronomy" are coreferential, referring to the same person; in the second sentence they are two distinct persons.

TEXT MODELING PROCESSES

Text modeling is the fourth step in comprehending units of increasing size; it is the construction of the overall meaning of extended text: that is, of a set of coherently related sentences or of a list of interrelated propositions. It is not enough that readers understand words, phrases, and sentences. The reader must construct an overall meaning of the total text. This is what is meant by text modeling or the building of a representation of extended text. The comprehension model which we have presented to this point and which we are about to complete is represented in Table 11-1.

One implication of Table 11-1 is that each stage of reading (word reading, phrase reading, sentence reading, etc.) requires a qualitatively different skill. Thus, paragraph reading requires skills beyond those of sentence reading. The major import of Table 11-1, however, is that text modeling depends on all of the processes that we have discussed thus far: the perceptual processes used to encode words (which was the concern of chapters 8 to 9), the lexical processes used to access word meaning and the encoding of the meaning that fits the context (which were the concern of chapter 10), and assembly and integration of propositions. It depends likewise on the referential processes, on schema activation, on use of context cues, on the monitoring of comprehension, and on inference processes which relate the text to the reader's schemata. And, as we shall see shortly, it requires an understanding of the text's coherence or organization.

The text modeling processes combine higher-level or schematic knowledge and inference processes with the output of semantic encoding and assembly and integration of the explicit propositions in text to construct a text model or a representation of text meaning (Just & Carpenter, 1987; Perfetti, 1985). Text modeling goes beyond simply making sense out of each sentence. It requires an understanding of each sentence's relationship to preceding and subsequent text and an awareness of intersentence relationships. It relies upon the ability to extract propositions from the text and to

TABLE 11-1: The Comprehension Process

Main Processes	Size of Text	Subprocesses
Lexical Access	Individual Word Meaning	Encoding of Words Referential Processes Schematic Processes
Semantic Encoding	Selecting the Meaning That Fits the Context	Contextual Processes Inferencing and Predictive Processes
Integration of Propositions	Phrase and Sentence Reading	Metacognitive Processes Assembly of Propositions Chunking Processes Microselection Processes
Text Modeling	Paragraph and Total Meaning	Integrative Processes and Global Coherence Processes

organize these propositions into a coherent and cohesive sequence. And, it requires the integration of the explicit propositions in text with the reader's schemata.

The reader in comprehending text is continually building a model of the text. The first sentence leads to a simple representation that the reader modifies with each succeeding sentence. Reading is a continually repeating process of predicting oneself through a line of print. The reader reads what is on the printed page, assembles and integrates the propositions from the words of text, makes inferences, and develops a representation of the text.

Perfetti (1985, p. 46) offers the following illustration of the interrelation of propositional encoding, schema activation, and text modeling:

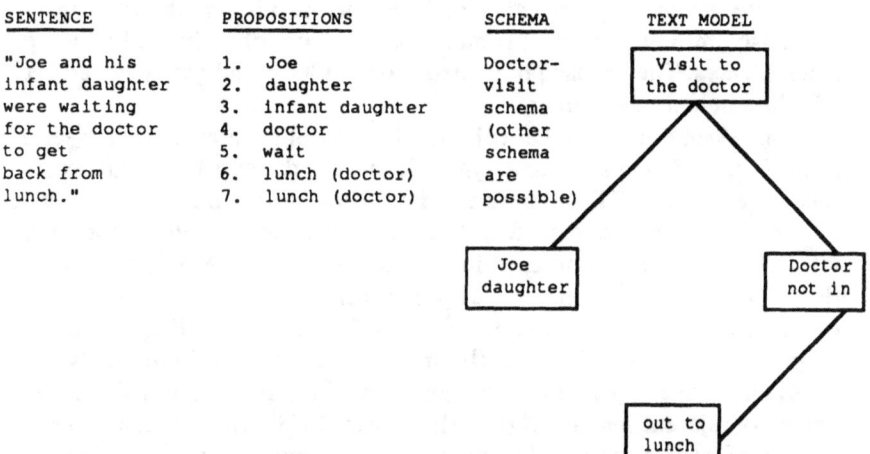

We present here only one sentence of the larger text presented by Perfetti. The process for the analysis of each sentence is the same. The text model, on the other hand, is constantly changing as new propositions and new relationships are added. As new information is processed, the text model remains the same, is modified in some slight manner, or is completely revised.

Kintsch (Kintsch, 1979, 1980; Kintsch & Greene, 1978; Kintsch & Van Dijk, 1978) notes that the degree of difficulty readers have in comprehending is in direct relation to the amount of searching they have to do to find a schema in their memory that matches the microstructure (i.e., individual words, the order of the words, the sentence structure, etc.) and the macrostructure of the text (i.e., topic, main idea, arrangement of ideas, organization, etc.). Kintsch suggests that processing of the microstructure or the intra-sentence relationships permits the reader to infer the macrostructure or the inter-sentence relationships. Kintsch observes that comprehension is a search of one's cognitive, informational, and linguistic schemas to effect a match with the text. If there is no match, the reader initiates a process of inferring or of a search of long-term memory.

Integration of Propositions: Local Coherence or Cohesion

We have delayed the discussion of integration of propositions, local coherence, or cohesion to this point because many (but not all) of the integrative processes function only at the multiple-sentence, paragraph, or total-text level. An important question in the comprehension of text is "How are sentences put together to form the meaning of the total text?" Obviously, meaning of a text is more than the sum of its individual words and sentences. The problem presented is one of local and global coherence, of cohesion and of coherence.

Irwin (1986b) observes that cohesion (i.e., local coherence) is "the set of structures, both semantic and syntactic, which directly link sentences to each other." (p. 31). Eye-movement data, showing extended processing at the end of sentences, demonstrate that intersentential integration is an integral part of the comprehension process (Irwin, 1986b). Cohesive ties that bind individual sentences together help the reader to establish a coherent memory representation of text (Moe & Irwin, 1986) and play a major role in comprehension (Irwin, 1986b). Irwin (1986b) adds that cohesion is "the psychologically significant links that tie individual sentences to adjacent sentences" (p. 57). Turner (1988) remarks that cohesion is a sort of intellectual glue that gives a piece of reading material unity in the mind of the reader.

Processes that conjoin or integrate sentences are a continuous and necessary part of developing a representation of text (Perfetti, 1985). Reading requires that propositions held in short-term memory be assembled and integrated in long-term memory. The recently formed propositions must be linked with successively occurring propositions into a representation that can survive in long-term memory. Integrative processes relate present text to earlier text or link one sentence with the next and thereby create textual unity. Readers can recall what they have read only if the individual ideas or propositions are connected or linked into a coherent whole.

Integration may be triggered (Perfetti, 1985) by any number of linguistic devices or cohesive linkages: by anaphora or pronoun referents, interclausal and intersentential connectives, the article *the*, redundancy or repetition of a proposition by using a noun or synonym, adding of additional text which keeps the information in active memory, punctuation, inferring causation and sequence, active memory search (as when a proposition or prior material is displaced from working memory and needs to be reinstated in memory), or making backward or bridging slot-filling inferences. Irwin notes that integration of simple sentences such as, "John went to the store. He was hungry," require the reader to infer that *he* refers to John, that John went to the store because he was hungry, and that the store sold food and John was going to buy some. Slot-filling inferences required to read these sentences and to relate one to the other are based upon the reader's ability to relate the sentences to prior text and real-world knowledge. The use of the article *the* (e.g., John drove his car very slowly. The old car has seen its better days.) often indicates connection.

Explicit cues that indicate how the ideas in text are related to each other are termed interclausal and intersentential connectives. They include (Just & Carpenter, 1987): cues that point to another item in the same series (also, again, another, finally, furthermore, likewise, moreover, similarly, too); cues that point to another item in a time series (afterwards, finally, later on, next, then); cues that point to an example or illustration (for instance, for example, specifically); cues that point to a consequence of what has been said (accordingly, as a result, consequently, hence, then, therefore, thus, so); cues that point to a restatement (in other words, that is to say, to put it differently); cues that point to a summary (all in all, altogether, finally, in conclusion); and cues pointing to a contrasting or opposing statement (but, however, on the other hand, on the contrary).

Sentence processing requires readers to compare the sentence input with their memory, to compare semantic information in memory with a semantic representation of the sentence, or to determine whether the sentence is a true description of the world (Perfetti, 1985). Thus processing of the sentence, "An apple is a fruit," involves encoding or assembling the propositions from the sentence (is apple, is fruit), retrieving the information from memory, and comparing the results. The research (Perfetti, 1985) shows that poor readers take more time than do good readers to process even such a simple sentence as "An apple is a fruit." They are even slower when the sentences demand integration. Sentence processing clearly differentiates between good and poor readers. A major factor in propositional integration is the working memory.

Perfetti (1985) observes that knowing word meanings enables the encoding of basic text units, that is, of propositions or sentences. As word meanings, including permanent memory nodes such as words and also the temporarily constructed links among nodes, are encoded, they are assembled into propositions in the working memory. Unfortunately, because of the limited capacity of the working memory, which can activate simultaneously only a few memory elements, only a few propositions can be assembled and held in working memory at a time.

Working memory stores partly processed sentences or phrases. Thus, if the reader cannot keep enough information active, propositional integration and indeed sentence comprehension are at risk. Poor readers do, in fact, have less memory capacity than do good readers. They must repeat even the most elementary propositional processes in the comprehension of text. They have a reduced ability to remember words just read. Conversely, good readers have a better memory for the words from the sentences they are currently processing and from the previous sentence (Perfetti, 1985). The end result is that poor readers assemble and integrate fewer propositions while good readers assemble and integrate more. Earlier assembled and successively occurring assembled propositions are vulnerable to memory loss in all readers, unless extra effort is applied at integrating the assembled propositions into a representation that can survive in long-term memory.

Understanding the Text's Global Coherence or Organization

In the section just completed, we referred to the integrative processes (i.e., local coherence or cohesion) and earlier to the role of the anaphora or cohesive ties in establishing cohesion or connectedness between sentences and total text and in creating text unity. A distinction needs to be drawn between local coherence and global coherence. Local coherence, cohesion, or integrative processing occurs when ideas are linked within and between sentences; global coherence or text organization happens when the content is integrated across entire paragraphs, chapters, sections, or books (Hittelman, 1988). The first of these is concerned with relating words to other words and sentences to other sentences.

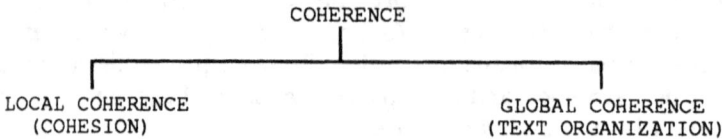

Global coherence is "the combined effect of all factors that contribute to textual unity, cohesion being one of them" (Irwin, 1986b, p. 32). Cohesion or local coherence is a text-related phenomenon; coherence is both text- and reader-related (Moe & Irwin, 1986).

Text modeling requires global coherence. Text modeling depends upon the ability to perceive the organization of the total text. Readers comprehend better when they can organize information around an overall organizational pattern (Irwin, 1986a), and when they can organize and synthesize individual idea units into a summary or a coherent whole. Reading is clearly a form of reasoning requiring categorization and synthesis.

Textual coherence and the ability to understand the coherence are vital in comprehending extended text. Just and Carpenter (1987) note that what distinguishes a text from a collection of unrelated sentences is the coherence of the underlying ideas. They add that to understand a text the reader must not only make sense of each sentence in itself, but must also determine its relation to the preceding portions of text, must determine the relations among the events, objects, and facts that are described by the text, and must construct a representation that integrates the information. When the reader's schemata match the writer's organizational patterns, the reader is more likely to comprehend and to remember what is being read.

The story schema provides a filing system for organizing the content of a story. The story schema is a frame-and-slots structure (or a mental framework containing a slot for each story component) that readers use to represent their knowledge of the story structure; story grammar is a rule-like specification of the hierarchical relations among the categories of story information (Just & Carpenter, 1987).

PARAGRAPH AND TOTAL-TEXT READING

Extended text involves the reading of multiple sentences or of multiple paragraphs and total text. We will focus first on paragraph reading, but the same processes and strategies operate in the reading of extended text. The reader is reminded particularly of the role played by the integrative processes (i.e., how sentences are integrated one with another) and of global or text coherence. Paragraph and total-text reading requires skills beyond those of phrase and sentence reading. Paragraphs are basically a series of sentences that are organized around one central idea. All the sentences are written in such a way that they relate to one another. Paragraph reading thus requires particularly the skills of reading for the main idea, reading for details (including directions and sequence), especially for how the details relate to the main idea, and inferring the relationships between sentences.

When readers are engaged in comprehension of a paragraph, they are engaged in discourse analysis. Discourse analysis is the study of the structure and function of language units longer than a single sentence. It goes beyond simple word recognition and understanding the sentence; it requires an awareness and an understanding of inter-sentence relationships, or the ability to relate the meaning of several sentences contained in a passage.

Undoubtedly, the most important skill required for comprehending a paragraph is the ability to identify the main idea of what one reads. Comprehension of a paragraph depends upon the ability to extract propositions from the text and to organize these propositions into a coherent and cohesive sequence. Unfortunately, the dynamics of converting single word meanings into the total thought of a paragraph are not sufficiently understood. Pupils who do not get the main ideas cannot identify the theme of a paragraph, do not understand the implied meanings, and usually cannot organize, integrate, or summarize what they have read. Reading for the main idea requires the pupil to distinguish between essentials and nonessentials and between the most important idea and subordinate details. Since it is a form of intellectual reasoning requiring categorization and synthesis, children with below-average intelligence have more difficulty in identifying the main idea than in identifying details.

In addition to reading for and stating the main idea, children must also be taught to read for details. Reading for details becomes especially important in functional reading and in study reading. Learning to follow directions and to identify sequence in printed materials is essentially reading for details. In directions every little step is significant. The pupil must give full attention and must look for a definite sequence of data. This process is particularly important in doing arithmetic and in carrying out experiments. Initially the pupil may be taught to arrange pictures in proper sequence to tell a story.

Subskills of Paragraph Comprehension

The subskills of paragraph comprehension are essentially the following:

1. Comprehension of words, phrases and sentences.
2. Comprehension of the main idea, including identification of the topic sentence and the words that cue the main idea. Can the pupil answer questions such as: What is this paragraph about? What do most of the key words point to? What idea is related to most of the supporting details? Can the pupil identify the words (e.g., first, last, the most important point) that cue the main idea? Can the pupil identify the topic sentence?
3. Comprehension of the details, whether a simple listing, a sequence (time order, space order, logical order) or directions.
4. Use of the title, subheadings, introductory statements, advance organizers, and the summary to infer the main idea, if it is not stated explicitly.

5. Comprehension of paragraph organization, (e.g., sequence, enumeration, cause-effect, problem-solution, comparison-contrast, main idea–details, etc.), of the organization of narratives (i.e., setting, plot, theme, and resolution), and of expository texts (i.e., superordinate, coordinate, and subordinate concepts).
6. Comprehension of the signal words that cue specific types of paragraph organization such as sequential or chronological order (e.g., first, second), comparison-contrast (although, but), cause-effect (because, consequently), enumeration or simple listing (e.g., one, two, next, finally), problem-solution, and so on.
7. Ability to summarize paragraphs, stories, chapter, and whole texts.
8. Use of outlining, semantic webbing, and pyramiding to identify paragraph organization. These strategies are discussed in chapter 12.
9. Identification of the paragraph as an introductory, transitional, content-bearing, or summarizing or concluding paragraph. Knowing whether the paragraph narrates, clarifies, describes, defines, illustrates, summarizes or compares.
10. Reading of the paragraph fluently and with expression.
11. Ability to use the additional context to relate one paragraph to another and to infer the larger unitary idea: Can the pupil use the topic sentences and the title or subtitles from various paragraphs to obtain the larger idea? Can the pupil use the structural words (connectives) to identify the interrelationships between paragraphs? Can the pupil organize propositions from the text into a coherent and cohesive sequence?

Reading for the Main Idea

Allusion has already been made to the importance of reading for the main idea whether in a sentence, in a paragraph, or in extended text. To identify the main idea the reader must organize information around a central focus. Unfortunately, even though well-written paragraphs usually contain a specific idea, identification of the main idea is not that simple. Fewer than 15% of expository paragraphs begin with a topic sentence, and half of such paragraphs do not contain an explicit statement of the main idea. The main idea may indeed be stated explicitly in a topic sentence at the beginning of the paragraph or even in a final sentence at the end of the paragraph, but it often is embedded in the middle of the paragraph or may be only implied. Indeed, at times, the paragraph is a continuation of a discussion centering about a main idea stated in an earlier paragraph. The main idea thus may be spread over two or three paragraphs, and paragraphs may well contain more than one main idea.

The main idea is the chief topic of a passage; it is what the paragraph is all about; it is what the story talks the most about; it is the central thought or theme; it is a statement in sentence form which gives the stated or implied major topic of a passage (Harris & Hodges, 1981). Rubin (1982) defines the main idea of a paragraph as the central thought or the common element that sentences share. The main idea is the one idea to which all the sentences relate.

The teacher can aid students in reading for the main idea by first of all modeling how to go about determining the main idea. The teacher needs to think out loud and demonstrate how and why certain details are not a part of the main idea (Johns, 1986). Johns (1986) suggests that the pupil be taught to:

1. Look for the topic: What is the sentence, paragraph, or passage about? What does most of the discussion refer to or what is it directed at?
2. Look for the most important idea: What is the most general statement made about the topic? What is emphasized or repeated? What is the central thought?

The main idea of a paragraph may also be identified by relating it to the details within the paragraph. Vacca and Vacca (1986, 1989) observe that the flow of meaning from author to reader is enhanced when the reader recognizes the structure of thought relationships in a text and when the reader can differentiate the important ideas from the less important ideas. Paragraphs in expository materials especially are generally structured around main ideas and details. The main idea usually does not stand alone. It generally is imbedded in or surrounded by details. It is the idea that the writer develops and supports with details. It includes and subsumes all the relevant details. Main ideas and details often are presented through specific organizational patterns (e.g., comparison and contrast, cause and effect, etc.). Thus, a comparison-contrast paragraph might have as the main idea the overall comparison and the details might be the points of similarity and dissimilarity.

The ability to attain the main idea is a gradually developing skill (Ross, 1984). Children at age 6 may well be able to identify the events, but have major difficulty in isolating central issues. Young children need to be helped in focusing their attention on the relevant information. Teachers should help children first to find the main idea in sentences (Ross, 1984). In sentences, the main idea is usually represented by the noun-verb relation.

Thus in the sentence, "The sleek airplane flew high in the sky far above the land below," the noun-verb combination, airplane flew, is the main idea.

Clark et al. (1984) recommend a visual imagery strategy designed to facilitate reading comprehension by requiring students to read a passage and to create visual images of the content of the passage.

Additional strategies for helping pupils to identify the main idea are:

1. Have pupils categorize objects or words as suggested in Chapter 10. This prepares the pupil for the cognitive strategies needed to comprehend main ideas (Richek, List, & Lerner, 1982).
2. Have pupils learn to identify the main idea of individual sentences by underlining key words, particularly the subject and verb.
3. Have pupils select the topic sentence, or the key sentence, which best identifies the main idea of a paragraph.
4. Have pupils write a title for a paragraph or story, or for a newspaper story. Have pupils read a newspaper story with the headline removed. Have pupils write a headline and then have them compare their headlines with the ones used in the paper.
5. Have pupils diagram the main idea and the supporting ideas:

"Transportation developed step by step. In the beginning people used logs to move down the stream. The lake or stream thus become the first roadway. Then people taught animals to pull heavy loads on sledges and the land became the natural roadway. Finally, people discovered the wheel. This led to the invention of the stagecoach."

Main idea	Transportation developed step by step.		
Supporting ideas:	Log Travel	Sledge Travel	Stagecoach Travel

The following activities are helpful in teaching pupils the skill of interrelating paragraphs.

1. Have pupil locate the topic sentences of all the paragraphs in an essay or story and relate these to obtain the larger idea conveyed in the selection.
2. Have pupils read the title, the subheads, and the summary of a chapter, then tell in a simple sentence what the chapter or selection is about.
3. Have pupils skim the chapter or selection in order to get a general idea of the selection.

4. After having read first one paragraph and then two other related paragraphs, have the pupil determine which of the last two supports and logically follows the first paragraph.

Reading for Details: Simple Listing, Sequence, and Directions

Comprehending the details is another important aspect in comprehending a paragraph. An important skill for pupils to learn is to differentiate the details of a paragraph from the main idea. A simple technique (Ross, 1984) has pupils graph the main idea and the details. A picture of a flower may be used (with the center as the main idea and each petal as the detail) or a picture of a tree (with the trunk as the main idea and the branches as the details). Outlining is another useful method for separating main idea from the details.

Details may be stated in the form of a simple listing or enumeration, as a sequence, or in direction form. One, two, first, second, next, finally, in addition, and, also, all signal a simple listing pattern. Sequence or chaining of events or ideas is an organization pattern that presents the steps of a process. It is distinct from enumeration or simple listening. When asking questions about sequence, the teacher needs to see to it that the pupil's answers clearly indicate a knowledge of the order of the events.

Burmeister (1974, 1983) notes that sequence can take a chronological or time order (flow chart, outline, time line, and tree chart), a spatial order (sketch, map, floor plan), an expository order (outline, chart, graph, etc.), a logical order as in stories with a theme, or an affective order or order of preference (comparison of likes or dislikes).

Words like first, second, before, then, after, finally, later, and now, signal chronological order, time patterns, or chronological sequence. Words like ahead, next to, nearby, behind, and to the left, signal a spatial order. Words like because, consequently, so, hence, thus, therefore, and as a result, signal a logical or cause-effect order.

Developing the pupil's ability to read for details, including reading for direction and sequence, may be accomplished through exercises such as the following:

1. Have the pupils look at a picture and then let them describe what they saw.
2. Have pupils identify the supporting details in simple paragraphs.
3. Have pupils analyze a written paragraph into its main and supporting ideas by making a formal outline of it.

4. Let pupils read and then carry out simple directions on how to do something or how to play a game. Have children develop direction or sequence charts. Common activities include how to care for a plant, pet, or garden; how to cook a simple dish; how to make a dictionary; or how to make a paper alligator.
5. Have pupils respond to directions such as:
   (a) Put a blue block in back of you (one direction activity);
   (b) Put a red block next to the blue block in back of you and put a white block on top of the red block (two directions);
   (c) Draw a circle around the longest word in this sentence;
   (d) Write the abbreviation for the third month of the year _____ ;
   (e) Write the following words in alphabetic order: bird, box, brush, bag, bench, bug.
6. After giving pupils a paragraph to read, ask specific questions about it that call for detail. Multiple choice, completion, and true-false questions are especially appropriate in eliciting answers concerning the details of a paragraph.
7. Use rebus stories to draw attention to details in a story (Burmeister, 1983, p. 312). For example, "The petting zoo had *rabbits* in one corner and a young *kangaroo* in another. The baby *lamb* was asleep, while the *anteater* was moving from one end of the cage to the other end." A rebus might be substituted for the words rabbit, kangaroo, lamb, and anteater.
8. Use comic strips to teach the pupil to read for sequence: have pupils put the frames in order to form a unified story. Use comics having few or no words. Mount the strips on pieces of oak tag and number each frame on the back. Then cut each comic strip apart, frame by frame, and place the pieces in an envelope. Have children put each comic strip back together in the correct sequence. Provide opportunities for children to tell or read the story to the group.
9. Use a sequence train with pockets: the pupil is required to put the events of a story (which have been transcribed onto cards) in proper order on the sequence train.

Comprehending Paragraph Organization

Paragraph and text organization are important aspects of comprehension and indeed of recall and retention (Meyer, 1984). Comprehension of textual coherence is vital in understanding paragraphs and extended text, especially of expository materials. In general, paragraphs have a similar organization. The writer usually provides introductory material, followed by informational or explanatory material, and ending with summary material. This basic organization allows the writer to present information in a coherent fashion. It allows for a logical interrelationship of ideas (Ringler and Weber, 1984). The same patterns which are used to organize paragraphs are also used to organize larger expository materials or total discourses. The larger selection, perhaps a chapter in a book, may well begin with an introductory paragraph, be followed by a series of paragraphs that become the body of the selection, and end with a concluding or summary paragraph.

Paragraph coherence or textual unity (this includes intersentential cohesion and paragraph organization) is a significant determinant of comprehension. Total-text modeling requires organization and a perception of the writer's organization. The reader comprehends better when he can organize information around an overall organizational pattern and when he can synthesize individual idea units into a summary or a coherent whole.

Understanding text organization or coherence depends upon understanding the macrostructure, story grammar, and the superordinate, coordinate, and subordinate structure of expository text; identifying the main or general ideas and of the supportive details; understanding organization patterns in expository materials (i.e., whether the paragraph defines, illustrates, compares, contrasts, etc.); and understanding the cues that signal organization such as though, consequently, and therefore. The end product of organization is the ability to outline the text, to synthesize individual idea units into a summary or organized series of related general ideas (Irwin, 1986a), and to represent the organization in a semantic web or structured overview. The organizational processes, that is, passage coherence and organization, are useful only to the degree in which the reader uses the writer's organization to organize his own memory representation of text (Irwin, 1986a).

Paragraphs exhibit the following types of paragraph organization (Cheek & Cheek, 1983a 1983b; Calfee, 1982; Calfee & Curley, 1984; Colwell & Helfeldt, 1983; Meyer & Rice, 1984; Zintz & Maggart, 1984):

1. Main idea/supporting details; main idea plus examples
2. Details/main idea or generalization
3. Examples/conclusion
4. Conclusion or generalization/supporting examples or details
5. Analogy pattern
6. Comparison/contrast pattern
7. Cause/effect or logical sequence
8. Effect/cause pattern
9. Enumerative or simple listing pattern
10. Time or chronological sequence pattern

11. Classification or categorization pattern
12. Organization by size, distance, position, or degree
13. General to specific pattern
14. Specific to general pattern
15. Problem-solution pattern; thesis-proof pattern
16. Narrative pattern
17. Explanation pattern
18. Clarification pattern
19. Topical pattern
20. Descriptive pattern
21. Definition pattern
22. Persuasion or argument pattern
23. Inductive pattern
24. Deductive pattern
25. Question-answer pattern

Cheek and Cheek (1983a, 1983b) singled out the enumeration pattern, the relationship pattern, the persuasive pattern, and the problem-solving pattern as being the most frequent forms:

1. Enumerator pattern: Organization may take the pattern of main idea, supporting information, and presentation of an example, illustration, or definition; that of presentation of a generalization with accompanying subtopics; or that of introduction of the topic and presentation of additional information to expand the topic.
2. Relationship pattern: Organization may take the pattern of cause-effect or comparison-contrast. Perception of these patterns is especially important in understanding social studies, science, and literature materials. To deal effectively with these patterns the pupil needs to use inferential comprehension skills and be proficient in the use of the signal words that cue comparison-contrast relationships (however, but, although, as well as) or that cue cause-effect relationships (because, since, therefore).
3. Persuasive pattern: This pattern uses propaganda techniques (glittering generalities, transfer, testimonials, plain folks, band-wagon, or card attacking) to sway the reader to accept or reject certain ideas. The pupil needs to read such materials in a critical fashion, using evaluative or critical comprehensive techniques.
4. Problem-solving or problem-solution pattern: This pattern is used especially in mathematics, science, business education, and vocational educational materials. The pupil needs to become familiar with the steps in problem solving. Mystery stories are particularly useful in teaching the problem-solving pattern.

The enumerative pattern encompasses the simple-listing pattern (a listing of items or ideas where the order of presentation of the items is not significant) and the temporal chronological sequence pattern, where the order of presentation does take on significance.

Piccolo (1987) suggests that the variant types of paragraph organization be taught in the following order: sequence, enumeration, cause-effect, description, problem-solution, and comparison-contrast. She also identifies the steps in teaching paragraph structure: (a) define and label the paragraph structures; (b) examine model paragraphs, presenting the model with a graphic organizer that identifies the critical attributes of each, including the signal words that clue the organization of the paragraph; (c) model the composition of an original paragraph; (d) have pupils compose an original paragraph; and (e) have pupils read expository text and identify the patterns used by various writers.

Cues Signaling Paragraph and Whole-Text Organization

Signaling of the structure of paragraphs and of larger expository materials also results in better comprehension and memory of what is read (Meyer, 1979). Authors signal or cue the structure by using some of the 300 structure or function words. Function words include prepositions, correlative (both, and, not only–but also, either-or) and subordinate (because, since, so that, if, whereas, etc.) conjunctions, conjunctive adverbs, relative pronouns, auxiliary and linking verbs, and articles. They are differentiated from content words which are nouns, verbs, adjectives, and adverbs. The structure words may signal that a particular syntactical pattern is to follow, indicate paragraph or total-text structure, cue coherence between subordinate ideas and the main ideas, establish relationships such as cause-effect, contrast, pairing of ideas, and time and space, and effect transitions from paragraph to paragraph. Function words do not take on inflectional endings, have no clear lexical meaning or concrete referent, and are readily confused because of the similarity of the physical features. Overlearning of them is a virtue. Understanding conjunctions and conjunctive adverbs, being able to identify the relationships that conjunctions signal, and using markers or structure words as cues to paragraph organization have a positive effect on reading comprehension. Key structural words assist the reader in following the author's transition from idea to idea and from paragraph to paragraph.

Shepherd (1973, 1978) grouped structure words or rhetorical terms of coherence as follows. Some additional words have been included.

ASSEMBLY AND INTEGRATION OF PROPOSITIONS

I. Structure words indicating additional ideas.
   A. Word pointing to or that signal supporting or coordinating ideas, adding to the total thought, or marking a pairing of ideas.

and	furthermore	besides	likewise	the main point is
also	plus	too	similarly	since then
another	otherwise	after that	again	not only, but also
in addition	moreover	as well as	since	both-and
alike	compared to	similar to	same as	either-or

   B. Words pointing to final or concluding ideas or that indicate that the point being made flows from previous statements.

consequently	in conclusion	then	thereupon
thus	in summation	to sum up	accordingly
hence	at last	in brief	as a consequence
therefore	finally	in the end	because

II. Structure words that signal contrast or a change in ideas, or that a contradictory statement is about to be introduced.

opposed to	on the other hand	nevertheless	whereas
in contrast	but	yet	while
to the contrary	in spite of	still	rather
conversely	although	even if	notwithstanding
however	either-or	if	except
even though	unless	unlike	not only ... but
meanwhile	different from	despite	also

III. Structure words that signal concrete application of a thought: cause-and-effect relationships, introduction of an example, classification, etc.

therefore	as a result	specifically	because of this
accordingly	hence	for instance	for this reason
it follows	consequently	provided	on account of this
in order that	since	because	if ... then
for example	so that	so	as
		thus	for

IV. Structure words pointing to relationships among and between ideas.
   A. Time relationships

in the first place	last	previously	afterward
at the same time	now	thereafter	during
thereafter	later	at last	in the mean time
in retrospect	after	at length	subsequently
meanwhile	before	following	always
finally	immediately	until	not long after
to begin with	initially	first	beyond
then	secondly	when	shortly
	next	in the end	

   B. Space relationships

here	far	under	westward
there	near	farther on	beneath
yonder	by	above	around
close	away	across	over
		to the east	everywhere

C. Relationships of degree

many	little	some	worst	greater
more	less	all	fewer	greatest
most	least	best	fewest	

D. Relationships of emphasis

| this | that | one | some |
| these | those | several | few |

The most difficult conjunctions are when, so, but, where, while, that, if; the easiest are and, how, for, and as. Such words as however, thus, which, although, and yet are difficult even in the intermediate years (Katz, 1968; Robertson, 1968).

There are other cueing systems within text. Previews, introductory statements, topic sentences, titles, subtitles, advance organizers, and structural overviews all relay organization and are perhaps the best cues available to the reader to infer the main idea.

Readers are aided also in paragraph comprehension when story structure or story grammar (setting, plot, theme, resolution) is made explicit by the writer and when readers can detect, identify, and comprehend this built-in paragraph and story structure. Smith (1988) rejects this view. He points out that if writers and readers are to connect, narratives must reflect the story schemata that readers have in their heads. He notes that having a sense of story structure in one's head is the basis of comprehension of text and also of one's memory for text.

Discourse structures and story grammars are perceived by Smith as part of one's cognitive structure, and the more the reader can anticipate and employ the formal structures that the author uses, the better the reader can comprehend and the more he will remember. Smith (1988) adds that meaningfulness requires a close match between the way a text is constructed and the organization of the reader's mind. Smith makes the controversial observations that repeating what was read does not prove that the reader understood and that making story structure explicit does not improve comprehension. Children, he observes, must be helped to understand the text in which story structures are employed. This is not the same as being taught the structures.

SUMMARY

Chapter 11 has dealt with the association of meanings with phrases, sentences, paragraphs, and extended texts. Earlier chapters stressed the importance of the sentence as the meaning-bearing unit, but if there is one inference to be drawn from this chapter it is that comprehension is cumulative and that the comprehension task is cumulative. The illustration below (Figure 11-6) suggests that understanding units of increasing size requires progressively higher levels of comprehending, involving increasingly more complex skills. Thus, comprehension of a phrase generally requires additional skills compared to comprehension of words.

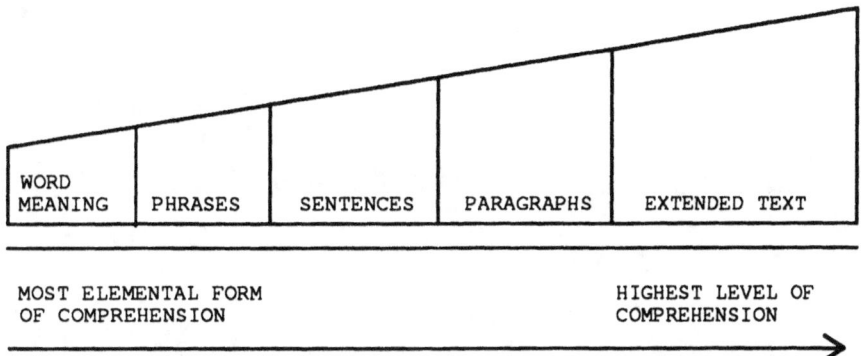

FIGURE 11-6: The Increasing Complexity of Comprehension

Chapter 11 emphasizes that the pupil must learn to reason with words, to interrelate words, and to become proficient in reading or comprehending increasingly larger units of context. Clearly, the sentence is the most appropriate level of discourse analysis, but this does not negate the fact that the total discourse (the paragraph, story, chapter) has elements distinct from the sentence structure. It is important to look at the total or macro-structure.

Chapter 12
Strategies for the Development of the Higher Levels of Comprehending

I. Introduction
II. Levels of Comprehension
III. Developing Literal and Denotative Comprehension
IV. Developing Organizational Comprehension
    A. Research Findings Concerning the Organization of Text
    B. Difficulties in Developing Organizational Comprehension
    C. Strategies for Developing Organizational Comprehension
        1. Sequence
        2. Categorization
        3. Story Grammar
        4. Expository Grammar or Textbook Organization
        5. Summarizing, Outlining, and Underlining
        6. Semantic Webbing
        7. DRA
V. Developing Inferential Comprehension
VI. Developing Evaluative Comprehension (Critical Reading)
VII. Developing Appreciative Comprehension
    A. Setting
    B. Theme
    C. Plot
    D. Resolution
    E. Genre
    F. Characterization
    G. Style
VIII. Developing Integrative Comprehension
    A. Content-Area Reading
    B. Rate of Comprehension
IX. Summary

CHAPTER 12
Strategies for the Development of Higher Levels of Comprehending

In the introduction to Part IV (Figure Part IV-1) the various facets of comprehension were outlined. One of these was identified as the ability to comprehend on different levels. Chapter 12 will focus on this aspect. To this point the discussion has focused on lexical access and semantic encoding (comprehending individual words) and on assembly and integration of propositions and text modeling (comprehending phrases, sentences, paragraphs, and the larger text). These are quantitative categories. Consider now a qualitative category.

The reader must learn to interpret words, sentences, paragraphs and total text, but the questions must also be asked: At what level? Is a literal interpretation needed? Or is an inferential, evaluative, or appreciative interpretation required?

Chapter 7, "Evaluating and Developing Comprehension," noted that asking questions, whether self- or teacher-generated, about what has been read is an important comprehension strategy, and it identified the different kinds of questions that can and should be asked to evaluate and enhance the pupil's comprehending ability. The significant element is that each of these questions is or can be a literal, organizational, or evaluative question, and the responses to the questions will require thinking of a higher sort or comprehending on qualitatively different levels. Clearly, comprehending behaviors can be ordered from easy to difficult in terms of the inferred thought requirements each category appears to demand (Tatham, 1978).

LEVELS OF COMPREHENSION

Writers have categorized the higher levels of comprehending into various levels. Barrett's (Barrett, 1974; Barrett & Smith, 1974, 1976, 1979) taxonomy includes literal comprehension, inferential comprehension, evaluation, and appreciation. To these we have added organizational comprehension and integrative comprehension or comprehending when reading for study purposes.

In general, pupils demonstrate their proficiency with the higher-level comprehension skills by (a) listing, telling, defining, identifying, restating, labeling, locating, recognizing, or recalling the basic facts (literal comprehension); (b) explaining, describing, interpreting, translating, comparing, concluding from, anticipating, or reading between the lines (interpretative comprehension); (c) summarizing, synthesizing, outlining, or illustrating the information (organizational comprehension); (d) judging, rating, criticizing, comparing, differentiating, distinguishing, evaluating, or appraising the information (evaluative comprehension); (e) identifying with the content, being emotionally involved with it, defending, rejecting, or stressing the points made (appreciative comprehension); and (f) demonstrating, applying, constructing, finding solutions, or solving problems (integrative comprehension).

Readers are constantly building a representation or a model of text. Comprehension occurs when words, phrases, sentences, and paragraphs are matched with slots in the reader's schemata (McNeil, 1987). When readers tap a representation of text that is explicitly stated in the text or when slots in the reader's schemata are filled with information that is explicitly stated in the text, readers are said to be processing the information on a literal level. When readers convert ideas into a coherent whole, when they build text unity, when they synthesize individual idea units into a summary or a semantic web, and when they attain intersentential and interparagraph integration, they are processing the text on an organizational level. When readers read between the lines predicting their way through print, integrating the explicit information in the text with prior knowledge, and when the information that fills the slots in the reader's schemata must be inferred, they are processing the text on an inferential level. Finally, when readers are required to judge, analyze, and evaluate what has been read, they are comprehending on an evaluative level.

Even though chapters 10 to 12 are organized, at least to some extent, on the basis of skills, it is important to remember that these skills are merely a manifestation of inner cognitive processes or of the comprehension process. They are outcomes or represent what results after comprehension has occurred (Hittelman, 1978). Table 12-1 identifies the processes that describe or identify each of the higher levels of comprehending.

TABLE 12-1: The Higher Levels of Comprehending

Level of Comprehending	Processes
Literal	Recognizing and recalling textually explicit, literal, or denotative meaning.
Organizational	Recognizing or inferring the writer's organization or the coherence within materials; identifying paragraph organization; developing intersentential and interparagraph integration; synthesizing, summarizing, and outlining what has been read; representing the organization in a semantic web, a flow chart, time line, a map, a graph, a circle story, etc.; identifying the overall organizational pattern (in narratives organizing them into setting, theme, plot, and resolution; in expository texts organizing them into superordinate, coordinate, and subordinate concepts); converting ideas into a coherent whole; and building text unity.
Inferential	Inferring information not specifically stated in text; inferring the textually implicit or connotative meaning (i.e., making a convergent inference); inferring the scriptally or schema-implicit meaning (i.e., making a divergent or slot-filling inference); drawing conclusions, predicting outcomes, inferring cause-effect relationships; and inferring referents for anaphora.
Evaluative	Making evaluative or critical judgments about the content; evaluating or passing personal judgments on the relevancy, adequacy, validity, logic, accuracy, truthfulness, and reliability of what is read; recognizing the author's intent or point of view; distinguishing facts from opinion or from fiction; questioning the writer's purpose; distinguishing between the denotative and connotative meanings of words; interpreting figures of speech; detecting the use of propaganda techniques; and evaluating the source of the material.
Appreciative	Identifying the mood, tone, or theme of the selection; interpreting the literary, semantic, rhetorical, and stylistic devices used by the writer; reacting to the writer's language and imagery; discriminating between the variant literary forms or genre, such as prose, poetry, drama, sonnets, essay, metaphors; and identifying in narratives the elements of setting, mood, plot, characterization, style, and theme.
Integrative	Comprehending for study purposes: ability to use the dictionary, to use an effective method of study-related reading, to locate information, to organize what one reads, to read maps, graphs, and charts, to read at an appropriate rate, and to read in the content areas.

Readers, if they are to become good comprehenders, must become proficient in each of the levels of comprehending. Examine now each of the levels more closely.

DEVELOPING LITERAL AND DENOTATIVE COMPREHENSION

A primary skill that the pupil needs to acquire when reading a sentence or paragraph is the ability to get the direct, literal or textually explicit meaning.

The pupil must be able to recognize and recall the ideas that are explicitly stated and must be able to answer questions about a sentence or paragraph calling for a literal, denotative meaning. Specifically, the reader must be able to:

1. Identify, understand, and recall the main idea.
2. Recognize, locate, and/or recall from memory significant facts, events, or details.
3. Follow the directions given in the material.
4. Recognize and recall the sequence of a passage.
5. Identify and recall explicitly stated expressions of relationships: cause-effect, contrast, comparison, etc.

Even though comprehension tasks often involve pupils in the retrieval of trivial factual data (Guszak, 1967), or in parroting back what they have read, literal comprehension is important. Literal comprehension is the basis of all the other higher-level comprehension skills. Literal comprehension is sometimes difficult for children because their knowledge of concepts and vocabulary or terminology is inadequate, because the syntax is too complex, or because the materials are too abstract. Figure 12-1 identifies the major difficulties in obtaining the literal meaning.

Basic types of exercises that teach literal- comprehension skills or that demonstrate that pupils are obtaining the literal or denotative meaning of units of increasing size (words, phrases, sentences, and paragraphs) are:

1. Have pupils change the information in the text into a different symbolic form or language: have them illustrate the story, act out the story, or draw a picture, map, chart, graph, diagram, detailing what was said. Teaching pupils to picture the action or to cartoon

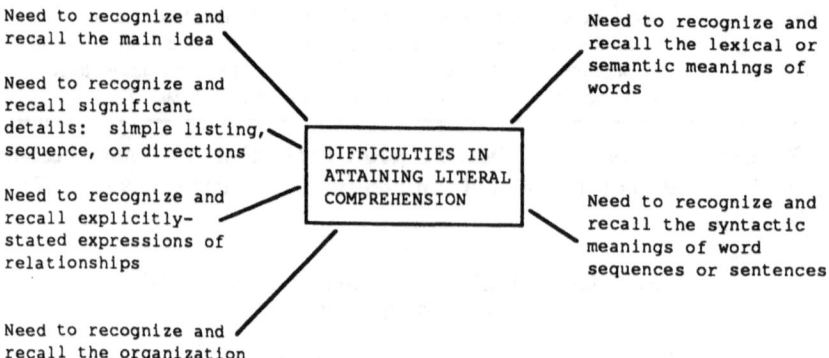

FIGURE 12-1. Difficulties in Attaining Literal Comprehension

the events told in a story with stick figures (Golinkoff, 1975) or to visualize what is read increases comprehension of what has been read. Burmeister (1983) suggests that the translations from the text may take the form of paraphrasing, syntactical transformation (sentence surfing), translation of the written account into a graph, chart, map, or diagram, acting out of the story, or defining or providing a synonym for a term used.
2. Have pupils retell or paraphrase the story or content: the emphasis should be on identifying the characters of the story, the characteristics of the characters, the events in the story, and the plot and theme of the story. The teacher can initiate free recall of text with questions such as (Ringler and Weber, 1984, p. 152): "Tell me what you have read using your own words." "What is this story all about?" "Tell me as much as you can about what you have just read."
3. Have pupils answer probe and teacher-made or textbook-structured questions over materials read that require them to identify, recall, or supply the names of the characters, to describe a very specific incident, to state the main idea, to state the order of events, and so forth. Following free recall, the teacher may ask probe questions (Ringler and Weber, 1984, p. 152) such as: "Tell me more about what happened and where it happened," and "Tell me more about the people about whom you just read."
4. Have pupils demonstrate the sequence of events in a story or identify the steps in a how-to-do article.
5. Have pupils match pictures with sentences.
6. Have pupils identify the main points or ideas in an article, and the writer's supporting material for the main points.
7. Have pupils identify the who, when, where, why, and how of a story.

DEVELOPING ORGANIZATIONAL COMPREHENSION

Good readers also comprehend the organization of narratives and expository text, classifying, synthesizing, organizing, and summarizing as they go along. They can tap into the writer's organization. They can identify the coherence within materials or can impose an organization upon the passage or total text. They can identify the propositions or idea units in text and can convert these into a coherent whole. They can organize and synthesize individual idea units into a summary by perceiving the relationship between the main idea and the supporting details and arranging them in some logical order, by understanding story grammar and the organization used in expository texts, and by understanding total passage organization or coherence. They not only understand text cohesion (i.e., local coherence between sentences and paragraphs), but total text organization (i.e., global coherence). They can build text unity. Efficient reading is a matter of perceiving the organizational patterns within written materials as one reads and responds to what one has read. It includes the ability to answer questions about a sentence or paragraph calling for an analysis, synthesis, summary, outline, and organization of ideas or information explicitly stated. It also includes the ability to infer the organization when it is not explicitly stated.

The emphasis in this text is that the reader must activate previously stored schemata to comprehend the events in a selection and to develop a coherent cognitive model of the meaning of the text. When this happens, the result is comprehension of what one is reading. What the reader brings to the text may, from this point of reference, be more important than what the reader finds in the text. However, to comprehend, the reader must also be helped by the text. The writer's organization of the text is an important comprehension aid. Organization processes are a key determinant of learning (Just & Carpenter, 1987).

Kintsch and Van Dijk (1978) in their comprehension model suggest that the first step of processing input information involves selecting a set of propositions or idea units to be held in short-term memory. When the next set of input propositions or idea units is processed, coherence is established by finding a shared semantic referent between the new idea units and the set retained in short-term memory. If no shared referent is found, a reinstatement or active search of the long-term memory of the previous text is required. Irwin (1986b) notes that the number of reinstatement searches required by a text provides a direct measure of coherence. Just and Carpenter (1987) note that text coherence depends upon:

1. Knowledge of the structure of the text genre: understanding, for example, that a story consists of a setting, plot, and resolution.
2. Knowledge of the referends.
3. Knowledge of the integrative cues within the text: for example, knowing how anaphora aid text integration.
4. Ability to focus on the causal or temporal chain of events in a narrative text and on the phenomena described and explained in an expository text.

Perfetti (1985) suggests that text integration depends upon repetition of the propositions or idea units through use of anaphora, through simple repetition of a word, through additional text, or through active memory search.

Irwin (1986a) identified three types of coherence or of integrative processes: understanding anaphora, understanding connectives, and slot-filling inferences (these are inferences that require the use of prior information). She identifies the process of synthesizing and organizing individual idea units into a summary as a separate process and terms it macroprocessing. Macroprocessing is analogous to organizational comprehension or global coherence. It requires the reader: (a) to identify the general ideas and to summarize the passage and (b) to identify the author's organizational pattern, and to use this information to organize one's own memory representation. Macroprocessing aids in general recall of what is read, but also in recall of details by "hooking" the details to more general ideas. Obvious forms of macroprocessing are understanding of the relationship between the main idea and the supporting details, understanding of story grammar, and identification of paragraph or total-passage organization (e.g., whether the paragraph follows a description, temporal-sequence, explanation, comparison-contrast, definition-example, problem-solution pattern, etc.).

Research Findings Concerning the Organization of Text

Textural coherence is obviously a vital text characteristic that pupils must identify and comprehend if they are to comprehend the text and that writers must provide for readers. It is this characteristic that makes a text a text rather than a haphazard collection of sentences (Chapman, 1984). Coherent text is text that is organized and structured.

Bruner (1966) early noted the importance of structure for learning. Structure makes it easier to understand by simplifying information and by increasing the manipulability of a body of knowledge. Without structure, knowledge is more readily forgotten. The key to retrieval (or recall of the information) is organization. Organization of information reduces the aggregate complexity of material by embedding it into a person's cognitive structure. Reading in the content areas and study-type or integrative reading especially depend upon proficiency in the organization skill.

The research generally indicates that:

1. Text structure and recognizing the writer's structure (i.e., knowing, identifying and perceiving the structure) help the reader to comprehend the text, to judge the importance of the information, to recall the text (Horowitz, 1985b; McGee & Richgels, 1985; Meyer, 1984), and to remember the content of the text.
2. Memory for stories is superior when the content is organized according to a well-known story grammar. Changing the struc-

ture, even when the content is left the same as it was, affects memory for the text.
3. Most intermediate pupils are not aware of how ideas are organized in a text (McGee, 1982a; Taylor & Samuels, 1983).
4. Good readers are better than poor readers in making use of text structure (McGee, 1982a; Pearson & Gallagher, 1983a, 1983b).
5. Pupils can be taught to identify text structure and this knowledge aids comprehension of text (Englert & Hiebert, 1984; Horowitz, 1985a).
6. Poor readers, more so than good readers, are aided by training in the use of text structure (Siedow & Fox, 1984). Graves, Cooke, and LaBerge (1983) found that seventh and eighth graders, reading significantly below grade level, when provided with previews, increased factual comprehension by 13% and inferential comprehension by 38%.
7. A major cause of inadequacies in organizing what one reads is often simple immaturity. The ability to capitalize on text structure is a late-developing skill (Baker & Brown, 1984b). Fifth-grade pupils are more aware of text structure than are third-grade readers (McGee, 1982a). The teacher may find that growth in organizational ability occurs only when the pupil arrives at the intellectual maturity to see interrelationships between the main idea and the supporting data. If organization of materials depends upon the ability to think abstractly, the pupil, who has a below-average IQ score, and who is under the age of 10 or 11, may have difficulty organizing what is read.
8. Top-level ideas (i.e., the writing plan of the writer) are retained and recalled better than lower-level ideas.
9. Writing is an effective way of teaching expository structure to intermediate-grade pupils (Flood, Lapp, & Farnan, 1986; Horowitz, 1985a, 1985b; McGee & Richgels, 1985). It develops the insight that writers organize their information to maximize the reader's comprehension and it helps the reader to recognize the organization pattern used by writers.
10. Readers need models that demonstrate the structure of different types of paragraphs (Flood, Lapp & Farnan, 1986).
11. Graphic organizers aid the reader in visualizing the text (McGee & Richgels, 1985; Slater, 1985). Other techniques for teaching relations and structures at the narrative or story level and at the expository text level include: summarizing and outlining, semantic webbing, multiple-choice cloze tests, story rewrites, and use of cued questions (Wittrock, 1987).

Difficulties in Developing Organizational Comprehension

Among the elements that cause pupils difficulty in comprehending the organization of what is read and that both singly and conjointly play a negative role in understanding text organization are the following:

1. Inadequate schemata.
2. Lack of text coherence.
3. Inability to identify the referent for anaphora.
4. Inability to identify the type or pattern of paragraph organization.
5. Lack of familiarity with story grammar.
6. Lack of familiarity with expository or textbook structure.
7. Difficulty in identifying and inferring the relationships between the main and subordinate ideas, and among the events, objects, and facts described in the text.
8. Difficulties with chronological and logical sequence.
9. Inability to identify and interpret the cues that signal organization or to understand the cueing function of cohesive ties.
10. Inadequate categorization skills.
11. Inability to use the writer's organization to structure one's own memory representation of text.
12. Inability to organize and synthesize individual idea units into a summary or to integrate the text into a coherent semantic representation.

There are surely other elements in text that make it difficult to organize and structure text (we identified some of these in chapter 7), but those listed seem to be most crucial.

Strategies for Developing Organizational Comprehension

The significance of the question strategy was affirmed in chapter 7 as a part of the DRA. Questions of an organizational type should check upon the pupil's ability to perceive sequence, to categorize, to understand story grammar, to identify organizational patterns and cues signaling organization, to summarize and outline what is read, and to use a circle diagram, semantic webbing, and pyramiding to organize what is being read. Other organizational strategies, which we have discussed in various parts of this text, include: underlining, paraphrasing, recalling the main idea, rereading, rehearsal and repetition, use of mnemonic devices, forming of mental images, and illustrations (Just & Carpenter, 1987). The writer also reveals his organization through the use of headings, italic print, and notations.

Sequence

Children's initial experience in organizational comprehension may involve grouping of a series of pictures in a logical or chronological order or arranging directions or ideas in a sequential order. Burmeister (1974) suggests that sequencing often takes the form of chronological order, spatial order, or expository order:

Chronological	Spatial	Expository
Flow Chart	Sketch	Outline
Outline	Map	Chart
Time Line	Floor Plan	Graph
Tree Chart		Map

Categorization

Categorizing or grouping is another early step in learning to comprehend the organization of what is written. We discussed in chapter 4 the significant role that categories play in the structure of nonvisual information or schemata classification. Smith (1988) believes that children are born with the ability to categorize. Categories are that part of the nonvisual information that is essential for making sense of the world. In chapter 10, we identified categorization as a significant element in teaching words in semantically and topically related sets, involving semantic association, semantic mapping, and semantic feature analysis. Categorization teaches the pupil the relatedness of words and concepts. Fortunately, almost all classroom materials lend themselves to exercises in classification. Sample exercises are:

1. Have pupils underline the word or object in a group of words or objects that does not belong:

purple	black	yellow	<u>shoes</u>	red
river	lake	<u>bridge</u>	ocean	sea

2. Have pupils group a series of objects (e.g., pencil, gloves, train, boat, boots, pen, crayon, plane, coat) into the appropriate

categories (e.g., things to ride in, things to write with, and things to wear).

Story Grammar

A special component of the reader's schemata is, or at least should be, knowledge of the different types of discourse or a generalized framework of how discourses are structured. Narrative schemata or story grammars generally consist of setting, theme, plot, and resolution. Narratives (Just & Carpenter, 1987) describe a series of events that are distributed over some time period and that are linked by a causal or thematic chain. They are organized in a special way, and pupils will be better comprehenders if they understand story structure or story grammar, if they understand the superstructure of a story, or if they possess a story map. Perhaps the simplest story structure is seen in the primary-level stories. Primary children quickly develop a sense of story structure, dividing stories into beginning, middle, and end of the story. Intermediate-grade pupils will add the elements of a setting, plot, and theme. Children develop a sense of story or story grammar through having stories read to them, through telling stories, and through reading.

Circle stories (Jett-Simpson, 1981; Vogel, 1987) may be used to teach story structure through visual diagramming of the story. The circle diagram is particularly effective with stories that have a main character begin at one location, and after a series of adventures, have the character return to the starting point to live happily ever after. *The Runaway Bunny* (Brown, 1942) is such a story. The teacher draws a large circle on the board or on butcher paper and divides it into as many segments as there are adventures in the story. At the top of the circle a house or cabin is drawn to represent the beginning and end of the story. After the story has been read, the teacher has the class recall the story and has them identify the sequence of adventures that the story describes. These adventures are then visualized and put into picture form, with different subgroups of children illustrating each of the adventures.

Another way to help children visualize story structure is to help them become familiar with the formal elements of the story structure. Just and Carpenter (1987) note that stories have both a content and a structure and both of these enter into the comprehension process. The structure of stories is known as story grammar. Just and Carpenter (1987) differentiate between story grammar and story schema. They observe that story grammar denotes the hierarchical relations among the components more directly than does a story schema. The story grammar resides in the text and is a framework with a number of slots that correspond to the various structural components of a story text. Whaley (1981b) uses the term story grammar more broadly and defines it as "a set of rules that defines both a story's structure and an individual's mental representation of the structure." Perfetti (1985) defines story grammar as a rule-based description of regularities in the structure of stories, predicated on the fact that stories conventionally have settings and episodes. We use the term story grammar to refer to a set of rules that spell out how stories are typically organized (Gordon & Braun, 1983). These rules specify the component parts of the stories, the types of information that occur at various locations of the story, and the relationship among parts. Story schema in this text refers to the idealized internal or mental representation of the parts of the story and the relationship among these parts (Mandler & Johnson, 1977). It is a set of expectations about the internal structure of stories.

A story schema can be thought of as a mental framework; it resides in the mind of the reader and consists of a labeled slot for each story component, such as setting or plot. As a person reads each component of the story, she fills in the schema slot for that component with the content of the story she is reading (Just & Carpenter, 1987). The story schema thus provides a filing system for organizing the content of a story. Readers use the story schema in comprehending and later in recalling the story.

The goal of teaching is: (a) to make story structure explicit and (b) to teach children to use the story structure as a metatextual aid in reading (Gordon & Braun, 1983). The major story elements (Gordon & Braun, 1983; Johnson & Mandler, 1980; Sadow, 1982; Stein & Glenn, 1979; Thorndyke, 1977) are setting, theme, plot (or episodes), and resolution. The plot consists of one or more episodes, with each episode composed of a setting (termed minor settings) and of the six facets of episode structure (initiating event, event itself, inner response, action, outcome, and the reaction to the earlier action). The plot or episode thus is the overall plan for the story and includes: (a) the initiating event or the beginning of the episode; (b) the problem or event itself; (c) the inner response—the main character's emotional reaction that causes him or her to initiate action and that sets up a goal; (d) the action—the effort or the plan to achieve the goal; (e) the outcome of the action or the consequence that gives the result of the attempt; and (f) the ending or reaction to the earlier action that is the concluding response to the situation (the main character's feelings about his or her goal attainment). The theme is the main idea that the writer wishes to convey. Figure 12-2 summarizes the story elements.

Even though not every story has the structure shown in Figure 12-2, knowledge of the component parts of the "ideal" story structure appears to enhance comprehension and to provide a framework for recalling events-through inference (Rand, 1984). Mandler (1978) notes that the more a story

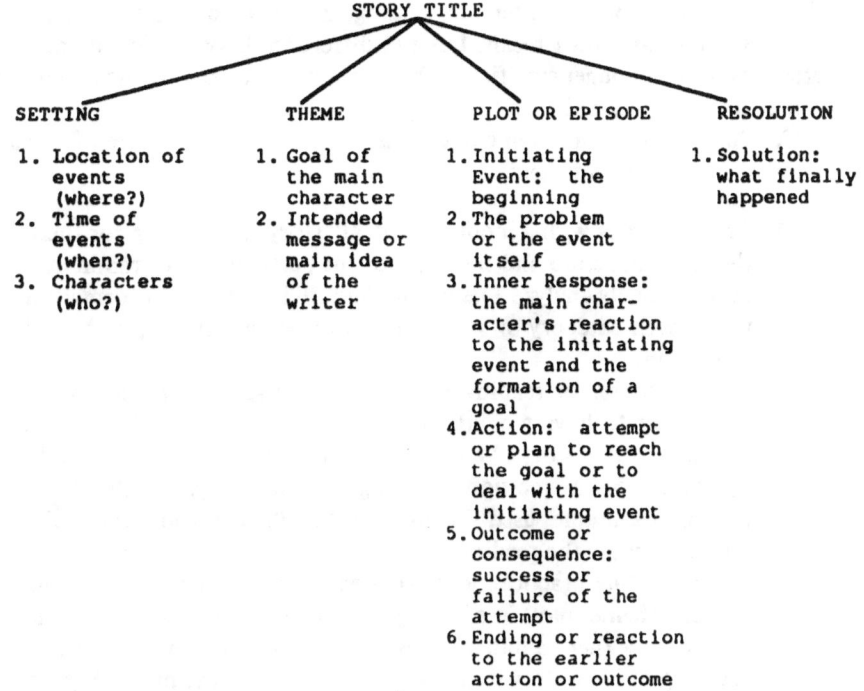

FIGURE 12-2. Schematic Representation of Story Structure

conforms to an ideal story structure, the better it will be comprehended, summarized, and recalled. Whaley (1981a) notes that readers of all ages come to expect certain structures in stories and that reading ability is related to an awareness of text structure. Bruce (1978) suggests that a failure to understand story structure may be an important factor in reading disability. McGee (1982a) found that the awareness of story structure develops with age, with older children having a better defined schema for stories than do younger children. Recall of stories is generally not developed until about the age of eight. Children clearly benefit and develop better schemata for stories when they have many experiences with well-formed stories, when they have many stories read to them (Rand, 1984), and when, as noted in chapter 7, story grammar is used as a framework for asking children questions about the setting, theme, plot, resolution, and characters before, during, and after reading the story. Mandler and Johnson (1977) found that first graders are better at recalling settings, beginnings, and outcomes, but their recall was poor on attempts, ending, and reactions. Fourth graders had a similar pattern of recall, but the difference between outcomes and their recall was poor on attempts, ending, and reactions. Fourth graders had a similar pattern of recall, but the difference between outcomes and attempts were no longer significant. Young children tend to stress outcomes rather than the internal events.

Teaching the skill of reading and comprehending the structure of stories may take the following steps:

1. Present pupils with a model or "ideal" story, identifying for them the story structure and the component parts of story grammar.
2. Have students analyze a new story and fill in the story information under each category of story structure: setting, theme, plot, and resolution.
3. Set a purpose for reading by asking story schema-related questions prior to having children read a story segment: What is the location of this story? Who are the characters? Who is the main character? Such questions can significantly improve the questioning technique used in the DRA. Elicit responses to the questions after the reading.
4. Have students practice identifying each of the story components (setting, theme, plot) in a variety of stories, emphasizing first one aspect and then another. Develop the pupil's overall understanding of ideal story structure. This will allow the pupil to grasp main ideas, summarize, recall, and understand relationships among story plots (Rand, 1984).
5. Ask story-specific questions, emphasizing not only literal questions, but also inferential questions.
6. Guide pupils in asking their own story-specific questions and in finding answers to their questions.

In the context of story structure, reading to children takes on new meaning. It expands children's vocabulary and develops their schemata, but it also develops their sense of story grammar.

Expository Grammar or Textbook Organization

The reader must also come to understand the organization of expository text. Textbooks and other expository materials generally share a similar organization (Ringler & Weber, 1984). This structure is substantially different from that of narratives. The writer provides introductory material, explanatory or informational material, and summary material. The topic sentence sets the theme of the paragraph. A sequence of details follows and the paragraph is concluded by a summarizing sentence. Expository materials thus generally are organized about superordinate, coordinate, and subordinate ideas (see Figure 12-3); they are structured about main ideas and details. This basic organization is used by the writer to present information in a coherent and logical fashion. If the target concept is reptiles, (see Figure 12-3), the superordinate concept is cold-blooded vertebrates (an even more general classification is animal); the coordinate concept is amphibians, and the subordinate concepts are alligators, snakes, or lizards (Tierney, Readance, & Dishner, 1985).

The reader of textbooks is significantly benefited when he uses the graphic representations (graphs, charts, tables, diagrams, illustrations, and figures), the typographical cues (chapter titles, headings, subheadings, boldface type, and italics), the questions at the beginning or end of the chapters, the terminal aids (the indexes, glossary, and tables), and the introductory and summary paragraphs (Ringler & Weber, 1984) to understand the organization of text.

Research indicates that readers who use the author's organization pattern to organize their own memory of a passage actually recall more than those who do not, and that good readers are more likely to do this than do poor readers (Irwin, 1986a). The evidence also suggests that awareness of organizational patterns in expository materials develops much later than does awareness of story structure. The reader must become especially proficient: (a) in developing either by himself or conjointly with the teacher a structured overview of the material to be read, (b) in understanding paragraph organization, and (c) in identifying and understanding the cues, the markers or structure words, that signal organization.

Sometimes writers signal the structure by explicitly stating the structure of organization. More commonly they present previews, make introductory statements, or write topic sentences that cue organization. They offer titles and subtitles, and may offer structural overviews or advance organizers. You may want to refresh your memory by reading in chapter 11 the section on "Comprehending Paragraph Organization."

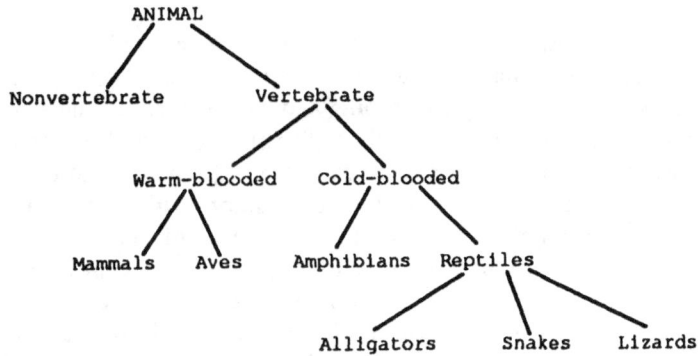

FIGURE 12-3. Reptiles

Summarizing, Outlining, and Underlining

Text modeling also requires the reader to synthesize individual propositions into a summary or into an organized series of related general ideas. These processes are useful only if the reader uses this organization to organize his own memory representation of text.

Summarizing. A reason poor readers or poor comprehenders often have so much difficulty in using sentence and paragraph structure to identify meaning is that they are unable to summarize and to outline the material. Summaries help to preserve the main ideas and the supporting details in capsule form. Often the topic sentence is a good summary of a paragraph. If the aim of the comprehension process is the reconstruction of what the writer wanted to say, then summarizing, having the pupil retell what he read in his own words, or paraphrasing becomes important. It is the only way teachers can know what the pupil's reconstruction or representations of the text is (Devine, 1984). Bromley (1985) found that summarizing or precise writing and outlining had equal value with fifth graders. McNeil and Donant (1982) found that teaching fifth graders to understand and use the rules of summarization had a positive effect on comprehension.

Usually five steps or operations (Brown & Day 1983a, 1983b) are recommended in summarizing text: (a) delete redundancy; (b) delete trivia; (c) substitute superordinates for a list of items or of actions (if the text speaks of cats, dogs, parrots, etc., one may want to substitute *pets*); (d) select topic sentences; and (e) invent topic sentences when they are not formally stated. Summaries are particularly useful when reading stories, essays, or social-science materials; they are not so useful in chemistry, physics, or biology. A summary, synthesis, or synopsis is all that may be necessary for retaining important information about the former. As for the latter, a summary may be longer than the original.

Outlining. Outlining is just another way of organizing information. It is closely related to summarizing. When readers own their books, they sometimes outline them by underlining and by using letters and numbers to designate main and subordinate points. The outline shows how main topics, subtopics, and details are related to each other. Pupils should be taught to look for the organization early in the primary grades. In their earliest picture reading, pupils learn to follow a sequence of events. In their first stories they learn to identify the main idea. Gradually, they will learn to put the story with its main idea and its supporting details into a simple outline. The outline should identify the major ideas and show the relation of supporting details in logical, sequential order. More formal outlining is usually taught during the middle grades.

To outline text, pupils must learn to select essential details, to ignore unimportant details, and to put the materials into an outline. They start by listing the major points. Points of lesser importance and that support the main ideas are indented. Indentation gives clues to the organization. Sometimes the pupil may want both to indent and to letter and number the headings. Roman numerals represent major headings or coordinate concepts; second-order headings represent subordinate concepts and are indented and prefaced by capital letters; headings or points that support second-order headings, hence third-order headings, are preceded by Arabic numerals; fourth-order concepts are preceded by lower-case letters:

TITLE (SUPERORDINATE CONCEPT)

I. Major topic, main idea, or coordinate concepts (major heading)
   A. Detail Supporting Major Topic 1 (Second-Order Heading)
   B. Detail Supporting Major Topic 1 (Second-Order Heading)
      1. Detail Supporting B (Third-Order Heading)
      2. Detail Supporting B (Third-Order Heading)
         a. Subordinate detail supporting 2 (Fourth-Order Heading)
         b. Subordinate detail supporting 2 (Fourth-Order Heading)
      3. Detail Supporting B
   C. Detail Supporting Major Topic I
II. Major topic (coordinate concept)
   A. Detail Supporting Major Topic II
   B. Detail Supporting Major Topic II
   C. Detail Supporting Major Topic II

The pupil should be taught to use the following steps in writing a basic outline:

1. Identify the title of the article: it tells what the main concept of the article is; it identifies the superordinate concept.
2. Write the main or major topics in order, starting each of them with the correct Roman numeral followed by a period. The first word of each main topic should begin with a capital letter, but no period should be placed at the end. These topics or ideas represent the coordinate concepts.
3. Identify the main supporting ideas and group them about the major topic. These are subordinate ideas.

Underlining. Another form of organizing information is underlining (McAndrew, 1983; Poostay, 1984). Many pupils use underlining of key words and phrases in a book to organize what they have read. Research shows that in underlining the Von Restorff effect is operative. The isolation of an item against a homogeneous background (as, for example, by printing one word in a different color) produces increased recall of that item. This is also true for preunderlining, as when the teacher provides handouts with certain materials underlined (McAndrew. 1983).

Semantic Webbing

Semantic webbing (Anderson & Armbruster, 1984; Clewell & Haidemos, 1983) or semantic mapping (Pearson & Johnson, 1978) is a visual display or diagram of categories and their interrelationships (Freedman & Reynolds, 1980); it is another aid to organizing and integrating concepts and events within a story or within expository materials. It helps the pupil to see the relationships within the reading material and to organize the concepts of the material (Flood & Lapp, 1988).

Semantic webbing defines text structure. It is a technique for figuring out the writer's organization and making it visual. It displays relationships visually through spatial configurations. It illustrates the similarities and differences among concepts. It establishes a relationship between the pupil's schema and the text's message (McNeil, 1984). And, it develops critical thinking skills.

Semantic maps or semantic organizers can be constructed before, during, or after reading. Reutzel (1985a) observes that semantic webs may be used as prereading organizers to guide the introduction of the reading material, as a visual device to help pupils summarize reflectively during reading, or as a device for discussing and reviewing what has been read. They clearly help pupils to organize, to integrate, and to comprehend both narrative and expository materials (Reutzel, 1985a). They appear to be especially effective with poor readers who cannot code (label) or synthesize (chunk) information for effective storage and retrieval (Sinatra et al., 1984). A semantic map that is completed before the reading occurs is a sort of prediction that pupils can modify, amend, or correct as they read.

The semantic web (Figure 12-4) consists of:

1. The core question: This is the title of the selection and is analogous to the establishing of a purpose for reading as recommended in Step 1 of the DRA. The title can be turned into a core question. It encourages the pupil to use a reading-thinking strategy.

    The core question is the focus of the web. From a predictive, reading-thinking point of reference, if the article is about baking a cake or about favorite pastimes, the core question may take the form of: "How does one make a cake?" or "What are some favorite past times?" The answers to these questions represent the web strands. They identify the main ideas.

2. Web strands are the answers to the core question. They are the main ideas that are grouped about the superordinate concept or the title. Thus the article on "Favorite Pastimes" includes five main ideas or coordinate concepts: bowling, travel, fishing, television, and reading (see Figure 12-4).
3. Strand supports are facts and details taken from the account that support and differentiate one web strand from another and that give validity to the strands. The strand supports are the subordinate concepts. Thus, reading as a pastime may involve reading of newspapers, journals, and books.
4. Strand ties are the relationships the strands have with one another. Strand ties may also be perceived as fourth-order or even fifth-order concepts.

The completed web demonstrates in a concrete way the process of comprehending print. The center of the web identifies the superordinate idea or concept. It identifies what the selection is all about. The spokes contain the related ideas. Figure 12-4 illustrates a semantic web for an article on

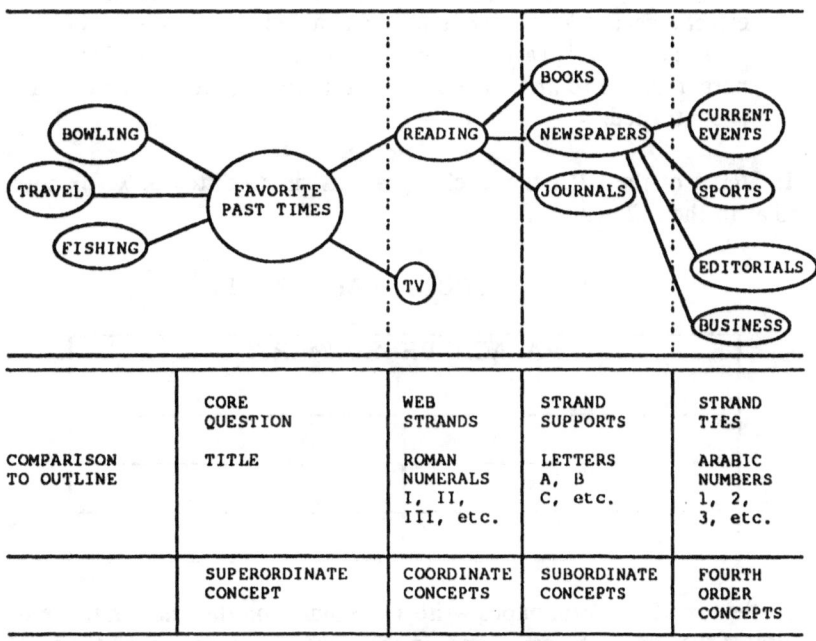

FIGURE 12-4. Semantic Web

"Favorite Pastimes" and shows relationships of the semantic web to outlines. Only the "Reading Strand" is presented with its detail. Observe that the strand ties can be broken down even further. Thus, the sports section of a newspaper may include hockey, football, tennis, volleyball, and so on. These would represent fifth-order concepts and would be represented in an outline as lower case letters: *a, b, c* and so on.

DRA

To help pupils organize what they are reading and to help them understand the writer's organization, the biggest modification in the DRA should occur in Steps 1 and 5 (Colwell & Helfeldt, 1983). In Step 1 of the DRA the teacher should:

1. Alert pupils to the writer's dominant style (paragraph organization) by providing several paragraphs of that type on the overhead projector. The teacher should lead a discussion into what type of a paragraph it is: cause-effect, comparison-contrast, etc.
2. Furnish pupils with a listing of the "signal" words that cue paragraph organization.
3. Distribute handouts containing paragraphs with various organizations and have students identify the organization of each.
4. Teach pupils, for example, to underline each cause once and each effect twice; to letter each item in a simple listing paragraph *a, b, c*, etc.; to number each item in a time-order, sequence or direction paragraph; or to underline once what is compared and twice what is contrasted.

In Step 5 of the DRA the teacher may distribute dittos or xerox copies similar to the following:

CAUSE–EFFECT PARAGRAPHS

PARAGRAPH SUMMARY	

At the top of the form pupils write a summary; on the lines on the left of the form they write the cause and on the right they record the effect.

COMPARISON/CONTRAST PATTERN

PARAGRAPH SUMMARY	

At the top of the form pupils write a summary of the paragraph; on the left of the form they write the first item and on the right they write the item that is bring contrasted or compared. The teacher should initially present and discuss exemplary paragraphs and should help students to write the summary statement. Students may then be subgrouped to work on each paragraph.

DEVELOPING INFERENTIAL COMPREHENSION

Inferential or interpretive comprehension, the third level of comprehending, goes beyond the printed page or beyond the explicitly stated content. Inference is "a reasoned assumption about information not explicitly stated in the text" (Leu & Kinzer, 1987, p. 198). Inferencing has a continuous role throughout the total text-modeling process. Specifically, readers use inferences:

1. To infer or to encode from context cues the meaning of unfamiliar single words and the specific meaning of the multiple meanings that can be associated with the word.
2. To infer referents for pronouns and adverbs.
3. To fill in the gaps in the text with inferences drawn from one's own background knowledge or to fill in the slots or the detail in the reader's schemata (slot-filling inferences) with information implicitly stated in the text. Readers must learn to make simple inferences or to read between the lines.
4. To infer the meaning of phrases whose meaning cannot be ascertained from the surface context (e.g., a run on the bank).
5. To infer the relationships or links between words, phrases, sentences, paragraphs, and total text.
6. To infer sequence and cause-effect relations among story parts.

7. To develop a basic understanding of stories. Beck and McKeown (1981, pp. 914–915) note that even the most basic understanding of a story requires the making of inferences as well as recall.
8. To make elaborative inferences or inferences not necessarily intended by the writer: e.g., making predictions about what might happen, responding affectively, etc.
9. To infer the main idea or the title of a story.
10. To draw conclusions.
11. To answer questions calling for inferential, interpretive, or connotative meaning, especially "why" questions calling for an inference.
12. To predict outcomes for story endings, to infer character traits, to infer mood, and to infer the author's purpose.

There are two types of inferences: (a) textually implicit or text-connecting inferences that connect two or more ideas given in the text and (b) scriptally implicit or slot-filling inferences that are made in order to fill in missing information or empty slots of meaning from one's background knowledge (Irwin, 1986a; Warren, Nicholas, & Trabasso, 1979). Just and Carpenter (1987) note that inferences are required when the text does not explicitly indicate how phrases and sentences are related to each other. Such inferences are termed text-connecting inferences (Warren, Nicholas, & Trabasso, 1979). They are required at the schematic level when the reader has to infer how a fact in the text fits a particular schema slot. Making schema-implicit inferences involves reading between and beyond the lines (McIntosh, 1985). Inference in this sense is a combination of conjecture and explanation based on a synthesis of the literal content, personal knowledge, intuition, and imagination. It goes beyond the printed page.

Most inferences are backward (other names for such inferencing are bridging inference, integrative inference, connective inference, or linking inference), linking the most recently read text to some portion of the text that came earlier. Forward inferences embellish the representation of the currently read text; they are variously termed predictive inference, extrapolative inference, or elaborative inference. Just and Carpenter (1987) note that such inferences are not essential to comprehension. Forward or elaborative inferences are inferences that were not intended by the writer. Readers do in fact often elaborate on the writer's intended message or embellish the text. Irwin (1986a) and McNeil (1987) refer to such inferencing as elaborative processing. Elaborative processing is manifested in such activities as making a prediction about what might happen; inferring a general concept (bird) from a specific concept (robin) or vice versa; paraphrasing the text in one's own language; relating what is read to one's own purposes; responding affectively; or responding with higher-level thinking processes.

Evaluative comprehension or critical reading, in which readers evaluate, judge statements for their logic, value, relevance, accuracy, and truthfulness, and in which they distinguish between propaganda and bias or between fact and opinion, are examples of elaborative inferencing. We will discuss the latter separately.

To be able to deal with inference, the pupil must first learn to handle convergent thinking or redefinition questions and open-ended or divergent thinking questions. Convergent thinking or convergent inference is involved in such skills as identifying topic sentences, determining sequence, and recalling details. It calls for some commonness of meaning or convergence between writer and reader. Convergent inferences are based principally upon information provided in the text. They cause the pupil to come to a specific correct answer or an agreed-upon hypothesis that may be verified through the data supplied by the writer.

Divergent inferences, on the other hand, call for imagination or creative thinking. A divergent inference is one that does not have to be judged as right or wrong. In divergent thinking, the individual develops alternative answers, none of which is necessarily correct but none of which is incorrect either. Divergent thinking is a synonym for creative thinking. When children are asked to give their interpretation of a poem, opinion of a character, or evaluation of a situation, their answer will, by definition, always be acceptable (Chester, 1976).

Divergent inferences, scriptally implicit inferences (Pearson, 1976), or schema-implicit inferences require an integration of one's prior knowledge with the text information. They bring the reader's own "scripts" or schemata to bear on reading between the lines. In this sense inference is the missing connection or link between the new knowledge and the reader's existing knowledge of the world (Anderson et al., 1977, 1978; Zintz & Maggart, 1984). Text is relatively more difficult and less readable as the need for inferencing or for searching one's schemata (i.e., one's long-term memory) increases (Kintsch, 1980; Perfetti, 1985; Stevens, 1982).

Irwin (1986b) observes that comprehension involves integrating a text into some sort of coherent semantic representation, and that cohesive relations (cohesive ties) contribute to this. In her view, the processing of noncohesive text is related to inference: "When a text lacks explicit links between sentence, a reader must infer those links" Irwin (1986b, p. 69). She adds: "If the inferring of these relations is an integral part of the comprehension process, then extensive training with questions focusing on the inference of cohesive relations might result in improved comprehension strategies" (1986b, p. 69).

Just and Carpenter (1987) also call attention to the effect that text and reader inferences have on coherence or organization. They note, "The comprehension of all types of texts involve inference making that uses previous knowledge of the text structure and content, conjointly with information in the text, (i.e., the text's structure), to produce coherence in the representation of the text" (p. 259). It is because the relations between events, objects, and facts in a text are often unstated that the reader must make inferences (Just & Carpenter, 1987).

The facts about inference were identified by McIntosh (1985) and are expanded upon here.

1. Studies of the reading abilities of 9-, 13-, and 17-year-olds (National Assessment of Education Progress, 1973, 1975, 1976, 1982, 1983, 1984, 1985, 1986) show that all age groups showed improvement in literal comprehension, but when the comprehension items became more difficult, either as a result of lengthy complex passages or because of questions that required some manipulation of the information, the 13- and 17-year-olds performed less well. The older pupils generally did not do as well on the inferential comprehension and reference (study) skill items. Schreiner and Shannon (1980) likewise found that poor readers consistently have more difficulty than good readers in answering inferential questions. Even so, in the general population the ability to infer, to understand and comprehend inferred relationships is developmental in nature (Tierney, Bridge, & Cera, 1978–79), improving with increased age.
2. The ability to infer can be enhanced through practice (Hansen & Pearson, 1983). Poor readers benefit more than good readers from training in answering inferential questions (Hansen & Pearson, 1982; Schmidt & Paris, 1983).
3. Kindergarten and first-grade children can make inferences only when the component premises or propositions are located together or right after one another (Johnson & Smith, 1981).
4. Aiding students in making connections and in understanding the logical connections between sentences enhances comprehension and retention of passages (Trabasso, 1981) and makes pupils more conscious of the need to search actively for meaning.
5. Drawing inferences always involves calling on one's world knowledge. Readers usually make inferences consistent with their schemata. The troubles of poor and very young readers in inferencing is directly related to their background deficiency (Holmes, 1983a). Background information has a greater effect on understanding implicit information than in understanding literal information.

Lipson (1984) observes that lack of background information accounts for text difficulty to a greater degree than do either sentence length or word frequency.
6. Probe questions elicit nearly three times the number of inferential statements as does the free recall of a story (Brown et al., 1977).
7. Children frequently overlook explicitly stated causal statements and form inferences that are totally incongruent with the text (Nicholson & Imlack, 1981).
8. Teachers ask literal questions five times as often as inferential questions (Hansen, 1981).
9. An inferential question ("What do you think the man was using?") whose answer is contained in one sentence ("The man was hitting the nail into the wall"), is more readily answered (the assumption is that the man is using a hammer) than is one, the answer to which requires information contained in several sentences (Paris & Upton, 1976).

Holmes (1963b) presents a confirmation strategy for filling in missing information, involving five steps:

1. Reading the passage: Pupils read the passage and an associated inferential question.

    "The more Roy walked, the darker it grew. He had to crouch to keep from bumping the damp rocks overhead. To his left ran a small underground brook. It was the only sound he heard besides his footsteps crunching over stones and earth. When he turned around, Roy saw the place where he had come in. It was a small, bright spot of light."

    Question: Where is Roy?

2. Hypothesizing an answer: Pupils generate tentative answers to the question (Roy was at the beach; on the mountain top; in a cave), using their prior knowledge and experiences.
3. Identifying key words: Pupils, beginning with the first sentence, identify key words such as walked, darker it grew, etc.
4. Formulating and answering yes/no questions: The teacher formulates yes/no questions based on the pupils' tentative answers and on the key words. For example, do the key words go along with the answer "at the beach?" If Roy is at the beach could he walk? Could it be getting darker? Could he be bumping damp rocks overhead? The answer to the last question is "no" and thus Roy could not be at the beach. Could Roy be in a cave?

5. Making a final confirmation: Pupils continue asking whether the key words go along with the tentative answers. When all the key words fit with one of the tentative answers (for example, "in a cave"), it is likely that the correct inference has been identified.

Additional strategies and activities useful in developing inferencing, hypothesizing, and predicting skill include the following:

1. Have pupils infer meaning form pictorial cues and from cartoons.
2. Have the pupil respond to and answer questions over the material read and calling for divergent or scriptally implicit inferences:
   a. How do you interpret this poem?
   b. What is your opinion of the main character?
   c. What might have been the motives of the main character?
   d. Could you provide a new ending?
   e. Do these people live in the way we do?
   f. Where do you think the incident took place?
3. Have pupils respond to questions asking for implied meaning or that require the pupil to infer meaning of a word from contextual cues: "It was so frigid outside that I quickly buttoned up my coat." What is the meaning of the word "frigid"? It is logical that the reason the person buttoned his or her coat was that it was cold and that frigid, therefore, is likely to mean cold.
4. Use the cloze procedure. The cloze technique usually involves the deletion of every fifth word and having the pupil predict what the deleted word is. An effective exercise is to require the pupil to fill in a blank: "The little _____ went chirp, chirp"; "When John opened the_____ , he found that someone had pilfered his safe and all his money." The teacher may cover up the context after the blank, have the pupil make a guess, and have the pupil then check the remainder of the sentence to see whether the result makes sense.
5. Have pupils read portions of a narrative (the title, subtitles, the initial sentence, and the illustrations, etc.) and make predictions about how the story will develop and end, and then read further to test the validity of their predictions. When finished reading, pupils need to evaluate which of their hypotheses were confirmed. The teacher may ask: "Can you predict what the story is about from the opening passage?" "Can you predict how the story will end?" "Are there other endings that are possible?"
6. Have pupils read a cause-effect paragraph and then have them respond to questions based on cause-effect relationship.
7. Teach children to identify the appropriate referents for pronouns and adverbs and for deleted words.

8. Have pupils read a paragraph and then have them make inferences about the character, reputation, or social standing of the main characters in the selection (Auckerman & Auckerman, 1981, p. 286).

"Yes, and you done more than that," said Injun Joe, approaching the doctor, who was now standing. "Five years ago you drove me away from your father's kitchen one night when I come to ask for something to eat, and you said I wasn't there for any good, and when I swore I'd get even with you if it took a hundred years, your father had me jailed as a vagrant. Did you think I'd forget?" (*Tom Sawyer* by Mark Twain).

   a. What can you infer about the doctor's character from the passage?
   b. What can you infer about the kind of man the doctor's father was?
   c. Was Injun Joe a forgiving man?

DEVELOPING EVALUATIVE COMPREHENSION (CRITICAL READING)

Evaluation or critical reading requires the reader to make evaluative judgements about the content, using external or internal criteria as points of reference. The external criteria might be the teacher or authorities on the subject; internal criteria might be the reader's personal experiences and knowledge or the internal logic or consistency of the passage or article. Harris and Hodges (1981) offer the following definition of critical reading:

> (1) The process of making judgements in reading, evaluating relevancy and adequacy of what is read; (2) an act of reading in which a questioning attitude, logical analysis, and inference are used to judge the worth of what is read according to an established standard; and (3) the judgment of validity or worth of what is read, based on sound criteria or standards developed through previous experience.

Critical reading or evaluative comprehension involves the higher order cognitive processes of analysis, synthesis, and evaluation (Flynn, 1989); it requires the making of reliable observations, the introducing of sound inferences, and the forming of reasonable hypotheses (Norris, 1985). It is a form of elaborative inferencing. Critical reading demands that the reader evaluate—pass personal judgment on the quality, logic, appropriateness, reasonableness, authenticity, adequacy, value, relevancy, timeliness, accuracy, completeness, and truthfulness of what is read. It involves the evaluation of the reliability and intellectual worthwhileness of printed materials. It means that the reader must be able to recognize the author's intent and point of view. The good reader looks for contradictory material, distinguishes reality from fantasy or fact from fiction or opinion, questions but tries to understand the author's motives, and goes beyond the facts to get the inferred meaning. Critical readers continuously test the writer's statements against their own observations, information, and experiences. Questioning and predicting, which, as was noted earlier, are basic to all comprehending, are particularly integral to drawing inferences and conclusions, to distinguishing fact from fiction, to sorting the significant from the insignificant, all key aspects of critical reading (Early & Sawyer, 1984).

Critical readers are as much interested in why something is said as in what is said. They are sensitive to how words are used and are slightly suspicious of the author's biases. They possess a critical attitude (Norris, 1985; Smith, 1988). They pay particular attention to words with several meanings and check the author's credentials and the publisher's past performance. Critical readers ask themselves: "How does what the author is saying compare with what I know and feel to be true about the subject, and does it compare with what authorities say about the subject?" (Burmeister, 1983, p. 303).

It is obvious that readers must prepare themselves so that they can detect generalities, oversimplification, distortion, fallacious reasoning, overgeneralization, inconsistency, inaccuracy, and unwarranted clichés. As citizens, as buyers of somebody's products, or as pupils in a classroom, individuals are constantly subjected to writings that attempt to make them think in a given way. They are asked to give allegiance to one thing and to turn against something else. "Resisting propaganda, discarding irrelevant information, choosing between two opinions when both are strongly supported, and being able to change one's thinking pattern when new evidence proves an old idea wrong or obsolete are all benefits of a well-developed critical reading ability" (Zintz and Maggart, 1984, p. 386).

Teachers should promote critical reading from first grade on. First graders can deal with such issues as whether a story is real or make-believe or whether an incident in a story could really have happened (e.g., "Can animals really talk?"). They can be taught to read pictures critically, perhaps to identify what is wrong in a picture.

Newspapers, especially the editorial section, offer numerous opportunities for practicing critical reading during the intermediate grades.

Teaching of critical reading skills may be accomplished with activities such as the following.

1. Have pupils compare editorials on similar subjects from two newspapers: Have them decide what the differences are and which view seems to be more logical and reasonable, based on the facts.

2. Have pupils interpret political cartoons.
3. Have pupils compare newspaper headlines and have them determine which fit the story and which do not.
4. Have pupils read a short paragraph containing an underlined statement of opinion and have them indicate: (a) if no evidence is given to support the opinion, (b) if supporting evidence is given, and (c) if supporting evidence is given by a qualified writer. Pupils need to learn the differences between fact (it is something that is known to exist; it is real or true; it is an actual event; one can prove it) and opinion (a belief, a judgment, a personal attitude). Pupils need to be able to determine which statements are fact and which are opinion (Johns, 1986). Pupils should also learn that words like I think, probably, maybe, appear, seems, I believe, could, and should are usually associated with the expression of opinion.
5. Have pupils read a story and then indicate whether it is real, fictional, or make-believe, whether it is truth or fantasy.
6. Have pupils stop before they come to the writer's conclusion and let them state all the possible solutions. Conclusions are reasoned deductions or inferences. Have pupils determine whether the conclusion, inference, or thesis flows from the facts presented.
7. Have pupils answer questions calling for an evaluative or critical response. Questions which require critical evaluation of what is read may take variant forms:
   a. Is this important?
   b. Is the writer evading the question?
   c. Is the writer trying to get me off the track or to divert my thinking from the main issue?
   d. Are these facts or simply opinions of the writer?
   e. What can you agree with and with what do you disagree? Does the story fit with what you know from past experiences?
   f. Is there another side of the story?
   g. Is this a true story?
   h. Did the writer omit important information?
8. Teach pupils the difference between connotative and denotative meanings of words. The critical reader understands the connotations or fine shades of meanings that words have in different contexts. The words, conservative, warmonger, isolationist, progressive educator, selfish, conformist, world-minded, idealist, overzealous, and liberal, mean different things to people.
9. Have pupils interpret figures of speech, indicating what the meaning of the underlined phrase is: "Grandma grinned like a cheshire cat when we yelled 'Surprise!' with a broad smile". Other similar phrases are: quiet as a mouse, like a ton of bricks, slow as molasses in winter,

busy as a beaver, clean as a whistle, sly as a fox, angry as a wet hen, light as a feather, a real cliffhanger, is a wet blanket, straight from the horse's mouth, blow one's stack, his hands are tied, (Jack) simmered down, bring home the bacon, let the cat out of the bag, be out of the woods, racking one's brain, to make light of, keep one's head, hot under the collar, don't want to be in your shoes, on top of the world, beating the pavement, stick in the mud, be on cloud nine, talk one's head off, snowed under with work, hit the ceiling, turn over a new leaf, shoot the breeze, sit tight, be down in the mouth, spill the beans, keep one's nose to the grindstone, live high off the hog, blow up at someone, lose one's marbles, take with a grain of salt, be dead on one's feet, it burns me up, to hit the hay, talk one's ear off, raise the roof, like the Rock of Gibraltar, and put one's foot in one's mouth.

10. Have pupils match the following propaganda techniques with statements used in printed materials:
   a. Citation of authority or testimonial and/or endorsements: getting some prominent person, a movie star or athlete, to endorse an idea or product in order to get others to act favorably to the product or idea: "Reggie Jackson uses Louisville Slugger bats."
   b. Bandwagon or "everybody is doing it" technique: "Everybody is getting a Johnny Carson suit for Christmas."
   c. Glittering generality: using a shred of truth or evidence as the basis for a sweeping generalization. Glittering generalizations are vague phrases that promise far beyond what is deliverable (e.g., "This action will benefit all Americans").
   d. Transfer technique: similar to testimonial, but supporting statement is not directly associated with what is being advocated. It is the association of a respected organization or symbol with a particular person, product, or idea, thus transferring that respect to the person or thing being promoted (Burns, Roe & Ross, 1984). For example: "President Reagan owns property just one mile from our new Pleasant Valley subdivision."
   e. Name-calling: using a derogatory term to create a negative attitude (e.g., "Who wants one of those gas guzzlers?"). In name-calling (calling a politician a crook or a fascist), it is the labels and not the facts that are used to get the desired reaction.
   f. Card-stacking: telling only one side of the story, using quotations out of context, using favorable statistics while supressing unfavorable ones, etc.
   g. Unwarranted inference or cliché.
   h. Begging the question.

i. Argument ad hominum: Getting the reader to accept a conclusion by ridiculing the opposition rather than by attacking the argument. Name-calling is such a technique.
11. The teacher can help pupils to analyze propaganda (Roe, Stoodt & Burns, 1983) by having pupils answer the following questions: What propaganda technique did the writer use? Who composed the propaganda? Why was the propaganda statement written? To what reader interests, emotions, and prejudices does the propaganda appeal? Will you allow yourself to be influenced by this propaganda?
12. Have pupils evaluate the source of the material. This includes the writer's qualification and reputation, background, experience, education, biases, purposes, and motives. Is the selection up to date? What is the source of this material? What is the copyright date? Is the writer qualified? What is the reputation of the publisher? Is this material reliable? Is there another side of the story? Is the writer biased or prejudiced? Is he making a one-sided presentation? Is he using questionable sampling? Faulty inference? Is he overgeneralizing? Is he oversimplifying? Is he jumping to quick solutions or conclusions? Is the writer employing undesirable propaganda techniques? Is the writer trying to get me off the track or to divert my attention from the main issue? The critical reader needs to be able to follow inductive and deductive argument, spot generalizations, and to be sensitive to analogies and such simple devices as guilt through association.
13. Have pupils evaluate the reliability of information by collecting several viewpoints from different sources on the same topic.
14. Teach pupils that one can react to what an author has written in many ways (agree or disagree with some or all of the reading, evaluate the author's attitudes or point of view, relate what the writer wrote to one's background and experiences, evaluate the validity of the author's arguments, etc.), present students with sentences and model the approach, and finally present sentences with which they are required to agree or disagree, which they must evaluate, or which they must relate to their own background of experiences (Johns, 1986).

DEVELOPING APPRECIATIVE COMPREHENSION

In addition to problems with inferencing and with reading critically, some pupils have difficulty identifying the mood, tone, or theme of a selection, seeing the intent or purpose of the writer, or perceiving the literary and semantic devices by means of which the writer accomplishes his or her purpose. Shaw (1958) observed that the writer's rhetorical and grammatical contrivances characterize his writing. "Like the ice cream cone, which is both container and confection, a writer's contrivances not only support ideas, but also are digestible themselves" (p. 239). Aesthetic reading involves qualities of language beyond the direct, specific meanings denoted by words (Cunningham et al., 1983).

Appreciation requires the reader to become aware of the literary techniques, forms, and styles employed by the writer to stimulate emotional response. It includes the emotional response to the plot or theme, identification with the characters and incidents, reactions to the author's use of language and imagery, but it also involves the recognition of and response to the artistry involved in developing stimulating plots, themes, settings, incidents, and characters and in selecting and using stimulating language. Unless the reader has at least some experience with the topic, is familiar with the specific rhetorical devices used in poems, plays, short stories, essays, novels, and biographies, and can process the language and stylistic features of the writer, it is unlikely that the reader will be able to make accurate predictions of the writer's meaning.

Reading in literature and reading of narratives best identifies the skills that are subsumed under appreciative comprehension. Reading in literature calls for special appreciation of the mood and style of the author; it requires the reader to respond to form, to connotative meanings, to rhyme, and to emotional overtones; and it requires appreciation of such literary forms as drama, the sonnet, the essay, and the metaphor. The reader of literature must analyze the characters, appreciate the style, or manner of expression, and digest the sequence of development (Tremonti & Alegero, 1967). Reading literature requires literal understanding, analysis, interpretative reading, critical insight, symbolic interpretation, aesthetic appreciation, and recognition of the relevance of literature to life. Readers of literature go beyond mere passive acceptance or simple literal comprehension; they do something with what is read (Simmons, 1965).

If the teacher is to facilitate the pupil's comprehension of literature, he must help the pupil to become knowledgeable about types of narratives. The term genre refers to the variant types: short stories, novels, plays, poetry, essays, fables, biographies, legends, and myths. Each literary form has its own mode of expression. Poetry adds the dimensions of rhythm, metrical form, metaphor, and rhyme. It is characterized by irregular syntax; the juxtaposition of words for auditory and aesthetic effects is peculiar; and the writing is littered with irregular constructions. Essays portray a variety of moods: formal, pedantic, humorous, satiric, philosophical, inspirational, persuasive, or political.

Whole stories usually form the basis for the classroom reading program (Ringler & Weber, 1984). And this is as it should be. What is read usually presents connected discourse organized around a particular idea, and the best reader-text interaction occurs when a complete narrative is read. The story grammar is especially useful as a framework for asking questions about a piece of narrative discourse or for scoring a pupil-generated retelling of the story. When retelling the story, children must focus on the total structure of the story, integrating all the information that is relevant (Marshall, 1984). They must construct a coherent representation of the entire story—a story which consists of a setting and one or more episodes and which can be evaluated for consistency. We earlier noted that pupils comprehend stories better if they have an understanding of story grammar or structure and if a story map or story grammar guides the teacher and the pupil in generating questions about the setting, plot, theme, and resolution, and also about characterization, mood, and style (Burns, Roe & Ross, 1984; Dechant, 1964, 1970, 1982; Pearson, 1982; Ringler & Weber, 1984).

The setting identifies the location or locale of the events (where?), the time of the events (when?), the chief characters (who?), and the customs and practices of the main people in the story. Questions about the setting may thus take the following form:

1. When and where did the story occur? Is this information important to the understanding of the story? How would the story change if the setting were changed?
2. How does the author describe when the story takes place?
3. How does the author describe where the story takes place?
4. Who are the main characters in the story?
5. Does the description of the characters and the language that they use fit the time and place when and where the story is said to have occurred?
6. How did the author reveal the setting?
7. Who is the main character?
8. What is the main character like?

An element of a story that relates to setting is the general mood of the story or the writer's point of view or perspective. It is the impression created by the setting, atmosphere, situation, and language. Questions directed to this aspect might be:

1. What is the general mood or tone of the writing?
2. Does the story capture the spirit and feeling of the place or time?
3. How does the story make you feel? What does the author do to make you feel this way?

The theme is the main idea or the meaning that the writer wishes to convey. Theme is the idea that holds the story together; it is the central meaning; it reveals the author's purpose and provides a dimension to the story that goes beyond the action of the plot (Huck, Hepler, & Hickman, 1987). Theme is the writer's intended message. It is the goal for which the main characters strive. Theme-related questions might take the following form:

1. What is the main point of the story?
2. Did the story have a moral? If so, what was it?
3. What does the main character need to do?
4. What does the story tell you about people?
5. What does the story tell you about the world?
6. How do the ideals portrayed fit your ideas and ideals?
7. What did the writer want the reader to learn from this story?

Themes or goals are often expressed as a part of the problem. The goal is usually the desire to alleviate the problem. To ascertain the theme of the story, the reader must be able to handle descriptive language, to identify the writer's purpose, to infer the main idea or general concept, and to formulate generalizations about the narrative.

The plot (or problem) is the overall plan for the story. It is the significant actions or related events which unfold in a specific order and lead to the story outcome. It includes a developing problem or conflict, a climax, and the resolution of the problem or conflict. The plot tells what the characters do and say and describes what happens to them. The plot is made up of a setting and one or more episodes (a series of events which focus upon a specific character). Each episode consists of the following parts: (a) the initiating event or problem which sets the story in motion; (b) the main character's reaction (reaction #1) to the initiating event or problem (this often leads to the formulation of a goal; it is the chief character's plan); (c) the action, attempt or plan to achieve the goal or to deal with the initiating event or problem; (d) the outcome or consequences (this is the success or failure of the attempt); (e) the ending (which is reaction #2 and is the response to the earlier action and outcome). Plot-related questions might be phrased thus:

I. Initiating event and problem or conflict
   A. What started the chain of events in the story?
   B. What is the main conflict, obstacle, or problem that the chief character faces and has to work out?
   C. Why was the main character in trouble?
   D. When did the problem begin?

E. How does the main character feel about the problem? (internal reaction)
F. What does the main character think about the problem? What was his or her reaction to the problem?

II. Attempt
A. What did the chief character do to try to solve the problem or to reach his or her goal?
B. What did the main character do first? Second?
C. Did the main character have to alter his or her goal because of the obstacle encountered?

III. Outcome The outcome is the result of the attempts to reach the goal; the ending, on the other hand, is the long-range consequences of the action and the final response of certain characters in the story (Lovitt, 1984).
A. Why did the main character fail to solve the problem?
B. What might the main character do next?
C. How was the problem solved?
D. What did the main character do to solve the problem?
E. Who solved the problem?

IV. Ending
A. What happened after the problem was solved?
B. Was there another way that the chief character might have solved the problem?
C. Does the end of the story fit with the rest of it?
D. Did the story end as you expected it would?
E. Did you like the ending?
F. How would you have changed the ending?
G. Did the writer use surprise, suspense, or mystery to keep you interested? Did the way the story was told hold you in suspense until the very end?

To ascertain the plot of the story the reader must be able to identify initiating events, to follow a sequence of events, to understand causality, and to pay special attention to anaphoric relations, especially to pronoun referents. In reading a story it is not enough to tap mere sequence (Pearson, 1982). The reader needs to understand that events are related causally. Pearson (1982) notes that "events often lead in some inevitable way toward one another; they do not simply precede and follow another."

The resolution represents the solution. It contains what finally happened. It may be expanded to include the moral.

Knowing how stories are constructed clearly helps pupils to understand narrative text. It helps them to sort out and tie together settings, characters, problems, goals, motivations, events, and resolutions in new stories that they encounter. And, as has been noted, it has the added value of developing within students an internal abstract sense of story, a story schema, that guides comprehension.

There are other aspects of narratives, besides those of setting, plot, theme, and resolution that need attention. From an appreciative comprehension perspective, pupils need to develop an appreciation for the story's genre, characterization, and the style and language used by the writer. Genre refers to the variant types of literature (short stories, novels, plays, poetry, essays, fables, biographies, myths, etc.). Questions such as the following are useful: What type of story is this? Is it fanciful or realistic literature? The reader must become familiar with the characteristics and structure of each type of narrative. Characterization refers to the way the writer makes the characteristics and motives of each person in the story evident to the reader (Burns, Roe, & Ross, 1984) through behavior, attitudes, feelings, language, and reactions of other people. Questions that get at characterization might be phrased thus:

1. What did you learn about the most important character in the story?
2. What did you learn about other characters in the story?
3. What words did the author use to describe the character?
4. Why do you think the author used these words to describe the character?
5. How do you know that the main character of the story is a real (imaginary) character?
6. Were the characters true to life?
7. If you were this character, what would you have done differently?
8. Which character do you like best? Which character would you like to be? Why? Which character did you like least?

To get at characterization the reader must pay attention to dialogue cues, must note comparison and contrast between actions and traits, must be able to draw conclusions about the character's behavior, must identify his or her own emotional reactions, must note the character's reactions and motives, should try to predict the character's behavior, and needs to understand anaphoric relations. In developing characterization skills the teacher must help pupils to see that writers describe the characters by: (a) telling about the character, (b) describing the character and the surroundings, (c) showing the character in action, (d) letting the character talk, (e) revealing the character's thoughts, (f) revealing what others say to the character, (g) narrating what others say about the character, (h) showing the reactions of others to the character, and (i) showing the character's reactions to others (Hook, 1963).

Style and language refers to the writer's mode of expressing thoughts in words or to the way a writer says something as opposed to the content of what is said. It includes tone, rhythm, word choice and usage, the order of words, use of connotative and denotative meanings, imagery, and use of figurative language. Questions that get at style and language might be phrased thus:

1. What did the author mean by (word, phrase, or sentence)?
2. What does the word _____ make you think of?
3. How did the connotations of selected words influence your feelings?
4. What figures of speech were used by the writer?
5. What word pictures did the writer paint?
6. How does this (word, phrase, sentence) make you feel?
7. Why does the author compare _____ to _____ ?
8. Could (description or figure of speech) really occur? Why does the author use this description?
9. Did the author tell the story from a personal point of view?
10. Is the story well written? How is it organized? What metaphors are used?

DEVELOPING INTEGRATIVE COMPREHENSION

Integrative comprehension, or comprehending when reading for learning or study purposes, includes all the previously discussed word recognition and comprehension skills, but puts special emphasis on the application of these skills in a learning context. Earlier chapters (chapters 7 and 10) have noted the importance of the metacognitive skills for reading comprehension. Integrative comprehension or reading for learning is clearly a metacognitive process (Schumacher, 1987). Irwin (1986a) divides the metacognitive process, as did Baker and Brown (1980), into those processes that are necessary for reading for recall or remembering. She observes that reading for remembering involves the application of those skills that have traditionally been called "study skills," such as previewing, self-questioning, rehearsing, reviewing, summarizing, noting the author's organization, outlining, underlining, and even elaborative interferencing which relates the text information to one's prior knowledge. We have discussed each of these in the course of this text.

Years ago Gray (1957) identified the steps of reading as recognition, understanding, reaction and integration. Reading consists of predicting, confirming, and integrating. In a very real sense, whenever children integrate what they are reading, they are studying. Gray (1957) points out that integration is the heart of the learning act in reading. The reading act is complete only when that which is read becomes assimilated with one's schemata.

Integrative reading or integrative comprehension is commonly identified with study-type reading. Herber (1969, 1970) defines study skills as work skills that produce useful knowledge for a learner; they are reading skills especially adapted to execute particular tasks. They help to develop ideas, to remember ideas, and to use ideas. Study skills teach pupils how to learn through reading or how to use reading as a vehicle for learning (Vacca, 1981).

Specific and new tasks face the reader when reading to learn. Figure 12-5 identifies specific skill areas that are required for effective study and for integrative reading.

Content-Area Reading

Content-area reading and rate of comprehension skills are separate areas of inquiry which have been discussed in numerous texts, including in Dechant (1982). Content-area reading involves the learning of a strategy of reading for information. It requires learning about the topic (Mason & Au, 1986). Content-area reading thus seeks to extend the pupil's reading proficiency (what might be described as growth in reading) and to expand the pupil's knowledge base through reading (growth through reading). The goals might be described as learning to read and reading to learn. A goal of the developmental reading program thus has to be the infusion of reading skills instruction into every subject area where reading is a prime medium for learning. It is difficult to be weak in reading and strong in the content areas.

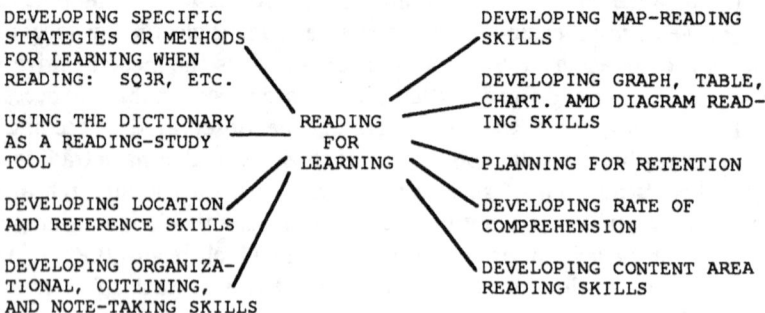

FIGURE 12-5. Cognitive Map: Reading for Learning

Rate of Comprehension

Another key reading skill, one that is also useful in developmental area reading, in study-type reading, and in reading in the content areas, is the ability to comprehend at an adequate rate. Good readers adjust their rate of reading to fit the purposes for reading and to fit the nature of the materials (Dechant, 1961, 1982). Adjusting and modifying one's rate of reading to fit the difficulty level of what one is reading is a metacognitive skill (Flippo & Lecheler, 1987). Rate of reading may be described as rate of comprehension or as speed in grasping the meanings intended by the writer. Rate of reading is not the primary goal in reading. The ultimate aim is comprehension. Rate has no meaning apart from comprehension. No one actually reads faster than he or she comprehends, but many read much more slowly than their comprehension permits. The central cognitive processes involving the storage of information in memory play a critical role in the performance of skilled readers.

Fast and slow readers are differentiated on the basis of the central processes. The speed reader's advantage is primarily conceptual. She can put information together better; she is better at inference making (Just & Carpenter, 1987). Smith (1988) observes that "reading is accelerated not by increasing the fixation rate but by reducing dependency on visual information, mainly through making use of meaning" (p. 86). It is not perceptual span differences that differentiate good from poor readers (Underwood & Zola, 1986), but rather the speed with which materials can be encoded and accessed in memory that determines reading speed (Jackson & McClelland, 1979; Rayner & Pollatsek, 1989). The size differences of the working memory appear to play a significant role in determining comprehension processes (Baddeley & Lewis, 1985).

The visual or perception span (the amount that is seen) can be increased both vertically and horizontally through tachistoscopic training. However, the tachistoscopic span (visual span) of the average reader is already much larger than the recognition span (the amount that is seen and understood). The evidence suggests that the span of recognition is relatively fixed and limited (Brozo & Johns, 1986). The span of recognition even for advanced readers is between 3 and 4 letter spaces to the left and about 15 letter spaces to the right of the center of the fixation point (Rayner & Pollatsek, 1989). It is wider (includes more information) when what is read is meaningful to the reader. Rate of reading can be increased by making fewer and shorter fixations, but most of the increase in speed is the result of making fewer fixations (Rayner & Pollatsek, 1989).

Flexibility in reading appears to be the critical difference between good and poor readers. Good readers set comprehension as their goal and adjust rate rather automatically. The poor reader mechanically plods from word to word. Efficiency in reading means simply this: With some purposes and some materials one should read slowly; with others, one should read more rapidly.

SUMMARY

Chapter 12 examined the difficulties that the reader has in moving from the literal to the higher levels of comprehending. It teaches that reading at times requires thinking of a higher sort or comprehending on qualitatively different levels. The pupil's comprehension can indeed be on a literal level (and this should not be devalued since it is the basis for all the higher levels of comprehending), but often readers comprehend adequately only if they can synthesize and organize what has been read (organizational comprehension), can read between the lines and can think on a convergent or divergent level (inferential comprehension), and can judge and analyze what has been read (evaluative comprehension). The concept of reading levels is based on fact: readers do in fact respond to meaning at various levels of abstraction and conceptualization (Vacca, 1981) and the various levels of comprehending reflect this. Although each of the specific higher-level comprehension levels reaches its culmination only in the upper grades, and frequently not even then, the teacher of reading, as indeed all teachers, must encourage the development of each level early in the primary grades. Even critical reading should begin in the primary grades.

References

Aaron, I. E., Chall, J. S., Durkin, D., Goodman, K., & Strickland, D. (1990). The present, past, future of literacy education: Comments from a panel of distinguished educators, Part I. *The Reading Teacher, 43,* 302-311.

Adams, M. J. (1990). *Beginning to read: Thinking and learning from print.* Cambridge, MA: MIT Press.

Adams, M. J., & Collins, A. (1979). A schema-theoretic view of reading. In R. Freedle (Ed.), *New directions in discourse processing.* Norwood, NJ: Ablex

Adams, M. J. & Collins, A. (1985). A schema theoretic view of reading. In H. Singer and R. Ruddell (Eds.), *Theoretical models and processes of reading* (pp. 404-425), Newark, D.E: International Reading Association.

Alexander, J .E. (Ed.). (1983, 1988). *Teaching reading.* Boston: Little, Brown.

Allen, E. G., Wright, J. P., & Laminack, L. L. (1988). Using language experience to alert pupil's critical thinking skills. *The Reading Teacher, 41,* 904-910.

Allen, E. G., & Laminack, L. L.. (1982). Language experience reading: It's a natural! *The Reading Teacher, 35,* 708-714.

Allen, R. V. (1976). *Language experiences in communication.* Boston: Houghton Mifflin.

Allen, R. V., & Allen, C. (1981, 1982). *Language experience activities.* Boston: Houghton Mifflin.

Allington, R. L. (1983). Fluency: The neglected reading goal. *The Reading Teacher, 36,* 556-561.

Altwerger, B., Edelsky, C., & Flores, B. M. (1987). Whole language: What's new? *The Reading Teacher, 41,* 145-154.

Alvermann, D. E., Smith, L. C., & Readance, J. E. (1985). Prior knowledge activation and the comprehension of compatible and incompatible text. *Reading Research Quarterly, 20,* 420-436.

Amble, B. R. (1967). Reading by phrases. *California Journal of Educational Research, 18,* 116-124.

Anderson, L., Dechant, E., Gullion, F. T., & Taylor, S. E. (1961). *Listen and read.* Huntington, NY: Educational Developmental Laboratories.

Anderson, R. C. (1984). Role of the reader's schema in comprehension, learning and memory.

In R. C. Anderson, J. Osborn, & R. J. Tierney (Eds.), *Learning to read in American schools: Basal readers and content texts* (pp. 243-258). Hillsdale, NJ: Lawrence Erlbaum Associates.

Anderson, R. C. & Freebody, P. (1981). Vocabulary knowledge. In J. Guthrie (Ed.), *Comprehension and teaching: Research reviews* (pp. 77-117). Newark, DE: International Reading Association.

Anderson, R. C., Hiebert, E. H., Scott, J. A., & Wilkinson, I. (1985). *Becoming a nation of readers: The report of the commission on reading.* Washington, DC: National Institute of Education.

Anderson, R. C., & Ortony, A. (1975). On putting apples into bottles: A problem in polysemy. *Cognitive Psychology, 7,* 167-180.

Anderson, R. C., & Pearson, P. D. (1984). A schema theoretic view of basic processes in reading comprehension. In P. D. Pearson (Ed.), *Handbook of reading research* (pp. 255-291). New York: Longman.

Anderson, R., Spiro, R., & Anderson, M. (1977). Schemata as scaffolding for the representation of information in connected discourse. Technical Report No. 24, University of Illinois.; *American Educational Research Journal, 15,* 433-440.

Anderson, T. H., & Armbruster, B. B. (1984). Studying. In P. D. Pearson (Ed.), *Handbook of reading research* (pp. 657-679). New York: Longman.

André, M. E. & Anderson, T. (1978-79). The development and evaluation of a self-questioning study technique. *Reading Research Quarterly, 14 (No. 4),* 605-623.

Ansara, A. (1982). The Orton-Gillingham approach to remediation in developmental dyslexia. In R. Malatesha & P. Aaron (Eds.), *Reading disorders: Varieties and treatments* (pp. 409-433). New York: Academic Press.

Anshen, R. N. (1957). Language as idea. In R. N. Anshen (Ed.), *Language: An inquiry into its meaning and function* (pp. 13). New York: Harper and Brothers.

Arnold, R. D. (1988). Teaching cohesive ties to children. *The Reading Teacher, 42,* 106-110.

Arnold, R., & Miller, John. (1976). Reading: Word recognition skills. In P. Lamb & R. Arnold (Eds.), *Reading* (pp. 320-361). Belmont, CA: Wadsworth Publishing Company.

Arnold, R. D., & Wist, A. H. (1970). Auditory discrimination abilities of disadvantaged Anglo-Mexican-American children. *The Elementary School Journal, 70,* 295-299.

Artley, A. S. (1975). Words, words, words. *Language Arts, 52,* 1067-1072.

Asher, S. R., Shelley, H. & Wigfield, A. (1976). *Children's comprehension of high-and-low-interest material and a comparison of two cloze scoring methods.* Urbana, IL: University of Illinois.

Asplund, B. B., & Sunal, C. S. (1980). *The effectiveness of the language experience approach as a supplement to a basal reader program* (ED 182 705). Washington, DC: ERIC Document Reproduction Services.

Atkinson, R. C. (1971). *Contemporary psychology.* San Francisco: W. H. Freeman and Company.

Aukerman, R. C. & Auckerman, L. R. (1981). *How do I teach reading.* New York: John Wiley and Sons.

Aulls, M. W. & Gelbart F. (1980). Effects of method of instruction and ability on Literal comprehension of short stories. *Research in the Teaching of English, 14,* 51-59.

Ausübel, D. P. (1960). The use of advance organizers in the learning and retention of meaningful verbal material. *Journal of Educational Psychology, 51,* 266-274. Ausübel, D. P. (1963). *The psychology of meaningful verbal learning.* New York: Gruen and Stratton. Ausübel, D. P. (1968). *Educational psychology: A cognitive view.* New York: Hold, Rinehart and Winston.

Ausübel, D. P., Novak, J. D., & Hanesian, H. (1978). *Educational psychology: A cognitive view* (2nd. ed.). New York: Holt, Rinehart and Winston.

Backman, J. E., Bruck, M., Herbert, M., & Seidenberg, M. S. (1984). Acquisition and use of spelling and sound correspondences in reading. *Journal of Experimental Child Psychology, 38*, 114–133.

Baddeley, A. D., & Lewis, V. (1985). Components of fluent reading. *Journal of Memory and Language, 24*, 119–131.

Bader, L. (1980). *Reading diagnosis and remediation in classroom and clinic.* New York: Macmillan.

Baker, L. & Brown, A. L. (1980). Metacognitive skills and reading (No. 188). Urbana, IL: Technical Report from the Center for the Study of Reading, University of Illinois.

Baker, L., & Brown, A. L. (1984a). Metacognitive skills and reading. In P. D. Pearson (Ed.), *Handbook of reading research* (pp. 353–394). New York: Longman.

Baker, L., & Brown, A. L. (1984b). Cognitive monitoring in reading. In J. Flood (Ed.), *Understanding reading comprehension* (pp. 21–44). Newark, DE: International Reading Association.

Balota, D. A., Pollatsek, A., & Rayner, K. (1985). The interaction of contextual constraints, and parafoveal visual information in reading. *Cognitive Psychology, 17*, 364–390.

Bannatyne, A. D. (1966). The color phonics system. In J. Money (Ed.), *The disabled reader* (pp. 193–214). Baltimore: Johns Hopkins Press.

Bannatyne, A. (1973). Reading: An auditory-vocal process. *Academic Therapy, 9*, 429–431.

Barnard, D. P., & Kendrick, R. (1980). *A new consciousness for integrating communication arts instruction* (Ginn Occasional papers, Number 6). Columbus: Ginn.

Barnitz, J. G. (1979). *Reading comprehension of pronoun-referent structures by children in grades two, four, and six* (Technical Report No. 117). Urbana, IL: University of Illinois, Urbana-Champaign.

Barnitz, J. G. (1980). Syntactic effects on the reading comprehension of pronoun-referent structures by children in grades two, four, and six. *Reading Research Quarterly, 15*, 268–289.

Barnitz, J. G. (1986). *The anaphora jigsaw puzzle in psycholinguistic and reading research* (pp. 45–56). Newark, NJ: International Reading Association.

Baron, J. & Treiman, R. (1980). Use of orthography in reading and learning to read. In J. F. Kavanagh & R. L. Venezky (Eds.), *Orthography, reading and dyslexia* (pp. 171–189). Baltimore, MD: University Park Press.

Barrett, T. C. (1965a). Visual discrimination tasks as predictors of first-grade reading achievement. *The Reading Teacher, 18*, 276–282.

Barrett, T. C. (1965b). The relationship between measures of pre-reading visual discrimination and first-grade achievement: A review of the literature. *Reading Research Quarterly, 1*, 51–76.

Barrett, T. C. (1967). Performances on selected prereading tasks and first-grade reading achievement. In *Vistas in reading* (pp. 461–464). Newark, DE: International Reading Association.

Barrett, T. C. (1972). Taxonomy of reading comprehension. In *Reading 360 Monograph.* Lexington, M.A.: Ginn; also in R. F. Smith & T. C. Barrett (Eds.), *Teaching reading in the middle grades* (1974). Reading, MA: Addison-Wesley.

Barrett, T. C., & Smith, R. J. (1974, 1976, 1979). *Teaching reading in the middle grades.* Reading, MA: Addison-Wesley.

Barron, R. F. (1969). The use of vocabulary as an advance organizer. In H. L. Herber & P. L. Sanders (Eds.), *Research in reading in the content areas: First report* (pp. 29–39). Syracuse, NY: Syracuse University and Language Arts Center.

Barron, R. W. (1979). Access to the meanings of printed words: Some implications for reading and for learning to read. In F. B. Murray (Ed.), *The Development of the reading process.* Newark, NJ: IRA.

Barron, R. W. (1980). Visual and phonological strategies in reading and spelling. In U. Frith (Ed.), *Cognitive processes in spelling* (pp. 195-213). New York: Academic Press.

Barron, R. W. (1981). Reading skill and reading strategies. In A. Lesgold and C. Perfetti (Eds.), *Interactive processes in reading* (pp. 299-325). Hillsdale, NJ: Lawrence Erlbaum Associates.

Barron, R. W. (1986). Word recognition in early reading: A review of the direct and indirect access hypothesis. *Cognition, 24*, 93-119.

Bartlett, F. C. (1932). *Remembering*. London: Cambridge University Press.

Baumann, J. F. (1984a). The effectiveness of a direct instruction paradigm for teaching main idea comprehension. *Reading Research Quarterly, 20*, 93-115.

Baumann, J. F. (1984b). Implications for reading instruction from the research on teacher and school effectiveness. *Journal of Reading, 28*, 109-115.

Baumann, J. F. (1988). Direct instruction reconsidered. *Journal of Reading, 31*, 712-718.

Baumann, J. F., & Stevenson, J. (1986a). Identifying types of anaphoric relationships. In J. W. Irwin (Ed.), *Understanding and teaching cohesion comprehension* (pp. 9-20). Newark, DE: International Reading Association.

Baumann, J. F., & Stevenson, J. (1986b). Teaching students to comprehend anaphoric relations. In J. W. Irwin (Ed.), *Understanding and teaching cohesion comprehension*. Newark, DE: International Reading Association.

Bax, M. C. O. & Whitmore, D. (1973). Neurodevelopmental screening in the school-entrant medical examination. *Lancet, 2*, 368-370.

Bean, T. W., & Peterson, J. (1980). Reading guides: Fostering reading in content areas. *Reading Horizons, 21*, 196-199.

Beck, I. L. (1984). Developing comprehension: The impact of the directed reading lesson. In R. C. Anderson, J. Osborn, & R. Tierney (Eds.), *Learning to read in American schools: Basal readers and content texts* (pp. 3-20). Hillsdale, NJ: Lawrence Erlbaum Associates.

Beck, I. L., McKeown, M. G., Omanson, R. C., & Pople, M. T. (1984). Improving the comprehensibility of stories: The effects of revisions that improve coherence. *Reading Research Quarterly, 19*, 263-277.

Beck, I. L., & McKeown, M. G. (1981). Developing questions that promote comprehension: The story map. *Language Arts, 58*, 913-918.

Beck, I. L., Perfetti, C. A. & McKeown, M. G. (1982). The effects of long-term vocabulary instruction on lexical access and reading comprehension. *Journal of Educational Psychology, 74*, 506-521.

Bellare, R. L. (1986). The integrated method of reading therapy. *Journal of Learning Disabilities, 19*, 271-273.

Benton, A. (1985). Visual factors in dyslexia: An unresolved issue. In D. D. Duane & C. K. Leong (Eds.), *Understanding learning disabilities* (pp. 87-96). New York: Plenum.

Betts, E. A. (1946). *Foundations of reading instruction*. New York: American Book Company.

Betts, E. A. (1961). Issues in teaching reading. *Controversial issues in reading*, Tenth Annual Reading Conference, Bethlehem, PA: Lehigh University.

Blair, S. M. (1977). Families of the lower case letters. *The Reading Teacher, 31*. 76.

Blanchard, H. E., McConkie, G. W., Zola, D., & Wolverton, G. S. (1984). Time course of visual information utilization during fixations in reading. *Journal of Experimental Psychology: Human Perception & Performance, 10*, 75-89.

Blanchard, H. E., Pollatsek, A., & Rayner, A. (1988). The acquisition of parafoveal word information in reading. Paper presented at Midwestern Psychological Association Annual Meeting, Chicago.

Blanton, W. E., Moorman, G. B., & Wood, K. D. (1986). A model of direct instruction applied to the basal skills lesson. *The Reading Teacher, 40*, 299-305.

Blanton, W. E., Wood, Karen D., & Moorman, G. B. (1990). The role of purpose in reading instruction. *The Reading Teacher, 43*, 486–493.

Blau, H. & Blau, H. (1969). A theory of learning to read by modality blocking. In J. Arena (Ed.), *Programming: Many points of view*. Pittsburg, PA: Association for Children with Learning Disabilities; also Blau, H., & Blau, H. (1968). A theory of learning to read. *The Reading Teacher, 22*, 126–129, 144.

Bloom, B. S. (Ed.). (1968). Taxonomy of Educational Objectives, Handbook I. *Cognitive domain*. New York: David McKay. (Original work published 1956)

Bloomfield, L. (1942). Linguistics and reading. *Elementary English Review, 19*, 125–130, 183–186.

Bloomfield, L., & Barnhart, C. L. (1961). *Let's read: A linguistic approach*. Detroit: Wayne State University Press.

Boehnlein, M. (1987). Reading intervention for high risk first-graders. *Educational Leadership, 44*, 32–37.

Bos, D. S. (1982). Getting past decoding: Assisted and repeating readings as remedial methods for learning disabled students. *Topics in Learning and Learning disabilities, 1*, 51–57.

Bradley, L. (1983). The organization of visual, phonological, and motor strategies in learning to read and to spell. In U. Kirk (Ed.), *Neuropsychology of language, reading, and spelling* (pp. 235–254). New York: Academic Press.

Bradley, L. & Bryant, P. E. (1985). *Rhyme and reason in reading and spelling*. Ann Arbor, MI: University of Michigan Press.

Bradley, L., & Bryant, P. E. (1983). Categorizing sounds and learning to read—A causal connection. *Nature, 301*, 419–421.

Bradley, L., Hulme, C., & Bryant, P. (1979). The connection between different verbal difficulties in a backward reader: A case study. *Developmental Medicine and Child Neurology, 21*, 790–795.

Breen, L. G. (1988). Context clues, structural analysis, and dictionary aids to pronunciation. In G. E. Alexander (Ed), *Teaching Reading* (pp. 104–126). Glenview, IL: Little, Brown.

Britton, B., & Glynn, S. M. (Eds.). (1987). *Executive control processes in reading*. Hillsdale, NJ: Lawrence Erlbaum Associates.

Bromley, K. D. (1985). Precis writing and outlining enhance content learning. *The Reading Teacher, 38*, 406–411.

Brown, A. (1981). Metacognition: The development of selective attention strategies for learning from texts. In M. Kamil (Ed.), *Directions in reading: Research and instruction* (pp. 21–43). Washington, DC: National Reading Conference.

Brown, A. L., & Day, J. D. (1983a). Macrorules for summarizing texts. *Journal of Verbal Learning and Verbal Behavior, 22*, 1–14.

Brown, A. L., and Day, J. D. (1983b). *Macrorules for summarizing text: The development of expertise* (Technical Report No. 270). Champaign, IL: Center for the Study of Reading, University of Illinois.

Brown, A. L., & Palincsar, A.S. (1982). Inducing strategic learning from texts by means of informed, self-control training. *Topics in Learning Disabilities, 2*, 1–7.

Brown, A. L., & Palincsar, A. S. (1985). *Reciprocal teaching of comprehension strategies* (Technical Report No. 334). Urbana, IL: University of Illinois, Center for the Study of Reading.

Brown, A. L., Palincsar, A. S., & Armbruster, B. B. (1984). Instructing comprehension fostering activities in interactive learning situations. In H. Mandl, N. Stein, & T. Trabasso (Eds.), *Learning from texts* (pp. 255–286). Hillsdale, NJ: Lawrence Erlbaum Associates.

Brown, A. L., Smiley, S. S., Day, J. D., Townsend, M. A. R., & Lawton, S. C. (1977). *Illustrations of a thematic idea in children's comprehension and retention of stories* (ED. 136, 189). Arlington, VA: ERIC Document Reproduction Service.

Brown, M. W. (1942). *The runaway bunny*. New York: Harper and Row.
Brozo, W. G., & Johns, J. L. (1986). A content and critical analysis of 40 speed reading books. *Journal of Reading, 30*, 242-247.
Bruce, B. (1978). What makes a good story. *Language Arts, 55*, 460-466.
Bruck, M. (1988). The word recognition and spelling of dyslexic children. *Reading Research Quarterly, 23*, 51-68.
Bruininks, R. H. (1968). Auditory and visual perceptual skills related to the reading performance of disadvantaged boys. *Perceptual and Motor Skills, 29*, 177-186.
Bruner, J. S. (1957a). Going beyond the information given. In H. E. Gruber, K. R. Hammond, & R. Jessor. (Eds). *Contemporary approaches to cognition*. (pp. 41-69). Cambridge: Harvard University Press.
Bruner, J. S. (1957b). On perceptual readiness. *Psychological Review, 64*, 123-152.
Bruner, J. S. (1966). *Toward a theory of instruction*. Cambridge: Harvard University Press.
Brunswick, E. (1957). Scope and aspects of the cognitive problem. In H. E. Gruber, K. R. Hammond, & R. Jessor. (Eds.), *Contemporary approaches to cognition* (pp. 5-32). Cambridge: Harvard University Press.
Burmeister, L. E. (1968a). The usefulness of phonic generalizations. *The Reading Teacher, 21*, 349-364.
Burmeister, L. E. (1968b). Vowel pairs. *The Reading Teacher, 21*, 445-452.
Burmeister, L. E. (1974). *Reading strategies for secondary school teachers*. Reading, MA: Addison-Wesley.
Burmeister, L. E. (1983). *Foundations and strategies for teaching children to read*. Reading, MA: Addison-Wesley.
Burns, P. C., Roe, B. D., & Ross, E. P. (1984, 1988). *Teaching reading in today's elementary schools*. Boston: Houghton Mifflin.
Buswell, G. T. (1922). *Fundamental reading habits: A study of their development* (Supplementary Education Monographs no. 21). Chicago: University of Chicago Press.
Buswell, G. T., (1947). Perceptual research and methods of learning. *The Scientific Monthly, 64*, 521-526.
Calanchini, P. R., & Trout, S. S. (1971, 1980). The neurology of learning disabilities. In L. Tarnopol (Ed.), *Learning disorders in children, diagnosis, mediation, education* (pp. 207-251). Boston: Little, Brown.
Calfee, R. (1982). Cognitive models of reading: Implications for assessment and treatment of reading disability. In R. Maletesha & P. Aaron (Eds.), *Reading disorders: Varieties and treatments* (pp. 151-176). New York: Academic Press.
Calfee, R. C. (1987). The school as a context for assessment of literacy. *The Reading Teacher, 40*, 738-743.
Calfee, R. C., & Curley, R. (1984). Structure of prose in the content areas. In J. Flood (Ed.), *Understanding reading comprehension* (pp. 161-180). Newark, DE: International Reading Association.
Calfee, R. C., & Pointkowski, D. C. (1981). The reading diary: Acquisition of decoding. *Reading Research Quarterly, 16*, 346-373.
Caramazza, A., & Berndt, R. A. (1978). Semantic and syntactic processes in aphasia: A review of the literature. *Psychological Bulletin, 85*, 898-918.
Carbo, M. (1980). *An analysis of the relationship between the modality preferences of kindergarteners and selected reading treatments as they effect the learning of a basic sight-word vocabulary*. Unpublished doctoral dissertation, St. John's University, Jamaica, NY.
Carbo, M. (1983). Research in reading and learning style: Implications for exceptional children. *Exceptional Children, 49*, 486-494.
Carnine, D. W. (1977). Phonics versus look-say: Transfer to new words. *Reading Teacher, 30*, 636-640.

Carnine, D. W. (1982). Direct instruction: A bottom-up skills approach to elementary instruction. In L. Reed & S. Ward (Eds.), *Basic skills: Issues and choices: Approaches to basic skills and instruction 2* (pp. 135-146). St. Louis: CEMREL.

Carnine, D. (1987). A response to false standards, a distorting and disintegrating effect on education, turning away from useful purposes, being inevitably unfulfilled, and remaining unrealistic and irrelevant. *Remedial and Special Education, 81*, 42-43.

Carnine, D., Kameenui, E. J., & Coyle, G. (1984). Utilization of contextual information in determining the meaning of unfamiliar words. *Reading Research Quarterly, 19*, 188-204.

Carnine, L., Carnine, D., & Gersten, R. (1984). Analysis of oral reading errors made by economically disadvantaged students taught with a synthetic-phonics approach. *Reading Research Quarterly, 17*, 343-356.

Carpenter, P. A., & Just, M. A. (1981). Cognitive processes in reading: Models based on reader's eye fixations. In A. M. Lesgold & C. A. Perfetti (Eds.), *Interactive processes in reading* (pp. 177-273). Hillsdale, NJ: Lawrence Erlbaum Associates.

Carroll, J. B. (1969). From comprehension to inference. 33rd . yearbook, Claremont Reading Conference. Claremont, CA: Claremont Graduate School.

Carroll, P., & Slowiaczek, M. L. (1986). Constraints on semantic priming in reading: A fixation time analysis. *Memory and Cognition, 14*, 509-522.

Casbergue, R. M., & Green, J. F. (1988). Persistent misconceptions about sensory perception and reading disability. *Journal of Reading, 32*, 196-203.

Cattell, J. M. (1885a). The inertia of the eye and brain. *Brain, 8*, 295-312.

Cattell, J. M. (1885b). Ueber die zeit der erkennung und benennung von schriftzeichen, bildern, und farben. *Philosophische Studien, 2*, 635-650.

Catts, H. W. (1986). Speech production/phonological deficits in reading disordered children. *Journal of Reading Disabilities, 19*, 504-507.

Chall, J. S. (1947). The influence of previous knowledge on reading ability. *Educational Research Bulletin, 26*, 225-230.

Chall, J. (1969). Research in linguistics and reading instruction. In J. A. Figurel (Ed.), *Reading and realism, Volume 13* (pp. 560-571). Newark, DE: International Reading Association Conference proceedings.

Chall, J. (1979). The great debate: Ten years later, with a modest proposal for reading stages. In L. B. Resnick & P. Weaver (Eds.), *Theory and practice of early reading, Volume 1*. Hillsdale, NJ: Lawrence Erlbaum.

Chall, J. S. (1967, 1983). *Learning to read: The great debate*. New York: McGraw-Hill.

Chall, J. (1987). Reading and early childhood education: The critical issues. *Principal, 66*, 6-9.

Chapman, L. J. (1984). Comprehending and the teaching of reading. In J. Flood (Ed.), *Promoting reading comprehension* (pp. 261-272). Newark, DE: International Reading Association.

Charnock, J. (1977). An alternative to the DRA. *The Reading Teacher, 31*, 269-271.

Cheek, E. H., & Cheek, M. C. (1983a). *Reading instruction through content teaching*. Columbus: Charles E. Merrill.

Cheek, E. H., & Cheek, M. C. (1983b). Organizational patterns: Untapped resources for better reading. *Reading World, 22*, 278-283.

Chester, R. D. (1976). Reading comprehension: A pragmatic approach to assessment and instruction. *Insights into why and how to read* (pp. 76-89). Newark: International Reading Association.

Chiesi, H. L., Spilich, G. J., & Voss, J. F. (1979). Acquisition of Domain-related information in relation to high and low domain knowledge. *Journal of Verbal Learning and Verbal Behavior, 18*, 257-274.

Chomsky, C. (1976). After decoding: What? *Language Arts, 53*, 288-296.

Chomsky, C. (1969). *The acquisition of syntax in children from 5 to 10.* Cambridge: MIT Press.

Chomsky, C. (1978). When you still can't read in third grade: After decoding, what? In S. J. Samuels (Ed.), *What research has to say about reading instructing instruction* (pp. 13–30). Newark NJ: International Reading Association.

Chomsky, C. (1979). *Consciousness is relevant to linguistic awareness.* Paper presented at the International Internion Reading Research Seminar On linguistic Awareness and Learning to Read, Victoria, B. C., Canada: University of Victoria.

Chomsky, N. (1969). Form and meaning in natural language. In J. D. Roslansky (Ed.), *Communication* (pp. 63–86). Amsterdam: North Holland Press.

Clark, C. H., & Bean, T. W. (1982). Improving advance organizer research: Persistent problems and future decisions. *Reading World, 22,* 2–10.

Clark, F., et al. (1984). Visual imagery and self-questioning: Strategies to improve comprehension of written material. *Journal of Learning Disabilities, 17,* 145–149.

Clewell, S. F. & Haidemos, J. (1983). Organizational strategies to increase comprehension. *Reading World, 22,* 314–321.

Colwell, C., & Hedfeldt, J. (1983). The paragraph as a semantic unit: Theory and practice. *Reading World, 22,* 332–345.

Content, A., Kolinsky, R., Morais, J., & Bertelson, P. (1986). Phonetic segmentation in prereaders: Effect of corrective information. *Journal of Experimental Child Psychology, 42,* 49–72.

Cooper, J. D. (1947) A procedure for teaching non-readers. *Education, 67,* 494–499.

Cooper, J. D. (1986). *Improving reading comprehension.* Boston: Houghton Mifflin.

Copple, C. E. (1975). Effects of three variables on the performance of middle-class and lower-class children in discriminating similar letters in words. *Journal of Educational Research, 68,* 226–229.

Cotman, C. W., & Lynch, G. S. (1988). The neurobiology of learning and memory. In J. F. Kavanagh & T. J. Truss, Jr. (Eds.), *Learning disabilities* (pp. 1–69). Parkton, MD: York Press.

Crafton, L. (1983). Learning from reading: What happens when students generate their own background knowledge. *Journal of Reading, 26,* 586–593.

Cromer, W. (1970). The difference model: A new explanation for some reading difficulties. *Journal of Educational Psychology, 61,* 471–483.

Cross, D. R., & Paris, S. G. (1988). Developmental and structural analysis of children's metacognition and reading comprehension. *Journal of Educational Psychology, 80,* 131–142.

Crowder, R. G. (1982). *The psychology of reading: An introduction.* New York: Oxford University Press.

Crystal, D. (1976). *Child language, learning, and linguistics.* London: Edward Arnold Publishers.

Cunningham, D., & Shablak, S. L. (1985). Selective reading guide-o-rama: The content teacher's best friend. *Journal of Reading, 18,* 380–382.

Cunningham, P. M. (1980). Teaching *were, with, what* and other four letter words. *The Reading Teacher, 34,* 160–233.

Cunningham, P. M., Moore, S. A., Cunningham, J. W., & Moore, D. (1983). *Reading in elementary classrooms.* New York: Longman.

Dahl, P. R., & Samuels, S. J. (1975). *Teaching high-speed word recognition and comprehension skills.* Unpublished paper, Minneapolis, MN: University of Minnesota.

Davey, B. (1983). Think aloud: Modeling the cognitive processes of reading comprehension. *Journal of Reading, 27,* 44–47.

Davey, B. (1986). Using textbook activity guides to help students learn from textbooks. *Journal of Reading, 29,* 489–494.

Davis, F. B. (1944). Fundamental factors of comprehension in reading. *Psychometrika, 9*, 185-197.
Davis, F. B. (1968). Research in comprehension in reading. *Reading Research Quarterly, 3*, 499-545.
Davis, F. B. (1972). Psychometric research on comprehension in reading. *Reading Research Quarterly, 7*, 628-678.
Dechant, E. (1961). Rate of comprehension—needed research. In J. A. Figurel (Ed.), *Changing concepts of reading instruction, Volume 6*. New York: Scholastic Magazines.
Dechant, E. (1964, 1970, 1982). *Improving the teaching of reading*. Englewood Cliffs, NJ: Prentice-Hall.
Dechant, E. (1965). The philosophy and sociology of reading. *The philosophical and sociological bases of reading* (pp. 9-20). Milwaukee: National Reading Conference Yearbook.
Dechant, E. (1968). *Diagnosis and remediation of reading disability*. West Nyack, NY: Parker Publishing.
Dechant, E. (1971). *Detection and correction of reading disability*. New York: Appleton-Century-Crofts.
Dechant, E. (1973). *Reading improvement in the secondary school*. Englewood Cliffs, NJ: Prentice-Hall.
Dechant, E. (1975). *The diagnostic process*. Hays, KS: Fort Hays State University.
Dechant, E. (1977). Motivation revisited. *Improving Instruction, 11*, 1-3.
Dechant, E. (1981a). *Diagnosis and remediation of reading disabilities*. Englewood Cliffs, NJ: Prentice-Hall.
Dechant, E. (1981b). *Teacher's directory of reading skill aids, techniques and materials*. West Nyach, NY: Parker Publishing.
Dechant, E. (1985). Teacher differences and reading method. *Education, 86*, 40-43.
Dechant, E., & Smith, H. P. (1977). *Psychology in teaching reading* Englewood Cliffs, NJ: Prentice-Hall.
De Hirsch, K., Jansky, J., & Langford, W. S. (1966). *Predicting reading failure*. New York: Harper and Row.
Dehn, N. (1984). An AI perspective on reading comprehension. In J. Flood (Ed.), *Understanding reading comprehension*. Newark, DE: International Reading Association.
Denburg, S. D. (1976-1977). The interaction of picture and print in reading instruction. *Reading Research Quarterly, 12*, 176-189.
Denckla, M. B., & Rudel, R. G. (1976). Rapid automatized naming (RAN): Dyslexia differentiated from other learning disabilities. *Neuropsychologia, 14*, 471-479.
Devine, T. G. (1984). What happens as students try to comprehend. *The NERA Journal*, 15-20.
Dillner, M. H., & Olson, J. P. (1977). *Personalizing reading instruction in middle, junior and senior high schools*. New York: Macmillan.
DiLollo, V., Hanson, D., & McIntyre, J. S. (1983). Initial stages of visual information processing in dyslexia. *Journal of Experimental Psychology: Human Perception and Performance, 9*, 923-935.
Doehring, D. G. (1968). *Patterns of impairment in specific reading disability: A neurological investigation*. Bloomington, IN: Indiana University Press.
Doehring, D. G. (1976). *Acquisition of rapid reading responses*. Monograph of the Society for Research in Child Development, Vol. 41, Serial No. 165, Chicago.
Dowhower, S. L. (1987). Effects of repeated reading on second-grade transitional readers' fluency and comprehension. *Reading Research Quarterly, 22*, 389-406.
Dowhower, S. L. (1989). Repeated reading: Research into practice. *The Reading Teacher, 42*, 502-507.
Downing, J., & Leong, C. K. (1982). *Psychology of reading*. New York: Macmillan.

DuCharme, C. (1987). Children as readers and writers in the classroom: An impossible dream. 51st. yearbook Claremont Reading Conference, Claremont, CA: 165-176.

Duffelmeyer, F. A. (1984). The effect of context on ascertaining word meaning. *Reading World, 24*, 103-107.

Duffelmeier, F. (1988). Word maps and student involvement. *The Reading Teacher, 41*, 968-969.

Duffy, G., & Roehler, L. (1982). Instruction as sense-making implications for teacher education. *Action in Teacher Education, 4*, 1-7.

Duffy, G. G., & Roehler, L. R. (1986). *Improving classroom reading instruction.* New York: Random House.

Duffy, G. G. Roehler, R., & Mason, J. (1984). *Comprehension instruction.* New York: Longman Incorporated.

Duffy, G., Roehler, L., Meloth, M., Vavrus, L., Book, C., Putnam, J., & Wesselman, R. (1986). The relationship between explicit verbal explanation during reading skill instruction and student awareness and achievement. *Reading Research Quarterly, 21*, 237-252.

Duffy, G. G., Roehler, L. R., & Herrmann, B. A. (1988). Modeling mental processes helps poor readers become strategic readers. *The Reading Teacher, 41* 762-767.

Duke-Elder, A., & Scott, G. I. (1971). *Neuroopthalmology.* St. Louis, MO: C. V. Mosby.

Dunn-Rankin, P. (1968). The similarity of lower case letters of the english alphabet. *Journal of Verbal Learning and Verbal Behavior, 7*, 990-995.

Dupuis, M. M., Lee, J. W., Badiali, B. J., & Askov, E. N. (1989). *Teaching reading and writing in the content areas.* Glenview, IL: Scott, Foresman, and Company.

Dupuis, M. M., & Snyder, S. L. (1983). Develop concepts through vocabulary: A strategy for reading specialists to use with content teachers. *Journal of Reading, 26*, 297-305.

Durkin, D. (1970, 1989). *Teaching them to read.* Boston: Allyn and Bacon.

Durkin, D. (1978-1979). What classroom observations reveal about reading comprehension instruction. *Reading Research Quarterly, 14*, 481-533. Also in Technical Report No. 106, Center for the Study of Reading, University of Illinois, 1978.

Durkin D. (1981). Reading comprehension instruction in five basal reader series. *Reading Research Quarterly, 16*, 515-544.

Durkin, D. (1981). What is the value of the new interest in reading comprehension? *Language Arts, 58*, 24-43. Also Report #19, Center for the Study of Reading, University of Illinois, Champaign, 1980. Also in S. J. Harris and E. Sipay (Eds.), (1984). *Readings in reading instruction* pp. 249-266). New York: Longman.

Durkin, D. (1984). Is there a match between what elementary teachers do and what basal reader manuals recommend? *The Reading Teacher, 37*, 734-744.

Early, M. & Sawyer, D. J. (1984). *Reading to learn in grades 5 to 12.* New York: Harcourt Brace Jovanovich.

Edfeldt, A. W. (1960). *Silent speech and silent reading.* Stockholm: Almquist and Wiksell; Chicago: University of Chicago Press.

Eads-Kniep, M. (1979). The frenetic frantic phonic backlash. *Language Arts, 56*, 909-917.

Eads, M. (1981). What to do when they don't understand what they read—Research-based strategies for teaching reading comprehension. *The Reading Teacher, 34*, 565-571.

Egeland, B. (1975). Effects of errorless training on teaching children to discriminate letters of the alphabet. *Journal of Applied Psychology, 60*, 533-536.

Eggen, P. D., & Kauchak, D. P. (1988). *Strategies for teachers: Teaching content and thinking skills.* Englewood Cliffs: Prentice-Hall.

Ehri, L. C. (1979). Linguistic insight: Threshold of reading acquisition. In T. G. Waller & G. E. MacKinnon (Eds.), *Research: Advances in theory and practice.* (pp. 63-114) New York: Academic press.

Ehri, L. C. (1980). The role of orthographic images in learning printed words. In J. Kavanagh & R. Venezky (Eds.), *Orthography, reading and dyslexia* (pp. 155-170). Baltimore:

University Park Press.
Ehri, L. C. (1983). A critique of five studies related to letter-name knowledge. In L. Gentile, M. Kamil, & J. Blanchard (Eds.), *Reading research revisited* (pp. 143-153). Columbus, Charles E. Merrill.
Ehri, L. C. (1984). How orthography alters spoken language competencies in children learning to read and spell. In J. Downing & R. Valtin (Eds.), *Language awareness and learning to read*. New York: Springer Verlag.
Ehri, L. (1987). Learning to read and spell words. *Journal of Reading Behavior, 19* 5-31.
Ehri, L. (1989). The development of spelling knowledge and its role in reading acquisition and reading disability. *Journal of Learning Disabilities, 22,* 356-365.
Ehri, L. C., & Roberts, K. T. (1979). Do beginners learn printed words better in context or in isolation? *Child Development, 50,* 675-685.
Ehri, L. C., & Wilce, L. S. (1979). The mnemonic value of orthography among beginning readers. *Journal of Educational Psychology, 71,* 26-40.
Ehri, L. C., & Wilce, L. S. (1980). Do beginners learn to read function words better in sentences or in lists? *Reading Research Quarterly, 15,* 451-476.
Ehri, L. C., & Wilce, L. S. (1985). Movement into reading: Is the first stage of printed word learning visual or phonetic? *Reading Research Quarterly, 20,* 163-179.
Ehri, L. C., & Wilce, L. S. (1987a). Cypher versus cue reading:An experiment in decoding acquisition. *Journal of Educational Psychology, 79,* 3-13.
Ehri, L. C., & Wilce, L. S. (1987b). Does learning to spell help beginning readers learn to read words? *Reading Research Quarterly, 18,* 47-65.
Ehrlich, S. F., & Rayner, K. (1981). Contextual effects on word perception and eye movements during reading. *Journal of Verbal Learning and Verbal Behavior, 20,* 641-655.
Eisner, E. (1983). The art and craft of teaching. *Educational Leadership,* 4-13.
Eldredge, J. L., & Butterfield, D. (1986). Alternatives to traditional reading instruction. *The Reading Teacher, 40,* 32-37.
Elkind, D. (1974). *Children and adolescents: Impressive essays on Jean Piaget* (2nd Ed.). New York: Oxford University Press.
Elkind, D. (1976). Cognitive development in reading. In H. Singer & R. B. Ruddell (Eds.), *Theoretical models and processes of reading* (pp. 113, 331-340). Newark, DE: International Reading Association.
Emans, R. (1968). Context clues. *In reading in the total curriculum.* (p. 13). Newark, D. E.: International Reading Association.
Englert, C. S., & Hiebert, E. (1984). Children's developing awareness of text structures in expository materials. *Journal of Educational Psychology, 76,* 65-74.
Erdmann, B., & Dodge, R. (1898). *Psychologische untersuchen ueber das lesen auf experimenteller grundlage.* Halle: Niemeyer.
Erickson, F. (1984). School literacy, reasoning, and civility. *Review of Educational Research, 54,* 525-546.
Estes, T. (1984). Paper presented at the Conference on Reading Research, Atlanta.
Farr, R., & Roser, N. (1979). *Teaching a child to read.* New York: Harcourt, Brace, Jovanovich.
Fernald, G. M. (1943, 1966). *Remedial techniques in basic school subjects.* New York: McGraw-Hill.
Fields, M., & Lee, D. (1987). *Let's begin reading right.* Columbus: Merrill.
Finn, P. J. (1985). *Helping children learn to read.* New York: Random House.
Fisher, E. (1980). Backwardness in reading and linguistic/memory deficits. *First Language, 1,* 223-226.
Flippo, R. F., & Lecheler, R. (1987). Adjusting reading rate: Metacognitive awareness. *The Reading Teacher, 40,* 712-713.
Flood, J. (1986). The text, the student, and the teacher; Learning from exposition in middle schools. *The Reading Teacher, 39,* 784-791.

REFERENCES

Flood, J. & Lapp, D. (1988). Conceptual mapping strategies for understanding information texts. *The Reading Teacher, 41,* 780–783.

Flood, J., Lapp, D., & Farnan, N. (1986). A reading-writing procedure that teaches expository paragraph structure. *The Reading Teacher, 39,* 556–562.

Flynn, L. L. (1989). Developing critical reading skills through cooperative problem solving. *The Reading Teacher, 42,* 664–668.

Foorman, B. R., & Liberman, D. (1989). Visual and phonological processing of words: A comparison of good and poor readers. *Journal of Learning Disabilities, 22,* 349–365.

Foss, D. J. (1982). A discourse on semantic priming. *Cognitive Psychology, 14,* 590–607.

Fowler, C. A. (1981). Some aspects of language perception by eye: The beginning reader. In O. Tzeng & H. Singer (Eds.), *Perception of print: Reading research in experimental psychology* (pp. 171–196). Hillsdale, NJ: Lawrence Erlbaum Associates.

Fox, B. & Routh, D. K. (1984). Phonemic analysis and synthesis as word attack skills: Revisited. *Journal of Educational Psychology, 76,* 1059–1064.

Frasure, N. E., & Entwisle, D. R. (1973). Semantic and syntactic development in children. *Developmental Psychology, 9,* 236–245.

Fredericksen, J. R. (1978). *Assessment of perceptual, decoding, and lexical skills and their relation to reading proficiency* (Technical Reports 1 and 2). Cambridge, MA: Bolt, Beranek, and Newman.

Fredericksen, C. H. (1979). Discourse comprehension and early reading. In L. Resnick & P. Weaver (Eds.), *Theory and practice in early reading* (Vol. 1) (pp. 155–186). Hillsdale, NJ: Lawrence Erlbaum Associates.

Fredericks, A. D. (1986). Mental imagery activities to improve comprehension. *The Reading Teacher, 40,* 78–81.

Freedman, G. & Reynolds, E. G. (1980). Enriching basal reader lessons with semantic webbing. *The Reading Teacher, 33,* 677–684.

Fries, C. C. (1963). *Linguistics and reading.* New York: Holt, Rinehart and Winston.

Frith, U. (1985). Beneath the surface of developmental dyslexia. In K. E. Patterson, J. C. Marshall, & M. Coltheart (Eds.), *Surface dyslexia* (pp. 301–330). Hillsdale, NJ: Lawrence Erlbaum Associates.

Fry, E. B., Fountoukidis, D., & Polk, J. K. (1985). *The reading teacher's book of lists.* Englewood Cliffs, N.J.: Prentice-Hall.

Gaardner, K. R. (1970). Eye movements and perception. In F. Young & D. Lindsley (Eds.), *Early experience and visual information processes in perceptual and reading disorders.* Washington, DC: National Academy of Sciences.

Gaddes, W. H. (1980, 1985). *Learning disabilities and brain function: A Neuropsychological approach.* New York: Springer-Verlag.

Gambrell, L. B., Pfeifer, W., & Wilson, R. (1985). The effects of retelling upon reading comprehension and recall of text information. *Journal of Education Research, 78,* 216–220.

Gardiner, B. (1986). *An analysis of selected teaching strategies at specific times of the school day and their effects on the social studies achievement scores of fourth grade low achieving students in an urban setting.* Unpublished doctoral dissertation, St. John's University, Jamaica, NY.

Garrison, J. W., & Hoskisson, K. (1989). Confirmation bias in predictive reading. *The Reading Teacher, 42,* 482–486.

Gates, L., & Lowry, H. (1983). A face lift for the silent e. *The Reading Teacher, 37,* 102.

Gazzaniga, M. S. (1973). *Fundamentals of psychology.* New York: Academic Press.

Gephart, W. J. (1970). *Application of the convergence technique to basic studies of the reading process* (Project No. 8-0737). Washington, DC: Office of Education.

Gersten, R., Carnine, D., & White, W. (1984). The pursuit of clarity: Direct instruction and applied behavior analysis. In W. L. Heward, T. E. Herron, D. S. Hill, & J. T. Porter (Eds.), *Focus on behavior analysis in education* (pp. 38–57). Columbus: Merrill.

Geschwind, N. (1979). Specialization of the human brain. *Scientific American, 24*, 180-201.
Gibson, E. J. (1969). *Principles of perceptual learning and development.* New York: Appleton-Century-Crofts.
Gibson, E. J. (1970). The ontogeny of reading. *American Psychologist, 25*, 136-143.
Gibson, E. J., & Levin, H. (1975). *The psychology of reading.* Cambridge: M.I.T. Press.
Gillett, J. W., & Temple, C. (1986, 1990). *Understanding reading problems.* Boston: Little, Brown.
Gillingham, A., & Stillmann, B. (1960, 1966, 1970, 1973). *Remedial training for children with specific disability in reading, spelling, and penmanship.* Cambridge, MA: Educators publishing Service.
Glass, G. G. (1967). The strange world of syllabication. *The Elementary School Journal, 67*, 403-405.
Glass, G. G. (1973a). *Teaching decoding as separate from reading.* Garden City, NY: Adelphi University Press.
Glass, G. G. (1973b). *Glass analysis for decoding only.* Garden City, NY: Easier to Learn Materials.
Glass, G. G., & Burton, E. H. (1973). How do they decode? Verbalizations and observed behaviors of successful decoders. *The Reading Teacher, 26*, 645.
Glushko, R. J. (1981). Principles of pronouncing print: The psychology of phonology. In A. Lesgold & C. Perfetti (Eds.), *Interactive process in reading.* Hillsdale, NJ: Lawrence Erlbaum Associates.
Goins, J. T. (1950). Visual and auditory perception in reading. *Reading Teacher, 13*, 9-13.
Goins, J. T. (1958). *Visual perceptual abilities and early reading progress* (Supplementary Educational Monograph No. 87). Chicago: University of Chicago Press.
Goldberg, H. K., Shiffman, G. B., & Bender, M. (1983). *Dyslexia: Interdisciplinary approaches to reading disability.* New York: Grune and Stratton.
Golinkoff, R. M. (1975-1976). A comparison of reading processes in good and poor comprehenders. *Reading Research Quarterly, 11*, 623-659.
Goodman, K. S. (1966). A psycholinguistic view of reading comprehension. In G. B. Schick & M. M. May (Eds.), *New frontiers in college-adult reading.* Milwaukee: National Reading Conference.
Goodman, K. S. (1967). Reading: A psycholinguistic guessing game. *Journal of the Reading Specialist, 6*, 126-135.
Goodman, K. S. (1969). Analysis of oral reading miscues: Applied psycholinguistics. *Reading Research Quarterly, 5*, 9-33.
Goodman, K. S. (1973). The 13th easy way to make learning to read difficult: A reaction to Gleitman and Rozin. *Reading Research Quarterly, 8*, 484-493.
Goodman, K. S. (1976a). Reading: A psycholinguistic guessing game. In H. Singer and R. Ruddell (Eds.), *Theoretical models and processes of reading* (2nd Ed.) (pp. 497-508). Newark, DE: International Reading Association.
Goodman, K. S. (1976b). The reading process. In E. B. Smith *et al* (Eds.), *Language and thinking in school*, 2nd . edition. New York: Holt, Rinehart, and Winston.
Goodman, K. S. (1981). Letter to the editors. *Reading Research Quarterly, 16*, 477-478.
Goodman, K. S. (1984). Unity in reading. In A. C. Purves & O. S. Niles (Eds.), *Becoming a reader in a complex society.* 83rd Yearbook of the National Society for the Study of Education (pp. 79-114). Chicago: University of Chicago Press.
Goodman, K. (1985). Unity in reading. In H. Singer & R. Ruddell (Eds.), *Theoretical Models and processes of reading.* Newark, DE: International Reading Association.
Goodman, K. (1986a). *What's whole in whole language.* Portsmouth, NH: Heinemann.
Goodman, K. S. (1986b). Basal readers: A call for action. *Language Arts, 63*, 358-363.
Goodman, K., & Goodman, Y. (1983). Reading and writing relationships: Pragmatic function. *Language Arts, 6*, 590-599.

Goodman, K. S., Shannon, P., Freeman, Y., & Murphy, S. (1988). *Report card on basal readers*. New York: Richard C. Owen.
Goodman, K. S., Smith, E. B., Meredith, R., & Goodman, Y. M. (1987). *Language and thinking in school*. New York: Richard C. Owen Publishers, Inc.
Goodman, Y. M., & Burke, C. (1972). *Reading miscue inventory*. New York: Macmillan.
Goodman, Y.M., & Burke, C. (1980). *Reading strategies: Focus on comprehension*. New York: Holt, Rinehart, & Winston.
Gordon, C. J., & Braun, C. (1983). Using story schema as an aid to reading and writing. *The Reading Teacher, 37*, 116-121.
Gordon, C., & Pearson, P. D. (1983). *The effects of instruction in metacomprehension and inferencing on children's comprehension abilities* (Technical Report No. 277). Urbana, IL: University of Illinois, Center for the Study of Reading.
Goswami, U. (1986). Children's use of analogy in learning to read: A developmental study. *Journal of Experimental Child Psychology, 42*, 73-83.
Gough, P. B. (1972). One second of reading. In J. F. Kavanagh & I. G. Mattingly (Eds.), *Language by ear and eye* (pp. 331-358). Cambridge: MIT Press.
Gough, P. B. (1976). One second of reading. In H. Singer & R. Ruddell (Eds.), *Theoretical models and processing of reading (2nd. ed., pp. 509-535)*. Newark, DE: International Reading Association.
Gough, P. B. (1984). Word recognition. In D. Pearson (Ed.), *Handbook of reading research* (pp. 225-254). New York: Longman.
Gough, P. B., Alford, J. A. & Holley-Wilcox, P. (1981). Words and contexts. In O. L. Tzeng & H. Singer (Eds.), *Perception of print: Reading research in experimental psychology*. Hillsdale, NJ: Erlbaum and Associates.
Gough, P. B. & Tunmer, W. E. (1986). Decoding, reading, and reading disability. *Remedial and Special Education, 7*, 6-10.
Gove, M. K. (1983). Clarifying teacher's beliefs about reading. *The Reading Teacher, 37*, 261-266.
Grabe, M., & Grabe, C. (1985). The microcomputer and the language experience approach. *The Reading Teacher, 38*, 508-511.
Graves, M. E. (1986). Vocabulary learning and instruction. In E. Z. Rothkopf (Ed.), *Review of research in education, 13*, 49-89.
Graves, M. F., Cooke, C. L., & Laberge, M., (1983). Effects of previewing difficult short stories on low ability junior high school students' comprehension, recall and attitudes. *Reading Research Quarterly, 18*, 262-276.
Gray, W. S. (1956). *The teaching of reading and writing*. Chicago: Scott Foresman.
Gray, W. S. (1957). *Is your reading program a good one?* Lawrence, KS: University of Kansas Conference of Reading, International Reading Association.
Gray, W. S. (1969). Reading and physiology and psychology of reading. In E. W. Harris (Ed.), *Encyclopedia of educational research* (2nd. ed.) (pp. 1186-1188). New York: Macmillan.
Gregory, J. F. (1986). Phrasing in the speech and reading of the hearing impaired. *Journal of Communication Disorders, 19*, 289-297.
Griffin, D. C., Walton, H. N., & Ives, V. (1974). Saccades as related to reading disorders. *Journal of Learning Disabilities, 7*, 52-58.
Groesbeck, H. G. (1961). *The comprehension of figurative language by elementary children: A study of transfer*. Unpublished doctoral dissertation, University of Oklahoma, Norman.
Groff, P. (1971). *The syllable*. Portland, OR: Northwest Regional Educational Laboratory.
Groff, P. (1984). Resolving the letter name controversy. *The Reading Teacher, 37*, 384-388.
Groff, P. (1986). The maturing of phonics instruction. *The Reading Teacher, 39*, 919-923.
Guszak, F. J. (1967). Teaching questioning and reading. *The Reading Teacher, 21*, 227-234, 252.

Guthrie, J. T. (1973). Models of reading and reading disability. *Journal of Educational Psychology, 65,* 9–18.

Guthrie, J. T. (1977). Reading comprehension processes and instruction. In J. T. Guthrie (Ed.), *Cognition, Curriculum, & Comprehension.* Newark, DE: International Reading Association.

Haber, L. R., Haber, R. N., & Furlin, D. R. (1983). Word length and word shape as sources of information in reading. *Reading Research Quarterly, 18,* 165–189.

Haddock, M. (1978). Teaching blending in beginning reading instruction is important. *The Reading Teacher, 31,* 654–658.

Hall, M. (1970, 1976, 1981). *Teaching reading as a language experience.* Columbus: Charles E. Merrill.

Hall, M. A. (1978). *The language experience approach for teaching reading* Newark, D. E.: International Reading Association.

Hall, W. S. (1989). Reading comprehension. *American Psychologist, 44,* 157–161.

Halliday, M. A. K., & Hasan, R. (1976). *Cohesion in English.* London: Longman.

Hanf, M. B. (1971). Mapping: A technique for translating reading into thinking. *Journal of Reading, 14,* 225–230.

Hansen, J. (1981). The effect of inference training and practice on young children's reading comprehension. *Reading Research Quarterly, 16,* 391–417.

Hansen, J. & Pearson, P. D. (1983). An instructional study: Improving the inferential comprehension of fourth grade good and poor readers. *Journal of Educational Psychology, 75,* 821–829.

Harber, J. D. (1983). The effects of illustrations on the reading performance of learning disabled and normal children. *Learning Disability Quarterly, 6,* 55–60.

Hardyck, C. D. & Petrinovich, L. F. (1970). Subvocal speech and comprehension level as a function of the difficulty level of reading material. *Journal of Verbal Learning and Verbal Behavior, 9,* 647–652.

Hargis, C. H., & Gickling, E. E. (1978). The function of imagery in word recognition development. *The Reading Teacher, 31,* 870–874.

Harp, B. (1989). When the principal asks: Why don't you ask comprehension questions? *The Reading Teacher, 42,* 638–639.

Harris, A. J., & Sipay, E. R. (1961, 1975, 1980, 1985). *How to increase reading ability.* New York: David McKay Company.

Harris, T. L., & Hodges, R. E. (Eds.) .(1981). *A dictionary of reading and related terms.* Newark, DE: International Reading Association.

Hart, L. A. (1983). Programs, patterns, and downshifting in learning to read. *The Reading Teacher, 37* 5–11.

Hayes, D. A. & Tierney, R. T. (1983). Developing readers' knowledge through analogy. *Reading Research Quarterly, 17,* 256–280.

Hebb, D. O. (1958). *A textbook of psychology.* Philadelphia: W. B. Saunders.

Heckelman, R. G. (1966). Using the neurological-impress remedial reading technique. *Academic Therapy Quarterly, 1,* 235–239.

Heckelman, R. G. (1969). A neurological-impress method of remedial reading instruction. *Academic Therapy, 4,* 272–282.

Heilman, A. W., Blair, T. R., & Rupley, W. R. (1961, 1972, 1981, 1986). *Practices of teaching reading.* Columbus: Charles E. Merrill.

Heller, M. E. (1988). Comprehending and composing through language experience. *The Reading Teacher, 42,* 130–135.

Henderson, E. H., & Beers, J. W. (Eds.). (1980). *Developmental and Cognitive aspects of learning to spell: A reflection of word knowledge.* Newark, DE: International Reading Association.

Henderson, E. H., & Templeton, S. (1986). A developmental perspective of formal spelling

instructions through alphabet pattern and meaning. *Elementary School Journal, 86,* 305-316.
Henk, W. A. (1983). Adapting the NIM to improve comprehension. *Academic Therapy, 19,* 97-101.
Herber, H. L. (1969). Study skills: Reading to develop, remember and use ideas. In H. L. Herber and P. L. Sanders (Eds.) *Reading in the content areas.* (pp. 13-21). Syracuse, NY: Syracuse University Press.
Herber, H. L. (1970). *Teaching reading in the content areas.* Englewood Cliffs, NJ: Prentice Hall.
Hermann, P. A., Anderson, R. C., Pearson, P. D., & Nagy, W. E. (1987). Incidental acquisition of word meaning from expositions with varied text features. *Reading Research Quarterly, 22,* 263-284.
Herrick, J. (1956). *The evolution of human nature.* Austin, TX: University of Texas Press.
Herrmann, B. A. (1988). Two approaches of helping poor readers become more strategic. *The Reading Teacher, 42,* 24-28.
Heshusius, L. (1989). The Newtonian mechanistic paradigm, special education and contours of alternatives: An overview. *Journal of Learning Disabilities, 22,* 403-415.
Heymsfeld, C. R. (1989). Filling the hole in whole language. *Educational Leadership, 46,* 65-68.
Hiebert, E. H., & Colt, J. (1989). Patterns of literature-based reading instruction. *Reading Teacher, 43,* 14-20.
Hildreth, G. (1958). *Teaching reading.* New York: Holt, Rinehart, and Winston.
Hinshelwood, J. (1917). *Congenital word blindness.* London: H. K. Lewis.
Hittelman, D. R. (1978). *Developmental reading: A psycholinguistic perspective.* Chicago: Rand McNally College Publishing.
Hittelman, D. R. (1988). *Developmental reading K-8: Teaching from a whole-language perspective.* Columbus: Merrill Publishing.
Hittelman, D. R., & Hittelman, C. G. (1983). *Developmental reading, K-8: Teaching from a psycholinguistic perspective.* Boston: Houghton-Mifflin.
Hochberg, J. (1970). Attention and perception in reading. In F. A. Young & D. B. Lindsley (Eds.), *Early experience and visual information processing in perceptual and reading disorders.* Washington, DC: National Academy of Sciences.
Hofler, D. B. (1981). Word lines: An approach to vocabulary development. *The Reading Teacher, 35.* 216-218.
Hofler, D. B. (1982). Vocabulary development—classifying homonyms, homophones, and other word terms. *Reading World, 22,* 58-59.
Hollander, S. K. (1975). Reading; process or product. *The Reading Teacher, 28,* 550-554.
Hollingsworth, P. M. (1978). An experimental approach to the impress method of teaching reading. *The Reading Teacher, 31,* 624-626.
Holmes, B. C. (1983a). The effect of prior knowledge on the question answering of good and poor readers. *Journal of Reading Behavior, 15,* 1-18.
Holmes, B. C. (1983b). A confirmation strategy for improving poor reader's ability to answer inferential questions. *The Reading Teacher, 37,* 144-148.
Hook, J. N. (1963). *Writing creatively.* Boston: D. C. Heath.
Horn, E. (1937). *Methods of instruction in the social studies.* New York: Charles Scribner's Sons.
Horowitz, R. (1985a). Text patterns: Part I. *Journal of Reading, 28,* 448-454.
Horowitz, R. (1985b). Text patterns: Part 2. *Journal of Reading, 28,* 534-541.
Hoskisson, K. (1979). Learning to read naturally. *Language Arts, 56,* 892-895.
Huck, C., Hepler, S., & Hickman, J. (1987). *Children's literature in the elementary school.* New York: Holt, Rinehart, and Winston.

Huey, E. B. (1908, 1912). *The psychology and pedagogy of reading.* New York: Macmillan; reprint: Cambridge: The MIT Press, 1968.

Hulme, C. (1981a). *Reading retardation and multisensory teaching.* Boston: Routledge and Kegan Paul.

Hulme, C. (1981b). The effects of manual tracing on memory in normal and retarded readers: Some implications for multi-sensory teaching. *Psychological Research, 43,* 179-191.

Hunter, M. (1989). *Mastery teaching.* El Segundo, CA: TIP Publications.

Inhoff, A. W. (1984). Two stages of word processing during eye fixations in the reading of prose. *Journal of Verbal Learning and Verbal Behavior, 23,* 612-624.

Inhoff, A. W., & Rayner, K. (1986). Parafoveal word processing during eye fixations in reading: Effects of word frequency. *Perception & Psychophysics, 40,* 431-439.

Irwin, J. W. (1986a). *Teaching reading comprehension processes.* Englewood Cliffs, NJ: Prentice-Hall.

Irwin, J. W. (1986b). *Understanding and teaching cohesion comprehension.* Newark: International Reading Association.

Irwin, J. W., & Baker, I. (1989). *Promoting active reading comprehension strategies.* Englewood Cliffs, NJ: Prentice Hall.

Jackson, M. D., & McClelland, J. L. (1979). Processing determinants of reading speed. *Journal of Experimental Psychology: General, 108,* 151-181.

Jacobs, J. (1887). Experiments in comprehension. *Mind, 12,* 75-79.

Jacobsen, E. (1932). Electrophysiology of mental activities. *American Journal of Psychology, 44,* 677-694.

James, W. (1890). *Principles of psychology.* New York: Holt, Rinehart and Winston.

James, W. (1920). *Talks to teachers on psychology.* New York: Holt, Rinehart, and Winston.

Javal, E. (1878). Essai sur la physiologie de la lecture. *Annales D'Oculistique, 82,* 242-253.

Jenkins, J. R., Bausell, R. B., & Jenkins, L. M. (1972). Comparisons of letter name and letter sound training as transfer variables. *American Educational Research Journal, 9,* 75-85.

Jenkins, J. R., & Dixon, R. (1983). Vocabulary Learning. *Contemporary Educational Psychology, 8,* 237-260.

Jenkins, J. R., Matlock, B., & Slocum, T. A. (1989). Two approaches to vocabulary instruction: The teaching of individual word meaning and practice in deriving word meaning from context. *Reading Research Quarterly, 24,* 215-235.

Jenkins, J. R., & Pany, D. (1981). Instructional variables in reading comprehension. In J. Guthrie (Ed.), *Comprehension and teaching: Research reviews* (pp. 163-202). Newark, DE: International Reading Association.

Jenkins, J. R., Stein, M. L., & Wysocki, K. (1984). Learning vocabulary through reading. *American Educational Research Journal, 21,* 767-788.

Jett-Simpson, M. (1981). Writing stories using model structures: The circle story. *Language Arts, 58,* 293-300.

Jewell, M. G. & Zintz, M. V. (1986). *Learning to read naturally.* Dubuque, IA: Kendall/Hunt Publishing.

Johns, J. L. (1986). *Handbook for remediation of reading difficulties.* Englewood Cliffs, NJ: Prentice-Hall.

Johnson, D. (1982). Knowledge structure, vocabulary and comprehension. Paper presented at the Ninth World Congress on Reading. Dublin, Ireland.

Johnson, D. D. (1983). *Three sound strategies for vocabulary development* (Paper No. 3). Columbus, OH: Ginn and Company.

Johnson, D. D., & Baumann, J. F. (1984). Word identification. In P. D. Pearson (Ed.), *Handbook of Reading Research.* New York: Longman.

Johnson, D. D., Pittelman, S. D., & Heimlieb, J. E. (1986). Semantic mapping. *The Reading Teacher, 39,* 778-783.

Johnson, D. J. (1969). Treatment approaches to dyslexia. In G. D. Spache (Ed)., *Reading disability and perception*. Newark, DE: International Reading Association.

Johnson, H., & Smith, L. (1981). Children's inferential abilities in the context of reading to understand. *Child Development, 52*, 1216-1223.

Johnson, N., & Mandler, J. (1980). A tale of two structures: Underlying and surface forms in stories. *Poetics, 9*, 51-86.

Johnston, W. R. (1988). Light on heteronyms. *Journal of Reading, 31*, 570-573.

Jolly, H. B., Jr. (1981). Teaching basic function words. *The Reading Teacher, 35*, 136-140.

Jones, K. J. (1965). Color as an aid to visual perception in early reading. *The British Journal of Educational Psychology, 35*, 21-27.

Jorm, A. F., & Share, D. L. (1983). Phonological recoding and reading acquisition. *Applied Psycholinguistics, 4*, 103-147.

Juel, C. (1980). Comparison of word identification strategies with varying context, word type, and reader skill. *Reading Research Quarterly, 15*, 358-376.

Juel, C. (1983). The development and use of mediated word recognition. *Reading Research Quarterly, 18*, 306-327.

Juel, C. (1988). Learning to read and write: A longitudinal study of fifty-four children from first through fourth grade. Paper presented at the annual meeting of the American Research Association, New Orleans.

Juel, C., Griffith, P. L., & Gough P. B. (1986). Acquisition of literacy: A longitudinal study of children in first and second grade. *Journal of Educational Psychology, 78*, 243-255.

Juel, C., & Roper-Schneider, D. (1982). *The influence of basal readers on first grade reading*. Paper presented at the American Educational Research Association Meeting.

Just, M. A. & Carpenter, P. A. (1980). A theory of reading: From eye fixations to comprehension. *Psychological Review, 87*, 329-354.

Just, M. A., & Carpenter, P. A. (1987). *The psychology of reading and language comprehension*. Boston: Allyn and Bacon.

Kachuck, B. (1981). Relative clauses may cause confusion for young readers. *The Reading Teacher, 34*, 372-377.

Kann, R. (1983). The method of repeated readings: Expanding the neurological impress method for use with disabled readers. *Journal of Learning Disabilities, 16*, 90-92.

Kardash, C. A. M., Royer, J. M., & Greene, B. A. (1988). Effects of schemata on both encoding and retrieval of information from prose. *Journal of Educational Psychology, 80*, 324-329.

Karlin, R. & Karlin, A. R. (1987). *Teaching elementary reading*. San Diego: Harcourt Brace Jovanovich.

Katz, E. W. (1968). Understanding connectives. *Journal of Verbal Learning and Verbal Behavior, 7*, 501-509.

Kaufman, J. M. (1987). Research in special education. *Remedial and Special Education, 8*, 57-62.

Keefe, D., & Meyer, V. (1988). Profiles of and instructional strategies for adult disabled readers. *Journal of Reading, 32*, 614-619.

Keller, H. (1920). *The story of my life*. New York: Doubleday.

Kendler, H. H. (1961). Stimulus-response psychology and audio-visual education. *AV Communication Review, 9*, 33-41.

Kimball, W. H., & Heron, T. E. (1988). Behavioral commentary on Poplin's discussion on reductionistic fallacy and holistic/constructivist principles. *Journal of Learning Disabilities, 21*, 425-428, 447.

Kimmel, S., & MacGinitie, W. H. (1984). Identifying children who use a perseverative processing strategy. *Reading Research Quarterly, 19*, 162-172.

Kintsch, W. (1977). On comprehending stories. In M. A. Just & P. A. Carpenter (Eds.),

Cognitive processes in comprehension. Hillsdale, NJ: Lawrence Erlbaum Associates.

Kintsch, W. (1979). On modeling comprehension. *Educational Psychologist, 14*, 3-14.

Kintsch, W. (1980). Learning from text, levels of comprehension or: Why anyone would read a story anyway. *Poetics, 9*, 87-98.

Kintsch, W., & Greene, E. (1978). The role of culture-specific schemata in the comprehension and recall of stories. *Discourse Processes, 1*, 1-13.

Kintsch, W., & Van Dijk, T. K. (1978). Toward a model of text comprehension and production. *Psychological Review, 85*, 363-394.

Kirk, U. (1983a). Introduction: Toward an understanding of the neuropsychology of language, reading, and spelling. In U. Kirk (Ed.), *Neuropsychology of language, reading, and spelling* (pp. 3-31). New York: Academic Press.

Kirk, U. (1983b). Language and the brain: Implications for education. In U. Kirk (Ed.), *Neuropsychology of language, reading, and spelling* (pp. 257-272). New York: Academic Press.

Kleiman, G. M., & Pumphrey, M. M. (1982). *Phonological representations in visual word recognition: The adjunct access model* (Technical Report No. 247). Champaign, IL: Center for the Study of Reading, University of Illinois.

Knafle, J. D. (1973). Word perception: Cues aiding structure detection. *Reading Research Quarterly, 8*, 502-524.

Kochnower, J., Richardson, E., & Di Benedetto, B. (1983). A comparison of the phonic-decoding ability of normal and learning disabled children. *Journal of Learning Disabilities, 16*, 348-351.

Koskinen, P. S., & Blum, I. H. (1986). Paired repeated reading: A classroom strategy for developing fluent reading. *The Reading Teacher, 40*, 70-75.

Koskinen, P. S., Gambrell, L. B., Kapinus, B. A., & Heathington, B. S. (1988). Retelling: A strategy for enhancing students' reading comprehension. *The Reading Teacher, 41*, 892-896.

Krashen, S. D. (1987). Encouraging Free Reading. 51st. *Claremont reading conference yearbook*, Claremont, CA: 1-10.

Kucer, S. B. (1987). The cognitive base of reading and writing. In J. R. Squire (Ed.), *The dynamics of language learning*. Urbana, IL.: National Council of the Teachers of English.

LaBerge, D., & Samuels, S. J. (1974). Toward a theory of automatic information processing in reading. *Cognitive Psychology, 6*, 293-323.

LaBerge, D., & Samuels, S. J. (1976, 1985). Toward a theory of automatic information processing in reading. In H. Singer & R. B. Ruddell (Eds.), *Theoretical models and processes of reading* (3rd. Ed.) (pp. 548-579, 689-718). Newark, DE: International Reading Association.

Labov, W. (1966). *Some sources of reading problems for negro speakers of non-standard English*. Bethesda, MD: National Cash Register Company.

Lamme, L. L. (1989). Authorship: A key facet of whole language. *The Reading Teacher, 42*, 704-710.

Lange, K. (1902). *Apperception: A monograph on psychology and pedagogy*, Boston, D. C. Heath.

Langer, J. A. (1981). From theory to practice: A prereading plan. *Journal of Reading, 25*, 2.

Langer, J. A. (1982). Facilitating text processing: The elaboration of prior knowledge. In J. A. Langer & M. T. Smith-Burke (Eds.), *Reader meets author: Bridging the gap* (pp. 149-162). Newark: International Reading Association.

Langer, J. A. (1986). *Children reading and writing*. Norwood, NJ: Ablex.

Langer, J. A., & Nicolich, M. (1981). Prior knowledge and its relationship to comprehension. *Journal of Reading Behavior, 13*, 373-379.

Langer, S. K. (1948). *Philosophy in a new key*. New York: Mentor Books New American Library.

Langford, K., Slade, K., & Barnett, A. (1974). An examination of impress techniques in remedial reading. *Academic Therapy, 9,* 309-319.

Langman, M. P. (1960). The reading process: A descriptive, interdisciplinary approach. *Genetic Psychology Monographs, 62,* 1-40.

Lanier, R. J., & Davis, A. P. (1972). Developing comprehension through teacher-made questions. *The Reading Teacher, 26,* 153-157.

Larrick, N. (1987). Illiteracy starts too soon. *Phi Delta Kappan* 69, 184-189.

Leal, L., Crays, N., & Moely, B. E. (1985). Training children to use a self-monitoring strategy in preparation for recall: Maintenance and generalization effects. *Child Development, 56,* 643-653.

Leary, B. E. (1950). Developing word perception skills in middle and upper grades. (pp. 22-27). In *Current problems in reading instruction.* Pittsburgh: University of Pittsburgh Press.

Lefevre, C. A. (1962). Reading our language patterns: A linguistic view — Contributions to a theory of reading. In *Challenge and experiment in reading* (Vol. 7, pp. 66-76). Newark, DE: International Reading Conference Proceedings.

Lefevre, C. A. (1964). *Linguistics and the teaching of reading.* New York: McGraw-Hill.

Lefton, L. A., Nagle, G. J., & Fisher, D. F. (1979). Eye movement dynamics of good and poor readers: Then and now. *Journal of Reading Behavior, 11,* 319-328.

Leong, C. K. (1989). The focus of so-called IQ test results in reading disabilities. *Journal of Reading Disabilities, 22,* 507-512.

Lerner, J. W. (1976, 1985). *Children with learning disabilities: Theories, diagnosis, and teaching strategies.* Boston: Houghton-Mifflin.

Lesgold., A. M., & Curtis, M. E. (1981). Learning to read words efficiently. In A. M. Lesgold & M. E. Curtis (Eds.), *Interactive processes in reading* (pp. 329-360). Hillsdale, NJ: Laurence Erlbaum Associates.

Lesgold, A., Resnick, L., & Hammond, K. (1985). Learning to read: A longitudinal study of word skill development in two curricula. In T. G. Waller & G. E. MacKinnon (Eds.), *Reading research: Advances in theory and practice* (Vol. 4) New York: Academic press.

Leu, D. J., Jr., & Kinzer, C. K. (1987). *Effective reading instruction in the elementary grades.* Columbus: Merrill Publishing.

Levin, H., & Turner, E. A. (1966). *Sentence structure and the eye-voice span* (Project No. B. R. 5-1213-9-OEC-6-10). Studies in oral reading, IX. ED 011 957.

Levine, S. G. (1984). USSR — A necessary component in teaching reading. *Journal of Reading, 27,* 394-400.

Liberman, I. Y. (1985). Should so-called modality preferences determine the nature of instruction for children with reading disabilities. In F. H. Duffy & N. Geschwind (Eds.), *Dyslexia: A neuroscientific approach to clinical evaluation.* Boston: Little, Brown.

Liberman, I. Y., Rubin, H., Duqués, S., & Carlisle, J. (1985). Linguistic abilities and spelling proficiency in kindergarteners and adult poor spellers. In D. B. Gray & J. F. Kavanagh (Eds.), *Biobehavioral measures of dyslexia* (pp. 163-176). Parkton, MD: York Press, Inc.

Liberman, I. Y., & Shankweiler, D. (1979). Speech, the alphabet and teaching to read. In L. B. Resnik & P. A. Weaver (Eds.), *Theory and practice of early reading,* (Vol. 2, pp. 109-134). Hillsdale, NJ: Laurence Erlbaum Associates.

Lipson, M. Y. (1982). Learning new information from text: The role of prior knowledge and reading ability. *Journal of Reading Behavior, 14,* 243-261.

Lipson, M. Y. (1984). Some unexpected issues in prior knowledge and comprehension. *The Reading Teacher, 37,* 760-764.

Lloyd, J. W. (1987). The art and science of research on teaching. *Remedial and Special Education, 8,* 44-46.

Lomax, R. G., & McGee, M. M. (1987). Young children's concepts about print and reading: Toward a model of reading acquisition. *Reading Research Quarterly, 22,* 237-256.

Lovitt, T. C. (1984). *Tactics for teaching.* Columbus: Charles E. Merrill.

Luiten, J., Ames, W., & Acherson, A. G. (1980). A meta-analysis of the effects of advance organizers on learning and retention. *American Educational Research Journal, 17,* 211-213.

Luria, A. R. (1973). *The working brain: An introduction to neuropsychology.* New York: Basic Books.

Luria, A. R. (1980). *Higher cortical functions in man.* New York: Basic Books.

Lyon, K. (1984). *The effect on comprehension of increasing the single-word recoding speed of poor readers.* Unpublished doctoral dissertation, State University of New York at Albany, Albany.

MacGinitie, W. H., Kimmel, S., & Marie, K. (1980). The role of cognitive strategies in certain reading comprehension disabilities. *The Forum, 6,* 10-13.

Mackworth, J. F. (1971). Some models of the reading process: Learners and skilled readers. In F. B. Davis (Ed.), *The literature of research with emphasis on models,* East Brunswick, NJ: Iris Corporation; also in *Reading Research Quarterly, 1972, 7:* 701-733.

MacLean, M., Bryant, P. E., & Bradley, L. (1987). Rhymes, nursery rhymes, and reading in early childhood. *Merrill-Palmer Quarterly, 33,* 255-281.

MacLean, R. (1988). Two paradoxes of phonics. *The Reading Teacher, 41,* 514-517.

Malicky, G., & Brake, M. D. (1983). Oral versus silent reading in programs for problem readers. *Reading—Canada—Lecture* (pp. 55-61).

Mallan, J., & Hersh, R. (1972). *No G. O. D. S. in the classroom: Inquiry into inquiry.* Philadelphia: W. B. Saunders.

Mandler, J. M. (1978). A code in the node: The use of story schema in retrieval. *Discourse Processes, 1,* 14-35.

Mandler, J. M. & Johnson, N. S. (1977). Remembrance of things parsed: Story structure and recall. *Cognitive Psychology, 9,* 111-151.

Manis, F. R. (1985). Acquisition of word identification skills in normal and disabled readers. *Journal of Educational Psychology, 77,* 78-90.

Mann, V. A. (1989). The learning mystique: A fair appraisal, a fruitful new direction. *Journal of Learning Disabilities, 22,* 283-286.

Manzo, A. V. (1969). The request procedure. *Journal of Reading, 13.* 123-126, 163.

Manzo, A. V. (1975). Guided reading procedure. *Journal of Reading, 18,* 287-291.

Manzo, A. V. (1985). Expansion modules for the Request, CAT, GRP, and REAP reading-study procedures. *Journal of Reading, 28,* 498-502.

Marcellesi, C. (1985). Les Difficultés d' apprentissage de la lecture sont-elles d' origine socio-culturelle? Un example: Étude contrastive en milieu urbain. *International Journal of the Sociology of Language, 54,* 99-115.

Marchbanks, G., & Levin, H. (1965). Cues by which children recognize words. *Journal of Educational Psychology, 56,* 57-61.

Marie, K., & MacGinitie, W. H. (1982). Reading comprehension disabilities: Knowledge structures and non-accommodating text processing strategies. *Annals of Dyslexia, 32,* 33-59.

Marr, M. B., & Gormley, K. (1982). Children's recall of familiar and unfamiliar text. *Reading Research Quarterly, 18,* 80-104.

Marsh, G., Friedman, M., Welch, V., & Desberg, P. (1981). A cognitive-development approach to reading acquisition. In T. G. Waller & G. E. MacKinnon (Eds.), *Reading research: Advances in theory and practice.* New York: Academic Press.

Marshall, J. C. (1985). On some relationships between acquired and developmental dyslexias. In F. H. Duffy & N. Geschwind (Eds.), *Dyslexia: A neuroscientific approach to clinical evaluation* (pp. 55-66). Boston: Little, Brown, & Company.

Marshall, N. (1984). Discourse analysis as a guide for informal assessment of comprehension. In J. Flood (Ed.), *Promoting reading comprehension* (pp. 79-96). Newark, DE: International Reading Association.

Marzano, R. J., Hagerty, P. J., Valencia, S. W., & Di Stefano, P. P. (1987). *Reading diagnosis and instruction: Theory and practice.* Englewood Cliffs, NJ: Prentice-Hall.

Mason, J. M. (1980). When do children begin to read: An exploration of four year old children's letter and word reading competencies. *Reading Research Quarterly, 15,* 203-227.

Mason, J. M., & Au, K. H. (1986, 1990). *Reading instruction for today.* Glenview, IL: Scott, Foresman and Company.

Mason, J., & Kendall, J. (1978). *Facilitating reading comprehension through text structure manipulation* (Technical Report No. 92). Champaign, IL: Center for the Study of Reading, University of Illinois.

Mason, J. M., Kniseley, E., & Kendall, J. (1979). Effects of polysemous words on sentence comprehension. *Reading Research Quarterly, 15,* 49-65.

Matthewson, G. C. (1976). The function of attitude in the reading process. In H. Singer & R. B. Ruddell (Eds.), *Theoretical models and processes of reading* (pp. 655-676). Newark, DE: International Reading Association. Also in (1985) *Theoretical models and processes of reading,* 3rd Edition, (pp. 841-856).

May, F. B. (1986). *Reading as communication.* Columbus, OH: Merrill Publishing.

McAndrew, D. A. (1983). Underlining and notetaking: Some suggestions from research. *Journal of Reading, 27,* 103-108.

McClelland, J. L. (1986). The programmable blackboard model of reading. In J. L. McClelland, D. E. Rumelhart, & the PDP Research Group (Eds.), *Parallel distributed processing: Explorations in the microstructure of cognition* (Vol. 2). Cambridge, MA: Bradford Books.

McConkie, G. W. (1982). *Studying the reader's perceptual processes by computer.* Reading Education Report No. 34, Champaign, IL: Center for the Study of Reading, University of Illinois.

McConkie, G. W., & Zola, D. (1984). *Eye movement control during reading: The effect of word units.* Technical Report No. 310. Champaign, IL: Center for the Study of Reading, University of Illinois.

McConkie, G. W., & Zola, D. (1985). Eye movement techniques in studying differences among developing readers. In D. B. Gray & J. F. Kavanagh (Eds.), *Behavioral measures of dyslexia* (pp. 245-259). Parkton, MD: York Press, Inc.

McCormick, S. (1987). *Remedial and clinical reading instruction.* Columbus, OH: Merrill.

McCusker, L. X., Bias, R. G., & Hillinger, M. L. (1981). Phonological recoding and reading. *Psychological Bulletin, 89,* 217-245.

McGaw, B., & Grotelueschen, A. (1972). Direction of the effects of questions in prose material. *Journal of Educational Psychology, 63,* 580-588.

McGee, L. M. (1982a). Awareness of text structure: Effects on children's recall of expository text. *Reading Research Quarterly, 17,* 581-590.

McGee, L. M. (1982b). The influence of metacognitive knowledge of expository text on discourse recall. In J. Niles & L. Harris (Eds.), *New inquiries in reading research and instruction.* Rochester, NY: National Reading Conference.

McGee, L. M., & Richgels, D. J. (1985). Teaching expository text structure to elementary students. *The Reading Teacher, 38,* 739-748.

McIntosh, M. E. (1985). What do practitioners need to know about current inference research? *The Reading Teacher, 38,* 755-761.

McKean, K. (1985). Intelligence: New ways to measure the wisdom of man. *Discover, 6,* 25-41.

McNeil, J. D. (1984, 1987). *Reading comprehension: New directions for classroom practice.* Glenview, IL: Scott, Foresman.

McNeil, J., & Donant, L. (1982). Summarization strategy for improving reading comprehension. In J. Miles & L. A. Harris (Eds.), *New inquiries in reading: Research and instruction* (pp. 215-219). Rochester, NY: National Reading Conference.

McNinch, G. T. (1981). A method for teaching sight words to disabled readers. *The Reading Teacher, 35*, 269-272.

Memory, D. M. (1983a). Constructing main idea questions: A test of a depth-of-processing perspective. In J. Niles & L. A. Harris (Eds.), *Searches for meaning in reading/language processing and instruction* (pp. 66-70). Rochester, NY: National Reading Conference.

Memory, D. M. (1983b). Main idea prequestions as adjunct aids with good and low average middle grade readers. *Journal of Reading Behavior, 15*, 37-48.

Merlin, S. B., & Rogers, S. F. (1981). Direct teaching strategies. *The Reading Teacher, 35*, 292-297.

Meyer, B. J. F. (1979). Structure of prose: *Implications for teachers of reading*. Research Report No. 3. Tempe, AZ: Arizona State University, Department of Educational Psychology.

Meyer, B. J. F. (1984). Organizational aspects of text: Effects on reading comprehension and applications for the classroom. In J. Flood (Ed.), *Promoting reading comprehension* (pp. 113-138). Newark, DE: International Reading Association.

Meyer, B. J. F., & Freedle, R. O. (1984). Effects of discourse type on recall. *American Educational Research Journal, 21*, 121-143.

Meyer, B. J. F., & Rice, G. E. (1984). The structure of text. In P. D. Pearson (Ed.), *Handbook of reading research* (pp. 319-351). New York: Longman.

Mezynski, K. (1983). Issues concerning the acquisition of knowledge: Effects of vocabulary training on reading comprehension. *Review of Educational Research, 53*, 253-279.

Miccinati, J. (1985). Using prosaic cues to teach oral reading. *The Reading Teacher, 39*, 206-212.

Michener, D. M. (1988). Testing your reading aloud IQ. *The Reading Teacher, 42*, 118-122.

Miles, T. R. (1983). *Dyslexia*. Springfield, IL: Charles C. Thomas.

Miller, L. (1989). Sometimes the tail should wag the dog. *The Reading Teacher, 42*, 428.

Moe, A. J., & Irwin, J. W. (1986). *Cohesion, coherence, and comprehension* (pp. 3-8). Newark, NJ: International Reading Association.

Moffett, J., & Wagner, B. J. (1976). *Student centered language arts and reading K-13* (2nd Ed.) Boston: Houghton, Mifflin.

Montgomery, D. (1977). Teaching prereading skills through training in pattern recognition. *The Reading Teacher, 30*, 616-623.

Morris, R. K. (1987). *Eye movement guidance in reading: The role of parafoveal letter and space information*. Amherst, MA: Unpublished master's thesis, University of Massachusetts.

Morrow, L. M. (1984). Effects of story retelling on young children's comprehension and sense of story structure. In J. A. Niles & L. A. Harris (Eds.), *Changing perspectives on research in reading/language processing and instruction*. 33rd yearbook of the National Reading Conference. Rochester, NY: National Reading Conference.

Morrow, L. M. (1985). Retelling stories: A strategy for improving young children's comprehension, concept of story structure, and oral language complexity. *Elementary School Journal, 75*, 647-661.

Morrow, L. M. (1986). Effects of story retelling on children's dictation of original stories. *Journal of Reading Behavior, 18*, 135-152.

Moyer, S. B. (1983). Repeated reading. *Journal of Learning Disabilities, 16*, 619-629.

Moyer, S. B., & Newcomer, P. L. (1977). Reversals in reading: Diagnosis and remediation. *Exceptional Children, 43*, 424-429.

Nagy, W. E., & Anderson, R. C. (1982). *The number of words in printed school English.* Technical Report No. 253. Champaign, IL: Center for the Study of Reading, University of Illinois.

Nagy, W. E., & Anderson, R. C. (1984). How many words are there in printed school English. *Reading Research Quarterly, 19,* 304–330.

Nagy, W. E., Herrmann, P. A., & Anderson, R. C. (1985). Learning words from context. *Reading Research Quarterly, 20,* 233–253.

Nagy, W. E., Anderson, R. C., & Herrmann, P. A. (1987). Learning word meanings from context during normal reading. *American Educational Research Journal, 24,* 237–270.

National Assessment of Educational Progress. (1973). *Reading: Released exercises* (Report 22-R-20). Denver, CO: Education Commission of the States.

National Assessment of Educational Progress. (1975). *Functional literacy: Basic reading performance* (Technical Summary of an Assessment of In-School 17-Year-Olds in 1974). Denver, CO: Education Commission of the States.

National Assessment of Educational Progress. (1982). *Reading comprehension of American youth: Do they understand what they read?* (Report No. 11-R-02). Denver, CO: Education Commission of the States.

National Assessment of Educational Progress. (1984). *Reading objectives 1983–84 Assessment* (Report No. 15-RL-10). Princeton, NJ: Educational Testing Service.

National Assessment of Educational Progress. (1985) .*The reading report card: Progress toward excellence in our schools, trends in reading over four national assessments, 1971–1984* (Report no. 15-R-01). Princeton, NJ: Educational Testing Service.

National Assessment of Educational Progress (1986). *Reading in America* (Reading Report No. 06-R-01, October 1976, Denver, 1976, 1983). Princeton, NJ: Educational Testing Service.

Nemko, B. (1984). Content versus isolation: Another look at beginning readers. *Reading Research Quarterly, 19,* 461.

Newton, M. J., Thomson, M. E., & Richards, I., (Eds.). (1979). *Readings in Dyslexia.* Wisbech: Learning Development Aids.

Nicholson, T. (1986). Reading is *NOT* a guessing game—The great debate revisited. *Reading Psychology, 7,* 197–210.

Nicholson, T., & Hill, D. (1985). Research revisited: Good readers don't guess—Taking another look at the issue of whether children read words better in context or in isolation. *Reading Psychology, 6,* 181–198.

Nicholson, T., & Imlack, R. (1981). Where do their answers come from? A study of the inferences which children make when answering questions about narrative stories. *Journal of Reading Behavior, 13,* 111–129.

Nicholson, T., Lillas, C., & Rzoska, M. A. (1988). Have we been misled by miscues? *The Reading Teacher, 42,* 6–9.

Niensted, S. (1968). A group use of the Fernald technique. *Journal of Reading, 11,* 435–437, 440.

Niles, O. S. (1974). Organization perceived. In H. L. Herber (Ed.), *Perspectives in reading: Developing study skills in secondary schools.* Newark, DE: International Reading Association.

Nolte, R. Y., & Singer, H. (1985). Active comprehension: Teaching a process of reading comprehension and its effect on reading achievement. *The Reading Teacher, 39,* 24–31.

Norberg, K. (1953). Perception research and audiovisual education. *Audio-Visual Communication Review, 1,* 18–29.

Norberg, K. (1956). Perception research and audio-visual education. In W. A. Fullagar, H. G. Lewis, & C. F. Cumbee (Eds.), *Readings for Educational Psychology* (pp. 26–36). New York: Thomas Y. Crowell.

Norris, S. P. (1985). Synthesis of research on critical thinking. *Educational Leadership, 42,* 40-45.

Nulman, J. A. H., & Gerber, M. M. (1984). Improving spelling performance by imitating a child's errors. *Journal of Learning Disabilities, 17,* 328-333.

O'Bruba, W. S. (1974). Basic principles for teaching remedial reading in the classroom. *Reading Improvement, 11,* 9-10.

Olson, R. K. (1985). Disabled reading processes and cognitive profiles. In D. B. Gray & J. F. Kavanagh (Eds.), *Biobehavioral measures of dyslexia* (pp. 215-243). Parkton, MD: York Press.

Olson, R., Wise, B., Conners, F., Rack, J., & Fulker, D. (1989). Specific deficits in component reading and language skills: Genetic and environmental influences. *Journal of Learning Disabilities, 22,* 339-348.

Olsen, W. C. (1952). *Seeking self-selection, and pacing in the use of books by children.* Boston: D.C. Health.

Orton, S. T. (1928). An impediment to learning to read: A neurological explanation of reading disability. *School and Society, 28,* 286-290.

Ortony, A. (1984). Understanding figurative language. In P. D. Pearson (Ed.), *Handbook of reading research* (pp. 453-470). New York: Longman.

O'Shea, L. J., & Sindelar, P. T. (1983). The effects of segmenting written discourse on the reading comprehension of low-and high-performance readers. *Reading Research Quarterly, 18,* 458-465.

Otto, W., White, S., & Campbell, K. (1980). Text comprehension research to classroom application: Developing an instructional technique. *Reading Psychology, 1,* 184-191.

Paivio, A. (1983). Strategies in language learning. In M. Pressley & J. R. Levin (Eds.), *Cognitive strategy research.* New York: Springer-Verlag.

Palincsar, A. S., & Brown, A. L. (1984). Reciprocal teaching of comprehension-fostering and comprehension-monitoring activities. *Cognition and instruction, 1,* pp. 117-175. Also in Technical Report No. 269, Champaign, IL: Center for the Study of Reading, University of Illinois.

Palincsar, A. S., & Ransom, K. (1988). From the mystery spot to the thoughtful spot: The instruction of metacognitive strategies. *The Reading Teacher, 41,* 784-789.

Pany, D., & McCoy, K. M. (1988). Effects of corrective feedback on word accuracy and reading comprehension of readers with learning disabilities. *Journal of Learning Disabilities, 21,* 546-547.

Paratore, J. R., & Indrisano, R. (1987). Intervention assessment of reading comprehension. *The Reading Teacher, 40,* 778-783.

Paris, S. G., & Jacobs, J. E. (1984). The benefits of informed instruction for children's reading awareness and comprehension skills. *Child Development, 55,* 2083-2093.

Paris, S., & Upton, L. (1976). Children's memory for inferential relationships in prose. *Child Development, 47,* 660-668.

Pavlidis, G. T. (1983). The dyslexia syndrome and its objective diagnosis by erratic eye movements. In K. Rayner (Ed.), *Eye movement in reading: Perceptual and language processing* (pp. 441-446). New York: Academic Press.

Pavlidis, G. (1985a). Eye movements in dyslexia: Their diagnostic significance. *Journal of Learning Disabilities, 18,* 42-50.

Pavlidis, G. T. (1985b). Eye movement differences between dyslexics, normal, and retarded readers while sequentially fixating digits. *American Journal of Optometry & Physiological Optics, 62,* 820-832.

Pearson, P. D. (1975). The effects of grammatical complexity of children's comprehension, recall, and conception of certain semantic relations. *Reading Research Quarterly, 10,* 155-192.

Pearson, P. D. (1978). Some practical applications of a psycholinguistic model of reading. In S. J. Samuels (Ed.), *What research has to say about reading instruction*. Newark, DE: International Reading Association.

Pearson, P. D. (1982). *Asking questions about stories* (Ginn Occasional Papers, No. 15. Columbus, OH: Ginn. Also in A. J. Harris & E. Sipay (Eds.), *Readings on reading instruction* (3rd ed., pp. 274-283). New York: Longman.

Pearson, P. D. (1984a). Direct explicit teaching of reading comprehension. In G. B. Duffy, L. R. Roehler, & J. Mason (Eds.), *Comprehension instruction: Perceptives and suggestions*. New York: Longman.

Pearson, P. D. (1984b). A context for instructional research on reading comprehension. In J. Flood (Ed.), *Learning to learn from text: A framework for improving classroom practice*. Newark, DE: International Reading Association.

Pearson, P. D. (1985). Changing the face of reading comprehension instruction. *The Reading Teacher, 38*, 724-738.

Pearson, P. D., & Dole, J. A. (1987). Explicit comprehension instruction: A review of research and a new conceptualization of instruction. *The Elementary School Journal, 88*, 151-165.

Pearson, P. D., & Fielding, L. (1983). *Instructional implications of listening comprehension research*. Reading Education Report No. 39. Urbana, IL: University of Illinois, Center for the Study of Reading.

Pearson, P. D., & Gallagher, M. C. (1983a). The instruction of reading comprehension. *Contemporary Educational Psychology, 8*, 317-344.

Pearson, P. D., & Gallagher, M. C. (1983b). *The instruction of reading comprehension*. Technical Report No. 297. (pp. 317-345). Champaign, IL: Center for the Study of Reading, University of Illinois.

Pearson, P. D., Hansen, J., & Gordon, C. (1979). The effect of background knowledge on young children's comprehension of explicit and implicit information. *Journal of Reading Behavior, 11*, 201-209.

Pearson, P. D., & Johnson, D. D. (1978). *Teaching reading comprehension*. New York: Holt, Rinehart, and Winston.

Perez, S. A. (1986). Children see, children do. *The Reading Teacher, 40*, 8-11.

Perfetti, C. A. (1985). *Reading ability*. New York: Oxford University Press.

Perfetti, C. A., Beverly, S., Bell, L. C., & Hughes, C. (1987). Phonemic knowledge and learning to read: A longitudinal study of first grade children. *Merrill-Palmer Quarterly, 33*, 283-319.

Perfetti, C. A., Finger, E., & Hogaboam, T. W. (1978). Sources of vocalization latency differences between skilled and less skilled young readers. *Journal of Educational Psychology, 70*, 730-739.

Perfetti, C. A., Goldman, S. R., & Hogaboam, T. W. (1979). Reading skill and the identification of words in discourse context. *Memory & Cognition, 7*, 273-282.

Perfetti, C. A., & Lesgold, A. M. (1979). Coding and comprehension in skilled reading and implications for reading instruction. In L. B. Resnick & P. A. Weaver (Eds.), *Theory and practice of early reading (Vol. 1*, pp. 57-84). Hillsdale, NJ: Lawrence Erlbaum Associates.

Perfetti, C. A., & McCutchen, D. (1982). Speech processes in reading. In N. Lass (Ed.), *Speech and language: Advances in basic research and practice* (pp. 237-269). New York: Academic Press.

Perfetti, C. A. ,& Roth, S. F. (1981). Some of the interactive processes in reading and their role in reading skill. In A. M. Lesgold & C. A. Perfetti (Eds.), *Interactive processes in reading* (pp. 269-297). Hillsdale, NJ: Lawrence Erlbaum Associates.

Peters, C. W. (1977). The comprehension process. In W. Otto, C. W. Peters, & N. Peters. (Eds.), *Reading problems: A multi-disciplinary perspective* (pp. 237-269). Reading, MA: Addison-Wesley.

Pflaum, S. W., & Pascarella, E. T. (1980). Interactive effects of prior reading achievement and training in context on the reading of learning disabled children. *Reading Research Quarterly, 16,* 138–158.

Piccolo, J. A. (1987). Expository text structure: Teaching and learning strategies. *The Reading Teacher, 40,* 838–847.

Pieronek, F. T. (1979). Using basal guide-books—The ideal integrated reading lesson plan. *The Reading Teacher, 33,* 167–172.

Pikulski, J. T. (1989). Questions and answers. *The Reading Teacher, 42,* 637.

Poostay, E. J. (1984). Show me your underlines: A strategy to teach comprehension. *The Reading Teacher, 37,* 828–830.

Pope, L. (1976). *Learning disabilities glossary.* Brooklyn, NY: Book Lab.

Poplin, M. S. (1988a). The reductionist fallacy in learning disabilities: Replicating the past by reducing the present. *Journal of Learning Disabilities, 21,* 389–400.

Poplin, M. S. (1988b). Holistic/constructivist principles of the teaching/learning process: Implications for the field of learning disabilities. *Journal of Learning Disabilities, 21,* 401–416.

Porter, W. E. (1958). Mass communication and education. *The National Elementary Principal, 37,* 12–16.

Pratt, A. C., & Brady, S. (1988). Relation of phonological awareness to reading disability in children and adults. *Journal of Educational Psychology, 80,* 319–323.

Prior, M., & McCorriston, M. (1983). Acquired and developmental spelling dyslexia. *Brain and Language, 20,* 263–285.

Pritchard, R. M. (1971). Stabilized images on the retina. In R. C. Atkinson (Ed.), *Contemporary Psychology* (pp. 117–123). San Francisco: W. H. Freeman and Company.

Purcell-Gates, V. (1989). What oral/written language differences can tell us about beginning instruction. *The Reading Teacher, 42,* 290–294.

Rabinovitch, R. D. (1968). Reading problems in children: Definition and classifications. In A. H. Keeney & V. T. Keeney (Eds.), *Dyslexia: Diagnosis and treatment of reading disorders* (pp. 1–10). St. Louis: C. V. Mosby.

Ramsey, W. (1972). *Evaluation of assumptions related to the testing of phonics skills.* Washington, DC: National Center for Educational Research & Development.

Rand, M. K. (1984). Story schema: Theory, research and practice:. *The Reading Teacher, 37,* 377–380.

Raphael, T. (1982a). *Improving question-answering performance through instruction.* Reading Education Report No. 32. Champaign, IL: Center for the Study of Reading, University of Illinois.

Raphael, T. E. (1982b). Question-answering strategies for children. *The Reading Teacher, 37,* 186–191.

Raphael, T. E. (1984). Teaching learners about sources of information for answering questions. *Journal of Reading, 27,* 303–311.

Raphael, T. E. (1986). Teaching question-answer relationships, revisited. *The Reading Teacher, 39,* 516–522.

Raphael, T. E., & McKinney, J. (1983). An examination of fifth and eighth-grade children's question-answering behavior: An instructional study in metacognition. *Journal of Reading Behavior, 15,* 67–86.

Raphael, T. E., & Gavelek, J. R. (1984). Question-related activities and their relationship to reading comprehension: Some instructional implications. In G. Duffy et al (Eds.), *Comprehension instruction: Perspectives and suggestions* (pp. 234–250). New York: Longman.

Raphael, T. E., & Pearson, P. D. (1985). Increasing students' awareness of sources of information for answering questions. *American Educational Research Journal, 22,* 217–236.

REFERENCES

Raphael, T. E., & Wonnacott, C. A. (1985). Metacognitive training in question-answering strategies: Implementation in a fourth-grade developmental reading program. *Reading Research Quarterly, 20,* 282–296.

Rash, J., Johnson, T. D., & Gleadon, N. (1984). Acquisition and retention of written words by kindergarten children under varying learning conditions. *Reading Research Quarterly, 19,* 452–460.

Rasinski, T. V. (1989). Fluency for everyone: Influency instruction in the classroom. *The Reading Teacher, 42,* 690–693.

Rayner, K. (1983a). Eye movements, perceptual spans, and reading disability. *Annals of Dyslexia, 33,* 163–173.

Rayner, K. (1983b). The perceptual span and eye movement control during reading. In K. Rayner (Ed.), *Eye movements in reading: Perceptual and language processes* (pp. 97–120). New York: Academic Press.

Rayner, K. (1983c). *Eye movements in reading: Perceptual and language processes.* New York: Academic Press.

Rayner, K. (1985). Do faulty eye movements cause dyslexia? *Developmental Neuropsychology, 1,* 3–15.

Rayner, K. (1986). Eye movements and the perceptual span in beginning and skilled readers. *Journal of Experimental Child Psychology, 41,* 211–236.

Rayner, K., & Bertera, J. H. (1979). Reading without a fovea. *Science, 206,* 468–469.

Rayner, K., & Pollatsek, A. (1989). *The psychology of reading.* Englewood Cliffs, NJ: Prentice-Hall.

Read, C. (1971). Preschool children's knowledge of English orthography. *Harvard Education Review, 41,* 1–41.

Read, D., Zhang, Y., Nie, H., & Ding, B. (1986). The ability to manipulate speech sounds depends on knowing alphabetic spelling. *Cognition, 24,* 31–44.

Readance, J. E., Baldwin, R. S., & Rickelman, R. J. (1983). Instructional sights into metaphors and similes. *The Journal of Reading, 27,* 109–112.

Readance, J. E., Bean, T. W., & Baldwin, R. S. (1981). *Content area reading.* Dubuque, IA: Kendall-Hunt.

Reicher, G. M. (1969). Perceptual as a function of meaningfulness of stimulus material. *Journal of Experimental Psychology, 81,* 275–280.

Reid, D. K. (1988). Reflections on the pragmatics of a paradigm shift. *Journal of Learning Disabilities, 21,* 417–420.

Reifman, B., Pascarella, E. T., & Larson, A. (1981). Effects of word bank instruction on sight word acquisitions: An experimental note. *Journal of Educational Research, 74,* 175–178.

Reitsma, P. (1988). Reading practice for beginners: Effects of guided reading, reading while listening, and independent reading with computer-based speech feedback. *Reading Research Quarterly, 23,* 219–235.

Rettinger, V., Walters, W., & Poplin, M. S. (1989). Constructing a response to responses. *Journal of Learning Disabilities, 22,* 309–313.

Reutzel, D. R. (1984). Story mapping: An alternative path to comprehension. *Reading World, 24,* 16–25.

Reutzel, D. R. (1985a). Story maps improve comprehension. *The Reading Teaching, 38,* 400–405.

Reutzel, D. R. (1985b). Reconciling schema theory and the basal reading lesson. *The Reading Teacher, 39,* 194–197.

Reutzel, R., & Parker, F. (1988). *A professor returns to the classroom: Implementing whole language.* Unpublished manuscript, Brigham Young University, Provo, Utah.

Reynolds, R. E., & Anderson, R. C. (1981). Influence of questions on the allocation of attention during reading. *Journal of Educational Psychology, 74,* 623–632.

Richek, M. S., List, L. K., & Lerner, J. W. (1982). *Reading problems: Diagnosis and remediation.* Englewood Cliffs, NJ: Prentice-Hall.

Richgels, D. J., & Hansen, R. (1984). Gloss: Helping students apply both skills and strategies in reading content texts. *Journal of Reading, 27,* 312-317.

Richgels, D. J., & Mateja, J. A. (1984). Gloss II: Integrating content and process for independence. *Journal of Reading, 27,* 424-431.

Rickards, J. P., & Hatcher, C. W. (1977-1978). Interpersonal meaningful learning questions as semantic cues for poor comprehenders. *Reading Research Quarterly, 13,* 538-553.

Ringler, L. J., & Weber, C. K. (1984). *A language-thinking approach to reading.* New York: Harcourt Brace Jovanovich.

Robeck, M. C. (1972). An ounce of prevention. In L. M. Schell & P. C. Burns (Eds.), *Remedial reading: Classroom and clinic.* Boston: Allyn & Bacon.

Robeck, M. C, & Wallace, R. R. (1990). *The psychology of reading.* Hillsdale, NJ: Lawrence Erlbaum Associates.

Robeck, M. C., & Wilson, J. A. R. (1974). *Psychology of reading.* New York: John Wiley.

Robertson, J. W. (1968). Pupil understanding of connectives. *Reading Research Quarterly, 3,* 387-417.

Robinson, F. P. (1941, 1946, 1970). *Effective study.* New York: Harper & Row.

Roe, B. D., Stoodt, B. D., & Burns, P. C. (1983). *Secondary school reading instruction: The content areas.* Geneva, IL: Houghton Mifflin.

Roehler, L. R., Duffy, G., Putnam, J., Wesselman, R., Sivan, E., Rackliffe, G., Book, C., Meloth, M., & Vavrus, L. (1987). *The effect of direct explanation of reading strategies on low group third graders' awareness and achievement.* Technical Report No. 181. East Lansing, MI: Institute for Research on Teaching, Michigan State University.

Rogers, C. (1961). *On becoming a person.* Boston: Houghton Mifflin.

Roney, C. R. (1984). Background experience is the foundation of success in learning to read. *The Reading Teacher, 2,* 196-199.

Rose, L. (1969). The reading process and some research implications. *Journal of Reading, 13,* 25-28.

Rose, M. C., Cundick, B. P., & Higbee, K. H. (1984). Verbal rehearsal and visual imagery: Mnemonic aids for learning disabled children. *Journal of Learning Disabilities, 16,* 353-354.

Rose, T. L. (1986). Effects of illustrations on reading comprehension of learning disabled students. *Journal of Learning Disabilities, 19,* 542-544.

Rose, T. L., & Furr, P. M. (1984). Negative effects of illustrations as word cues. *Journal of Learning Disabilities, 17,* 334-337.

Roser, N. L. (1987). Research currents: Relinking literature and literacy. *Language Arts, 64,* 90-97.

Rosenshine, B. V. (1979). Content, time, and direct instruction. In P. L. Peterson & H. J. Walberg (Eds.), *Research on teaching: Concepts, findings, and implications.* Berkeley, CA: McCutchan.

Rosner, S. L., Abrams, J. C., Daniels, P. R., & Schiffman, G. (1981). Dealing with the reading needs of the learning disabled child. *Journal of Learning Disabilities, 14,* 436-450, 492.

Ross, E. (1984). Teaching—Not just testing the main idea. *Reading World, 24,* 84-89.

Ross, E. P. (1986). Classroom experiments with oral reading. *The Reading Teacher, 40,* 270-275.

Rosso, B. R., & Emans, R. (1981). Children's use of phonic generalizations. *The Reading Teacher, 34,* 653-658.

Roth, K. J., Smith, E. L., & Anderson, C. W. (1984). Verbal patterns of teachers: Comprehension instruction in the content areas. In G. Duffy, R. Roehler, & J. Mason (Eds.),

Comprehension instruction: Perspectives and suggestions (pp. 281-293). New York: Longman.
Rothkopf, E. Z. (1970). The concept of mathemagenic activities. *Review of Educational Research, 40*, 325-336.
Rowe, D. W., & Rayford, L. (1987). Activating background knowledge in reading comprehension assessment. *Reading Research Quarterly, 22*, 160-176.
Rubenstein, H. L., & Rubenstein, M. A. (1971). Evidence for phonetic recoding in visual word recognition. *Journal of Verbal Learning and Verbal Behavior, 10*, 647-657.
Rubin, D. (1982). *Diagnosis and correction in reading instruction*. NY: Holt, Rinehart, and Winston.
Rude, R. T. (1986). *Teaching reading using microcomputers*. Englewood Cliffs, NJ: Prentice-Hall.
Rudel, R. G. (1985). The definition of dyslexia: Language and motor deficits. In F. H. Duffy & N. Geschwind (Eds.), *Dyslexia: A neuroscientific approach to clinical evaluation* (pp. 33-54). Boston: Little, Brown, and Company.
Rumelhart, D. E. (1975). Notes on a schema for stories. In D. G. Bobrow & A. M. Collins (Eds.), *Representation and understanding: Studies in cognitive science*. New York: Academic Press.
Rumelhart, D. E. (1976). *Toward an interactive model of reading* (Technical Report No. 56). San Diego, CA: Center for Human Information Processing; also in (1977). pp. 573-603. S. Dornic (Ed.), *Attention and performance VI*. Hillsdale, NJ: Lawrence Erlbaum Associates.
Rumelhart, D. E. (1980). Schemata: The building blocks of cognition. In R. Spiro, B. Bruce, & W. Brewer (Eds.), *Theoretical issues in reading comprehension* .(pp. 33-58). Hillsdale, NJ: Lawrence Erlbaum Associates.
Rumelhart, D. E. (1981). Schemata: The building blocks of cognition. In J. T. Guthrie, (Ed.), *Comprehension and teaching: Research Reviews* (pp. 3-26). Newark, DE: International Reading Association.
Rumelhart, D. E. (1984). Understanding understanding. In J. Flood (Ed.), *Understanding reading comprehension* (pp. 1-20). Newark, DE: International Reading Association.
Rumelhart, D. E., & McClelland, J. L. (1981). Interactive processing through spreading activation. In A. Lesgold & C. Perfetti (Eds.), *Interactive processes in reading* (pp. 37-60). Hillsdale, NJ: Lawrence Erlbaum Associates.
Rumelhart, D. E., & McClelland, J. L. (1982). An interactive model of context effects in letter perception II. *Psychological Review, 89*, 60-94.
Rumelhart, D. E., & Ortony, A. (1977). The representation of knowledge in memory. In R. C. Anderson, R. J. Sprio, & W. E. Montague (Eds.), *Schooling and the acquisition of knowledge* pp. 99-135. Hillsdale, NJ: Lawrence Erlbaum Associates.
Russell, S. (1989). Commentary: Reading visions. *Reading Today, 7*, 2.
Ryan, E. B., Short, E. J., & Weed, K. A. (1986). The role of cognitive strategy training in improving the academic performance of learning disabled children. *Journal of Learning Disabilities, 19*, 521-629.
Sadow, M. W. (1982). The use of story grammar in the design of questions. *The Reading Teacher, 35*, 518-522.
Sadowski, M. (1983). An exploratory study of the relationships between reported imagery and the comprehension and recall of a story. *Reading Research Quarterly, 19*, 110-121.
Samuels, S. J. (1967). Attentional processes in reading: The effects of pictures on the acquisition of reading responses. *Journal of Educational Psychology, 58*, 337-342.
Samuels, S. J. (1970). Effects of pictures on learning to read. *Review of Educational Research, 40*, 397-407.
Samuels, S. J. (1972). The effect of letter-name knowledge on learning to read. *American Educational Research Journal, 9*, 65-74.

Samuels, S. J. (1973). Success and failure in learning to read. *Reading Research Quarterly, 8*, 200-239.
Samuels, S. J. (1976a). Automatic decoding and reading comprehension. *Language Arts, 53*, 323-325.
Samuels, S. J. (1976b). Hierarchical subskills in the reading acquisition process. In J. T. Guthrie (Ed.), *Aspects of reading acquisition* (pp. 141-161). Baltimore, MD: John Hopkins University Press.
Samuels, S. J. (1979). The method of repeated readings. *The Reading Teacher, 32*, 403-408.
Samuels, S. J. (1985). Automaticity and repeated reading. In J. Osborn, P. Wilson, & R. C. Anderson (Eds.), *Reading education*. Lexington, MA: D.C. Heath.
Samuels, S. J. (1987). Information processing abilities and reading. *Journal of Learning Disabilities, 20*, 18-22.
Samuels, S. J. (1988). Decoding and automaticity: Helping poor readers become automatic at word recognition. *The Reading Teacher, 41*, 756-760.
Samuels, S. J., & LaBerge, D. (1983). Critique of a theory of automaticity in reading. Looking Back: A retrospective analysis of the LaBerge-Samuels reading Model. In L. Gentile, M. Kamil, & J. Blanchard (Eds.), *Reading research revisited*. Columbus: Charles E. Merrill.
Samuels, S. J., & Kamil, M. L. (1984). Models of the reading process. In P. D. Pearson (Ed.), *Handbook of reading research* (pp. 185-224). New York: Longman.
Santa, C. M. (1977). Spelling patterns and the development of flexible word recognition strategies. *Reading Research Quarterly, 12*, 125-144.
Schatz, E. K., & Baldwin, R. S. (1986). Context clues are unreliable predictors of word meanings. *Reading Research Quarterly, 21*, 439-453.
Schlieper, A. (1977). Oral reading errors in relation to grade and level of skill. *The Reading Teacher, 31*, 283-287.
Schmidt, C. R., & Paris, S. G. (1983). Children's use of successive clues to generate and monitor inferences. *Child Development, 54*, 742-759.
Schmitt, M. C., & Baumann, J. F. (1986). How to incorporate comprehension monitoring strategies into basal reader instruction. *The Reading Teacher, 40*, 28-31.
Schreiner, R., & Shannon, P. (1980). *The recall of explicit and implied propositions by good and poor readers using three types of assessment procedure*. Paper presented at the International Reading Association Annual Convention, St. Louis.
Schumacher, G. M. (1987). Executive control in studying. In B. Britton & S. M. Glynn (Eds.), *Executive control processes in reading* (pp. 107-144). Hillsdale, NJ: Lawrence Erlbaum Associates.
Schwartz, R. M., & Raphael, T. E. (1985). Concept of definition: A key to improving students' vocabulary. *Reading Teacher, 39*, 198-205.
Searfoss, L. W., & Readence, J. E. (1989). *Helping children learn to read*. Englewood Cliffs, NJ: Prentice-Hall.
Seidenberg, M. S., Waters, G. S., Barnes, M. A., & Tanenhaus, M. K. (1984). When does irregular spelling or pronunciation influence word recognition? *Journal of Verbal Learning and Verbal Behavior, 23*, 383-404.
Semelmeyer, M. (1957). Can Johny Read? *Education, 77*, 505-512.
Shanahan, T. (1984). The nature of the reading-writing relation: An exploratory multivariate analysis. *Journal of Educational Psychology, 76*, 466-477.
Shanahan, T. (1988). The reading-writing relationship: Seven Instructional principles. *The Reading Teacher, 41*, 636-647.
Shankweiler, D., & Liberman, I. Y. (1972). Misreading: A search for causes. In J. F. Kavanagh & I. G. Mattingly (Eds.), *Language by ear and by eye: The relationship between speech and reading* (pp. 293-317). Cambridge, MA: MIT Press.

Share, D. L., Jorm, A. F., Maclean, R., & Matthews, R. (1984). Sources of individual differences in reading acquisition. *Journal of Educational Psychology, 76,* 1309-1324.

Shaw, P. (1958). Rhetorical guides to reading comprehension. *The Reading Teacher, 11,* 239-243.

Sheikh, A. A. (Ed.). (1983). *Imagery: Current theory, research, and application.* New York: John Wiley and Sons.

Shepherd, D. (1973, 1978). *Comprehensive high school reading methods.* Columbus, OH: Charles E. Merrill.

Short, E. J., Yeates, K. O., Feagans, L., & McKinney, J. D. (1983). *The effects of story grammar strategy training on comprehension monitorying* . Unpublished manuscript, University of North Carolina, Durham.

Short, E. J., & Ryan, E. B. (1984). Metacognitive differences between skilled and less skilled readers: Remediating deficits through story grammar and attribution training. *Journal of Educational Psychology, 76,* 225-235.

Siedow, M. D., & Fox, B. J. (1984). Effect of training on good and poor readers' use of top level structure. *Reading World, 23,* 340-346.

Siegel, L. A. (1989). I.Q. is irrelevant to the definition of learning disabilities. *Journal of Learning Disabilities, 22,* 468-478, 486.

Silvernail, L. A. (1987). *The effect of cross-age tutoring and language experience activities on the reading and language achievement scores of third and seventh graders.* Unpublished doctoral dissertation, Auburn University, Auburn, AL.

Simmons, J. S. (1965). Reasoning through reading. *Journal of Reading, 8,* 311-314.

Sinatra, R. C., Stahl-Gemake, J., & Berg, D. N. (1984). Improving reading comprehension of disabled readers through semantic mapping. *The Reading Teacher, 38,* 22-29.

Singer, H. (1978). Active comprehension from answering to asking questions. *The Reading Teacher, 31,* 901-908.

Singer, H., & Donlan, D. (1980). *Reading and learning from text.* Boston: Little, Brown.

Singer, H., Samuels, S. J., & Spiroff, J. (1973-1974). The effect of pictures and contextual conditions on learning responses to printed words. *Reading Research Quarterly, 9,* 555-567.

Slater, W. (1985). Teaching expository text structure with structural organizers. *Journal of Reading, 28,* 712-718.

Slaghuis, W. L., & Lovegrove, W. J. (1985). Spatial-frequency-dependent visible persistence and specific reading disability. *Brain and Cognition, 4,* 219-240.

Smith, C. B. (1989a). Emergent literacy—An environmental concept. *The Reading Teacher, 42,* 528.

Smith, C. (1989b). Prompting critical thinking. *The Reading Teacher, 42,* 424.

Smith, F. (1973). *Psycholinguistics and reading.* New York: Holt, Rinehart and Winston.

Smith, F. (1975). *Comprehension and learning.* New York: Holt, Rinehart and Winston.

Smith, F. (1977). Making sense of reading—And of reading instruction. *Harvard Educational Review, 47,* 386-395.

Smith, F. (1971, 1978, 1982, 1988). *Understanding reading: A psycholinguistic analysis of reading and learning to read.* New York: Holt, Rinehart and Winston; Hillsdale, NJ: Lawrence Erlbaum Associates.

Smith, H. P. (1956). The sociology of reading. In *Exploring the goals of college reading programs, fifth yearbook of the Southwest Reading Conference for Colleges and Universities* (pp. 23-28) Fort Worth: Texas Christian University Press.

Smith, H. (1962). The perceptual nature of the reading process. *Bulletin of Education* (pp. 60-69). Lawrence, KS: University of Kansas.

Smith, H. P., & Dechant, E. V. (1961). *Psychology in teaching reading.* Englewood Cliffs, NJ: Prentice-Hall.

Smith, M. & Bean, T. W. (1983). Four strategies that develop children's story comprehension and writing. *The Reading Teacher, 37,* 295-301.

Smith, R. J., & Barrett, T. C. (1974, 1979). *Teaching reading in the middle grades.* Reading, MA: Addison-Wesley.
Spache, G. (1976). *Diagnosing and correcting reading disabilities.* Boston: Allyn and Bacon.
Spache, G., & Spache, E. B. (1986). *Reading in the elementary school.* Boston: Allyn and Bacon.
Spencer, L. P. (1946). The reading process and types of reading. In 11th yearbook, *Claremont college reading conference* yearbook. Claremont, CA: pp. 19-20.
Spilich, G. J., Vesonder, G. T., Chiesi, H. L., & Voss, J. F. (1979). Text processing of domain-related information for individuals with high and low domain knowledge. *Journal of Verbal Learning and Verbal Behavior, 18,* 275-290.
Spiro, R. J., Bruce, B. C., & Brewer, W. F. (Eds.). (1980). *Theoretical issues in reading comprehension: Perspectives from cognitive psychology, linguistics, artificial intelligence, and education.* Hillsdale, NJ: Lawrence Erlbaum Associates.
Spring, H. T. (1985). Teacher decisionmaking: A metacognitive approach. *The Reading Teacher, 39,* 290-295.
Squire, J. (1983). Composing and comprehending: Two sides of the same basic process. *Language Arts, 60,* 581-589.
Stanley, G., & Hall, R. (1973). Short-term visual information in dyslexics. *Child Development, 44,* 841-844.
Stanovich, K. E. (1980). Toward an interactive compensatory model of individual differences in the development of reading fluency. *Reading Research Quarterly, 15,* 32-71.
Stanovich, K. E. (1981). Attentional and automatic context effects in reading. In A. Lesgold & C. Perfetti (Eds.), *Interactive processes in reading* (p. 241-267). Hillsdale, NJ: Lawrence Erlbaum Associates.
Stanovich, K. E. (1986). Matthew effects on reading: Some consequence of individual differences in the acquisition of literacy. *Reading Research Quarterly, 21,* 360-406.
Stanovich, K. E. (1987). Perspectives on segmental analysis and alphabetical literacy. *Cahiers de psychologie cognitive, 7,* 514-519.
Stanovich, K. E. (1988). Explaining the differences between the dyslexic and the garden-variety poor reader: The phonological-core variable-difference model. *Journal of Learning Disabilities, 21,* 590-604.
Stanovich, K. E., Cunningham, A. F., & Feeman, D. J. (1984). Relation between early reading acquisition and word decoding with and without context: A longitudinal study of first-grade children. *Journal of Educational Psychology, 76,* 668-677.
Stanovich, K. E., Cunningham, A., & Feeman, D. J. (1984). Intelligence, cognitive skills, and early reading progress. *Reading Research Quarterly, 19,* 278-303.
Stanovich, K. E., & West, R. F. (1983). The generalizability of context effects on word recognition: A reconsideration of the roles of parafoveal priming and sentence context. *Memory and Cognition, 11,* 49-58.
Stanovich, K. E., & West, R. F. (1983). On priming by a sentence context. *Journal of Experimental Psychology: General, 112,* 1-36.
Stauffer, R. (1969). *Directing reading maturity as a cognitive process.* New York: Harper and Row.
Stauffer, R. (1975). *Directing the reading-thinking process.* New York: Harper and Row.
Stedman, L., & Kaestle, C. (1987). Literacy and reading performance in the United States from 1880 to the present. *Reading Research Quarterly, 22,* 8-46.
Stein, J. F., & Fowler, S. (1984). Ocular motor problems of learning to read. In A. G. Gale & F. Johnson (Eds.), *Theoretical and applied aspects of eye movement research.* Amsterdam: North Holland Press.
Stein, N. L., & Glenn, C. G. (1979). An analysis of story comprehension in elementary school children. In R. O Freedle (Ed.), *New directions in discourse processing* (pp. 53-120). Norwood, NJ: Ablex.

REFERENCES

Stein, M. L. & Jenkins, J. R. (1989). *The effect of multiple exposures on learning vocabulary from context.* Seattle, WA: University of Washington.

Steiner, R., Morton, W., & Cromer, W. (1971). Comprehension training and identification for poor and good readers. *Journal of Educational Psychology, 62,* 506-513.

Steinheiser, R., & Guthrie, J. T. (1977). Perceptual and linguistic processing of letters and words by normal and disabled readers. *Journal of Reading Behavior, 9,* 217-225.

Sternberg, R. (1987). Most vocabulary is learned from context. In M. C. McKeown & M. E. Curtis (Eds.), *The nature of vocabulary acquisition* (pp. 89-105). Hillsdale, NJ: Lawrence Erlbaum Associates.

Sternberg, R., Powell, J. S., & Kaye, D. B. (1983). Teaching vocabulary building skills: A contextual approach. In A. C. Wilkinson (Ed.), *Communicating with computers in the classroom.* New York: Academic Press.

Stevens, K. C. (1980). The effect of background knowledge on the reading comprehension of ninth graders. *Journal of Reading Behavior, 12,* 151-154.

Stevens, K. C. (1981). Chunking material as an aid to reading comprehension. *Journal of Reading, 25,* 126-129.

Stevens, K. C. (1982). Can we improve reading by teaching background information? *Journal of Reading, 25,* 326-329.

Sticht, T. G., & James, J. H. (1984). Listening and reading. In P. D. Pearson, R. Barr, M. L. Kamil, & P. Mosenthal (Eds.), *Handbook of reading research.* New York: Longman.

Stoodt, B. (1989). *Reading instruction.* New York: Harper & Row.

Stotsky, S. (1983). Research on reading/writing relationships: A synthesis and suggested direction. *Language Arts, 60,* 627-642.

Stott, D. J. (1973). Some less obvious cognitive aspects of learning to read. *The Reading Teacher, 26,* 374-383.

Strange, M. (1980). Instructional implications of a conceptual theory of reading comprehension. *The Reading Teacher, 33,* 391-397.

Straus, A., & Lehtinen, L. E. (1947). *Psychopathology and education of the brain injured child.* New York: Grune and Stratton.

Sulzby, E., & Teale, W. H. (1985). Writing development in early childhood. *Educational Horizons, 64,* 8-12.

Swaby, B. (1984). *Teaching and learning reading.* Boston: Little, Brown.

Swalm, J. E. (1972). A comparison of oral reading, silent reading, and listening comprehension. *Education, 92,* 111-115.

Swanson, H. L. (1984). Phonological reading and suppression effects in children's sentence comprehension. *Reading Research Quarterly, 19,* 393-403.

Swanson, H. L. (1989). Phonological processes and other routes. *Journal of Learning Disabilities, 22,* 493-497.

Swenson, I. (1975). Word-recognition cues used in matching verbal stimuli within and between auditory and visual modalities. *Journal of Educational Psychology, 67,* 409-415.

Taft, M. (1985). The decoding of words in lexical access: A review of the morphological approach. In D. Besner, T. G. Waller, & G. E. MacKinnon (Eds.), *Reading research: Advances in theory and practice* (Vol. 5). New York: Academic Press.

Tatham, S. M. (1978). Comprehension taxonomies: Their uses and abuses. *The Reading Teacher, 32,* 190-194.

Taylor, B. M., & Beach, R. W. (1984). The effects of text structure instruction on middle grade students' comprehension and production of expository text. *Reading Research Quarterly, 19,* 134-161.

Taylor, B. M., & Samuels, S. J. (1983). Children's use of text structure in the recall of expository material. *American Educational Research Journal, 20,* 517-528.

Taylor, E. A. (1959). *Eyes, visual anomalies and the fundamental reading skill.* New York: Reading and Study Skills Center.

Taylor, S. E. (1962). *Speed reading vs. improved reading efficiency*. Huntington, NY: Educational Developmental Laboratories.

Taylor, S. E., Frackenpohl, H., & Pettee, I. L. (1960). *Grade level norms for the components of the fundamental reading skill*. Bulletin 3. Huntington, NY: Educational Developmental Laboratories.

Taylor, W. (1953). Cloze procedure: A new tool for measuring readability. *Journalism Quarterly, 30*, 415-433.

Teale, W. H., Hiebert, E. H., & Chittenden, E. A. (1987). Assessing young children's literacy development. *The Reading Teacher, 40*, 772-777.

Terman, S., & Walcutt, C. C. (1958). *Chaos and cure*. New York: McGraw-Hill.

Thelen, J. (1982). Preparing students for content reading assignments. *Journal of Reading, 25*, 544-549.

Thompson, G. B. (1981). Toward a theoretical account of individual differences in the acquisition of reading skill. *Reading Research Quarterly, 15*, 596-599.

Thorndike, E. L. (1913). *The psychology of learning*. New York: Teachers College Press.

Thorndike, E. L. (1917). Reading as reasoning: A study of mistakes in paragraph reading. *Journal of Educational Psychology, 8*, 323-332.

Thorndyke, P. W. (1977). Cognitive structures in comprehension and memory of narrative discourse. *Cognitive Psychology, 9*, 77-110.

Tierney, R., Bridge, C., & Cera, M. J. (1978-1979). The discourse operations of children. *Reading Research Quarterly, 14 (No. 4)*, 539-573.

Tierney, R. J., & Cunningham, J. W. (1984). Research on teaching reading comprehension. In P. D. Pearson (Ed.), *Handbook of reading research* (pp. 609-655). New York: Longman.

Tierney, R., & Leys, M. (1984). *What is the value of connecting reading and writing?*. Reading Education Report No. 55. Champaign, IL: Center for the Study of Reading.

Tierney, R., & Leys, M. (1986). What is the value of connecting reading and writing? In B. Peterson (Ed.), *Convergences: Transactions in reading and writing*. Urbana, IL: National Council of Teachers of English.

Tierney, R. J., & Pearson, P. D. (1983). Toward a composing model of reading. *Language Arts, 60*, 568-580.

Tierney, R. J., Readance, J. E., & Dishner, E. K. (1980, 1985). *Reading strategies and practices: A guide for improving instruction*. Boston: Allyn and Bacon.

Tolman, E. C. (1945). A stimulus-expectancy need cathexis psychology. *Science, 101*, 16-166.

Tolman, E. C. (1951). *Collected papers in psychology*. Berkeley, CA: University of California Press.

Tonjes, M. J., & Zintz, M. V. (1981). *Teaching reading/thinking study skills in context classrooms*. Dubuque IA: William C. Brown Company.

Topping, K. (1989). Peer tutoring and paired reading: Combining two powerful techniques. *The Reading Teacher, 42*, 488.

Torgesen, J. (1985). Memory processes in reading disabled children. *Journal of Learning Disabilities, 18*, 350-357.

Torgesen, J. (1986). Computers and cognition in reading: A focus in decoding fluency. *Exceptional Children, 53*, 151-162.

Torgesen, J. K. (1986). Learning disabilities theory: Its current state and future prospects. *Journal of Learning Disabilities, 19*, 399-407.

Torneus, M. (1984). Phonological awareness and reading: A chicken and egg problem. *Journal of Educational Psychology, 76*, 1346-1358.

Trabasso, T. (1981). On the making of inferences during reading and their assessment. In J. Guthrie (Ed.), *Comprehension and Teaching: Research Reviews* (pp. 56-76). Newark, DE: International Reading Association.

Trachtenberg, P. (1990). Using children's literature to enhance phonics instruction. *The Reading Teacher, 43*, 648-652.

Traynelis-Yurek, E. (1985). Preferred versus non-preferred hand: A comparative study. *Academic Therapy, 21,* 29-36.

Treiman, R., & Baron, J. (1983). Phonemic analysis training helps children benefit from spelling-sound rules. *Memory and Cognition, 11,* 382-389.

Trelease, J. (1985). *The read-aloud handbook.* New York: Viking/Penguin.

Tremonti, J. B., & Alegero, C. (1967). Reading and study habits in content areas. *Reading Improvement, 4,* 54-57.

Tunmer, W. E., & Nesdale, A. R. (1985). Phonemic segmentation skill and beginning reading. *Journal of Educational Psychology, 77,* 417-427.

Tunnell, M. O. (1986). The natural act of reading: An affective approach. *The Advocate, 5,* 146-164.

Tunnell, M. O., & Jacobs, J. S. (1989). Using real books: Research findings on literature based reading instruction. *The Reading Teacher, 42,* 470-477.

Turner, T. N. (1988). Comprehension reading for meaning. In J. E. Alexander (Ed.), *Teaching reading* (pp. 158-182). Glenview, IL: Scott, Foresman.

Turner, T. N. (1988). Higher levels of comprehension: Inference, critical reading, and creative reading. In J. E. Alexander (Ed.), *Teaching reading* (pp. 182). Glenview, IL: Scott Foresman.

Underwood, N. R., & Zola, D. (1986). The span of letter recognition of good and poor readers. *Reading Research Quarterly, 21,* 6-19.

Vacca, J. A. L., Vacca, R. T., & Gove, M. K. (1987). *Reading and learning to read.* Boston: Little, Brown.

Vacca, R. T. (1981). *Content area reading.* Boston: Little, Brown.

Vacca, R. T., & Jones, J. L. (1976). $R > S_1 + S_2 \ldots S_n$. *Reading Horizons, 17,* 9-13.

Vacca, R. T., & Vacca, J. A. L. (1986, 1989). *Content area reading.* Boston: Little, Brown.

Valencia, S., & Pearson, P. D. (1987). Reading assessment: Time for a change. *Reading Teacher, 40,* 726-733.

VanOrden, G. C. (1987). A rose is a rose: Spelling, sound, and reading. *Memory and Cognition, 15,* 181-198.

Vaughan, S., Crawley, S., & Mountain, L. (1979). A multiple-modality approach to word study: Vocabulary scavenger hunts. *The Reading Teacher, 32,* 434-437.

Veatch, J. (1984). *Reading in the elementary school.* New York: R. C. Owen.

Veatch, J. (1986-1987). Reflections: Teaching without texts. *Journal of Clinical Reading, 2,* 32-35.

Veatch, J. (1987). Return to reason: Individualized reading. 51st *Claremont reading conference yearbook* (pp. 177-181). Claremont, CA.

Veatch, J., & Acinapuro, P. J. (1978). *Reading in the elementary school.* New York: John Wiley.

Veatch, J., Sawicki, F., Elliott, G., Barnette, E., & Blakey, J. (1979). *Key words to reading: The language experience approach.* Columbus, OH: Charles C. Merrill.

Vellutino, F. (1979). *Dyslexia: Theory and research.* Cambridge, MA: MIT Press.

Vellutino, F. (1980). Dyslexia: Perceptual deficiency or perceptual inefficiency. In J. F. Kavanagh & R. L. Venezky (Eds.), *Orthography, reading, and dyslexia* (pp. 251-270). Baltimore: University Park Press.

Vellutino, F. (1987). Dyslexia. *Scientific American, 256,* 34-44.

Vellutino, F. R., & Scanlon, D. M. (1985). Verbal memory in poor and normal readers: Developmental differences in the use of linguistic codes. In D. B. Gary & J. F. Kavanagh (Eds.), *Biobehavioral measures of dyslexia* (pp. 177-214). Parkton, MD: York Press, Inc.

Vellutino, F. R., & Scanlon, D. M. (1987). Phonological coding, phonological awareness, and reading ability: Evidence from a longitudinal and experimental study. *Merrill-Palmer Quarterly, 33,* 321-363.

Venezky, R. L. (1983). *Issues in the design of phonics instruction, Number 14*. Columbus, OH: Ginn and Company.

Vogel, J. A. (1987). Story circles teach sequence. *The Reading Teacher, 414*, 250–251.

Wagner, L. (1980). The effects of TV on reading. *Journal of Reading, 34*, 201–206. Also in A. J. Harris & E. Sipay (Eds.), (1984), *Readings on reading instruction, third edition* (pp. 358–362). New York: Longman.

Wagner, R. K., & Torgesen, J. K. (1987). The nature of phonological processing and its causal role in the acquisition of reading skills. *Psychological Bulletin, 101*, 192–212.

Walcutt, C. C., Lamport, J., & McCracken, G. (1974). *Teaching reading*. New York: Macmillan.

Wallach, L., & Wallach, M. A. (1982). Phonemic analysis training in the teaching of reading. In W. M. Cruickshank & J. W. Lerner (Eds.), *Coming of Age*. Syracuse, NY: Syracuse University Press.

Walsh, D. J., Price, G. G., & Gillingham, M. G. (1988). The critical but transitory importance of letter naming. *Reading Research Quarterly, 23*, 108–122.

Warren, W. H., Nicholas, D. W., & Trabasso, T. (1979). Event chains and inferences in understanding narratives. In R. O. Freedle (Ed.), *New dimensions in discourse processing* (Vol. 2). Hillsdale, NJ: Lawrence Erlbaum Associates.

Watson, J. B. (1920). Is thinking merely the action of the language mechanism? *British Journal of Psychology, 11*, 87–104.

Weaver, C. (1988). *Reading process and practice from sociopsycholinguistics to whole language*. Portsmouth, NH: Heinmann.

Weinberg, F. (1983). *An experimental investigation of the interaction between sensory modality preference and mode of presentation in the instruction of arithmetic concepts to third-grade underachievers*. Unpublished doctoral dissertation, St. John's University, Jamaica, NY.

Weinstein, C. E. (1987). Fostering learning autonomy through the use of learning strategies. *Journal of Reading, 30*, 590–595.

Weinstein, C. F., & Mayer, R. F. (1986). The teaching of learning strategies. In M. C. Wittrock (Ed.), *Handbook of research on teaching* (pp. 315–327). New York: Macmillan.

Weiss, D. S. (1983). The effects of text segmentation on children's reading comprehension. *Discourse Processes. 6*: 77–89.

West, R. F., & Stanovich, K. E. (1978). Automatic contextual facilitation in readers of three ages. *Child Development, 49*, 717–727.

Whaley, J. F. (1981a). Readers' expectations for story structure. *Reading Research Quarterly, 17*, 90–114.

Whaley, J. F. (1981b). Story grammars and reading instruction. *The Reading Teacher, 34*, 762–771.

Wheeler, R. (1983). *An investigation of the degree of academic achievement evidenced when second grade, learning disabled students' perceptual preferences are matched and mismatched with complimentary sensory approaches to beginning reading instruction*. Unpublished doctoral dissertation, St. John's University, Jamaica, NY.

Wheelock, W. H., & Silvaroli, N. J. (1967). Visual discrimination training for beginning readers. *The Reading Teacher, 21*, 115–120.

White, J. H., Vaughan, J. L., & Rorie, I. L. (1986). Picture of a classroom where reading is for real. *The Reading Teacher, 40*, 84–86.

White, T. G., Sowell, J., & Yanagihara, A. (1989). Teaching elementary students to use word-part clues. *The Reading Teacher, 42*, 302–308.

Widomski, C. L. (1983). Building foundations for reading comprehension. *Reading World, 22*, 306–313.

Wiesendanger, K. D., & Bader, L. A. (1987). Teaching easily confused words: Timing makes the difference. *The Reading Teacher, 41*, 328–332.

REFERENCES

Wigg, E., Semel, E., & Abele, E. (1981). Perception and interpretation of ambiguous sentences by learning disabled twelve-year-olds. *Learning Disability Quarterly, 4*, 3-12.

Williams, J. (1984). Phonemic analysis and how it relates to reading. *Journal of Learning Disabilities, 17*, 240-245.

Wilson, C. R. (1983). Teaching reading comprehension by connecting the known to the new. *The Reading Teacher, 36*, 382-390.

Wilson, R. M., & Cleland, C. J. (1985). *Diagnostic and remedial reading for classroom and clinic (5th ed.)*. Columbus, OH: Charles E. Merrill.

Wittrock, M. C. (1983). Writing and the teaching of reading. *Language Arts, 60*, 600-606.

Wittrock, M. C. (1987). Process oriented measures of comprehension. *The Reading Teacher, 40*, 734-737.

Wixson, K. K. (1982). *Level of importance of post-questions and children's learning from text*. Paper presented at the National Reading Conference, Clearwater Beach, FL.

Wixson, K. K. (1983a). Postreading question-answer interactions and children's learning from text. *Journal of Educational Psychology, 30*, 413-423.

Wixson, K. K. (1983b). Questions about a text: What you ask about is what children learn. *The Reading Teacher, 37*, 287-294.

Wixson, K. K., Peters, C. W., Weber, E. M., & Roeber, E. D. (1987). New directions in statewide reading assessment. *The Reading Teacher, 40*, 749-755.

Wolpert, E. M. (1972). Length, imagery values and word recognition. *The Reading Teacher, 26*, 180-186.

Wong, B. Y. L., & Jones, W. (1982). Increasing metacomprehension in learning disabled and normally achieving students through self-questioning training. *Learning Disability Quarterly, 5*, 228-240.

Wood, K. (1983). Variation on an old theme: Four way oral reading. *The Reading Teacher, 37*, 38-43.

Wood, K. D. (1988). Guiding students through informational text. *The Reading Teacher, 41*, 912-920.

Wood, K. D., & Mateja, J. A. (1983). Adapting secondary level strategies for use in elementary classrooms. *The Reading Teacher, 36*, 492-496.

Woolfolk, A. E. (1990). *Educational psychology*. Englewood Cliffs, NJ: Prentice-Hall.

Wynn, S. J. (1988). Developing a sight vocabulary. In J. E. Alexander (Ed.), *Teaching reading* (pp. 53-73). Glenview, IL: Scott, Foresman.

Yekovich, F. R., & Walker, C. H. (1987). The activation and use of scripted knowledge in reading about routine activities. In B. Britton & S. M. Glynn (Eds.), *Executive control processes in reading* (pp. 145-171). Hillsdale, NJ: Lawrence Erlbaum Associates.

Yelland, G., & Bradley, D. (1985). *Children's exploration of word and sentence contexts: The influence of reading training*. Manuscript submitted for publication.

Yule, W., & Rutter, M. (1976). Epidemiology and social implications of specific reading retardation. In R. M. Knights & D. J. Bakker (Eds.), *The neuropsychology of learning disorders: Theoretical approaches* (pp. 25-39). Baltimore: University Park Press.

Zanjano, N. C. (1977). *Broncos reading improvement project 1976-77. Final evaluation report*. Burrillville, RI: ERIC Document Reproduction Service.

Zintz, M. V. (1972, 1977). *Corrective reading*. Dubuque, IA: William C. Brown Company.

Zintz, M. V., & Maggart, Z. R. (1989). *The reading process: The teacher and the learner*. Dubuque: William C. Brown Company.

Author Index

A

Aaron, I. E., 99, 186
Abele, E., 400
Abrams, J. C., 160, 356
Acherson, A. G., 203
Acinapura, P. J., 175
Adams, M. J., 33, 254, 257, 270, 275, 277, 281, 282
Alegero, C., 458
Alexander, J. E., 262
Alford, J. A., 151
Allen, C., 168–169
Allen, E. G., 172
Allen, R. V., 168–169
Allington, R. L., 227, 287–288
Altwerger, B., 177
Alvermann, D. E., 125
Amble, B. R., 393
Ames, W., 203
Anderson, C. W., 203, 358
Anderson, M., 116, 449
Anderson, R. C., 6, 14, 116, 120, 148, 150, 198, 218, 340, 350, 363, 365, 449
Anderson, T. H., 218, 444
André, M. E., 218
Ansara, A., 286, 355
Anshen, R. N., 99
Armbruster, B. B., 228–229, 444
Arnold, R., 142, 403

Artley, A. S., 377
Asher, S. R., 197
Askov, E. N., 105, 115
Asplund, B. B., 172
Atkinson, R. C., 87
Au, A. H., 117, 231, 271, 358, 464
Aukerman, L. R., 374, 453
Aukerman, R. C., 374, 453
Aulls, M. W., 227, 288
Ausübel, D. P., 111, 117, 119, 202–203

B

Backman, J. E., 261
Baddeley, A. D., 465
Bader, L., 74, 264
Badiali, J. W., 105, 115
Baker, L., 119, 121, 212, 215, 232, 353, 434, 463
Baldwin, R. S., 148, 202, 385
Balota, D. A., 152
Bannatyne, A. D., 8, 76, 289
Barnard, D. P., 169
Barnes, M. A., 33
Barnette, E., 169
Barnhart, C. L., 258
Barnitz, J. G., 401, 405
Baron, J., 272
Barrett, T. C., 189, 254, 326, 328

505

Barron, R. F., 209, 210
Barron, R. W., 33, 34, 261
Bartlett, F. C., 114
Baumann, J. F., 205, 209, 215, 228, 230
Bausell, R. B., 255
Bax, M. C. O., 54
Beach, R. W., 208
Bean, T. W., 202–203
Beck, I. L., 202, 218, 350, 357, 366, 448
Beers, J. W., 282
Bell, L. C., 275
Bellare, R. L., 240
Bender, M., 51
Benton, A., 55
Berg, D. N., 444
Berndt, R. A., 395
Bertelson, P., 275
Betts, E. A., 195
Beverly, S., 275
Blair, S. M., 249
Blair, T. R., 209, 210, 395
Blakey, J., 169
Blanchard, H. E., 59
Blanton, W. E., 199, 200, 230, 231
Blau, H., 285
Bloom, B. S., 189
Bloomfield, L., 258
Blum, I. H., 287–288
Boehnlein, M., 184
Book, C., 232
Bos, D. S., 287
Bradley, L., 275–277, 281–282, 284, 296
Brady, S., 275
Brake, M. D., 125
Braun, C., 438
Breen, L. G., 139, 374
Britton, B., 216
Bromley, K. D., 441
Brower, W. F., 26
Brown, A. L., 119, 121, 212, 215–216, 228–229, 232, 253, 434, 442, 451, 463
Brown, M. W., 437
Brozo, W. G., 465
Bruce, B., 26, 439
Bruck, M., 34, 261
Bruner, J. S., 102, 111, 274, 433
Brunswick, E., 90
Bryant, P. E., 265–277, 281–282, 296
Burke, C., 297
Burmeister, L. E., 190, 310, 317, 326, 368, 381, 416–417, 431, 454

Burns, P. C., 201–202, 208, 456, 457, 459, 462
Burton, E. H., 281
Buswell, G. T., 35, 62
Butterfield, D., 184, 287

C

Calfee, R. C., 248, 273, 418
Caramazza, A., 395
Carbo, M., 285
Carlisle, J., 91, 238, 290
Carnine, D. W., 149, 160, 180, 189, 296, 349–350
Carnine, L., 149
Carpenter, P. A., 12, 14, 17, 21, 31, 33, 36, 57, 68, 81, 87, 93, 117, 135–136, 144, 149, 151–152, 156, 160, 248, 281, 329, 343, 345, 351–352, 356, 372, 378, 389–391, 406, 409, 411, 431, 436–438, 448–449
Carroll, J. B., 354
Carroll, P., 152
Casbergue, R. M., 65
Cattell, J. M., 267
Catts, H. W., 96, 276
Cera, M. J., 450
Chall, J. S., 99, 116, 186, 254, 277
Chapman, L. J., 433
Charnock, J., 223
Cheek, E. H., 418–419
Cheek, M. C., 418–419
Chester, R. D., 449
Chiesi, H. L., 117
Chittenden, E. A., 94, 98
Chomsky, C., 282, 288
Chomsky, N., 399–400
Clark, C. H., 203
Clark, F., 213, 415
Cleland, C. J., 91
Clewell, S. F., 444
Collins, A., 115
Colt, J., 184–185, 231–232
Colwell, C., 418–446
Conners, F., 276
Content, A., 217
Cooke, C. L., 434
Cooper, J. D., 205, 230–231, 285, 340
Copple, C. E., 251
Cotman, C. W., 40
Coyle, G., 349–350
Crafton, L., 204

AUTHOR INDEX 507

Crawley, S., 363–369
Crays, N., 216
Cromer, W., 139, 392
Cross, D. R., 215
Crystal, D., 88, 351
Cundick, B. P., 223
Cunningham, D., 209
Cunningham, J. W., 22, 205, 458
Cunningham, P. M., 264, 458
Curley, R., 418
Curtis, M. A., 255

D

Dahl, P. R., 287
Daniels, P. R., 160, 356
Davey, B., 209–342
Davis, A. P., 189
Davis, F. B., 189, 339, 342, 350
Day, J. D., 442, 451
Dechant, E., 6, 20, 25, 75, 93, 100, 102, 109–110, 199, 201, 251, 254, 267, 295, 297, 331, 363, 389, 397, 459, 464–465
Dehn, N., 202
Denburg, S. D., 141, 149
Denckla, M. B., 255
Desberg, P., 137, 140, 154, 248, 259, 277
Devine, T. G., 442
DiBenedetto, B., 277
Dillner, M. H., 381
Ding, B., 275
DiLollo, V., 71
Dishner, E. K., 200, 202, 227, 441
DiStefano, P. P., 12
Dixon, R., 149, 160
Doehring, D. G., 34, 76, 269
Dole, J. A., 228
Donant, L., 442
Donlan, D., 209
Dowhower, S. L., 287–288
Downing, J., 33, 174, 189, 349, 392
DuCharme, C., 232
Duffelmeyer, F. A., 149, 358
Duffy, G., 6, 231, 232
Duke-Elder, A., 49
Dunn-Rankin, P., 250
Dupuis, M. M., 105, 115, 363
Durkin, D., 117, 120, 186, 203, 217–218, 255, 286, 403

E

Early, M., 196, 201, 334, 340, 362, 368, 454
Edelsky, C., 177
Edfeldt, A. W., 32
Eeds-Kniep, M., 198, 229
Egeland, B., 251
Eggen, P. D., 119
Ehri, L. C., 34, 156, 254–255, 264, 270, 273, 275–276, 282
Ehrlich, S. F., 152
Eisner, E., 189
Eldredge, J. L., 184, 287
Elkind, D., 98, 121
Emans, R., 153, 296
Englert, C. S., 434
Entwisle, D. R., 22, 400
Erdmann, B., 267
Erickson, F., 183
Estes, T., 202

F

Farnan, N., 434
Farr, R., 142
Feagans, L., 216
Feeman, D. J., 240, 275
Fernald, G. M., 264, 283–284
Fielding, L., 227
Fields, M., 176
Finger, E., 240
Finn, P. J., 248
Fisher, D. F., 65
Fisher, E., 68
Flippo, R. F., 465
Flood, J., 90, 201, 434, 444
Flores, B. M., 177
Flynn, L. L., 453
Foorman, B. R., 260, 276
Foss, D. J., 153
Fowler, C. A., 34
Fowler, S., 55
Fox, B. J., 275, 434
Frackenpohl, H., 62
Frasure, N. E., 22, 400
Fredericksen, C. H., 248
Fredericksen, J. R., 355
Fredericks, A. D., 216
Freebody, P., 350
Freedle, R. O., 208

Freedman, G., 444
Friedman, M., 137, 140, 149, 154, 248, 259, 277
Fries, C. C., 278
Frith, U., 259
Fulker, D., 276
Furlin, D. R., 265
Furr, P. M., 141

G

Gaardner, K. R., 59
Gaddes, W. H., 35
Gallagher, M. C., 434
Gambrell, L. B., 91, 221
Gardiner, B., 285
Garrison, J. W., 131
Gates, L., 131
Gavelek, J. R., 218
Gazzaniga, M. S., 47
Gelbart, F., 227, 288
Gephart, W. J., 9
Gerber, M. M., 279
Gersten, R., 189
Gibson, E. J., 249, 274, 281, 340
Gickling, E. E., 381
Gillett, J. W., 6, 119, 201, 214
Gillingham, A., 284
Gillingham, M. G., 255
Glass, G. G., 281
Gleadon, N., 263
Glenn, C. G., 438
Glushko, R. J., 260
Glynn, S. M., 216
Goins, J. T., 256
Goldberg, H. K., 51
Goldman, S. R., 140
Golinkoff, R. M., 134, 392, 431
Goodman, K. S., 9, 16, 18, 23, 26, 97, 99, 129, 150, 175, 177, 188–189, 196, 340
Goodman, Y. M., 9, 97, 177, 188, 297
Gordon, C. J., 438
Gormley, K., 117–118
Goswami, U., 137
Gough, P. B., 23, 35, 151, 270, 275
Gove, M. K., 23–25
Grabe, C., 172
Grabe, M., 173
Graves, M. E., 148
Graves, M. F., 434
Gray, W. S., 142, 463–464
Green, B. A., 117, 124

Green, J. F., 65
Greene, E., 407
Gregory, J. F., 288
Griffin, D. C., 54, 65, 67–68
Griffith, P. L., 275
Groesbeck, H. G., 385
Groff, P., 255, 281, 296, 312
Grotelueschen, A., 218
Guszak, F. J., 430
Guthrie, J. T., 121, 189, 248

H

Haber, L. R., 265
Haber, R. N., 265
Haddock, M., 171
Haidemos, J., 444
Hall, M., 171
Hall, W. S., 57, 62, 81
Halliday, M. A. K., 401
Hammond, K., 240
Hansen, J., 116, 202, 228, 232, 450–451
Hanson, D., 71
Harber, J. D., 141
Hardyck, C. D., 36
Hargis, C. H., 381
Harp, B., 177
Harris, A. J., 6, 94, 102, 145, 203, 391
Harris, T. L., 414, 453
Hart, L. A., 274
Hasan, R., 401
Hatcher, C. W., 218
Heathington, B. S., 91
Hebb, D. O., 120
Heckelman, R. G., 227, 287
Hedfeldt, J., 418, 446
Heilman, A. W., 158, 209–210, 396
Heimlieb, J. E., 208
Heller, M. E., 169
Henderson, E. H., 282
Hepler, S., 460
Herber, H. L., 464
Herbert, M., 261
Hermann, P. A., 148, 231, 363, 365
Herrick, J., 129, 377
Herron, J. E., 190
Heshusius, L., 180–181, 183
Heymsfeld, C. R., 186–187
Hickman, J., 460
Hiebert, E. H., 6, 94, 98, 150, 184–185, 198, 231–232, 434
Higbee, K. H., 223

Hildreth, G., 15
Hillinger, M. L., 277
Hittelman, D. R., 9, 98, 118, 171, 195, 199, 206, 214, 221, 396, 398, 410, 428
Hochberg, J., 340, 400
Hodges, R. E., 414, 453
Hofler, D. B., 367
Hogaboam, T. W., 140, 240
Hollander, S. K., 20
Holley-Wilcox, P., 151
Hollingsworth, P. M., 287
Holmes, B. C., 121, 450–451
Hook, J. N., 463
Horn, E., 110
Horowitz, R., 433–434
Hoskisson, K., 131, 227
Huck, C., 460
Huey, E. B., 14, 32, 257, 395
Hughes, C., 275
Hulme, C., 281, 285
Hunter, M., 230

I

Imlach, R., 451
Indrisano, R., 219
Inhoff, A. W., 57, 61, 64
Irwin, J. W., 182, 201, 204–205, 212, 220, 243, 389, 391–393, 407, 410–411, 418, 433, 441, 448–449, 463
Ives, V., 54, 65, 67–68

J

Jackson, M. D., 465
Jacobs, J. E., 216
Jacobs, J., 76, 184, 185
Jacobsen, E., 32
James, J. H., 93
James, W., 110
Javal, E., 56
Jenkins, J. R., 148–149, 160, 190, 255, 372
Jenkins, L. M., 255
Jett-Simpson, M., 437
Jewell, M. G., 97, 137, 140, 172, 198
Johns, J. L., 414, 455, 457, 465
Johnson, D. D., 205, 208, 340, 366, 369, 444
Johnson, D. J., 76
Johnson, H., 450
Johnson, N., 438, 439

Johnson, T. D., 263
Jolly, H. B., 264
Jones, K. J., 251
Jones, W., 216
Jorm, A. F., 34, 275, 290, 296
Juel, C., 160
Just, M. A., 12, 14, 17, 21, 31, 33–36, 57, 59, 61, 68, 81, 87, 90, 92, 117, 135–136, 144, 149, 151, 153, 156, 160, 248, 281, 329, 343, 345, 351–352, 356, 372, 378, 389–391, 406, 409–411, 431, 436–438, 446, 449, 465

K

Kachuck, B., 398
Kamil, M. L., 270, 278
Kann, R., 287
Kapinus, B. A., 91
Kardash, C. A. M., 117, 124
Karlin, A. R., 28
Karlin, R., 28
Katz, E. W., 422
Kauchak, D. P., 119
Kaufman, J. M., 180
Kaye, D. B., 355, 379
Keefe, D., 50
Kendall, J., 362, 392
Kendrick, R., 169
Kimball, W. H., 180, 190
Kimmel, S., 119
Kintsch, W., 390–391, 407, 432, 449
Kinzer, C. K., 28, 400, 447
Kirk, U., 85
Kleiman, G. M., 33
Knafle, J. D., 307
Kniseley, E., 362
Kochnower, J., 277
Kolinski, R., 275
Koskinen, P. S., 91, 287–288
Krashen, S. D., 197–198, 232
Kucer, S. B., 97

L

LaBerge, D., 23, 205, 240, 288
LaBerge, M., 434
Labov, W., 380
Laminack, L. L., 172
Lamme, L. L., 186
Lamport, J., 255
Lange, K., 89, 110

Langer, J. A., 99, 117, 202
Langer, S. K., 95
Langford, K., 287
Langman, M. P., 9, 102
Lanier, R. J., 189
Lapp, D., 434, 444
Larrick, N., 184
Lawton, S. C., 451
Leal, L., 216
Leary, B. E., 129, 142
Lecheler, R., 465
Lee, D., 176
Lee, J. W., 105, 115
Lehtinen, L. E., 284
Lefevre, C. A., 21, 97, 395
Lefton, L. A., 65
Leong, C. K., 31, 33, 189, 349
Lerner, J. W., 74, 290, 330, 389, 399, 415
Lesgold, A. M., 240, 255, 342
Leu, D. J., 28, 400, 447
Levin, H., 62, 248, 274, 340
Levine, S. G., 100–102
Lewis, V., 465
Leys, M., 97
Liberman, D., 260, 276
Liberman, I. Y., 91, 95, 238, 248, 266, 290
Lillas, C., 150
Lipson, M. Y., 120, 125, 451
List, L. K., 290, 330, 398–399, 415
Lloyd, J. W., 180
Lomax, R. G., 155, 161
Lovegrove, W. J., 71
Lovitt, T. C., 250–251, 283, 285
Lowry, H., 316
Luiten, J., 203
Luria, A. R., 72
Lynch, G. S., 40
Lyon, K., 242

M

MacGinitie, W. H., 119
Mackworth, J. F., 345
MacLean, M., 275, 276
MacLean, R., 275, 276
Maggart, Z. R., 312, 381, 418, 449, 454
Malicky, G., 125
Mallan, J., 195
Mandler, J. M., 438–439
Manis, F. R., 275
Manzo, A. V., 195, 221

Marcellesi, C., 117
Marchbanks, G., 248
Marie, K., 119
Marr, M. B., 117–118
Marsh, G., 137, 140, 149, 154, 248, 259, 277
Marshall, J. C., 15
Marshall, N., 459
Marzano, R. J., 12
Mason, J. M., 117, 140, 154, 231, 271, 358, 362, 392, 464
Mateja, J. A., 202, 209
Matlock, B., 148, 372
Matthews, R., 275, 296
Matthewson, G. C., 197
May, F. B., 350
Mayer, R. F., 215
McAndrew, D. A., 443–444
McClelland, J. L., 23, 26, 465
McConkie, G. W., 57, 59, 61, 65
McCormick, S., 28
McCorriston, M., 282
McCoy, K. M., 226, 235
McCracken, G., 255
McCusker, L. X., 277
McCutchen, D., 34
McGaw, B., 218
McGee, L. M., 433–434, 439
McGee, M. M., 155, 261
McIntosh, M. E., 200, 202, 204, 448
McIntyre, J. S., 71
McKean, K., 183
McKeown, M. G., 202, 350, 357, 448
McKinney, J. D., 216, 229
McNeil, J. D., 103, 115, 119, 339, 351, 353–354, 397, 428, 441, 444
McNinch, G. T., 264
Meloth, M., 232
Memory, D. M., 217
Meredith, R., 177–188
Merlin, S. B., 264
Meyer, B. J. F., 208, 417–418
Meyer, V., 50
Mezynski, K., 350
Miccinati, J., 227
Michener, D. M., 198
Miles, T. R., 266, 286
Miller, J., 142
Miller, L., 313
Moe, A. J., 408, 410
Moely, B. E., 216
Moffett, J., 282

Montgomery, D., 249, 257
Moore, S. A., 458
Moorman, G. B., 199–200, 230–231
Morais, J., 275
Morrow, L. M., 223
Mountain, L., 363, 369
Moyer, S. B., 253, 287
Murphy, S., 175

N

Nagle, G. J., 65
Nagy, W. E., 148, 363, 365
National Assessment of Educational Progress, 393, 450
Nemko, B., 264
Nesdale, A. R., 275
Newcomer, P. L., 253
Nicholas, D. W., 448
Nicholson, T., 17, 98, 275, 451
Nicolich, M., 117
Nie, H., 275
Niensted, S., 285
Niles, O. S., 208
Nolte, R. Y., 213
Norberg, K., 129, 159
Norris, S. P., 453–454
Nulman, J. A. H., 279

O

Olsen, W. C., 75
Olson, J. P., 381
Olson, R. K., 37, 65, 69, 92, 137, 276
Orton, S. T., 252
Ortony, A., 14, 114
O'Shea, L. J., 393

P

Paivio, A., 380
Palincsar, A. S., 216, 228, 229
Pany, D., 190, 226, 235
Paratore, J. R., 219
Paris, S. G., 215–216, 450–451
Pascarella, E. T., 160
Pavlidis, G. T., 65, 68
Pearson, P. D., 92, 97, 120, 126, 148, 189, 201–202, 207, 227–229, 232, 340, 350, 366, 434, 444, 449–450, 459, 461
Perez, S. A., 198

Perfetti, C. A., 6, 13–15, 17, 23, 26, 28–29, 33–35, 57, 60, 84, 95, 117, 121, 122, 129, 140, 149–151, 153–154, 158, 202, 216, 238, 240, 275, 340, 342–343, 350, 353–355, 357, 371, 376–378, 389, 406–410, 432, 438, 449
Peters, C. W., 189, 350, 357
Peterson, J., 202
Petrinovich, L. F., 36
Pettee, J. L., 62
Pfeifer, W., 223
Pflaum, S. W., 160
Piccolo, J. A., 420
Pieronek, F. T., 199
Pittelman, S. D., 208
Pollatsek, A., 14, 17–18, 23–25, 26, 29, 32–36, 37, 46, 50, 55–70, 112, 115, 125, 140, 145, 149–154, 180, 249, 259–261, 266–267, 273, 275, 289, 313, 333, 335, 355, 357, 378, 395, 398, 401, 465
Pointkowski, D. C., 248
Poostay, E. J., 443
Pope, L., 55
Poplin, M. S., 111–113, 121, 178–180, 182–183, 187, 189
Porter, W. E., 89
Pratt, A. C., 275
Prior, M., 282
Pritchard, R. M., 57
Purcell-Gates, V., 95
Pumphrey, M. M., 33
Putnam, J., 232

R

Rabinovitch, R. D., 282
Rack, J., 276
Rackliffe, G., 232
Ramsey, W., 290
Rand, M. K., 438–440
Raphael, T., 218, 219, 229, 232, 358
Rash, J., 263
Rasinski, T. V., 287
Rayford, L., 199
Rayner, K.,
Read, C., 98
Read, D., 275
Readance, J. E., 102, 125, 200, 202, 227, 385, 441
Reicher, G. M., 267
Reid, D. K., 187

Reifman, B., 172
Reitsma, P., 288
Resnick, L., 240
Rettinger, V., 180, 186
Reutzel, D. R., 200, 204, 208, 444
Reynolds, E. G., 444
Reynolds, R. E., 218
Rice, G. E., 418
Richek, M. S., 290, 330, 397, 399, 415
Richards, I., 76, 92, 282
Richardson, E., 277
Richgels, D. J., 433–434
Rickards, J. P., 218
Ringler, L. J., 96, 137, 169, 211, 306, 327, 359, 373, 404–405, 418, 431, 440–441, 458–459
Robeck, M. C., 72, 73, 95, 141, 255
Roberts, K. T., 264
Robertson, J. W., 422
Roe, B. D., 201–202, 208, 456–457, 459, 462
Roeber, E. D., 189
Roehler, L. R., 6, 231, 232
Rogers, S. F., 264
Roper-Schneider, D., 238
Rorie, I. L., 184
Rose, L., 35, 269
Rose, M. C., 223
Roser, N. L., 142, 185
Rosenshine, B. V., 365
Rosner, S. L., 160, 356
Ross, E., 414, 416, 456, 459, 462
Rosso, B. R., 296
Roth, K. J., 203, 358
Roth, S. F., 26, 140, 154
Rothkoph, E. Z., 217–218
Routh, D. K., 275
Rowe, D. W., 199
Royer, J. M., 117, 124
Rubenstein, H. L., 272
Rubenstein, M. A., 272
Rubin, H., 91, 238, 290
Rude, R. T., 313
Rudel, R. G., 94, 255
Rumelhart, D. E., 23, 26, 113–115, 120–121
Rupley, W. R., 209–210, 395
Russell, S., 98
Rutter, M., 92, 282
Ryan, E. B., 213, 216
Rzosko, M. A., 150

S

Sadow, M. W., 438
Sadowski, M., 216
Samuels, S. J., 134, 141, 174, 205, 227, 229, 240, 255, 264, 270, 287–288, 434
Santa, C. M., 281
Sawicki, F. E., 169
Sawyer, D. J., 196, 201, 334, 340, 362, 368, 454
Scanlon, D., 91–92, 276
Schatz, E. K., 148
Schiffman, G., 160, 356
Schlieper, A., 145
Schmidt, C. R., 450
Schmitt, M. C., 209, 215
Schreiner, R., 450
Schumacher, G. M., 215, 463
Schwartz, R. M., 358
Scott, G. I., 49
Scott, J. A., 6, 150, 198
Seidenberg, M. S., 33, 261
Semel, E., 400
Semelmeyer, M., 102
Shanahan, T., 99, 171
Shankweiler, D., 91, 95, 248
Shannon, K. S., 175
Shannon, P., 450
Share, D. L., 34, 275, 290, 296
Shaw, P., 458
Sheikh, A. A., 380
Shelley, H., 197
Shepherd, D., 420
Short, E. J., 213, 216
Seidow, M. D., 434
Siegel, L. A., 276
Silvaroli, N. J., 250
Silvernail, L. A., 168, 172
Simmons, J. S., 458
Sinatra, R. C., 444
Sindelar, P. T., 393
Singer, H., 141, 199, 209, 213, 264
Sipay, E. R., 6, 94, 102, 145, 203, 391
Sivan, E., 232
Slater, W., 434
Slaghuis, W. L., 71
Slocum, T. A., 148, 372
Slowiaczek, M. L., 152
Smiley, S. S., 451
Smith, C. B., 71

Smith, E. B., 177, 188
Smith, E. L., 203, 358
Smith, F., 10-14, 16, 18, 22-23, 26, 33, 35, 39-40, 45, 55, 59, 61, 64-65, 71, 83-87, 94, 101, 115-116, 122-124, 130-133, 140, 145-149, 158, 177-178, 180-182, 184-189, 197, 217-218, 232, 237, 249-250, 254-255, 267-269, 278, 281-283, 300-301, 340, 400, 422, 436, 454, 465
Smith, H. P., 19, 20, 25, 109-110
Smith, L., 125, 450
Smith, M., 450
Smith, R. J., 189, 326, 428
Snyder, S. L., 363
Sowell, J., 331
Spache, G., 52, 76
Spencer, L. P., 6
Spilich, G. J., 117
Spiro, R. J., 26, 116, 449
Spiroff, J., 141, 264
Spring, H. T., 216
Squire, J., 98
Stahl-Gemake, J., 444
Stanley, G., 83
Stanovich, K. E., 18, 27, 34, 137, 140, 151, 152, 240, 275-277
Stauffer, R., 195, 221
Stedman, L., 32
Stein, J. F., 55, 32
Stein, M. L., 148, 372
Stein, N. L., 438
Steiner, R., 438
Steinheiser, R., 248
Sternberg, R., 349, 355, 379
Stevens, K. C., 121, 189, 392-393, 449
Stevenson, J., 402
Sticht, T. G., 95
Stillman, B., 284
Stoodt, B., 18, 40, 184, 201-202, 208, 457
Stotsky, S., 97
Stott, D. J., 196, 253
Strange, M., 120
Straus, A., 284
Strickland, D., 99, 186
Sulzby, E., 98
Sunal, C. S., 172
Swaby, B., 203, 271
Swalm, J. E., 94
Swanson, H. L., 272
Swenson, I., 158, 281

T

Taft, M., 31
Tannenhaus, M. K., 33
Tatham, S. M., 427
Taylor, B. M., 208, 434
Taylor, E. A., 65
Taylor, S. E., 55, 62
Taylor, W., 376
Teale, W. H., 94, 108
Temple, C., 6, 119, 201, 214
Terman, S., 266
Thelen, J., 210
Thomson, M. E., 76, 92, 282
Thorndike, E. L., 15, 129, 196
Thorndyke, P. W., 438
Tierney, R., 97, 200, 202, 205, 227, 441, 450
Tolman, E. C., 129-130
Topping, K., 287
Torgesen, J., 235, 275-276
Torneus, M., 275
Townsend, M. A. R., 451
Trabasso, T., 448, 450
Trachtenberg, P., 184, 186
Traynelis-Yurek, E., 285
Treiman, R., 272
Trelease, J., 185
Tremonti, J. B., 458
Tunmer, W. E., 275
Tunnel, M. O., 184, 185
Turner, E. A., 62
Turner, T. N., 408

U

Underwood, N. R., 465

V

Vacca, J. A. L., 24, 120-121, 142, 195, 202-203, 211, 342, 363, 371, 375, 414
Vacca, R. T., 24, 120-121, 142, 195, 202-203, 209, 211, 217, 342, 363, 371, 375, 381, 414, 464
Valencia, S., 12, 189
Van Dijk, T. K., 390-391, 407, 432
Van Orden, G. C., 31, 34
Vaughan, J. L., 184
Vaughan, S., 363, 369
Vavrus, L., 232

Veatch, J., 168-169, 175
Vellutino, F., 55, 65, 82, 85, 91-92, 157-158, 253, 269, 276
Venezky, R. L., 296, 323
Vesonder, G. T., 117
Vogel, J. A., 437
Voss, J. F., 117

W

Wagner, B. J., 282
Wagner, L., 218
Wagner, R. K., 275
Walcutt, C. C., 255, 266
Walker, C. H., 111-112, 115, 117, 123, 216
Wallace, R. R., 72, 73, 95
Wallach, L., 289, 290
Wallach, M. A., 289-290
Walsh, D. J., 255
Walters, W., 180
Walton, H. N., 54, 65, 67-68
Warren, W. H., 448
Waters, G. S., 33
Watson, J. B., 32
Weaver, C., 184
Weber, C. K., 96, 137, 169, 210, 306, 327, 359, 373, 404-405, 418, 431, 440-441, 458-459
Weber, E. M., 189
Weed, K. A., 213
Weinberg, F., 285
Weinstein, C. E., 354
Weinstein, C. F., 215
Weiss, D. S., 393
Welch, V., 137, 140, 149, 154, 248, 259, 276
Wesselman, R., 232
West, R. F., 151-152
Whaley, J. F., 439
Wheeler, R., 285
Wheelock, W. H., 250

White, J. H., 184
White, T. J., 331
White, W., 189
Whitmore, D., 54
Widomski, C. L., 114
Wiesendanger, K. D., 264
Wigfield, A., 197
Wigg, E., 400
Wilce, L. S., 156, 264, 282
Williams, J., 277
Wilson, C. R., 115
Wilson, J. A. R., 141, 255
Wilson, R. M., 91, 223
Wise, B., 276
Wist, A. H., 74
Wittrock, M. C., 97, 434
Wixson, K. K., 189, 219-220
Wolpert, E. M., 381
Wong, B. Y. L., 216
Wonnacott, C. A., 229
Wood, K., 199-200, 202, 209, 227, 230-231
Wollfolk, A. E., 82, 215, 250, 390
Wright, J. P., 172
Wysocki, K., 372

Y

Yanagihara, A., 331
Yeates, K. O., 216
Yekovich, F. R., 111-112, 115, 118, 123, 216
Yule, W., 92, 282

Z

Zanjano, N. C., 172
Zhang, Y., 275
Zintz, M. V., 97, 137, 140, 172, 176, 198, 212, 376, 382, 418, 449, 454
Zola, D., 57, 59, 465

Subject Index

A

Accentuation, 335-337
Accommodation (schema), 118-121
Acronyms, 382
Advance organizers, 202-203
Affixes, 21, 136, 329, 331-332
Allegory, 384
Alliteration, 275
Allusion, 384
Alphabet method, 258
Alphabetic principle (code), 18, 188, 237, 260, 272-276, 300
Analogy cues, 37, 137, 260
Analytic phonics, 258
Anaphora, 354, 401-405
Aniseikonia, 54
Anticipation Guide, 202
Antithesis, 384
Apostrophe, 384
Apposition, 398
Appreciative Comprehension, 457
Articulation, 270
Articulatory deficits, 96
Assimilation (schema), 118-121
Association (and reading), 365
Astereopsis, 54
Astigmatism, 53
Attention, 40, 82, 134, 196, 240, 268-269

Auditory: 71-77
 Acuity, 71
 Deficits, 72
 Discrimination, 74-76
 Figure-ground perception, 76-77
 Memory, 76
 Neural pathways, 71-72
 Perception, 74
 Processes (in reading), 71-77
 Processing difficulties, 77
Authorship, 186
Automaticity (in word identification), 204-205, 236, 240, 289
Automatic semantic activation, 34-35, 132, 139, 151, 153-154, 157-158, 160
Automatic semantic priming, 152

B

Basal reading program, 164, 173-175
Binocular coordination, 69
Binocular difficulties, 53-54
Blending, 275, 290-291
Bottom-up model, 18, 23-25, 103, 143, 154, 180-183, 187, 250
Brainstorming, 202
Broca's area, 32

C

Cataphora, 401
Categorization, 123–124, 249, 356, 436
Category system, 123–124, 249
Cell assembly, 120
Choral reading, 170, 227, 287
Chunking, 82, 84–86
Clause(s):
  Markers, 396
  Nonrestrictive, 398
  Restrictive, 398
Cognition, 15, 86–90, 110
Cognitive disequilibrium, 183
Cognitive field, 88, 100–101
Cognitive learning models, 214
Cognitive strategies, 215
Cognitive structure, 111–112, 117, 123, 134
Coherence, 408–411, 418, 431–433
  Global (organization), 408–411, 431–433
  Local (cohesion), 408–411, 432
Cohesion, 408–411, 432
Communication, 7, 9, 11, 14, 99–103
Compound words, 329
Composition (in writing), 97–98
Comprehension, 9–13, 16, 20, 26, 90, 102, 111, 113, 115, 120–123, 131–133, 177, 185, 213–217, 221–222, 228, 235, 339–467
  Appreciative, 457
  Definition of, 12, 102, 133, 217, 339
  Development of, 217, 339–467
  Evaluative, 428, 453–457
  Failures of, 121–122
  F. Smith's view of, 10
  Higher levels of, 12, 221–222, 428–429
  Inferential, 346, 428–429, 447–453
  Integrative, 463
  Literal, 345, 429–431
  Monitoring of, 213–217
  Organizational, 345, 428–429, 431–447
  Processes (and subprocesses), 341–344, 406
  Rate of, 465
  Taxonomies, 428
Concept development, 356–358
Conceptualization, 15, 160, 356
Configuration cues, 155, 256, 265–266
Connotative meaning, 359–362
Cooperative learning, 185
Consonant grapheme/phoneme correspondences, 300–313

Content materials, 464
Context: 17–18, 20, 27–29, 129, 132, 138–141, 143, 145–154, 159, 221, 371–377
  F. Smith's view of, 145–149
  Inferring meaning from, 29, 132, 138–140, 149–153, 159, 371–376
  Rayner-Pollatsek view of, 149
  Semantic context (cues) 12, 16–17, 19–22, 27, 101, 114, 116–117, 134–146, 352–353
  Syntactic context (cues), 12, 16–17, 19–22, 28, 101, 114, 116–117, 134–146
  Within-mind, 20, 135, 139, 143–144, 149–151, 153
  Within-text, 20, 135, 139, 143–144
Contractions, 329–330
Convergent inference, 449

D

Declarative knowledge, 112, 123, 215, 244
Decoding (see comprehension), 12–14, 16, 26, 132, 397
Deep structure, 12–14, 16, 26, 132, 397
Denotative meaning, 359–362, 430
Dictionary cues, 137
Directed Reading Activity (DRA), 195–244, 446
Directed Reading-Thinking Activity (DR-TA), 163–164, 195, 212, 221–222
Direct visual access (to meaning), 5, 24, 30, 35–37, 261, 272
Disambiguation, 378
Discourse analysis, 411
Discussion strategy, 221–222
Distal stimulus, 88
Divergent inference, 449

E

Echoic memory, 82
Ellipses, 401, 403
Encoding, 7–8, 11–12, 97, 98
Epigram, 384
Eponyms, 361
Errors (in reading), 183, 214, 239, 242
Esophoria, 54
Etymology, 381
Euphemism, 384
Evaluative comprehension, 428, 453–457

SUBJECT INDEX   517

Exophoria, 54
Expectancy, 128-130
Experience and reading, 19-20
Expository grammar, 201, 413-414, 440-441
Expository materials:
    Organization of, 201, 413-414, 440-441
    Reading of, 167, 207-210, 219, 221
Eye fixation, 24
Eye memory span, 63, 68
Eye movements, 24-70, 248, 345
    Causes of eye-movement difficulties, 68-70
    Components of, 66
    Control, 58
    Deficits of, 65-68
    Difficulties of, 68-69
    Rayner-Pollatsek model, 58, 70
    Word-identification model of, 58
Eye-voice span, 63, 68, 226
Eyes: structure and functions of, 16-54

F

Farsightedness, 51-52
Feature detection, 249-250, 267
Figurative expressions, 360, 383-386
Fixations, 24-25, 47, 57-60, 67, 101, 149, 152
Fixation frequency, 62
Fixation time, 57, 60-61
Fluency (in reading), 164, 171, 177, 225, 227-229, 287-288, 355, 393
Foveal word processing, 24, 46, 51, 70, 154
Free recall questions, 219, 431
Function words, 136, 350, 396, 398, 420-422

G

Gaze (eye movement), 24, 152
Generalizations, 356
Genre, 133, 432
Global coherence, 408-411, 431-433
Global questions, 199, 211, 220
Gloss procedure, 209
Grammar (Story), 133, 167, 201-202, 219, 411, 422, 437-440, 458-463
Grammar (syntax), 96-97
Grapheme information (cues), 8, 27, 35, 136-138, 155, 259, 298
Grapheme-phoneme correspondences (see phonics)

Graphic awareness, 262
Graphic cues, 7-8, 12, 16, 99, 129
Graphic organizers, 209-210, 434
Guided reading, 211-217
Guided Reading Procedure, 195, 222-223
Guided Reading-Thinking Procedure, 195, 222-223

H

Hearing, 71, 269
    Conductive loss, 72
    Sensori-neural loss, 72, 73
Heschl's gyrus, 71-72
Heteronyms, 360-379
Heterophoria, 54
High-imagery words, 380
Holistic constructivism, 112, 180-184, 187-189
Homographs, 360, 379
Homonyms, 360, 379-380
Homophones, 360, 379
How-to-learn strategies, 215
Hyperbole, 384
Hypermetropia, 52
Hyperopia, 51-52
Hyphenation, 331

I

Iconic memory, 82-83
Idiomatic expressions, 360, 383-386
Imitative method, 227, 287
Incus, 72
Individualized reading, 175-176
Inferencing processes, 117, 138, 142, 228, 353-354, 409, 447-453
    Convergent, 449
    Divergent, 449
    Elaborative, 138
    Schema-implicit, 448
    Slot-filling, 354, 409
    Textually explicit, 448
    Textually implicit, 448
Inferential Comprehension, 346, 428-429, 447-453
Inflectional changes, 328
Inflectional endings, 327-328
Information processing, 81-82, 180
Information theory, 11-12
Inner hearing, 32
Inner speech, 24, 33, 36-37

518 SUBJECT INDEX

Instructional level, 206, 226
Integrative Reading Method (IRM), 187, 257-289
Integrative comprehension, 463
Interactive model of reading, 26-29, 116, 143, 161, 186, 258
Interest (in reading), 185-186, 196-199
Interference (role of, in memory), 85
Intonation, 136
Invented spelling, 98, 282
Irony, 384

K

Kinesthetic method, 258

L

Language, 15, 90-99, 137, 177, 180
  Definition of, 137
  Natural, 177, 180, 184-185
Language arts (and reading), 163-164, 171, 177, 191
Language experience story, 163-164, 167-173, 207
  Advantages of, 171-173
  Steps of, 169-170
Lateral geniculate nuclei, 49
Letters: 248-268
  Developing of letter recognition, 248-251
  Letter-by-letter identification, 266-267
  Naming of, 254-255
  Orientation of, 251-254
  Parallel processing of, 266-268
  Writing of, 255-256
Learning theory, 178-179, 181-184, 187
Learning-thinking strategies, 214
Lexical access, 24, 27, 70, 82, 149, 152-154, 205, 349-376 (see meaning)
  And context, 29, 132, 138-140, 149-153, 159, 371-376
  Conceptualization and, 356-358
  Development of, 362-365
  Difficulties in, 358-362
  Pupil difficulties in, 354-356
Lexicon, 24, 30
Linguistic method, 257-258
Listening, 93-94, 185, 227-228
  Relationship to reading, 185
Literacy learning, 177
Literal comprehension, 345, 429-431
Literature-based reading, 184-186

Local coherence, 408-411, 432
Logographic cues, 27, 136, 155, 259, 276
Long-term memory, 24, 81-82, 85, 111-112, 117, 123, 134, 153, 349, 408-410

M

Macrostructure (of text), 407-408
Main idea, 413-416
Malleus, 72
Meaning (meaning cues), 10-14, 18-20, 27-28, 30, 86, 88-89, 100-102, 129, 131-132, 134, 138-153, 154, 158, 181-184, 187-188, 200, 238, 264
  Direct visual access to, 5, 24, 30-31, 35-37, 261, 272
  Inferring – from context, 29, 132, 138-140, 149-153, 159, 371-376
  Morphemic cues to, 27, 31, 136-137, 157-158, 379
  Phonological route to, 24, 30-37
  Role of, 112-113
Memory: 81-86
  Long-term, 24, 81-82, 85-86, 111-112, 117, 123, 134, 149, 153, 408-410
  Sensory store, 83
  Short-term (working), 24, 29, 33, 36, 82-85, 122, 152, 240, 277, 409-410
Mental imagery, 415
Metacognitive processes, 122, 164, 180, 213-217, 231, 354
Metalinguistic awareness, 261-262
Metaphor, 384
Metonyms, 361
Metonomy, 384
Microselection, 392-393, 396
Minimum difference strategy, 272, 278-279
Microstructure (of text), 407-408
Modeling:
  of skills, 229-231
  of text, 405-407, 414
Morphemes:
  Bound, 326
  Free, 326
  Lexical, 326
  Relational, 326
Monitoring of comprehension, 213-217
Morphemic:
  Analysis skills, 243-256, 325-337
  Cues, 27, 31, 136-137, 157-158, 379
  Decomposition, 31, 379
Morphology, 96, 298, 325-327

SUBJECT INDEX 519

Motivation, 40, 196–198
Motivational strategies, 215
Moving of lips (in reading), 32
Myopia, 52

N

Narratives, 167, 201–202, 219, 413, 437–440, 458–463
Natural language, 180, 184–185
Negative markers, 396
Neurological impress method, 185, 227, 287
Nonvisual information, 10, 82, 133–134, 138, 151, 159, 188, 219
Noun markers, 396
Numerical concepts, 382–383
Nystagmus, 57

O

Occipital lobe, 48, 50, 69
Optic chiasma, 46
Optic Nerve, 46
Oral reading, 224–227
Oral reading errors, 183, 214, 225–226, 239, 242, 297
Organizational comprehension, 345, 428–429, 431–447
Orthographic cues, 15, 18, 27, 35, 129, 136, 155, 237, 260, 267
Orthography, 15, 17, 91, 155, 273, 276–277, 299
Outlining, 418, 442
Ownership, 181, 187
Oxymoron, 384

P

Paired cooperative learning, 185
Paired reading, 227, 287–288
Palindromes, 361
Parafoveal word processing, 24, 46, 58–59, 68, 70, 152
Paranyms, 361
Paragraph organization, 413–433
  Comprehending of, 417–420
  Cues signaling, 420–423
  Types of, 419–420
Paragraph reading, 411–417
Parallel processing, 28, 29, 155, 260–261, 265–268
Peer tutoring, 185

Perception, 86–90
  Definition of, 46
  Validity of, 377
Perceptual field, 88
Perceptual span, 24, 59, 70
Peripheral word processing, 46, 51, 52, 58–59, 68, 152
Personification, 384
Phonemes, 8, 274, 298
Phonemics, 298
Phonetic coding, 37
Phonetics, 298
Phonics, 27, 37, 137–138, 156–157, 186–188, 259–262, 277, 295–337, 365
  Analytic, 258
  Definition of, 299
  Developing of, 277, 295–337
  Direct teaching of, 297
  Incidental teaching of, 297
  Phonogram teaching, 305–308
  Synthetic, 289–292
  Teaching consonants, 300–312
  Teaching consonant clusters, 307
  Teaching vowels, 313–325
  Terminology, 297–299
Phonograms, 35, 260, 280–281, 291, 305, 307–308
Phonological awareness, 254, 262, 275–277, 290
Phonological coding (see recoding), 5, 85, 91, 92, 111, 157, 272–274
  Postlexical, 36–37, 260
  Prelexical, 33–35, 72
Phonological cues, 137, 156–157
Phonological route to meaning, 24, 72, 239, 261, 272, 273
Phonological segmentation, 98, 157, 254, 275–276, 290
Phonology, 298
Phrase reading, 12, 82, 84–86, 227, 392–394
Phrase structure grammar, 393
Picture cues, 135, 140–141
Polysemy, 378
Practice (guided), 231
Prediction: 10, 16, 17, 19, 22, 26, 117, 129–166, 200, 207, 211–213, 222, 353
  Focal, 129, 132–134, 138–139, 146, 151, 154
  Global, 129, 132–134, 138–139, 151
Prefixes, 21, 329–331
Pre-Reading Plan, 202
Previewing, 201, 208–210

SUBJECT INDEX

Procedural knowledge, 123, 215, 244
Propositions: 390–411
  Assembly of, 390–391
  Chunking of, 391–393
  Integration of, 392, 408–412
  Microselection of, 392–393, 396
Prosody, 36, 288
Proximal stimuli, 46, 88
Psycholinguistic guessing game, 16–18, 151–152, 157, 160, 266
Psycholinguistics, 16–19
Punctuation, 396, 400–401
Pupillary adjustment, 54–55
Purpose in reading, 115, 181, 199–201, 211

Q

Question (questioning), 199, 202, 206, 207, 209, 212–213, 216, 217–224, 228
  Benefits of, 217
  Comprehension monitoring, 220
  Free-recall, 219, 431
  Global, 119, 211, 220
  Markers, 396
  Organizational type, 220
  Prediction, 220
  Probe, 219
  Process, 220
  QAR, 219, 229
  Scriptally-implicit, 220
  Structured, 219
  Structured overview, 220
  Textually explicit, 220
  Textually implicit, 220
  Vocabulary, 220

R

Rate: improvement of, 65, 465
Rayner-Pollatsek Bottom-up model, 23–25, 26, 29
Reader and text interaction, 103, 111, 115–116, 119–120, 122, 126, 131, 143, 146, 189, 202, 216, 340, 343
Reading:
  As a communicative process, 39, 99–103
  As a high-level thinking process, 14–16
  As a language process, 15–19, 39, 90
  As a meaning-getting process, 16, 33, 140
  As a memory process, 39
  As a perceptual-cognitive process, 39, 86, 90
  As a psycholinguistic process, 15–19
  As construction of meaning, 16, 33, 180–184, 187
  As information processing, 39
  As interpretation of experience, 5–6
  As interpretation of graphic symbols, 6–7
  Definition of, 5–7, 10, 16, 22, 26, 88, 90, 102, 112, 201
  Enabling skills and, 39, 42, 196–210, 226
  Errors in, 183, 214, 225–226, 239, 242, 297
  Habit, 197
  Models of, 23, 29–30
    Bottom-up, 18, 23–25, 103, 116, 143, 149, 154, 170, 180–183, 185, 187, 250
    Interactive, 26–29, 116, 143, 161, 186, 258
    Top-down, 10, 16, 25–26, 29, 103, 116, 138–139, 143, 145, 149, 170, 184, 237–238
  Rate of, 465
  Readiness for, 39, 196–210
Reading achievement, correlates of, 39–42, 196–210
Reading aloud (to children), 185, 198
Reading disability, causes of, 40–42, 157, 182, 276–277
Reading lesson:
  Steps of, 196–244
  Structuring of, 163–244
Reading readiness, 39–42, 196–210
Reading-writing connection, 186
Recoding, 17–18, 26, 34–35, 37, 65, 71, 129, 133–134, 137–138, 150, 155–156, 160, 184, 229, 235–241, 258–291, 296–297, 355, 361
  Hierarchical, 155, 259–260
  Sequential, 155, 259–260
Recognition span, 61–62, 67
Reduction of uncertainty, 10–12, 21, 130–132, 146, 148, 158, 185, 300, 341
Reductionism, 178–180, 188
Redundancy, 101, 136, 138, 146, 268
  Distributional, 146
  Sequential, 146, 268
Referent, 21–22, 123, 262, 351, 353
Referential processes, 351–353
Regression, 25, 57–59, 64, 70
Rehearsal, 82, 85
Repeated readings, 185, 227, 287–288
Retelling, 223
Retrieval, 83, 86

SUBJECT INDEX 521

Return sweep, 57, 65, 68
Reversals: 251-254
  Static, 252
  Kinetic, 252
  Transpositions, 252
  Inversions, 252
  Causes of, 254
Review, 209, 233
Rhyming, 275-276, 305
Root words, 329-332

S

Saccade: 24, 55-56, 58, 61, 67-68
  Definition of, 24
  Duration of, 61
  Length of, 61
Schema theory, 28, 88, 105, 109, 111, 115, 121, 123, 124, 139, 143, 159, 168, 171, 196
Schema (schemata), 15, 16, 25, 88, 97, 102-103, 105, 109-126, 183-184, 341, 350-352
  Accommodation, 118-121
  Activation, 126, 200-203
  Assimilation, 118-121
  Building of, 203-207
  Definition of, 113-114, 118
  Expository, 201, 440
  Narrative, 167, 201, 219
  Networks, 86, 352-358
  Restructuring, 119
  Role of, 113
  Shift, 121
  Slots, 117-118, 120, 123, 138, 353, 428
  Storing and retrieval of, 117
Scripted knowledge, 112
Segmentation of text, 211
Self-concept, 40, 182, 198
Self-selection (of materials), 163, 175, 184, 186
Semantic association, 366
Semantic context (cues), 12, 16-17, 19-22, 27, 101, 114, 116-117, 134-135, 138, 141-144, 352-353
Semantic encoding, 82, 122, 350, 371, 376-379
Semantic feature analysis, 369-371
Semantic mapping, 208-209, 367-369, 444-446
Semantic networks, 91, 112
Semantic processing, 19-21

Sensation, 46, 87
Sensory store, 83
Sentence method, 257
Sentence reading, 12, 395-399
Sequence, 416-417, 436
Serial models, 28
Short-term memory, 24, 29, 33, 36, 82-85, 152
Sight-configuration method, 257-258
Sight words, 35, 242-243, 257, 271, 296
Simultaneous listening and reading, 227-228
Skills teaching, 177-178, 186-190, 228-232
Social interaction, 181, 184
Specification of text, 131, 133
Spelling, 98, 281-283
Spelling patterns, 273, 279-280, 312
Spiral of learning, 111, 113
Stapes, 72
Story grammar, 133, 167, 201-202, 219, 411, 422, 437-440, 458-463
Story schema, 411, 437-438
Storytelling, 364
Strabismus, 54
Strategy instruction, 187, 189
Structured overview, 209-210, 434
Study guides, 209
Subgrouping, 223
Subvocalization, 32, 36
Suffixes, 21, 329-332
Summarizing, 411, 418, 442
Surface structure, 12-14, 16, 131-132, 397
Syllabication, 331-335
Syllable:
  Closed, 333
  Definition of, 332
  Open, 333
Synecdoche, 384
Syntactic analysis, 391, 395-401
Syntactic context (cues), 12, 16-17, 19, 21-22, 28, 101, 114, 116-117, 134-138, 144-145
Syntactic structure, 399-400
Syntax, 21-22, 96-97
Synthetic phonics, 289-292

T

Text and reader interaction, 103, 111, 115-116, 119-120, 122, 126, 131, 143, 146, 189, 202, 216, 340, 343
Textbook organization, 201, 413-414, 440-441

Text-modeling, 405–412
Text organization, 410–411
Text processing, 23
Textually-explicit questions, 448
Textually-implicit questions, 448
Thought-unit reading, 63
Time concepts, 382–383
Top-down model, 10, 16, 25–26, 29, 103, 138–139, 143, 145, 149, 170, 237–238
Topic sentence, 413–415
Total-text reading, 405–412
Tracing, 283–286
Transformational grammar, 12, 22, 393

U

Underlining, 443–444

V

Veridicality, 90, 126
Verb markers, 396
Visual memory, 265–266, 269, 272, 277, 284–285, 296
Visual processes, 10, 45–56, 69
    Accommodation, 54–55
    Acuity, 46, 51
    Binocular coordination, 69
    Convergence, 53–55
    Defects of, 50–56
    Discrimination, 8, 50, 251
    Divergence, 54–55
    Nystagmus, 54, 57
    Perception, 70–71
    Pursuit, 54–55
    Tracking, 65
Vocabulary: 349
    Direct experience and, 357–386
    Direct instruction of, 365
    Development of, 357–386
    Ownership of, 366
    Vicarious experience and, 363–364, 377
    Wide reading and, 365
Vowel correspondences, 313–324

W

Whole language, 163–164, 171, 174–191
Whole-part relationship, 187–190
Whole-word method, 257–258
Within-word cues, 17, 134, 136–137, 140, 154–160, 236, 263, 273
Word-by-word reading, 340, 389, 392
Word class, 327
Word concept, 12, 87, 351
Word identification: 7–9, 18, 28, 46, 50, 146–147, 150, 153–155, 235–292, 342, 355
    And letter sequence, 256–257
    Automaticity in, 204–205, 236, 240, 289
    Definition of, 231, 241
    Development of, 257–288
    Difficulties of, 241–242
    Goals of, 271
    Hearing and, 269
    In isolation, 264
    Instant recognition from context, 264, 295
    Integration of – cues, 158–161
    Letter-by-letter, 266–267
    Meaning cues and, 135–136, 138–153
    Methods, 187, 257–258
    Naming and, 270
    Need for, 236–240
    Outline of, 243
    Spelling and, 281
    Stages of, 258–262
    Strategies of, 133–149
    Subsets of, 7
Word maps, 357–358
Word meaning: 15, 205–206, 350
    Connotative, 359–362
    Denotative, 359–362, 430
    Difficulties with, 358–362
    Expansion in breadth, 350, 355
    Expansion in depth, 350, 355
Word percept, 36, 81, 87
Working memory, 24, 29, 33, 36, 82–85, 122, 152, 240, 277, 409–410
Writing, 97–99, 171, 180, 233, 283–286